Imaging Beyond the Pinhole Camera

Computational Imaging and Vision

This comprehensive book series embraces state-of-the-art expository works and advanced research monographs on any aspect of this interdisciplinary field.

Topics covered by the series fall in the following four main categories:

- Imaging Systems and Image Processing
- Computer Vision and Image Understanding
- Visualization
- Applications of Imaging Technologies

Only monographs or multi-authored books that have a distinct subject area, that is where each chapter has been invited in order to fulfill this purpose, will be considered for the series.

Volume 33

Imaging Beyond the Pinhole Camera

Edited by

Kostas Daniilidis

University of Pennsylvania, Philadelphia, PA, U.S.A.

and

Reinhard Klette

The University of Auckland, New Zealand

Springer

A C.I.P. Catalogue record for this book is available from the Library of Congress.

ISBN-10 1-4020-4893-9 (HB)
ISBN-13 978-1-4020-4893-7 (HB)
ISBN-10 1-4020-4894-7 (e-book)
ISBN-13 978-1-4020-4894-4 (e-book)

Published by Springer,
P.O. Box 17, 3300 AA Dordrecht, The Netherlands.

www.springer.com

Printed on acid-free paper

Contents

Contributors

Mongi Abidi
The Imaging, Robotics, and Intelligent Systems Laboratory
The University of Tennessee, Knoxville, 334 Ferris Hall
Knoxville, TN 37996-2100, USA

Elli Angelopoulou
Stevens Institute of Technology
Department of Computer Science
Castle Point on Hudson
Hoboken, NJ 07030, USA

Antonis A. Argyros
Institute of Computer Science
FORTH Vassilika Vouton, P.O. Box 1385
GR-711-10, Heraklion, Crete, Greece

João P. Barreto
Institute of Systems and Robotics
Department of Electrical and Computer Engineering
Faculty of Sciences and Technology of the University of Coimbra
3030 Coimbra, Portugal

John Barron
Department of Computer Science
University of Western Ontario
London, Ontario, Canada, N6A 5B7

Stephen S. Beauchemin
Department of Computer Science
University of Western Ontario
London, Ontario, Canada, N6A 5B7

Kostas E. Bekris
Computer Science Department, Rice University
Houston, TX, 77005, USA

Ryad Benosman
University of Pierre and Marie Curie
4 place Jussieu 75252 Paris cedex 05, France

Kostas Daniilidis
GRASP Laboratory, University of Pennsylvania
Philadelphia, PA 19104, USA

Christopher Geyer
University of California, Berkeley, USA

D. Griesbach
German Aerospace Center DLR, Competence Center
Berlin, Germany

H. O. Hamshari
Department of Computer Science
University of Western Ontario
London, Ontario, Canada, N6A 5B7

Fay Huang
Electronic Engineering Department
National Ilan University
I-Lan, Taiwan

Sio-hoi Ieng
University of Pierre and Marie Curie
4 place Jussieu 75252, Paris cedex 05, and
Lab. of Complex Systems Control, Analysis and Comm.
E.C.E, 53 rue de Grenelles, 75007 Paris, France

Atsushi Imiya
Institute of Media and Information Technology
Chiba University, Chiba 263-8522, Japan

Lydia E. Kavraki
Computer Science Department, Rice University
Houston, TX, 77005, USA

Reinhard Klette
Department of Computer Science and CITR
The University of Auckland
Auckland, New Zealand

Andreas Koschan
The Imaging, Robotics, and Intelligent Systems Laboratory
The University of Tennessee, Knoxville, 334 Ferris Hall
Knoxville, TN 37996-2100, USA

M. T. Kotb
Department of Computer Science
University of Western Ontario
London, Ontario, Canada, N6A 5B7

GEOMETRY OF A CLASS OF CATADIOPRIC SYSTEMS

AKIHIKO TORII
School of Science and Technology
Chiba University, Chiba 263-8522, Japan

AKIHIRO SUGIMOTO
National Institute of Informatics
Tokyo 101-8430, Japan

TOMOYA SAKAI
Institute of Media and Information Technology
Chiba University, Chiba 263-8522, Japan

ATSUSHI IMIYA
Institute of Media and Information Technology
Chiba University, Chiba 263-8522, Japan

Abstract. Images observed by a catadioptric system with a quadric mirror are considered as images on a quadric surface which is determined by a mirror of the system. In this paper, we propose a unified theory for the transformation from images observed by catadioptric systems to images on a sphere. Images on a sphere are functions on a Riemannian manifold with the positive constant curvature. Mathematically, spherical images have similar analytical and geometrical properties with images on a plane. This mathematical property leads to the conclusion that spherical image analysis provides a unified approach for the analysis of images observed through a catadioptric system with a quadric mirror. Therefore, the transformation of images observed by the systems with a quadric mirror to spherical images is a fundamental tool for image understanding of omnidirectional images. We show that the transformation of omnidirectional images to spherical images is mathematically a point to point transformation among quadric surfaces. This geometrical property comes from the fact that the intersection of a double cone in a four-dimensional Euclidean space and a three-dimensional linear manifold yields a surface of revolution employed as a mirror for the catadioptric imaging system with a quadric mirror.

Key words: geometries of catadioptric cameras, central and non-central cameras, spherical camera model, spherical images

K. Daniilidis and R. Klette (eds.), Imaging Beyond the Pinhole Camera, 3–20.

1. Introduction

In this paper, we propose a unified theory for the transformation from images observed by catadioptric systems with a quadric mirror, say catadioptric images, to images on a sphere, say spherical images. The transformed spherical images are functions on a Riemannian manifold with the positive constant curvature. Mathematically, spherical images have similar analytical and geometrical properties with images on a plane. For the development of new algorithms in the computer vision, we analyze the spherical images. The spherical image analysis provides a unified approach for the analysis of catadioptric images. Therefore, the transformation of images observed by the systems with a quadric mirror to spherical images is a fundamental tool for image understanding of omnidirectional images.

In the computer-vision communities, traditional algorithms and their applications are developed based on the pinhole-camera systems. An ideal pinhole camera has no limitation of the region of images. However, the actual camera practically has limitation of the region of images. The pinhole camera can observe objects in the finite region. Therefore, the established algorithms employing sequential and multi-view images implicitly yield the restriction, that is, the observed images share a common region in a space. For the construction of practical systems applying the computer vision methods, this implicit restriction yields the geometrical configuration among cameras, objects, and scenes. If the camera systems practically observe the omnidirectional region in a space, this geometrical configuration problem are solved. Furthermore, the omnidirectional camera systems enable us to notate the simple and clear algorithms for the multiple view geometry (Svoboda et al., 1998; Dahmen, 2001), ego-motion analysis (Dahmen, 2001; Vassallo et al., 2002; Makadia and Daniilidis, 2003), et al.

For the generation of the image which practically express the omnidirectional scenes in a space, the camera system must project the scene on a sphere (ellipsoid). The construction of the camera system, which employs the geometrical configuration of CCD sensors and traditional lenses, is still impractical. Consequently, some researchers developed the camera system constructed by the combination of a quadric-shaped mirror and a general pinhole camera (Nayar, 1997; Baker and Nayar, 1998). Since this catadioptric camera system generates the image on a plane collecting the reflected rays from the mirror, the back-projection of this planar image enables us to transform to the images on the quadric surface as described in Section 2. Furthermore, all the quadric images are geometrically converged to the spherical images as described in Section 3. The application of the spherical camera systems enables us to develop unified algorithms for the different types of catadioptric camera systems. Moreover, one of

Suresh Lodha
Department of Computer Science
University of California, Santa Cruz, USA

Ameesh Makadia
GRASP Laboratory
Department of Computer and Information Science
University of Pennsylvania

Takashi Matsuyama
Graduate School of Informatics, Kyoto University
Sakyo, Kyoto, 606-8501, Japan

Rana Molana
University of Pennsylvania, USA

Jin-Choon Ng
The Imaging, Robotics, and Intelligent Systems Laboratory
The University of Tennessee, Knoxville, 334 Ferris Hall
Knoxville, TN 37996-2100, USA

Robert Pless
Department of Computer Science and Engineering
Washington University in St. Louis, USA

Srikumar Ramalingam
Department of Computer Science
University of California, Santa Cruz, USA

Ralf Reulke
Humboldt University Berlin
Institute for Informatics, Computer Vision
Berlin, Germany

Tomoya Sakai
Institute of Media and Information Technology
Chiba University, Chiba 263-8522, Japan

Karsten Scheibe
Optical Information Systems
German Aerospace Center (DLR)
Rutherfordstr. 2, D-12489 Berlin, Germany

Peter Sturm
INRIA Rhône-Alpes
655 Avenue de l'Europe, 38330 Montbonnot, France

Hironobu Sugaya
School of Science and Technology
Chiba University, Chiba 263-8522, Japan

Akihiro Sugimoto
National Institute of Informatics
Tokyo 101-8430, Japan

Akihiko Torii
School of Science and Technology
Chiba University
Yayoi-cho 1-33, Inage-ku, Chiba 263-8522, Japan

Rene Vidal
Center for Imaging Science, Department of Biomedical Engineering
Johns Hopkins University
308B Clark Hall, 3400 N. Charles Street
Baltimore MD 21218, USA

A. Wehr
Institute for Navigation, University of Stuttgart
Stuttgart, Germany

Shou-Kang Wei
Presentation and Network Video Division
AVerMedia Technologies, Inc.
Taipei, Taiwan

Preface

"I hate cameras. They are so much more sure than I am about everything."

John Steinbeck (1902 - 1968)

The world's first photograph was taken by Joseph Nicephore Niépce (1775–1833) in 1826 on his country estate near Chalon-sur-Saône, France. The photo shows parts of farm buildings and some sky. Exposure time was eight hours. Niépce used a pinhole camera, known as camera obscura, and utilized pewter plates as the support medium for the photographic process. The camera obscura, the basic projection model of pinhole cameras, was first reported by the Chinese philosopher Mo-Ti (5th century BC): light rays passing through a pinhole into a darkened room create an upside-down image of the outside world.

Cameras used since Niépce are basically following the pinhole camera principle. The quality of projected images improved due to progress in optical lenses and silver-based film, the latter one replaced today by digital technologies. Pinhole-type cameras are still the dominating brands, and also used in computer vision for understanding 3D scenes based on captured images or videos.

However, different applications have pushed for designing alternative architectures of cameras. For example, in photogrammetry cameras are installed in planes or satellites, and a continuous stream of image data can also be created by capturing images just line by line, one line at a time. As a second example, robots require to comprehend a scene in full 360° to be able to react to obstacles or events; a camera looking upward into a parabolic or hyperbolic mirror allows this type of omnidirectional viewing. The development of alternative camera architectures also requires understanding related projective geometries for the purpose of camera calibration, binocular stereo, or static or dynamic scene comprehension.

This book reports about contributions given at a workshop at the international computer science center in Dagstuhl (Germany) addressing basics and applications of alternative camera technologies, in particular in the context of computer vision, computer graphics, visualisation centers, camera producers, or application areas such as remote sensing, surveillance, ambient intelligence, satellite or super-high resolution imaging. Examples of subjects are geometry and image processing on plenoptic modalities, multiperspective image acquisition, panoramic imaging, plenoptic sampling and editing, new camera technologies and related theoretical issues.

The book is structured into five parts, each containing three or four chapters on (1) sensor geometry for different camera architectures, also adressing calibration, (2) applications of non-pinhole cameras for analyzing motion, (3) mapping of 3D scenes into 3D models, (4) navigation of robots using new camera technologies, and (5) on specialized aspects of new sensors and other modalities.

The success of this workshop at Dagstuhl is also due to the outstanding quality of the provided facilities and services at this centre, supporting a relaxed and focused academic atmosphere.

Kostas Daniilidis
Reinhard Klette

Philadelphia and Auckland, February 2006

the fundamental problems for the omnidirectional camera system is the visualization of numerical results computed using computer vision and image processing techniques such as optical flow and snakes. The transform of sphere is historically well-studied in the field of the map projections (Berger, 1987; Pearson, 1990; Yang et al., 2000). The techniques of the map projections enable us to transform the computational results on a sphere preserving the specific features such as angles, areas, distances, and their combinations.

It is possible to develop algorithms on the back-projected quadric surfaces (Daniilidis et al., 2002). However, the algorithms depend on the shapes of the quadric mirror. For the development of unified omnidirectional image analysis, a unified notation of the catadioptric and dioptric cameras are proposed (Barreto and Daniilidis, 2004; Ying and Hu, 2004; Corrochano and Fraco, 2004). In this study, we propose a unified formula for the transformation of omnidirectional images to spherical images, say quadric-to-spherical image transform. Our unified formulas enable us to transform different kinds of omnidirectional images observed by catadioptric camera systems to the spherical images. We show that the transformation of omnidirectional images to spherical images is mathematically a point-to-point transformation among quadric surfaces. This geometrical property comes from the fact that the intersection of a double cone in a four-dimensional Euclidean space and a three-dimensional linear manifold yields a surface of revolution employed as a mirror for the catadioptric imaging system with a quadric mirror.

Furthermore, the traditional computer vision techniques are developed on a planar images where the curvature always equals to zero. The new computer vision techniques for the catadioptric camera systems are required to develop the image analysis methodology on the quadric surfaces (Makadia and Daniilidis, 2003), where the curvature is not zero, since the combination of a pin-hole camera and a quadric mirror provides the omnidirectional images. The geometrical analysis of the catadioptric camera system leads that the planar omnidirectional image is identically transformed to the image on the quadric surface. For the first step of our study on omnidirectional systems, we develop the algorithms to image analysis on the sphere where the curvature is always positive and constant.

2. Spherical Camera Model

As illustrated in Figure 1, the center $\boldsymbol{C}$ of the spherical camera is located at the origin of the world coordinate system. The spherical imaging surface is expressed as

$$S : x^2 + y^2 + z^2 = r^2, \tag{1}$$

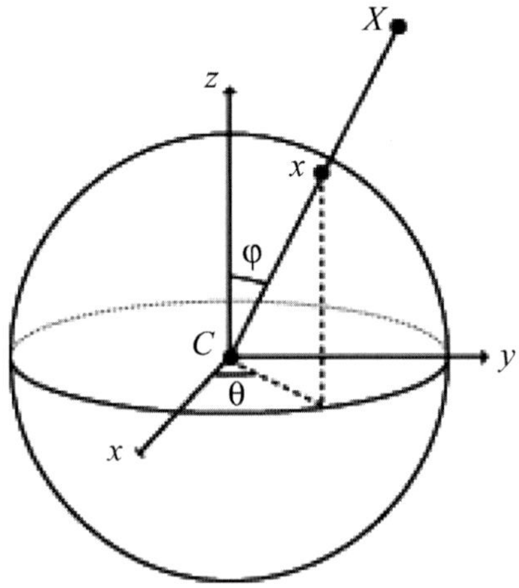

Figure 1. Spherical-camera model.

where r is the radius of the sphere. The spherical camera projects a point $\boldsymbol{X} = (X, Y, Z)^\top$ to the point $\boldsymbol{x} = (x, y, z)^\top$ on S according to the formulation,

$$\boldsymbol{x} = r\frac{\boldsymbol{X}}{|\boldsymbol{X}|}. \tag{2}$$

The spherical coordinate system expresses a point $\boldsymbol{x} = (x, y, z)$ on the sphere as

$$\begin{pmatrix} x \\ y \\ z \end{pmatrix} = \begin{pmatrix} r\cos\theta\sin\varphi \\ r\sin\theta\sin\varphi \\ r\cos\varphi \end{pmatrix}, \tag{3}$$

where $0 \leq \theta < 2\pi$ and $0 \leq \varphi < \pi$. Hereafter, we assume $r = 1$. Therefore, the spherical image is also expressed as $I(\theta, \varphi)$.

3. Catadioptric-to-Spherical Transform

As illustrated in Figure 2, a catadioptric camera system generates an image following the two step. A point $\boldsymbol{X} \in \mathbf{R}^3$ is transformed to a point $\boldsymbol{x} \in C^2$ by nonlinear function f:

$$f : \boldsymbol{X} \to \boldsymbol{x}. \tag{4}$$

The point $\boldsymbol{x} \in C^2$ is projected by a pinhole or orthogonal camera to a point $\boldsymbol{m} \in \mathbf{R}^2$.

$$P : \boldsymbol{x} \to \boldsymbol{m}. \tag{5}$$

We assume that the parameter of the catadioptric camera system is known. As illustrated in Figure 3, locating the center of a spherical camera at the

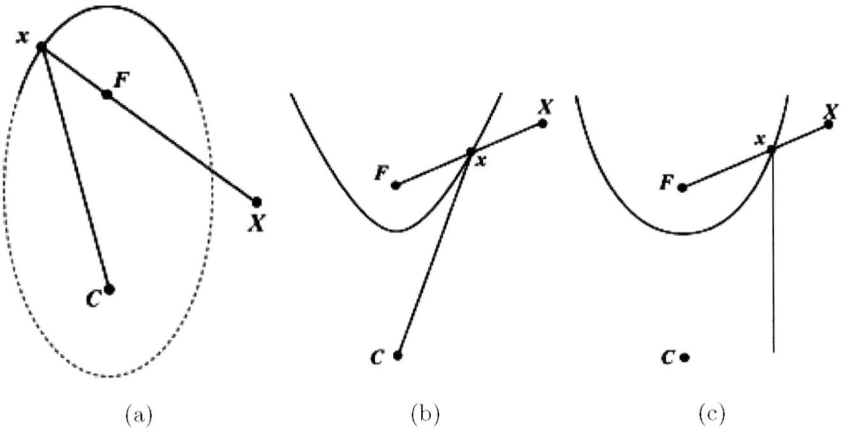

Figure 2. Transform of a point in space to a point on a quadric mirror.

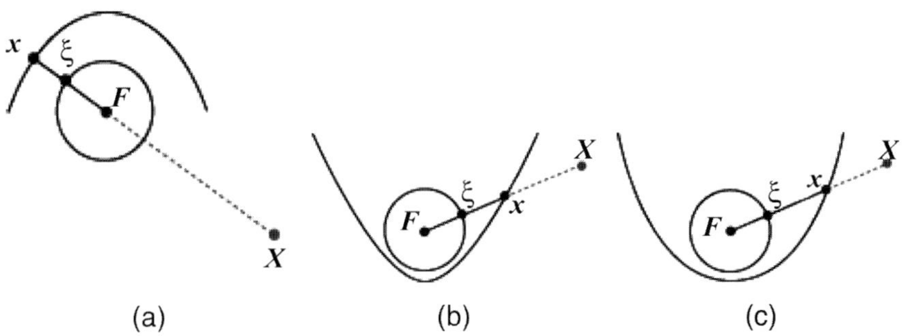

Figure 3. Transform of a point on a quadric mirror to a point on a unit sphere.

focal point of the quadric surface, a nonlinear function transform g a point $\boldsymbol{\xi} \in S^2$ on the unit sphere to the point $\boldsymbol{x} \in C^2$:

$$g : \boldsymbol{\xi} \rightarrow \boldsymbol{x}. \tag{6}$$

This nonlinear function is the catadioptric-to-spherical (CTS) transform.

3.1. HYPERBOLIC(PARABOLIC)-TO-SPHERICAL IMAGE TRANSFORM

In this section, we describe the practical image transform. We assume that all the parameters of catadioptric camera system are known. As illustrated in Figure 4(a), the focus of the hyperboloid (paraboloid) C^2 is located at the point $\boldsymbol{F} = (0,0,0)^\top$. The center of the pinhole camera is located at the point $\boldsymbol{C} = (0,0,-2e)$ ($\boldsymbol{C} = (0,0,-\infty)$). The hyperbolic(parabolic)-camera axis l is the line which connects $\boldsymbol{C}$ and $\boldsymbol{F}$. We set the hyperboloid (paraboloid) C^2:

$$\tilde{\boldsymbol{x}}^\top \mathbf{A}\tilde{\boldsymbol{x}} = (x,y,z,1)\begin{pmatrix} \frac{1}{a^2} & 0 & 0 & 0 \\ 0 & \frac{1}{a^2} & 0 & 0 \\ 0 & 0 & -\frac{1}{b^2} & -\frac{e}{b^2} \\ 0 & 0 & -\frac{e}{b^2} & -\frac{e^2}{b^2}+1 \end{pmatrix}\begin{pmatrix} x \\ y \\ z \\ 1 \end{pmatrix} = 0. \tag{7}$$

$$(\tilde{\boldsymbol{x}}^\top \mathbf{A}\tilde{\boldsymbol{x}} = (x,y,z,1)\begin{pmatrix} \frac{1}{4c} & 0 & 0 & 0 \\ 0 & \frac{1}{4c} & 0 & 0 \\ 0 & 0 & 0 & -1 \\ 0 & 0 & -1 & -1 \end{pmatrix}\begin{pmatrix} x \\ y \\ z \\ 1 \end{pmatrix} = 0). \tag{8}$$

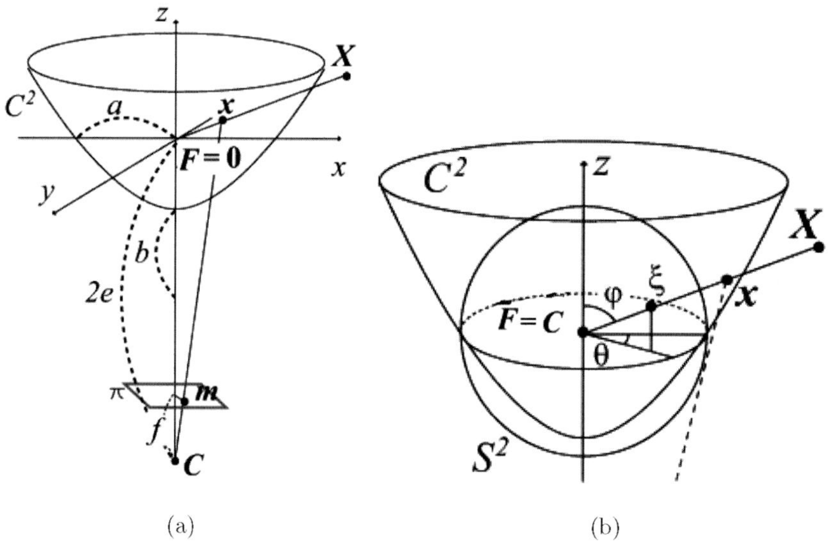

Figure 4. Transformation among hyperbolic- and spherical-camera systems. (a) illustrates a hyperbolic-camera system. The camera $\boldsymbol{C}$ generates the omnidirectional image π by the central projection, since all the rays collected to the focal point $\boldsymbol{F}$ are reflected to the single point. A point $\boldsymbol{X}$ in a space is transformed to the point $\boldsymbol{x}$ on the hyperboloid and $\boldsymbol{x}$ is transformed to the point $\boldsymbol{m}$ on image plane. (b) illustrate the geometrical configuration of hyperbolic- and spherical-camera systems. In this geometrical configuration, a point $\boldsymbol{\xi}$ on the spherical image and a point $\boldsymbol{x}$ on the hyperboloid lie on a line connecting a point $\boldsymbol{X}$ in a space and the focal point $\boldsymbol{F}$ of the hyperboloid.

where $e = \sqrt{a^2 + b^2}$ (c is the parameter of the paraboloid). We set a point $\boldsymbol{X} = (X, Y, Z)^\top$ in a space, a point on the hyperboloid (paraboloid) C^2, and $\boldsymbol{m} = (u, v)^\top$ on the image plane π. The nonlinear transform in Equation (4) is expressed as:

$$\boldsymbol{x} = \chi \boldsymbol{X}, \tag{9}$$

where

$$\chi = \frac{\pm a^2}{b|\boldsymbol{X}| \mp eZ} \qquad (\chi = \frac{2c}{|\boldsymbol{X}| - Z}). \tag{10}$$

The projection in Equation (5) is expressed as:

$$\begin{pmatrix} \boldsymbol{m} \\ 1 \end{pmatrix} = \frac{1}{z + 2e} \begin{pmatrix} f & 0 & 0 & 0 \\ 0 & f & 0 & 0 \\ 0 & 0 & 1 & 0 \end{pmatrix} \begin{pmatrix} \boldsymbol{x} \\ 1 \end{pmatrix} \tag{11}$$

$$\left(\begin{pmatrix} \boldsymbol{m} \\ 1 \end{pmatrix} = \begin{pmatrix} 1 & 0 & 0 & 0 \\ 0 & 1 & 0 & 0 \\ 0 & 0 & 0 & 1 \end{pmatrix} \begin{pmatrix} \boldsymbol{x} \\ 1 \end{pmatrix} \right). \tag{12}$$

Accordingly, a point $\boldsymbol{X} = (X, Y, Z)^\top$ in a space is transformed to the point $\boldsymbol{m}$ as

$$u = \frac{fa^2 X}{(a^2 \mp 2e^2)Z \pm 2be|\boldsymbol{X}|} \qquad (u = \frac{2cX}{|\boldsymbol{X}| - Z}), \tag{13}$$

$$v = \frac{fa^2 Y}{(a^2 \mp 2e^2)Z \pm 2be|\boldsymbol{X}|} \qquad (v = \frac{2cY}{|\boldsymbol{X}| - Z}). \tag{14}$$

For the next step, we show the hyperbolic-to-spherical (parabolic-to-spherical) image transform. As illustrated in Figure 4 (b) (Figure 5 (b)), Setting $\boldsymbol{\xi} = (\xi_x, \xi_y, \xi_z)$ to be the point on a sphere, the spherical-camera center $\boldsymbol{C}_s$ and the the focal point $\boldsymbol{F}$ of the hyperboloid (paraboloid) C^2 are $\boldsymbol{C}_s = \boldsymbol{F} = \boldsymbol{0}$. (Therefore, $\boldsymbol{q} = \boldsymbol{0}$ in Equation (31).) Furthermore, $\boldsymbol{l}_s$ denotes the axis connecting $\boldsymbol{C}_s$ and north pole of the spherical surface. For the axis $\boldsymbol{l}_s$ and the hyperbolic-camera (parabolic-camera) axis $\boldsymbol{l}$ we set $\boldsymbol{l}_s = \boldsymbol{l} = k(0, 0, 1)^\top$ for $k \in \mathbf{R}$, that is, the directions of $\boldsymbol{l}_s$ and $\boldsymbol{l}$ are the direction of the z axis. For the configuration of the spherical camera and the hyperbolic (parabolic) camera which share axes $\boldsymbol{l}_s$ and $\boldsymbol{l}$ as illustrated in Figure 4(b) (Figure 5(b)), the nonlinear function in Equation (6) is expressed as:

$$\boldsymbol{x} = \mu \boldsymbol{\xi}, \tag{15}$$

where

$$\mu = \frac{\pm a^2}{b \mp e\xi_z} \qquad (\mu = \frac{2c}{1 - \xi_z}). \tag{16}$$

Applying the spherical coordinate systems, the point $\boldsymbol{m}$ on the hyperbolic (parabolic) image and the point $\boldsymbol{\xi}$ on the sphere derives the equations:

$$u = \frac{fa^2 \cos\theta \sin\varphi}{(a^2 \mp 2e^2)\cos\varphi \pm 2be} \quad (u = 2c\cos\theta\cot(\frac{\varphi}{2})), \tag{17}$$

$$v = \frac{fa^2 \sin\theta \sin\varphi}{(a^2 \mp 2e^2)\cos\varphi \pm 2be} \quad (v = 2c\sin\theta\cot(\frac{\varphi}{2})). \tag{18}$$

Setting $I(u,v)$ and $I_S(\theta,\varphi)$ to be the hyperbolic (parabolic) image and the spherical image, respectively, the hyperbolic(parabolic)-to-spherical image transform is expressed as follows:

$$I_S(\theta,\varphi) = I(\frac{fa^2 \cos\theta \sin\varphi}{(a^2 \mp 2e^2)\cos\varphi \pm 2be}, \frac{fa^2 \sin\theta \sin\varphi}{(a^2 \mp 2e^2)\cos\varphi \pm 2be}) \tag{19}$$

$$(I_S(\theta,\varphi) = I(2c\cos\theta\cot(\frac{\varphi}{2}), 2c\sin\theta\cot(\frac{\varphi}{2})), \tag{20}$$

for $I(u,v)$ which is the image of the hyperbolic- (parabolic) camera.

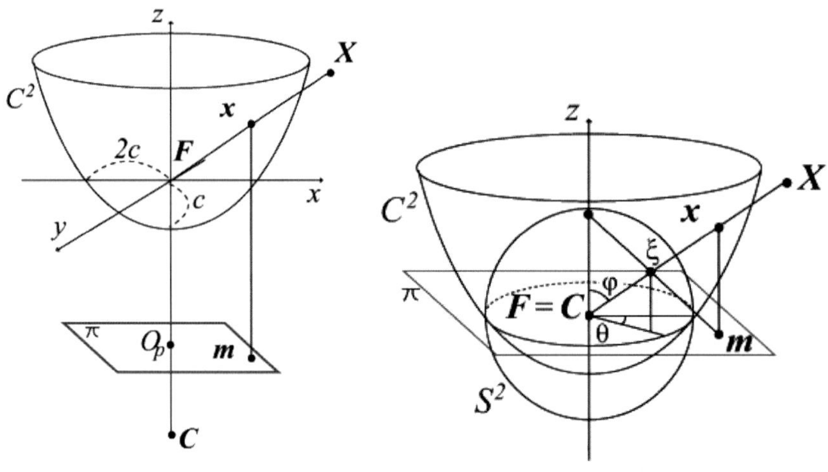

(a) (b)

Figure 5. Transformation among parabolic- and spherical-camera systems. (a) illustrates a parabolic-camera system. The camera $\boldsymbol{C}$ generates the omnidirectional image π by the orthogonal projection, since all the rays collected to the focal point $\boldsymbol{F}$ are orthogonally reflected to the imaging plane. A point $\boldsymbol{X}$ in a space is transformed to the point $\boldsymbol{x}$ on the paraboloid and $\boldsymbol{x}$ is transformed to the point $\boldsymbol{m}$ on image plane. (b) illustrate the geometrical configuration of parabolic- and spherical-camera systems. In this geometrical configuration, a point $\boldsymbol{\xi}$ on the spherical image and a point $\boldsymbol{x}$ on the paraboloid lie on a line connecting a point $\boldsymbol{X}$ in a space and the focal point $\boldsymbol{F}$ of the paraboloid.

3.2. ELLIPTIC-TO-SPHERICAL TRANSFORM

We set that the focus of the ellipsoid C^2 is located at the point $\boldsymbol{F} = (0,0,0)^\top$. The center of the pinhole camera is located at the point $\boldsymbol{C} = (0,0,-2e)$. The elliptic-camera axis l is the line which connects $\boldsymbol{C}$ and $\boldsymbol{F}$. We set the hyperboloid S:

$$\tilde{\boldsymbol{x}}^\top \mathbf{A}\tilde{\boldsymbol{x}} = (x,y,z,1)\begin{pmatrix} \frac{1}{a^2} & 0 & 0 & 0 \\ 0 & \frac{1}{a^2} & 0 & 0 \\ 0 & 0 & \frac{1}{b^2} & -\frac{e}{b^2} \\ 0 & 0 & -\frac{e}{b^2} & \frac{e^2}{b^2} - 1 \end{pmatrix}\begin{pmatrix} x \\ y \\ z \\ 1 \end{pmatrix} = 0 \qquad (21)$$

where $e = \sqrt{b^2 - a^2}$. Employing the same strategy for the hyperbolic-to-spherical image transform, the elliptic image $I(u,v)$ and the spherical image $I_S(\theta,\varphi)$ satisfy the equation

$$I_S(\theta,\varphi) = I(\frac{fa^2\cos\theta\sin\varphi}{(a^2 \pm 2e^2)\cos\varphi \pm 2be}, \frac{fa^2\sin\theta\sin\varphi}{(a^2 \pm 2e^2)\cos\varphi \pm 2be}). \qquad (22)$$

3.3. A UNIFIED FORMULATION OF CTS TRANSFORM

We express quadric surfaces in the homogeneous form as:

$$\tilde{\boldsymbol{x}}^\top \mathbf{A}\tilde{\boldsymbol{x}} = 0, \qquad (23)$$

where

$$\tilde{\boldsymbol{x}} = (x,y,z,1)^\top, \qquad (24)$$

and

$$\mathbf{A} = \{a_{ij}\}, i,j = 1,2,3,4. \qquad (25)$$

The matrix $\mathbf{A}$ satisfies the relation

$$\mathbf{A}^\top = \mathbf{A}. \qquad (26)$$

A quadric surface is also expressed as:

$$\boldsymbol{x}^\top \mathbf{A}_0\boldsymbol{x} + 2\boldsymbol{b}^\top\boldsymbol{x} + a_{44} = 0, \qquad (27)$$

where

$$\boldsymbol{x} = (x,y,z)^\top, \qquad (28)$$

$$\mathbf{A}_0 = \{a_{ij}\}, i,j = 1,2,3, \qquad (29)$$

and

$$\boldsymbol{b} = (a_{41}, a_{42}, a_{43})^{\top}. \tag{30}$$

The eigenvalues λ_m and σ_n, for $m = 1, 2, 3, 4$ and $n = 1, 2, 3$, of the matrix $\mathbf{A}$ and $\mathbf{A}_0$, respectively.

THEOREM 1. *If λ_m and σ_n satisfy the two conditions, the quadric surface represent the revolution surface of quadratic curve, that is, a ellipsoid of revolution, a hyperboloid of two sheets, a paraboloid of revolution. One is that the signs of λ_i are three positives and one negative, and vice versa. The other is $\sigma_1 = \sigma_2$ and $\sigma_3 \in \mathbf{R}$.*

A quadric surfaces, which satisfy Theorem 1, has two focal points. If we can locate a focal point of quadric mirror at one focal point and a center of camera at the other focal point, all the rays reflected on the quadric mirror pass through the camera center. (In case of $\sigma_3 = 0$, a camera center is the point at infinity. The projection becomes orthogonal.) Furthermore, locating the center of sphere at the focus of quadric mirror, all the rays, which pass through the focus of quadric mirror and the sphere, are identical. Therefore, the nonlinear transform g in Equation (6) is expressed as:

$$\boldsymbol{x} = \mu \boldsymbol{p} + \boldsymbol{q}, \tag{31}$$

where $\boldsymbol{p} = \boldsymbol{\xi}$ and $\boldsymbol{q}$ is the focal point of the quadric mirror, and

$$\mu = \frac{-\beta \pm \sqrt{\beta^2 - \alpha\gamma}}{\alpha}, \tag{32}$$

where

$$\alpha = \sum_{j=1}^{4} \sum_{i=1}^{4} p_j a_{ij} p_i,$$

$$\beta = \sum_{j=1}^{4} \sum_{i=1}^{4} p_j a_{ij} q_i,$$

$$\gamma = \sum_{j=1}^{4} \sum_{i=1}^{4} q_j a_{ij} q_i,$$

and $p_4 = 0$ and $q_4 = 1$. The sign of μ depends on the geometrical configuration of the surface and ray.

4. Applications of Spherical Camera Model

4.1. LINE RECONSTRUCTION IN SPACE

As illustrated in Figure 6, we set a spherical camera center $\boldsymbol{C}$ at the origin of the world coordinate system. In the spherical camera system, a line $\boldsymbol{L}$ is always projected to a great circle $\boldsymbol{r}$ by the intersection of the plane π and the sphere S^2. If the normal vector $\boldsymbol{n} = (n_1, n_2, n_3)^\top$ of π satisfies

$$n_1^2 + n_2^2 + n_3^2 = 1, \tag{33}$$

$$\boldsymbol{n}^\top \boldsymbol{X} = 0 \tag{34}$$

expresses the great circle $\boldsymbol{r}$ on the sphere S^2.

The dual space of S^2 is S^2, we denote the dual of S^2 as S^{2*}. The dual vector of $\boldsymbol{n} \in S^2$ is $\boldsymbol{n}^* \in S^{2*}$ such that

$$\boldsymbol{n}^\top \boldsymbol{n}^* = 0. \tag{35}$$

A vector on S^2 defines a great circle corresponded to $\boldsymbol{n}$, we express the great circle as $\boldsymbol{n}^*$. Therefore, voting the vector $\boldsymbol{n}^*$ in S^{2*}, we can estimate the great circle on S^2 as illustrated in Figure 7. Equivalently, voting $\boldsymbol{n}_{ij}^* = \boldsymbol{n}_i \times \boldsymbol{n}_j$ to S^{2*}, we can estimate a great circle in S^2 due to select the peak in S^{2*} as illustrated in Figure 8.

As illustrated in Figure 9, the centers of three spherical cameras are located at $\boldsymbol{C}_a = \boldsymbol{0}$, $\boldsymbol{C}_b = \boldsymbol{t}_b$ and $\boldsymbol{C}_c = \boldsymbol{t}_c$. We assume that the rotation

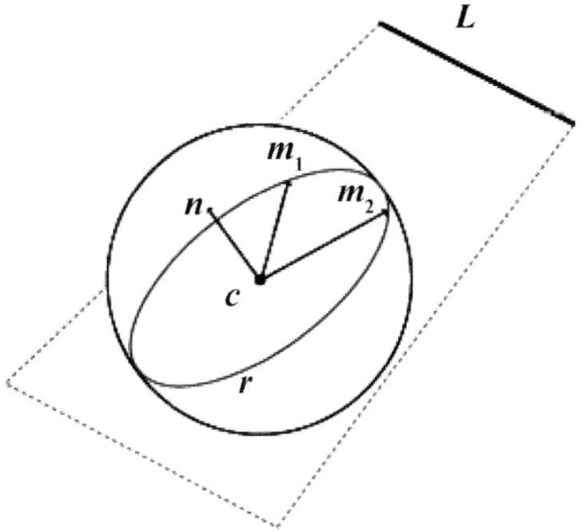

Figure 6. A line in a space and a spherical image. A line in a space is always projected to a great circle on a spherical image as the intersection of the plane π and the sphere S^2.

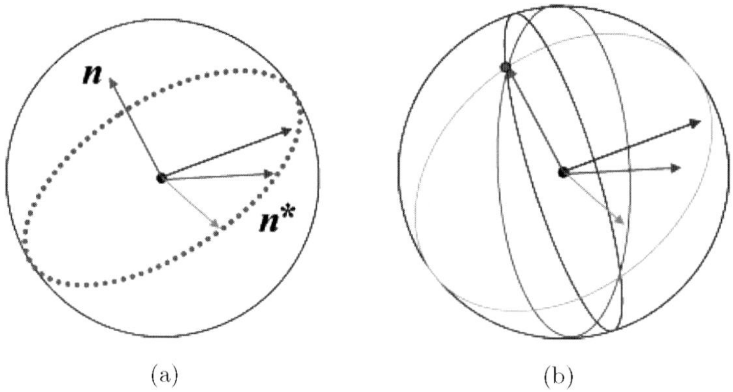

Figure 7. Estimation of a great circle on a spherical image by Hough Transform.

R_b, and R_c among these cameras and the world coordinate system are calibrated. Employing the random Hough transform, we obtain three normal vectors $\boldsymbol{n}_a$, $\boldsymbol{n}_b$, and $\boldsymbol{n}_c$, that is, great circles $\boldsymbol{r}_a$ on S_a, $\boldsymbol{r}_b$ on S_b, and $\boldsymbol{r}_c$ on S_c. Simultaneously, we obtain three planes in a space. The intersection of the three planes yields the line in a space as follows.

$$\boldsymbol{n}_a^\top(\boldsymbol{X}) = 0, \tag{36}$$
$$(R_b\boldsymbol{n}_b)^\top(\boldsymbol{X} - \boldsymbol{t}_b) = 0, \tag{37}$$
$$(R_c\boldsymbol{n}_c)^\top(\boldsymbol{X} - \boldsymbol{t}_c) = 0. \tag{38}$$

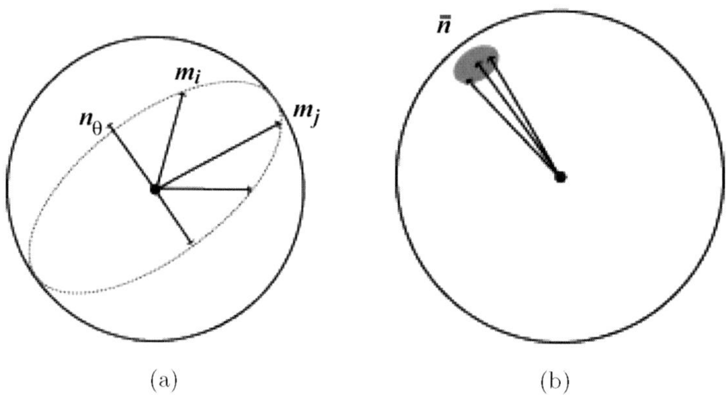

Figure 8. Estimation of a great circle on a spherical image by random Hough Transform.

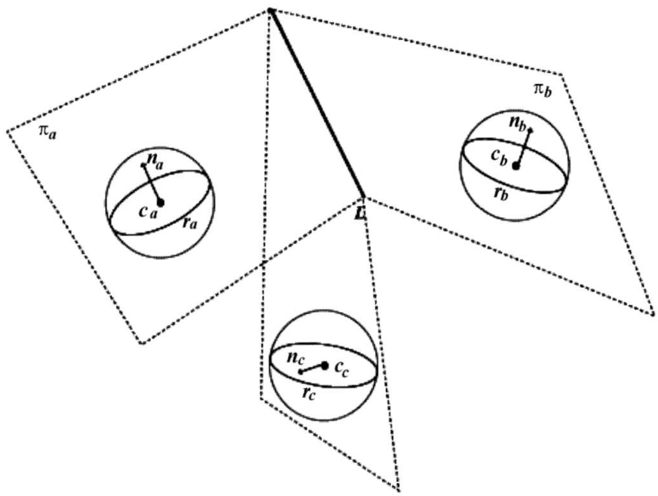

(a)

Figure 9. Reconstruction of a line in a space using three spherical cameras. If the three planes, which are yielded by the great circles, intersect at a single line in a space, then, we have a collect circle-correspondence-triplet.

By employing homogeneous coordinates, these equations are expressed as

$$\mathbf{M}\tilde{\boldsymbol{X}} = \mathbf{0}, \tag{39}$$

where

$$\mathbf{M} = \begin{pmatrix} \boldsymbol{n}_a & R_b\boldsymbol{n}_b & R_c\boldsymbol{n}_c \\ 0 & -(R_b\boldsymbol{n}_b)^\top\boldsymbol{t}_b & -(R_c\boldsymbol{n}_c)^\top\boldsymbol{t}_c \end{pmatrix}^\top \tag{40}$$

If the circles corresponds to the line $\boldsymbol{L}$, the rank of $\mathbf{M}$ equals to two. Therefore, these relations are the constraint for a line reconstruction employing three spherical cameras.

4.2. THREE-DIMENSIONAL RECONSTRUCTION USING FOUR SPHERICAL CAMERAS

We proposed the efficient geometrical configurations of panoramic (omnidirectional) cameras (Torii et al., 2003) for the reconstruction of points in a space. In this section, we extend the idea for four spherical cameras.

We consider the practical imaging region observed by the transformed two spherical cameras which are configurated parallel axially, single axially and oblique axially. The parallel-axial and the single-axial stereo cameras yield images which have a large feasible region compared with the oblique-axial stereo ones. Therefore, for the geometric configuration of four panorama cameras, we assume that the four panorama-camera centers are on the corners of a square vertical to a horizontal plane. Furthermore, all of the camera axes are parallel.

Therefore, the panorama-camera centers are $\boldsymbol{C}_a = (t_x, t_y, t_z)^\top$, $\boldsymbol{C}_b = (t_x, t_y, -t_z)^\top$, $\boldsymbol{C}_c = (-t_x, -t_y, t_z)^\top$ and $\boldsymbol{C}_d = (-t_x, -t_y, -t_z)^\top$. This configuration is illustrated in Figure 10. Since the epipoles exist on the panorama images and correspond to the camera axes, this camera configuration permits us to eliminate the rotation between the camera coordinate and the world coordinate systems.

For a point $\boldsymbol{X}$, the projections of the point $\boldsymbol{X}$ to cameras $\boldsymbol{C}_a$, $\boldsymbol{C}_b$, $\boldsymbol{C}_c$ and $\boldsymbol{C}_d$ are $\boldsymbol{x}_a = (\cos\theta, \sin\theta, \tan a)^\top$, $\boldsymbol{x}_b = (\cos\theta, \sin\theta, \tan b)^\top$, $\boldsymbol{x}_c = (\cos\omega, \sin\omega, \tan c)^\top$ and $\boldsymbol{x}_d = (\cos\omega, \sin\omega, \tan d)^\top$, respectively, on the cylindrical-image surfaces. These four points are the corresponding-point quadruplet. The points $\boldsymbol{x}_a$, $\boldsymbol{x}_b$, $\boldsymbol{x}_c$ and $\boldsymbol{x}_d$ are transformed to $\boldsymbol{p}_a = (\theta, a)^\top$, $\boldsymbol{p}_b = (\theta, b)^\top$, $\boldsymbol{p}_c = (\omega, c)^\top$ and $\boldsymbol{p}_d = (\omega, d)^\top$, respectively, on the rectangular panoramic images. The corresponding-point quadruplet yields six epipolar planes. Using homogeneous coordinate systems, we represent $\boldsymbol{X}$ as $\boldsymbol{\xi} = (X, Y, Z, 1)^\top$. Here, these six epipolar planes are formulated as $\mathbf{M}\boldsymbol{\xi} = 0$,

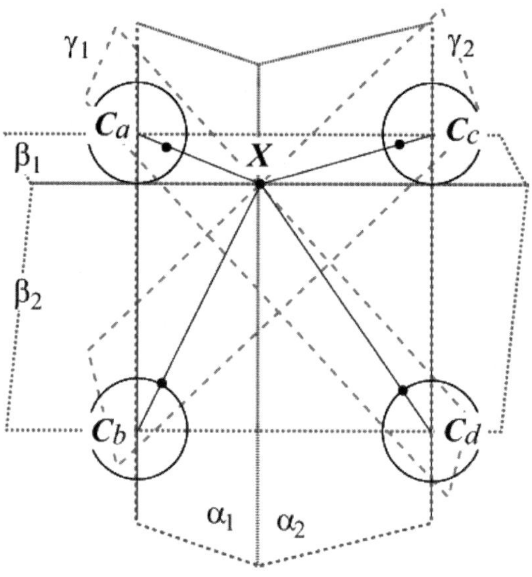

Figure 10. The four spherical-camera system. A corresponding-point quadruplet yields six epipolar plane. It is possible to reconstruct a point in a space using the six epipolar planes. Furthermore, using the six epipolar planes, we can derive a numerically stable region for the reconstruction of a point in a space.

where $\mathbf{M} = (\boldsymbol{m}_1, \boldsymbol{m}_2, \boldsymbol{m}_3, \boldsymbol{m}_4, \boldsymbol{m}_5, \boldsymbol{m}_6)^\top$,

$$\boldsymbol{m}_1 = \begin{pmatrix} \sin\theta \\ -\cos\theta \\ 0 \\ -\sin\theta t_x + \cos\theta t_y \end{pmatrix},$$

$$\boldsymbol{m}_2 = \begin{pmatrix} \sin\omega \\ -\cos\omega \\ 0 \\ \sin\omega t_x \ - \cos\omega t_y \end{pmatrix},$$

$$\boldsymbol{m}_3 = \begin{pmatrix} \tan c \sin\theta - \tan a \sin\omega \\ \tan a \cos\omega - \tan c \cos\theta \\ \sin(\omega - \theta) \\ -\sin(\omega - \theta) t_z \end{pmatrix},$$

$$\boldsymbol{m}_4 = \begin{pmatrix} \tan d \sin\theta - \tan b \sin\omega \\ \tan b \cos\omega - \tan d \cos\theta \\ \sin(\omega - \theta) \\ \sin(\omega - \theta) t_z) \end{pmatrix},$$

$$\boldsymbol{m}_5 = \begin{pmatrix} \tan d \sin\theta - \tan a \sin\omega \\ \tan a \cos\omega - \tan d \cos\theta \\ \sin(\omega - \theta) \\ 0 \end{pmatrix},$$

and

$$\boldsymbol{m}_6 = \begin{pmatrix} \tan c \sin\theta - \tan b \sin\omega \\ \tan b \cos\omega - \tan c \cos\theta \\ \sin(\omega - \theta) \\ 0 \end{pmatrix}.$$

Since these six planes intersect at the point $\boldsymbol{X}$ in a space, the rank of the matrix $\mathbf{M}$ is three. Therefore, the matrix $\mathbf{M}_R$,

$$\mathbf{M}_R = \begin{pmatrix} m_{i1} & m_{i2} & m_{i3} & m_{i4} \\ m_{j1} & m_{j2} & m_{j3} & m_{j4} \\ m_{k1} & m_{k2} & m_{k3} & m_{k4} \end{pmatrix} = \begin{pmatrix} \boldsymbol{m}_i^\top \\ \boldsymbol{m}_j^\top \\ \boldsymbol{m}_k^\top \end{pmatrix}, \tag{41}$$

is constructed from three row vectors of the matrix $\mathbf{M}$. If and only if the rank of the matrix $\mathbf{M}_R$ is three, $\mathbf{M}_R$ satisfies the equation $\mathbf{M}_R\boldsymbol{\xi} = 0$. The point $\boldsymbol{X}$ is derived by the equation

$$\boldsymbol{X} = \bar{\mathbf{M}}^{-1}\boldsymbol{m}_4 \tag{42}$$

where

$$\bar{\mathbf{M}} = \begin{pmatrix} m_{i1} & m_{i2} & m_{i3} \\ m_{j1} & m_{j2} & m_{j3} \\ m_{k1} & m_{k2} & m_{k3} \end{pmatrix}, \ \bar{\boldsymbol{m}}_4 = \begin{pmatrix} -m_{i4} \\ -m_{j4} \\ -m_{k4} \end{pmatrix}. \tag{43}$$

Equation (42) enable us to reconstruct the point $\boldsymbol{X}$ uniquely from any three row vectors selected from the matrix $\mathbf{M}$.

5. Discussions and Concluding Remarks

DEFINITION 1. *Convex Cone in* $\mathbf{R}^n$*; Let* $\mathcal{M}$ *to be a closed finite convex body in* $\mathbf{R}^{n-1}$*. We set* $\mathcal{M}\boldsymbol{a} = \mathcal{M} + \boldsymbol{a}$ *for* $\boldsymbol{a} \in \mathbf{R}^n$*. (It is possible to set* $\boldsymbol{a} = \lambda \boldsymbol{e}_i$*.) For* $\boldsymbol{x} \in \mathcal{M}\boldsymbol{a}$*,*

$$C(\mathcal{M}, \boldsymbol{a}) = \{\boldsymbol{x} \mid \boldsymbol{x} = \lambda \boldsymbol{y}, \ {}^{\forall}\lambda \in \mathbf{R}, \ \boldsymbol{y} \in \mathcal{M}\boldsymbol{a}\} \tag{44}$$

is the convex cone in $\mathbf{R}^n$*.*

Figure 11 illustrates a convex cone in $\mathbf{R}^n$.

DEFINITION 2. *Conic Surface in* $\mathbf{R}^{n-1}$*; Let* $\mathcal{L}$ *to be a linear manifold in* $\mathbf{R}^n$*, that is,*

$$\mathcal{L} = \mathcal{P} + \boldsymbol{b} \tag{45}$$

for $\boldsymbol{b} \in \mathbf{R}^n$ *and* $\mathcal{P}$ *is a* $n-1$ *dimensional linear subspace in* $\mathbf{R}^n$*.*

$$\mathcal{L} \cap C(\mathcal{M}, \boldsymbol{a}) \tag{46}$$

is a conic surface in $\mathbf{R}^{n-1}$*.*

For $n = 3$ and $\mathcal{M} = S$, $\mathcal{L} \cap C(\mathcal{M}, \boldsymbol{a})$ is a planar conic. This geometrical property derives the following relations.

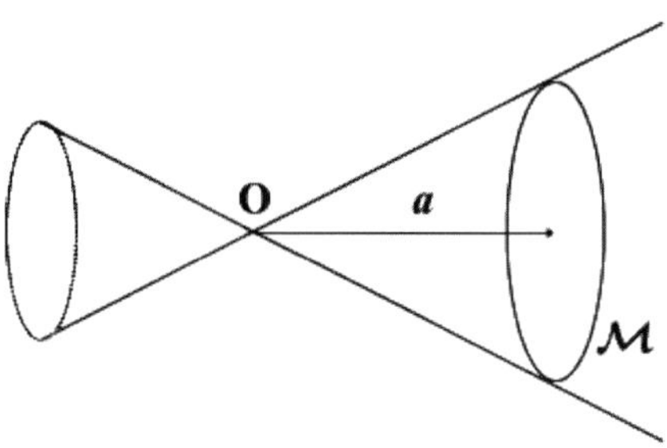

(a)

Figure 11. Definition of a convex cone in $\mathbf{R}^n$.

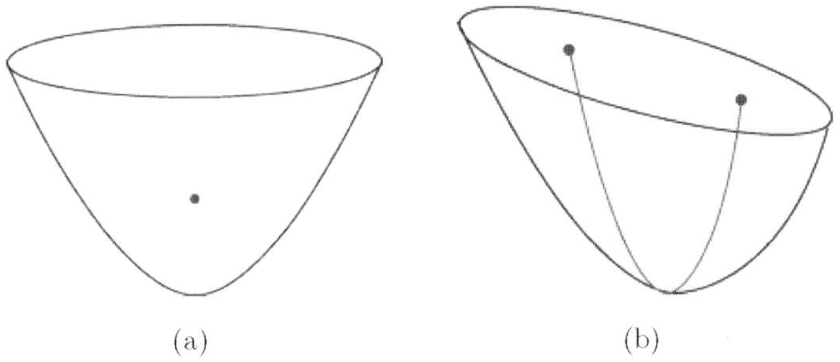

Figure 12. Central and non-central catadioptric cameras. It is possible to classify non-central cameras in two classes. One has a focal line as illustrated in (b) and the other has a focal surface (ruled surface).

1. For $n = 4$ and $\mathcal{M} = S^2$, we have a conic surface of revolution.
2. For $n = 4$ and $\mathcal{M} = \mathcal{E}^2(ellipsoid)$ in $\mathbf{R}^2$, we have an ellipsoid of revolution.

For the cone in the class (ii), it is possible to transform ellipsoid $\mathcal{E}^2$ to S^2. Therefore, vectors on $\mathcal{L} \cap C(\mathcal{M}, \boldsymbol{a})$ is equivalent to vectors on S^{n-1}. This geometrical property leads that images observed through a catadioptric camera system with quadric mirror is equivalent to images on the sphere.

Catadioptric camera systems are classified into central and non-central cameras depending on the shape of mirrors. Our observation using the cone intersection in $\mathbf{R}^n$ leads that it is possible to classify non-central catadioptric cameras into two classes. One has a focal line and the other has a focal surface (ruled surface).

Acknowledgments

This work is in part supported by Grant-in-Aid for Scientific Research of the Ministry of Education, Culture, Sports, Science and Technology of Japan under the contract of 14380161 and 16650040. The final manuscript prepared while the first author was at CMP at CTU in Prague. He expresses great thanks to the hospitality of Prof. V. Hlaváč and Dr. T. Pajdla.

References

Svoboda, T., Pajdla, T., and Hlaváč, V.: Epipolar geometry of panoramic cameras. In Proc. *ECCV*, Volume A, pages 218–231, 1998

Dahmen, H. -J., Franz, M. O., and Krapp, H. G.: Extracting egomotion from optic flow: limits of accuracy and neural matched filters. In *Motion vision: computational, neural and ecological constraints* (J.M. Zanker and J. Zeil, editors), pages 143–168, Springer, Berlin, 2001.

Vassallo, R. F., Victor, J. S., and Schneebeli, H. J.: A general approach for egomotion estimation with omnidirectional images. In Proc. *OMNIVIS*. pages 97-103, 2002.

Makadia, A. and Daniilidis, K.: Direct 3D-rotation estimation from spherical images via a generalized shift theorem. In Proc. *CVPR*, Volume 2, pages 217-224, 2003.

Nayar, S. K.: Catadioptric omnidirectional camera. In Proc. *CVPR*, pages 482–488, 1997.

Baker, S. and Nayar, S. K.: A theory of catadioptric image formation. In Proc. *ICCV*, pages 35-42, 1998.

Berger, M.: *Geometry I & II*. Springer, 1987.

Pearson, F.: *Map Projections: Theory and Applications*. CRC Press, 1990.

Yang, Q., Snyder, J. P., and Tobler, W. R.: *Map Projection Transformation: Principles and Applications*. Taylor & Francis, 2000.

Daniilidis, K., Makadia, A., and Bülow, T.: Image processing in catadioptric planes: spatiotemporal derivatives and optical flow computation. In Proc. *OMNIVIS*, pages 3–10, 2002.

Barreto, J. P. and Daniilidis, K.: Unifying image plane liftings for central catadioptric and dioptric cameras. In Proc. *OMNIVIS*, pages 151–162, 2004.

Ying, X. and Hu, Z.: Can we consider central catadioptric cameras and fisheye cameras within a unified model. In Proc. *ECCV*, LNCS 3021, pages 442–455, 2004.

Corrochano, E. B-. and Fraco, C. L-.: Omnidirectional vision: unified model using conformal geometry. In Proc. *ECCV*, LNCS 3021, pages 536–548, 2004.

Geyer, C. and Daniilidis, K. Catadioptric projective geometry. *Int. J. Computer Vision*, **43**: 223–243, 2001.

Torii, A., Sugimoto, A., Imiya, A. Mathematics of a multiple omni-directional system. In Proc. *OMNIVIS*, CD-ROM, 2003.

UNIFYING IMAGE PLANE LIFTINGS FOR CENTRAL CATADIOPTRIC AND DIOPTRIC CAMERAS

JOÃO P. BARRETO
Institute of Systems and Robotics
Dept. of Electrical and Computer Engineering
Faculty of Sciences and Technology, University of Coimbra
3030 Coimbra, Portugal

Abstract. In this paper, we study projection systems with a single viewpoint, including combinations of mirrors and lenses (catadioptric) as well as just lenses with or without radial distortion (dioptric systems). Firstly, we extend a well-known unifying model for catadioptric systems to incorporate a class of dioptric systems with radial distortion. Secondly, we provide a new representation for the image planes of central systems. This representation is the lifting through a Veronese map of the original image plane to the 5D projective space. We study how a collineation in the original image plane can be transferred to a collineation in the lifted space and we find that the locus of the lifted points which correspond to projections of world lines is a plane in parabolic catadioptric systems and a hyperplane in case of radial lens distortion.

Key words: central catadioptric cameras, radial distortion, lifting of coordinates, Veronese maps

1. Introduction

A vision system has a single viewpoint if it measures the intensity of light traveling along rays which intersect in a single point in 3D (the projection center). Vision systems satisfying the single viewpoint constraint are called central projection systems. The perspective camera is an example of a central projection system. The mapping of points in the scene into points in the image is linear in homogeneous coordinates, and can be described by a 3×4 projection matrix $\mathbf{P}$ (pin-hole model). Perspective projection can be modeled by intersecting a plane with a pencil of lines going through the scene points and the projection center $\mathbf{O}$.

There are central projection systems whose geometry can not be described using the conventional pin-hole model. In (Baker and Nayar, 1998)

K. Daniilidis and R. Klette (eds.), Imaging Beyond the Pinhole Camera, 21–38.

Baker et al., derive the entire class of catadioptric systems verifying the single viewpoint constraint. Sensors with a wide field of view and a unique projection center can be built by combining a hyperbolic mirror with a perspective camera, and a parabolic mirror with an orthographic camera (paracatadioptric system). However the mapping between points in the 3D world and points in the image is non-linear. In (Svoboda and Pajdla, 2002) it is shown that in general the central catadioptric projection of a line is a conic section. A unifying theory for central catadioptric systems has been proposed in (Geyer and Daniilidis, 2000). It is proved that central catadioptric image formation is equivalent to a projective mapping from a sphere to a plane with a projection center on a sphere axis perpendicular to the plane. Perspective cameras with non-linear lens distortion are another example of central projection systems where the relation in homogeneous coordinates between scene points and image points is no longer linear. True lens distortion curves are typically very complex and higher-order models are introduced to approximate the distortion during calibration (Brown, 1966; Willson and Shaffer, 1993). However, simpler low-order models can be used for many computer vision applications where an accuracy in the order of a pixel is sufficient. In this chapter the radial lens distortion is modeled after the division model proposed in (Fitzgibbon, 2001). The division model is not an approximation to the classical model in (Brown, 1966), but a different approximation to the true curve. In this chapter, we present two main novel results:

1. The unifying model of central catadioptric systems proposed (Geyer and Daniilidis, 2000) can be extended to include radial distortions. It is proved, that the projection in perspective cameras with radial distortion is equivalent to a projective mapping from a paraboloid to a plane, orthogonal to the paraboloid's axis, and with projection center in the vertex of the paraboloid. It is also shown that, assuming the division model, the image of a line is in general a conic curve.

2. For both catadioptric and radially distorted dioptric systems, we establish a new representation through lifting of the image plane to a five-dimensional projective space. In this lifted space, a collineation in the original plane corresponds to a collineation of the lifted points. We know that world line project to conic sections whose representatives in the lifted space lie on a quadric. We prove that in the cases of parabolic catadioptric projection and radial lens distortion this quadric degenerates to a hyperplane.

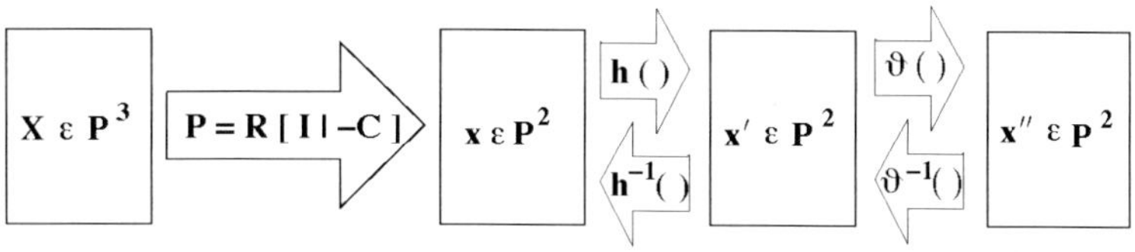

Figure 1. Steps of the unifying image formation model. The 3D point $\mathbf{X}$ is projected into point $\mathbf{x} = \mathbf{PX}$ assuming the conventional pin-hole model. To each point $\mathbf{x}$ corresponds an intermediate point $\mathbf{x}'$ which is mapped in the final image plane by function $\eth$. Depending on the sensor type, functions $\hbar$ and $\eth$ can represent a linear transformation or a non-linear mapping (see Table I).

2. A Unifying Model for Perspective Cameras, Central Catadioptric Systems, and Lenses with Radial Distortion

In (Geyer and Daniilidis, 2000), a unifying model for all central catadioptric systems is proposed where conventional perspective imaging appears as a particular case. This section reviews this image formation model as well as the result that in general the catadioptric image of a line is a conic section (Svoboda and Pajdla, 2002). This framework can be easily extended to cameras with radial distortion where the division model (Fitzgibbon, 2001) is used to describe the lens distortion.

This section shows that conventional perspective cameras, central catadioptric systems, and cameras with radial distortion underly one projection model. Figure 1 is a scheme of the proposed unifying model for image formation. A point in the scene $\mathbf{X}$ is transformed into a point $\mathbf{x}$ by a conventional projection matrix $\mathbf{P}$. Vector $\mathbf{x}$ can be interpreted both as a 2D point expressed in homogeneous coordinates, and as a projective ray defined by points $\mathbf{X}$ and $\mathbf{O}$ (the projection center). Function $\hbar$ transforms $\mathbf{x}$ in the intermediate point $\mathbf{x}'$. Point $\mathbf{x}'$ is related with the final image point $\mathbf{x}''$ by function $\eth$. Both $\hbar$ and $\eth$ are transformations defined in the two dimensional oriented projective space. They can be linear or non-linear depending on the type of system, but they are always injective functions with an inverse. Table I summarizes the results derived along this section.

2.1. PERSPECTIVE CAMERA AND CENTRAL CATADIOPTRIC SYSTEMS

The image formation in central catadioptric systems can be split in three steps (Barreto and Araujo, 2005) as shown in Figure 1: world points are mapped into an oriented projective plane by a conventional 3×4 projection matrix $\mathbf{P}$; the oriented projective plane is transformed by a non-linear function $\hbar$ [see Equation (1)]; the last step is a collineation in the plane $\mathbf{H_c}$ [see Equation (2)]. In this case, the function $\eth$ is a linear transformation

Perspective Camera ($\xi = 0$, $\psi = 0$)	
$\hbar(\mathbf{x}) = (x, y, z)^t$; $\hbar^{-1}(\mathbf{x}') = (x', y', z')^t$;	$\eth(\mathbf{x}') = \mathbf{K}\mathbf{x}'$ $\eth^{-1}(\mathbf{x}'') = \mathbf{K}^{-1}\mathbf{x}''$
Hyperbolic Mirror ($0 < \xi < 1$)	
$\hbar(\mathbf{x}) = (x, y, z + \xi\sqrt{x^2 + y^2 + z^2})^t$; $\hbar^{-1}(\mathbf{x}') = (x', y', z' - \frac{(x'^2+y'^2+z'^2)\xi}{z'\xi+\sqrt{z'^2+(1-\xi^2)(x'^2+y'^2)}})^t$;	$\eth(\mathbf{x}') = \mathbf{H_c}\mathbf{x}'$ $\eth^{-1}(\mathbf{x}'') = \mathbf{H_c}^{-1}\mathbf{x}''$
Parabolic Mirror ($\xi = 1$)	
$\hbar(\mathbf{x}) = (x, y, z + \sqrt{x^2 + y^2 + z^2})^t$; $\hbar^{-1}(\mathbf{x}') = (2x'z', 2y'z', z'^2 - x'^2 - y'^2)^t$;	$\eth(\mathbf{x}') = \mathbf{H_c}\mathbf{x}'$ $\eth^{-1}(\mathbf{x}'') = \mathbf{H_c}^{-1}\mathbf{x}''$
Radial Distortion ($\xi < 0$)	
$\eth(\mathbf{x}') = (2x', 2y', z' + \sqrt{z'^2 - 4\xi(x'^2 + y'^2)})^t$, $\eth^{-1}(\mathbf{x}'') = (x''z'', y''z'', z''^2 + \xi(x''^2 + y''^2))^t$,	$\hbar(\mathbf{x}) = \mathbf{K}\mathbf{x}$ $\hbar^{-1}(\mathbf{x}') = \mathbf{K}^{-1}\mathbf{x}'$;

depending on the camera intrinsics $\mathbf{K_c}$, the relative rotation between the camera and the mirror $\mathbf{R_c}$, and the shape of the reflective surface. As discussed in (Geyer and Daniilidis, 2000; Barreto and Araujo, 2005), parameters ξ and ψ in Equations (1) and (2), only depend on the system type and shape of the mirror. For paracatadioptric systems $\xi = 1$, while in the case of conventional perspective cameras $\xi = 0$. If the mirror is hyperbolic then ξ takes values in the range $[0, 1]$.

$$\mathbf{x}' = \hbar(\mathbf{x}) = (x, y, z + \xi\sqrt{x^2 + y^2 + z^2})^t \tag{1}$$

$$\mathbf{x}'' = \underbrace{\mathbf{K}\mathbf{R_c}\begin{bmatrix} \psi - \xi & 0 & 0 \\ 0 & \xi - \psi & 0 \\ 0 & 0 & 1 \end{bmatrix}}_{\mathbf{H_c}} \hbar(\mathbf{x}) \tag{2}$$

The non-linear characteristics of the mapping are isolated in $\hbar$ which has a curious geometric interpretation. Since $\mathbf{x}'$ is a homogeneous vector representing a point in an oriented projective plane, $\lambda\mathbf{x}'$ represents the same point whenever $\lambda > 0$ (Stolfi, 1991). Assuming $\lambda = 1/\sqrt{x^2 + y^2 + z^2}$ we obtain from Equation (1) that

$$\begin{cases} x' = \frac{x}{\sqrt{x^2+y^2+z^2}} \\ y' = \frac{y}{\sqrt{x^2+y^2+z^2}} \\ z' - \xi = \frac{z}{\sqrt{x^2+y^2+z^2}} \end{cases} \tag{3}$$

Assume $\mathbf{x}$ and $\mathbf{x}'$ as projective rays defined in two different coordinates systems in $\Re^3$. The origin of the first coordinate system is the effective

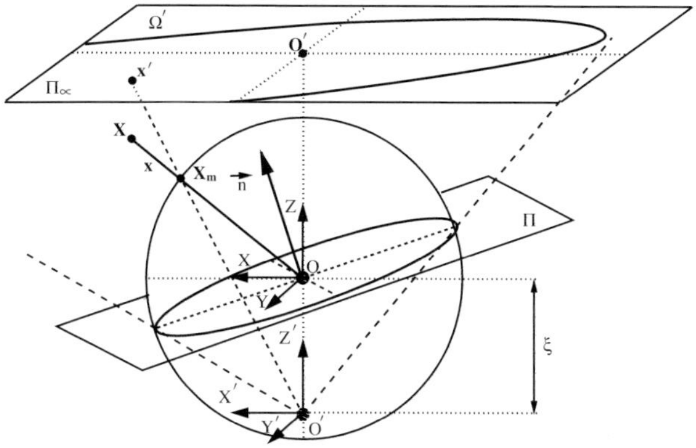

Figure 2. The sphere model for central catadioptric image formation. Projective ray $\mathbf{x}$ intersects the unitary sphere centered on the projection center $\mathbf{O}$ at point $\mathbf{X_m}$. The new projective point $\mathbf{x}'$ is defined by $\mathbf{O}'$ and $\mathbf{X_m}$. The distance between the origins $\mathbf{O}$ and $\mathbf{O}'$ is ξ which depends on the mirror shape

viewpoint $\mathbf{O}$ and $\mathbf{x}$ is a projective ray going through $\mathbf{O}$. In a similar way $\mathbf{x}'$ represents a projective ray going through the origin $\mathbf{O}'$ of the second reference frame. According to the previous equation to each ray $\mathbf{x}$ corresponds one, and only one, projective ray $\mathbf{x}'$. The correspondence is such that a pencil of projective rays $\mathbf{x}$ intersects a pencil of rays $\mathbf{x}'$ in a unit sphere centered in $\mathbf{O}$. The equation of the sphere in the coordinate system with origin in $\mathbf{O}'$ is

$$x'^2 + y'^2 + (z' - \xi)^2 = 1 \tag{4}$$

We have just derived the well known sphere model derived in (Geyer and Daniilidis, 2000) and shown in Figure 2. The homogeneous vector $\mathbf{x}$ can be interpreted as a projective ray joining a 3D point in the scene with the effective projection center $\mathbf{O}$, which intersects the unit sphere in a single point $\mathbf{X_m}$. Consider a point $\mathbf{O}'$ in $\Re^3$, with coordinates $(X, Y, Z) = (0, 0, -\xi)^t$ $(\xi \in [0, 1])$. To each $\mathbf{x}$ corresponds an oriented projective ray $\mathbf{x}'$ joining $\mathbf{O}'$ with the intersection point $\mathbf{X_m}$ in the sphere surface. The non-linear mapping $\hbar$ corresponds to projecting the scene in the unit sphere and then re-projecting the points on the sphere into a plane from a novel projection center $\mathbf{O}'$. Points in the image plane $\mathbf{x}''$ are obtained after a collineation $\mathbf{H_c}$ of the 2D projective points $\mathbf{x}'$ [see Equation (2)].

Consider a line in space lying on a plane $\mathbf{\Pi}$ with normal $\mathbf{n} = (n_x, n_y, n_z)^t$, which contains the effective viewpoint $\mathbf{O}$ (Figure 2). The 3D line is projected into a great circle on the sphere surface. The great circle is obtained by intersecting plane $\mathbf{\Pi}$ with the unit sphere. The projective rays $\mathbf{x}'$, joining $\mathbf{O}'$ with points in the great circle, form a central cone. The central cone, with vertex in $\mathbf{O}'$, projects into the conic $\mathbf{\Omega}'$ in the canonical image plane. The equation of $\mathbf{\Omega}'$ is provided in (5) and depends both on the normal $\mathbf{n}$ and

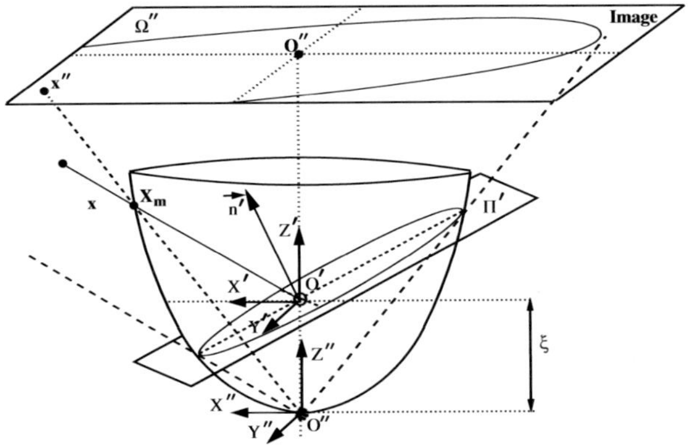

Figure 3. The paraboloid model for image formation in perspective cameras with lens with radial distortion. The division model for lens distortion is isomorphic to a projective mapping from a paraboloid to a plane with projection center on the vertex $\mathbf{O}''$. The distance between $\mathbf{O}''$ and the effective viewpoint is defined by the distortion parameter ξ

on the parameter ξ (Geyer and Daniilidis, 2000; Barreto and Araujo, 2005). The original 3D line is projected in the catadioptric image on a conic section $\mathbf{\Omega}''$, which is the projective transformation of $\mathbf{\Omega}'$ ($\mathbf{\Omega}'' = \mathbf{H_c}^{-t}\mathbf{\Omega}'\mathbf{H_c}^{-1}$) (Geyer and Daniilidis, 2000; Svoboda and Pajdla, 2002).

$$\mathbf{\Omega}' = \begin{bmatrix} n_x^2(1-\xi^2) - n_z^2\xi^2 & n_x n_y(1-\xi^2) & n_x n_z \\ n_x n_y(1-\xi^2) & n_y^2(1-\xi^2) - n_z^2\xi^2 & n_y n_z \\ n_x n_z & n_y n_z & n_z^2 \end{bmatrix} \quad (5)$$

Notice that the re-projection center $\mathbf{O}'$ depends only on mirror shape. For the case of a parabolic mirror $\mathbf{O}'$ lies in the sphere surface and the re-projection is a stereographic projection. For hyperbolic systems $\xi \in (0, 1)$ and point $\mathbf{O}'$ is inside the sphere in the negative Z-axis. The conventional perspective camera is a degenerate case of central catadioptric projection where $\xi = 0$ and $\mathbf{O}'$ is coincident with $\mathbf{O}$.

2.2. DIOPTRIC SYSTEMS WITH RADIAL DISTORTION

In perspective cameras with lens distortion the mapping between points in the scene and points in the world can no longer be described in a linear way. In this chapter the radial distortion is modeled using the so called division model (Fitzgibbon, 2001). According to the well known pin-hole model, to each point in the scene $\mathbf{X}$ corresponds a projective ray $\mathbf{x} = \mathbf{PX}$ which is transformed into a 2D projective point $\mathbf{x}' = \mathbf{Kx}$. Point $\mathbf{X}$ is projected in the image on point $\mathbf{x}''$, which is related with $\mathbf{x}'$ by a non-linear transformation that models the radial distortion. This transformation, originally introduced in (Fitzgibbon, 2001), is provided in Equation (6) where parameter ξ

quantifies the amount of radial distortion. If $\xi = 0$ then points $\mathbf{x}'$ and $\mathbf{x}''$ are the same, and the camera is modeled as a conventional pin-hole. Equation (6) corresponds to the inverse of function $\eth$ (see Figure 1), which isoates the non-linear characteristics of the mapping. In the case of dioptric systems with radial distortion function $\hbar$ is a linear transformation $\mathbf{K}$ (matrix of intrinsic parameters). Notice that the model of Equation (6) requires that points $\mathbf{x}'$ and $\mathbf{x}''$ are referenced in a coordinate system with origin in the image distortion center. If the distortion center is not known in advance, we can place it at the image center without significantly affect the correction (Willson and Shaffer, 1993).

$$\mathbf{x}' = \eth^{-1}(\mathbf{x}'') = (x''z'', y''z'', z''^2 + \xi(x''^2 + y''^2))^t \tag{6}$$

Transformation $\eth$ has a geometric interpretation similar to the sphere model derived for central catadioptric image formation. As stated $\mathbf{x}'$ and $\lambda\mathbf{x}'$ represent the same point whenever λ is a positive scalar (Stolfi, 1991). Assuming $\lambda = 1/\sqrt{x''^2 + y''^2}$ in Equation (6) yields

$$\begin{cases} x' = \frac{x''z''}{x''^2+y''^2} \\ y' = \frac{y''z''}{x''^2+y''^2} \\ z' - \xi = \frac{z''^2}{x''^2+y''^2} \, . \end{cases} \tag{7}$$

Reasoning as in the previous section, $\mathbf{x}'$ and $\mathbf{x}''$ can be interpreted as projective rays going through two distinct origins $\mathbf{O}'$ and $\mathbf{O}''$. From Equation (7) follows that the two pencils of rays intersect on a paraboloid with vertex in $\mathbf{O}''$. The equation of this paraboloid in the coordinate system attached to the origin $\mathbf{O}'$ is

$$x'^2 + y'^2 - (z' - \xi) = 0 \tag{8}$$

The scheme of Figure 3 is the equivalent to Figure 2 for the situation of lens with radial distortion. It shows an intuitive 'concrete' model for the non-linear transformation $\eth$ (Table I) based on the paraboloid derived above. Since in this case the ξ parameter is always negative (Fitzgibbon, 2001), the effective projection center $\mathbf{O}'$ lies inside the parabolic surface. The projective ray $\mathbf{x}'$ goes through the viewpoint $\mathbf{O}'$ and intersects the paraboloid at point $\mathbf{X_m}$. By joining $\mathbf{X_m}$ with the vertex $\mathbf{O}''$ we obtain the projective ray associated with the distorted image point $\mathbf{x}''$. This model is in accordance the fact that the effects of radial distortion are more noticeable in the image periphery than in the image center. Notice that the paraboloid of reference is a quadratic surface in $\wp^3$ which is tangent to the plane at infinity on point $(X', Y', Z', W')^t = (0, 0, 1, 0)^t$. If the angle between the projective ray $\mathbf{x}'$ and the Z' axis is small, then the intersection point $\mathbf{X_m}$ is close to infinity. In this case the rays associated with $\mathbf{x}'$ and $\mathbf{x}''$ are almost coincident and the effect of radial distortion can be neglected.

Consider a line in the space that, according to the conventional pinhole model, is projected into a line $\mathbf{n}' = (n'_x, n'_y, n'_z)^t$ in the projective plane. Points $\mathbf{x}'$, lying on line $\mathbf{n}'$, are transformed into image points $\mathbf{x}''$ by the non-linear function $\eth$. Since $\mathbf{n}'^t\mathbf{x}' = 0$ and $\mathbf{x}' = \eth^{-1}(\mathbf{x}'')$, then $\mathbf{n}'^t\eth^{-1}(\mathbf{x}'') = 0$. After some algebraic manipulation the previous equality can be written in the form $\mathbf{x}''^t\boldsymbol{\Omega}''\mathbf{x}'' = 0$ with $\boldsymbol{\Omega}''$ given by Equation (9). In a similar way to what happens for the central catadioptric systems, the non-linear mapping $\eth$ transforms lines $\mathbf{n}'$ into a conic sections $\boldsymbol{\Omega}''$ (see Figure 3).

$$\boldsymbol{\Omega}'' = \begin{bmatrix} \xi n'_z & 0 & \frac{n'_x}{2} \\ 0 & \xi n'_z & \frac{n'_y}{2} \\ \frac{n'_x}{2} & \frac{n'_y}{2} & n'_z \end{bmatrix} \tag{9}$$

3. Embedding $\wp^2$ into $\wp^5$ Using Veronese Maps

Perspective projection can be formulated as a transformation of $\Re^3$ into $\Re^2$. Points $\mathbf{X} = (X, Y, Z)^t$ are mapped into points $\mathbf{x} = (x, y)^t$ by a non-linear function $f(\mathbf{X}) = (X/Z, Y/Z)^t$. A standard technique used in algebra to render a nonlinear problem into a linear one is to find an embedding that lifts the problem into a higher dimensional space. For conventional cameras, the additional homogeneous coordinate linearizes the mapping function and simplifies most of the mathematic relations. In the previous section we established a unifying model that includes central catadioptric sensors and lens with radial distortion. Unfortunately the use of an additional homogeneous coordinate does no longer suffice to cope with the non-linearities in the image formation.

In this chapter, we propose the embedding of the projective plane into a higher dimensional space in order to study the geometry of general single viewpoint images in a unified framework. This idea has already been explored by other authors to solve several computer vision problems. Higher-dimensional projection matrices are proposed in (Wolf and Shashua, 2001) for the representation of various applications where the world is no longer rigid. In (Geyer and Daniilidis, 2003), lifted coordinates are used to obtain a fundamental matrix between paracatadioptric views. Sturm generalizes this framework to analyze the relations between multiple views of a static scene where the views are taken by any mixture of paracatadioptric, perspective or affine cameras (Sturm, 2002).

The present section discusses the embedding of the projective plane $\wp^2$ in $\wp^5$ [see Equation (10)] using Veronese mapping (Sample and Kneebone, 1998; Sample and Roth, 1949). This polynomial embedding preserves homogeneity and is suitable to represent quadratic relations between image points (Feldman et al., 2003; Vidal et al., 2003). Moreover there is a natural duality between lifted points $\widetilde{\mathbf{x}}$ and conics which is advantageous when dealing with catadioptric projection of lines. It is also shown that projective transformations in $\wp^2$ can be transposed to $\wp^5$ in a straightforward manner.

$$\mathbf{x} \in \wp^2 \longrightarrow \widetilde{\mathbf{x}} = (x_0, x_1, x_2, x_3, x_4, x_5)^t \in \wp^5 \tag{10}$$

3.1. LIFTING POINT COORDINATES

Consider an operator $\mathbf{\Gamma}$ which transforms two 3×1 vectors $\mathbf{x}$, $\bar{\mathbf{x}}$ into a 6×1 vector as shown in Equation (11)

$$\mathbf{\Gamma}(\mathbf{x}, \bar{\mathbf{x}}) = (x\bar{x}, \frac{x\bar{y} + y\bar{x}}{2}, y\bar{y}, \frac{x\bar{z} + z\bar{x}}{2}, \frac{y\bar{z} + z\bar{y}}{2}, z\bar{z})^t \tag{11}$$

The operator $\mathbf{\Gamma}$ can be used to map pairs of points in the projective plane $\wp^2$, with homogeneous coordinates $\mathbf{x}$ and $\bar{\mathbf{x}}$, into points in the 5D projective space $\wp^5$. To each pair of points $\mathbf{x}$, $\bar{\mathbf{x}}$ corresponds one, and only one, point $\widetilde{\mathbf{x}} = \mathbf{\Gamma}(\mathbf{x}, \bar{\mathbf{x}})$ which lies on a primal $\mathbf{S}$ called the cubic symmetroid (Sample and Kneebone, 1998). The cubic symmetroid $\mathbf{S}$ is a non-linear subset of $\wp^5$ defined by the following equation

$$x_0x_2x_5 + 2x_1x_3x_4 - x_0x_4^2 - x_2x_3^2 - x_5x_1^2 = 0, \forall_{\widetilde{\mathbf{x}} \in \mathbf{S}} \tag{12}$$

By making $\bar{\mathbf{x}} = \mathbf{x}$ the operator $\mathbf{\Gamma}$ can be used to map a single point in $\wp^2$ into a point in $\wp^5$. In this case the lifting function becomes

$$\mathbf{x} \longrightarrow \widetilde{\mathbf{x}} = \mathbf{\Gamma}(\mathbf{x}, \mathbf{x}) = (x^2, xy, y^2, xz, yz, z^2)^t. \tag{13}$$

To each point $\mathbf{x}$ in the projective plane corresponds one, and only one, point $\widetilde{\mathbf{x}}$ lying on a quadratic surface $\mathbf{V}$ in $\wp^5$. This surface, defined by the triplet of Equations (14), is called the Veronese surface and is a sub-set of the cubic symmetroid $\mathbf{S}$ (Sample and Kneebone, 1998; Sample and Roth, 1949). The mapping of Equation (13) is the second order Veronese mapping that will be used to embed the projective plane $\wp^2$ into the 5D projective space.

$$x_1^2 - x_0x_2 = 0 \ \wedge \ x_3^2 - x_0x_5 = 0 \ \wedge \ x_4^2 - x_2x_5 = 0, \forall_{\widetilde{\mathbf{x}} \in \mathbf{V}}. \tag{14}$$

3.2. LIFTING LINES AND CONICS

A conic curve in the projective plane $\wp^2$ is usually represented by a 3×3 symmetric matrix $\mathbf{\Omega}$. Point $\mathbf{x}$ lies on the conic if, and only if, equation $\mathbf{x}^t\mathbf{\Omega}\mathbf{x} = 0$ is satisfied. Since a 3×3 symmetric matrix has 6 parameters, the conic locus can also be represented by a 6×1 homogeneous vector $\widetilde{\boldsymbol{\omega}}$ [see Equation (15)]. Vector $\widetilde{\boldsymbol{\omega}}$ is the representation in lifted coordinates of the planar conic $\mathbf{\Omega}$

$$\mathbf{\Omega} = \begin{bmatrix} a & b & d \\ b & c & e \\ d & e & f \end{bmatrix} \longrightarrow \widetilde{\boldsymbol{\omega}} = (a, 2b, c, 2d, 2e, f)^t. \tag{15}$$

Point $\mathbf{x}$ lies on conic the conic locus $\mathbf{\Omega}$ if, and only if, its lifted coordinates $\widetilde{\mathbf{x}}$ are orthogonal to vector $\widetilde{\boldsymbol{\omega}}$ and $\widetilde{\boldsymbol{\omega}}^t.\widetilde{\mathbf{x}} = 0$. Moreover, if points $\mathbf{x}$ and $\bar{\mathbf{x}}$ are harmonic conjugates with respect to the conic then $\mathbf{x}^t\mathbf{\Omega}\bar{\mathbf{x}} = 0$ and $\widetilde{\boldsymbol{\omega}}^t.\mathbf{\Gamma}(\mathbf{x}, \bar{\mathbf{x}}) = 0$. In the same way as points and lines are dual entities in $\wp^2$, there is a duality between points and conics in the lifted space $\wp^5$. Since the general single viewpoint image of a line is a conic [see Equations (5) and (9)], this duality will prove to be a nice and useful property.

Conic $\mathbf{\Omega} = \mathbf{m}.\mathbf{l}^t + \mathbf{l}.\mathbf{m}^t$ is composed of two lines $\mathbf{m}$ and $\mathbf{l}$ lying on the projective plane $\wp^2$. In this case the conic is said to be degenerate, the 3×3 symmetric matrix $\mathbf{\Omega}$ is rank 2, and Equation (15) becomes

$$\mathbf{\Omega} = \mathbf{m}\mathbf{l}^t + \mathbf{l}\mathbf{m}^t \longrightarrow \widetilde{\boldsymbol{\omega}} = \underbrace{\begin{bmatrix} 1 & 0 & 0 & 0 & 0 & 0 \\ 0 & 2 & 0 & 0 & 0 & 0 \\ 0 & 0 & 1 & 0 & 0 & 0 \\ 0 & 0 & 0 & 2 & 0 & 0 \\ 0 & 0 & 0 & 0 & 2 & 0 \\ 0 & 0 & 0 & 0 & 0 & 1 \end{bmatrix}}_{\widetilde{\mathbf{D}}} . \ \mathbf{\Gamma}(\mathbf{m}, \mathbf{l}) \tag{16}$$

In a similar way a conic locus can be composed of a single line $\mathbf{n} = (n_x, n_y, n_z)^t$. Matrix $\mathbf{\Omega} = \mathbf{n}.\mathbf{n}^t$ has rank 1 and the result of Equation (15) can be used to establish the lifted representation of a line

$$\mathbf{n} \rightarrow \widetilde{\mathbf{n}} = \widetilde{\mathbf{D}}.\mathbf{\Gamma}(\mathbf{n}, \mathbf{n}) = (n_x^2, 2n_xn_y, n_y^2, 2n_xn_z, 2n_yn_z, n_z^2)^t \tag{17}$$

Consider a point $\mathbf{x}$ in $\wp^2$ lying on line $\mathbf{n}$ such that $\mathbf{n}^t.\mathbf{x} = 0$. Point $\mathbf{x}$ is on the line if, and only if, its lifted coordinates $\widetilde{\mathbf{n}}$ are orthogonal to the homogeneous vector $\widetilde{\mathbf{n}}$ ($\widetilde{\mathbf{n}}^{\mathbf{t}}\widetilde{\mathbf{x}} = 0$). Points and lines are dual entities in $\wp^2$ as well as in the lifted space $\wp^5$. By embedding the projective plane into $\wp^5$ lines and conics are treated in a uniform manner. The duality between points and lines is preserved and extended for the case of points and conics.

The space of all conics is the dual 5D projective space $\wp^{5*}$, because each point $\tilde{\omega}$ corresponds to a conic curve $\mathbf{\Omega}$ in the original 2D plane. The set of all lines $\mathbf{n}$ is mapped into a non-linear subset $\mathbf{V}^*$ of $\wp^{5*}$, which is the projective transformation of the Veronese surface $\mathbf{V}$ by $\widetilde{\mathbf{D}}$ [see Equation (17)].

3.3. LIFTING CONIC ENVELOPES

Each point conic $\mathbf{\Omega}$ has dual conic $\mathbf{\Omega}^*$ associated with it (Sample and Kneebone, 1998). The line conic $\mathbf{\Omega}^*$ is usually represented by a 3×3 symmetric matrix and a generic line $\mathbf{n}$ belongs to the conic envelope whenever satisfies $\mathbf{n}^t\mathbf{\Omega}^*\mathbf{n} = 0$. The conic envelope can also be represented by a 6×1 homogeneous vector $\tilde{\omega}^*$ like the one provided in Equation (18). In this case line $\mathbf{n}$ lies on $\mathbf{\Omega}^*$ if, and only if, the corresponding lifted vector $\tilde{\mathbf{n}}$ [see Equation (17)] is orthogonal to $\tilde{\omega}^*$.

$$\mathbf{\Omega}^* = \begin{bmatrix} a^* & b^* & d^* \\ b^* & c^* & e^* \\ d^* & e^* & f^* \end{bmatrix} \longrightarrow \tilde{\omega}^* = (a^*, b^*, c^*, d^*, e^*, f^*)^t. \tag{18}$$

If matrix $\mathbf{\Omega}^*$ is rank deficient then the conic envelope is said to be degenerate. There are two possible cases of degeneracy: when the line conic is composed by two pencils of lines going through a pair of points $\mathbf{x}$ and $\bar{\mathbf{x}}$, and when the conic envelope is composed by a single pencil of lines. In the former case $\mathbf{\Omega}^* = \mathbf{x}\bar{\mathbf{x}}^t + \bar{\mathbf{x}}\mathbf{x}^t$ and the lifted representation becomes

$$\mathbf{\Omega}^* = \mathbf{x}\bar{\mathbf{x}}^t + \bar{\mathbf{x}}\mathbf{x}^t \longrightarrow \tilde{\omega}^* = \mathbf{\Gamma}(\mathbf{x}, \bar{\mathbf{x}}) \tag{19}$$

If the line conics is a single pencil going through point $\mathbf{x}$ then $\mathbf{\Omega}^* = \mathbf{x}\mathbf{x}^t$ and

$$\mathbf{\Omega}^* = \mathbf{x}\mathbf{x}^t \longrightarrow \tilde{\omega}^* = \mathbf{\Gamma}(\mathbf{x}, \mathbf{x}) \tag{20}$$

3.4. LIFTING LINEAR TRANSFORMATIONS

On the previous sections we discussed the representation of points, lines, conics and conic envelopes in the 5D projective space $\wp^5$. However a geometry is defined not only by a set of objects but also by the group of transformations acting on them (Klein, 1939). This section shows how a linear transformation on the original space $\wp^2$ can be coherently transferred to the lifted space $\wp^5$.

Consider a linear transformation, represented by a 3×3 matrix $\mathbf{H}$, which maps any two points $\mathbf{x}$, $\bar{\mathbf{x}}$ into points $\mathbf{H}\mathbf{x}$, $\mathbf{H}\bar{\mathbf{x}}$. Both pairs of points can be lifted to $\wp^5$ using the operator $\mathbf{\Gamma}$ of Equation (11). We wish to obtain a new operator $\mathbf{\Lambda}$ that has the following characteristic

$$\mathbf{\Gamma}(\mathbf{Hx}, \mathbf{H\bar{x}}) = \mathbf{\Lambda}(\mathbf{H}).\mathbf{\Gamma}(\mathbf{x}, \mathbf{\bar{x}}) \tag{21}$$

The desired result can be derived by developing Equation (21) and performing some algebraic manipulation. The operator $\mathbf{\Lambda}$, transforming a 3×3 matrix $\mathbf{H}$ into a 6×6 matrix $\widetilde{\mathbf{H}}$, is provided in Equation (22) with $\mathbf{v_1}$, $\mathbf{v_2}$ and $\mathbf{v_3}$ denoting the columns of the original matrix $\mathbf{H}$.

$$\mathbf{\Lambda}(\underbrace{\begin{bmatrix} \mathbf{v_1} & \mathbf{v_2} & \mathbf{v_3} \end{bmatrix}}_{\mathbf{H}}) = \underbrace{\begin{bmatrix} \mathbf{\Gamma}(\mathbf{v_1}, \mathbf{v_1})^t \\ \mathbf{\Gamma}(\mathbf{v_1}, \mathbf{v_2})^t \\ \mathbf{\Gamma}(\mathbf{v_2}, \mathbf{v_2})^t \\ \mathbf{\Gamma}(\mathbf{v_1}, \mathbf{v_3})^t \\ \mathbf{\Gamma}(\mathbf{v_2}, \mathbf{v_3})^t \\ \mathbf{\Gamma}(\mathbf{v_3}, \mathbf{v_3})^t \end{bmatrix} \widetilde{\mathbf{D}}}_{\widetilde{\mathbf{H}}} \tag{22}$$

It can be proved that $\mathbf{\Lambda}$, not only satisfies the relation stated on Equation (21), but also has the following properties

$$\begin{aligned} \mathbf{\Lambda}(\mathbf{H}^{-1}) &= \mathbf{\Lambda}(\mathbf{H})^{-1} \\ \mathbf{\Lambda}(\mathbf{H}.\mathbf{B}) &= \mathbf{\Lambda}(\mathbf{H}).\mathbf{\Lambda}(\mathbf{B}) \\ \mathbf{\Lambda}(\mathbf{H}^t) &= \widetilde{\mathbf{D}}^{-1}.\mathbf{\Lambda}(\mathbf{H})^t.\widetilde{\mathbf{D}} \\ \mathbf{\Lambda}(\mathbf{I}_{3\times 3}) &= \mathbf{I}_{6\times 6} \end{aligned} \tag{23}$$

From Equation (21) comes that if $\mathbf{x}$ and $\mathbf{y}$ are two points in $\wp^2$ such that $\mathbf{y} = \mathbf{Hx}$ then $\widetilde{\mathbf{y}} = \mathbf{\Lambda}(\mathbf{H}).\widetilde{\mathbf{x}}$ where $\widetilde{\mathbf{x}}$ and $\widetilde{\mathbf{y}}$ are the lifted coordinates of the points. The operator $\mathbf{\Lambda}$ maps the linear transformation $\mathbf{H}$ in the plane into the linear transformation $\widetilde{\mathbf{H}} = \mathbf{\Lambda}(\mathbf{H})$ in $\wp^5$. The transformation of points, conics and conic envelopes are transferred to the 5D projective space in the following manner

$$\begin{aligned} &\mathbf{y} = \mathbf{Hx} && \longrightarrow \quad \widetilde{\mathbf{y}} = \widetilde{\mathbf{H}}\widetilde{\mathbf{x}} \\ &\mathbf{\Psi} = \mathbf{H}^{-t}\mathbf{\Omega}\mathbf{H}^{-1} && \longrightarrow \quad \widetilde{\boldsymbol{\psi}} = \widetilde{\mathbf{H}}^{-t}\widetilde{\boldsymbol{\omega}} \\ &\mathbf{\Psi}^* = \mathbf{H}\mathbf{\Omega}^*\mathbf{H}^t && \longrightarrow \quad \widetilde{\boldsymbol{\psi}}^* = \widetilde{\mathbf{H}}\widetilde{\boldsymbol{\omega}}^* \end{aligned} \tag{24}$$

The operator $\mathbf{\Lambda}$ can be applied to obtain a lifted representations for both collineations and correlations. A correlation $\mathbf{G}$ in $\wp^2$ transforms a point $\mathbf{x}$ into a line $\mathbf{n} = \mathbf{Gx}$. From Equations (13) and (17) the lifted coordinates for $\mathbf{x}$ and $\mathbf{n}$ are respectively $\widetilde{\mathbf{x}}$ and $\widetilde{\mathbf{n}}$. It comes in a straightforward manner that the lifted vectors are related in $\wp^5$ by $\widetilde{\mathbf{n}} = \widetilde{\mathbf{D}}\widetilde{\mathbf{G}}\widetilde{\mathbf{x}}$. Thus the correlation $\mathbf{G}$ in $\wp^2$ is represented in the 5D projective space by $\widetilde{\mathbf{D}}\widetilde{\mathbf{G}}$ with $\widetilde{\mathbf{G}} = \mathbf{\Lambda}(\mathbf{G})$ and $\widetilde{\mathbf{D}}$ the diagonal matrix of Equation (16).

We just proved that the set of linear transformations in $\wp^2$ can be mapped into a subset of linear transformations in $\wp^5$. Any transformation, represented by a singular or non-singular 3×3 matrix $\mathbf{H}$, has a correspondence in $\widetilde{\mathbf{H}} = \mathbf{\Lambda}(\mathbf{H})$. However note that there are linear transformations in $\wp^5$ without any correspondence in the projective plane.

4. The Subset of Line Images

This section applies the established framework in order to study the properties of line projection in central catadioptric systems and cameras with radial distortion. If it is true that a line is mapped into a conic in the image, it is not true that any conic can be the projection of a line. It is shown that a conic section $\widetilde{\boldsymbol{\omega}}$ is the projection of a line if, and only if, it lies in a certain subset of $\wp^5$ defined by the sensor type and calibration. This subset is a linear subspace for paracatadioptric cameras and cameras with radial distortion, and a quadratic surface for hyperbolic systems.

4.1. CENTRAL CATADIOPTRIC PROJECTION OF LINES

Assume that a certain line in the world is projected into a conic section $\mathbf{\Omega}''$ in the catadioptric image plane. As shown in Figure 2 the line lies in plane $\mathbf{\Pi}$ that contains the projection center $\mathbf{O}$ and is orthogonal to $\mathbf{n} = (n_x, n_y, n_z)^t$. The catadioptric projection of the line is $\mathbf{\Omega}'' = \mathbf{H_c}^{-t}\mathbf{\Omega}'\mathbf{H_c}^{-1}$ where $\mathbf{H_c}$ is the calibration matrix. The conic $\mathbf{\Omega}'$ is provided in Equation (5) and depends on the normal $\mathbf{n}$ and the shape of the mirror.

The framework derived in the previous section is now used to transpose to $\wp^5$ the model for line projection discussed in Section 2.1. Conic $\mathbf{\Omega}'$ is mapped into $\boldsymbol{\omega}'$ in the 5D projective space. As shown in Equation (5) the conic depends on the normal $\mathbf{n}$ and on parameter ξ. This dependence can be represented in $\wp^5$ by $\widetilde{\boldsymbol{\omega}}' = \widetilde{\mathbf{\Delta}}_\mathbf{c}\widetilde{\mathbf{n}}$ with $\widetilde{\mathbf{\Delta}}_\mathbf{c}$ given by Equation (25). The lifted coordinates of the final image of the line are $\widetilde{\boldsymbol{\omega}}'' = \widetilde{\mathbf{H}}_\mathbf{c}\widetilde{\mathbf{\Delta}}_\mathbf{c}\widetilde{\mathbf{n}}$. Hence forth, if nothing is said, the collineation $\widetilde{\mathbf{H}}_\mathbf{c}$ is ignored and we will work directly with $\widetilde{\boldsymbol{\omega}}' = \widetilde{\mathbf{H}}_\mathbf{c}^{-1}\widetilde{\boldsymbol{\omega}}''$.

$$\underbrace{\begin{bmatrix} a' \\ 2b' \\ c' \\ 2d' \\ 2e' \\ f' \end{bmatrix}}_{\widetilde{\boldsymbol{\omega}}'} = \underbrace{\begin{bmatrix} 1-\xi^2 & 0 & 0 & 0 & 0 & -\xi^2 \\ 0 & 1-\xi^2 & 0 & 0 & 0 & 0 \\ 0 & 0 & 1-\xi^2 & 0 & 0 & -\xi^2 \\ 0 & 0 & 0 & 1 & 0 & 0 \\ 0 & 0 & 0 & 0 & 1 & 0 \\ 0 & 0 & 0 & 0 & 0 & 1 \end{bmatrix}}_{\widetilde{\mathbf{\Delta}}_c} \underbrace{\begin{bmatrix} n_x^2 \\ 2n_xn_y \\ n_y^2 \\ 2n_xn_z \\ 2n_yn_z \\ n_z^2 \end{bmatrix}}_{\widetilde{\mathbf{n}}} \tag{25}$$

Notice that the linear transformation $\widetilde{\mathbf{\Delta}}_{\mathbf{c}}$, derived from Equation (5), does not have an equivalent transformation in the projective plane [see Equation (22)]. The catadioptric projection of a line, despite of being non-linear in $\wp^{\mathbf{2}}$, is described by a linear relation in $\wp^{\mathbf{5}}$.

As stated in Section 3.2, a line $\mathbf{n}$ in the projective plane is lifted into a point $\widetilde{\mathbf{n}}$ which lies on the quadratic surface $\mathbf{V}^*$ in $\wp^{\mathbf{5*}}$. From Equation (25) it follows that conic $\widetilde{\boldsymbol{\omega}}'$ is the catadioptric projection of a line if, and only if, $\widetilde{\mathbf{\Delta}}_{\mathbf{c}}^{-1}\widetilde{\boldsymbol{\omega}}' \in \mathbf{V}^*$. Since surface $\mathbf{V}^*$ is the projective transformation of the Veronese surface $\mathbf{V}$ [see Equation (14)] by $\widetilde{\mathbf{D}}$, then $\widetilde{\boldsymbol{\omega}}' = (a', 2b', c', 2d', 2e', f')^t$ is the projection of a line if, and only if,

$$\begin{cases} d'^2(1-\xi^2) - f'(a' + f'\xi^2) = 0 \\ e'^2(1-\xi^2) - f'(c' + f'\xi^2) = 0 \, , \ \forall_{\widetilde{\boldsymbol{\omega}}' \in \boldsymbol{\zeta}} \\ b'^2 - (a' + f\xi^2)(c' + f'\xi^2) = 0 \end{cases} \tag{26}$$

Equation (26) defines a quadratic surface $\boldsymbol{\zeta}$ in the space of all conics. The constraints of Equation (26) have been recently introduced in (Ying and Hu, 2003) and used as invariants for calibration purposes.

4.2. LINE PROJECTION IN PARACATADIOPTRIC CAMERAS

Let's consider the situation of paracatadioptric cameras where $\xi = 1$. In this case point $\mathbf{O}'$ lies on the sphere surface (Figure 2) and the re-projection from the sphere to the plane becomes a stereographic projection (Geyer and Daniilidis, 2000). Equation (27) is derived by replacing ξ in Equation (26). For the particular case of paracatadioptric cameras the quadratic surface $\boldsymbol{\zeta}$ degenerates to a linear subspace $\boldsymbol{\varphi}$ which the set of all line projections $\widetilde{\boldsymbol{\omega}}'$.

$$a' + f' = 0 \ \wedge \ c' + f' = 0 \ \wedge \ b'^2 = 0, \forall_{\widetilde{\boldsymbol{\omega}}' \in \boldsymbol{\varphi}} \tag{27}$$

Stating this result in a different way, the conic $\boldsymbol{\Omega}'$ is is the paracatadioptric projection of a line if, and only if, the corresponding lifted representation $\widetilde{\boldsymbol{\omega}}'$ is on the null space of matrix $\mathbf{N_p}$.

$$\underbrace{\begin{bmatrix} 1 & 0 & 0 & 0 & 0 & 1 \\ 0 & 0 & 1 & 0 & 0 & 1 \\ 0 & 1 & 0 & 0 & 0 & 0 \end{bmatrix}}_{\mathbf{N_p}} \widetilde{\boldsymbol{\omega}}' = 0 \tag{28}$$

We have already seen that if point $\mathbf{x}'$ is on conic $\boldsymbol{\Omega}'$ then $\widetilde{\boldsymbol{\omega}}'^t\widetilde{\mathbf{x}}' = 0$. In $\wp^{\mathbf{5}}$ the lifted coordinates $\widetilde{\mathbf{x}}'$ must lie on the prime orthogonal to $\widetilde{\boldsymbol{\omega}}'$ (Sample and Kneebone, 1998). However, not all points in this prime are lifted coordinates of points in $\wp^{\mathbf{2}}$. Section 3.1 shows that only points lying on the Veronese surface $\mathbf{V}$ have a correspondence on the projective plane. Thus, points $\mathbf{x}'$ lying on $\mathbf{\Omega}'$ are mapped into a subset of $\wp^5$ defined by the intersection of the prime orthogonal to $\widetilde{\boldsymbol{\omega}}'$ with the Veronese surface $\mathbf{V}$.

Consider the set of all conic sections $\mathbf{\Omega}'$ corresponding to paracatadioptric line projections. If this conic set has a common point $\mathbf{x}'$ then its lifted vector $\widetilde{\mathbf{x}}'$ must be on the intersection of $\mathbf{V}$ with the hyperplane orthogonal to φ. Points $\widetilde{\mathbf{I}}'$ and $\widetilde{\mathbf{J}}'$ are computed by intersecting the range of matrix $\mathbf{N_p}^t$ (the orthogonal hyperplane) with the Veronese surface defined in Equation (14). These points are the lifted coordinates of the circular points in the projective plane where all paracatadioptric line images $\mathbf{\Omega}'$ intersect.

$$\begin{cases} \widetilde{\mathbf{I}}' = (1, i, -1, 0, 0, 0)^t \\ \widetilde{\mathbf{J}}' = (1, -i, -1, 0, 0, 0)^t \end{cases} \rightarrow \begin{cases} \mathbf{I}' = (1, i, 0)^t \\ \mathbf{J}' = (1, -i, 0)^t \end{cases} \tag{29}$$

In a similar way, if there is a pair of points $\mathbf{x}$, $\bar{\mathbf{x}}$ that are harmonic conjugate with respect to all conics $\mathbf{\Omega}'$ then, the corresponding vector $\mathbf{\Gamma}(\mathbf{x}, \bar{\mathbf{x}})$, must be in the intersection of $\mathbf{S}$ with the range of $\mathbf{N_p}^t$. The intersection can be determined from Equations (12) and (28) defining the cubic symmetroid $\mathbf{S}$ and matrix $\mathbf{N_p}$. The result is presented in Equation (30) where λ is a free scalar.

$$\begin{cases} \widetilde{\mathbf{P}'\mathbf{Q}'} = (-\lambda, 1, \lambda, 0, 0, 0)^t \rightarrow \begin{cases} \mathbf{P}' = (1 + \sqrt{1+\lambda^2}, \lambda, 0)^t \\ \mathbf{Q}' = (1 - \sqrt{1+\lambda^2}, \lambda, 0)^t \end{cases} \\ \\ \widetilde{\mathbf{R}'\mathbf{T}'} = (1, \lambda, \lambda^2, 0, 0, 1+\lambda^2)^t \rightarrow \begin{cases} \mathbf{R}' = (1, \lambda, -i\sqrt{1+\lambda^2})^t \\ \mathbf{T}' = (1, \lambda, i\sqrt{1+\lambda^2})^t \end{cases} \end{cases} \tag{30}$$

According to Equation (29), any paracatadioptric projection of a line must go through the circular points. This is not surprising, since the stereographic projection of a great circle is always a circle (see Figure 2). However, not all circles correspond to the projection of lines. While points $\mathbf{P}', \mathbf{Q}'$ are harmonic conjugate with respect to a all circles, the same does not happen with the pair $\mathbf{R}', \mathbf{T}'$. Thus, a conic $\mathbf{\Omega}'$ is the paracatadioptric image of a line if, and only if, it goes through the circular points and satisfies $\mathbf{R}'^t\mathbf{\Omega}'\mathbf{T}' = 0$. This result has been used in (Barreto and Araujo, 2003b; Barreto and Araujo, 2003a) in order to constrain the search space and accurately estimate line projections in the paracatadioptric image plane.

4.3. LINE PROJECTION IN CAMERAS WITH RADIAL DISTORTION

We have already shown that for catadioptric cameras the model for line projection becomes linear when the projective plane is embedded in $\wp^5$. A similar derivation can be applied to dioptric cameras with radial distortion. According to the conventional pin-hole model a line in the scene is mapped into a line $\mathbf{n}'$ in the image plane. However, and as discussed on Section 2.2, the non-linear effect of radial distortion transforms $\mathbf{n}'$ into a conic curve $\mathbf{\Omega}''$. If $\widetilde{\omega}''$ and $\widetilde{\mathbf{n}}''$ are the 5D representations of $\mathbf{\Omega}''$ and $\mathbf{n}'$ it comes from Equation (9) that

$$\underbrace{\begin{bmatrix} a'' \\ 2b'' \\ c'' \\ 2d'' \\ 2e'' \\ f'' \end{bmatrix}}_{\widetilde{\omega}''} = \underbrace{\begin{bmatrix} 0 & 0 & 0 & 0 & 0 & \xi \\ 0 & 0 & 0 & 0 & 0 & 0 \\ 0 & 0 & 0 & 0 & 0 & \xi \\ 0 & 0 & 0 & 0.5 & 0 & 0 \\ 0 & 0 & 0 & 0 & 0.5 & 0 \\ 0 & 0 & 0 & 0 & 0 & 1 \end{bmatrix}}_{\widetilde{\mathbf{\Delta}}_r} \underbrace{\begin{bmatrix} n_x'^2 \\ 2n_x' n_y' \\ n_y'^2 \\ 2n_x' n_z' \\ 2n_y' n_z' \\ n_z'^2 \end{bmatrix}}_{\widetilde{n}'} \tag{31}$$

Consider matrix $\widetilde{\mathbf{\Delta}}_c$ for the paracatadioptric camera situation with $\xi = 1$. The structure of $\widetilde{\mathbf{\Delta}}_r$ and $\widetilde{\mathbf{\Delta}}_c$ is quite similar. It can be proved that a conic section $\widetilde{\omega}''$ is the distorted projection of a line if, and only if, it lies on a hyperplane ς defined as follows

$$a'' - \xi f'' = 0 \ \wedge \ c'' - \xi f'' = 0 \ \wedge \ b''^2 = 0, \forall_{\widetilde{\omega}' \in \varsigma} \tag{32}$$

Repeating the reasoning that we did for the paracatadioptric camera, it can be shown that conic $\mathbf{\Omega}''$ is the distorted projection of a line if, and only if, it goes through the circular points of Equation (29) and satisfies the condition $\mathbf{M}''^t \mathbf{\Omega}'' \mathbf{N}'' = 0$ with $\mathbf{M}''$ and $\mathbf{N}''$ given below

$$\widetilde{\mathbf{M}''\mathbf{N}''} = (1, \lambda, \lambda^2, 0, 0, -\xi(1+\lambda^2))^t \rightarrow \begin{cases} \mathbf{M}'' = (1, \lambda, \sqrt{\xi(1+\lambda^2)})^t \\ \mathbf{N}'' = (1, \lambda, -\sqrt{\xi(1+\lambda^2)})^t \end{cases} \tag{33}$$

5. Conclusion

In this chapter we studied unifying models for central projection systems and representations of projections of world points and lines. We first proved that the two step projection model through the sphere, equivalent to perspective cameras and all central catadioptric systems, can be extended to cover the division model of radial lens distortion. Having accommodated all central catadioptric as well as radial lens distortion models under one formulation, we established a representation of the resulting image planes in the five-dimensional projective space through the Veronese mapping. In this space, a collineation of the original plane corresponds to a collineation of the lifted space. Projections of lines in the world correspond to points in the lifted space lying in the general case on a quadric surface. However, in the cases of paracatadioptric and radial lens distortions, liftings of the projections of world lines lie on hyperplanes. In ongoing work, we study the epipolar geometry of central camera systems when points are expressed in this lifted space.

Acknowledgments

The authors are grateful for support through the following grants: NSF-IIS-0083209, NSF-IIS-0121293, NSF-EIA-0324977, NSF-CNS-0423891, NSF-IIS-0431070 and ARO/MURI DAAD19-02-1-0383. Generous funding was also supplied by the Luso-American Foundation for Development.

References

Baker, S. and S. Nayar: A theory of catadioptric image formation. In Proc. *ICCV*, 1998.

Barreto, J.P. and H. Araujo: Direct least square fitting of paracatadioptric line images. In Proc. *Workshop on Omnidirectional Vision and Camera Networks*, Madison, Wisconsin, June 2003.

Barreto, J.P. and H. Araujo: Paracatadioptric camera calibration using lines. In Proc. *ICCV*, 2003.

Barreto, J.P. and H. Araujo: Geometric properties of central catadioptric line images and its application in calibration. *IEEE Trans. Pattern Analysis Machine Intelligence*, **27**: 1327–1333, 2005.

Klein, F.: *Elementary Mathematics from an Advanced Standpoint.* Macmillan, New York, 1939

Brown, D.C.: Decentering distortion of lens. *Photogrammetric Engineering*, **32**: 444–462, 1966.

Feldman, D., Padjla, T. and D. Weinshall: On the epipolar geometry of the crossed-slits projection. In Proc. *ICCV*, 2003.

Fitzgibbon, A.: Simultaneous linear estimation of multipleview geometry and lens distortion. In Proc. *Int. Conf. Computer Vision Pattern Recognition*, 2001.

Geyer, C. and K. Daniilidis: An unifying theory for central panoramic systems and practical implications. In Proc. *European Conf. Computer Vision*, pages 445–461, 2000.

Geyer, C. and K. Daniilidis: Mirrors in motion. epipolar geometry and motion estimation. In Proc. *ICCV*, 2003.

Sample, J.G. and G.T. Kneebone: *Algebraic Projective Geometry.* Claredon Press, 1998.

Sample, J.G. and L. Roth: *Algebraic Geometry.* Claredon Press, 1949.

Stolfi, J.: *Oriented Projective Geometry.* Academic Press, 1991.

Sturm, P.: Mixing catadioptric and perspective cameras. In Proc. *IEEE Workshop on Omnidirectional Vision*, Copenhagen, Denmark, July 2002.

Svoboda, T., and T. Pajdla: Epipolar geometry for central catadioptric cameras. *Int. J. Computer Vision*, **49**: 23–37, 2002.
Vidal, R., Ma, Y. and S. Sastry: Generalized principal component analysis (gpca). In Proc. *CVPR*, 2003.
Willson, R. and S. Shaffer: What is the center of the image? In Proc. *CVPR*, 1993.
Wolf, L. and A. Shashua: On projection matrices $\mathbf{P^k} \rightarrow \mathbf{P^2}$, and their applications in computer vision. In Proc. *ICCV*, 2001.
Ying, X. and Z. Hu: Catadioptric camera calibration using geometric invariants. In Proc. *ICCV*, 2003.

GEOMETRIC CONSTRUCTION OF THE CAUSTIC SURFACE OF CATADIOPTRIC NON-CENTRAL SENSORS

SIO-HOI IENG
University of Pierre and Marie Curie
4 place Jussieu 75252, Paris cedex 05, and
Lab. of Complex Systems Control, Analysis and Comm.
E.C.E, 53 rue de Grenelles, 75007 Paris, France

RYAD BENOSMAN
University of Pierre and Marie Curie
4 place Jussieu 75252 Paris cedex 05, France

Abstract. Most of the catadioptric cameras rely on the single viewpoint constraint that is hardly fulfilled. There exists many works on non single viewpoint catadioptric sensors satisfying specific resolutions. In such configurations, the computation of the caustic curve becomes essential. Existing solutions are unfortunately too specific to a class of curves and need heavy computation load. This paper presents a flexible geometric construction of the caustic curve of a catadioptric sensor. Its extension to the 3D case is possible if some geometric constraints are satisfied. This introduces the necessity of calibration that will be briefly exposed. Tests and experimental results illustrate the possibilities of the method.

Key words: caustic curve, non-central catadioptric camera

1. Introduction

The caustic curves are an optical phenomenon studied since Huygens and (Hamilton, 1828). They are envelopes of the reflected or diffracted light. Most of the existing vision systems are designed in order to achieve the convergence of the incident rays of light at a single point called 'effective viewpoint'.

Such a configuration of sensors can be seen as a degenerated form of the caustic reduced to a single point. The catadioptric sensors are divided into two categories, the ones fulfilling the single viewpoint constraint (SVC)

K. Daniilidis and R. Klette (eds.), Imaging Beyond the Pinhole Camera, 39–54.

where the caustic is reduced to a point and the none SVC that need the computation of the caustic. The single viewpoint constraint (Rees, 1970; Yamazawa et al., 1993; Nalwa, 1996; Nayar, 1997; Peri and Nayar, 1997; Baker and Nayar, 1998; Gluckman and Nayar, 1999) provides easier geometric systems and allows the generation of correct perspective images. However it requires a high precision assembly of the devices that is hardly fulfilled practically (Fabrizio et al., 2002) and it also faces the problem of uniformity of resolution. The problem of designing a catadioptric sensor that results in improved uniformity of resolution compared to the conventional sensor has been studied by several approaches (Chahl and Srinivasan, 1997; Backstein and Padjla, 2001; Conroy and Moore, 1999; Gaetcher and Pajdla, 2001; Hicks and Bajcsy, 2000; Hicks et al., 2001; Ollis et al., 1999). These solutions rely on the resolution of differential equations that are in most cases solved numerically providing a set of sampled points.

There are many ways to compute the caustic of a smooth curve, generally they are too specific to a finite class of curves and/or to a particular position of the light source (Bellver-Cebreros et al., 1994). More complex methods based on the illumination computation (the flux-flow model) are studied in geometric optics (Burkhard and Shealy, 1973). They are highly applied in computer graphics when a realistic scene rendering is required (Mitchell and Hanrahan, 1992; Jensen, 1996). A method for determining the locus of the caustic is derived from this flux-flow model, analysis and tests are carried out on conic shape mirrors in (Swaminathan et al., 2001), in order to extract the optical properties of the sensor.

In this chapter we study a method allowing the computation of the caustic based on a simple geometric constructions as related in (Bruce et al., 1981). The interest of the approach is its moderate computational load and its great flexibility toward unspecified smooth curves. We will show that its extension to the third dimension is possible if we consider the problem as a planar one in the incident plane and by assuming that the surface has a symmetry axis. We will show that the geometric construction can be applied if the light source is placed on this axis. This highlights the problem of ensuring the alignment between the camera and the mirror and points out the importance of a robust and accurate calibration that will be briefly introduced. Finally experimental results carried out on analytically defined mirrors and non explicit equation mirrors are presented.

2. The Caustic Curve: Definition and Construction

The catadioptric sensor that does not comply with the single viewpoint constraint, require the knowledge of the caustic surface if one expects to calibrate it. Defined as the envelope of the reflected rays, the caustic curve gives the direction of any incident ray captured by the camera.

In this section, we present in detail two methods applied to the caustic curve computation for systems combining a mirror and a linear camera. The first method derives from the flux-flow computation detailed in (Burkhard and Shealy, 1973). (Swaminathan et al., 2001) used this technique on conical based catadioptric sensors. A detailed analysis and relevant results are obtained.

The second method is based only on geometrical properties of the mirror curve. Caustic surface point is determined by approximating locally the curve by a conic where both the light source and the caustic point are foci of this conic.

2.1. FLUX-FLOW MODEL

The vanishing constraint on the Jacobian is applied to the whole class of conical mirrors. Though it can be applied for any regular curves, work examples exposed here are smooth curves discussed in (Swaminathan et al., 2001).

We define $\mathbf{N}$, $\mathbf{V_i}$ and $\mathbf{V_r}$ as respectively the normal, the incident and the reflected unit vectors, at the point P of the mirror M. The three vectors are functions of the point P, then if M is parametrized by t, they are functions of t.

According to the reflection laws, we have:

$$\mathbf{V_r} - \mathbf{V_i} = 2(\mathbf{V_r}.\mathbf{N})\mathbf{N} \Rightarrow \mathbf{V_i} = \mathbf{V_r} - 2(\mathbf{V_r}.\mathbf{N})\mathbf{N}$$

Assuming the point P to be the point of reflection on M, if we set P_c as the associated caustic point then P_c satisfies:

$$P_c - P + r\mathbf{V_i}$$

r is a parameter and since P and $\mathbf{V_i}$ depend on t, P_c is a function of (t, r). If the parametric equation of M is given as:

$$M : \begin{cases} z(t) \\ \gamma(t) \end{cases}$$

Then, the the Jacobian of P_c is:

$$J(P_c) = \begin{vmatrix} \frac{\partial P_z}{\partial t} & \frac{\partial P_z}{\partial r} \\ \frac{\partial P_\gamma}{\partial t} & \frac{\partial P_\gamma}{\partial r} \end{vmatrix} = \begin{vmatrix} \dot{P}_z + r\dot{V}_{iz} & V_{iz} \\ \dot{P}_\gamma + r\dot{V}_{i\gamma} & V_{i\gamma} \end{vmatrix} \tag{1}$$

$J(P_c)$ must vanish, thus we solve the equation $J(P_c) = 0$ for r:

$$r = \frac{\dot{P}_z V_{i\gamma} - \dot{P}_\gamma V_{iz}}{V_{iz}\dot{V}_{i\gamma} - V_{i\gamma}\dot{V}_{iz}} \tag{2}$$

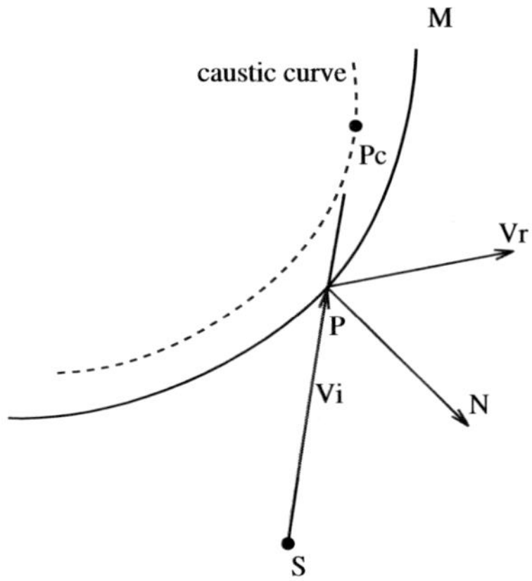

Figure 1. Catacaustic or caustic by reflection: the dashed curve shows the locus of the reflected rays envelope.

Obviously r is a function of t. Then we can have the parametrized form of the caustic.

In the case of conical curve M, we can parametrize it by t, according to the following form:

$$M : \begin{cases} z(t) = t \\ \gamma(t) = \sqrt{C - Bt - At^2} \end{cases}$$

Where A,B and C are constant parameters. The implicit equation of M can be deduced:

$$f(x, y) = Az^2 + \gamma^2 + Bz - C = 0$$

Explicit solutions and details for these curves can be found in (Swaminathan et al., 2001). The same method is extended to three dimensional curves. M is then a smooth surface and its caustic surface relatively to the light source can be determined by solving a three by three matrix determinant.

Remark 1: Parametrized equation of M is known.

Assuming the profile of M known, one can expect an important preprocessing step. First because of the computation of the Jacobian then the resolution for r according to the vanishing constraint.

Analytical resolution of r will provide exact solution for the caustic. However, if equation $J(P_c) = 0$ can be solved for conical class curves, we are not always able to solve it analytically for any smooth curves.

Remark 2: The profile of the mirror is not known.

This is the most general case we have to face. M is given by a set of points, then the computation of r must be numerical. This can be difficult to handle with, especially when we extend the problem to three dimension curves where r is root of a quadratic equation.

Bearing in mind the advantages and weaknesses of the Jacobian method, we present here another technique to compute the caustic curve, where only local mathematical properties of M are taken into account.

The caustic of a curve M, is function of the source light S. The basic idea is to consider a conic where S is placed on one of its foci. A simple physical consideration shows that any ray emitted by S should converge on the other focus F. It is proved in (Bruce et al., 1981) that for any P on M, there is only one caustic with properties mentioned above so that F is the caustic point of M, relative to S, at P.

A detailed geometric construction of F will be described here, first for plane curves then followed by an extension to three dimensional ones.

2.2. GEOMETRICAL CONSTRUCTION

DEFINITION 3.1. *Considering a regular(i.e smooth) curve M, a light source S and a point P of M, we construct Q as the symmetric of S, relative to the tangent to M at P. The line (QP) is the reflected ray (see Figure 2). When P describes M, Q describes a curve W where (QP) is normal to it at Q. W is known as the orthotomic of M, relatively to S. The physical interpretation of W is the wavefront of the reflected wave.*

It is equivalent to define the caustic curve C of M, relative to S as:

- *The evolute of W i.e. the locus of its centers of curvature, see (*Rutter, 2000*).*
- *The envelope of the reflected rays.*

DEFINITION 3.2. *Given two regular curves f and g of class C^n, with a common tangent at a common point P, taken as $(0\ 0)^t$ and the abscissa*

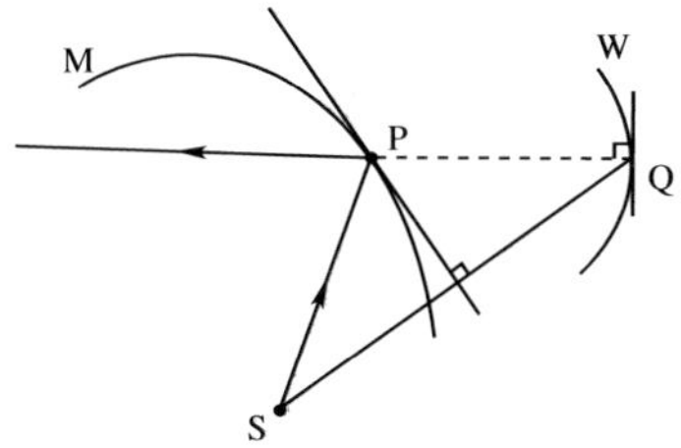

Figure 2. Illustration of the orthotomic W of the curve M, relative to S. W is interpreted as the wavefront of the reflected wave.

axis as the tangent. Then this point is an n-order point of contact if:

$$\begin{cases} f^{(k)}(0) = g^{(k)}(0) = 0 & \textit{if} \quad 0 \leq k < 2 \\ f^{(k)}(0) = g^{(k)}(0) & \textit{if} \quad 2 \leq k \leq n-1 \\ f^{(n)}(0) \neq g^{(n)}(0) \end{cases}$$

There is only one conic $\mathcal{C}$ of at least a 3-point contact with M at P, where S and F are the foci. F is the caustic point of M at P, with respect to S.

For the smooth curve M, we consider the parametrized form:

$$M : \begin{cases} x = t \\ y = f(t) \end{cases} \tag{3}$$

where $P = (x\ y)^t \in M$. The curvature of a M at P is given by:

$$k = \frac{|P^{'}P^{''}|}{|P|^3} = \frac{f^{''}(t)}{\sqrt{1 + f^{'}(t)^2}^3} \tag{4}$$

with

$$|P^{'}P^{''}| = \begin{vmatrix} x^{'} & x^{''} \\ y^{'} & y^{''} \end{vmatrix}$$

With regard to these definitions, we can deduce that M and $\mathcal{C}$ have the same curvature at P. If k is known, we are able to build the caustic C independently of W.

For more details and proofs of these affirmations, reader should refer to (Bruce et al., 1981). We give here the geometrical construction of the focus F, with respect to the conic $\mathcal{C}$ complying with the properties described above. Figure 3 illustrates the geometrical construction detailed below.

- Compute O, center of curvature of M at P, according to $r = \frac{1}{k}$, radius of curvature at P. O satisfies:

$$O = P + |r|\mathbf{N} \tag{5}$$

- Project orthogonally O to (SP) at u.
  Project orthogonally u to (PO) at v.
  (Sv) is the principal axis of C.
- Place F on (Sv) so that (OP) is bisectrix of $\widehat{SPF}$.

  Depending on the value taken by k, $\mathcal{C}$ can be an ellipse, a hyperbola or a parabola. For the first two, F is at finite distance of S ($\mathcal{C}$ has a center) and $k \neq 0$. If $k = 0$, F is at infinity and $\mathcal{C}$ is a parabola. — We consider here only the case where S is at a finite distance from M. If S is placed at infinity or projected through a telecentric camera, the incident rays are parallel and the definition of the caustic is slightly different.

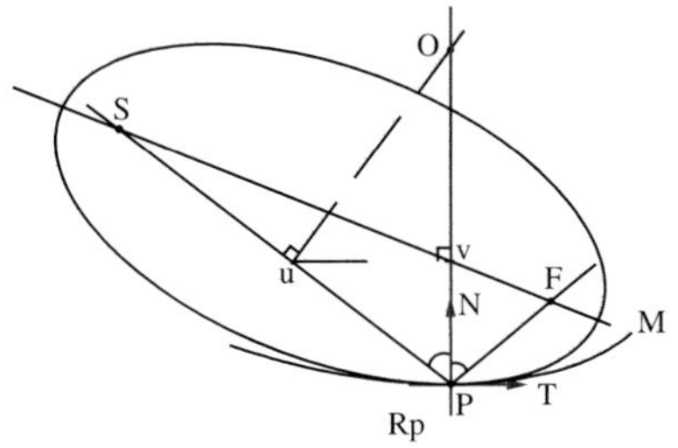

Figure 3. Geometric construction of the caustic point expressed in the local Frenet's coordinates system $\mathcal{R}_\mathcal{P}$

It is more simple to express the curves using the local Frenet's coordinates system at P and denoted $\mathcal{R}_P$. Hence P is the origin of $\mathcal{R}_P$ and we have $O = (0\ |r|)^t$ since $\mathbf{N}$ is the direction vector of the ordinate axis. — One can easily prove that the generic implicit equation of $\mathcal{C}$ in $\mathcal{R}_P$ is

$$ax^2 + by^2 + 2hxy + y = 0 \tag{6}$$

and that the curvature is $k = -\frac{1}{2a}$. However, it is obvious to see that the construction of F does not require the computation of the parameters of Equation (6).

We can write down the coordinates of F in R_p if we express analytically the cartesian equation of each line of Figure 3.

$$\mathcal{C} : \begin{cases} x_f = -\frac{y_s^2 x_s |r|}{2y_s(x_s^2+y_s^2)-y_s^2|r|} \\ y_f = \frac{y_s^2|r|}{2(x_s^2+y_s^2)-y_s|r|} \end{cases} \tag{7}$$

The generic expression of the coordinates of F depend only on the source S and the curve M through r.

2.3. EXTENSION TO THE THIRD DIMENSION

Given a three dimension surface $\mathcal{M}$, we decompose it into planar curves M which are the intersections of $\mathcal{M}$ with the incident planes. According to the Snell's law of reflection, the incident and the reflected rays are coplanar and define the plane of incidence Π_P. Since the caustic point associated to S and the point P belongs to (PQ) (see Figure 2.2), can we expect to apply the geometric construction to M? (See Figure 4 for a general illustration.)

A problem could arise if we consider a curve generated by a plane containing the incident ray and intersecting the mirror, then the normals to the generated curve may not be the normal to the surface, the computed rays are then not the reflected ones.

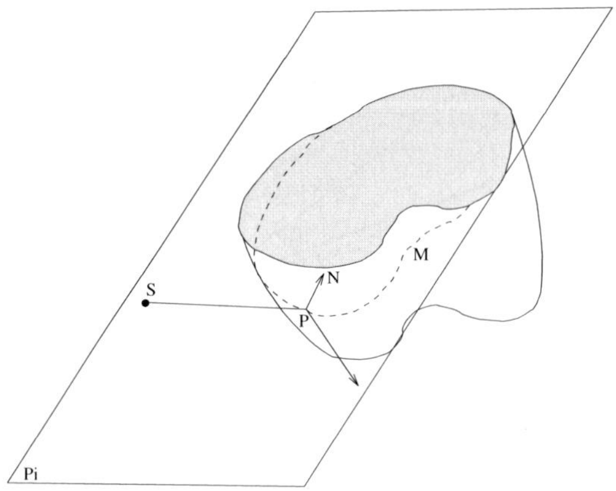

Figure 4. Generic case of a three dimension curve: can it be decomposed into planes and solved as planar curves for each point P of M?

We will now apply the construction on $\mathcal{M}$ a surface that has a revolution axis with S lying on it (see Figure 5).

Step 1: $(\Omega z) \in \Pi_P$ with respect to $S \in (\Omega z)$.

Given the standard parametrization of the surface of revolution $\mathcal{M}$, expressed in an arbitrary orthogonal basis $E = (\Omega, \mathbf{x}, \mathbf{y}, \mathbf{z})$ such that (Ωz) is the revolution axis of $\mathcal{M}$:

$$\mathcal{M} : \begin{cases} x(t,\theta) = r(t)\cos\theta \\ y(t,\theta) = r(t)\sin\theta \\ z(t,\theta) = k(t) \end{cases} \tag{8}$$

The normal unit vector to $\mathcal{M}$ at $P = \begin{pmatrix} x & y & z \end{pmatrix}^t$ can be defined as:

$$\mathbf{N} = \frac{\mathbf{A} \wedge \mathbf{B}}{|\mathbf{A} \wedge \mathbf{B}|} \text{ where } \wedge \text{ is the cross product, } \mathbf{A} = \begin{pmatrix} x_t \\ y_t \\ z_t \end{pmatrix} \text{ and } \mathbf{B} = \begin{pmatrix} x_\theta \\ y_\theta \\ z_\theta \end{pmatrix}$$

and the subscripts t and θ referee to the partial derivatives with respect to t and θ.

Thus,

$$\mathbf{N} = \frac{1}{|\mathbf{A} \wedge \mathbf{B}|} \begin{pmatrix} r' \cos\theta \\ r' \sin\theta \\ k' \end{pmatrix} \wedge \begin{pmatrix} -r\sin\theta \\ r\cos\theta \\ 0 \end{pmatrix} = \frac{1}{\sqrt{r'^2 + k'^2}} \begin{pmatrix} -k' \cos\theta \\ -k' \sin\theta \\ r' \end{pmatrix}.$$

Let us consider now the rotation along (Ωz), given by the rotation matrix:

$$R = \begin{pmatrix} \cos\theta & \sin\theta & 0 \\ -\sin\theta & \cos\theta & 0 \\ 0 & 0 & 1 \end{pmatrix}$$

if the rotation angle is assumed to be θ.

We then define $B = (\Omega, \mathbf{u}, \mathbf{v}, \mathbf{z})$ as the orthogonal coordinates system obtained by applying R to E. The coordinates of $\mathbf{N}$ in B is:

$$R.\mathbf{N} = \frac{1}{\sqrt{r'^2 + k'^2}} R \begin{pmatrix} -k' \cos\theta \\ -k' \sin\theta \\ r' \end{pmatrix} = \frac{1}{\sqrt{r'^2 + k'^2}} \begin{pmatrix} -k' \\ 0 \\ r' \end{pmatrix} \tag{9}$$

$\mathbf{N}$ has a null component along $\mathbf{v}$, hence the line $(P, \mathbf{N})$ belongs to the plane $\Pi = (\Omega, \mathbf{u}, \mathbf{z})$. Moreover, since $S \in (\Omega z)$, one can deduce that $\Pi = (S, (P, \mathbf{N})) = \Pi_P$.

Step 2: $\mathbf{N} = \mathbf{n}$

With respect to the hypotheses made above, we compute $\mathbf{n}$ according to the parametric equation of M, expressed in the coordinate system (Ω, u, z):

$$M : \begin{cases} u = r(t) \\ z = k(t) \end{cases} \tag{10}$$

Thus the tangent to M at P is defined as $T = \begin{pmatrix} r' \\ k' \end{pmatrix}$ end the unit normal vector is:

$$\mathbf{n} = \frac{1}{\sqrt{r'^2 + k'^2}} \begin{pmatrix} -k' \\ r' \end{pmatrix} \tag{11}$$

By combining Equations (9) and (11), we have the equality $\mathbf{N} = \mathbf{n}$.

This proves that in particular configurations that involve an on-axis reflection, N is normal to $\mathcal{M}$ and to M at P, then the geometric construction holds.

3. Ensuring Alignment Mirror/Camera: Catadioptric Calibration

Most of the catadioptric sensors rely on a mirror having a surface of revolution. In general most of the applications assume the perfect alignment between the optical axis of the camera and the revolution axis of the reflector. As shown in the previous sections, the perfect alignment between the two axes introduce a simplification in the computation of the caustic surface. We may wonder how realistic is this condition and if it still holds in the real case? It then appears the necessity of an accurate and robust calibration procedure to retrieve the real position of the mirror with respect to the camera.

Calibration in general relies on the use of a calibration pattern to ensure a known structure or metric in the scene. Due to the non linear geometry

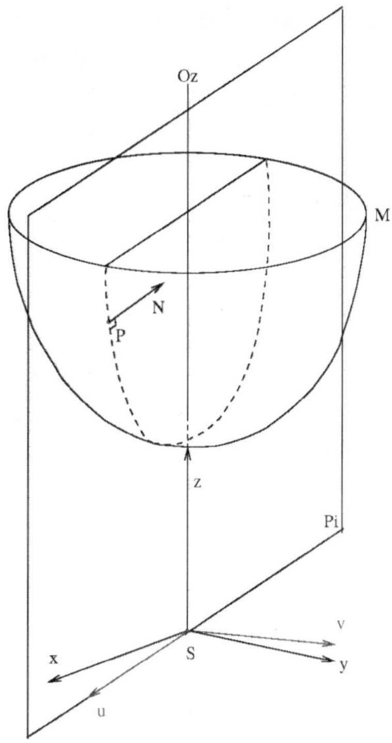

Figure 5. If the source light S is placed on the revolution axis, the geometric construction can be applied on each slices of incident planes.

of catadioptric sensors, the computation of the parameters (position camera/mirror, intrinsics of the camera, ...) can turn into a major non linear problem. Previous calibration works are not numerous and are in general connected to the shape of the mirror.

A much simpler approach would be to consider the mirror as a calibration pattern. The mirror is generally manufactured with great care (precision less than 1 micron) and its shape and surface are perfectly known. Using the mirror as a calibration pattern avoids the non linearity and turns the calibration problem into a linear one. The basic idea is to assume the surface parameters of the mirror as known and to use the boundaries of the mirror as a calibration pattern (Fabrizio et al., 2002). As a major consequence the calibration becomes robust as the mirror is always visible, the calibration is then independent from the content of the scene and can be performed anytime needed. The calibration relies on one or two homographic mapping (according to the design of the mirror) between the mirror borders and their corresponding images. To illustrate this idea let us consider a catadioptric sensor developed by (Vstone Corp., 2004) that has an interesting property. A little black needle is mounted at the bottom of the mirror to avoid unexpected reflections. The calibration method is based on the principle used in (Gluckman and Nayar, 1999). This approach is known as the two grid calibration. Two different 3D parallel planes P_1 and P_2 are required (see Figure 6). The circular sections of the lower and upper mirror boundaries C_1 and C_2 are respectively projected as ellipses E_1 and E_2. Homographies H_1 and H_2 are estimated using the correspondence between C_1/E_1 and C_2/E_2. The distance between the two parallel planes P_1 and P_2 respectively containing C_1 and C_2 being perfectly known, the position of the focal point is then computed using both H_1 and H_2 by back projecting a set of n image points on each plane. In a second stage the pose of the camera is estimated. We then have the complete pose parameters between the mirror and the camera and the intrinsic parameters of the camera. The reader may refer to (Fabrizio et al., 2002) for a complete overview of this method.

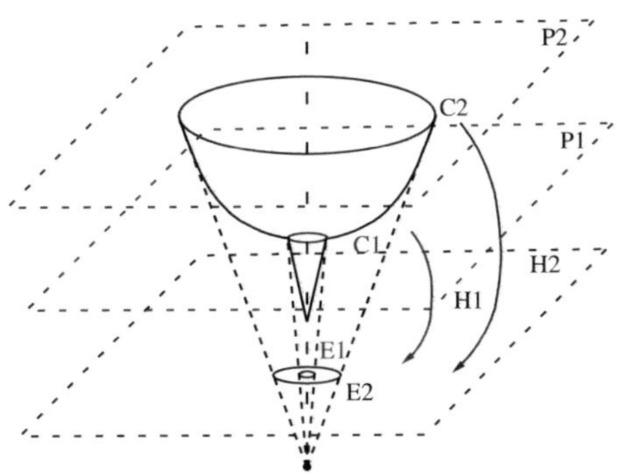

Figure 6. Calibration using parallel planes corresponding to two circular sections of the mirror

The same idea can be used if only one plane is available. In that case only the image E_2 of the upper boundary of the mirror C_2 is available. The homography H_2 can then be estimated. There is a projective relation between the image plane and the plane P_2. The classic perspective projection matrix is $P = K(R \mid t)$ with K the matrix containing the intrinsics and R,t the extrinsics. The correspondence between E_2 and C_2 allows an identification of P with H_2. The only "scene" points available for calibration all belong to the same plane P_2. P can then be reduced to the following form $P = K(r_1\ r_2\ t)$, where $r_1 r_2$ correspond to the first two columns vectors of the rotation matrix R. As a consequence the matrix $H_2 = (h_{21}\ h_{22}\ h_{23})$ can be identified with $P = K(r_1\ r_2\ t)$ giving :

$$(h_{21}\ h_{22}\ h_{23}) \sim K(r_1\ r_2\ t) \tag{12}$$

The matrix H_2 is constrained to be a perspective transform by the rotation R giving the two following relations :

$$\begin{array}{l} h_1^T K^{-T} K^T h_2 = 0 \\ h_1^T K^{-T} K^T h_1 = h_2^T K^{-T} K^T h_2 = 0 \end{array} \quad (13)$$

If an estimate of K is available it becomes possible to compute R and t using Equation (12). The reader may refer to (Sturm 2001; Zhang 2002) for a complete overview of this computation.

The two presented approaches allow a full calibration of catadioptric sensors and can ensure if the geometry of the sensor fulfills the desired alignment between the camera and the mirror. It becomes then possible to choose the adequate computation method. These methods are not connected to the shape of the mirror and can then be applied to all catadioptric sensors. It is interesting to notice that catadioptric sensors have an interesting property as they carry their own calibration pattern.

4. Experimental Results

The geometrical construction is illustrated here with smooth curves examples. Their profiles are defined by the parametrized equations. As we can see in Section 3.2, only Equation (4) is specific to M, the curvature at P implies only the first two derivatives at P with respect to t. Hence, if the profile of M is given only as a set of sampled points, the algorithm can handle it if the sampling step is small enough.

4.1. PLANE CURVES

Example 1: Let M be the conic defined by its parametrized and implicit equations:

$$M : \begin{cases} x(t) = t \\ y(t) = b\sqrt{1 + \frac{t^2}{a^2}} - c \end{cases} \quad (14)$$

and

$$f(x, y) = \frac{(y - c)^2}{b^2} - \frac{x^2}{a^2} - 1 = 0 \quad (15)$$

The first and second derivatives with respect to the parameter t are:

$$M' : \begin{cases} x'(t) = 1 \\ y'(t) = \frac{bt}{a^2\sqrt{1+\frac{t^2}{a^2}}} \end{cases} \quad (16)$$

$$M'' : \begin{cases} x''(t) = 0 \\ y''(t) = \frac{b}{a^2} \frac{1}{\left(1+\frac{t^2}{a^2}\right)^{\frac{3}{2}}} \end{cases} \quad (17)$$

Compute r at P according to Equation (4):

$$r = \frac{1}{k} = \frac{\sqrt{a^2(a^2+t^2)+b^2t^2}^3}{a^4 b} \tag{18}$$

then change the coordinate system to the Frenet's local coordinate system at P for an easier construction of F.

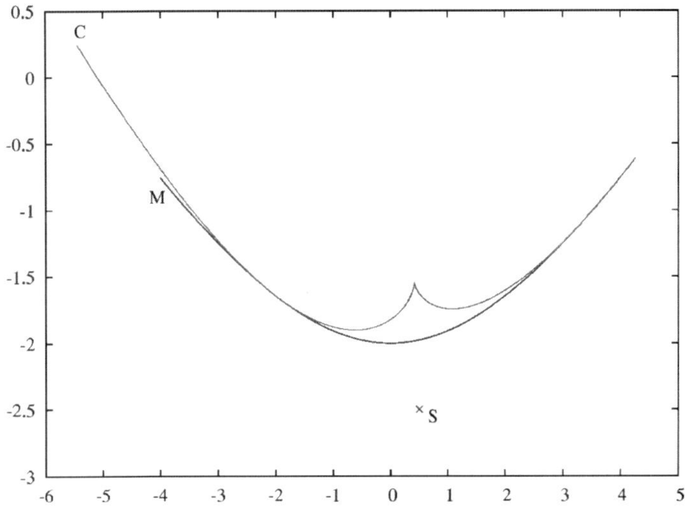

Figure 7. Caustic of a hyperbola for an off-axis reflection.

Figure 7 shows the plot of the caustic for an off-axis reflection i.e. P is not on the symmetry axis of M. The parameters are $a = 4$, $b = 3$, and $c = 5$ and $S = [0.5\ 0.25]^t$.

Example 2: This is the most general case we have to face: the reflector is given only by a set of sampled points, no explicit equation is known. The curvature at each point is numerically computed, providing a numerical estimation of the caustic.

The mirror tested has a symmetric axis and the camera is placed arbitrarily on it. We computed the caustic curve relative to this configuration (see Figure 8). The catadioptric sensor has been calibrated using a method similar to (Fabrizio et al., 2002), the sensor is then fully calibrated. Given a set of points taken from a scene captured by this sensor, we reproject the rays on the floor in order to check the validity of the method of construction. As illustrated in Figure 9, the geometry of the calibration pattern is accurately reconstructed retrieving the actual metric (the tiles on the floor are squares of 30 x 30 cm). The reconstruction shows that the farther we are from the center of the optical axis, the less accurate we are which is an expected result as the mirror was not computed to fulfill this property.

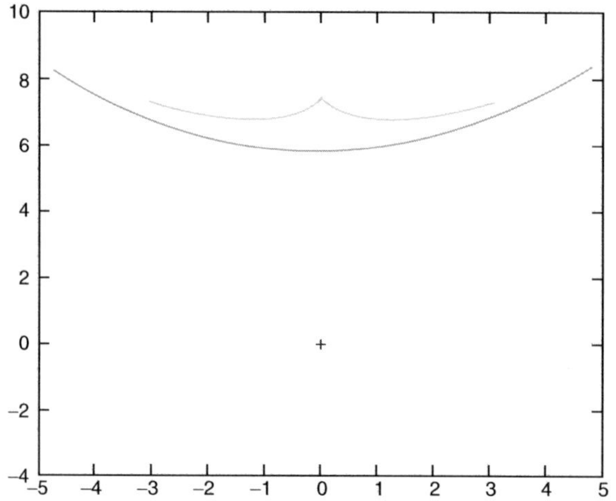

Figure 8. Caustic curve of the sampled mirror. The camera is placed at the origin of the coordinates system, represented by the cross.

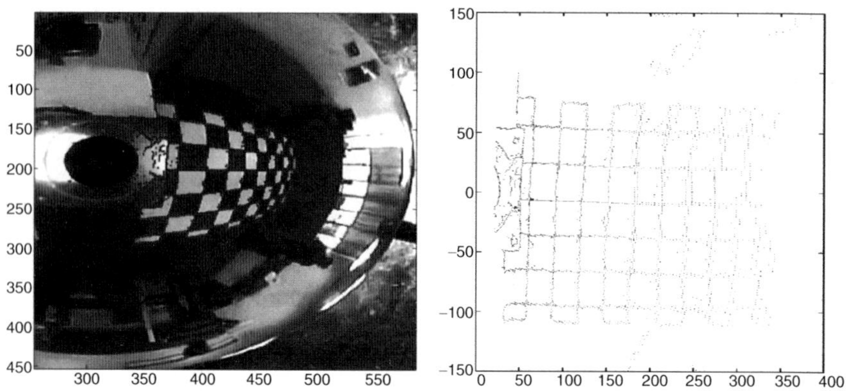

Figure 9. A scene captured by the sensor. The blue dots are scene points that are reprojected on the floor, illustrated on the left plot.

5. Conclusion

This chapter presented a geometric construction of caustic curves in the framework of catadioptric cameras. When the single viewpoint constraint cannot be fulfilled, the caustic becomes essential if calibration and reconstruction are needed.

Existing methods imply heavy preprocessing work that can lead to an exact solution of the caustic if the mirror profile is known, however this is not guaranteed for general cases. The presented geometric construction is a very flexible computational approach as it relies only on local properties of the mirror.

Since no special assumption is made on the mirror curve, except its smoothness, the presented work is able to solve cases of either known mirror profile or curves defined by a set of sample points fulfilling the aim of flexibility. The extension to 3D is possible under certain geometric restrictions.

Acknowledgments

We would like to thank Professor P.J. Giblin for his relevant advices and help and Mr. F. Richard for providing us some test materials.

References

Hamilton, W.R.: Theory of systems of rays. *Trans. Royal Irish Academy*, **15**: 69–174, 1828.

Rees, D.: Panoramic television viewing system. *United States Patent No.3,505,465*, April 1970.

Burkhard, D.G. and D.L. Shealy: Flux density for ray propagation in geometric optics. *J. Optical Society of America*, **63**: 299–304, 1973.

Bruce, J.W., P.J. Giblin, and C.G. Gibson: On caustics of plane curves. *American Mathematical Monthly*, **88**: 651–667, 1981.

Mitchell, D. and P. Hanrahan: Illumination from curved reflectors. In Proc. *SIGGRAPH*, pages 283–291, 1992.

Yamazawa, K., Y. Yagi, and M. Yachida: Omnidirectional imaging with hyperboloidal projection. In Proc. *Int. Conf. Intelligent Robots and Systems*, pages 1029–1034, 1993

Bellver-Cebreros, C., E. Gómez-González, and M. Rodríguez-Danta. Obtention of meridian caustics and catacaustics by means of stigmatic approximating surfaces. *Pure Applied Optics*, **3**: 7–16, 1994.

Jensen, H.W.: Rendering caustics on non-Lambertian surfaces. In Proc. *Graphics Interface*, pages 116–121, 1996.

Nalwa, V.: A true omnidirectional viewer. Technical report, Bell Laboratories, Holmdel, NJ 07733, U.S.A., February 1996.

Nayar, S.: Catadioptric omnidirectional cameras. In Proc. *CVPR*, pages 482–488, 1997.

Peri, V. and S.K. Nayar: Generation of perspective and panoramic video from omnidirectional video. In Proc. *DARPA-IUW*, vol. I, pages 243–245, December 1997.

Chahl, J.S. and M.V. Srinivasan: Reflective surfaces for panoramic imaging: *Applied Optics*, **36**: 8275–8285, 1997.

Baker, S. and S.K. Nayar: A theory of catadioptric image formation. In Proc. *ICCV*, pages 35–42, 1998.

Vstone Corporation, Japan: http://www.vstone.co.jp/ (last visit: 12 Feb. 2006).

Gluckman, J. and S.K. Nayar: Planar catadioptric stereo: geometry and calibration. In Proc. *CVPR*, Vol. I, pages 22–28, 1999.

Baker, S. and S.K. Nayar: A theory of single-viewpoint catadioptric image formation. *Int. J. Computer Vision*, **35**: 175–196, 1999.

Conroy, J. and J. Moore: Resolution invariant surfaces for panoramic vision systems. In Proc. *ICCV*, pages 392–397, 1999.

Ollis, M., H. Herman, and S. Singh: Analysis and design of panoramic stereo vision using equi-angular pixel cameras. Technical Report, The Robotic Institute, Carnegie Mellon University, 5000 Forbes Avenue Pittsburgh, PA 15213, 1999.

Rutter, J.W.: *Geometry of Curves*, Chapman & Hall/CRC, 2000.

Hicks, R.A. and R. Bajcsy: Catadioptric sensors that approximate wide-angle perspective projections. In Proc. *CVPR*, pages 545–551, 2000.

Swaminathan, R., M.D. Grossberg, and S.K. Nayar: Caustics of catadioptric cameras. In Proc. *ICCV*, pages 2–9, 2001.

Backstein, H. and T. Padjla: Non-central cameras: a review. In Proc. *Computer Vision Winter Workshop*, Ljubljana, pages 223–233, 2001.

Gaetcher, S. and T. Pajdla: Mirror design for an omnidirectional camera with space variant imager. In Proc. *Workshop on Omnidirectional Vision Applied to Robotic Orientation and Nondestructive Testing*, Budapest, 2001.

Hicks, R. A., R. K. Perline, and M. Coletta: Catadioptric sensors for panoramic viewing. In Proc. *Int. Conf. Computing Information Technology*, 2001.

Fabrizio, J., P. Tarel, and R. Benosman: Calibration of panoramic catadioptric sensors made easier. In Proc. *IEEE Workshop on Omnidirectional Vision*, June 2002.

CALIBRATION OF LINE-BASED PANORAMIC CAMERAS

FAY HUANG
Department of Computer Science and Information Engineering, National Taipei University of Technology
Taipei, Taiwan

SHOU-KANG WEI
Presentation and Network Video Division
AVerMedia Technologies, Inc., Taipei, Taiwan

REINHARD KLETTE
Computer Science Department
The University of Auckland, Auckland, New Zealand

Abstract. The chapter studies the calibration of four parameters of a rotating CCD line sensor, which are the effective focal length and the principal row (which are part of the intrinsic calibration), and the off-axis distance and the principal angle (which are part of the extrinsic calibration). It is shown that this calibration problem can be solved by considering two independent subtasks, first the calibration of both intrinsic parameters, and then of both extrinsic parameters. The chapter introduces and discusses different methods for the calibration of these four parameters. Results are compared based on experiments using a super-high resolution line-based panoramic camera. It turns out that the second subtask is solved best if a straight-segment based approach is used, compared to point-based or correspondence-based calibration methods; these approaches are already known for traditional (planar) pinhole cameras, and this chapter discusses their use for calibrating panoramic cameras.

Key words: panoramic imaging, line-based camera, rotating line sensor, camera calibration, performance evaluation

1. Introduction

Calibration of a standard perspective camera (pinhole camera) is divided into intrinsic and extrinsic calibration. Intrinsic calibration specifies the imager and the lens. Examples of intrinsic parameters are the effective focal length or the center of the image (i.e., the intersection point of the optical axis with the ideal image plane). Extrinsic calibration has to do with the

K. Daniilidis and R. Klette (eds.), Imaging Beyond the Pinhole Camera, 55–84.

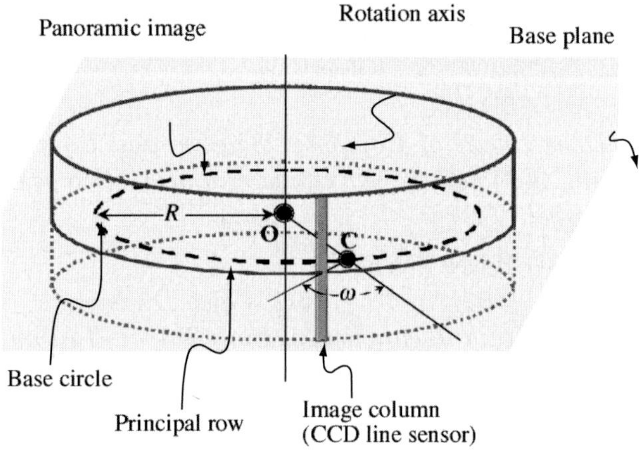

Figure 1. Illustration of all four parameters of interest: the effective focal length is the distance between focal point **C** on the base circle and the cylindrical panoramic image, the principle row is the assumed location (in the panoramic image) of all principal points, the off-axis distance R specifies the distance between rotation axis (passing through **O** and orthogonal to base plane) and base circle, and the viewing angle ω describes the constant tilt of the CCD line sensor during rotation.

positioning of the camera with respect to the world reference frame, and is normally solved by determining parameters of an affine transform, defined by rotation and translation.

This chapter discusses calibration of a camera characterized by a rotating line sensor (see Figure 1). Such a panoramic camera consists of one or multiple linear CCD sensor(s); a panoramic image is captured by rotating the linear photon-sensing device(s) about a *rotation axis*. See Figure 1 for a camera with two (symmetrically positioned) line sensors.

We focus on four parameters, which define major differences to standard perspective cameras. Instead of a single center of an image, here we have to calibrate a sequence of principle points (one for each position of a rotating line sensor), and this task is inherently connected with calibrating the effective focal length. As an additional challenge, off-axis distance and viewing angle also define the positioning of each of the rotating line sensors with respect to a world reference frame.

Calibration results for a rotating line sensor are fundamental for stereo reconstruction, stereo viewing, or mapping of panoramic image data on surface models captured by a range finder. See (Klette and Scheibe, 2005) for these 3D reconstruction and visualization issues, and also for calibrating affine transforms for positioning a panoramic camera or a range finder in a 3D world frame. Intrinsic parameter calibration is very complex for these

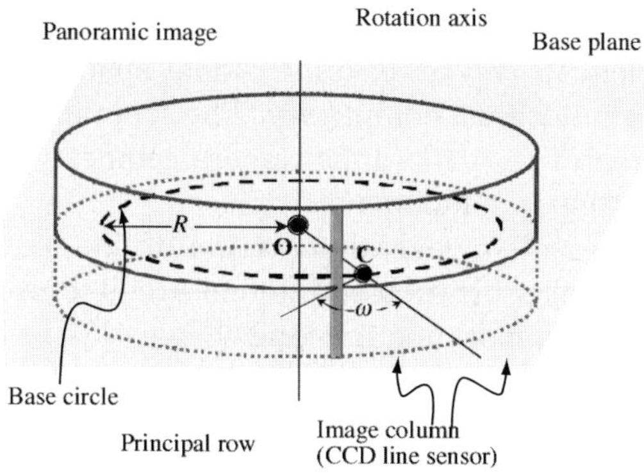

Figure 2. A rotating line camera with two line sensors (viewing angles ω and $-\omega$).

high-resolution rotating line sensors; see the calibration section in (Klette et al., 2001) for production-site facilities for geometric and photometric sensor calibration.

Two essential parameters of a line-based panoramic camera that do not exist in traditional pinhole cameras are *off-axis distance* R, and *principal angle* ω. The off-axis distance specifies how far the linear sensor is away from the rotation axis, and the principal angle describes the orientation of the sensor. These two camera parameters can be dynamically adjusted for different scene ranges of interest and application-specific requirements, allowing optimizations with respect to scene parameters (Wei et al., 2001).

Due to differences in camera geometries, previously developed calibration approaches for pinhole cameras cannot be used for calibrations of panoramic cameras. Although the general calibration scenario (calibration objects, localization of calibration marks, calculation of intrinsic and extrinsic camera parameters, etc.), and some of the used procedures (e.g., detection of calibration marks) may be similar for both planar and cylindrical images, differences in camera architectures (e.g., multiple projection centers, and a nonplanar image projection surface) require the design of new calibration methods for rotating line cameras.

This chapter reports about on-site camera calibration methods for line-based panoramic cameras, and these methods are in contrast to production-site camera calibration (e.g., for photometric and geometric parameters of the used line sensor, see (Klette et al., 2001)).

The calibration process of the selected four parameters can be divided into two steps. First we calibrate the effective focal length and the principal row. The second step uses the obtained results and calibrates R and ω. This splitting allows to separate linear geometric features from non-linear geometric features; we factorize a high-dimensional space and solve the calibration problem in two lower-dimensional spaces, which finally allows to reduce the computational complexity. The separability of the calibration process also characterizes panoramic camera geometry to be a composition of linear and non-linear components.

The chapter presents a general definition of line-based panoramic cameras, which allows a classification of different architectures and image acquisition approaches in panoramic imaging. Then three different approaches are elaborated for the calibration of the specified four parameters of line-based panoramic cameras, and they are compared with respect to various performance criteria.

2. Generalized Cylindrical Panoramas

A panorama may cover spatial viewing angles of a sphere (i.e., a 4π solid angle) as studied by (Nayar and Karmarkar, 2000), a full 2π circle (Chen, 1995), or an angle which is less than 2π, but still wider than the viewing angle of a traditional planar image. Moreover, there are various geometric forms of panoramic image surfaces. This chapter always assumes cylindrical 2π panoramas acquired by a line-based panoramic camera.

Traditionally, the camera model of a panorama has a single projection center[1]. In this section, a general camera model of a cylindrical panorama associated with multiple projection centers is discussed. We introduce the coordinate systems of panoramic camera and the acquired image, which are fundamental for our calculations of image projection formulas in Section 3. Finally, a classification of multiple cylindrical panoramas is given in this section.

2.1. CAMERA MODEL

Our camera model is an abstraction from existing line-based cameras. It formalizes the basic projective geometry of forming a cylindrical panorama, but avoids the complexity of optical systems. This is justified because the optics of a line sensor are calibrated at production sites of line-based cameras. The main purpose of the camera model is the specification of the projection geometry of a cylindrical panorama assuming an ideal line sensor without optical distortion.

Our camera model has multiple projection centers and a cylindrical image surface. The geometry of the camera model is illustrated in Figure 1. **C** (possibly with subscripts i) denotes the different projection centers. These

[1] It is also known as a 'nodal' point because it is the intersection of the optical axis and the rotation axis.

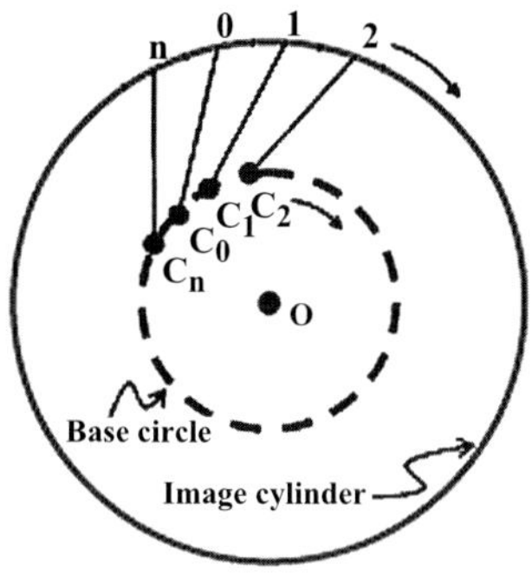

Figure 3. A one-one mapping between indices of projection centers and image columns (Note: ω is constant).

are uniformly distributed on a circle called *base circle*, drawn as a bold and dashed circle. The plane where all the projection centers lie on (i.e., the plane incident with the base circle) is called *base plane*. Here, $\mathbf{O}$ denotes the center of the base circle and the off-axis distance R describes the radius of the base circle. The cylindrical image surface is called *image cylinder*. The center of the base circle coincides with the center of the image cylinder.

The angle which describes the constant angular distance between any pair of adjacent projection centers on the base circle with respect to $\mathbf{O}$ is called the *angular unit*, and it is denoted as γ. Let $\mathbf{C}_i$ and $\mathbf{C}_{i+1}$ be two adjacent projection centers as shown in Figure 3. The angular unit γ is given by the angle $\angle \mathbf{C}_i \mathbf{O} \mathbf{C}_{i+1}$. In the (theoretical) case of infinitely many projection centers on the base circle, the value of γ would be equal to zero.

For a finite number of the projection centers, an image cylinder is partitioned into *image columns* of equal width which are parallel to the axis of the image cylinder. The number of image columns is equal to the number of projection centers on the base circle. The number of image columns is the *width* of a cylindrical panorama, and denoted by W. Obviously, we have $W = \frac{2\pi}{\gamma}$. There is a one-to-one ordered mapping between those image columns and the projection centers, see Figure 3.

The distance between a projection center and its associated image column is called the *effective focal length* of a panoramic camera, and is denoted as f (see Figure 1). Principal angle ω is the angle between a projection ray which lies in the base plane and intersects the base circle at a focal point $\mathbf{C}_i$, and the normal vector of the base circle at this point $\mathbf{C}_i$ (see Figure 3). To be precise: the angle ω is defined starting from the normal of the base circle in clockwise direction (as seen from the top) over the valid interval $[0, 2\pi)$. When the value of ω exceeds this range (in some calculations later on), it is considered modulo 2π.

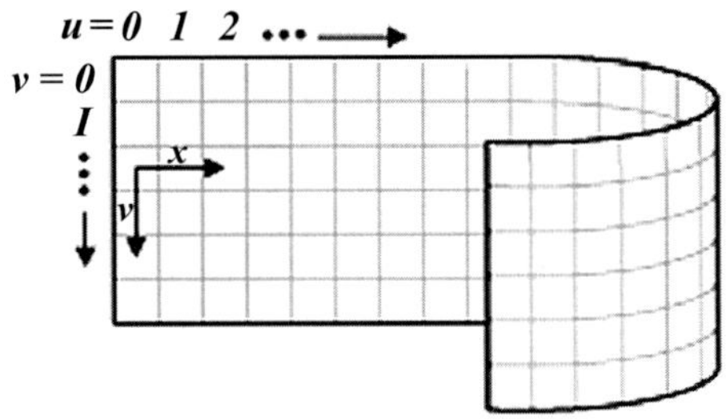

Figure 4. Unfolded panorama and its discrete and Euclidean image coordinate systems.

Altogether, the four parameters, R, f, ω, and γ are the defining parameters of our camera model. The values of these parameters characterize how a panoramic image is acquired. For a panoramic image $E_{\mathcal{P}}$ we write $E_{\mathcal{P}}(R, f, \omega, \gamma)$ to specify its camera parameters. Actually, $E_{\mathcal{P}}$ defines a functional into the set of all panoramic images assuming a fixed rotation axis in 3D space and a fixed center **O** on this axis.

2.2. COORDINATE SYSTEMS

Discrete and Euclidean Image Coordinate Systems
Each image pixel has its coordinates denoted as (u, v), where u and v indicate the image column and image row respectively and are both integers as shown in Figure 4. Let the origin of the image coordinate system be at the top-left corner of the image.

We also define a 2D Euclidean image coordinate system for each panoramic image. Every image point has its coordinates denoted as (x, y). The x-axis is defined to be parallel to the image rows, and the y-axis is aligned with the image columns as shown in Figure 4. Let the origin of the image coordinate system be at the centroid of the square pixel with image coordinates $(u, v) = (0, v_c)$, where the v_cth image row is assumed to be the intersection of the image cylinder with the base plane and is called *principal row*.

The relation between the discrete and continuous image coordinate systems is described as follows:

$$\begin{pmatrix} x \\ y \end{pmatrix} = \begin{pmatrix} u\mu \\ (v - v_c)\mu \end{pmatrix}, \tag{1}$$

where μ is the pixel size. Note that image pixels are assumed to be squares.

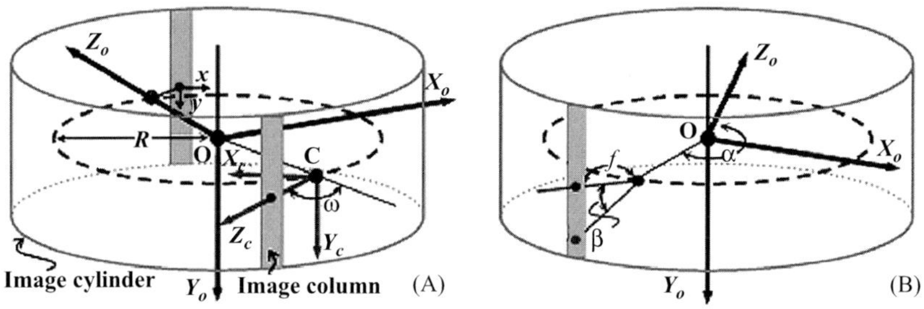

Figure 5. (A) Camera (in black) and optical (in gray) coordinate systems originate at **O** and **C** respectively. (B) Definitions of angular image coordinates α and β in a camera model.

Camera and Optical Coordinate Systems

A 3D *camera coordinate system* is defined for each panoramic camera model, as depicted in Figure 5(A). The origin of a camera coordinate system coincides with the center of the base circle of the panoramic camera model, and is denoted as **O**. The coordinates are denoted as (X_o, Y_o, Z_o). The y-axis of a camera coordinate system coincides with the axis of the image cylinder of the panoramic camera model. The z-axis of a camera coordinate system passes through the projection center associated with the initial image column (i.e., $x = 0$). The x-axis of a camera coordinate system is defined by the right-hand rule.

We also define a 3D *optical coordinate system* for each optical center of the panoramic camera model, as shown in Figure 5(A). The origin of the optical coordinate system, denoted as **C**, coincides with one of the projection centers of the camera model. The coordinates are denoted as (X_c, Y_c, Z_c). The y-axis of an optical coordinate system is parallel to the y-axis of the camera coordinate system. The z-axis of an optical coordinate system, which is also called *optical axis* of the optical center, lies on the base plane of the camera model and passes through the center of the associated image column. The x-axis of an optical coordinate system is also defined by the right-hand rule. The xz-planes of an optical coordinate system and the camera coordinate system are both coplanar with the base plane of the camera model.

Angular Image Coordinate System

Another way of expressing an image point (x, y) is defined by an *angular image coordinate system*. The coordinates are denoted as (α, β), where α is the angle between the z-axis of the camera coordinate system and the line segment $\overline{\mathbf{OC}}$ (see Figure 5(A)), and β is the angle between the z-axis of the optical coordinate system and the line passing through both the associated optical center and the image point (x, y). Figure 5 (B) depicts the definitions of α and β in the camera model.

The conversion between image coordinates (x, y) and angular image coordinates (α, β) is defined by

$$\begin{pmatrix} \alpha \\ \beta \end{pmatrix} = \begin{pmatrix} \frac{2\pi x}{W\mu} \\ \arctan\left(\frac{y}{f}\right) \end{pmatrix}, \tag{2}$$

where f is the effective focal length of a panoramic camera and W is the number of image columns of a panoramic image.

2.3. CLASSIFICATION

Multiple panoramas have been widely used in image technology fields, such as stereoscopic visualization (Huang and Hung, 1998; Peleg and Ben-Ezra, 1999; Wei et al., 1999), stereo reconstruction (Ishiguro et al., 1992; Murray, 1995; Kang and Szeliski, 1997; Huang et al., 1999; Shum and Szeliski, 1999; Huang et al., 2001), walk-through or virtual reality (Chen, 1995; McMillan and Bishop, 1995; Kang and Desikan, 1997; Szeliski and Shum, 1997; Rademacher and Bishop, 1998; Shum and He, 1999), multimedia and teleconferencing (Rademacher and Bishop, 1998; Nishimura et al., 1997), localization, route planning or obstacle detection in robot-navigation or mobile vehicle contexts (Yagi, 1990; Hong, 1991; Ishiguro et al., 1992; Zheng and Tsuji, 1992; Ollis et al., 1999; Yagi, 1999), or tracking and surveillance in 3D space (Ishiguro et al., 1997). This subsection classifies existing multiple-panorama approaches based on our camera model, which allows a specification of used camera geometries. Figure 6 sketches the resulting classes.

Polycentric Panoramas: A set of panoramas, whose rotation axes and centers $\mathbf{O}$ may be somewhere in 3D space, is called a (set of) *polycentric panorama(s)*. Note that the camera parameters associated with each of the panoramas in this set may differ from one to the others. An example of polycentric panoramas is depicted in Figure 6 (A). Basically, polycentric panoramas represent a very general notion for describing the geometry of multiple cylindrical panoramas. Geometric studies based on polycentric panoramas (e.g., their epipolar geometry (Huang et al., 2001)) not only allow exploring geometric behaviors of multiple panoramas in a general sense, but are also useful for studies of more specific types of multiple panoramas, [e.g., Figure 6 (B∼E)].

Parallel-axis and Leveled Panoramas: A set of polycentric panoramas whose associated axes are all parallel is called *parallel-axis panoramas*. Such a set is illustrated by Figure 6 (B). In particular, if the associated axes of parallel-axis panoramas are all orthogonal to the sea level (of course,

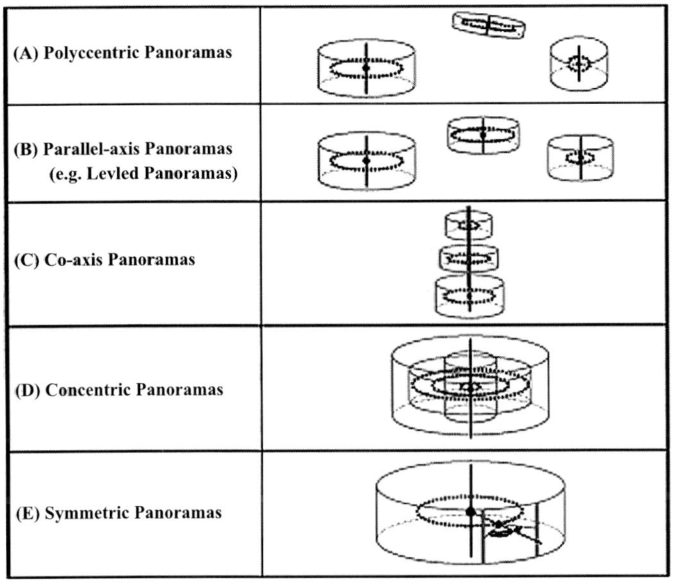

Figure 6. Different classes of multiple panoramas.

assuming a local planar approximation of the sea level) and the centers **O** are all at the same height above sea level, then they are called *leveled panoramas.* Leveled panoramas are often used for visualization and/or reconstruction of a complex scene (e.g., in a museum). There are four reasons supporting their usage:

1. Scene objects in the resulting panoramas are acquired in natural orientation corresponding to human vision experience.

2. The overlap of common fields of view in multiple panoramas is maximized.

3. It is practically achievable (i.e., with a leveler).

4. The dimensionality of the relative-orientation of multiple panoramas is reduced from three dimensions to one dimension (e.g., expressed by orthogonal distances of centers **O** from a straight line).

Co-axis Panoramas: A set of polycentric panoramas whose associated axes coincide is called (a set of) *co-axis panoramas.* Figure 6 (C) shows examples of three co-axis panoramas with different camera parameter values and different centers **O** on this axis. If the camera parameter values of two co-axis panoramas are identical, then the epipolar geometry is quite simple, namely, the epipolar lines are the corresponding image columns.

This special feature simplifies the stereo matching process. In addition, the implementation of such a configuration is reasonably straightforward. This is why this conceptual configuration is widely shared by different panoramic camera architectures, such as, for instance the catadioptric approaches (Southwell et al., 1996; Nene and Nayar, 1998; Petty et al., 1998).

Concentric Panoramas: A set of panoramas where not only their axes coincide but also their associated centers, is called a (set of) *concentric panorama(s)*. An example is given in Figure 6(D). A complete 360-degree scan of a matrix camera of image resolution $H \times W$ generates W different panoramas with different camera parameters (i.e., different effective focal length and principal angle). All these panoramas are in fact concentric panoramas (Shum and He, 1999).

Symmetric Panoramas: Two concentric panoramas, $E_{\mathcal{P}_R}(R, f, \omega, \gamma)$ and $E_{\mathcal{P}_L}(R, f, (2\pi - \omega), \gamma)$ respectively, are called *symmetric panoramas* or a *symmetric pair*. The word 'symmetric' is for describing that their principal angles are symmetric to the associated normal vector of the base circle. An example of a symmetric panorama is shown in Figure 6(E). Due to this epipolar property, the resultant stereo panoramas are directly stereoscopic-viewable (Peleg and Ben-Ezra, 1999). Moreover, this property also supports 3D reconstruction applications by using the same stereo-matching algorithms that were previously developed for binocular stereo images (Shum et al., 1999).

3. Calibration

This section presents methods for calibrating off-axis distance R and principal angle ω. These two parameters are characterizing the 'non-linear component' of a panorama, and their calibration is the new challenge. The other two parameters, effective focal length f_μ (in pixels) and principal row v_c, are pre-calibrated using the calibration method discussed first in Subsection 3.1. The calibration of these two parameters characterizing the 'linear component' of a panorama, is provided for completeness reasons.

This section specifies then to what degree commonly known, or adopted geometric information is useful for calibrating off-axis distance R and principal angle ω. We present three different approaches, which all have been used or discussed already for planar pinhole camera calibration, but not yet for cylindrical panoramic camera calibration. The question arises, how these concepts developed within the planar pinhole camera context can be applied to cylindrical panoramic cameras, and what performance can be achieved. In particular, we are looking for possibilities of using linear geometric features which may reduce the dimensionality and complexity of panoramic camera calibration.

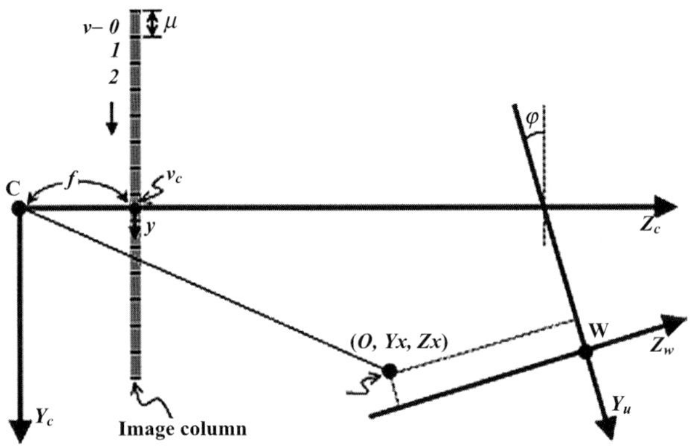

Figure 7. Geometric interpretation for the first step of panoramic camera calibration.

3.1. CALIBRATING EFFECTIVE FOCAL LENGTH AND PRINCIPAL ROW

The first step of the camera calibration process for a line-based panoramic camera is to calibrate the effective focal length f measured in pixels and the *principal row*[2] v_c. The projection geometry can be modeled as the same way as already applied for traditional pinhole cameras of planar images (Tsai, 1987; Faugeras, 1993) except that only one image column is considered in our case. In this case, given a calibration object we may then calibrate the camera effective focal length f and the principal row v_c of a line-based panoramic camera by minimizing the differences between actual and ideal projections of known 3D points on a calibration object.

A 2D space is sufficient to describe all the necessary geometrical relations. All the coordinate systems used here are therefore defined on a 2D plane. The geometry of a single image column of the panorama is depicted in Figure 7. The associated optical center is denoted as **C**. A world coordinate system originated at **W** is defined on the calibration object.

The relation between a calibration point $(0, Y_w, Z_w)$ in world coordinates and its projection v in image coordinates can be expressed as follows:

$$\begin{pmatrix} sv \\ s \end{pmatrix} = \begin{bmatrix} f_\mu & v_c \\ 0 & 1 \end{bmatrix} \begin{bmatrix} \cos(\varphi) & -\sin(\varphi) & t_y \\ \sin(\varphi) & \cos(\varphi) & t_z \end{bmatrix} \begin{pmatrix} Y_w \\ Z_w \\ 1 \end{pmatrix}.$$

The value v can be calculated by the following Equation (12):

$$v = \frac{Y_w(f_\mu \cos(\varphi) + v_c \sin(\varphi)) + Z_w(v_c \cos(\varphi) - f_\mu \sin(\varphi)) + (f_\mu t_y + v_c t_z)}{Y_w \sin(\varphi) + Z_w \cos(\varphi) + t_z}$$

[2] The image row where the panorama intersects with the base plane.

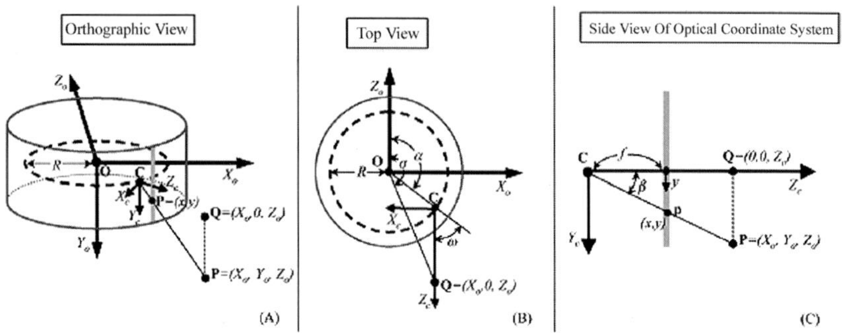

Figure 8. Projection geometry of a cylindrical panorama.

The values of f_μ and v_c can therefore be determined by given a set of calibration points and their corresponding projections. Equation (12) can be rearranged in a linear equation of five unknowns denoted as X_i, where $i = 1, 2, \ldots, 5$:

$$Y_w X_1 + Z_w X_2 - vY_w X_3 - vZ_w X_4 + X_5 = v,$$

where

$$X_1 = \frac{f_\mu \cos(\varphi) + v_c \sin(\varphi)}{t_z}, \quad X_2 = \frac{v_c \cos(\varphi) - f_\mu \sin(\varphi)}{t_z},$$
$$X_3 = \frac{\sin(\varphi)}{t_z}, \quad X_4 = \frac{\cos(\varphi)}{t_z}, \quad \text{and} \quad X_5 = \frac{(f_\mu t_y + v_c t_z)}{t_z}.$$

Hence, at least five pairs of calibration points and their projections are necessary to determine f_μ and v_c. The values of f_μ and v_c can be calculated as follows:

$$\begin{pmatrix} f_\mu \\ v_c \end{pmatrix} = \begin{bmatrix} X_4 & X_3 \\ -X_3 & X_4 \end{bmatrix}^{-1} \begin{pmatrix} X_1 \\ X_2 \end{pmatrix}.$$

3.2. POINT-BASED APPROACH

A straightforward (traditional) camera calibration approach is to minimize the difference between ideal projections and actual projections of known 3D points, such as on calibration objects, or localized 3D scene points. The same concept is applied in this section for the calibration of off-axis distance R and principal angle ω.

3.2.1. *Nonlinear Least Square Optimization*

In the following, a parameter with a hat '^' indicates that this parameter may contain an error.

THEOREM 4.1. *Given a set of known 3D points* (X_{wi}, Y_{wi}, Z_{wi}) *in world coordinates and their actual projections* $(\hat{u}_i, \hat{v}_i)$ *in image coordinates, where* $i = 1, 2, \ldots, n$. *The values of* R *and* ω *can be estimated by solving the following minimization:*

$$min \sum_{i=1}^{n} \left(\sin\left(\frac{2\hat{u}_i\pi}{W} + \omega\right) - \frac{X_{oi}A + Z_{oi}R\sin\omega}{X_{oi}^2 + Z_{oi}^2} \right)^2 + \left(\hat{v}_i - \frac{f_\mu Y_{oi}}{A - R\cos\omega} + v_c \right)^2 \quad (3)$$

where $A = \sqrt{X_{oi}^2 + Z_{oi}^2 - R^2\sin^2\omega}$ *and*

$$\begin{pmatrix} X_{oi} \\ Y_{oi} \\ Z_{oi} \end{pmatrix} = \begin{pmatrix} X_{wi}t_{11} + Y_{wi}t_{12} + Z_{wi}t_{13} + t_{14} \\ X_{wi}t_{21} + Y_{wi}t_{22} + Z_{wi}t_{23} + t_{24} \\ X_{wi}t_{31} + Y_{wi}t_{32} + Z_{wi}t_{33} + t_{34} \end{pmatrix}.$$

Proof The derivation of the objective function as shown in Equation (3) follows from the projection formula for our camera model: consider a known 3D point **P**, whose coordinates are (X_w, Y_w, Z_w) with respect to the world coordinate system. A point **P** is transformed into the camera coordinate system before calculating its projection on the image. We denote the coordinates of **P** with respect to the camera coordinate system as (X_o, Y_o, Z_o). Let $\mathbf{R_{wo}}$ be the 3×3 rotation matrix and $\mathbf{T_{wo}}$ be the 3×1 translation vector which describes the orientation and the position of the camera coordinate system with respect to the world coordinate system, respectively. We call the 3×4 matrix $[\mathbf{R_{wo}} \quad -\mathbf{R_{wo}}\mathbf{T_{wo}}]$ transformation matrix and denote it by twelve parameters t_{ij}, where $i = 1, 2, 3$ and $j = 1, 2, 3, 4$.

The projection of (X_o, Y_o, Z_o) can be expressed in image coordinates (u, v). The values of u and v can be determined separately. To determine the value of u, we obtain the angular coordinate α. From Equation (2) and Equation (1) we may derive that

$$u = \frac{\alpha W}{2\pi}. \quad (4)$$

Consider a 3D point **P** with coordinates (X_o, Y_o, Z_o). Its projection on the xz-plane of the camera coordinate system is denoted as **Q**, as shown in Figure 8(A). Thus, point **Q** has coordinates $(X_o, 0, Z_o)$ with respect to the camera coordinate system. From Figure 8(B), the top view of the projection geometry, the angular coordinate α can be calculated by $\alpha = \sigma - \angle\mathbf{COQ} = \sigma - \omega + \angle\mathbf{CQO}$. Hence, we have

$$\alpha = \arctan\left(\frac{X_o}{Z_o}\right) - \omega + \arcsin\left(\frac{R\sin\omega}{\sqrt{X_o^2 + Z_o^2}}\right)$$

$$= \arcsin\left(\frac{X_o}{\sqrt{X_o^2+Z_o^2}}\right) - \omega + \arcsin\left(\frac{R\sin\omega}{\sqrt{X_o^2+Z_o^2}}\right)$$

$$= \arcsin\left(\frac{X_o}{\sqrt{X_o^2+Z_o^2}}\sqrt{1-\frac{R^2\sin^2\omega}{X_o^2+Z_o^2}} + \frac{R\sin\omega}{\sqrt{X_o^2+Z_o^2}}\sqrt{1-\frac{X_o^2}{X_o^2+Z_o^2}}\right)$$
$$-\omega$$

$$= \arcsin\left(\frac{X_o\left(\sqrt{X_o^2+Z_o^2-R^2\sin^2\omega}\right)+Z_oR\sin\omega}{X_o^2+Z_o^2}\right) - \omega. \quad (5)$$

To determine the value of v, we need to find the value of the angular coordinate β as shown in Figure 8 (C). It is understood from Equation (2) that $y = f\tan\beta$, where y is Euclidean image coordinate. Similar to the case of calculating u, the value of v can be obtained by Equation (1) as

$$v = \frac{f\tan\beta}{\mu} + v_c = f_\mu \tan\beta + v_c, \quad (6)$$

where f_μ is the camera effective focal length measured in pixels and v_c is the principal row.

Points $\mathbf{P}$ and $\mathbf{Q}$ have coordinates $(0, Y_c, Z_c)$ and $(0, 0, Z_c)$ with respect to the optical coordinate system, respectively, where $Y_c = Y_o$. From the side view of the optical coordinate system originated at $\mathbf{C}$, as shown in Figure 8 (C), the angular coordinate β can be calculated by

$$\beta = \arctan\left(\frac{Y_c\sin\omega}{\overline{\mathbf{OQ}}\sin(\angle\mathbf{COQ})}\right).$$

Thus, we have

$$\tan\beta = \frac{Y_o\sin\omega}{\sqrt{X_o^2+Z_o^2}\sin\left(\omega - \arcsin\left(\frac{R\sin\omega}{\sqrt{X_o^2+Z_o^2}}\right)\right)}$$

$$= \frac{Y_o\sin\omega}{\sqrt{X_o^2+Z_o^2}\left(\sin\omega\sqrt{1-\frac{R^2\sin^2\omega}{X_o^2+Z_o^2}} - \cos\omega\left(\frac{R\sin\omega}{\sqrt{X_o^2+Z_o^2}}\right)\right)}$$

$$= \frac{Y_o}{\sqrt{X_o^2+Z_o^2-R^2\sin^2\omega} - R\cos\omega}. \quad (7)$$

When n points are given, we want to minimize the following:

$$min \sum_{i=1}^{n} (\hat{u}_i - u_i)^2 + (\hat{v}_i - v_i)^2,$$

Approaches	Number of Image Required	Pre-process	Complexity	Dimensionality	Initial Value Dependence	Error Sensitivity	Estimated R	Estimated ω
Point-based	one	identifying projections of 3D points	nonlinear form e.g. sine, fractions and square roots	14 unknowns [R|T]* unavoidable	high	exponential growing	actual	actual
Image Correspondence	two	searching image corresponding points	linear form	four unknowns [R|T]* not required	ignorable	exponential growing	ratio	actual
Parallel-line-based	one	identifying projections of lines	linear form	three unknowns [R|T]* avoidable	ignorable	linear growing	actual	actual

* [R|T] is a matrix that characterizes camera extrinsic parameters, where **R** is a rotation matrix and **T** is a translation vector.

Figure 9. Summaries of the performances of three different camera calibration approaches under selected criteria.

where the value of u_i can be obtained from Equations (4) and (5). The value of v_i can be obtained by Equations (6) and (7). After a minor rearrangement, it is equivalent to the minimization shown in Theorem 4.1. □

3.2.2. *Discussion*

In Theorem 4.1, the parameters f_μ and v_c are assumed to be pre-calibrated. Therefore, there are 14 parameters in total to be estimated using a nonlinear least square optimization method (Gill et al., 1991). These 14 parameters consist of the targeted parameters R, ω, and the twelve unknowns in the transformation matrix.

The objective function in Equation (3) is rather complicated. The parameters to be estimated are enclosed in sine functions and square roots involved in both numerator and denominator of the fractions. The dimensionality is high due to the fact that the extrinsic parameters in $\mathbf{R}_{\mathbf{wo}}$ and $\mathbf{T}_{\mathbf{wo}}$ are unavoidable in this approach. Hence, a large set of 3D points is needed for a reasonably accurate estimation.

The quality of calibration results following this approach highly depends on the given initial values for parameter estimation. Our error sensitivity analysis shows an exponentially growing trend. All above mentioned assessments are summarized in Figure 9 and the poor result motivates us to explore other options for better performances with respect to those criteria in the table.

We claim that the most critical problem of the point-based approach is the high dimensionality of the objective function. Therefore, it is necessary to look for an approach that is able to avoid the involvement of camera extrinsic parameters in the calibration process. In the next section, we investigate the possibility of camera calibration from image correspondences.

3.3. IMAGE CORRESPONDENCE APPROACH

In this subsection, we investigate the possibility of calibrating the off-axis distance R and the principal angle ω using the information of corresponding image points in two panoramas. Since this approach requires neither scene measures nor calibration object, thus avoiding a dependency from camera extrinsic parameters in the calibration process, it is surely of interest to see to what extent the camera parameters can be calibrated.

Epipolar curve equations are used to link the provided corresponding image points, and estimation of parameters is based on this. For the camera calibration, we should choose a geometrical representation to be as simple as possible for describing the relation between two panoramas such that a more stable estimation can be obtained. We choose the geometry of a concentric panoramic pair for detailing an image-correspondence based approach.

The concentric panoramic model was explained in Subsection 2.3. The effective focal length and the angular unit are assumed to be identical for both images. The concentric panoramic pair can be acquired in various ways (e.g., using different or the same off-axis distances, and/or different or the same principal angle). The authors studied all these options and obtained that the configuration that consists of different off-axis distances, say $R_1$and R_2, and the same principal angle ω, gives the best performance for image-correspondence based calibration. This subsection elaborates camera calibration using a concentric panoramic pair under such a configuration.

3.3.1. *Objective Function*

THEOREM 4.2. *Given n pairs of corresponding image points (x_{1i}, y_{1i}) and (x_{2i}, y_{2i}), where $i = 1, 2, \ldots, n$, in a concentric pair of panoramas $E_{\mathcal{P}_1}(R_1, f, \omega, \gamma)$ and $E_{\mathcal{P}_2}(R_2, f, \omega, \gamma)$. The ratio $R_1 : R_2$ and ω can be calibrated by minimizing the following cost function:*

$$min \sum_{i=1}^{n} (y_{i2} \sin \sigma_i X_1 + (y_{i2} \cos \sigma_i - y_{i1}) X_2 \\ - y_{i1} \sin \sigma_i X_3 + (y_{i1} \cos \sigma_i - y_{i2}) X_4)^2$$

subject to the equality constraint $X_1 X_4 = X_2 X_3$, where $\sigma_i = \frac{\gamma}{\mu} \cdot (x_{1i} - x_{2i})$, μ is the pixel size, and $X_1 = R_2 \cos \omega$, $X_2 = R_2 \sin \omega$, $X_3 = R_1 \cos \omega$, and $X_4 = R_1 \sin \omega$.

Once the values of X_1, X_2, X_3, and X_4 are obtained, $\frac{R_1}{R_2}$ and ω can be calculated by

$$\frac{R_1}{R_2} = \frac{\sqrt{X_3^2 + X_4^2}}{\sqrt{X_1^2 + X_2^2}} \quad \text{and} \quad \omega = \arccos\left(\frac{X_1}{\sqrt{X_1^2 + X_2^2}}\right).$$

Proof Let (x_1, y_1) and (x_2, y_2) be a pair of corresponding image points in a concentric pair of panoramas $E_{\mathcal{P}_1}(R_1,\ f,\ \omega,\ \gamma)$ and $E_{\mathcal{P}_2}(R_2,\ f,\ \omega,\ \gamma)$. Given x_1 and y_1, by the epipolar curve equation in (Huang et al., 2001) we have

$$y_2 = \frac{y_1 \left(\frac{f}{f}\right)(R_2 \sin\omega - R_1 \sin(\alpha_2 + \omega - \alpha_1))}{R_2 \sin(\alpha_1 + \omega - \alpha_2) - R_1 \sin\omega}, \tag{8}$$

where $\alpha_1 = \frac{2\pi x_1}{\mu W_1} = \frac{\gamma x_1}{\mu}$ and similarly for $\alpha_2 = \frac{2\pi x_2}{\mu W_2} = \frac{\gamma x_2}{\mu}$. The equation can be rearranged as follows:

$$y_2 R_2 \sin((\alpha_1 - \alpha_2) + \omega) - y_2 R_1 \sin\omega + y_1 R_1 \sin((\alpha_2 - \alpha_1) + \omega) - y_1 R_2 \sin\omega = 0$$

Let $(\alpha_1 - \alpha_2) = \sigma$. We have

$$y_2 \sin\sigma R_2 \cos\omega + (y_2 \cos\sigma - y_1) R_2 \sin\omega - y_1 \sin\sigma R_1 \cos\omega$$
$$+ (y_1 \cos\sigma - y_2) R_1 \sin\omega = 0$$

We observe from the equation that only the ratio $R_1 : R_2$ and ω can be calibrated. The actual values of R_1 and R_2 are not computable following this approach alone.

Given n pairs of corresponding image points (x_{1i}, y_{1i}) and (x_{2i}, y_{2i}), where $i = 1, 2, \ldots, n$, it is thus to minimize the objective function given in Theorem 4.2. □

3.3.2. *Experiments and Discussion*

The objective function of this correspondence-based approach is in linear form and there are only four unknowns to be estimated, namely X_1, X_2, X_3, and X_4 in Equation (4.2). In this case, at least four pairs of corresponding image points are required. This can be considered to be a great improvement compared to the point-based approach. However, the results of estimated values for real scene data remain to be very poor, in general far from the known parameter values. An experiment using a real scene and a concentric panoramic pair is illustrated in Figure 3.3.2, and there are 35 pairs of corresponding image points identified manually, marked by crosses and indexed by numbers. We use the optimization method of sequential quadratic programming (Gill et al., 1991) for estimating $\frac{R_1}{R_2}$ and ω. This experimental result stimulated further steps into the analysis of error sensitivity.

The authors analyzed the error sensitivity by a simulation of synthetic data. The ground-truth data are generated in correspondence to a real case, and the errors are simulated by additive random noise in normal distribution, perturbating the coordinates of ideal corresponding image point-pairs.

(A)

(B)

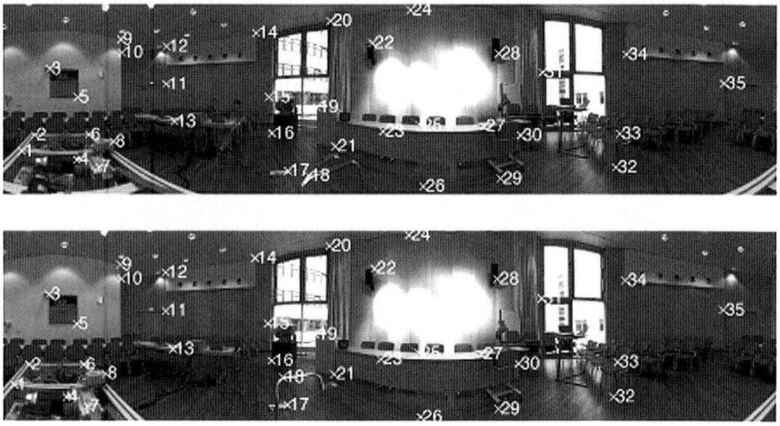

Figure 10. A concentric pair with 35 corresponding image points for the calibration of the camera parameters, off-axis distance ratio R_1/R_2, and principal angle ω.

Calibration results after adding errors are shown in Figure 10. We see that the estimated result is rather sensitive to these errors. The errors of the estimated parameters increase exponentially with respect to the input errors. These results may serve as guidance for studies of error behavior of calibration results for real image and scene data.

One of the reasons why this image correspondence approach is sensitive to error is that the values of the coefficients of the objective function are likely very close upon the selected corresponding points. Possible ways for improving such an error-sensitive characteristic, without relying on the 'robustness' of numerical methods in (Gill et al., 1991), include first increase the number of pairs of corresponding image points, and second place a calibration object closer to the camera for producing greater disparities.

Input data error in pixel	Estimated ω error in (%)
0.0	0.00
0.5	0.17
1.0	0.52
1.5	2.78
2.0	10.34
3.0	28.14
4.0	68.25
5.0	155.62

Figure 11. Error sensitivity results of the camera calibration based on the image correspondence approach.

Regarding the first improvement suggestion, we found that only minor improvements are possible.

Despite the error problem, the correspondence-based approach is unable to recover the actual value of R, which is (of course) one of the main intentions of the intended calibration process. The assessments of this approach is also summarized in Figure 9.

3.4. PARALLEL-LINE-BASED APPROACH

In this section, we discuss another possible approach that has been widely used for planar pinhole camera calibration, which we call the parallel-line-based approach. The main intention is to find a single linear equation that links 3D geometric scene features to the camera model such that by providing sufficient scene measurements we are able to calibrate the values of R and ω with good accuracy. This approach is presented by exploring the related geometric properties such as distances, lengths, orthogonalities of the straight lines, and formulating them as constraints for estimating the camera parameters.

This section starts with the assumptions for this approach. We assume that there are more than two straight lines in the captured real scene (e.g., a special object with straight edges), which are parallel to the axis of the associated image cylinder.

For each straight line, we assume that there are at least two points on this line which are visible and identifiable in the panoramic image, and that the distance between these two points and the length of the projected line segment on the image are measurable (i.e., available input data). Furthermore, for each straight line we assume either there exists another parallel straight line where the distance between these two lines is known, or there exist two other parallel straight lines such that these three lines are orthogonal. The precise definition of orthogonality of three lines is given in Subsection 3.4.2.

Two possible geometric constraints are proposed, namely a distance constraint and an orthogonality constraint. Each constraint allows calibrating the camera parameters of the off-axis distance R and the principal angle ω. The experiments are conducted and comparing the calibration performances of both constraints. The comparisons to the other two approaches are summarized in Figure 11.

3.4.1. *Constraint 1: Distance*

All straight lines (e.g., straight edges of objects) measured in the 3D scene are denoted as $\mathcal{L}$ and indexed by a subscript for the distinction of multiple lines. The (Euclidean) distance between two visible points on a line $\mathcal{L}_i$ is

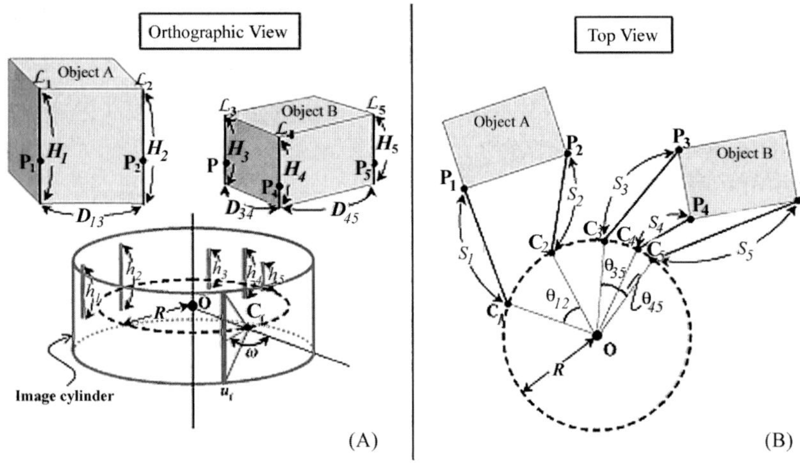

Figure 12. Geometrical interpretations of the parallel-line-based camera calibration approach.

denoted as H_i. The length of a projection of a line segment on an image column u can be determined from the input image, denoted as h in pixels. Examples of H_i and its corresponding h_i values are depicted in Figure 3.4.1 (A) where $i = 1, 2, \ldots, 5$.

The distance between two lines $\mathcal{L}_i$ and $\mathcal{L}_j$ is the length of a line segment that connects and is perpendicular to both lines $\mathcal{L}_i$ and $\mathcal{L}_j$. The distance is denoted as D_{ij}. If the distance between two straight lines is measured (in the 3D scene), then we say that both lines form a *line pair*. One line may be paired up with more than one other line. Figure 3.4.1 (A) shows examples of three line pairs, namely ($\mathcal{L}_1$, $\mathcal{L}_2$), ($\mathcal{L}_3$, $\mathcal{L}_4$), and ($\mathcal{L}_4$, $\mathcal{L}_5$).

Consider two straight lines $\mathcal{L}_i$ and $\mathcal{L}_j$ in 3D space and the image columns of their projections, denoted as u_i and u_j respectively, on a panoramic image. The camera optical centers associated with image columns u_i and u_j, respectively, are denoted as $\mathbf{C}_i$ and $\mathbf{C}_j$. Let the distance between the two associated image columns be equal to $d_{ij} = |u_i - u_j|$ in pixels. The angular distance of two associated image columns of lines $\mathcal{L}_i$ and $\mathcal{L}_j$ is the angle defined by line segments $\overline{\mathbf{C}_i\mathbf{O}}$ and $\overline{\mathbf{C}_j\mathbf{O}}$, where $\mathbf{O}$ is the center of the base circle. We denote the angular distance of a line pair ($\mathcal{L}_i$, $\mathcal{L}_j$) as θ_{ij}. Examples of angular distances for some line pairs are given in Figure 3.4.1 (B). The angular distance θ_{ij} can be calculated in terms of d_{ij}, that is $\theta_{ij} = \frac{2\pi d_{ij}}{W}$, where W is the width of a panorama in pixels.

The distance between a line $\mathcal{L}_i$ and the associated camera optical center (which 'sees' the line $\mathcal{L}_i$) is defined by the length of a line segment starting from the optical center and ending at one point on $\mathcal{L}_i$ such that the line segment is perpendicular to the line $\mathcal{L}_i$. The distance is denoted as S_i. We can infer the distance S_i by $S_i = \frac{f_\mu H_i}{hi}$, where f_μ is the pre-calibrated effective focal length of the camera.

THEOREM 4.3. *Given n pairs of $(\mathcal{L}_{it}, \mathcal{L}_{jt})$, where $t = 1, 2, \ldots, n$. The values of R and ω can be estimated by solving the following minimization:*

$$min \sum_{t=1}^{n} (K_{1t}X_1 + K_{2t}X_2 + K_{3t}X_3 + K_{4t})^2 , \tag{9}$$

subject to the equality constraint $X_1 = X_2^2 + X_3^2$, where $K_{st}, s = 1, 2, 3, 4$, are coefficients, and $X_s, s = 1, 2, 3$ are three linearly independent variables. We have $X_1 = R^2$, $X_2 = R\cos\omega$, and $X_3 = R\sin\omega$. Moreover, we have

$$\begin{aligned} K_{1t} &= 1 - \cos\theta_{ijt} \, , \\ K_{2t} &= (S_{it} + S_{jt})(1 - \cos\theta_{ijt}), \\ K_{3t} &= -(S_{it} - S_{jt})\sin\theta_{ijt}, \qquad \textit{and} \\ K_{4t} &= \frac{S_{it}^2 + S_{jt}^2 - D_{ijt}^2}{2} - S_{it}S_{jt}\cos\theta_{ijt}, \end{aligned}$$

which can be calculated based on the measurements from real scenes and the image.

The values of R and ω can be found uniquely by

$$R = \sqrt{X_1} \quad \textit{and} \quad \omega = \arccos\left(\frac{X_2}{\sqrt{X_1}}\right).$$

Proof For any given pair of $(\mathcal{L}_i, \mathcal{L}_j)$, a 2D coordinate system is defined on the base plane depicted in Figure 3.4.1, which is independent from the camera coordinate system. Note that even though all the measurements are defined in 3D space, the geometrical relation can be described on a plane, since all the straight lines are assumed to be parallel to the axis of the image cylinder. The coordinate system is originated at $\mathbf{O}$, and the z-axis passes through the camera focal point $\mathbf{C}_i$ while the x-axis is orthogonal to the z-axis and lies on the base plane. This coordinate system is analogous to the camera coordinate system previously defined without y-axis, and more importantly the coordinate system is defined for each line pair.

The position of $\mathbf{C}_i$ can then be described by coordinates $(0, R)$ and the position $\mathbf{C}_j$ can be described by coordinates $(R\sin\theta_{ij}, R\cos\theta_{ij})$. The intersection point of line $\mathcal{L}_i$ and the base plane, denoted as $\mathbf{P}_i$, can be expressed by a sum vector of $\overrightarrow{\mathbf{OC}_i}$ and $\overrightarrow{\mathbf{C}_i\mathbf{P}_i}$. Thus, we have

$$\mathbf{P}_i = \begin{pmatrix} S_i \sin\omega \\ R + S_i \cos\omega \end{pmatrix}.$$

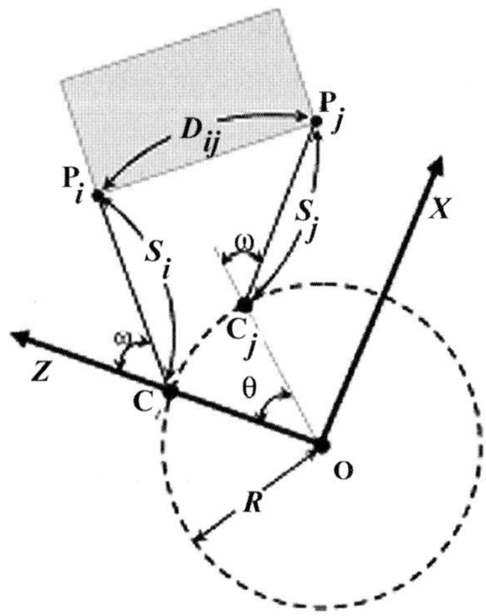

Figure 13. The coordinate system of a line pair.

Similarly, the intersection point of line $\mathcal{L}_j$ and the base plane, denoted as $\mathbf{P}_j$, can be described by a sum vector of $\overrightarrow{\mathbf{OC}_j}$and $\overrightarrow{\mathbf{C}_j\mathbf{P}_j}$. We have

$$\mathbf{P}_j = \begin{pmatrix} R\sin\theta_{ij} + S_j \sin(\theta_{ij} + \omega) \\ R\cos\theta_{ij} + S_j \cos(\theta_{ij} + \omega) \end{pmatrix}$$

As the distance between points $\mathbf{P}_i$ and $\mathbf{P}_j$ is pre-measured, denoted by D_{ij}, thus we have the following equation

$$D_{ij}^2 = (S_i \sin\omega - R\sin\theta_{ij} - S_j \sin(\omega+\theta_{ij}))^2 + (R + S_i \cos\omega - R\cos\theta_{ij} - S_j \cos(\omega+\theta_{ij}))^2$$

This equation can then be expanded and rearranged as follows:

$$\begin{aligned} D_{ij}^2 &= S_i^2 \sin^2\omega + R^2 \sin^2\theta_{ij} + S_j^2 \sin^2(\omega + \theta_{ij}) - 2S_i R \sin\omega \sin\theta_{ij} \\ &\quad -2S_i S_j \sin\omega \sin(\omega + \theta_{ij}) + 2RS_j \sin\theta_{ij} \sin(\omega + \theta_{ij}) \\ &\quad +R^2 + S_i^2 \cos^2\omega + R^2 \cos^2\theta_{ij} + S_j^2 \cos^2(\omega + \theta_{ij}) \\ &\quad +2RS_i \cos\omega - 2R^2 \cos\theta_{ij} - 2RS_j \cos(\omega + \theta_{ij}) - 2S_i R \cos\omega \cos\theta_{ij} \\ &\quad -2S_i S_j \cos\omega \cos(\omega + \theta_{ij}) + 2RS_j \cos\theta_{ij} \cos(\omega + \theta_{ij}) \\ &= S_i^2 + 2R^2 + S_j^2 + 2RS_i \cos\omega - 2R^2 \cos\theta_{ij} \\ &\quad -2S_j R \cos(\omega + \theta_{ij}) - 2S_i R(\sin\omega \sin\theta_{ij} + \cos\omega \cos\theta_{ij}) \\ &\quad -2S_i S_j (\sin\omega \sin(\omega + \theta_{ij}) + \cos\omega \cos(\omega + \theta_{ij})) \\ &\quad +2S_j R(\sin\theta_{ij} \sin(\omega + \theta_{ij}) + \cos\theta_{ij} \cos(\omega + \theta_{ij})) \\ &= S_i^2 + S_j^2 + 2R^2(1 - \cos\theta_{ij}) + 2(S_i + S_j)R\cos\omega \\ &\quad -2(S_i + S_j)R\cos\omega\cos\theta_{ij} - 2(S_i - S_j)R\sin\omega\sin\theta_{ij} - 2S_i S_j \cos\theta_{ij} \end{aligned}$$

Finally, we obtain

$$0 = (1-\cos\theta_{ij})R^2 + (S_i+S_j)(1-\cos\theta_{ij})R\cos\omega - (S_i-S_j)\sin\theta_{ij}R\sin\omega + \frac{S_i^2+S_j^2-D_{ij}^2}{2} - S_iS_j\cos\theta_{ij} \tag{10}$$

In Equation (10), the values of S_i, S_j, D_{ij}, and θ_{ij} are known. Thus Equation (10) can be arranged into the following linear form

$$K_1X_1 + K_2X_2 + K_3X_3 + K_4 = 0$$

If more than three equations are provided, then linear least-square techniques may be applied. The values of R and ω may be found by

$$R = \sqrt{X_1} \quad \text{or} \quad \sqrt{X_2^2+X_3^2}$$

and

$$\omega = \arccos\left(\frac{X_2}{\sqrt{X_1}}\right) \text{ or } \arcsin\left(\frac{X_3}{\sqrt{X_1}}\right) \text{ or } \arccos\left(\frac{X_2}{\sqrt{X_2^2+X_3^2}}\right)$$

Because of the dependency among the variables X_1, X_2, and X_3, there are multiple solutions of R and ω. To tackle this multiple-solutions problem, we may constrain the parameter estimation further by the inter-relation among X_1, X_2, and X_3, which is

$$X_1^2 = X_2^2 + X_3^2$$

because of

$$R^2 = (R\cos\omega)^2 + (R\sin\omega)^2.$$

Hence Theorem 4.3 is shown. □

Note that even though the additional constraint forced us to use a non-linear optimization method, we still have the expected linear parameter estimation quality.

3.4.2. *Constraint 2: Orthogonality*

We say that three parallel lines $\mathcal{L}_i$, $\mathcal{L}_j$, and $\mathcal{L}_k$ are *orthogonal* iff the plane defined by lines $\mathcal{L}_i$ and $\mathcal{L}_j$ and the plane defined by lines $\mathcal{L}_j$ and $\mathcal{L}_k$ are orthogonal. It follows that the line $\mathcal{L}_j$ is the intersection of these two planes. For example, in Figure 3.4.1 (A), lines $\mathcal{L}_3$, $\mathcal{L}_4$, and $\mathcal{L}_5$ are orthogonal lines.

THEOREM 4.4. *For any given orthogonal lines ($\mathcal{L}_i$, $\mathcal{L}_j$, $\mathcal{L}_k$), we may derive a liner relation which is the same as in the distance-based approach except that the expressions of the four coefficients are different. Hence, the minimization of Equation (9) and the calculations of R and ω in the distance-based approach also apply to this modified approach.*

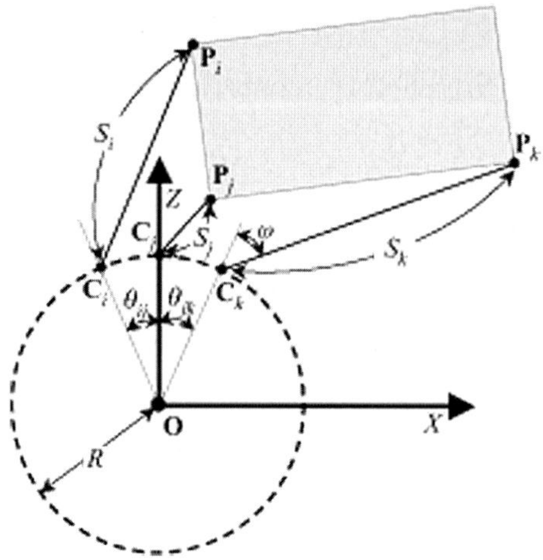

Figure 14. The coordinate system of three orthogonal lines.

Proof Consider three orthogonal lines $\mathcal{L}_i$, $\mathcal{L}_j$, and $\mathcal{L}_k$ in 3D space. The measures of S_i, S_j, S_k, θ_{ij}, and θ_{jk} are defined and obtained in the same way as in the case of the distance constraint. A 2D coordinate system is defined for each group of orthogonal lines in the similar way as in the distance constraint case. Figure 3.4.2 illustrates the 2D coordinate system for the three orthogonal lines ($\mathcal{L}_i$, $\mathcal{L}_j$, $\mathcal{L}_k$).

The position of $\mathbf{C}_j$ can be described by coordinates $(0, R)$, the position of $\mathbf{C}_i$ by coordinates $(-R\sin\theta_{ij}, R\cos\theta_{ij})$, and the position of $\mathbf{C}_k$ by coordinates $(R\sin\theta_{jk}, R\cos\theta_{jk})$. The intersection points of lines $\mathcal{L}_i$, $\mathcal{L}_j$, and $\mathcal{L}_k$ with the base-plane are denoted as $\mathbf{P}_i$, $\mathbf{P}_j$, and $\mathbf{P}_k$, respectively. We have

$$\mathbf{P}_i = \begin{pmatrix} -R\sin\theta_{ij} + S_i\sin(\omega - \theta_{ij}) \\ R\cos\theta_{ij} + S_j\cos(\omega - \theta_{ij}) \end{pmatrix}, \quad \mathbf{P}_j = \begin{pmatrix} S_j\sin\omega \\ R + S_j\cos\omega \end{pmatrix},$$

and

$$\mathbf{P}_k = \begin{pmatrix} R\sin\theta_{jk} + S_k\sin(\theta_{jk} + \omega) \\ R\cos\theta_{jk} + S_k\cos(\theta_{jk} + \omega) \end{pmatrix}.$$

Since the vector $\overrightarrow{\mathbf{P}_i\mathbf{P}_j}$ and vector $\overrightarrow{\mathbf{P}_j\mathbf{P}_k}$ are orthogonal, thus we have the following equation

$$\begin{aligned} 0 \;=\; & (-R\sin\theta_{ij} + S_i\sin(\omega-\theta_{ij}) - S_j\sin\omega) \\ & \times\; (R\sin\theta_{jk} + S_k\sin(\omega+\theta_{jk}) - S_j\sin\omega) \\ & +\; (R\cos\theta_{ij} + S_j\cos(\omega-\theta_{ij}) - R - S_j\cos\omega) \\ & \times\; (R\cos\theta_{jk} + S_k\cos(\omega+\theta_{jk}) - R - S_j\cos\omega). \end{aligned}$$

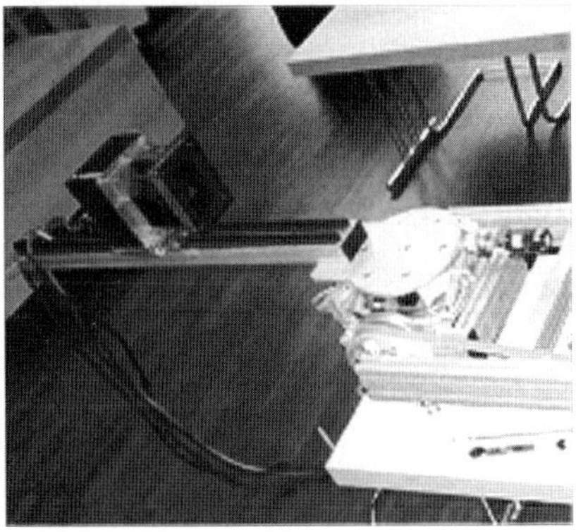

Figure 15. Line-based panoramic camera at the Institute of Space Sensor Technology and Planetary Exploration, German Aerospace Center (DLR), Berlin.

This equation can be rearranged to as follows:

$$\begin{aligned} 0 = \quad & (1 - \cos\theta_{ij} - \cos\theta_{jk} + \cos(\theta_{ij} + \theta_{jk}))R^2 \\ & + (2S_j - (S_j + S_k)\cos\theta_{ij} - (S_i + S_j)\cos\theta_{jk} \\ & + (S_i + S_k)\cos(\theta_{ij} + \theta_{jk}))R\cos\omega + ((S_k - S_j)\sin\theta_{ij} \\ & + (S_j - S_i)\sin\theta_{jk} + (S_i - S_k)\sin(\theta_{ij} + \theta_{jk}))R\sin\omega + S_j^2 \\ & + S_i S_k \cos(\theta_{ij} + \theta_{jk}) - S_i S_j \cos\theta_{ij} - S_j S_k \cos\theta_{jk}. \end{aligned} \tag{11}$$

Equation (11) can can be described by the following linear form

$$K_1 X_1 + K_2 X_2 + K_3 X_3 + K_4 = 0,$$

where $K_i, i = 1, 2, 3, 4$, are coefficients as

$$\begin{aligned} K_1 &= 1 - \cos\theta_{ij} - \cos\theta_{jk} + \cos(\theta_{ij} + \theta_{jk}) \\ K_2 &= 2S_j - (S_j + S_k)\cos\theta_{ij} - (S_i + S_j)\cos\theta_{jk} + (S_i + S_k)\cos(\theta_{ij} + \theta_{jk}) \\ K_3 &= (S_k - S_j)\sin\theta_{ij} + (S_j S_i)\sin\theta_{jk} + (S_i - S_k)\sin(\theta_{ij} + \theta_{jk}) \quad \text{and} \\ K_4 &= S_j^2 + S_i S_k \cos(\theta_{ij} + \theta_{jk}) - S_i S_j \cos\theta_{ij} - S_j S_k \cos\theta_{jk} \ . \end{aligned}$$

Moreover, we have $X_1 = R^2$, $X_2 = R\cos\omega$, and $X_3 = R\sin\omega$, which is the same as in case of the distance-based approach. □

3.4.3. *Experimental Results*

DLR Berlin-Adlershof provided the line camera WAAC, see Figure 15, for a experiments with real images, scenes and panoramic images. The specifications of the WAAC camera are as follows: each image line has 5184 pixels, the effective focal length of the camera is 21.7 mm for the center image line, the selected CCD line of WAAC for image acquisition defines a

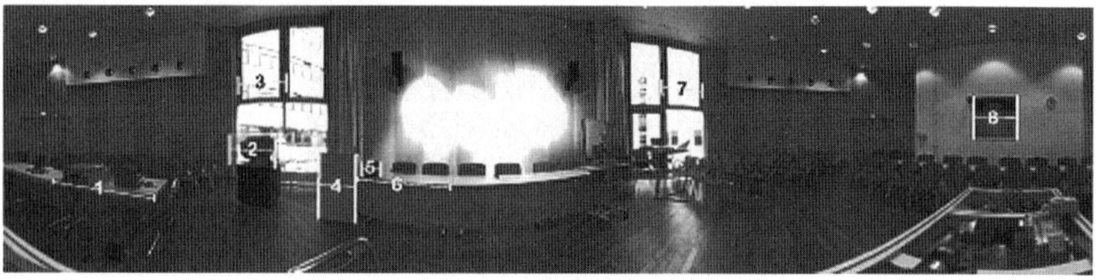

Figure 16. A test panorama image (a seminar room at DLR Berlin-Adlershof) with indexed line-pairs.

principal angle ω of 155° and has an effective focal length of 23.94 mm, the CCD cell size is 0.007×0.007 mm^2, and thus the value of f_μ is equal to 3420 pixels in this case. The camera was mounted on a turntable supporting an extension arm with values of R up to 1.0 m. The value of R was set to be 10 cm in our experiments.

Figure 16 shows one of the panoramic images taken in a seminar room of the DLR-Institute of Space Sensor Technology and Planetary Exploration at Berlin. The size of the seminar room is about 120 m^2. The image has a resolution of $5,184 \times 21,388$ pixels. The pairs of lines (eight pairs in total) are highlighted and indexed. The lengths of those lines are also manually measured, with an expected error of no more than 0.5% of their readings. The data of these sample lines used for the camera calibration are summarized in Figure 17. These pairs of lines are used for estimating R and ω, but in this case, only the distance constraint is applied.

We use the optimization method of sequential quadratic programming (Gill et al., 1991) for estimating R and ω. We minimize Equation (9). The results are summarized as follows: when all pairs are used, we obtain R = 10.32 cm and ω = 161.68°. If we select pairs {2,3,4,7,8}, we have R =

Index	$H_1 = H_1$(m)	h_1 (pixel)	h_2 (pixel)	D_α (m)	d_x (pixel)
1	0.0690	91.2	133.8	1.4000	1003.1
2	0.6320	600.8	683.0	1.0000	447.3
3	0.5725	351.4	367.4	1.5500	490.5
4	1.0860	1269.0	1337.6	0.6000	360.9
5	0.2180	273.0	273.6	0.2870	180.1
6	0.0690	81.8	104.2	1.5500	910.5
7	0.5725	318.0	292.0	1.5500	398.2
8	1.3300	831.2	859.4	1.3400	422.5

Figure 17. Parallel-line-based panoramic camera calibration measurements associate with the panorama shown in Figure 16.

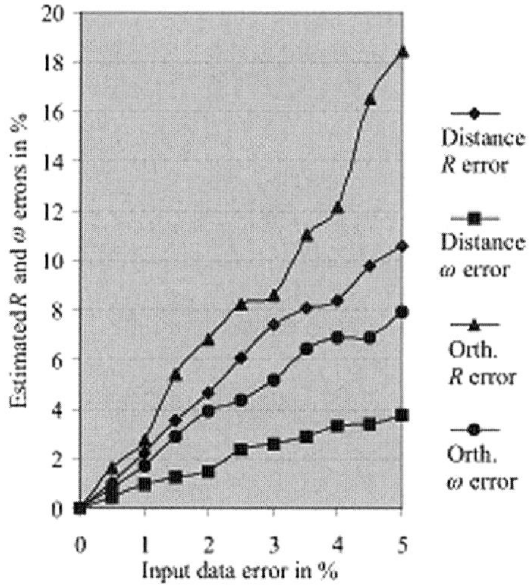

Figure 18. Error sensitivity results of parallel-line-based approach.

10.87 cm and $\omega = 151.88°$. If we only use the pairs $\{2,4,8\}$, then $R = 10.83$ cm and $\omega = 157.21°$. This indicates influences of sample selections and of the quality of sample data onto the calibration results; more detailed experiments should follow.

We also tested error sensitivity for both constraints: errors in the measured distance between two parallel lines, and in the orthogonality of three lines, and the impact of these errors onto the estimated parameters. Ground-truth data was synthetically generated, in correspondence with the previously used values for real data (i.e., $R = 10$ cm and $\omega = 155°$). Errors in values of S_i, D_{ij}, and θ_{ij} are introduced to the ground-truth data independently with a maximum of 5% additive random noise in normal distribution. The range of S_i is from 1 m to 8 m, and the range of θ_{ij} is from 4° to 35°. The sample size is eight. The average results of 100 trials are shown in Figure 18. The results suggest that estimated parameters using the orthogonality constraint are more sensitive to errors than in the case of using the distance constraint. The errors of the estimated parameters increase linearly with respect to the input errors for both cases.

The distance-based and the orthogonality-based approaches discussed in this section share the same form in their objective functions. Thus, these two geometric features can be used together for further potential improvements. The overall performance comparisons for all three approaches, namely point-based, image-correspondence-based, and parallel-line-based approach, is given in Figure 9.

4. Conclusions

We subdivided the calibration process for a panoramic camera into two steps. The first step calibrates the effective focal length and the principal row, and this is discussed in the Appendix. The second step calibrates the two essential panorama parameters: off-axis distance, and principal angle. The separability of the calibration process is an interesting feature of panoramic camera geometry, showing that this combines linear and non-linear components.

We presented three different approaches for the second step of panoramic camera calibration. The number of parameters which needs to be estimated for each approach is summarized in Figure 9. In the first approach, the point-based approach, there are a total of 14 parameters to be estimated, consisting of the target parameters R, ω, and the other twelve unknowns in the transformation matrix, due to the fact that extrinsic camera parameters are unavoidable. The second approach reduces the dimensions down to four by utilizing information from image correspondences between panoramic images and through avoiding the inclusion of extrinsic camera parameters. In the third approach (i.e., the parallel-line-based approach), linear geometric features are used. As a result, only three parameters need to be estimated in this case. Not surprisingly, the third approach gives the best results among all also shown in our practical and simulation experiments.

The point-based approach involves non-linear features, such as fractions, square roots etc., and hence results in unstable estimations. The other two approaches, the image-correspondence-based and the parallel-line-based approaches, allow the objective functions to be in linear form and improve the stability of estimation results in comparison to the point-based approach.

The parallel-line-based approach allowed the most accurate calibration results as well as the best numerical stability among these three studied approaches. We found for both of the geometric properties of parallel lines (i.e., distance and orthogonality), there is a single linear equation that links those 3D geometric scene features of parallel lines to the camera model. Therefore, after providing sufficient scene measurements, we are able to calibrate the values of R and ω with good accuracy. The errors in the estimated parameters for both geometric property constraints increase linearly with respect to the input errors. More specifically, the estimated parameters obtained by using the orthogonality constraint are more sensitive to errors than those in the case of using the distance constraint.

Overall, the reduction of dimensionality, the simplification of computational complexity, and being less sensitive to errors are attributes of the linear geometric feature approach. It will be of interest to continue these explorations by using other possible geometric features (e.g., triangles or squares), properties (e.g., point ratios), or 'hybrid' such that the followings can be achieved: (1) loosening the assumption that the rotation axis must be parallel to the calibration lines, (2) improving the robustness to error, and (3) reducing the current two calibration steps to just a single step.

Acknowledgment:

The authors thank the colleagues at DLR Berlin for years of valuable collaboration.

References

Chen, S. E.: QuickTimeVR - an image-based approach to virtual environment navigation. In Proc. *SIGGRAPH*, pages 29–38, 1995.

Faugeras, O.: *Three-Dimensional Computer Vision: A Geometric Viewpoint.* The MIT Press, London, 1993.

Gill, P. E., W. Murray, and M. H. Wright: *Practical Optimization.* Academic Press, London, 1981.

Hong, J.: Image based homing. In Proc. *Int. Conf. Robotics and Automation*, pages 620–625, 1991.

Huang, F., S.-K. Wei, and R. Klette: Depth recovery system using object-based layers. In Proc. *Image Vision Computing New Zealand*, pages 199–204, 1999.

Huang, F., S.-K. Wei, and R. Klette: Geometrical fundamentals of polycentric panoramas. In Proc. *Int. Conf. Computer Vision*, pages I: 560–565, 2001.

Huang, F., S.-K. Wei, and R. Klette: Stereo reconstruction from polycentric panoramas. In Proc. *Robot Vision 2001*, pages 209–218, LNCS 1998, Springer, Berlin 2001.

Huang, H.-C. and Y.-P. Hung: Panoramic stereo imaging system with automatic disparity warping and seaming. *GMIP*, **60**: 196–208, 1998.

Ishiguro, H., T. Sogo, and T. Ishida: Human behavior recognition by a distributed vision system. In Proc. *DiCoMo Workshop*, pages 615–620, 1997.

Ishiguro, H., M. Yamamoto, and S. Tsuji: Omni-directional stereo. *IEEE Trans. PAMI*, **14**: 257–262, 1992.

Kang, S.-B. and P. K. Desikan: Virtual navigation of complex scenes using clusters of cylindrical panoramic images. Technical Report CRL 97/5, DEC, Cambridge Research Lab, September 1997.

Kang, S.-B. and R. Szeliski: 3-d scene data recovery using omnidirectional multibaseline stereo. *IJCV*, **25**: 167–183, 1997.

Klette, R., G. Gimel'farb, and R. Reulke: Wide-angle image acquisition, analysis, and visualisation. Invited talk, in Proc. *Vision Interface*, pages 114–125, 2001 (see also CITR-TR-86).

Klette, R. and K. Scheibe: Combinations of range data and panoramic images new opportunities in 3D scene modeling. Keynote, In Proc. IEEE Int. Conf. Computer Graphics Imaging Vision. Beijing, July 2005 (to appear, see also CITR-TR-157).

McMillan, L. and G. Bishop: Plenoptic modeling: an image-based rendering system. In Proc. *SIGGRAPH*, pages 39–46, 1995.

Murray, D. W.: Recovering range using virtual multicamera stereo. *CVIU*, **61**: 285–291, 1995.

Nayar, S. K. and A. Karmarkar: 360 x 360 mosaics. In Proc. *CVPR'00*, volume II, pages 388–395, 2000.

Nene, S. A. and S. K. Nayar: Stereo with mirrors. In Proc. *Int. Conf. Computer Vision*, pages 1087–1094, 1998.

Nishimura, T., T. Mukai, and R. Oka: Spotting recognition of gestures performed by people from a single time-varying image. In Proc. *Int. Conf. Robots Systems*, pages 967–972, 1997.

Ollis, M., H. Herman, and S. Singh: Analysis and design of panoramic stereo vision using equi-angular pixel cameras. Technical Report CMU-RI-TR-99-04, The Robotics Institute,Carnegie Mellon University, Pittsburgh, USA, 1999.

Peleg, S. and M. Ben-Ezra: Stereo panorama with a single camera. In Proc. *CVPR*, pages 395–401, 1999.

Petty, R., M. Robinson, and J. Evans: 3d measurement using rotating line-scan sensors. *Measurement Science and Technology*, **9**: 339–346, 1998.

Rademacher, P. and G. Bishop: Multiple-center-of-projection images. In Proc. *SIGGRAPH*, pages 199–206, 1998.

Shum, H., A. Kalai, and S. Seitz: Omnivergent stereo. In Proc. *Int. Conf. Computer Vision*, pages 22–29, 1999.

Shum, H.-Y. and L.-W. He: Rendering with concentric mosaics. In Proc. *SIGGRAPH*, pages 299–306, 1999.

Shum, H.-Y. and R. Szeliski: Stereo reconstruction from multiperspective panoramas. In Proc. *Int. Conf. Computer Vision*, pages 14–21, 1999.

Southwell, D., J. Reyda, M. Fiala, and A. Basu: Panoramic stereo. In Proc. *ICPR*, pages A: 378–382, 1996.

Szeliski, R. and H.-Y. Shum: Creating full view panoramic image mosaics and environment maps. In Proc. *SIGGRAPH'97*, pages 251–258, 1997.

Tsai, R.Y.: A versatile camera calibration technique for high-accuracy 3d machine vision metrology using off-the-shelf tv cameras and lenses. *IEEE J. Robotics and Automation*, **3**: 323–344, 1987.

Wei, S.-K., F. Huang, and R. Klette: Three-dimensional scene navigation through anaglyphic panorama visualization. In Proc. *Computer Analysis Images Patterns*, pages 542–549, LNCS 1689, Springer, Berlin, 1999.

Wei, S.-K., F. Huang, and R. Klette: Determination of geometric parameters for stereoscopic panorama cameras. *Machine Graphics Vision*, **10**: 399–427, 2001.

Yagi, Y.: Omnidirectional sensing and its applications. *IEICE Transactions on Information and Systems*, **E82-D**: 568–579, 1999.

Yagi, Y. and S. Kawato: Panoramic scene analysis with conic projection. In Proc. *IROS*, pages 181–187, 1990.

Zheng, J.-Y. and S. Tsuji: Panoramic representation for route recognition by a mobile robot. *IJCV*, **9**: 55–76, 1992.

Part II

Motion

ON CALIBRATION, STRUCTURE FROM MOTION AND MULTI-VIEW GEOMETRY FOR GENERIC CAMERA MODELS

PETER STURM
INRIA Rhône-Alpes
655 Avenue de l'Europe, 38330 Montbonnot, France

SRIKUMAR RAMALINGAM
Department of Computer Science
University of California, Santa Cruz, USA

SURESH LODHA
Department of Computer Science
University of California, Santa Cruz, USA

Abstract. We consider calibration and structure from motion tasks for a previously introduced, highly general imaging model, where cameras are modeled as possibly unconstrained sets of projection rays. This allows to describe most existing camera types (at least for those operating in the visible domain), including pinhole cameras, sensors with radial or more general distortions, catadioptric cameras (central or non-central), etc. Generic algorithms for calibration and structure from motion tasks (pose and motion estimation and 3D point triangulation) are outlined. The foundation for a multi-view geometry of non-central cameras is given, leading to the formulation of multi-view matching tensors, analogous to the fundamental matrices, trifocal and quadrifocal tensors of perspective cameras. Besides this, we also introduce a natural hierarchy of camera models: the most general model has unconstrained projection rays whereas the most constrained model dealt with here is the central model, where all rays pass through a single point.

Key words: calibration, motion estimation, 3D reconstruction, camera models, non-central cameras

1. Introduction

Many different types of cameras including pinhole, stereo, catadioptric, omnidirectional and non-central cameras have been used in computer vision. Most existing camera models are parametric (i.e. defined by a few intrinsic parameters) and address imaging systems with a single effective

K. Daniilidis and R. Klette (eds.), Imaging Beyond the Pinhole Camera, 87–105.

viewpoint (all rays pass through one point). In addition, existing calibration or structure from motion procedures are often taylor-made for specific camera models, see examples e.g. in (Barreto and Araujo, 2003; Hartley and Zisserman, 2000; Geyer and Daniilidis, 2002).

The aim of this work is to relax these constraints: we want to propose and develop calibration and structure from motion methods that should work for any type of camera model, and especially also for cameras without a single effective viewpoint. To do so, we first renounce on parametric models, and adopt the following very general model: a camera acquires images consisting of pixels; each pixel captures light that travels along a ray in 3D. The camera is fully described by (Grossberg and Nayar, 2001):

- the coordinates of these rays (given in some local coordinate frame).
- the mapping between rays and pixels; this is basically a simple indexing.

This general imaging model allows to describe virtually any camera that captures light rays travelling along straight lines. Examples are (see Figure 1):

- a camera with any type of optical distortion, such as radial or tangential.
- a camera looking at a reflective surface, e.g. as often used in surveillance, a camera looking at a spherical or otherwise curved mirror (Hicks and Bajcsy, 2000). Such systems, as opposed to central catadioptric systems (Baker and Nayar, 1999; Geyer and Daniilidis, 2000) composed of cameras and parabolic mirrors, do not in general have a single effective viewpoint.
- multi-camera stereo systems: put together the pixels of all image planes; they "catch" light rays that definitely do not travel along lines that all pass through a single point. Nevertheless, in the above general camera model, a stereo system (with rigidly linked cameras) is considered as a **single** camera.
- other acquisition systems, many of them being non-central, see e.g. (Bakstein, 2001; Bakstein and Pajdla, 2001; Neumann et al., 2003; Pajdla, 2002b; Peleg et al., 2001; Shum et al., 1999; Swaminathan et al., 2003; Yu and McMillan, 2004), insect eyes, etc.

In this article, we first review some recent work on calibration and structure from motion for this general camera model. Concretely, we outline basics for calibration, pose and motion estimation, as well as 3D point triangulation. We then describe the foundations for a multi-view geometry of the general, non-central camera model, leading to the formulation of multi-view matching tensors, analogous to the fundamental matrices, trifocal and quadrifocal tensors of perspective cameras. Besides this, we also

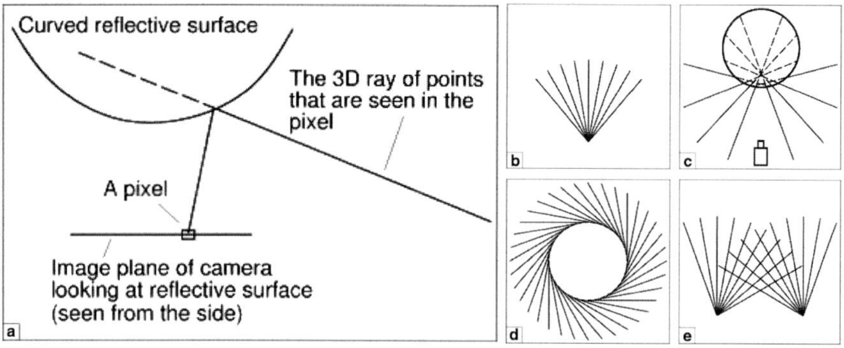

Figure 1. Examples of imaging systems. (a) Catadioptric system. Note that camera rays do not pass through their associated pixels. (b) Central camera (e.g. perspective, with or without radial distortion). (c) Camera looking at reflective sphere. This is a non-central device (camera rays are not intersecting in a single point). (d) Omnivergent imaging system. (e) Stereo system (non-central) consisting of two central cameras.

introduce a natural hierarchy of camera models: the most general model has unconstrained projection rays whereas the most constrained model dealt with here is the central model, where all rays pass through a single point. An intermediate model is what we term *axial cameras*: cameras for which there exists a 3D line that cuts all projection rays. This encompasses for example x-slit projections, linear pushbroom cameras and some non-central catadioptric systems. Hints will be given how to adopt the multi-view geometry proposed for the general imaging model, to such axial cameras.

The chapter is organized as follows. Section 2 explains some background on Plücker coordinates for 3D lines, which are used to parameterize camera rays in this work. A hierarchy of camera models is proposed in Section 3. Sections 4 to 7 deal with calibration, pose estimation, motion estimation, as well as 3D point triangulation. The multi-view geometry for the general camera model is given in Section 8. A few experimental results on calibration, motion estimation and 3D reconstruction are shown in Section 9.

2. Plücker Coordinates

We represent projection rays as 3D lines, via Plücker coordinates. There exist different definitions for them, the one we use is explained in the following.

Let **A** and **B** be two 3D points given by homogeneous coordinates, defining a line in 3D. The line can be represented by the skew-symmetric 4×4 Plücker matrix

$$
\begin{aligned}
\mathsf{L} &= \mathbf{A}\mathbf{B}^{\mathsf{T}} - \mathbf{B}\mathbf{A}^{\mathsf{T}} \\
&= \begin{pmatrix}
0 & A_1B_2 - A_2B_1 & A_1B_3 - A_3B_1 & A_1B_4 - A_4B_1 \\
A_2B_1 - A_1B_2 & 0 & A_2B_3 - A_3B_2 & A_2B_4 - A_4B_2 \\
A_3B_1 - A_1B_3 & A_3B_2 - A_2B_3 & 0 & A_3B_4 - A_4B_3 \\
A_4B_1 - A_1B_4 & A_4B_2 - A_2B_4 & A_4B_3 - A_3B_4 & 0
\end{pmatrix}
\end{aligned}
$$

Note that the Plücker matrix is independent (up to scale) of which pair of points on the line are chosen to represent it.

An alternative representation for the line is by its Plücker coordinate vector of length 6:

$$
\mathbf{L} = \begin{pmatrix}
A_4B_1 - A_1B_4 \\
A_4B_2 - A_2B_4 \\
A_4B_3 - A_3B_4 \\
A_3B_2 - A_2B_3 \\
A_1B_3 - A_3B_1 \\
A_2B_1 - A_1B_2
\end{pmatrix} \tag{1}
$$

The Plücker coordinate vector can be split in two 3-vectors **a** and **b** as follows:

$$
\mathbf{a} = \begin{pmatrix} L_1 \\ L_2 \\ L_3 \end{pmatrix} \qquad \mathbf{b} = \begin{pmatrix} L_4 \\ L_5 \\ L_6 \end{pmatrix}
$$

They satisfy the so-called Plücker constraint: $\mathbf{a}^{\mathsf{T}}\mathbf{b} = 0$. Furthermore, the Plücker matrix can now be conveniently written as

$$
\mathsf{L} = \begin{pmatrix} [\mathbf{b}]_\times & -\mathbf{a} \\ \mathbf{a}^{\mathsf{T}} & 0 \end{pmatrix}
$$

where $[\mathbf{b}]_\times$ is the 3×3 skew-symmetric matrix associated with the cross-product and defined by: $\mathbf{b} \times \mathbf{y} = [\mathbf{b}]_\times \mathbf{y}$.

Consider a metric transformation defined by a rotation matrix R and a translation vector $\mathbf{t}$, acting on points via:

$$
\mathbf{C} \to \begin{pmatrix} \mathsf{R} & \mathbf{t} \\ \mathbf{0}^{\mathsf{T}} & 1 \end{pmatrix} \mathbf{C}
$$

Plücker coordinates are then transformed according to

$$
\begin{pmatrix} \mathbf{a} \\ \mathbf{b} \end{pmatrix} \to \begin{pmatrix} \mathsf{R} & 0 \\ -[\mathbf{t}]_\times \mathsf{R} & \mathsf{R} \end{pmatrix} \begin{pmatrix} \mathbf{a} \\ \mathbf{b} \end{pmatrix}
$$

3. A Natural Hierarchy of Camera Models

A **non-central camera** may have completely unconstrained projection rays, whereas for a **central camera**, there exists a point – the **optical center** – that lies on all projection rays. An intermediate case is what we call **axial cameras**, where there exists a line that cuts all projection rays – the **camera axis** (not to be confounded with optical axis). Examples of cameras falling into this class are pushbroom cameras (if motion is translational) (Hartley and Gupta, 1994), x-slit cameras (Pajdla, 2002a; Zomet, 2003), and non-central catadioptric cameras of the following construction: the mirror is any surface of revolution and the optical center of the central camera (can be any central camera, i.e. not necessarily a pinhole) looking at the mirror lies on its axis of revolution. It is easy to verify that in this case, all projection rays cut the mirror's axis of revolution, i.e. the camera is an axial camera, with the mirror's axis of revolution as camera axis.

These three classes of camera models may also be defined as: existence of a linear space of d dimensions that has an intersection with all projection rays. In this sense, $d = 0$ defines central cameras, $d = 1$ axial cameras and $d = 2$ general non-central cameras.

Intermediate classes do exist. X-slit cameras are a special case of axial cameras: there actually exist 2 lines in space that both cut all projection rays. Similarly, central 1D cameras (cameras with a single row of pixels) can be defined by a point and a line in 3D. Camera models, some of which do not have much practical importance, are summarized in the following table.

Points/lines cutting the rays	Description
None	Non-central camera
1 point	Central camera
2 points	Camera with a single projection ray
1 line	Axial camera
1 point, 1 line	Central 1D camera
2 skew lines	X-slit camera
2 coplanar lines	Union of non-central 1D camera and central camera
3 coplanar lines without a common point	Non-central 1D camera

It is worthwhile to consider different classes due to the following observation: the usual calibration and motion estimation algorithms proceed by first estimating a matrix or tensor by solving linear equation systems (e.g. the calibration tensors in (Sturm and Ramalingam, 2004) or the essential matrix (Pless, 2003)). Then, the parameters that are searched for (usually, motion parameters), are extracted from these. However, when estimating for example the 6×6 essential matrix of *non-central* cameras based on image correspondences obtained from *central* or *axial* cameras, then the associated linear equation system does not give a unique solution. Consequently, the algorithms for extracting the actual motion parameters, can not be applied without modification. This is the reason why in (Sturm and Ramalingam, 2003; Sturm and Ramalingam, 2004) we already introduced generic calibration algorithms for both, central and non-central cameras.

In the following, we only deal with central, axial and non-central cameras. Structure from motion computations and multi-view geometry, will be formulated in terms of the Plücker coordinates of camera rays. As for *central cameras*, all rays go through a single point, the optical center. Choosing a local coordinate system with the optical center at the origin, leads to projection rays whose Plücker sub-vector $\mathbf{b}$ is zero, i.e. the projection rays are of the form:

$$\mathbf{L} = \begin{pmatrix} \mathbf{a} \\ \mathbf{0} \end{pmatrix}$$

This is one reason why the multi-linear matching tensors, e.g. the fundamental matrix, have a "base size" of 3.

As for *axial cameras*, all rays touch a line, the camera axis. Again, by choosing local coordinate systems appropriately, the formulation of the multi-view relations may be simplified, as shown in the following. Assume that the camera axis is the Z-axis. Then, all projection rays have Plücker coordinates with $L_6 = b_3 = 0$:

$$\mathbf{L} = \begin{pmatrix} \mathbf{a} \\ b_1 \\ b_2 \\ 0 \end{pmatrix}$$

Multi-view relations can thus be formulated via tensors of "base size" 5, i.e. the essential matrix for axial cameras will be of size 5×5 (see in later sections).

As for *general non-central cameras*, no such simplification occurs, and multi-view tensors will have "base size" 6.

4. Calibration

We briefly review a generic calibration approach developed in (Sturm and Ramalingam, 2004), an extension of (Champleboux et al., 1992; Gremban et al., 1988; Grossberg and Nayar, 2001), to calibrate different camera systems. As mentioned, calibration consists in determining, for every pixel, the 3D projection ray associated with it. In (Grossberg and Nayar, 2001), this is done as follows: two images of a calibration object with known structure are taken. We suppose that for every pixel, we can determine the point on the calibration object, that is seen by that pixel. For each pixel in the image, we thus obtain two 3D points. Their coordinates are usually only known in a coordinate frame attached to the calibration object; however, if one knows the motion between the two object positions, one can align the coordinate frames. Then, every pixel's projection ray can be computed by simply joining the two observed 3D points.

In (Sturm and Ramalingam, 2004), we propose a more general approach, that does not require knowledge of the calibration object's displacement. In that case, three images need to be taken at least. The fact that all 3D points observed by a pixel in different views, are on a line in 3D, gives a constraint that allows to recover both the motion and the camera's calibration. The constraint is formulated via a set of trifocal tensors, that can be estimated linearly, and from which motion, and then calibration, can be extracted. In (Sturm and Ramalingam, 2004), this approach is first formulated for the use of 3D calibration objects, and for the general imaging model, i.e. for non-central cameras. We also propose variants of the approach, that may be important in practice: first, due to the usefulness of planar calibration patterns, we specialized the approach appropriately. Second, we propose a variant that works specifically for central cameras (pinhole, central catadioptric, or any other central camera). More details are given in (Sturm and Ramalingam, 2003).

5. Pose Estimation

Pose estimation is the problem of computing the relative position and orientation between an object of *known* structure, and a calibrated camera. A literature review on algorithms for pinhole cameras is given in (Haralick, 1994). Here, we briefly show how the minimal case can be solved for general cameras. For pinhole cameras, pose can be estimated, up to a finite number of solutions, from 3 point correspondences (3D-2D) already. The same holds for general cameras. Consider 3 image points and the associated projection rays, computed using the calibration information. We parameterize generic points on the rays as follows: $\mathbf{A}_i + \lambda_i \mathbf{B}_i$.

We know the structure of the observed object, meaning that we know the mutual distances d_{ij} between the 3D points. We can thus write equations on the unknowns λ_i, that parameterize the object's pose:

$$\|\mathbf{A}_i + \lambda_i \mathbf{B}_i - \mathbf{A}_j - \lambda_j \mathbf{B}_j\|^2 = d_{ij}^2 \quad \text{for } (i,j) = (1,2), (1,3), (2,3)$$

This gives a total of 3 equations that are quadratic in 3 unknowns. Many methods exist for solving this problem, e.g. symbolic computation packages such as MAPLE allow to compute a resultant polynomial of degree 8 in a single unknown, that can be numerically solved using any root finding method.

Like for pinhole cameras, there are up to 8 theoretical solutions. For pinhole cameras, at least 4 of them can be eliminated because they would correspond to points lying behind the camera (Haralick, 1994). As for general cameras, determining the maximum number of feasible solutions requires further investigation. In any case, a unique solution can be obtained using one or two additional points (Haralick, 1994). More details on pose estimation for non-central cameras are given in (Faugeras and Mourrain, 2004; Nistér, 2004).

6. Motion Estimation

We describe how to estimate ego-motion, or, more generally, relative position and orientation of two calibrated general cameras. This is done via a generalization of the classical motion estimation problem for pinhole cameras and its associated centerpiece, the essential matrix (Longuet-Higgins, 1981). We briefly summarize how the classical problem is usually solved (Hartley and Zisserman, 2000). Let R be the rotation matrix and $\mathbf{t}$ the translation vector describing the motion. The essential matrix is defined as $\mathsf{E} = -[\mathbf{t}]_\times \mathsf{R}$. It can be estimated using point correspondences $(\mathbf{x}_1, \mathbf{x}_2)$ across two views, using the epipolar constraint $\mathbf{x}_2^\mathsf{T} \mathsf{E} \mathbf{x}_1 = 0$. This can be done linearly using 8 correspondences or more. In the minimal case of 5 correspondences, an efficient non-linear minimal algorithm, which gives exactly the theoretical maximum of 10 feasible solutions, was only recently introduced (Nistér, 2003). Once the essential matrix is estimated, the motion parameters R and $\mathbf{t}$ can be extracted relatively straightforwardly (Nistér, 2003).

In the case of our general imaging model, motion estimation is performed similarly, using pixel correspondences $(\mathbf{x}_1, \mathbf{x}_2)$. Using the calibration information, the associated projection rays can be computed. Let them be represented by their Plücker coordinates, i.e. 6-vectors $\mathbf{L}_1$ and $\mathbf{L}_2$. The epipolar constraint extends naturally to rays, and manifests itself by a 6×6 essential matrix, see (Pless, 2003) and Section 8.3:

$$\mathsf{E} = \begin{pmatrix} -[\mathbf{t}]_\times \mathsf{R} & \mathsf{R} \\ \mathsf{R} & 0 \end{pmatrix}$$

The epipolar constraint then writes: $\mathbf{L}_2^\mathsf{T} \mathsf{E} \mathbf{L}_1 = 0$ (Pless, 2003). Once E is estimated, motion can again be extracted straightforwardly (e.g., R can simply be read off E). Linear estimation of E requires 17 correspondences.

There is an important difference between motion estimation for central and non-central cameras: with central cameras, the translation component can only be recovered up to scale. Non-central cameras however, allow to determine even the translation's scale. This is because a single calibrated non-central camera already carries scale information (via the distance between mutually skew projection rays). One consequence is that the theoretical minimum number of required correspondences is 6 instead of 5. It might be possible, though very involved, to derive a minimal 6-point method along the lines of (Nistér, 2003).

7. 3D Point Triangulation

We now describe an algorithm for 3D reconstruction from two or more calibrated images with known relative position. Let $\mathbf{C} = (X, Y, Z)^{\mathsf{T}}$ be a 3D point that is to be reconstructed, based on its projections in n images. Using calibration information, we can compute the n associated projection rays. Here, we represent the ith ray using a starting point $\mathbf{A}_i$ and the direction, represented by a unit vector $\mathbf{B}_i$. We apply the mid-point method (Hartley and Sturm, 1997; Pless, 2003), i.e. determine $\mathbf{C}$ that is closest in average to the n rays. Let us represent generic points on rays using position parameters λ_i. Then, $\mathbf{C}$ is determined by minimizing the following expression over X, Y, Z and the λ_i: $\sum_{i=1}^{n} \|\mathbf{A}_i + \lambda_i \mathbf{B}_i - \mathbf{C}\|^2$.

This is a linear least squares problem, which can be solved e.g. via the Pseudo-Inverse, leading to the following explicit equation (derivations omitted):

$$\begin{pmatrix} \mathbf{C} \\ \lambda_1 \\ \vdots \\ \lambda_n \end{pmatrix} = \underbrace{\begin{pmatrix} n\mathtt{I}_3 & -\mathbf{B}_1 & \cdots & -\mathbf{B}_n \\ -\mathbf{B}_1^{\mathsf{T}} & 1 & & \\ \vdots & & \ddots & \\ -\mathbf{B}_n^{\mathsf{T}} & & & 1 \end{pmatrix}^{-1}}_{\mathsf{M}} \begin{pmatrix} \mathtt{I}_3 & \cdots & \mathtt{I}_3 \\ -\mathbf{B}_1^{\mathsf{T}} & & \\ & \ddots & \\ & & -\mathbf{B}_n^{\mathsf{T}} \end{pmatrix} \begin{pmatrix} \mathbf{A}_1 \\ \vdots \\ \mathbf{A}_n \end{pmatrix}$$

where $\mathtt{I}_3$ is the identity matrix of size 3×3. Due to its sparse structure, the inversion of the matrix M in this equation, can actually be performed in closed-form. Overall, the triangulation of a 3D point using n rays, can by carried out very efficiently, using only matrix multiplications and the inversion of a symmetric 3×3 matrix (details omitted).

8. Multi-View Geometry

We establish the basics of a multi-view geometry for general (non-central) cameras. Its cornerstones are, as with perspective cameras, matching tensors. We show how to establish them, analogously to the perspective case.

Here, we only talk about the calibrated case; the uncalibrated case is nicely treated for perspective cameras, since calibrated and uncalibrated cameras are linked by projective transformations. For non-central cameras however, there is no such link: in the most general case, every pair (pixel, camera ray) may be completely independent of other pairs.

8.1. REMINDER ON MULTI-VIEW GEOMETRY FOR PERSPECTIVE CAMERAS

We briefly review how to derive multi-view matching relations for perspective cameras (1995). Let P_i be projection matrices and $\mathbf{q}_i$ image points. A set of image points are matching, if there exists a 3D point $\mathbf{Q}$ and scale factors λ_i such that:

$$\lambda_i \mathbf{q}_i = \mathsf{P}_i \mathbf{Q}$$

This may be formulated as the following matrix equation:

$$\underbrace{\begin{pmatrix} \mathsf{P}_1 & \mathbf{q}_1 & \mathbf{0} & \cdots & \mathbf{0} \\ \mathsf{P}_2 & \mathbf{0} & \mathbf{q}_2 & \cdots & \mathbf{0} \\ \vdots & \vdots & \vdots & \ddots & \vdots \\ \mathsf{P}_n & \mathbf{0} & \mathbf{0} & \cdots & \mathbf{q}_n \end{pmatrix}}_{\mathsf{M}} \begin{pmatrix} \mathbf{Q} \\ -\lambda_1 \\ -\lambda_2 \\ \vdots \\ -\lambda_n \end{pmatrix} = \begin{pmatrix} 0 \\ 0 \\ \vdots \\ 0 \end{pmatrix}$$

The matrix M, of size $3n \times (4+n)$ has thus a null-vector, meaning that its rank is less than $4+n$. Hence, the determinants of all its submatrices of size $(4+n) \times (4+n)$ must vanish. These determinants are multi-linear expressions in terms of the coordinates of image points $\mathbf{q}_i$.

They have to be expressed for any possible submatrix. Only submatrices with 2 or more rows per view, give rise to constraints linking all projection matrices. Hence, constraints can be obtained up to n views with $2n \leq 4+n$, meaning that only for up to 4 views, matching constraints linking all views can be obtained.

The constraints for n views take the form:

$$\sum_{i_1=1}^{3} \sum_{i_2=1}^{3} \cdots \sum_{i_n=1}^{3} q_{1,i_1} q_{2,i_2} \cdots q_{n,i_n} T_{i_1,i_2,\cdots,i_n} = 0 \tag{2}$$

where the multi-view matching tensor T of dimension $3 \times \cdots \times 3$ depends on and partially encodes the cameras' projection matrices P_i.

Note that as soon as cameras are calibrated, this theory applies to any central camera: for a camera with radial distortion for example, the above formulation holds for distortion-corrected image points.

8.2. MULTI-VIEW GEOMETRY FOR NON-CENTRAL CAMERAS

Here, instead of projection matrices (depending on calibration and pose), we deal with pose matrices:

$$\mathsf{P}_i = \begin{pmatrix} \mathsf{R}_i & \mathbf{t}_i \\ \mathbf{0}^\mathsf{T} & 1 \end{pmatrix}$$

These express the similarity transformations that map a point from some global reference frame, into the camera's local coordinate frames (note that since no optical center and no camera axis exist, no assumptions about the local coordinate frames are made). As for image points, they are now replaced by camera rays. Let the ith ray be represented by two 3D points $\mathbf{A}_i$ and $\mathbf{B}_i$.

Eventually, we will to obtain expressions in terms of the rays' Plücker coordinates, i.e. we will end up with matching tensors T and matching constraints of the form (2), with the difference that tensors will have size $6 \times \cdots \times 6$ and act on Plücker line coordinates:

$$\sum_{i_1=1}^{6}\sum_{i_2=1}^{6}\cdots\sum_{i_n=1}^{6} L_{1,i_1} L_{2,i_2} \cdots L_{n,i_n} T_{i_1,i_2,\cdots,i_n} = 0 \tag{3}$$

In the following, we explain how to derive such matching constraints.

Consider a set of n camera rays and let them be defined by two points $\mathbf{A}_i$ and $\mathbf{B}_i$ each; the choice of points to represent a ray is not important, since later we will fall back onto the ray's Plücker coordinates.

Now, a set of n camera rays are matching, if there exist a 3D point $\mathbf{Q}$ and scale factors λ_i and μ_i associated with each ray such that:

$$\lambda_i \mathbf{A}_i + \mu_i \mathbf{B}_i = \mathsf{P}_i \mathbf{Q}$$

i.e. if the point $\mathsf{P}_i\mathbf{Q}$ lies on the line spanned by $\mathbf{A}_i$ and $\mathbf{B}_i$.

Like for perspective cameras, we group these equations in matrix form:

$$\underbrace{\begin{pmatrix} \mathsf{P}_1 & \mathbf{A}_1 & \mathbf{B}_1 & \mathbf{0} & \mathbf{0} & \cdots & \mathbf{0} & \mathbf{0} \\ \mathsf{P}_2 & \mathbf{0} & \mathbf{0} & \mathbf{A}_2 & \mathbf{B}_2 & \cdots & \mathbf{0} & \mathbf{0} \\ \vdots & \vdots & \vdots & \vdots & \vdots & \ddots & \vdots & \vdots \\ \mathsf{P}_n & \mathbf{0} & \mathbf{0} & \mathbf{0} & \mathbf{0} & \cdots & \mathbf{A}_n & \mathbf{B}_n \end{pmatrix}}_{\mathsf{M}} \begin{pmatrix} \mathbf{Q} \\ -\lambda_1 \\ -\mu_1 \\ -\lambda_2 \\ -\mu_2 \\ \vdots \\ -\lambda_n \\ -\mu_n \end{pmatrix} = \begin{pmatrix} \mathbf{0} \\ \mathbf{0} \\ \vdots \\ \mathbf{0} \end{pmatrix}$$

As above, this equation shows that M must be rank-deficient. However, the situation is different here since the P_i are of size 4×4 now, and M of size $4n \times (4+2n)$. We thus have to consider submatrices of M of size $(4+2n)\times(4+2n)$. Furthermore, in the following we show that only submatrices with 3 rows or more per view, give rise to constraints on all pose matrices. Hence, $3n \leq 4+2n$, and again, $n \leq 4$, i.e. multi-view constraints are only obtained for up to 4 views.

Let us first see what happens for a submatrix of M where some view contributes only a single row. The two columns corresponding to its base points $\mathbf{A}$ and $\mathbf{B}$, are multiples of one another since they consist of zeroes only, besides a single non-zero coefficient, in the single row associated with the considered view. Hence, the determinant of the considered submatrix of M is always zero, and no constraint is available.

In the following, we exclude this case, i.e. we only consider submatrices of M where each view contributes at least two rows. Let N be such a matrix. Without loss of generality, we start to develop its determinant with the columns containing $\mathbf{A}_1$ and $\mathbf{B}_1$. The determinant is then given as a sum of terms of the following form:

$$(A_{1,j}B_{1,k} - A_{1,k}B_{1,j}) \det \bar{\mathsf{N}}_{jk}$$

where $j,k \in \{1..4\}$, $j \neq k$, and $\bar{\mathsf{N}}_{jk}$ is obtained from N by dropping the columns containing $\mathbf{A}_1$ and $\mathbf{B}_1$ as well as the rows containing $A_{1,j}$ etc.

We observe several things:

- The term $(A_{1,j}B_{1,k} - A_{1,k}B_{1,j})$ is nothing else than one of the Plücker coordinates of the ray of camera 1 (see Section 2). By continuing with the development of the determinant of $\bar{\mathsf{N}}_{jk}$, it becomes clear that the total determinant of N can be written in the form:

$$\sum_{i_1=1}^{6}\sum_{i_2=1}^{6}\cdots\sum_{i_n=1}^{6} L_{1,i_1}L_{2,i_2}\cdots L_{n,i_n}T_{i_1,i_2,\cdots,i_n} = 0$$

  i.e. the coefficients of the $\mathbf{A}_i$ and $\mathbf{B}_i$ are "folded together" into the Plücker coordinates of camera rays and T is a matching tensor between the n cameras. Its coefficients depend exactly on the cameras' pose matrices.
- If camera 1 contributes only two rows to N, then the determinant of N becomes of the form:

$$L_{1,x}\left(\sum_{i_2=1}^{6}\cdots\sum_{i_n=1}^{6} L_{2,i_2}\cdots L_{n,i_n}T_{i_2,\cdots,i_n}\right) = 0$$

  i.e. it only contains a single coordinate of the ray of camera 1, and the tensor T does not depend at all on the pose of that camera. Hence, to obtain constraints between all cameras, every camera has to contribute at least three rows to the considered submatrix.

# cameras	central M	central useful submatrices	non-central M	non-central useful submatrices
2	6×6	3-3	8×8	4-4
3	9×7	3-2-2	12×10	4-3-3
4	12×8	2-2-2-2	16×12	3-3-3-3

We are now ready to establish the different cases that lead to useful multi-view constraints. As mentioned above, for more than 4 cameras, no constraints linking all of them are available: submatrices of size at least $3n \times 3n$ would be needed, but M only has $4 + 2n$ columns. So, only for $n \leq 4$, such submatrices exist.

The table above gives all useful cases, both for central and non-central cameras. These lead to two-view, three-view and four-view matching constraints, encoded by essential matrices, trifocal and quadrifocal tensors.

8.3. THE CASE OF TWO VIEWS

We have so far explained how to formulate bifocal, trifocal and quadrifocal matching constraints between non-central cameras, expressed via matching tensors of dimension 6×6 to $6 \times 6 \times 6 \times 6$. To make things more concrete, we explore the two-view case in some more detail in the following. We show how the bifocal matching tensor, or essential matrix, can be expressed in terms of the motion/pose parameters. This is then specialized from non-central to axial cameras.

8.3.1. *Non-Central Cameras*

For simplicity, we assume here that the global coordinate system coincides with the first camera's local coordinate system, i.e. the first camera's pose matrix is the identity. As for the pose of the second camera, we drop indices, i.e. we express it via a rotation matrix R and a translation vector $\mathbf{t}$. The matrix M is thus given as:

$$\mathsf{M} = \begin{pmatrix} 1 & 0 & 0 & 0 & A_{1,1} & B_{1,1} & 0 & 0 \\ 0 & 1 & 0 & 0 & A_{1,2} & B_{1,2} & 0 & 0 \\ 0 & 0 & 1 & 0 & A_{1,3} & B_{1,3} & 0 & 0 \\ 0 & 0 & 0 & 1 & A_{1,4} & B_{1,4} & 0 & 0 \\ R_{11} & R_{12} & R_{13} & t_1 & 0 & 0 & A_{2,1} & B_{2,1} \\ R_{21} & R_{22} & R_{23} & t_2 & 0 & 0 & A_{2,2} & B_{2,2} \\ R_{31} & R_{32} & R_{33} & t_3 & 0 & 0 & A_{2,3} & B_{2,3} \\ 0 & 0 & 0 & 1 & 0 & 0 & A_{2,4} & B_{2,4} \end{pmatrix}$$

For a matching pair of lines, M must be rank-deficient. In this two-view case, this implies that its determinant is equal to zero. As for the determinant, it can be developed to the following expression, where the Plücker coordinates $\mathbf{L}_1$ and $\mathbf{L}_2$ are defined as in Equation (1):

$$\mathbf{L}_2^\mathsf{T} \begin{pmatrix} -[\mathbf{t}]_\times \mathsf{R} & \mathsf{R} \\ \mathsf{R} & 0 \end{pmatrix} \mathbf{L}_1 = 0 \qquad (4)$$

We find the essential matrix E and the epipolar constraint that were already mentioned in Section 6.

8.3.2. *Axial Cameras*
As mentioned in Section 3, we adopt local coordinate systems where camera rays have $L_6 = 0$. Hence, the epipolar constraint (4) can be expressed by a reduced essential matrix of size 5×5:

$$\begin{pmatrix} L_{2,1} & \cdots & L_{2,5} \end{pmatrix} \begin{pmatrix} -[\mathbf{t}]_\times \mathsf{R} & \begin{pmatrix} R_{11} & R_{12} \\ R_{21} & R_{22} \\ R_{31} & R_{32} \end{pmatrix} \\ \begin{pmatrix} R_{11} & R_{12} & R_{13} \\ R_{21} & R_{22} & R_{23} \end{pmatrix} & 0_{2\times 2} \end{pmatrix} \begin{pmatrix} L_{1,1} \\ \vdots \\ L_{1,5} \end{pmatrix} = 0$$

Note that this essential matrix is in general of full rank (rank 5), but may be rank-deficient. It can be shown that it is rank-deficient exactly if the two camera axes cut each other. In that case, the left and right null-vectors of E represent the camera axes of one view in the local coordinate system of the other one (one gets the Plücker vectors when adding a zero between second and third coordinates).

8.3.3. *Central Cameras*
As mentioned in Section 3, we here deal with camera rays of the form $(L_1, L_2, L_3, 0, 0, 0)^\mathsf{T}$. Hence, the epipolar constraint (4) can be expressed by a reduced essential matrix of size 3×3:

$$\begin{pmatrix} L_{2,1} & L_{2,2} & L_{2,3} \end{pmatrix} \begin{pmatrix} -[\mathbf{t}]_\times \mathsf{R} \end{pmatrix} \begin{pmatrix} L_{1,1} \\ L_{1,2} \\ L_{1,3} \end{pmatrix} = 0$$

We actually find here the "classical" 3×3 essential matrix $-[\mathbf{t}]_\times \mathsf{R}$ (Hartley and Zisserman, 2000; Longuet-Higgins, 1981).

9. Experimental Results

We describe a few experiments on calibration, motion estimation and 3D reconstruction, on the following three indoor scenarios:

- A house scene, captured by an omnidirectional camera and a stereo system.
- A house scene, captured by an omnidirectional and a pinhole camera.
- A scene consisting of a set of objects placed in random positions as shown in Figure 3(b), captured by an omnidirectional and a pinhole camera.

9.1. CALIBRATION

We calibrate three types of cameras here: pinhole, stereo, and omnidirectional systems.

Pinhole Camera: Figure 2(a) shows the calibration of a pinhole camera using the single center assumption (Sturm and Ramalingam, 2004).

Stereo camera: Here we calibrate the left and right cameras separately as two individual pinhole cameras. In the second step we capture an image of a same scene from left and right cameras and compute the motion between them using the technique described in Section 6. Finally using the computed motion we obtain both the rays of left camera and the right camera in the same coordinate system, which essentially provides the required calibration information.

Omni-directional camera: Our omnidirectional camera is a Nikon Coolpix-5400 camera with an E-8 Fish-Eye lens. Its field of view is 360×183. In theory, this is just another pinhole camera with large distortions. The calibration results are shown in Figure 2. Note that we have calibrated only a part of the image because three images are insufficient to capture the whole image in an omnidirectional camera. By using more than three boards it is possible to cover the whole image.

9.2. MOTION AND STRUCTURE RECOVERY

Pinhole and Omni-directional: Pinhole and omnidirectional cameras are both central. Since the omnidirectional camera has a very large field of view and consequently lower resolution compared to pinhole camera, the images taken from close viewpoints from these two cameras have different resolutions as shown in Figure 3. This poses a problem in finding correspondences between keypoints. Operators like SIFT (Lowe, 1999), which are scale invariant, are not camera invariant. Direct application of SIFT failed to provide good results in our scenario. Thus we had to manually give the correspondences. One interesting research direction would be to work on the automatic matching of feature points in these images.

Stereo system and Omni-directional: A stereo system can be considered as a non-central camera with two centers. The image of a stereo system

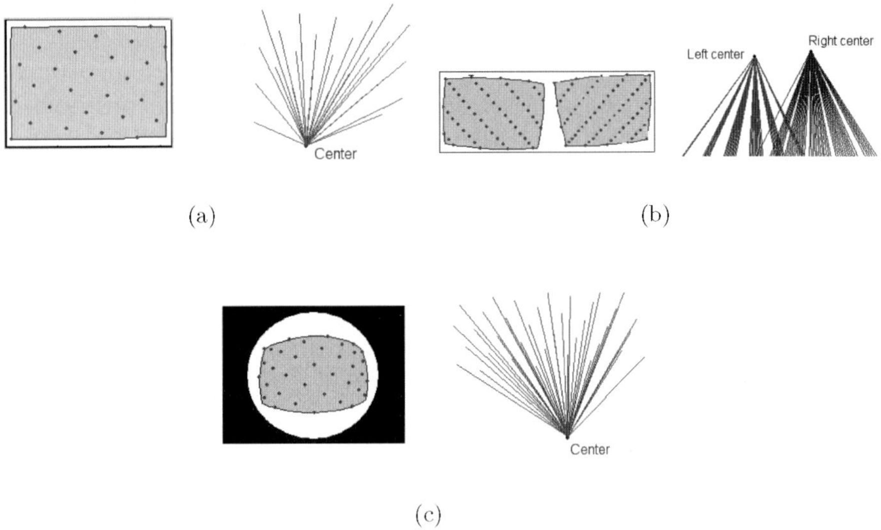

Figure 2. (a) Pinhole. (b) Stereo. (c) Omni-directional (fish-eye). The shading shows the calibrated region and the 3D rays on the right correspond to marked image pixels.

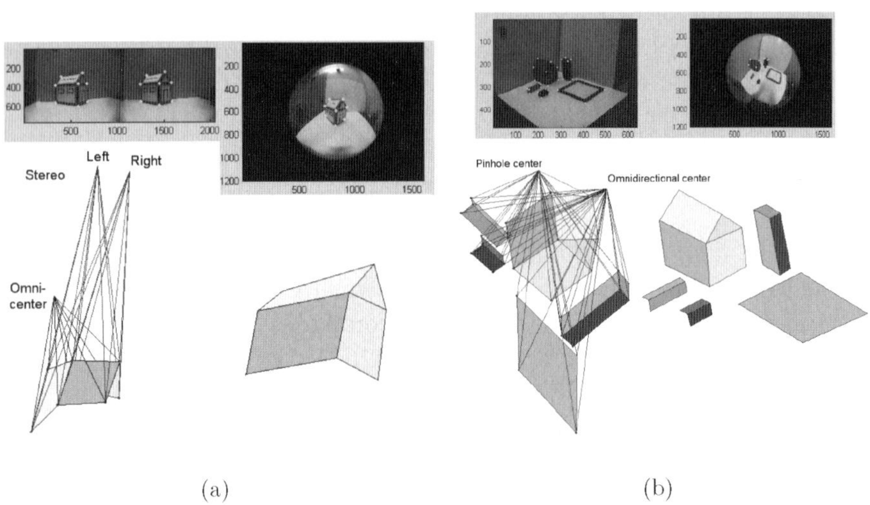

Figure 3. (a) Stereo and omnidirectional. (b) Pinhole and omnidirectional. We intersect the rays corresponding to the matching pixels in the images to compute the 3D points.

is a concatenated version of left and right camera images. Therefore the same scene point appears more than once in the image. While finding image correspondences one keypoint in the omnidirectional image may correspond to 2 keypoints in the stereo system as shown in Figure 3(a). Therefore in the ray-intersection we intersect three rays to find one 3D point.

10. Conclusion

We have reviewed calibration and structure from motion tasks for the general non-central camera model. We also proposed a multi-view geometry for non-central cameras. A natural hierarchy of camera models has been introduced, grouping cameras into classes depending on, loosely speaking, the spatial distribution of their projection rays.

Among ongoing and future works, there is the adaptation of our calibration approach to axial and other camera models. We also continue our work on bundle adjustment for the general imaging model, see (Ramalingam et al., 2004), and the exploration of hybrid systems, combining cameras of different types (Sturm, 2002; Ramalingam et al., 2004).

Acknowledgements

This work was partially supported by the NSF grant ACI-0222900 and by the Multidisciplinary Research Initiative (MURI) grant by Army Research Office under contract DAA19-00-1-0352.

References

S. Baker and S.K. Nayar. A theory of single-viewpoint catadioptric image formation. *IJCV*, **35**: 1–22, 1999.

H. Bakstein. Non-central cameras for 3D reconstruction. Technical Report CTU-CMP-2001-21, Center for Machine Perception, Czech Technical University, Prague, 2001.

H. Bakstein and T. Pajdla. An overview of non-central cameras. In Proc. *Computer Vision Winter Workshop*, Ljubljana, pages 223–233, 2001.

J. Barreto and H. Araujo. Paracatadioptric camera calibration using lines. In Proc. *Int. Conf. Computer Vision*, pages 1359–1365, 2003.

G. Champleboux, S. Lavallée, P. Sautot and P. Cinquin. Accurate calibration of cameras and range imaging sensors: the NPBS method. In Proc. *Int. Conf. Robotics Automation*, pages 1552–1558, 1992.

C.-S. Chen and W.-Y. Chang. On pose recovery for generalized visual sensors. *IEEE Trans. Pattern Analysis Machine Intelligence*, **26**: 848–861, 2004.

O. Faugeras and B. Mourrain. On the geometry and algebra of the point and line correspondences between N images. In Proc. *Int. Conf. Computer Vision*, pages 951–956, 1995.

C. Geyer and K. Daniilidis. A unifying theory of central panoramic systems and practical applications. *Europ. Conf. Computer Vision*, Volume II, pages 445–461, 2000.

C. Geyer and K. Daniilidis. Paracatadioptric camera calibration. *IEEE Trans. Pattern Analysis Machine Intelligence*, **24**: 687–695, 2002.

K.D. Gremban, C.E. Thorpe and T. Kanade. Geometric camera calibration using systems of linear equations. In Proc. *Int. Conf. Robotics Automation*, pages 562–567, 1988.

M.D. Grossberg and S.K. Nayar. A general imaging model and a method for finding its parameters. In Proc. *Int. Conf. Computer Vision*, Volume 2, pages 108-115, 2001.

R.M. Haralick, C.N. Lee, K. Ottenberg, and M. Nolle. Review and analysis of solutions of the three point perspective pose estimation problem. *Int. J. Computer Vision*, **13**: 331-356, 1994.

R.I. Hartley and R. Gupta. Linear pushbroom cameras. *Europ. Confe. Computer Vision*, pages 555–566, 1994.

R.I. Hartley and P. Sturm. Triangulation. *Computer Vision Image Understanding*, **68**: 146–157, 1997.

R.I. Hartley and A. Zisserman. *Multiple View Geometry in Computer Vision*. Cambridge University Press, 2000.

R.A. Hicks and R. Bajcsy. Catadioptric sensors that approximate wide-angle perspective projections. In Proc. *Int. Conf. Computer Vision Pattern Recognition*, pages 545–551, 2000.

H.C. Longuet-Higgins. A computer program for reconstructing a scene from two projections. *Nature*, **293**: 133–135, 1981.

D.G. Lowe. Object recognition from local scale-invariant features. In Proc. *Int. Conf. Computer Vision*, pages 1150–1157, 1999.

J. Neumann, C. Fermüller, and Y. Aloimonos. Polydioptric camera design and 3D motion estimation. In Proc. *Int. Conf. Computer Vision Pattern Recognition*, Volume II, pages 294–301, 2003.

D. Nistér. An efficient solution to the five-point relative pose problem. In Proc. *Int. Conf. Computer Vision Pattern Recognition*, Volume II, pages 195–202, 2003.

D. Nistér. A minimal solution to the generalized 3-point pose problem. In Proc. *Int. Conf. Computer Vision Pattern Recognition*, Volume 1, pages 560–567, 2004.

T. Pajdla. Geometry of two-slit camera. Technical Report CTU-CMP-2002-02, Center for Machine Perception, Czech Technical University, Prague, 2002.

T. Pajdla. Stereo with oblique cameras. *Int. J. Computer Vision*, **47**: 161–170, 2002.

S. Peleg, M. Ben-Ezra, and Y. Pritch. OmniStereo: panoramic stereo imaging. *IEEE Trans. Pattern Analysis Machine Intelligence*, **23**: 279–290, 2001.

R. Pless. Using many cameras as one. In Proc. *Int. Conf. Computer Vision Pattern Recognition*, Volume II, pages 587–593, 2003.

S. Ramalingam, S. Lodha, and P. Sturm. A generic structure-from-motion algorithm for cross-camera scenarios. In Proc. *Workshop Omnidirectional Vision, Camera Networks and Non-Classical Cameras*, pages 175–186, 2004.

H.-Y. Shum, A. Kalai, and S.M. Seitz. Omnivergent stereo. In Proc. *Int. Conf. Computer Vision*, pages 22–29, 1999.

P. Sturm. Mixing catadioptric and perspective cameras. In Proc. *Workshop Omnidirectional Vision*, pages 60–67, 2002.

P. Sturm and S. Ramalingam. A generic calibration concept-theory and algorithms. Research Report 5058, INRIA, 2003.

P. Sturm and S. Ramalingam. A generic concept for camera calibration. In Proc. *Europ. Conf. Computer Vision*, pages 1–13, 2004.

R. Swaminathan, M.D. Grossberg, and S.K. Nayar. A perspective on distortions. *Int. Conf. Computer Vision Pattern Recognition*, Volume II, pages 594–601, 2003.

J. Yu and L. McMillan. General linear cameras. In Proc. *Europ. Conf. Computer Vision*, pages 14–27, 2004.

A. Zomet, D. Feldman, S. Peleg, and D. Weinshall. Mosaicking new views: the crossed-slit projection. *IEEE Trans. Pattern Analysis Machine Intelligence*, **25**: 741–754, 2003.

MOTION ESTIMATION WITH ESSENTIAL AND GENERALIZED ESSENTIAL MATRICES

RANA MOLANA
University of Pennsylvania, USA

CHRISTOPHER GEYER
University of California, Berkeley, USA

Abstract. Recent advances with camera clusters, mosaics, and catadioptric systems led to the notion of generalized images and general cameras, considered as the rigid set of viewing rays of an imaging system, known also as the domain of the plenoptic function. In this paper, we study the recovery of rigid 3D camera motion from ray correspondences in both cases when all rays intersect (central) or do not intersect (non-central) at a single viewpoint. We characterize the manifold associated with the central essential matrices and we show that the non-central essential matrices are permutations of SE(3). Based on such a group-theoretic parameterization, we propose a non-linear minimization on the central and non-central essential manifold, respectively. The main contribution of this paper is a unifying characterization of two-view constraints in camera systems and a computational procedure based on this framework. Current results include simulations verifying priorly known facts for the central case and showing the sensitivity in the transition from central to non-central systems.

Key words: essential matrices, central catadioptric, non-central catadioptric, generalized essential matrices

Introduction

During the past three decades, structure from motion research has mainly dealt with central camera systems characterized by the pinhole model. In the last decade, the confluence of vision and graphics has resulted to more general notions of imaging like the lightfield (Levoy and Hanrahan, 1996) or the lumigraph (Gortler et al., 1996). In both cases as well as in cases associated with catadioptric systems, we can speak of realizations of what Adelson and Bergen (Adelson and Bergen, 1991) have called the plenoptic function which associates with each light ray an intensity or color value. In this paper, we will not deal with a particular lightfield implementation but

K. Daniilidis and R. Klette (eds.), Imaging Beyond the Pinhole Camera, 107–123.

rather with an arbitrary sampling of rays as the domain of the plenoptic function. In case of two views we assume that for the same point in space there will exist at least one ray per view going through this point. We also assume that there exists a procedure for mapping image input to that ray space like the ones proposed in (Grossberg and Nayar, 2001; Sturm and Ramalingam, 2004). Two views with a non-central camera system have been studied by Seitz, Kim (Seitz, 2001) and Pajdla (Pajdla, 2002) who characterize the epipolar surfaces of such systems. A particular plenoptic system being able to capture any ray in space has been considered in (Neumann et al., 2002) where it has been shown that a generalized brightness change constraint can linearly be solved for 3D velocities without involving depth as is the case in central cameras. A simultaneous calibration and motion estimation has recently been proposed in (Sturm and Ramalingam, 2004). The most relevant study to ours has been done by Pless (Pless, 2002) who is the first who proposed an epipolar constraint for non-central systems and this is exactly the constraint we analyze here.

The study of general camera systems has stimulated a revisiting of camera systems with a unique viewpoint. In particularly, central omnidirectional images can be mapped to spherical images when calibration is known and structure from motion can be formulated on the basis of correspondences on the spheres. The representation of the data on spheres has given us insight on the structure of the manifold of essential matrices which we first studied in (Geyer and Daniilidis, 2003). Here, together with the structure of the epipolar constraint in non-central systems, we revisit and give a formal proof of the structure of classical essential matrices. In particularly, we prove that (1) the set of essential matrices is a homogeneous space with the cross-product of rotations as an acting group. It is a manifold of dimension 5 as expected. (2) The non-central essential matrix is a permutation of SE(3).

We propose nonlinear minimization schemes involving a Gauss-Newton iteration on manifolds (Taylor and Kriegman, 1994). Such iterations on the central case but with a different characterization of the essential manifold have been proposed by Soatto et al. (Soatto and Perona, 1998) and Ma et al. (Ma et al., 2001). We tested our algorithms on simulations. We are aware that by no means such simulations are sufficient to characterize the success of the algorithms. In a mainly theoretical paper like this, the main motivation was to use simulations to verify existing experimental findings in the central case and to study non-central systems at the practical case when the non-central epipolar constraint degenerates to the central epipolar term.

1. Calibrated General Camera Model

Various versions of the general camera concept exist in recent literature (Grossberg and Nayar, 2001; Seitz, 2001; Pajdla, 2002; Pless, 2002; Yu and McMillan, 2004). Whilst the notions are similar in principle, the realizations vary according to the devices used. In this paper, being concerned with overall geometric properties, we use an idealization of rays as unoriented lines in space. The general camera we consider is an unrestricted sampling of the plenoptic function. It consists of a *ray set* (a rigid subset of the set of all lines in space, fixed relative to a camera coordinate system) and a *calibration function* that maps each pixel from the image input, for example a catadioptric image or a lightfield, to a single ray in the ray set. Note that this projection function from pixels to rays may be one-to-one or many-to-one, and it is not required to be continuous or differentiable.

We use the terms *central* and *non-central* indicate camera systems where the ray set consists of a 2D pencil and where it does not, respectively. By a *calibrated general camera* we mean a general camera whose calibration function is known. Methods for calibrating general cameras are outlined in (Grossberg and Nayar, 2001; Sturm and Ramalingam, 2004).

Since rays here are lines, they may be parameterized in various ways, including as a pair of points, a point and a direction, or the intersection of two planes. We choose the Plücker coordinate parameterization of 3D lines, primarily because it provides a concise and insightful representation of line transformations. The Plücker parameterization is used frequently in robotics and kinematics and computer graphics and was recently applied by Pless to formulate discrete and continuous generalized epipolar constraints (Pless, 2002).

Plücker coordinates of a line with respect to an origin consist of 6 coefficients that are often grouped as a pair of 3-vectors. In particular, rays in our general camera are represented by $(\mathbf{d}, \mathbf{m})$, where $\mathbf{d}$ is a unit vector in the direction of the ray (from camera to scene), and $\mathbf{m}$ is a vector normal to the plane containing the ray and the origin, such that $\mathbf{m} = \mathbf{P} \times \mathbf{d}$ for any point $\mathbf{P}$ on the line. Here, we choose a Euclidean as opposed to projective or affine framework, so that the coordinates of a line must obey the two equations

$$|\mathbf{d}| = 1 \tag{1}$$
$$\mathbf{m}^\top \mathbf{d} = 0. \tag{2}$$

Thus the six coefficients of a line have only four degrees of freedom.

We shall use the fact that two distinct lines with Plücker coordinates

$(\mathbf{d}_a, \mathbf{m}_a)$ and $(\mathbf{d}_b, \mathbf{m}_b)$ intersect if and only if

$$\begin{pmatrix} \mathbf{d}_b \\ \mathbf{m}_b \end{pmatrix}^\top \begin{pmatrix} 0 & I \\ I & 0 \end{pmatrix} \begin{pmatrix} \mathbf{d}_a \\ \mathbf{m}_a \end{pmatrix} = 0. \tag{3}$$

1.1. GENERALIZED EPIPOLAR CONSTRAINT

Given calibrated cameras, image correspondences can be translated into ray correspondences, and each ray correspondence provides a constraint on the rigid body transformation between the cameras' coordinate systems. We say ray $(\mathbf{d}_1, \mathbf{m}_1)$ from camera C1 *corresponds* to ray $(\mathbf{d}_2, \mathbf{m}_2)$ from camera C2 if these two lines intersect; at their intersection lies the point being imaged. This intersection condition can be expressed by writing both rays with respect to the same coordinate system: the resulting equation is the so-called generalized epipolar constraint (Pless, 2002). We repeat its derivation here, since it will be our starting point for motion estimation.

General cameras C1 and C2 view a scene, see Figure 1. The two camera coordinate systems are related by a rigid body transformation $\langle R, \mathbf{t} \rangle$ such that the coordinates of a world point $\mathbf{P}$ with respect to C1 and with respect to C2 are related as

$$^{\mathbf{2}}\mathbf{P} = R\,^{\mathbf{1}}\mathbf{P} + \mathbf{t}.$$

The Plücker coordinates of ray $(\mathbf{d}_1, \mathbf{m}_1)$ from C1 are represented as $(^{\mathbf{2}}\mathbf{d_1}, {}^{\mathbf{2}}\mathbf{m_1})$ with respect to the C2 coordinate frame. The effect of the base transformation on the line coordinates is as follows:

$$\begin{pmatrix} ^{\mathbf{2}}\mathbf{d_1} \\ ^{\mathbf{2}}\mathbf{m_1} \end{pmatrix} = \underbrace{\begin{pmatrix} R & 0 \\ [\mathbf{t}]_\times R & R \end{pmatrix}}_{H} \begin{pmatrix} \mathbf{d}_1 \\ \mathbf{m}_1 \end{pmatrix}.$$

We call H the *Line Motion Matrix.*

Now $(^{\mathbf{2}}\mathbf{d_1}, {}^{\mathbf{2}}\mathbf{m_1})$ and $(\mathbf{d}_2, \mathbf{m}_2)$ are Plücker coordinates of two distinct lines with respect to the same coordinate system, and if the rays intersect then they must obey Equation (3) to give

$$\begin{aligned} \begin{pmatrix} \mathbf{d}_2 \\ \mathbf{m}_2 \end{pmatrix}^\top \begin{pmatrix} 0 & I \\ I & 0 \end{pmatrix} \begin{pmatrix} ^{\mathbf{2}}\mathbf{d_1} \\ ^{\mathbf{2}}\mathbf{m_1} \end{pmatrix} &= 0 \\ \Rightarrow \begin{pmatrix} \mathbf{d}_2 \\ \mathbf{m}_2 \end{pmatrix}^\top \underbrace{\begin{pmatrix} [\mathbf{t}]_\times R & R \\ R & 0 \end{pmatrix}}_{G} \begin{pmatrix} \mathbf{d}_1 \\ \mathbf{m}_1 \end{pmatrix} &= 0. \end{aligned} \tag{4}$$

We call G the *Generalized Essential Matrix.*

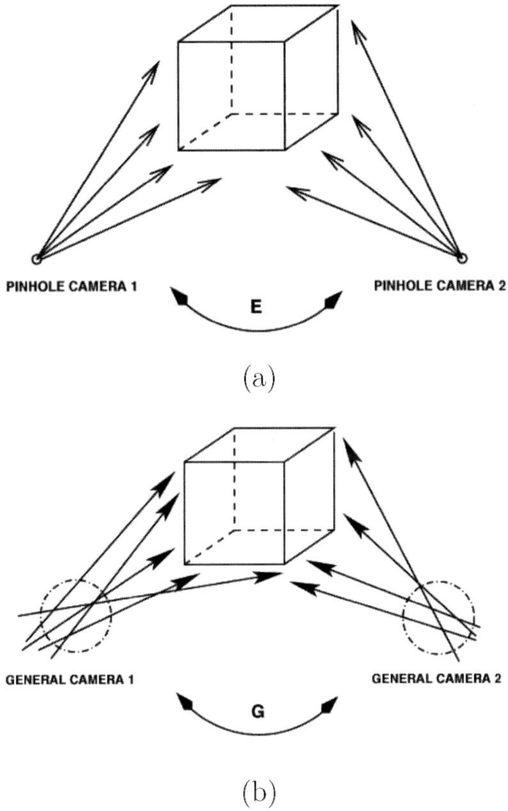

Figure 1. Two cameras viewing a static scene. (a) For central cameras the corresponding rays satisfy a bilinear form with the Essential Matrix E. (b) For two non-central cameras corresponding rays satisfy a bilinear form with the General Essential Matrix G. The centrality of the cameras is encapsulated by the locus of viewpoints which models how much the rays bunch up.

Expanding the matrix multiplication in Equation (4) gives

$$\mathbf{d}_2{}^\top [\mathbf{t}]_\times R\mathbf{d}_1 + \mathbf{d}_2{}^\top R\mathbf{m}_1 + \mathbf{m}_2{}^\top R\mathbf{d}_1 \;=\; 0. \tag{5}$$

This equation is linear homogeneous in the nine elements of rotation matrix R and linear, but not homogeneous, in the three elements of translation vector $\mathbf{t}$. Since the scale of R is fixed by the constraint that it must have determinant one, and since the equation is not homogeneous in $\mathbf{t}$, it follows that the scale of $\mathbf{t}$ is normally recoverable. An important exception where the epipolar constraint becomes homogeneous in $\mathbf{t}$ is when $\mathbf{m}_1 = \mathbf{m}_2 = \mathbf{0}$, giving

$$\mathbf{d}_2{}^\top [\mathbf{t}]_\times R\mathbf{d}_1 = 0.$$

This is the well-known pinhole camera case, where $E = [\mathbf{t}]_\times R$ is called the *Essential Matrix.*

2. The Essential Matrix

In this section we consider the properties of the set $\mathcal{E}$ of all 3×3 Essential matrices, defined[1] as

$$\mathcal{E} = \left\{ E \in \mathbb{R}^{3\times 3} \mid E = [\mathbf{t}]_\times R,\ \mathbf{t} \in \mathrm{S}^2,\ R \in \mathrm{SO}(3) \right\}. \tag{6}$$

We recall that a matrix $E \in \mathbb{R}^{3\times 3}$ is Essential (i.e., $E \in \mathcal{E}$) if and only if E has rank 2 and the two non-zero singular values are both equal to 1. We wish to reinterpret this well known SVD characterization of Essential Matrices. We shall follow the group theoretic approach of (Geyer and Daniilidis, 2003) and construct a group action on the set of Essential matrices.

2.1. A GROUP ACTION ON $\mathcal{E}$

Let $\mathrm{K} = \mathrm{O}(3) \times \mathrm{O}(3)$. Since K is a direct product group, its elements are pairs of orthogonal matrices and the group operation is pairwise matrix multiplication, given by

$$(P_1, Q_1)\,(P_2, Q_2) = (P_1 P_2, Q_1 Q_2)\,.$$

The identity element of the group K is $I_\mathrm{K} = (I, I)$. Consider the differentiable map $\varphi : \mathrm{K} \times \mathcal{E} \longrightarrow \mathcal{E}$ that is defined by

$$\varphi\left((P, Q)\,, E\right) = PEQ^\top.$$

We note that the differentiable map φ satisfies the two properties of a group action:

- Identity: $\varphi\,(I_\mathrm{K}, E) = E$ for all $E \in \mathcal{E}$.
- Associativity: $\varphi\,((P_2, Q_2),\ \varphi\,((P_1, Q_1)\,, E)) = \varphi\,((P_2, Q_2)\,(P_1, Q_1)\,,\ E)$.

[1] Essential matrices could equally well be defined as $\mathcal{E}_2 = \left\{ E \in \mathbb{R}^{3\times 3} \mid E = [\mathbf{t}]_\times R,\right.$ where $\left.\mathbf{t} \in \mathrm{S}^2 \text{ and } R \in \mathrm{O}(3) \right\}$. This definition differs to that in (6) because here R is only required to be an orthogonal matrix, rather than special orthogonal. Obviously, $\mathcal{E} \subseteq \mathcal{E}_2$. In fact, the two sets are identical, i.e., $\mathcal{E} = \mathcal{E}_2$, because given an Essential matrix decomposition where $det(R) = -1$ we can always multiply by $(-1)^2$ so that $E = [\mathbf{t}]_\times R = [-\mathbf{t}]_\times(-\mathrm{R})$, and whenever we have $\det(R) = -1$ then $\det(-\mathrm{R}) = 1$. Hence, the definition in (6) simply reduces the ambiguity of the underlying $[\mathbf{t}]_\times R$ decomposition. In fact, the decomposition of an Essential matrix as $[\mathbf{t}]_\times R$ for $R \in \mathrm{SO}(3)$ is still not unique, as shown in (Maybank, 1993) and elsewhere.

Furthermore, the action φ is easily shown to be transitive meaning that for any $E_1, E_2 \in \mathcal{E}$ there is some $(P, Q) \in \mathrm{K}$ such that $PE_1Q^\top = E_2$. The fact that any group - in this case K - acts transitively on the set of Essential matrices, $\mathcal{E}$, means that $\mathcal{E}$ is a homogeneous space.

We can pick a canonical form, $E_0 \in \mathcal{E}$, for Essential matrices. For convenience, we choose

$$E_0 = \begin{pmatrix} 1 & 0 & 0 \\ 0 & 1 & 0 \\ 0 & 0 & 0 \end{pmatrix}.$$

The orbit of E_0 will be the entire space $\mathcal{E}$, such that any matrix in Essential space can be mapped to E_0. In other words, we have a surjection $\pi : \mathrm{K} \to \mathcal{E}$ given by $\pi(g) = \varphi(g, E_0)$. Effectively, this allows a global parameterization of Essential matrices by pairs of orthogonal matrices, albeit with some redundancy. To determine the redundancy of the parameterization, we consider the isotropy group (also known as stabilizer) of E_0, which we denote by K_{E_0}. This is defined as the set

$$\mathrm{K}_{E_0} = \{g \in \mathrm{K} \mid \varphi(g, E_0) = E_0\}$$

and it follows from the definition that K_{E_0} is a subgroup of K. We derive the structure of this group below.

Consider a path in K_{E_0} that is parameterized by t and passes through the identity at $t = 0$. Let the path be given by $(P(t), Q(t)) : \mathbb{R} \to \mathrm{K}_{E_0}$, so that $(P(0), Q(0)) = I_G$.

Since the K_{E_0} is the isotropy group of E_0, we must have

$$P(t)E_0Q(t)^\top = E_0 \qquad \text{for all } t \in \mathbb{R}.$$

Differentiating this with respect to t gives

$$P'(t)E_0Q(t)^\top + P(t)E_0Q'(t)^\top = 0.$$

Setting $t = 0$ we have $P(0) = Q(0) = I$. Moreover, being members of the Lie algebra of O(3), we know that $P'(0)$ and $Q'(0)$ are skew-symmetric matrices, which gives

$$\begin{aligned} P'(0)E_0 + E_0Q'(0)^\top &= 0 \\ \Rightarrow \quad P'(0)E_0 &= E_0Q'(0) \\ \Rightarrow \quad P'(0) = Q'(0) &= [\mathbf{z}]_\times. \end{aligned}$$

Since the tangent space to K_{E_0} at the identity is spanned by $(P'(0), Q'(0))$ - this is the Lie algebra of K_{E_0}. Hence, the group K_{E_0} can be constructed by exponentiating its Lie algebra as follows

$$\mathrm{K}_{E_0} = \left\{ \left(e^{\lambda[\mathbf{z}]_\times}, e^{\lambda[\mathbf{z}]_\times} \right) \mid \lambda \in \mathbb{R}, \, \mathbf{z} = (0,0,1)^\top \right\}.$$

Thus, the isotropy group of E_0 is the one-dimensional group of z-rotations. Note that K_{E_0} is in fact a Lie subgroup of K.

2.2. THE ESSENTIAL HOMOGENEOUS SPACE

We note from (Boothby, 1975) that if $\varphi : \mathrm{K} \times \mathrm{X} \longrightarrow \mathrm{X}$ is a transitive action of a group K on a set X, then for every $x \in \mathrm{X}$ we have a bijection, $\pi_x : \mathrm{K}/\mathrm{K}_x \longrightarrow \mathrm{X}$, where K_x is the isotropy group of x. Moreover, K/K_x carries an action of K, which is then termed the natural action.

In our case, then, we have a one-to-one correspondence between the quotient space $\mathrm{K}/\mathrm{K}_{E_0}$ and the Essential homogeneous space $\mathcal{E}$.

Since K is a Lie group and K_{E_0} is a Lie subgroup the quotient space is a manifold whose dimension can be calculated as

$$\dim \mathrm{K}/\mathrm{K}_{E_0} = \dim \mathrm{K} - \dim \mathrm{K}_{E_0} = 6 - 1 = 5$$

Thus, being identified with $\mathrm{K}/\mathrm{K}_{E_0}$, the Essential homogeneous space $\mathcal{E}$ must be a five-dimensional manifold.

3. Estimating E: Minimization on $\mathrm{O}(3) \times \mathrm{O}(3)$

Let $\mathbf{f}(U, V)$ be the $m \times 1$ vector of epipolar constraints. Then

$$f_i(U, V) = {\mathbf{d}_2^{(i)}}^\top U \begin{pmatrix} 1 & 0 & 0 \\ 0 & 1 & 0 \\ 0 & 0 & 0 \end{pmatrix} V^\top \mathbf{d}_1^{(i)},$$

where $U, V \in \mathrm{O}(3)$ and $\mathbf{d}_1, \mathbf{d}_2 \in \mathrm{S}^2$. The objective function to be minimized with respect to $U, V \in \mathrm{O}(3)$ is the residual, given by

$$F(U, V) = \frac{1}{2}||\mathbf{f}(U, V)||^2.$$

We apply non-linear minimization on the Lie group $\mathrm{O}(3) \times \mathrm{O}(3)$ using a local parameterization at each step, similar to the method in (Taylor and Kriegman, 1994). We use the quadratic model of the Gauss-Newton so that only first-order terms are computed(Gill et al., 1981).

Consider the objective function at the kth iteration of the algorithm, that is locally parameterized by $\mathbf{u}, \mathbf{v} \in \mathbb{R}^3$ as

$$F_k(\mathbf{u}, \mathbf{v}) = \frac{1}{2} \sum_{i=1}^{m} \left({\mathbf{d}_2^{(i)}}^\top U_k \mathrm{e}^{[\mathbf{u}]_\times} E_0 \mathrm{e}^{[-\mathbf{v}]_\times} V_k^\top \mathbf{d}_1^{(i)} \right)^2.$$

The Jacobian of $\mathbf{f}$ will be an $m \times 6$ matrix which, since there is a redundancy in the parameterization, is normally of rank 5. Then the minimization algorithm is as follows:

Algorithm *MinE*: Minimizing E on $\mathrm{O}(3) \times \mathrm{O}(3)$

Initialization

Set $k = 0$. Let $U_0 = V_0 = I$.

Step 1

Compute the Jacobian J_k of $\mathbf{f}_k$ with respect to the local parameterization $\langle \mathbf{u}, \mathbf{v} \rangle$.

Compute the gradient as $\mathbf{g}_k = \nabla F_k = J_k^\top \mathbf{f}_k$.

Step 2

Test convergence. If $|\mathbf{g}_k| < \tau$ for some threshold $\tau > 0$ then end.

Step 3

Compute the minimization step using the pseudoinverse of the Jacobian J_k^* and enforcing rank $= 5$ since the parameterization is redundant, so that

$$\begin{pmatrix} \mathbf{u}^* \\ \mathbf{v}^* \end{pmatrix} = -J_k^* \mathbf{g}_k.$$

Step 4

Update

$$U_{k+1} = U_k \mathrm{e}^{[\mathbf{u}]_\times} \qquad \text{and} \qquad V_{k+1} = V_k \mathrm{e}^{[\mathbf{v}]_\times}.$$

Set $k = k + 1$ and go to step 1.

4. The Generalized Essential Matrix

In this section we consider the properties of the set $\mathcal{G}$ of all 6×6 Generalized Essential matrices, defined as

$$\mathcal{G} = \left\{ G \in \mathbb{R}^{6\times 6} \mid G = \begin{pmatrix} [\mathbf{t}]_\times R & R \\ R & 0 \end{pmatrix}, \mathbf{t} \in \mathbb{R}^3, R \in \mathrm{SO}(3) \right\}. \tag{7}$$

In order to facilitate discussion, we define the group H of 6×6 Line Motion matrices as

$$\mathrm{H} = \left\{ H \in \mathbb{R}^{6\times 6} \mid H = \begin{pmatrix} A & 0 \\ [\mathbf{a}]_\times A & A \end{pmatrix}, \mathbf{a} \in \mathbb{R}^3, A \in \mathrm{SO}(3) \right\}. \tag{8}$$

Matrices in H describe a rigid body transformation applied to Plücker coordinates. It is straightforward to see that the Line Motion matrices form a group. In fact, these Line Motion matrices also form an *adjoint representation* of SE(3), as described in (R.M. Murray and Sastry, 1993) and so H is itself a 6-dimensional manifold, and thus a Lie group. We note that since H is homomorphic to SE(3) it also has subgroups corresponding to SO(3) and $\mathbb{R}^3$ as can be seen from the following decomposition

$$\begin{pmatrix} R & 0 \\ [\mathbf{t}]_\times R & R \end{pmatrix} = \underbrace{\begin{pmatrix} I & 0 \\ [\mathbf{t}]_\times & I \end{pmatrix}}_{\in \mathbb{R}^3} \underbrace{\begin{pmatrix} R & 0 \\ 0 & R \end{pmatrix}}_{\in \mathrm{SO}(3)}.$$

We can parameterize matrices in H by $\langle \omega, \mathbf{t} \rangle$ as follows

$$H(\omega, \mathbf{t}) = \begin{pmatrix} \mathrm{e}^{[\omega]_\times} & 0 \\ [\mathbf{t}]_\times \mathrm{e}^{[\omega]_\times} & \mathrm{e}^{[\omega]_\times} \end{pmatrix}.$$

Now, we wish to characterize Generalized Essential space $\mathcal{G}$.

PROPOSITION 6.1. *A General Essential matrix right-multiplied by Line Motion matrices remains Generalized Essential.*
Proof:
Let $G \in \mathcal{G}$, parameterized by $\mathbf{t} \in \mathbb{R}^3$ and $R \in \mathrm{SO}(3)$. Let $H \in \mathrm{H}$, parameterized by $\mathbf{a} \in \mathbb{R}^3$ and $A \in \mathrm{SO}(3)$. Then, right-multiplication of G by H gives

$$\begin{aligned} GH &= \begin{pmatrix} [\mathbf{t}]_\times R & R \\ R & 0 \end{pmatrix} \begin{pmatrix} A & 0\mathbf{a} > \mathbf{a} \\ {}_\times A & A \end{pmatrix} \\ &= \begin{pmatrix} [\mathbf{t} + R\mathbf{a}]_\times RA & RA \\ RA & 0 \end{pmatrix} \end{aligned}$$

Hence, $GH \in \mathcal{G}$. □

PROPOSITION 6.2. *A General Essential matrix left-multiplied by the transpose of Line Motion matrices remains Generalized Essential.*
Proof:
Let $G \in \mathcal{G}$, parameterized by $\mathbf{t} \in \mathbb{R}^3$ and $R \in \mathrm{SO}(3)$. Let $H \in \mathrm{H}$, parameterized by $\mathbf{a} \in \mathbb{R}^3$ and $A \in \mathrm{SO}(3)$. Then, left-multiplication of G by $H^\top$ gives

$$\begin{aligned} H^\top G &= \begin{pmatrix} A^\top & -A^\top [\mathbf{a}]_\times \\ 0 & A^\top \end{pmatrix} \begin{pmatrix} [\mathbf{t}]_\times R & R \\ R & 0 \end{pmatrix} \\ &= \begin{pmatrix} [A^\top \mathbf{t}]_\times A^\top R & A^\top R \\ A^\top R & 0 \end{pmatrix} \end{aligned}$$

Hence, $H^\top G \in \mathcal{G}$. □

Following the group theoretic approach for Essential Matrices, we can define a right action of the Line Motion matrix group H on the space of Generalized Essential matrices $\mathcal{G}$ as right-multiplication by H. It is trivial to see that H acts transitively and faithfully on $\mathcal{G}$. Consequently, we can pick a canonical form for Generalized Essential matrices. For convenience we choose

$$G_0 = \begin{pmatrix} 0 & I \\ I & 0 \end{pmatrix}.$$

We can then parameterize Generalized Essential matrices by elements of H, since for any $G \in \mathcal{G}$ there exists a unique $H \in \mathrm{H}$ such that $G = G_0 H$. Since the isotropy group of G_0 is just the 6×6 identity matrix of H, there is no redundancy in this parameterization and clearly $\mathcal{G}$ is isomorphic to H. Alternatively, we can note that Generalized Essential matrices are themselves merely a permutation of the Line Motion matrix, and as such $\mathcal{G}$ is also a 6-dimensional manifold (though it is *not* a matrix group because Generalized Essential matrices are not closed under matrix multiplication).

5. Estimating G: Minimization on SE(3)

Let $\mathbf{f}(R, \mathbf{t})$ be the $m \times 1$ vector of epipolar constraints. Then

$$f_i(R, \mathbf{t}) = {\mathbf{q}_2^{(i)}}^\top \begin{pmatrix} [\mathbf{t}]_\times R & R \\ R & 0 \end{pmatrix} \mathbf{q}_1^{(i)},$$

where $R \in \mathrm{SO}(3)$ and $\mathbf{t} \in \mathbb{R}^3$ and the Euclidean Plücker coordinates of the lines are of the form

$$\mathbf{q}_1 = \begin{pmatrix} \mathbf{d}_1 \\ \mathbf{m}_1 \end{pmatrix} \quad \text{and} \quad \mathbf{q}_2 = \begin{pmatrix} \mathbf{d}_2 \\ \mathbf{m}_2 \end{pmatrix}.$$

The objective function to be minimized with respect to $R \in \mathrm{SO}(3)$ and $\mathbf{t} \in \mathbb{R}^3$ is the residual, given by

$$F(R, \mathbf{t}) = \frac{1}{2} ||\mathbf{f}(R, \mathbf{t})||^2.$$

We apply non-linear minimization on the Lie group H using a local parameterization at each step, similar to the method in (Taylor and Kriegman, 1994). We use the quadratic model of the Gauss-Newton so that only first-order terms are computed and the Hessian is approximated (Gill et al., 1981). Consider the objective function at the kth iteration of the algorithm, that is locally parameterized by $\omega, \mathbf{t} \in \mathbb{R}^3$ as

$$F_k(\omega, \mathbf{t}) = \frac{1}{2} \sum_{i=1}^{m} \left({\mathbf{q}_2^{(i)}}^\top \begin{pmatrix} 0 & I \\ I & 0 \end{pmatrix} H_k H(\omega, \mathbf{t})\, \mathbf{q}_1^{(i)} \right)^2$$

where

$$H_k = \begin{pmatrix} R_k & 0\mathbf{t}_k > \mathbf{t}_k \\ {}_\times R_k & R_k \end{pmatrix} \quad \text{and}$$

Algorithm *MinG*: Minimizing G on SE(3)

Initialization

Set $k = 0$. Let $H_0 = \begin{pmatrix} I & 0 \\ 0 & I \end{pmatrix}$.

Step 1

Compute the Jacobian J_k of $\mathbf{f}_k$ with respect to the local parameterization $\langle \omega, \mathbf{t} \rangle$.

Compute the gradient as $\mathbf{g}_k = \nabla F_k = J_k^\top \mathbf{f}_k$.

Approximate the Hessian as $G_k = \nabla^2 F_k \approx J_k^\top J_k$.

Step 2

Test convergence. If $|\mathbf{g}_k| < \tau$ for some threshold $\tau > 0$ then end.

Step 3

Compute the minimization step, whilst ensuring that $|\omega^*| < \pi$, as

$$\begin{pmatrix} \omega^* \\ \mathbf{t}^* \end{pmatrix} = -G_k^{-1} \mathbf{g}_k.$$

Step 4

Update

$$H_{k+1} = H_k \begin{pmatrix} e^{[\omega^*]_\times} & 0\mathbf{t}^* > \mathbf{t}^* \\ {}_\times e^{[\omega^*]_\times} & e^{[\omega^*]_\times} \end{pmatrix}.$$

Set $k = k + 1$ and go to step 1.

Figure 2. Minimization algorithm.

$$H(\omega, \mathbf{t}) = \begin{pmatrix} e^{[\omega]_\times} & 0\mathbf{t} > \mathbf{t} \\ {}_\times e^{[\omega]_\times} & e^{[\omega]_\times} \end{pmatrix}.$$

The Jacobian of $\mathbf{f}$ will be an $m \times 6$ matrix which, since there is no redundancy in the parameterization, is normally of rank 6 Then the minimization algorithm is as in Figure 2.

6. Simulation Results

We test the algorithms using simulated data. For both the central and non-central cases, the test situation consists of two cameras observing 100 3D points in a cube with sides of length 2m. Each result is an average over 100 runs.

6.1. CENTRAL CASE

For the central case, a pinhole camera model is used. The 3D points are projected into the image planes and corrupted by additive Gaussian noise. Algorithm *MinE* is then used to estimate E from the noisy data. The Essential matrix is decomposed into $\mathbf{t}$ and R using the standard technique of reconstructing a single point to disambiguate the 4 possible solutions (Hartley and Zisserman, 2000).

We study the results from *MinE* when the ground truth and field of view (FOV) are varied. We consider translations of 1m in the xz-plane, going from a pure x-translation of [1000 0 0]mm to a pure z-translation of [0 0 1000]mm with ground truth rotation fixed at 3 degrees about y. The variation of error with translation direction is shown in Figure 3. Results using the eight point algorithm are shown for comparison. We are interested in the behavior with changing FOV. We keep the cube of 3D points at the same size and maintain the same focal length but change the distance of the cameras from the cube. It is evident from Figure 3 that with a small FOV *MinE* confuses the tx and tz components of the translation. This is consistent with the behavior of the Eight Point algorithm on the same data, and is to be expected (Daniilidis and Spetsakis, 1996; Fermüller and Aloimonos, 1998).

6.2. NON-CENTRAL CASE

For the non-central case, we model a general camera by its locus of viewpoints (LOV) as depicted in Figure 1. We consider this to be a sphere of a certain radius. The viewpoints of the camera are a randomly chosen set of

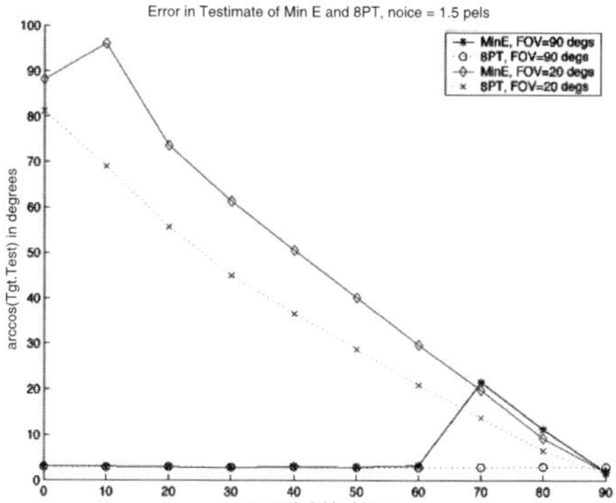

Figure 3. The error in the t estimate for the MinE algorithm and the Eight Point algorithm shown for FOV = 90deg and FOV = 20deg. The ground truth is Ry = 3deg and translation is varied from 1m in the pure x-direction to 1m in the pure z-direction. The starting point is fixed at R = I and t = [1000 0 0]mm

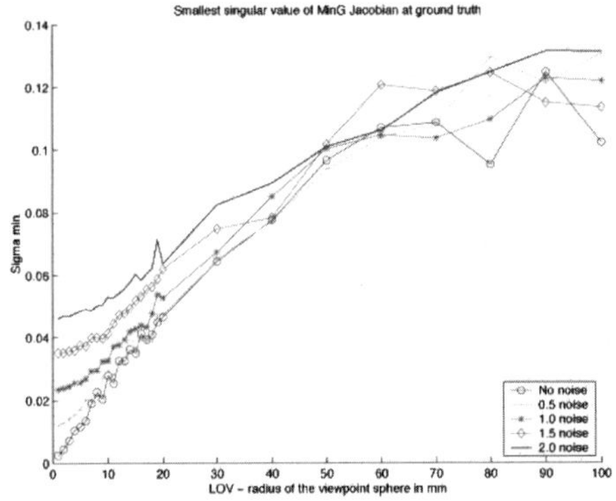

Figure 4. The smallest singular value of the Jacobian of MinG evaluated at the ground truth, which is Ry = 3deg and t = [1000 0 0]mm.

points within the sphere, and a viewpoint paired with a viewed 3D point defines a ray in the camera, enabling the moment and direction vectors to be calculated. Noise is added to the rays by perturbing the viewpoints and perturbing the direction of the rays. The LOV effectively models the non-centralness of the camera: the smaller the sphere of viewpoints, the closer the rays will be to intersecting at a single point.

Figure 4 plots the smallest singular value of the Jacobian of *MinG* calculated at the ground truth as the LOV of the camera is increased from 1mm to 10cm. It is evident that the closer the actual camera is to the single viewpoint case, the smaller this singular value becomes, indicating that the algorithm *MinG* will return poorer solutions when the problem approaches a single viewpoint situation. Figure 5 plots the smallest singular value of the

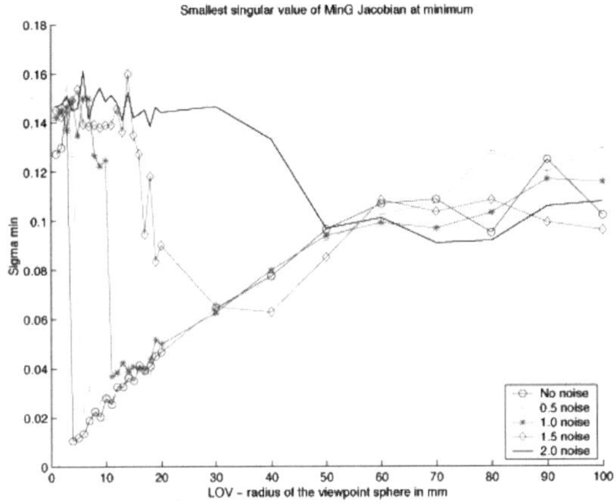

Figure 5. The smallest singular value of the Jacobian of MinG evaluated at the optimized minimum, when the ground truth is Ry = 3deg and t = [1000 0 0]mm.

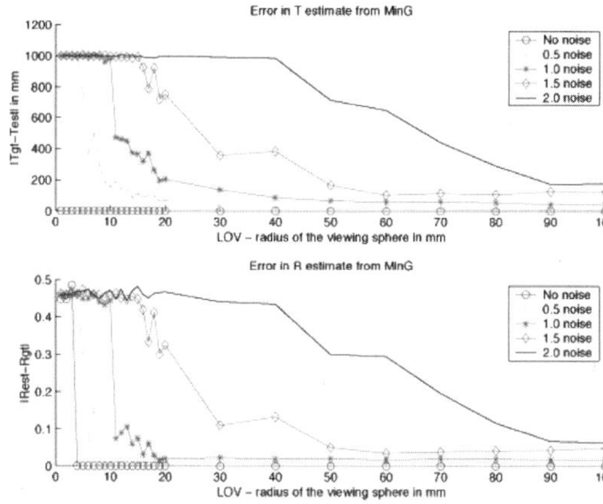

Figure 6. The error in the t and R estimates from the MinG algorithm, as the radius of the Locus of Viewpoints is varied.

Jacobian of *MinG* calculated at the converged minimum. These are much larger than at the ground truth which indicates that *MinG* will converge on an incorrect solution when the LOV is very small. Indeed this theory is confirmed by analyzing the errors in estimates plotted in Figure 6.

6.3. TESTING THE NON-CENTRALITY

Finally, for fixed sets of rays from cameras with LOV ranging between 1mm and 100mm, we consider applying two solutions. We first test *MinG* using the Plücker correspondences. Results are shown in Figure 7. We then discard the moment vector information and run the Eight Point algorithm

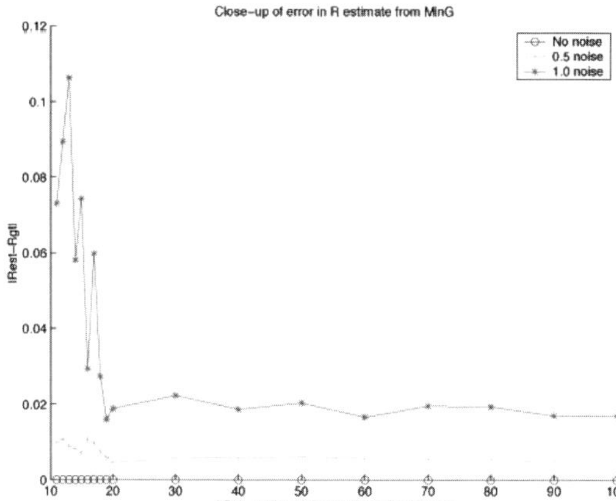

Figure 7. The error in the t estimates from the MinG algorithm, as the radius of the Locus of Viewpoints is varied.

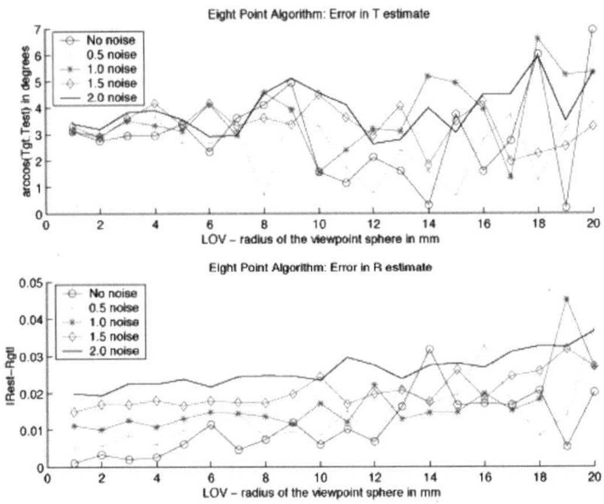

Figure 8. The error in the t and R estimates found from applying the Eight Point algorithm to the direction vector correspondences of a non-central general camera, as the radius of the Locus of Viewpoints is varied.

on the direction vectors only, with results shown in Figure 8. Although the Eight Point algorithm does not model the non-centrality, the errors in its rotation estimates are comparable to those obtained from *MinG*. In fact, the Eight Point algorithm treats the non-centrality as it would treat any noise, which is why the results for different noise values are not easily discernible in Figure 8. This indicates that for correspondence data with a small underlying LOV making a single viewpoint approximation should still give good results, comparable to optimal estimates. Of course, a problem with this approach is that by discarding the moment vectors the magnitude of the translation becomes immeasurable.

7. Conclusions

In this paper, we studied the structure of the essential matrices in central and non-central two-view constraints. We proved that the central essential matrices comprise a homogeneous space which is a manifold of degree 5 and that the non-central essential matrices are permutations of rigid motion representations. We provided computation algorithms based on the principle of iteration on manifolds. Simulations among other results show is in which cases we are safe to use a non-central system to estimate all six degrees of rigid motion as opposed to using central methods which cannot estimate the translation magnitude. In our current work, we study the two-view constraint for particular non-central camera realizations and we extend it to include calibration of such systems.

Acknowledgments

The authors are grateful for support through the following grants: NSF-IIS-0083209, NSF-IIS-0121293, NSF-EIA-0324977, NSF-CNS-0423891, and ARO/MURI DAAD19-02-1-0383.

References

Adelson, E.H. and Bergen, J.R.: The plenoptic function and the elements of early vision. In *Computational Models of Visual Processing* (Landy, M. and Movshon, J. A., editors), MIT Press, 1991.

Boothby, W.M.: *An Introduction to Differentiable Manifolds and Riemannian Geometry.* Academic Press, 1975.

Daniilidis, K. and Spetsakis, M.: Understanding noise sensitivity in structure from motion. In *Visual Navigation* (Aloimonos, Y., editor), pages 61–88, Lawrence Erlbaum Associates, Hillsdale, NJ, 1996.

Fermüller, C. and Aloimonos, Y.: Ambiguity in structure from motion: sphere vs. plane. *Int. J. Computer Vision*, **28**: 137–154, 1998.

Geyer, C. and Daniilidis, K.: Mirrors in motion: epipolar geometry and motion estimation. In Proc. *Int. Conf. Computer Vision*, pages 766–773, 2003.

Gill, P., Murray, W., and Wright, M.: *Practical Optimization.* Academic Press Inc., 1981.

Gortler, S., Grzeszczuk, R., Szeliski, R., and Cohen, M.: The lumigraph. In Proc. *SIGGRAPH*, pages 43–54, 1996.

Grossberg, M.D. and Nayar, S.K.: A general imaging model and a method for finding its parameters. In Proc. *Int. Conf. Computer Vision*, Volume 2, pages 108–115, 2001.

Hartley, R. and Zisserman, A.: *Multiple View Geometry in Computer Vision.* Cambridge University Press, 2000.

Levoy, M. and Hanrahan, P.: Lightfield rendering. In Proc. *SIGGRAPH*, pages 31–42, 1996.

Ma, Yi, Kosecka, Jana, and Sastry, Shankar S.: Optimization criteria and geometric algorithms for motion and structure estimation. *Int. J. Computer Vision*, **44**: 219–249, 2001.

Maybank, S.: *Theory of Reconstruction from Image Motion.* Springer, 1993.

Neumann, J., Fermüller, C., and Aloimonos, Y.: Eyes from eyes: new cameras for structure from motion. In Proc. *IEEE Workshop Omnidirectional Vision*, pages 19–26, 2002.

Pajdla, T.: Stereo with oblique cameras. *Int. Journal Computer Vision*, **47**: 161–170, 2002.

Pless, R.: Discrete and differential two-view constraints for general imaging systems. In Proc. *IEEE Workshop Omnidirectional Vision*, pages 53–59, 2002.

Murray, R.M., Li, Z.and Sastry, S.S.: *A Mathematical Introduction to Robotic Manipulation.* CRC Press, 1993.

Seitz, S.M.: The space of all stereo images. In Proc. *Int. Conf. Computer Vision*, Volume 1, pages 26–33, 2001.

Soatto, S. and Perona, P.: Reducing "structure from motion": a general framework for dynamic vision. *IEEE Trans. Pattern Analysis Machine Intelligence*, **20**: 933–942, 1998.

Sturm, P. and Ramalingam, S.: A generic concept for camera calibration. In Proc. *ECCV*, pages 1–13, 2004.

Taylor, C.J. and Kriegman, D.J.: Minimization on the Lie group so(3) and related manifolds. Technical report, Yale University, 1994.

Yu, J. and McMillan, L.: General linear cameras. In Proc. *ECCV*, pages 14–27, 2004.

SEGMENTATION OF DYNAMIC SCENES TAKEN BY A MOVING CENTRAL PANORAMIC CAMERA

RENE VIDAL
Center for Imaging Science, Dep. of Biomedical Engineering
Johns Hopkins University
308B Clark Hall, 3400 N. Charles Street
Baltimore MD 21218, USA

Abstract. We present an algebraic geometric solution to the problem of segmenting an unknown number of rigid-body motions from optical flow measurements taken by a moving central panoramic camera. We first show that the central panoramic optical flow generated by a rigidly moving object lives in a complex six-dimensional subspace of a high-dimensional linear space, hence motion segmentation is equivalent to segmenting data living in multiple complex subspaces. We solve this problem in closed form using complex Generalized PCA. Our approach involves projecting the optical flow measurements onto a seven-dimensional subspace, fitting a complex polynomial to the projected data, and differentiating this polynomial to obtain the motion of each object relative to the camera and the segmentation of the image measurements. Unlike previous work for affine cameras, our method does not restrict the motion of the objects to be full-dimensional or fully independent. Instead, our approach deals gracefully with all the spectrum of possible motions: from low-dimensional and partially dependent to full-dimensional and fully independent. We test our algorithm on two real sequences. For a sequence with two mobile robots, we also compare the estimates of our algorithm with GPS measurements gathered by the mobile robots.

Key words: multibody structure from motion, motion segmentation, central panoramic optical flow, Generalized Principal Component Analysis (GPCA)

1. Introduction

The panoramic field of view offered by omnidirectional cameras makes them ideal candidates for many vision-based mobile robot applications, such as autonomous navigation, localization, formation control, pursuit evasion games, etc. A problem that is fundamental to most of these applications is multibody motion estimation and segmentation, which is the problem of estimating the number of independently moving objects in the scene;

K. Daniilidis and R. Klette (eds.), Imaging Beyond the Pinhole Camera, 125–142.

the motion of each one of the objects relative to the camera; the camera motion; and the segmentation of the image measurements according to their associated motion.

The problem of estimating the 3-D motion of a moving central panoramic camera imaging a single static object has received a lot of attention over the past few years. Researchers have generalized many two-view structure from motion algorithms from perspective projection to central panoramic projection, both in the case of discrete (Geyer and Daniilidis, 2001) and differential motion (Gluckman and Nayar, 1998; Vassallo et al., 2002). For instance, in (Gluckman and Nayar, 1998; Vassallo et al., 2002) the image velocity vectors are mapped to a sphere using the Jacobian of the transformation between the projection model of the camera and spherical projection. Once the image velocities are on the sphere, one can apply well-known ego-motion algorithms for spherical projection. In a more recent approach (Daniilidis et al., 2002), the omnidirectional images are stereographically mapped onto the unit sphere and the image velocity field is computed on the sphere. Again, once the velocities are known on the sphere, one may apply any ego-motion algorithm for spherical projection. In (Shakernia et al., 2002), we proposed the first algorithm for motion estimation from *multiple* central panoramic views. Our algorithm does not need to map the image data onto the sphere, and is based on a rank constraint on the central panoramic optical flows which naturally generalizes the well-known rank constraints for orthographic (Tomasi and Kanade, 1992), and affine and paraperspective (Poelman and Kanade, 1997) cameras.

The more challenging problem of estimating the 3-D motion of multiple moving objects observed by a moving camera, without knowing which image measurements correspond to which moving object, has only been addressed in the case of affine and perspective cameras. In the case of perspective cameras, early studies concentrated on simple cases such as multiple points moving linearly with constant speed (Han and Kanade, 2000; Shashua and Levin, 2001), multiple points moving in a plane (Sturm, 2002), reconstruction of multiple translating planes (Wolf and Shashua, 2001a), or two-object segmentation from two views (Wolf and Shashua, 2001b). The case of multiple objects in two views was recently studied in (Vidal and Sastry, 2003; Vidal et al., 2006), where a generalization of the 8-point algorithm based on the so-called *multibody epipolar constraint* and its associated *multibody fundamental matrix* was proposed. The method simultaneously recovers multiple fundamental matrices using multivariate polynomial factorization, and can be extended to most two-view motion models in computer vision, such as affine, translational and planar homographies, by fitting and differentiating complex polynomials (Vidal and Ma, 2004). The case of multiple objects in three views has also been recently solved by exploiting the algebraic and geometric properties of the *multibody trifocal tensor* (Hartley and Vidal, 2004). The case of multiple moving objects seen in multiple views has only been studied in the case of discrete measurements taken by an affine camera (Boult and Brown, 1991; Costeira and Kanade, 1998), and differential measurements taken by a perspective camera (Vidal et al., 2002; Machline et al., 2002). These works exploit the fact that when the motion of the objects are independent and full-dimensional, motion segmentation can be achieved by thresholding the entries of a certain similarity matrix built from the image measurements. Unfortunately, these methods are very sensitive to noise as shown in (Kanatani, 2001; Wu et al., 2001). Furthermore, they cannot deal with degenerate or partially dependent motions as pointed out in (Zelnik-Manor and Irani, 2003; Kanatani and Sugaya, 2003; Vidal and Hartley, 2004).

1.1. CONTRIBUTIONS OF THIS PAPER

In this paper, we present an algorithm for infinitesimal motion segmentation from multiple central panoramic views. Our algorithm estimates the number of independent motions, the segmentation of the image data and the motion of each object relative to the camera from measurements of central panoramic optical flow in multiple frames. We exploit the fact that the optical flow measurements generated by one rigid-body motion live in a six-dimensional complex subspace of a high-dimensional linear space, hence motion segmentation is achieved by segmenting data living in multiple complex subspaces. Inspired by the method of (Vidal and Hartley, 2004) for affine cameras, we solve this problem in closed form using a combination of complex PCA and complex GPCA. Our method is provably correct both in the case of full-dimensional and fully independent motions, as well as in the case of low-dimensional and partially dependent motions. It involves projecting the complex optical flow measurements onto a seven-dimensional complex subspace using complex PCA, fitting a complex polynomial to the projected data, and differentiating this polynomial to obtain the motion of each object relative to the camera and the segmentation of the image measurements using complex GPCA. We test our algorithm on two real sequences. For a sequence with two mobile robots, we also compare the estimates of our algorithm with GPS measurements gathered by the mobile robots.

Paper Outline: In Section 2 we describe the projection model for central panoramic cameras, derive the optical flow equations, and show that after a suitable embedding in the complex plane, the optical flow measurements live in a six-dimensional complex subspace of a higher dimensional space. In Section 3 we present an algorithm for segmenting multiple independently moving objects from multiple central panoramic views of a scene. In Section 4 we present experimental results evaluating the performance of the algorithm, and we conclude in Section 5.

2. Single Body Motion Analysis

In this section, we describe the projection model for a central panoramic camera and derive the central panoramic optical flow equations for a single rigid-body motion. We then show that after a suitable embedding into the complex plane, the optical flow measurements across multiple frames live in a six-dimensional subspace of a high-dimensional complex space.

2.1. PROJECTION MODEL

Catadioptric cameras are realizations of omnidirectional vision systems that combine a curved mirror and a lens. Examples of catadioptric cameras are a parabolic mirror in front of an orthographic lens and a hyperbolic mirror in front of a perspective lens. In (Baker and Nayar, 1999), an entire class of catadioptric systems containing a single effective focal point is derived. A single effective focal point is necessary for the existence of epipolar geometry that is independent of the scene structure (Svoboda et al., 1998).

Camera systems with a unique effective focal point are called *central panoramic cameras*. It was shown in (Geyer and Daniilidis, 2000) that all central panoramic cameras can be modeled by a mapping of a 3-D point onto a sphere followed by a projection onto the image plane from a point in the optical axis of the camera. According to the unified projection model (Geyer and Daniilidis, 2000), the image point $(x, y)^T$ of a 3-D point $\boldsymbol{X} = (X, Y, Z)^T$ obtained through a central panoramic camera with parameters (ξ, m) is given by:

$$\begin{bmatrix} x \\ y \end{bmatrix} = \frac{\xi + m}{-Z + \xi\sqrt{X^2 + Y^2 + Z^2}} \begin{bmatrix} s_x X \\ s_y Y \end{bmatrix} + \begin{bmatrix} c_x \\ c_y \end{bmatrix}, \tag{1}$$

where $0 \leq \xi \leq 1$, m and (s_x, s_y) are scales that depend on the geometry of the mirror, the focal length and the aspect ratio of the lens, and $(c_x, c_y)^T$ is the mirror center. By varying two parameters (ξ, m), one can model all catadioptric cameras that have a single effective viewpoint. The particular values of (ξ, m) in terms of the shape parameters of different types of mirrors are listed in (Barreto and Araujo, 2002).

As central panoramic cameras for $\xi \neq 0$ can be easily calibrated from a single image of three lines, as shown in (Geyer and Daniilidis, 2002; Barreto and Araujo, 2002), from now on we will assume that the camera has been calibrated, i.e. we know the parameters $(s_x, s_y, c_x, c_y, \xi, m)$. Therefore, without loss of generality, we consider the following *calibrated* central panoramic projection model:

$$\begin{bmatrix} x \\ y \end{bmatrix} = \frac{1}{\lambda}\begin{bmatrix} X \\ Y \end{bmatrix}, \quad \lambda \triangleq -Z + \xi\sqrt{X^2 + Y^2 + Z^2} \tag{2}$$

which is valid for $Z < 0$. It is direct to check that $\xi = 0$ corresponds to perspective projection, and $\xi = 1$ corresponds to paracatadioptric projection (a parabolic mirror in front of an orthographic lens).

2.2. BACK-PROJECTION RAYS

Since central panoramic cameras have a unique effective focal point, one can efficiently compute the *back-projection ray* (a ray from the optical center in the direction of the 3-D point being imaged) associated with each image point.

One may consider the central panoramic projection model in equation (2) as a simple projection onto a curved virtual retina whose shape depends on the parameter ξ. We thus define the *back-projection ray* as the *lifting* of the image point $(x, y)^T$ onto this retina. That is, as shown in Figure 1, given an image $(x, y)^T$ of a 3-D point $\boldsymbol{X} = (X, Y, Z)^T$, we define the back-projection rays as:

$$\boldsymbol{x} \triangleq (x, y, z)^T, \tag{3}$$

where $z = \boldsymbol{f}_\xi(x, y)$ is the height of the virtual retina. We construct $\boldsymbol{f}_\xi(x, y)$ in order to re-write the central panoramic projection model in (2) as a simple scaling:

$$\lambda \boldsymbol{x} = \boldsymbol{X}, \tag{4}$$

where the unknown scale λ is lost in the projection. Using equations (4) and (2), it is direct to solve for the height of the virtual retina as:

$$z \triangleq \boldsymbol{f}_\xi(x, y) = \frac{-1 + \xi^2(x^2 + y^2)}{1 + \xi\sqrt{1 + (1 - \xi^2)(x^2 + y^2)}}. \tag{5}$$

Notice that in the case of paracatadioptric projection $\xi = 1$ and the virtual retina is the parabola $z = \frac{1}{2}(x^2 + y^2 - 1)$.

2.3. CENTRAL PANORAMIC OPTICAL FLOW

If the camera undergoes a linear velocity $v \in \mathbb{R}^3$ and an angular velocity $\omega \in \mathbb{R}^3$, then the coordinates of a static 3-D point $\boldsymbol{X} \in \mathbb{R}^3$ evolve in the camera frame as $\dot{\boldsymbol{X}} = \widehat{\omega}\boldsymbol{X} + v$. Here, for $\omega \in \mathbb{R}^3$, $\widehat{\omega} \in so(3)$ is the

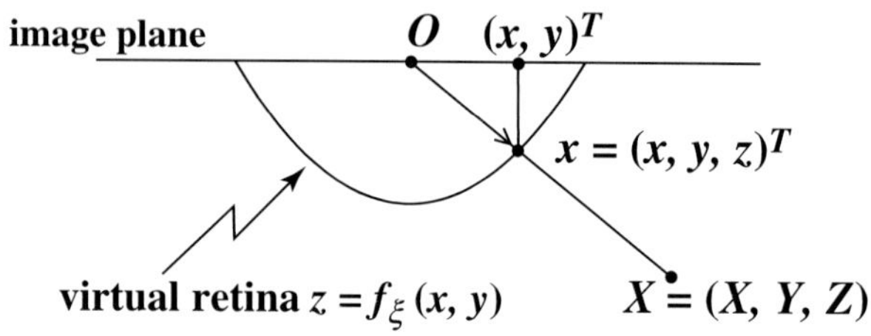

Figure 1. Showing the curved virtual retina in central panoramic projection and back-projection ray $\boldsymbol{x}$ associated with image point $(x, y)^T$.

skew-symmetric matrix generating the cross product by ω. Then, after differentiating equation (4), we obtain:

$$\dot{\lambda}\boldsymbol{x} + \lambda\dot{\boldsymbol{x}} = \lambda\widehat{\omega}\boldsymbol{x} + v, \tag{6}$$

where $\lambda = -e_3^T\boldsymbol{X} + \xi r$, $e_3 \triangleq (0,0,1)^T$ and $r \triangleq \|\boldsymbol{X}\|$. Now, using $\boldsymbol{X} = \lambda\boldsymbol{x}$, we get $r = \lambda(1+e_3^T\boldsymbol{x})/\xi$. Also, it is clear that $\dot{\lambda} = -e_3^T(\widehat{\omega}\boldsymbol{X}+v)+\xi\boldsymbol{X}^Tv/r$. Thus, after replacing all these expressions into (6), we obtain the following expression for the velocity of the back-projection ray in terms of the relative 3-D camera motion:

$$\dot{\boldsymbol{x}} = -(I + \boldsymbol{x}e_3^T)\widehat{\boldsymbol{x}}\omega + \frac{1}{\lambda}\left(I + \boldsymbol{x}e_3^T - \frac{\xi^2\boldsymbol{x}\boldsymbol{x}^T}{1 + e_3^T\boldsymbol{x}}\right)v. \tag{7}$$

Since the first two components of the back-projection ray are simply $(x, y)^T$, the first two rows of (7) give us the expression for *central panoramic optical flow:* (Shakernia et al., 2003)

$$\begin{bmatrix}\dot{x}\\ \dot{y}\end{bmatrix} = \begin{bmatrix} xy & z - x^2 & -y\\ -(z-y^2) & -xy & x\end{bmatrix}\omega + \frac{1}{\lambda}\begin{bmatrix}1-\rho x^2 & -\rho xy & (1-\rho z)x\\ -\rho xy & 1-\rho y^2 & (1-\rho z)y\end{bmatrix}v, \tag{8}$$

where $\lambda = -Z+\xi\sqrt{X^2+Y^2+Z^2}$, $z = \boldsymbol{f}_\xi(x,y)$, and $\rho \triangleq \xi^2/(1+z)$. Notice that when $\xi = 0$, then $\rho = 0$ and (8) becomes the well-known equation for the optical flow of a perspective camera. When $\xi = 1$, then $\rho = 1/(x^2+y^2)$, and (8) becomes the equation for the optical flow of a paracatadioptric camera, which can be found in (Shakernia et al., 2002).

2.4. CENTRAL PANORAMIC MOTION SUBSPACE

Consider now the optical flow of multiple pixels in multiple frames. To this end, let $(x_p, y_p)^T$, $p = 1, \ldots, P$, be a pixel in the zeroth frame and let $\boldsymbol{u}_{fp} = \dot{x}_{fp} + j\dot{y}_{fp} \in \mathbb{C}$ be its *complex* optical flow in frame $f = 1, ..., F$, relative to the zeroth frame. If we stack all these measurements into a $F \times P$ *complex optical flow* matrix

$$W = \begin{bmatrix} \boldsymbol{u}_{11} & \cdots & \boldsymbol{u}_{1P} \\ \vdots & & \vdots \\ \boldsymbol{u}_{F1} & \cdots & \boldsymbol{u}_{FP} \end{bmatrix} \in \mathbb{C}^{F\times P}, \tag{9}$$

we obtain that $\operatorname{rank}(W) \leq 6$, because W can be factored as the product of a *motion matrix* $M \in \mathbb{R}^{F\times 6}$ and a *structure matrix* $S \in \mathbb{C}^{6\times P}$ as

$$W = MS = \begin{bmatrix} \omega_1^T & v_1^T \\ \vdots & \vdots \\ \omega_F^T & v_F^T \end{bmatrix} \begin{bmatrix} x_1y_1 - j(z_1 - y_1^2) & \cdots & x_Py_P - j(z_P - y_P^2) \\ z_1 - x_1^2 - jx_1y_1 & \cdots & z_P - x_P^2 - jx_Py_P \\ -y_1 + jx_1 & \cdots & -y_P + jx_P \\ \frac{1-\rho_1(x_1^2+jx_1y_1)}{\lambda_1} & \cdots & \frac{1-\rho_P(x_P^2+jx_Py_P)}{\lambda_P} \\ \frac{-\rho_1x_1y_1+j(1-\rho_1y_1^2)}{\lambda_1} & \cdots & \frac{-\rho x_Py_P+j(1-\rho_Py_P^2)}{\lambda_P} \\ \frac{(1-\rho_1z_1)(x_1+jy_1)}{\lambda_1} & \cdots & \frac{(1-\rho_Pz_P)(x_P+jy_P)}{\lambda_P} \end{bmatrix}. \tag{10}$$

Therefore, the central panoramic optical flow measurements generated by a single rigid-body motion live in a six-dimensional subspace of $\mathbb{C}^F$.

REMARK 7.1. (Real versus complex optical flow). *As demonstrated in (Shakernia et al., 2003), one can derive a rank constraint* $\operatorname{rank}(W_r) \leq 10$ *on the real optical flow matrix* $W_r \in \mathbb{R}^{2F\times P}$. *However, as we will see shortly, working with motion subspaces of dimension* 10, *rather than* 6, *increases the computational complexity of the motion segmentation algorithm we are about to present from* $O(n^6)$ *to* $O(n^{10})$, *where* n *is the number of motions.*

REMARK 7.2. (Calibrated versus uncalibrated cameras). *In our derivation of the optical flow equations we have assumed that the central panoramic camera has been previously calibrated. In the uncalibrated case, the optical flow equations are essentially the same, except for an scaling factor. While such a scale will necessarily effect motion estimation, it will not effect motion segmentation, because the rank of the measurements matrix is still* 6 *for a single rigid-body motion.*

3. Multibody Motion Analysis

In this section, we propose an algebraic geometric solution to the problem of segmenting an unknown number of rigid-body motions from optical flow measurements in multiple central panoramic views. We assume we are given a matrix $W \in \mathbb{C}^{F\times P}$ containing P image measurements in F frames.

From our analysis in the previous section, we know that when the image measurements are generated by a single rigid-body motion the columns of W span a subspace of $\mathbb{C}^F$ of dimension at most six. Therefore, if the image measurements are generated by n independently moving objects, then the columns of W must live in a collection of n subspaces $\{S_i \subset \mathbb{C}^F\}_{i=1}^n$ of dimension at most six.

3.1. SEGMENTING FULLY INDEPENDENT MOTIONS

Let us first consider the case in which the motion subspaces are fully independent, i.e. $S_i \cap S_\ell = \{0\}$, and full-dimensional, i.e. $\dim(S_i) = 6$. If the columns of W were ordered according to their respective motion subspaces, then we could decompose it as:

$$W = [W_1 \cdots W_n] = [M_1 \cdots M_n] \begin{bmatrix} S_1 & & 0 \\ & \ddots & \\ 0 & & S_n \end{bmatrix} = MS, \tag{11}$$

where $M \in \mathbb{R}^{F\times 6n}$, $S \in \mathbb{C}^{6n\times P}$, $M_i \in \mathbb{R}^{F\times 6}$, $S_i \in \mathbb{C}^{6\times P_i}$, P_i is the number of pixels associated with object i for $i = 1, \dots, n$, and $P = \sum_{i=1}^n P_i$ is the total number of pixels. Since in this paper we assume that the segmentation of the image points is unknown, the rows of W may be in a different order. However, the reordering of the rows of W will not affect its rank. Therefore, we must have $\text{rank}(W) = 6n$, provided that $F \geq 6n$ and $P \geq 6n$. This rank constraint on W allows us to determine the number of independent motions directly from the image measurements as

$$n = \frac{\text{rank}(W)}{6}. \tag{12}$$

Furthermore, it was shown in (Kanatani, 2001) that if the subspaces are independent, though not necessarily full-dimensional, then the so-called *shape interaction* matrix $Q = VV^T \in \mathbb{C}^{P\times P}$, where $W = USV^T$ is the SVD of W, is such that

$$Q_{pq} = \begin{cases} 0 & \text{if } p \text{ and } q \text{ correspond to the same subspace} \\ \text{any number} & \text{otherwise} \end{cases} \tag{13}$$

Therefore, one can obtain the number of motions and the segmentation of the image measurements by thresholding the entries of the shape interaction matrix Q and then permuting its rows and columns, as suggested by the work of (Costeira and Kanade, 1998) for affine cameras, which deals with real subspaces of dimension at most four.

Unfortunately, the Costeira and Kanade algorithm is very sensitive to noise as pointed out in (Kanatani, 2001; Wu et al., 2001) where various improvements were proposed. Furthermore, equation (13) holds if and only if the motion subspaces are linearly independent, hence the segmentation scheme is not provably correct for most practical motion sequences which usually exhibit partially dependent motions, such as when two objects have the same rotational but different translational motion relative to the camera, or vice versa.

In order to obtain an algorithm that deals with both independent and/or partially dependent motions, we need to assume only that the motion subspaces are different, i.e. $S_i \neq S_\ell$ for all $i \neq \ell = 1, \ldots, n$, or equivalently $\dim(S_i \cup S_\ell) > \max\{\dim(S_i), \dim(S_\ell)\}$, as we do in the next section.

3.2. SEGMENTING INDEPENDENT AND/OR PARTIALLY DEPENDENT MOTIONS

In this section we present an algorithm that is probably correct not only for full-dimensional and fully independent motions, but also for low-dimensional and partially dependent motions,[1] or any combination thereof. This is achieved by a combination of complex PCA and complex GPCA which leads to the following purely geometric solution to the multiframe motion segmentation problem:

1. Project the image measurements onto a seven-dimensional subspace of $\mathbb{C}^F$. A byproduct of this projection is that our algorithm requires a minimum number of *seven* views for *any* number of independent motions. Furthermore, the projection allows us to deal with noise and outliers in the data by robustly fitting the seven dimensional subspace.
2. Estimate all the motion subspaces by fitting a complex homogeneous polynomial to the projected data and segment the motion subspaces by taking the derivatives of this polynomial. We deal with noisy data by optimally choosing the points at which to evaluate the derivatives.

The following subsections describe our algorithm in greater detail.

3.2.1. *Projecting onto a Seven-Dimensional Subspace*

The first step of our algorithm is to project the point trajectories (columns of W) from $\mathbb{C}^F$ to $\mathbb{C}^7$. In choosing a projection, it makes sense to lose as little information as possible by projecting into a dominant eigensubspace, which we can do simply by computing the SVD of $W = U_{F\times 7}V_{7\times P}$, and then defining a new data matrix $Z = V \in \mathbb{C}^{7\times P}$. At a first sight, it may seem

---

[1] Two motions are said to be fully independent if $\dim(S_i \cup S_\ell) = \dim(S_i) + \dim(S_\ell)$ or equivalently $S_i \cap S_\ell = \{0\}$. Two motions are said to be partially dependent if $\max\{\dim(S_i), \dim(S_\ell)\} < \dim(S_i \cup S_\ell) < \dim(S_i) + \dim(S_\ell)$ or equivalently $S_i \cap S_\ell \neq S_i \neq S_\ell \neq \{0\}$

counter-intuitive to perform this projection. For instance, if we have $F = 12$ frames of $n = 2$ independent six-dimensional motions, then we can readily apply an modified version of the Costeira and Kanade algorithm, because we are in a nondegenerate situation. However, if we first project onto $\mathbb{C}^7$, the motion subspaces become partially dependent because $\text{rank}(Z) = 7 < 6 + 6 = 12$. What is the reason for projecting then? The reason is that the clustering of data lying on multiple subspaces is preserved by a generic linear projection. For instance, if one is given data lying on two lines in $\mathbb{R}^3$ passing through the origin, then one can first project the two lines onto a plane in general position[2] and then cluster the data inside that plane. More generally the principle is (Vidal et al., 2003; Vidal et al., 2005):

THEOREM 7.1. (Cluster-Preserving Projections). *If a set of vectors* $\{\boldsymbol{z}^j\}$ *all lie in n linear subspaces of dimensions* $\{d_i\}_{i=1}^n$ *in* $\mathbb{C}^D$, *and if* π_S *represents a linear projection into a subspace S of dimension* D', *then the points* $\{\pi_S(\boldsymbol{z}^j)\}$ *lie in at most n linear subspaces of S of dimensions* $\{d_i' \leq d_i\}_{i=1}^n$. *Furthermore, if* $D > D' > d_{\max}$, *then there is an open and dense set of projections that preserve the separation and dimensions of the subspaces.*

The same principle applies to the motion segmentation problem. Since we know that the maximum dimension of each motion subspace is six, then projecting onto a generic seven-dimensional subspace preserves the segmentation of the motion subspaces. Loosely speaking, in order for two different motions to be distinguishable from each other, it is enough for them to be different along one dimension, i.e. we do not really need to have the subspaces be different in all six dimensions. It is this key observation the one that enable us to treat *all* partially dependent motions as well as *all* independent motions in the same framework: segmenting subspaces of dimension one through six living in $\mathbb{C}^7$.

Another advantage of projecting the data onto a seven-dimensional space is that, except for the projection itself, the complexity of the motion segmentation algorithm we are about to present becomes independent on the number of frames, because we only need seven frames to perform the above projection. Furthermore, one can deal with noise and outliers in the data by robustly fitting the seven-dimensional subspace. This can be done using, e.g., Robust PCA (De la Torre and Black, 2001).

3.2.2. *Fitting Motion Subspaces using Complex GPCA*

We have reduced the motion segmentation problem to finding a set of linear subspaces in $\mathbb{C}^7$, each of dimension at most six, which contain the data

[2] A plane perpendicular to any of the lines or perpendicular to the plane containing the lines would fail.

points (or come close to them). The points in question are the columns of the projected data matrix Z. We solve this problem in closed form by adapting the Generalized GPCA algorithm in (Vidal et al., 2003; Vidal et al., 2004; Vidal et al., 2005) to the complex domain.

To this end, let $Z \in \mathbb{C}^{7\times P}$ be the matrix of projected data and let $\boldsymbol{z} \in \mathbb{C}^7$ be any of its columns. Since $\boldsymbol{z}$ must belong to one of the projected subspaces, say S_i,[3] then there exists a vector $\boldsymbol{b}_i \in \mathbb{C}^7$ normal to subspace S_i such that $\boldsymbol{b}_i^T\boldsymbol{z} = 0$. Let $\{\boldsymbol{b}_i\}_{i=1}^n$ be a collection of n different vectors in $\mathbb{C}^7$ such that $\boldsymbol{b}_i$ is orthogonal to S_i but not orthogonal to S_ℓ for $\ell \neq i = 1,\dots,n$. Then $\boldsymbol{z}$ must satisfy the following homogeneous polynomial of degree n in 7 variables

$$p_n(\boldsymbol{z}) = (\boldsymbol{b}_1^T\boldsymbol{z})(\boldsymbol{b}_2^T\boldsymbol{z})\cdots(\boldsymbol{b}_n^T\boldsymbol{z}) = \sum c_{n_1,\dots,n_7} z_1^{n_1}\cdots z_7^{n_7} = \boldsymbol{c}_n^T\nu_n(\boldsymbol{z}) = 0, \quad (14)$$

where $\nu_n : \mathbb{C}^7 \to \mathbb{C}^{M_n(7)}$ is the *Veronese map* of degree n (Harris, 1992) which is defined as $\nu_n : [z_1,\dots,z_7]^T \mapsto [\dots, z_1^{n_1}z_2^{n_2}\cdots z_7^{n_7},\dots]^T$, where $0 \leq n_\ell \leq n$, for $\ell = 1,\dots,7$, $n_1+n_2+\cdots+n_7 = n$, and $M_n(7) = \begin{pmatrix} n+6 \\ 6 \end{pmatrix}$.

Since any column of the projected data matrix $Z = [\boldsymbol{z}_1,\cdots,\boldsymbol{z}_P]$ must satisfy $p_n(\boldsymbol{z}) = 0$, the vector of coefficients $\boldsymbol{c}_n$ must be such that

$$\boldsymbol{c}_n^T L_n = \boldsymbol{c}_n^T[\nu_n(\boldsymbol{z}_1)\cdots\nu_n(\boldsymbol{z}_P)] = 0, \quad (15)$$

where $L_n \in \mathbb{R}^{M_n(7)\times P}$. This equation allows us to simultaneously solve for the number of motions n, the vector of coefficients $\boldsymbol{c}_n$, the normal vectors $\{\boldsymbol{b}_i\}_{i=1}^n$ and the clustering of the columns of Z as follows:

1. If the number of independent motions n is known, one can linearly solve for the coefficients $\boldsymbol{c}_n$ of p_n from the least squares problem $\min \|\boldsymbol{c}_n^T L_n\|^2$. The solution is given by the singular vector of L_n associated with the smallest singular value. Notice that the minimum number of pixels required is $P \geq M_n(7) - 1 \sim O(n^6)$. That is $P = 27$, 209 and 923 pixels for $n = 2$, 4 and 6 independent motions, which is rather feasible in practice. Notice also that the solution to $\boldsymbol{c}_n^T L_n = 0$ is unique only if the motion subspaces are full-dimensional, because in this case there is a unique normal vector associated with each motion subspace. If a subspace is of dimension strictly less than six, there is more than one normal vector defining the subspace, hence there is more than one polynomial of degree n fitting the data. In such cases, we can choose any generic vector $\boldsymbol{c}_n$ in the left null space of L_n. Each choice defines a surface passing through all the points and the derivative of the surface

[3] With an abuse of notation, we use S_i to denote both the original and the projected motion subspace

at a data point gives a vector normal to the surface at that point. Therefore, if $\boldsymbol{z}$ corresponds to motion subspace S_i, then the derivative of p_n at $\boldsymbol{z}$ gives a normal vector $\boldsymbol{b}_i$ to subspace S_i up to scale factor, i.e.

$$\boldsymbol{b}_i = \frac{Dp_n(\boldsymbol{z})}{\|Dp_n(\boldsymbol{z})\|}. \tag{16}$$

In order to find a normal vector to each one of the motion subspaces we can choose n columns of Z, $\{\tilde{\boldsymbol{z}}_i\}_{i=1}^n$, such that each one belongs each one of the n subspaces, and then obtain the normal vectors as $\boldsymbol{b}_i \sim Dp_n(\tilde{\boldsymbol{z}}_i)$. We refer the reader to (Vidal and Ma, 2004) for a simple method for choosing such points. Given the normal vectors $\{\boldsymbol{b}_i\}$, we can immediately cluster the columns of Z by assigning $\boldsymbol{z}_p$ to the ith motion subspace if

$$i = \arg \min_{\ell=1,\ldots,n} \{(\boldsymbol{b}_\ell^T \boldsymbol{z}_p)^2\}. \tag{17}$$

2. If the number of independent motions n is unknown, we need to determine both the degree n and the coefficients $\boldsymbol{c}_n$ of a polynomial p_n that vanishes on all the columns of Z. Unfortunately, it is possible to find a polynomial of degree $m \leq n$ that vanishes on the data. For example, consider the case of data lying on $n = 3$ subspaces of $\mathbb{R}^3$: one plane and two lines through the origin. Then we can fit a polynomial of degree $m = 2$ to all the points, because the data can also be fit with two subspaces: the plane containing the two lines and the given plane. More generally, let $m \leq n$ be the degree of the polynomial of minimum degree fitting the data and let $\boldsymbol{c}_m \in \mathbb{C}^{M_m(7)}$ be its vector of coefficients. Since $p_m(\boldsymbol{z}) = \boldsymbol{c}_m^T \nu_m(\boldsymbol{z})$ is satisfied by all the columns of Z, we must have $\boldsymbol{c}_m^T L_m = 0$. Therefore, we can determine the minimum degree m as

$$m = \min\{i : \text{rank}(L_i) < M_i(7)\}, \tag{18}$$

where L_i is computed by applying the Veronese map of degree i to the columns of Z. Since the polynomial $p_m(\boldsymbol{z}) = \boldsymbol{c}_m^T \nu_m(\boldsymbol{z})$ must represent a union of m subspaces of $\mathbb{C}^7$, as before, we can partition the columns of Z into m groups by looking at the derivatives of p_m. Then we can repeat the same procedure of polynomial fitting and differentiation to each one of the m groups to partition each subspace into subspaces of smaller dimensions, whenever possible. This recursive procedure stops when none of the current subspaces can be further partitioned, yielding automatically the number of motions n and the segmentation of the data. With minor modifications, the algorithm can also handle noisy data, as described in (Huang et al., 2004).

In summary, the motion segmentation problem is solved by recursively fitting a polynomial to the columns of Z and computing the derivatives of this polynomial to assign each column to its corresponding motion subspace.

4. Experiments

We first evaluate the performance of the proposed motion segmentation algorithm on an indoor sequence taken by a moving paracatadioptric camera observing a moving poster. We grabbed 30 images of size 640×480 pixels at a frame rate of 5Hz. Figure 2 shows the first and last frames. Rather than computing the optical flow, we extracted a set of $P = 358$ point correspondences, 50 on the poster and 308 on the background, using the algorithm in (Chiuso et al., 2002). From the set of point correspondences, $\{\boldsymbol{x}_{fp}\}$, we approximated the optical flow measurements as $\boldsymbol{u}_{fp} = \boldsymbol{x}_{fp} - \boldsymbol{x}_{0p}$. We then applied complex GPCA with $n = 2$ motions to the 7 principal components of the complex optical flow matrix. The algorithm achieved a percentage of correct classification of 83.24%. The ground truth segmentation was computed manually.

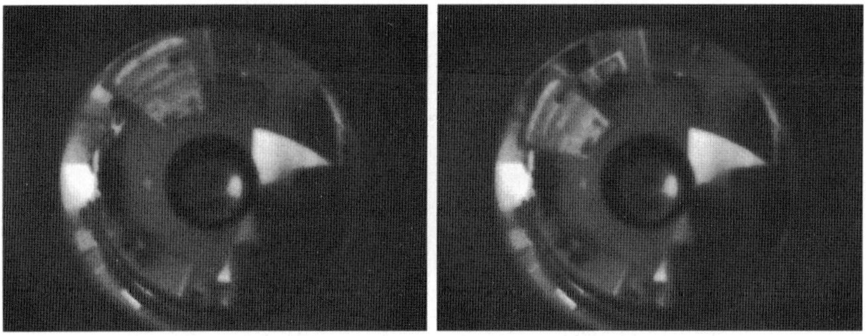

Figure 2. First and last frame of an indoor sequence taken by a moving camera observing a moving poster.

We also evaluated the performance of the proposed motion segmentation algorithm in an outdoor scene consisting of two independently moving mobile robots viewed by a static paracatadioptric camera. We grabbed 18 images of size 240×240 pixels at a frame rate of 5Hz. The optical flow was computed directly in the image plane using Black's algorithm available at http://www.cs.brown.edu/people/black/ignc.html. Since the motion is planar, then the motion of each robot spans a 3-dimensional subspace of $\mathbb{C}^F$. Therefore, we projected the complex optical flow data onto the first four principal components and then applied complex GPCA to the projected data to fit $n = 2$ motion models. Figure 3 shows the motion segmentation results. On the left, the optical flow generated by the two moving robots is shown, and on the right is the segmentation of the pixels corresponding to the independent motions. The two moving robots are segmented very well from the static background.

Given the segmentation of the image measurements, we estimated the motion parameters (rotational and translational velocities) for each one of the two robots using our factorization-based motion estimation algorithm (Shakernia et al., 2003). Figure 4 and Figure 5 plot the estimated translational (v_x, v_y) and rotational velocity ω_z for the robots as a function of time in comparison with the values obtained by the on-board GPS sensors, which have a 2cm accuracy. Figure 6 shows the root mean squared error for the motion estimates of the two robots. The vision estimates of linear velocity are within 0.15 m/s of the GPS estimates. The vision estimates of angular velocity are more noisy than the estimates of linear velocity, because the optical flow due to rotation is smaller than the one due to translation.

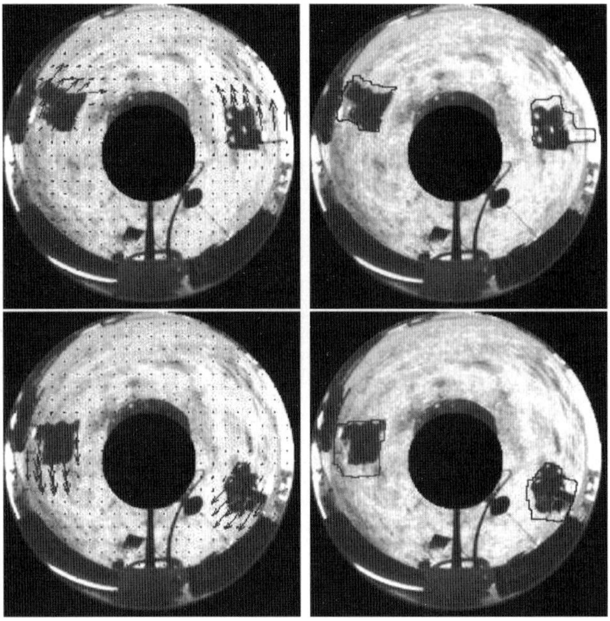

Figure 3. Showing an example of motion segmentation based on central-panoramic optical flow.

5. Conclusions

We have presented an algorithm for infinitesimal motion estimation and segmentation from multiple central panoramic views. Our algorithm is a

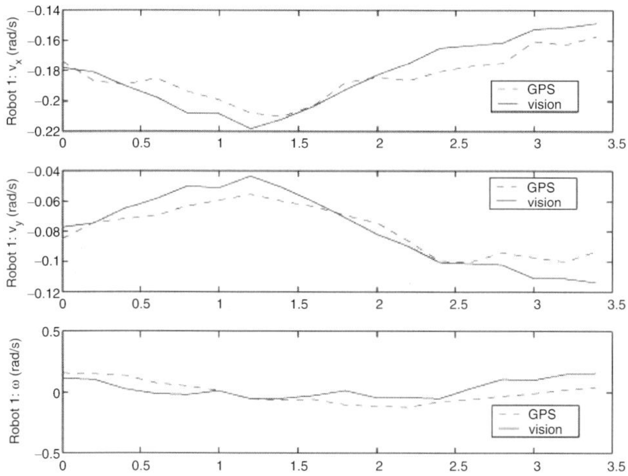

Figure 4. Comparing the output of our vision-based motion estimation algorithm with GPS data for robot 1.

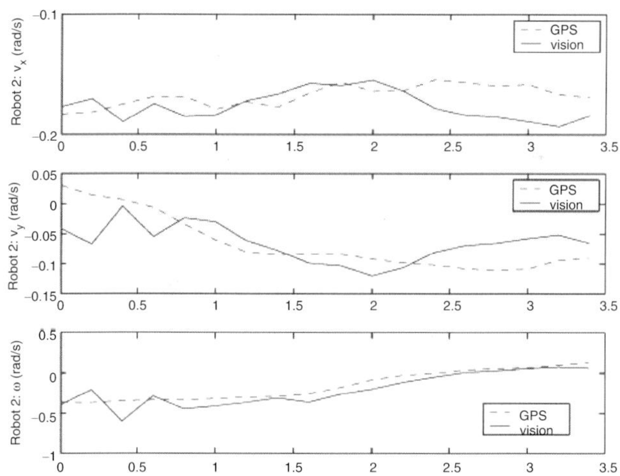

Figure 5. Comparing the output of our vision-based motion estimation algorithm with GPS data for robot 2.

factorization approach based on the fact that optical flow generated by a rigidly moving object across many frames lies in a six-dimensional subspace of a higher-dimensional space. We presented experimental results that show that our algorithm can effectively segment and estimate the motion of multiple moving objects from multiple catadioptric views.

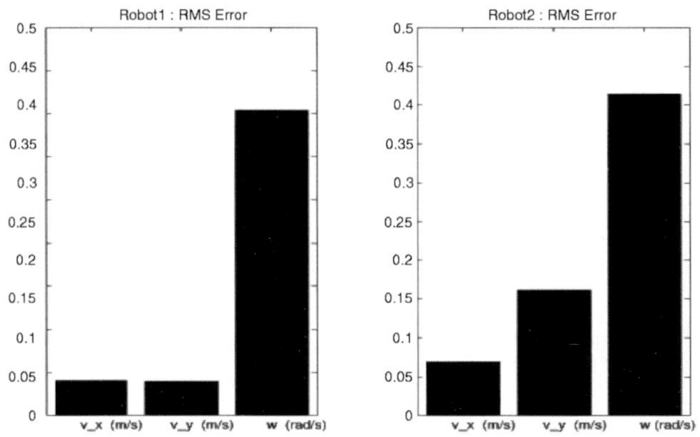

Figure 6. Showing the RMS error for the motion estimates of the two robots.

Acknowledgments

The author wishes to thank Dr. O. Shakernia for his contribution to this work, and Drs. Y. Ma, and R. Hartley for insightful discussions.

References

Baker, S. and Nayar, S.: A theory of single-viewpoint catadioptric image formation. *Int. J. Computer Vision*, **35**: 175–196, 1999.

Barreto, J. and Araujo, H.: Geometric properties of central catadioptric line images. In Proc. *Europ. Conf. Computer Vision*, pages 237–251, 2002.

Boult, T. and Brown, L.: Factorization-based segmentation of motions. In Proc. *IEEE Workshop Motion Understanding*, pages 179–186, 1991.

Chiuso, A., Favaro, P., Jin, H., and Soatto, S.: Motion and structure causally integrated over time. *IEEE Trans. Pattern Analysis Machine Intelligence*, **24**: 523–535, 2002.

Costeira, J. and Kanade, T.: A multibody factorization method for independently moving objects. *Int. J. Computer Vision*, **29**: 159–179, 1998.

Daniilidis, K., Makadia, A., and Blow, T.: Image processing in catadioptric planes: Spatiotemporal derivatives and optical flow computation. In Proc. *IEEE Workshop Omnidirectional Vision*, pages 3–10, 2002.

De la Torre, F. and Black, M. J.: Robust principal component analysis for computer vision. In Proc. *IEEE Int. Conf. Computer Vision*, pages 362–369, 2001.

Geyer, C. and Daniilidis, K.: A unifying theory for central panoramic systems and practical implications. In Proc. *Europ. Conf. Computer Vision*, pages 445–461, 2000.

Geyer, C. and Daniilidis, K.: Structure and motion from uncalibrated catadioptric views. In Proc. *Int. Conf. Computer Vision Pattern Recognition*, pages 279–286, 2001.

Geyer, C. and Daniilidis, K.: Paracatadioptric camera calibration. *IEEE Trans. Pattern Analysis Machine Intelligence*, **24**: 1–10, 2002.

Gluckman, J. and Nayar, S.: Ego-motion and omnidirectional cameras. In Proc. *Int. Conf. Computer Vision*, pages 999–1005, 1998.

Han, M. and Kanade, T.: Reconstruction of a scene with multiple linearly moving objects. In Proc. *Int. Conf. Computer Vision Pattern Recognition*, Volume 2, pages 542–549, 2000.

Harris, J.: *Algebraic Geometry: A First Course*. Springer, 1992.

Hartley, R. and Vidal, R.: The multibody trifocal tensor: Motion segmentation from 3 perspective views. In Proc. *Int. Conf. Computer Vision Pattern Recognition*, Volume 1, pages 769–775, 2004.

Huang, K., Ma, Y., and Vidal, R.: Minimum effective dimension for mixtures of subspaces: A robust GPCA algorithm and its applications. In Proc. *Int. Conf. Computer Vision Pattern Recognition*, 2004.

Kanatani, K.: Motion segmentation by subspace separation and model selection. In Proc. *Int. Conf. Computer Vision*, Volume 2, pages 586–591, 2001.

Kanatani, K. and Sugaya, Y.: Multi-stage optimization for multi-body motion segmentation. In Proc. *Australia-Japan Advanced Workshop on Computer Vision*, pages 335–349, 2003.

Machline, M., Zelnik-Manor, L., and Irani, M.: Multi-body segmentation: Revisiting motion consistency. In Proc. *ECCV Workshop on Vision and Modeling of Dynamic Scenes*, 2002.

Poelman, C. J. and Kanade, T.: A paraperspective factorization method for shape and motion recovery. *IEEE Trans. Pattern Analysis Machine Intelligence*, **19**: 206–18, 1997.

Shakernia, O., Vidal, R., and Sastry, S.: Infinitesimal motion estimation from multiple central panoramic views. In Proc. *IEEE Workshop Motion Video Computing*, pages 229–234, 2002.

Shakernia, O., Vidal, R., and Sastry, S.: Multi-body motion estimation and segmentation from multiple central panoramic views. In Proc. *IEEE Int. Conf. Robotics and Automation*, 2003.

Shashua, A. and Levin, A.: Multi-frame infinitesimal motion model for the reconstruction of (dynamic) scenes with multiple linearly moving objects. In Proc. *Int. Conf. Computer Vision*, Volume 2, pages 592–599, 2001.

Sturm, P.: Structure and motion for dynamic scenes - the case of points moving in planes. In Proc. *Europ. Conf. Computer Vision*, pages 867–882, 2002.

Svoboda, T., Pajdla, T., and Hlavac, V.: Motion estimation using panoramic cameras. In Proc. *IEEE Conf. Intelligent Vehicles*, pages 335–350, 1998.

Tomasi, C. and Kanade, T.: Shape and motion from image streams under orthography. *Int. J. Computer Vision*, **9**: 137–154, 1992.

Vassallo, R., Santos-Victor, J., and Schneebeli, J.: A general approach for egomotion estimation with omnidirectional images. In Proc. *IEEE Workshop Omnidirectional Vision*, pages 97–103, 2002.

Vidal, R. and Hartley, R.: Motion segmentation with missing data by PowerFactorization and Generalized PCA. In Proc. *Int. Conf. Computer Vision Pattern Recognition*, Volume 2, pages 310–316, 2004.

Vidal, R. and Ma, Y.: A unified algebraic approach to 2-D and 3-D motion segmentation. In Proc. *Europ. Conf. Computer Vision*, pages 1–15, 2004.

Vidal, R., Ma, Y., and Piazzi, J.: A new GPCA algorithm for clustering subspaces by fitting, differentiating and dividing polynomials. In Proc. *Int. Conf. Computer Vision Pattern Recognition*, Volume 1, pages 510–517, 2004.

Vidal, R., Ma, Y., and Sastry, S.: Generalized principal component analysis (GPCA). In Proc. *Int. Conf. Computer Vision Pattern Recognition*, Volume 1, pages 621–628, 2003.

Vidal, R., Ma, Y., and Sastry, S.: Generalized principal component analysis (GPCA). *IEEE Trans. Pattern Analysis Machine Intelligence*, **27**: 1–15, 2005.

Vidal, R., Ma, Y., Soatto, S., and Sastry, S.: Two-view multibody structure from motion. *Int. J. Computer Vision*, 2006.

Vidal, R. and Sastry, S.: Optimal segmentation of dynamic scenes from two perspective views. In Proc. *Int. Conf. Computer Vision Pattern Recognition*, Volume 2, pages 281–286, 2003.

Vidal, R., Soatto, S., and Sastry, S.: A factorization method for multibody motion estimation and segmentation. In Proc. *Annual Allerton Conf. Communication Control Computing*, pages 1625–1634, 2002.

Wolf, L. and Shashua, A.: Affine 3-D reconstruction from two projective images of independently translating planes. In Proc. *Int. Conf. Computer Vision*, pages 238–244, 2001a.

Wolf, L. and Shashua, A.: Two-body segmentation from two perspective views. In Proc. *Int. Conf. Computer Vision Pattern Recognition*, pages 263–270, 2001b.

Wu, Y., Zhang, Z., Huang, T., and Lin, J.: Multibody grouping via orthogonal subspace decomposition. In Proc. *Int. Conf. Computer Vision Pattern Recognition*, Volume 2, pages 252–257, 2001.

Zelnik-Manor, L. and Irani, M.: Degeneracies, dependencies and their implications in multi-body and multi-sequence factorization. In Proc. *Int. Conf. Computer Vision Pattern Recognition*, Volume 2, pages 287–293, 2003.

OPTICAL FLOW COMPUTATION OF OMNI-DIRECTIONAL IMAGES

ATSUSHI IMIYA
Institute of Media and Information Technology
Chiba University, Chiba 263-8522, Japan

AKIHIKO TORII
School of Science and Technology
Chiba University, Chiba 263-8522, Japan

HIRONOBU SUGAYA
School of Science and Technology
Chiba University, Chiba 263-8522, Japan

Abstract. This paper focuses on variational image analysis on Riemannian manifolds. Since a sphere is a closed Riemannian manifold with the positive constant curvature and no holes, the sphere has similar geometrical properties with a plane, whose curvature is zero. Images observed through a catadioptric system with a conic mirror is transformed to images on the sphere. As an application of image analysis on Riemannian manifolds, we develop an accurate algorithm for the computation of optical flow of omni-directional images. The spherical motion field on the spherical retina has some advantages for ego-motion estimation of autonomous mobile observer. Our method provides a framework for motion field analysis on the spherical retina, since views observed by a quadric-mirror-based catadioptric system are transformed to views on the spherical and semi-spherical retinas.

Keywords: variational principle, Riemannian manifold, optical flow, statistical analysis, numerical method, omnidirectional image

1. Introduction

The spherical motion field on the spherical retina has some advantages for ego-motion estimation of an autonomous mobile observer (Nelson et al., 1988; Fermüller et al., 1998). For motion field analysis on the spherical retina, we are required to establish optical-flow computation algorithms to images on the curved surface. The omnidirectional views observed by

K. Daniilidis and R. Klette (eds.), Imaging Beyond the Pinhole Camera, 143–162.

a quadric-mirror-based catadioptric systems are transformed to views on the spherical retina. Therefore, we can construct an emulation system of spherical views using these catadioptric observing systems. In this paper, we establish a method in the computation of optical flow on the curved retina. This method allows us to accurately analyze the motion field observed by the spherical retina and the semi-spherical retina systems.

Variational methods enjoy a unified framework for image analysis, such as optical flow computation, noise removal, edge detection, and in-painting (Morel and Solimini, 1995; Aubert and Kornprobst, 2002; Sapiro, 2001; Osher et al., 2003). The fundamental nature of the variational principle governed by the minimization of Hamiltonians for problems allows us to describe the problems of image analysis in coordinate-free forms. This mathematical property implies that variational-method-based image analysis is the most suitable strategy for image analysis on Riemannian manifolds. This paper focuses on variational image analysis on Riemannian manifolds.

Conic-mirror-based omnidirectional imaging systems (Benosman and Kang, 2001; Baker and Nayer, 1999; Geyer and Daniilidis, 2001; Svoboda and Pajdla, 2002) capture images on convex Riemannian manifolds (Morgan, 1993). This class of images on convex Riemannian manifolds can be transformed to images on a sphere. A sphere has mathematically important geometrical properties (Berger, 1987).

1. A sphere is a closed manifold without any holes.
2. The mean curvature on a sphere is constant and positive. Therefore, spherical surfaces and planes, which are the manifold with zero curvature, have geometrically similar properties (Berger, 1987; Zdunkowski and Bott, 2003).
3. Functions on a sphere are periodic.
4. The stereographic projection provides a one-to-one correspondence between points on a plane and on a sphere.

In Figure 1, we show the geometric drawings of a manifold, a sphere and a plane, respectively. As an application of image analysis on Riemannian manifolds, we develop an accurate algorithm for the computation of optical flow of omnidirectional images. Classical image analysis and image processing deal with images on planes, which are the Riemannian manifolds with zero mean curvature. Therefore, as an extension of classical problems in image analysis and image processing, the analysis of images on a sphere is geometrically the next step. This paper is organized as follows. In Section 2, we introduce three minimization criteria for the detection of optical flow on Riemannian manifolds. Section 3 derives numerical schemes for the computation of optical flow of images on manifolds. In Section 4, we briefly review the geometries of conic-mirror-based omnidirectional imaging systems and the transformation from images observed by conic mirror to images observed by the spherical retina. In Section 5, some numerical results are shown for both synthetic and real-world images. These numerical examples show the possibility and validity of variational-method image analysis on Riemannian manifolds.

2. Image Analysis on Manifolds

Considering the optical flow detection problem, we show the validity of variational method of image analysis on Riemannian manifolds.

Setting $\boldsymbol{y} = \phi^{-1}(\boldsymbol{x})$ to be the invertible transformation from $\mathbf{R}^n$ to Riemannian manifold $\mathbf{M}$ embedded in $\mathbf{R}^{n+1}$, we define $\hat{f}(\boldsymbol{y}) = f(\phi(\boldsymbol{y}))$ and $f(\boldsymbol{x}) = \hat{f}(\phi^{-1}(\boldsymbol{x}))$. Setting $\nabla_{\mathbf{M}}$ to be the gradient operator on Riemannian manifold $\mathbf{M}$ (Morgan, 1993) and $\boldsymbol{M}$ to be the metric tensor on manifold $\mathbf{M}$, the gradient of function f on this manifold satisfies the relation

$$\nabla f = \boldsymbol{M}^{-1}\nabla_{\mathbf{M}}\hat{f}, \tag{1}$$

where ∇f is the gradient on $\mathbf{R}^n$.

For the case that $n = 2$, the spatio-temporal gradient of temporal function $f(\boldsymbol{x}, t)$ satisfies the relation

$$\nabla f^{\top}\dot{\boldsymbol{x}} + \frac{\partial f}{\partial t} = \left(\boldsymbol{M}^{-1}\nabla_{\mathbf{M}}\hat{f}\right)^{\top}\dot{\boldsymbol{y}} + \frac{\partial \hat{f}}{\partial t}, \tag{2}$$

assuming that tensor $\boldsymbol{M}$ is time independent. Here, we call $\dot{\boldsymbol{x}}$ and $\dot{\boldsymbol{y}}$ optical flow and optical flow on the Riemannian manifold, respectively.

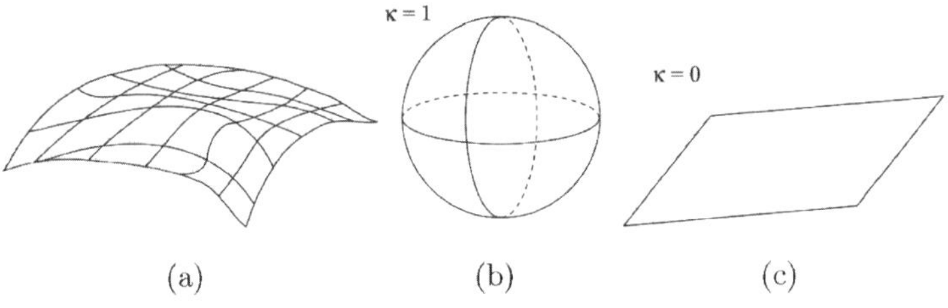

Figure 1. Manifolds: A general manifold in two-dimensional Euclidean space is a curved surface as shown in (a) A sphere shown in (b) is a closed finite manifold with positive constant curvature $\kappa = 1$. A spherical surface has similar geometries with those of a plane in (c), which is a infinite manifold with zero curvature.

Introducing a matrix and vectors such that

$$\boldsymbol{A} = \begin{pmatrix} \boldsymbol{M} & \boldsymbol{o} \\ \boldsymbol{o}^\top & 1 \end{pmatrix}, \quad \boldsymbol{u} = (\dot{\boldsymbol{x}}^\top, 1)^\top, \quad \boldsymbol{v} = (\dot{\boldsymbol{y}}^\top, 1)^\top, \tag{3}$$

$$\nabla_t f = (\nabla f^\top, f_t)^\top, \quad \nabla_{\mathbf{M}t} \hat{f} = (\nabla_{\mathbf{M}} \hat{f}^\top, \hat{f}_t)^\top, \tag{4}$$

Equation (2) is expressed as

$$\nabla_t f^\top \boldsymbol{u} = \langle \nabla_{\mathbf{M}t} \hat{f}, \boldsymbol{v} \rangle, \tag{5}$$

where $\langle \boldsymbol{a}, \boldsymbol{b} \rangle = \boldsymbol{a}^\top \boldsymbol{A}^{-1} \boldsymbol{b}$.

Since $\nabla_t f^\top \boldsymbol{v} = 0$, our task for the detection of optical flow on the Riemannian manifold is described as the next problem.

PROBLEM 1. *Find* $\dot{\boldsymbol{y}}$ *which fulfils the equation*

$$\langle \nabla_{\mathbf{M}t} \hat{f}, \boldsymbol{v} \rangle = 0. \tag{6}$$

Since this problem is an ill-posed problem, we need some additional constrains to solve the problem. According to the classical problem on a plane, we have the following three constrains.

1. Lucas-Kanade criterion (Barron et al., 1994). Minimize

$$J_{LK}(\dot{\boldsymbol{y}}) = \int_{\Omega(\boldsymbol{y})} \int_{\boldsymbol{M}} |\langle \nabla_{\mathbf{M}t} \hat{f}, \boldsymbol{v}|\rangle|^2 d\boldsymbol{m}, \tag{7}$$

assuming that that $\dot{\boldsymbol{y}}$ is constant in a small region $\Omega(\boldsymbol{y})$, which is the neighborhood of $\boldsymbol{y}$.

2. Horn-Schunck criterion(Barron et al., 1994; Horn and Schunck, 1981). Minimize the functional

$$\begin{aligned} J_{HS}(\dot{\boldsymbol{y}}) &= \int_{\mathbf{M}} |\langle \nabla_{\mathbf{M}t} \hat{f}, \boldsymbol{v} \rangle|^2 d\boldsymbol{m} \\ &\quad + \alpha \int_{\mathbf{M}} (|\langle \nabla_{\mathbf{M}} y_1 \rangle|^2 + |\langle \nabla_{\mathbf{M}} y_2 \rangle|^2) d\boldsymbol{m}. \end{aligned} \tag{8}$$

3. Nagel-Enkelmann criterion (Barron et al., 1994; Nagel, 1987). Minimize

$$\begin{aligned} J_{NE}(\dot{\boldsymbol{y}}) &= \int_{\mathbf{M}} |\langle \nabla_{\mathbf{M}t} \hat{f}, \boldsymbol{v} \rangle|^2 \\ &\quad + \alpha \int_{\mathbf{M}} (\langle \nabla_{\mathbf{M}} y_1, \boldsymbol{N} \nabla_{\mathbf{M}} y_1 \rangle + \langle \nabla_{\mathbf{M}} y_2, \boldsymbol{N} \nabla_{\mathbf{M}} y_2 \rangle) d\boldsymbol{m} \end{aligned} \tag{9}$$

for a positive symmetry matrix

$$\boldsymbol{N} = \frac{1}{|\boldsymbol{M}^{-1} \nabla_{\mathbf{M}} \hat{f}|^2 + 2\lambda} \nabla_{\mathbf{M}} \hat{f}^\perp (\nabla_{\mathbf{M}} \hat{f}^\perp)^\top + \lambda \boldsymbol{I}, \tag{10}$$

where $\langle \nabla_{\mathbf{M}} \boldsymbol{f}, \nabla_{\mathbf{M}} \boldsymbol{f}^\perp \rangle = 0$.

These three functionals are expressed as

$$J(\dot{\boldsymbol{y}}) = \int_{\mathbf{M}} \langle \nabla_{\mathbf{M}t}\hat{f}, \boldsymbol{v}\rangle|^2 d\boldsymbol{m} + \alpha \int_{\mathbf{M}} F(\nabla_{\mathbf{M}}y_1, \nabla_{\mathbf{M}}y_2) d\boldsymbol{m}, \tag{11}$$

where $F(\cdot,\cdot)$ is an appropriate symmetry function, such that $F(x,y) = F(y,x)$

Setting for spatio-temporal structure tensor $\boldsymbol{S}$ of $\hat{f}$ as

$$\boldsymbol{L} = \boldsymbol{A}^{-1}\boldsymbol{S}\boldsymbol{A}^{-\top},\ \boldsymbol{S} = \int_{\Omega(\boldsymbol{y})} \nabla_{\mathbf{M}t}\hat{f}\nabla_{\mathbf{M}t}\hat{f}^{\top} d\boldsymbol{m}, \tag{12}$$

the solution of the Lucas-Kanade constraint is the vector associated with the zero eigenvalue of $\boldsymbol{L}$, that is, $\boldsymbol{L}\boldsymbol{v} = 0$, since $J_{LK}(\mathbf{y}) = \boldsymbol{v}^{\top}\boldsymbol{L}\boldsymbol{v} \geq 0$ for $\boldsymbol{y} = const.$ in $\Omega(\boldsymbol{y})$.

For the second and third conditions, the Euler-Lagrange equations are

$$\nabla_{\mathbf{M}}^{\top}\nabla_{\mathbf{M}}\dot{\boldsymbol{y}} = \frac{1}{\alpha}\langle \nabla_{\mathbf{M}t}\hat{f}, \boldsymbol{v}\rangle\nabla_{\mathbf{M}}\hat{f}, \tag{13}$$

$$\nabla_{\mathbf{M}}^{\top}\boldsymbol{N}\nabla_{\mathbf{M}}\dot{\boldsymbol{y}} = \frac{1}{\alpha}\langle \nabla_{\mathbf{M}t}\hat{f}, \boldsymbol{v}\rangle\nabla_{\mathbf{M}}\hat{f}, \tag{14}$$

where $\nabla_{\mathbf{M}}^{\top}$ is the divergent operation on the manifold $\mathbf{M}$.

The solutions of these equations are $\lim_{t\to\infty}\dot{\boldsymbol{y}}(\boldsymbol{y},t)$ of the solutions of the diffusion-reaction system of equations on manifold $\mathbf{M}$,

$$\frac{\partial}{\partial t}\dot{\boldsymbol{y}} = \nabla_{\mathbf{M}}^{\top}\nabla_{\mathbf{M}}\dot{\boldsymbol{y}} - \frac{1}{\alpha}\langle \nabla_{\mathbf{M}t}\hat{f}, \boldsymbol{v}\rangle\nabla_{\mathbf{M}}\hat{f}, \tag{15}$$

$$\frac{\partial}{\partial t}\dot{\boldsymbol{y}} = \nabla_{\mathbf{M}}^{\top}\boldsymbol{N}\nabla_{\mathbf{M}}\dot{\boldsymbol{y}} - \frac{1}{\alpha}\langle \nabla_{\mathbf{M}t}\dot{f}, \boldsymbol{v}\rangle\nabla_{\mathbf{M}}\hat{f}. \tag{16}$$

3. Numerical Scheme

The Euler type discretization scheme with respect to the argument t,

$$\frac{\dot{\boldsymbol{y}}^{n+1} - \dot{\boldsymbol{y}}^{n}}{\Delta\tau} = \nabla_{\mathbf{M}}^{\top}\boldsymbol{N}\nabla_{\mathbf{M}}\dot{\boldsymbol{y}} - \frac{1}{\alpha}\langle \nabla_{\mathbf{M}t}\dot{f}, \boldsymbol{v}^n\rangle\nabla_{\mathbf{M}}\hat{f}, \tag{17}$$

$$\boldsymbol{v}^n = (\boldsymbol{y}^{n+1}, 1)^{\top}, \tag{18}$$

derives the iteration form

$$\dot{\boldsymbol{y}}^{n+1} = \dot{\boldsymbol{y}}^{n} + \Delta\tau\left(\nabla_{\mathbf{M}}^{\top}\boldsymbol{N}\nabla_{\mathbf{M}}\dot{\boldsymbol{y}} - \frac{1}{\alpha}\langle \nabla_{\mathbf{M}t}\dot{f}, \boldsymbol{v}^n\rangle\nabla_{\mathbf{M}}\hat{f}\right). \tag{19}$$

The next step is the discretization of the spatial operation $\nabla_{\mathbf{M}}$. The discretization of $\nabla_{\mathbf{M}}$ depends on topological structures in the neighborhood.

On the sphere, we express positions using longitude and latitude. Adopting the 8-neighborhood on the discretized manifold, for $\boldsymbol{y} = (u, v)$, we have the relation

$$\begin{array}{lll}\nabla_{\mathbf{M}}^{\top}\boldsymbol{N}\nabla_{\mathbf{M}} = & & \\ \beta_1\hat{f}(u-\Delta u, v-\Delta v, t) & +\beta_2\hat{f}(u, v-\Delta v, t) & +\beta_3\hat{f}(u+\Delta u, v-\Delta v, t) \\ +\beta_4\hat{f}(u-\Delta u, v, t) & +\beta_5\hat{f}(u, v, t) & +\beta_6\hat{f}(u+\Delta u, v, t) \\ +\beta_7\hat{f}(u-\Delta u, v+\Delta v, t) & +\beta_8\hat{f}(u, v+\Delta v, t) & +\beta_9\hat{f}(u+\Delta u, v+\Delta v, t).\end{array}$$

Coefficients $\{\beta_i\}_{i=1}^{9}$for the Horn-Schunck criterion, we have the relations $\beta_5 = -\frac{1}{8}$ and $\beta_i = 1$ for $i \neq 5$. Furthermore, for the Nagel-Enkelmann criterion coefficients depending on the matrix $\boldsymbol{N}$ are

$$\beta_1 = -\beta_3 = -\beta_7 = \beta_9 = \Delta\tau\frac{n_{12}}{2\sin\theta\Delta\theta\Delta\phi}$$

$$\beta_2 = \Delta\tau\left(\frac{n_{22}}{\sin^2\theta(\Delta\phi)^2} - \frac{n_{12}\cos\theta}{2\sin^2\theta\Delta\phi}\right)$$

$$\beta_4 = \beta_6 = \Delta\tau\frac{n_{11}}{(\Delta\theta)^2}$$

$$\beta_5 = -\Delta\tau\left(\frac{2n_{11}}{(\Delta\theta)^2} + \frac{2n_{22}}{\sin^2\theta(\Delta\phi)^2}\right)$$

$$\beta_8 = \Delta\tau\left(\frac{n_{22}}{\sin^2\theta(\Delta\phi)^2} + \frac{n_{12}\cos\theta}{2\sin^2\theta\Delta\phi}\right).$$

In Figure 2, (a), (b), and (c) show grids on a curved manifold, on a plane, and on a sphere, respectively. Although these grids are topologically equivalent, except at the poles of the sphere, the area measure in the neighborhood of the grids are different. These differences depend on the metric and curvature on the manifolds. Since $\dot{\boldsymbol{y}}$ is a function of time t, we accept the smoothed function

$$\dot{\boldsymbol{y}}(t) := \int_{t-\tau}^{t+\tau} w(\tau)\dot{\boldsymbol{y}}(\tau)d\tau, \quad \int_{t-\tau}^{t+\tau} w(\tau)d\tau = 1, \tag{20}$$

as a solution.

M-estimator in the form

$$J_\rho(\dot{\boldsymbol{y}}) = \int_{\mathbf{M}} \rho(|\langle\nabla_{\mathbf{M}t}\hat{f}, \boldsymbol{v}\rangle|^2)d\boldsymbol{m} + \alpha\int_{\mathbf{M}} F(\nabla_{\mathbf{M}}y_1, \nabla_{\mathbf{M}}y_2)d\boldsymbol{m}, \tag{21}$$

is a common method to avoid outliers, where $\rho(\cdot)$ is an appropriate weight function. Instead of Equation (21), we adopt the criterion

$$\dot{\boldsymbol{y}}^* = \text{argument}\left(\text{median}_{\Omega(\boldsymbol{y})}\left\{|\dot{\boldsymbol{y}}| \leq T|\text{median}_{\mathbf{M}}(\min J(\dot{\boldsymbol{y}}))|\right\}\right). \tag{22}$$

We call this operation defined by Equation (22) the double-median operation.

If we can have the operation Ψ, such that

$$\int_{\mathbf{M}} \rho(|\langle \nabla_{\mathbf{M}t} \hat{f}, \boldsymbol{v} \rangle|^2) d\boldsymbol{m} = \Psi \left(\int_{\mathbf{M}} |\langle \nabla_{\mathbf{M}t} \hat{f}, \boldsymbol{v} \rangle|^2 d\boldsymbol{m} \right) \tag{23}$$

and

$$\int_{\mathbf{M}} F(\nabla_{\mathbf{M}} y_1, \nabla_{\mathbf{M}} y_2) d\boldsymbol{m} = \Psi \left(\int_{\mathbf{M}} F(\nabla_{\mathbf{M}} y_1, \nabla_{\mathbf{M}} y_2) d\boldsymbol{m} \right), \tag{24}$$

it is possible to achieve the minimization operation before statistical operation. We accept the double-median operation of Equation (22) as an approximation of the operation Ψ. Therefore, after computing the solution of the Euler-Lagrange equation at each point, we apply the following statistical operations.

1. Compute the median of the norm of the solution vectors on the manifold, and set it as $\dot{\boldsymbol{y}}^m$.
2. Accept the solution at each point if $|\dot{\boldsymbol{y}}| \leq T|\dot{\boldsymbol{y}}^m|$, for an appropriate constant T.
3. For the 5×5 neighborhood of each point, accept the solution whose length is the median in this region.

Figure 3 shows the operations of Ψ. For the Lucas-Kanade criterion, before the application of the double median operation, the minimization derives the median of the lengths of the vectors in the window and accepts it as the solution of the flow at the center of the neighborhood as shown in Figure 3(c).

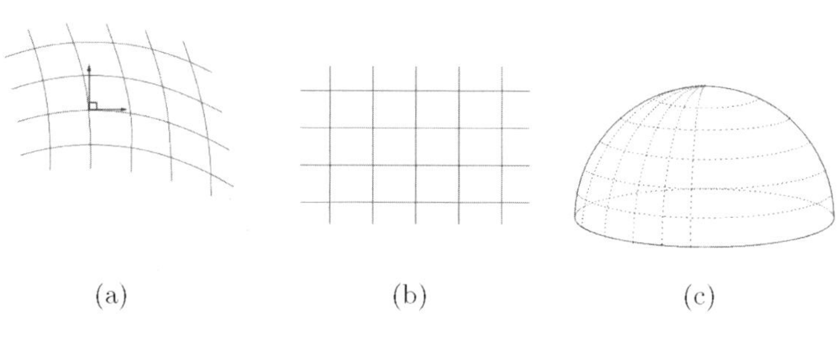

Figure 2. Discretization on manifolds: (a), (b), and (c) are orthogonal grids on a manifold, on a sphere and on a curved manifolds, respectively. On the curved orthogonal coordinate systems, the metric tensor becomes diagonal tensor.

4. Conic-to-Spherical Image Transform

As illustrated in Figure 4(a) [Figure 5(a)], the focal point of the hyperboloid (paraboloid) S is located at the point $\boldsymbol{F} = (0,0,0)^\top$. The center of the pinhole camera is located at the point $\boldsymbol{C} = (0,0,-2e)$. The hyperbolic-camera (parabolic-camera) axis l is the line which connects $\boldsymbol{C}$ and $\boldsymbol{F}$. We set the hyperboloid (paraboloid) as

$$S : \frac{x^2+y^2}{a^2} - \frac{(z+e)^2}{b^2} = -1 \quad \Big(S : z = \frac{x^2+y^2}{4c} - c\Big), \tag{25}$$

where $e = \sqrt{a^2+b^2}$ (c is the parameter of the paraboloid). A point $\boldsymbol{X} = (X,Y,Z)^\top$ in a space is projected to the point $\boldsymbol{x} = (x,y,z)^\top$ on the hyperboloid (paraboloid) S according to the relation,

$$\boldsymbol{x} = \lambda \boldsymbol{X}, \tag{26}$$

where

$$\lambda = \frac{\pm a^2}{b|\boldsymbol{X}| \mp eZ} \qquad \lambda = \Big(\frac{2c}{|\boldsymbol{X}| - Z}\Big). \tag{27}$$

This relation between $\boldsymbol{X}$ and $\boldsymbol{x}$ is satisfied, if the line, which connects the focal point $\boldsymbol{F}$ and the point $\boldsymbol{X}$, and the hyperboloid (paraboloid) S have at least one real common point. Furthermore, the sign of parameter λ depends on the geometrical position of the point $\boldsymbol{X}$. Hereafter, we assume

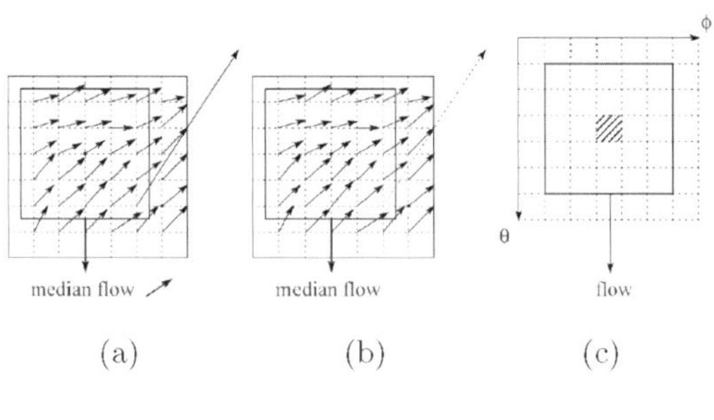

Figure 3. The double median operation: First, for the solutions, the operation computes the median of the length of the vectors in the whole domain as shown in (a). Second, the operator accepts vectors whose lengths are smaller than T times of the median in the whole domain as the solutions, where T is an appropriate positive constant. Finally, the operator admits the vector whose length is the median of the vectors in a window. As shown in (b), this operation eliminates the vector expressed by the dashed line. For the Lucas-Kanade criterion, the minimization derives the median of the lengths of the vectors in the window and accepts it as the solution of the flow at the center of the neighborhood as shown in (c).

that Equation (27) is always satisfied. Setting $\boldsymbol{m} = (u, v)^\top$ to be a point on the image plane π, point $\boldsymbol{x}$ on S is projected to point $\boldsymbol{m}$ according to

$$u = f\frac{x}{z+2e} \quad (u = x), \tag{28}$$

$$v = f\frac{y}{z+2e} \quad (v = y), \tag{29}$$

where f is the focal length of the pinhole camera. Therefore, a point $\boldsymbol{X} = (X, Y, Z)^\top$ in a space is transformed to point $\boldsymbol{m}$ as

$$u = \frac{fa^2X}{(a^2 \mp 2e^2)Z \pm 2be|\boldsymbol{X}|} \quad u = \Big(\frac{2cX}{|\boldsymbol{X}| - Z}\Big), \tag{30}$$

$$v = \frac{fa^2Y}{(a^2 \mp 2e^2)Z \pm 2be|\boldsymbol{X}|} \quad v = \Big(\frac{2cY}{|\boldsymbol{X}| - Z}\Big). \tag{31}$$

For the hyperbolic-to-spherical (parabolic-to-spherical) image transform, setting $S_s : x^2 + y^2 + z^2 = r^2$, the spherical-camera center $\boldsymbol{C}_s$ and the the focal point $\boldsymbol{F}$ of the hyperboloid (paraboloid) S are $\boldsymbol{C}_s = \boldsymbol{F} = \boldsymbol{0}$. Furthermore, $\boldsymbol{l}_s$ denotes the axis connecting $\boldsymbol{C}_s$ and the north pole of the spherical surface. For the axis $\boldsymbol{l}_s$ and the hyperbolic-camera (parabolic-camera) axis $\boldsymbol{l}$ we set $\boldsymbol{l}_s = \boldsymbol{l} = k(0, 0, 1)^\top$ for $k \in \mathbf{R}$, that is, the directions of $\boldsymbol{l}_s$ and $\boldsymbol{l}$ are the direction of the z axis. The spherical coordinate system expresses a point $\boldsymbol{x}_s = (x_s, y_s, z_s)$ on the sphere as

$$x_s = r\sin\theta\cos\varphi, \; y_s = r\sin\theta\sin\varphi, \; z_s = r\cos\theta, \tag{32}$$

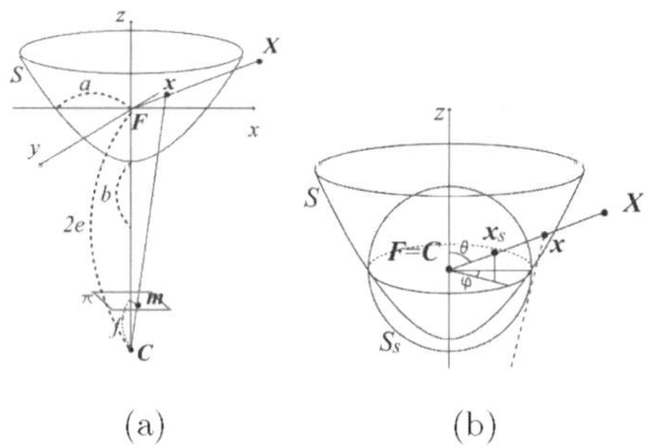

Figure 4. Transformation among hyperbolic- and spherical-camera systems. (a) illustrates a hyperbolic-camera system. The camera $\boldsymbol{C}$ generates the omnidirectional image π by the central projection, since all the rays corrected to the focal point $\boldsymbol{F}$ are reflected to the single point. A point $\boldsymbol{X}$ in a space is transformed to the point $\boldsymbol{x}$ on the hyperboloid and $\boldsymbol{x}$ is transformed to the point $\boldsymbol{m}$ on image plane. (b) illustrate the geometrical configuration of hyperbolic- and spherical-camera systems. In this geometrical configuration, a point $\boldsymbol{x}_s$ on the spherical image and a point $\boldsymbol{x}$ on the hyperboloid lie on a line connecting a point $\boldsymbol{X}$ in a space and the focal point $\boldsymbol{F}$ of the hyperboloid.

where $0 \leq \theta < 2\pi$ and $0 \leq \varphi < \pi$. For the configuration of the spherical camera and the hyperbolic (parabolic) camera which share axes $\boldsymbol{l}_s$ and $\boldsymbol{l}$ as illustrated in Figure 4 (b) (Figure 5 (b)), the point $\boldsymbol{m}$ on the hyperbolic (parabolic) image and the point $\boldsymbol{x}_s$ on the sphere satisfy

$$u = \frac{fa^2 \sin\theta \cos\varphi}{(a^2 \mp 2e^2)\cos\theta \pm 2be} \quad u = \Big(2c\frac{\sin\theta\cos\varphi}{1-\cos\varphi}\Big), \tag{33}$$

$$v = \frac{fa^2 \sin\theta \sin\varphi}{(a^2 \mp 2e^2)\cos\theta \pm 2be} \quad v = \Big(2c\frac{\sin\theta\sin\varphi}{1-\cos\varphi}\Big). \tag{34}$$

Setting $I(u, v)$ and $I_S(\theta, \varphi)$ to be the hyperbolic (parabolic) image and the spherical image, respectively, these images satisfy

$$I_S(\theta,\varphi) = I\Big(\frac{fa^2 \sin\theta \cos\varphi}{(a^2 \mp 2e^2)\cos\theta \pm 2be}, \frac{fa^2 \sin\theta \sin\varphi}{(a^2 \mp 2e^2)\cos\theta \pm 2be}\Big) \tag{35}$$

$$(I_S(\theta,\varphi) = I\ \Big(c\frac{\sin\theta\cos\varphi}{1-\cos\varphi}, 2c\frac{\sin\theta\sin\varphi}{1-\cos\varphi}\Big)), \tag{36}$$

for $I(u, v)$, which is the image on the hyperboloid (paraboloid).

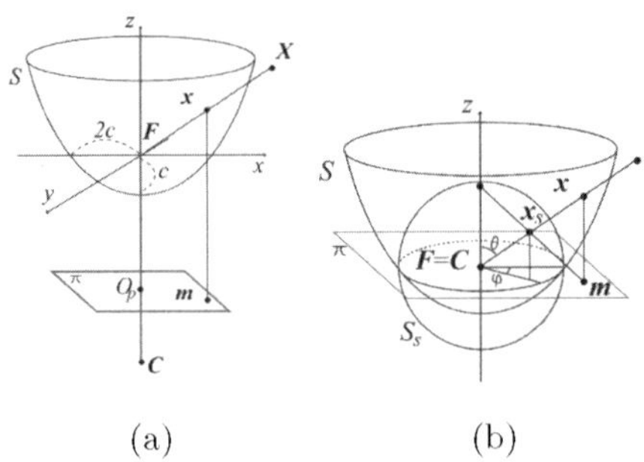

Figure 5. Transformation among parabolic- and spherical-camera systems. (a) illustrates a parabolic-camera system. The camera $\boldsymbol{C}$ generates the omnidirectional image π by the orthogonal projection, since all the rays corrected to the focal point $\boldsymbol{F}$ are orthogonally reflected to the imaging plane. A point $\boldsymbol{X}$ in a space is transformed to the point $\boldsymbol{x}$ on the paraboloid and $\boldsymbol{x}$ is transformed to the point $\boldsymbol{m}$ on image plane. (b) illustrate the geometrical configuration of parabolic- and spherical-camera systems. In this geometrical configuration, a point $\boldsymbol{x}_s$ on the spherical image and a point $\boldsymbol{x}$ on the paraboloid lie on a line connecting a point $\boldsymbol{X}$ in a space and the focal point $\boldsymbol{F}$ of the paraboloid.

5. Numerical Examples

In this section, we show examples of optical flow detection for omnidirectional images to both synthetic and real-world image sequences. We have generated synthetic test patterns of image sequence for the evaluation of algorithms on the flow computation of omnidirectional images. Since a class of omnidirectional camera using conic-mirror-based catadioptric systems observes middle-latitude images on a sphere, we accept direct numerical differentiation for numerical computation of the system of diffusion-reaction equations. In meteorology (Zdunkowski and Bott, 2003), to avoid the pole problem in the discretization of partial differential equations on a sphere, the discrete spherical harmonic transform (Freeden et al., 1997; Swarztrauber and Spotz, 2000) and quasi-equi-areal domain decomposition are common (Randol, 2002; Schröder and Swelden, 1995). However, in our problem, imaging systems do not capture images in the neighborhood of the poles, since the pole on a sphere is the blind spot of a class of catadioptric imaging systems.

Since the metric tensor on a sphere is

$$\boldsymbol{M} = \begin{pmatrix} 1, & 0 \\ 1, & \sin\theta \end{pmatrix}, \tag{37}$$

we have

$$\begin{pmatrix} 1 + \Delta\tau\frac{1}{\alpha}(\frac{\partial I_S}{\partial\theta})^2 & \Delta\tau\frac{1}{\alpha\sin\theta}\frac{\partial I_S}{\partial\phi}\frac{\partial I_S}{\partial\theta} \\ \Delta\tau\frac{1}{\alpha\sin\theta}\frac{\partial I_S}{\partial\phi}\frac{\partial I_S}{\partial\theta} & 1 + \Delta\tau\frac{1}{\alpha\sin^2\theta}(\frac{\partial I_S}{\partial\phi})^2 \end{pmatrix} \begin{pmatrix} \dot{\theta}^{n+1} \\ \dot{\phi}^{n+1} \end{pmatrix}$$
$$= \begin{pmatrix} \dot{\theta}^n + \Delta\tau\nabla_S^\top \boldsymbol{N}\nabla_S\dot{\theta}^n - \Delta\tau\frac{1}{\alpha}\frac{\partial I_S}{\partial\theta}\frac{\partial I_S}{\partial t} \\ \dot{\phi}^n + \Delta\tau\nabla_S^\top \boldsymbol{N}\nabla_S\dot{\phi}^n - \Delta\tau\frac{1}{\alpha\sin\theta}\frac{\partial I_S}{\partial\phi}\frac{\partial I_S}{\partial t} \end{pmatrix}, \tag{38}$$

where I_s, $\dot{\boldsymbol{q}}$, and ∇_S are an image on a sphere, the flow vectors on this sphere, and the spherical gradient, respectively. For the Horn-Schunck criterion, we set $\boldsymbol{N} = \boldsymbol{I}$.

In these examples, the algorithm first computed optical flow vectors of each point for three successive intervals using the for successive images. Second it computed the weighted average at each point selecting weight as 1/4, 1/2, and 1/4. Third the double median operation with $T = 4$ is applied.

We set the parameters of discretization as shown in Table 1 for the synthetic data. In tables, L-K, H-S, and N-E are abbreviations of the Lucas-Kanade, Horn-Schunck, and Nagel-Enkelmann criteria, respectively.

Table 2 and Figure 5 show error distribution and average and median errors for various image sequences. The results for the rotational motion and side view of the translation are acceptable for image analysis from

Iteration time		2000
Grid length	$\Delta\tau$	0.002
Parameter	α of H-S and N-E	1000
Parameter	λ^2 of N-E	10000
Parameter	T of L-K	10
Grid pitch	$\Delta\theta$	0.25°
Grid pitch	$\Delta\phi$	0.25°
Image size on sphere	$(\phi \times \theta)$	1440×360

Table 1. Discretization parameters for synthetic data.

optical flow. In these experiments, the optical axis of the camera in the catadioptric omnidirectional imaging system is perpendicular to the floor. For translational motion, the camera system moves a line parallel to the

Side View of Translation						
Operation	H-S av.	N-E av.	L-K av.	H-S med.	N-E med.	L-K med.
frames 1,2 a	37.9°	36.0°	14.3°	26.7°	24.2°	2.72°
frames 1,2 b	23.9°	21.8°	7.03°	16.0°	13.7°	1.56°
frames 0-3 a	28.9°	26.5°	3.71°	21.1°	17.4°	1.74°
frames 0-3 b	16.9°	17.3°	2.94°	15.3°	14.6°	1.66°
Front View of Translation						
Operation	H-S av.	N-E av.	L-K av.	H-S med.	N-E med.	L-K med.
frames 1,2 a	21.2°	27.9°	50.2°	19.2°	25.4°	28.0°
frames 1,2 b	18.3°	19.0°	44.8°	18.6°	18.6°	28.9°
frames 0-3 a	19.8°	21.4°	41.5°	19.5°	21.1°	30.4°
frames 0-3 b	19.6°	20.9°	41.6°	19.6°	20.6°	32.8°
Whole View of Rotation						
Operation	H-S av.	N-E av.	L-K av.	H-S med.	N-E med.	L-K med.
frames 1,2 a	35.6°	45.9°	19.9°	13.0°	36.8°	1.46°
frames 1,2 b	27.3°	37.4°	1.08°	7.10°	11.4°	0.25°
frames 0-3 b	28.2°	38.0°	0.85°	6.45°	14.2°	0.24°
frames 0-3 b	9.40°	21.9°	0.66°	2.09°	3.49°	0.24°

Table 2. Errors of the operations. av. and med. mean the average and median of the data over the whole domain. For frames 1 and 2, a and b are the results without the double median operation and with the double median operation. For frames 0-3, we computed the weighted average of the flow vectors over 4 frames. Furthermore, for frames 0-3, a and b are the results after eliminating vectors whose norms were smaller than 0.01 and 0.5 pixels, respectively.

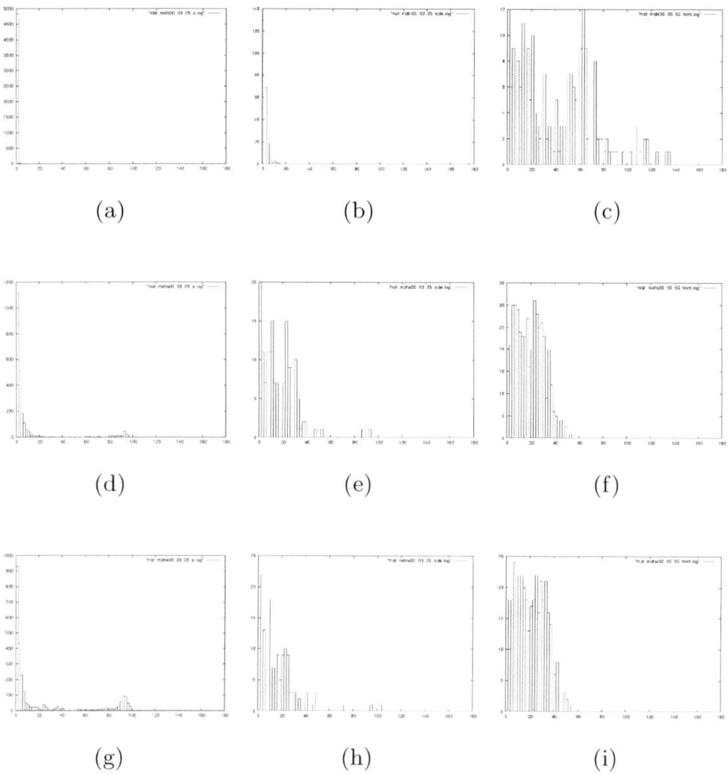

Figure 6. Error analysis. For the Lucas-Kanade, Horn-Schunck, and Nagel-Enkelmann criteria, respectively, (a), (d), and (g) show the bin counts of the angles between the theoretical and numerical optical flows at each point for rotation. For Lucas-Kanade, Horn-Schunck, and Nagel-Enkelmann criteria, respectively, (b), (e), and (h) show the bin counts of the angles between the theoretical and numerical optical flows at each point for the side view of translation. For the Lucas-Kanade, Horn-Schunck, and Nagel = Enkelmann criteria, respectively, (c), (f), and (i) show the bin counts of the angles between the theoretical and numerical optical flows at each point for the front view of translation.

grand flow. For rotational motion, the camera rotation axis is the optical axis of the camera. In this geometrical configuration of the motion of the camera and the optical axis of the camera, during the rotation, the sizes of objects around the camera do not markedly deform. This geometrical property of the objects around the camera is satisfied for the side view of translational motion, if the speed of the moving camera is slow. However, in the front view of the translating camera, the sizes of the objects change and the shape of objects deformed on the sphere. This geometrical property of

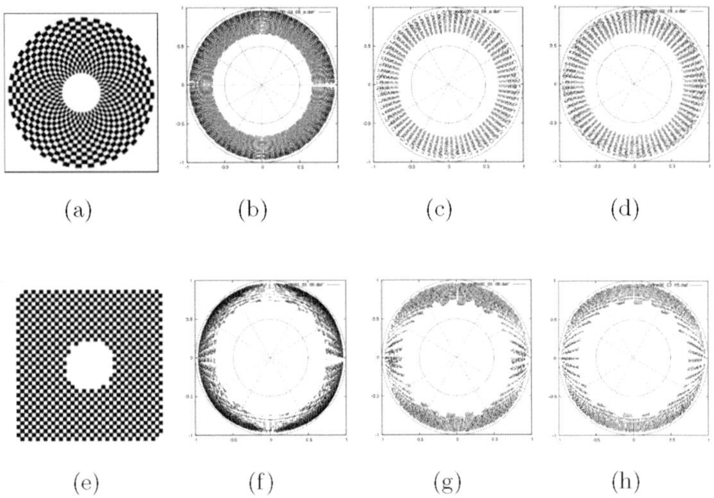

Figure 7. Optical flow of the synthetic images. (a) A circle chessboard. A catadioptric system rotates around the axis perpendicular to the board. (b), (c), and (d) are optical flow fields computed by Lucas-Kanade, Horn-Schunck, and Nagel-Enkelmann criteria, respectively. (e) A regular chessboard. A catadioptric system translates along a line parallel to one axis of the pattern. (f), (g), and (h) are optical flow fields computed by Lucas-Kanade, Horn-Schunck, and Nagel-Enkelmann criteria, respectively.

the front view of the translationally moving camera causes the errors shown in the tables and figures. In these experiments, the front view is between $15°$ to the left and $15°$ to the right of the direction of motion. Furthermore, the side view is $90° \pm 15°$ to the direction of the motion. as show in Figure 5.

In Tables 3 and 4, we list the dependence of errors on the parameters in the regularization terms of the minimization problems for the detection of optical flow caused by rotational motion. These tables show that for a

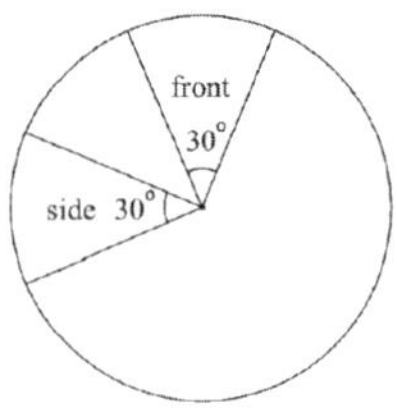

Figure 8. View angles of the front and side views. The front view is between $15°$ to the left and $15°$ to the right of the the direction of motion. The side view is $90° \pm 15°$ to the direction of motion.

average					
$\alpha = 10$	$\alpha = 100$	$\alpha = 500$	$\alpha = 1000$	$\alpha = 2000$	$\alpha = 10000$
53.5°	46.6°	39.1°	35.6°	31.9°	23.3°
median					
$\alpha = 10$	$\alpha = 100$	$\alpha = 500$	$\alpha = 1000$	$\alpha = 2000$	$\alpha = 10000$
59.1°	35.6°	17.2°	13.0°	11.2°	9.4°

Table 3. Parameters of the Horn-Schunck criterion for rotation detection.

uniform motion such as rotation, the appropriate value of the parameter α of the Horn-Schunck criterion is 1000, if we adopt the double median operation for the robust estimation of the flow vectors. Furthermore, for the Nagel-Enkelmann criterion a small value of the parameter λ guarantees accurate solutions.

In Figure 5, we show the detected optical flow in the spherical representations for the Lucas -Kanade, the Horn -Schunck, and Nagel -Enkelmann criteria from left to right. The first and second columns show results with the thresholds 0.01 and 0.5 pixels. These results indicate that, as expected, the Nagel-Enkelmann method detect the boundary of moving objects, although the method fails the detection of small motion. The Lucas-Kanade method requires to design appropriate windows since the local stationarity on the flow vectors is assumed. Furthermore, these results show the validity of embedding of Horn-Schunck method to the system of diffusion-reaction equations.

Finally, Figure 6 shows optical flow computed with Horn-Schunck criterion images of real-world images for the cases that objects move around a

average			
	$\alpha = 100$	$\alpha = 1000$	$\alpha = 10000$
$\lambda = 10$	52.3°	44.6°	30.0°
$\lambda = 100$	54.1°	45.9°	36.8°
$\lambda = 1000$	54.2°	46.4°	36.9°
median			
	$\alpha = 100$	$\alpha = 1000$	$\alpha = 10000$
$\lambda = 10$	65.6°	30.0°	21.7°
$\lambda = 100$	74.3°	36.8°	24.3°
$\lambda = 1000$	75.0°	38.6°	25.3°

Table 4. Parameters of the Nagel-Enkelmann criterion for rotation detection.

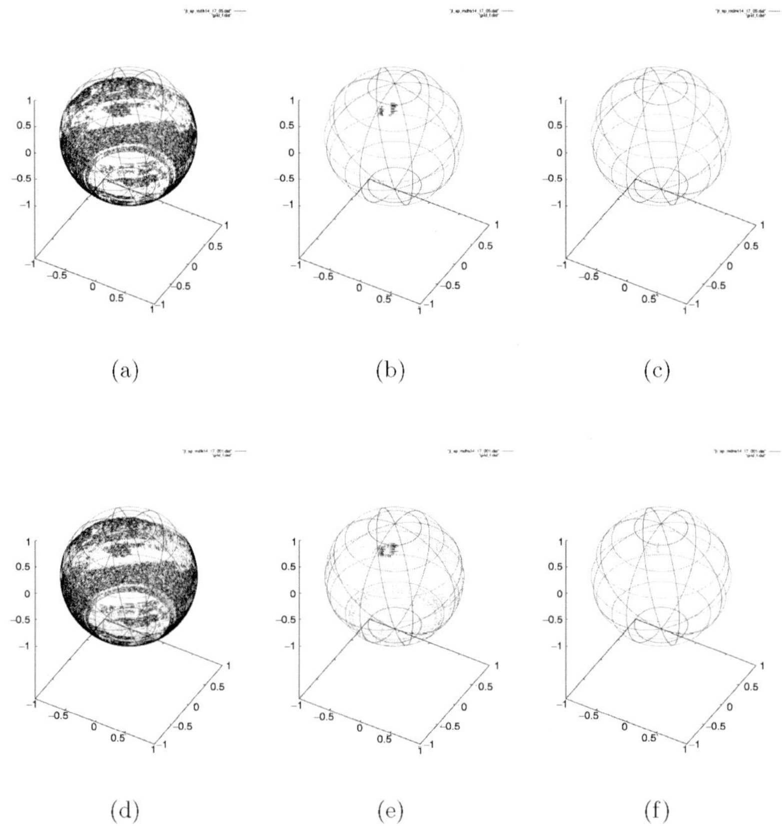

Figure 9. Results of real-world images: (a) and (d) are the spherical expressions of computed flow by the Lucas-Kanade criterion, for thresholds are 0.01 and 0.5 pixels, respectively. (b) and (e)are the spherical expressions of computed flow by the Horn-Schunck criterion, for thresholds are 0.01 and 0.5 pixels, respectively. (c) and (f)are the spherical expressions of computed flow by the Nagel-Enkelmann criterion, for thresholds are 0.01 and 0.5 pixels, respectively.

stationary camera and that the camera system moves in a stationary environment. These results show that objects in the environment and markers used for the navigation exhibit the typical flow patterns observed in the synthetic patterns.

These results lead to the conclusion that flow vectors computed by our method are suitable for the navigation of a mobile robot with a catadioptric imaging system which captures omnidirectional images.

Iteration time		2000
Grid length	$\Delta\tau$	0.002
Parameter (H-S, N-E)	α	1000
Parameter(N-E)	λ^2	10000
Parameter(L-K)	T	4
Parameters of (a) in Figure 9.		
Grid pitch	$\Delta\theta$	0.20°
Grid pitch	$\Delta\phi$	0.20°
Image size on the sphere	$(\phi \times \theta)$	1800 × 900
Parameters for (c) in Figure 9.		
Grid pitch	$\Delta\theta$	0.40°
Grid pitch	$\Delta\phi$	0.40°
Image size on the sphere	$(\phi \times \theta)$	900 × 450
Parameters for (e) (g) in Figure 9.		
Grid pitch	$\Delta\theta$	0.20°
Grid pitch	$\Delta\phi$	0.20°
Image Size	$(\phi \times \theta)$	1800 × 900

Table 5. Discretization parameters for real-world images.

6. Concluding Remarks

In this chapter, we showed that for the analysis and understanding of images on Riemannian manifolds, the variational principle provides a unified framework. We applied the method to optical flow computation. The method permits us a method for an accurate tracking of object and navigation of robots using omnidirectional images.

Appendix

For the Lucas-Kanade criterion, an appropriate spatio-temporal pre-smoothing is usually operated. Setting symmetry functions $w(t)$ and $u(\boldsymbol{x})$ to be temporal and spatial weight functions, respectively, the constraint on a plane is expressed as

$$J_{LK}(\dot{\boldsymbol{x}}) = \int_{\Omega} \frac{1}{2a} \int_{\mathbf{R}^2} \int_{t-a}^{t+a} w(\tau)^2 u(x-x', y-y')^2 |f_x \dot{x} + f_y \dot{y} + f_t|^2 d\boldsymbol{x}' d\boldsymbol{x} d\tau.$$

The matrix form of the minimization equation becomes

$$J_{LK}(\dot{x}, \dot{y}; \boldsymbol{W}) = \boldsymbol{u}^\top \boldsymbol{W} \boldsymbol{S}_a \boldsymbol{W} \boldsymbol{u}, \ \ \boldsymbol{u} = (\dot{x}, \dot{y}, 1)^\top,$$

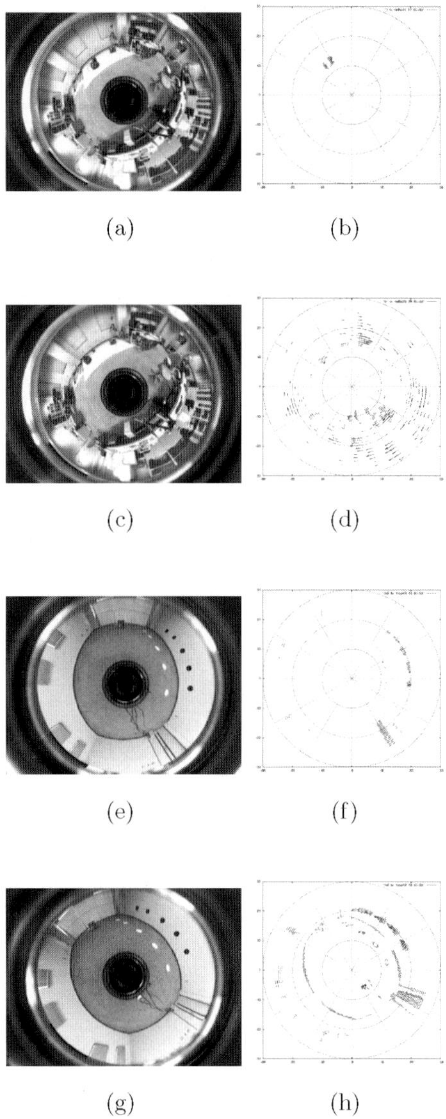

Figure 10. Optical flow of real-world images computed with the Horn-Schunck criterion: (a) an image from a sequence when an object moves in radial direction to the mirror, and (b) the optical flow in this case; (c) an image from a sequence when an object moves in direction orthogonal to the radial direction of the mirror, and (d) the optical flow in this case; (e) an image observed from a translating robot, and (f) the optical flow in this case; (g) an image observed from a rotating robot, and (h) the optical flow in this case.

where $\boldsymbol{S}_a$ and $\boldsymbol{W}$ are structure tensor of

$$g(x,y,t) = \frac{1}{2a}\int_{t-a}^{t+a} f(x,y,\tau)d\tau$$

and a symmetry weighting matrix defined by $u(x,y)$, respectively. Setting $\boldsymbol{W} = \boldsymbol{I}$, we have a quadric minimization form without any spatial presmoothing operations. The selection of an appropriate weighting function on the sphere is an open problem.

Regression model fitting for planar sample points $\{(x_i, y_i)^\top\}_{i=1}^n$for $x_1 < x_2 < \cdots < x_n$ is achieved, for example (Silverman, 1985), by minimizing the criterion

$$J_\rho(f) = \sum_{i=1}^{n} \rho(|y_i - f(x_i)|) + \alpha \sum_{i=1}^{n-1} \int_{x_i}^{x_{i+1}} \left|\frac{d^2 f(\tau)}{d\tau^2}\right|_{\tau=x}^2 dx,$$

where $\rho(\tau)$ is a positive symmetry function. We adopt Equation (21) as an extension of this regression model. Furthermore, we accept the exchange of the operation order for the minimization and statistical operation as

$$J_\Psi(f) = \Psi\left(\sum_{i=1}^{n} |y_i - f(x_i)|^2 + \alpha \sum_{i=1}^{n-1} \int_{x_i}^{x_{i+1}} \left|\frac{d^2 f(\tau)}{d\tau^2}\right|_{\tau=x}^2 dx\right),$$

for a operation Ψ and a class of functions.

References

Nelson, R. C., and Y. Aloimonos: Finding motion parameters from spherical flow fields (or the advantage of having eyes in the back of your head), Biological Cybernetics, **58**: 261–273, 1988.

Fermüller, C., and Y. Aloimonos: Ambiguity in structure from motion: sphere versus plane, Int. J. Computer Vision, **28**: 137–154, 1998.

Morel, J.-M., and S. Solimini: *Variational Methods in Image Segmentation*, Birkhaäuser, 1995.

Aubert, G., and P. Kornprobst: *Mathematical Problems in Image Processing: Partial Differential Equations and the Calculus of Variations*, Springer, 2002.

Sapiro, G.: *Geometric Partial Differential Equations and Image Analysis*, Cambridge University Press, 2001.

Osher, S., and N. Paragios (editors): *Geometric Level Set Methods in Imaging, Vision, and Graphics*, Springer, 2003.

Benosman, R., and S.-B. Kang (editors): *Panoramic Vision, Sensor, Theory, and Applications*, Springer, 2001.

Baker, S., and S. Nayer: A theory of single-viewpoint catadioptric image formation, Int. J. Computer Vision, **35**: 175–196, 1999.

Geyer, C., and K. Daniilidis: Catadioptric projective geometry, Int. J. Computer Vision, **45**: 223–243, 2001.

Svoboda, T., and T. Pajdla: Epipolar geometry for central catadioptric cameras, Int. J. Computer Vision, **49**: 23–37, 2002.

Morgan, F.: *Riemannian Geometry: A Beginner's Guide*, Jones and Bartlett Publishers, 1993.

Berger, M.: *Geometry I & II*, Springer, 1987.

Horn, B. K. P., and B. G. Schunck: Determining optical flow, Artificial Intelligence, **17**: 185–204, 1981.

Nagel, H.-H.: On the estimation of optical flow: Relations between different approaches and some new results, Artificial Intelligence, **33**: 299–324, 1987.

Barron, J. L., D.J. Fleet, and S. S. Beauchemin: Performance of optical flow techniques, Int. J. Computer Vision, **12**: 43–77, 1994.

Schröder, P., and W. Swelden: Spherical wavelet: Efficiently representing functions on the sphere, In Proc. SIGGRAPH, pages 161–172, 1995.

Freeden, W., M. Schreiner, and R. Franke: A survey on spherical spline approximation, Surveys on Mathematics for Industry, **7**, 1997.

Swarztrauber, P. N., and W. S. Spotz: Generalized discrete spherical harmonic transform, J. Computational Physics, **159**: 213-230, 2000 [see also Electronic Transactions on Numerical Analysis, **16**: 70–92, 2003].

Zdunkowski, W., and A. Bott: *Dynamics of the Atmosphere*, Cambridge University Press, 2003.

Randol, D. *et al*: Climate modeling with spherical geodesic grids, IEEE Computing in Science and Engineering, **4**: 32–41, 2002.

Silverman, B. W.: Some aspects of the spline smoothing approach to non-parametric regression curve fitting, J. R. Statist. Soc. B. **47**: 1–52, 1985.

Part III

Mapping

MOBILE PANORAMIC MAPPING USING CCD-LINE CAMERA AND LASER SCANNER WITH INTEGRATED POSITION AND ORIENTATION SYSTEM

R. REULKE
Humboldt University Berlin
Institute for Informatics, Computer Vision
Berlin, Germany

A. WEHR
Institute for Navigation, University of Stuttgart
Stuttgart, Germany

D. GRIESBACH
German Aerospace Center DLR, Competence Center
Berlin, Germany

Abstract. The fusion of panoramic camera data with laser scanner data is a new approach and allows the combination of high-resolution image and depth data. Application areas are city modelling, virtual reality and documentation of the cultural heritage. Panoramic recording of image data is realized by a CCD-line, which is precisely rotated around the projection centre. In the case of other possible movements, the actual position of the projection centre and the view direction has to be measured. Linear moving panoramas e.g. along a wall are an interesting extension of such rotational panoramas. Here, the instantaneous position and orientation determination can be realized with an integrated navigation system comprising differential GPS and an inertial measurement unit. This paper investigates the combination of a panoramic camera and a laser scanner with a navigation system for indoor and outdoor applications. First, laboratory experiments it are reported, which were carried out to obtain valid parameters about the surveying accuracy achievable with both sensors panoramic camera and laser scanner respectively. Thereafter, outdoor surveying results using a position and orientation system as navigation sensor are presented and discussed.

Key words: digital panoramic camera, laser scanner, data fusion, mobile mapping

K. Daniilidis and R. Klette (eds.), Imaging Beyond the Pinhole Camera, 165–183.

1. Introduction

Generation of city models offering a high realistic visualization potential requires three-dimensional imaging sensors with high 3D resolution and high image quality. Today commonly used sensors offer either a high image quality or high depth accuracy. This paper describes the hard- and software integration of independent measurement systems. For the acquisition of high resolution image and depth data from extended objects, e.g. building facades, a high resolution camera for the image information and a laser scanner for the depth information can be applied synchronously.

High resolution images can be acquired by CCD-matrix and line sensors. The main advantage of line sensors is the generation of high resolution images without merging or stitching of image patches like in frame imaging. A problem is an additional sensor motion of the CCD-line to achieve the second image dimension. An obvious solution is the accurate reproducible rotation around CCD-line axis on a turntable as used in panoramic imaging. The 3-dimensional information of the imaged area can be acquired very precisely in a reasonable short time with laser scanners. However, these systems very often sample only depth data with poor horizontal resolution. Some of them offer monochrome intensity images of poor quality in the spectral range of the laser beam (e.g. NIR). Very few commercial laser scanners use additional imaging color sensors for obtaining colored 3D images.

However, with regard to building surveying and setting up cultural heritage archives, the imaging resolution of laser scanner data must be improved. This can be achieved by combining data from a high-resolution digital 360° panoramic camera with data from a laser scanner. Fusing these image data with 3D information of laser scanning surveys very precise 3D models with detailed texture information will be obtained. This approach is related to the 360° geometry. Large linear structures like city facades can be acquired in the panoramic mode only from different standpoints with variable resolution of the object. To overcome this problem, laser-scanner and panoramic camera should be linearly moved along e.g. a building facade. In applying this technique, the main problem is georeferencing and fusing the two data sets of the panoramic camera and the laser scanner respectively. For each measured CCD- and laser-line the position and orientation must be acquired by a position and orientation system (POS).

The experimental results shown in the following will deal with this problem and will lead to an optimum surveying setup comprising a panoramic camera, a laser scanner and a POS. This surveying and documentation system will be called POSLAS-PANCAM (POS supported laser scanner panoramic camera).

To verify this approach first experiments were carried out in the laboratory and in the field with the digital 360° panoramic camera (M2), the 3D-Laserscanner (3D-LS) and a POS. The objectives of the experiments are to verify the concepts and to obtain design parameters for a compact and handy system for combined data acquisition and inspection. In Chapter 2 the components of the combined system are described. Calibration and fusion of the system and the data is explained in Chapter 3. Some indoor- and outdoor-applications are discussed in Chapter 4.

2. System

The measurement system consists of a combination of an imaging system, a laser scanner and a system for position and attitude determination.

2.1. DIGITAL 360° PANORAMIC CAMERA (M2)

The digital panoramic camera EYESCAN will be primarily used as a measurement system to create high-resolution 360° panoramic images for photogrammetry and computer vision (Scheibe et al., 2001; Klette et al., 2001). The sensor principle is based on a CCD-line camera, which is mounted on a turntable with CCD-line parallel to the rotation direction. Moving the turntable generates the second image direction. This generates a special image geometry which makes additional correction and transformations for further processing necessary. To reach highest resolution and a large field of view a CCD-line with more than 10000 pixels is used. This CCD is a RGB triplet and allows acquiring true color images. A high SNR electronic design allows a short capture time for a 360° scan.

EYESCAN is designed for rugged everyday field use as well as for the laboratory measurement. Combined with a robust and powerful portable PC it becomes easy to capture seamless digital panoramic pictures. The sensor system consists of the camera head, the optical part (optics, distance dependent focus adjustment) and the high precision turntable with DC-gear-system motor.

The first table summarizes the principle features of the camera: the camera head is connected to the PC with a bidirectional fiber link for data transmission and camera control. The camera head is mounted on a tilt unit for vertical tilts of ±30° with 15° stops. Axis of tilt and rotation are in the needlepoint.

The pre-processing of the data consists of data correction and a (non linear) radiometric normalization to cast the data from 16 to 8 bit. All these procedures can be run in real time or off line. Additional software parts are responsible for real-time visualization of image data, a fast preview for scene selection and a quick look during data recording.

Table 1. Technical parameters of the digital panoramic camera.

Number of Pixel	3*10200 (RGB)
Radiometric dynamic/resolution	14 bit / 8 bit per channel
Shutter speed	4ms up to infinite
Data rate	15 Mbytes / s
Data volume 360° (optics f = 60mm)	3 GBytes
Acquisition time	4 min
Power supply	12 V

2.2. THE LASER SCANNER 3D-LS

In the experiments M2 images were supported by the 3D-LS depth data. This imaging laser scanner carries out the depth measurement by side-tone ranging (Wehr, 1999). This means that the optical signal emitted from a semiconductor laser is modulated by high frequency signals. As the laser emits light continuously such a laser system is called continuous wave (cw) laser system. The phase difference between the transmitted and received signal is proportional to the two-way slant range. Using high modulation frequencies, e.g. 314MHz, resolutions down to the tenth of a millimetre are possible.

Besides depth information these scanners sample for each measurement point the backscattered laser light with a 13 bit resolution. Therefore, the user obtains 3D surface images. The functioning of the laser scanner is explained in (Wehr, 1999). For technical parameters, see the second table.

2.3. APPLANIX POS-AV 510

The attitude measurement is the key problem of this combined approach. Inertial measurement systems (s. Figure 1 are normally fixed with respect to a body coordinate system, which coincides with the principal axes of the platform movement. Strapdown systems measure directly the linear accelerations in x-, y- and z-direction by three orthogonal mounted accelerometers and the three angular rates about the same axes by gyros which are three mechanical gyros or either three laser or fiber optical gyros. From the measured accelerations and angular rates a navigation computer calculates the instantaneous position and orientation in a body coordinate system.

The so computed inertial heading and attitude data are necessary for

Table 2. Technical parameter of 3D-LS.

Laser power	0.5 mW
Optical wavelength	670 nm
Inst. field of view (IFOV)	0.1°
Field of view (FOV)	30° × 30°
Scanning pattern	- 2-dimensional line - vertical line scan - free programmable pattern
Pixels per image	max. 32768 × 32768 pixels
Range	¡ 10 m
Ranging accuracy	0.1 mm (for diffuse reflecting targets, ρ=60%, 1 m distance)
Measurement rate	2 kHz (using on side tone) 600 Hz (using two side tones)

the transformation into the navigation or object coordinate system, which is in our case a horizontal system.

For demonstration we use the airborne attitude measurement system POS AV 510 from Applanix, which is designed for those applications that require both excellent absolute accuracy and relative accuracy. An example of this would be a high altitude, high resolution digital line scanner.

The absolute measurement accuracy after post processing is 5-30 cm in position, $\delta\theta = \delta\phi = 0.005°$ for pitch or roll and $\delta\psi = 0.008°$ for heading.

For an object distance D the angle dependent spatial accuracy d is therefore:

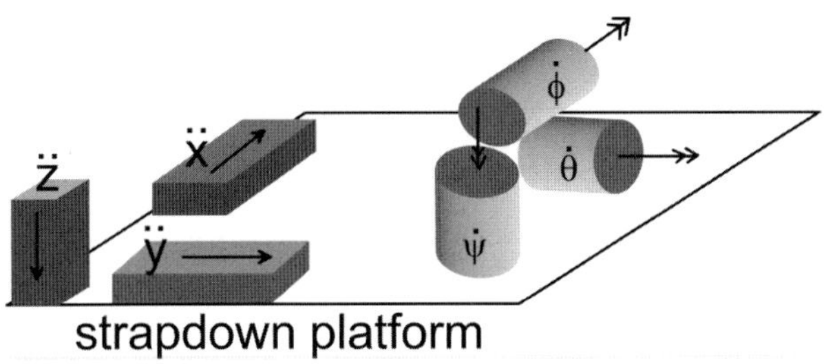

Figure 1. Strapdown navigation system.

$$d = D \cdot \delta \tag{1}$$

For an object distance $D = 10\ m$ the spatial accuracy is $d \cong 1\ mm$ and appropriate for verification of a mobile mapping application.
For a future mobile mapping systems a sufficient attitude measurement is necessary, which is also less expensive. For this purpose we expect new gyro developments and improved post processing algorithms in the next few years .

2.4. POSLAS-PANCAM

Figure 2 shows the mechanical integration of the three sensor systems. In the following POSLAS-PANCAM will be abbreviated to PLP-CAM. This construction allows a precise relation between 3D-LS and panoramic data which is the main requirement for data fusion. The 3D-LS data are related to the POS data as the lever arms are minimized with regard to the laser scanner and are well defined by the construction.

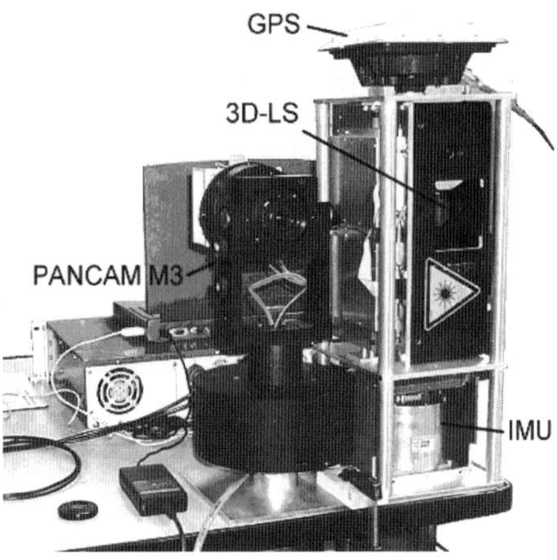

Figure 2. PLP-CAM.

The different items of PLP-CAM have to be synchronized exactly, because each system works independently. The block chart in Figure 3 shows the approach. Using event markers solves the problem by generating time stamps. These markers are stored by POS and combine a measurement event with absolute GPS-time (e.g. starting a scanning line).

The determination of the exterior orientation of each system must be determinate independently. For data fusion a misalignment correction for geometrical adjusting is necessary.

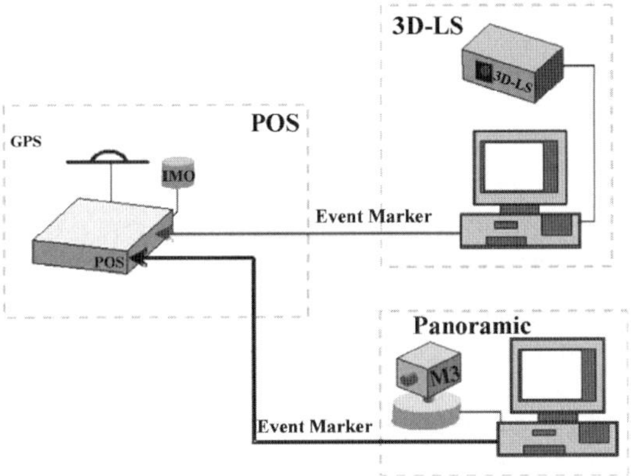

Figure 3. Synchronization.

3. Calibration and Fusion of M2 AND 3D-LS DATA

To investigate the fusion of panoramic and laser data, first experiments were carried out in a laboratory environment. Here, only the panoramic camera M2 and 3D-LS were used.

3.1. EXPERIMENTAL SET-UP

In order to study the problems arising from fusion of data sets of the panoramic camera and the 3D-LS, both instruments took an image of a special prepared scene, which are covered with well-defined control points as shown in Figure 4. The panoramic camera (Figure 5) was mounted on a tripod. To keep the same exterior orientation the camera and the 3D-LS were mounted on the tripod without changing the tripod's position. 3D-LS were used in the imaging mode scanning a field of view (FOV) of $40° \times 26°$ comprising 1600×1000 pixels. Each pixel is described by the quadruple Cartesian coordinates plus intensity (x, y, z, I). The M2-image covered a FOV of approximately $30° \times 60°$ with 5000×10000 pixels.

More than 70 control points were available at a distance of 6 m. Lateral resolution of laser and panoramic scanner is 3 mm and 1 mm respectively, which is a suitable value for fusion of the data sets. The coordinate determination of the signalized points was done by using image data from a monochrome digital frame camera (DCS 460) and a software package for the close range digital photogrammetry (Australis, www.sli.unimelb.edu.au/australis). Applying the bundle block adjustment on the image data of the frame camera, the position of the control points can be determined. The lateral accuracy of about 0.5 mm and depth accuracy about 3 mm.

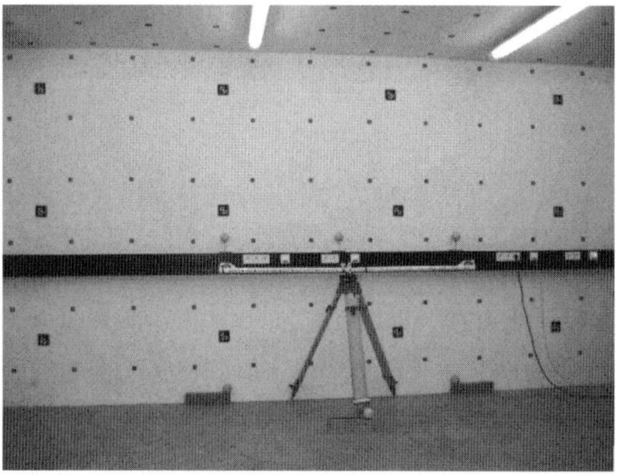

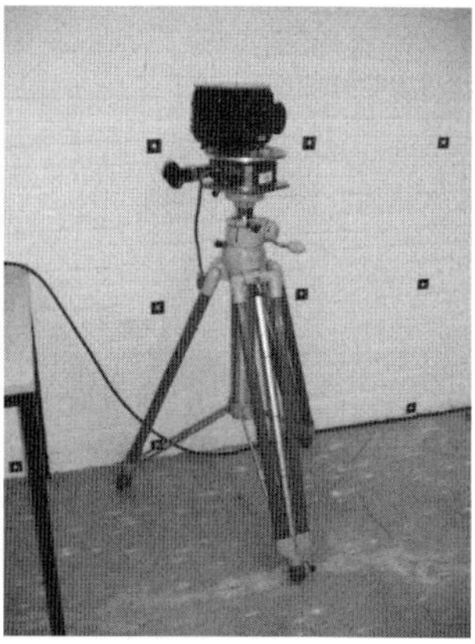

Figure 5. PANCAM on tripod.

3.2. MODELLING AND CALIBRATION

Laser scanner and panoramic camera work with different coordinate systems and must be adjusted one to each other. The laser scanner delivers Cartesian coordinates; whereas M2 puts out data in a typical photo image projection. Although, both devices are mounted at the same position one has to regard that the projection center of both instruments are not located exactly at the same position. Therefore a model of panoramic imaging and a calibration with known target data is required.

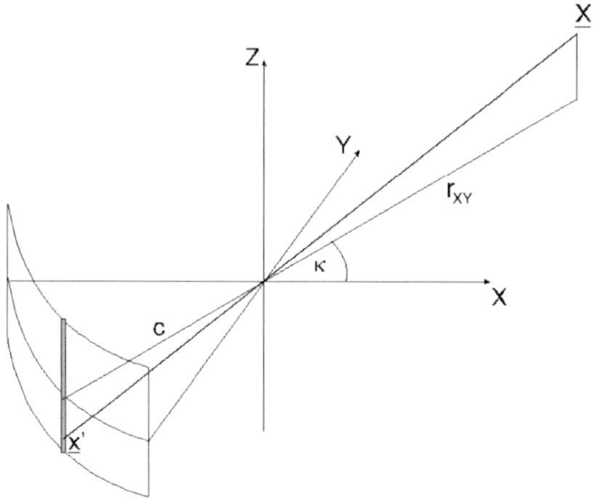

Figure 6. Panoramic imaging.

The imaging geometry of the panoramic camera is characterized by the rotating CCD-line, assembled perpendicular to the $x-y$ plane and forming an image by rotation around the z-axis. The modelling and calibration of panoramic cameras was investigated and published recently (Schneider and Maas, 2002; Schneider, 2003; Klette et al., 2001; Klette et al., 2003).

For camera description and calibration we use the approach shown in Figure 6. The CCD-line is placed in the focal plane perpendicular to the z'-axis and shifted with respect to the y'–z' coordinate origin by (y'_0, z'_0). The focal plane is mounted in the camera at a distance x', which is suitable to the object geometry. If the object is far from the camera the CCD is placed in the focal plane of the optics at $x' = c$ (the focal length) on the x'-axis behind the optics (lower left coordinate system). To form an image, the camera is rotated around the origin of a (x, y) coordinate system.

To derive the relation between object point $\underline{X}$ and a pixel x' in an image the collinearity equation can be applied.

$$\underline{X} - \underline{X}_0 = \lambda \cdot (\underline{x}' - \underline{x}'_0) \tag{2}$$

$\underline{X}_0$ and $\underline{x}'_0$ are the projection centers for the object and the image space. Object points of a panoramic scenery can be imagined as a pixel in the focal plane if the camera is rotated by an angle of κ around z-axis. For the simplest case $(y'_0 = 0)$ the result is:

$$\begin{aligned}
(\underline{X} - \underline{X}_0) &= \lambda \cdot \underline{\underline{R}}^T \cdot (\underline{x}' - \underline{x}'_0) \\
&= \lambda \cdot \begin{bmatrix} \cos\kappa & -\sin\kappa & 0 \\ \sin\kappa & \cos\kappa & 0 \\ 0 & 0 & 1 \end{bmatrix} \cdot \begin{bmatrix} -c \\ 0 \\ z' - z'_0 \end{bmatrix} \\
&= \lambda \cdot \begin{bmatrix} -c \cdot \cos\kappa \\ -c \cdot \sin\kappa \\ z' - z'_0 \end{bmatrix}.
\end{aligned} \tag{3}$$

To derive some key parameters of the camera, a simplified approach is used. The unknown scale factor can be calculated from the square of the $x - y$ components of this equation:

$$\lambda = \frac{r_{XY}}{c} \qquad r_{XY} = \sqrt{(X - X_0)^2 + (Y - Y_0)^2} \tag{4}$$

The meaning of r_{XY} can easily be seen in Figure 6. This result is a consequence of the rotational symmetry. By dividing the first two equations and using the scale factor for the third, the following equations deliver an obvious result, which can be geometrically derived from Figure 6:

$$\begin{aligned}
\frac{\Delta Y}{\Delta X} &= \tan\kappa, \\
\Delta Z &= r_{XY} \cdot \frac{\Delta z'}{c}
\end{aligned} \tag{5}$$

The image or pixel coordinates (i, j) are related to the angle κ and the z-value. Because of the limited image field for this investigation, only linear effects (with respect to the rotation and image distortions) should be taken into account:

$$\begin{aligned} i &= \frac{1}{\delta\kappa} \cdot \arctan \frac{\Delta Y}{\Delta X} + i_0, \\ j &= \frac{c}{\delta z} \cdot \frac{\Delta Z}{r_{XY}} + j_0 \end{aligned} \tag{6}$$

δz pixel distance
$\delta\kappa$ angle of one rotation step
c focal length

The unknown or not exactly known parameters $\delta\kappa$, i_0, c and j_0 can be derived from known marks in the image field.

For calibration we used signalized point field (Figure 7). The analyzing of the resulting errors in the object space shows, that the approaches (5) and (6) must be extended. Following effects should be investigated first:

- Rotation of the CCD (around x-axis)
- Tilt of the camera (rotation around y-axis)

These effects can be incorporated into Equation (3). In case the variation of the angels φ and ω are small ($sin\varphi = \varphi$, $cos\varphi = 1$ and $sin\omega = \omega$, $cos\omega = 1$):

$$\begin{aligned} (\underline{x}' - \underline{x}'_0) &= \lambda^{-1} \cdot \underline{\underline{R}} \cdot (\underline{X} - \underline{X}_0) \\ &= \lambda \cdot \begin{bmatrix} \cos\kappa & \sin\kappa & \omega \cdot \sin\kappa - \varphi \cdot \cos\kappa \\ -\sin\kappa & \cos\kappa & \omega \cdot \sin\kappa + \varphi \cdot \sin\kappa \\ \varphi & -\omega & 1 \end{bmatrix} \cdot \begin{bmatrix} X - X_0 \\ Y - Y_0 \\ Z - Z_0 \end{bmatrix} \end{aligned} \tag{7}$$

For this special application the projection center of the camera is $(X_0, Y_0, Z_0) \cong (0, 0, 0)$. With a spatial resection approach, based on Equation (7), the unknown parameter of the exterior orientation can be derived. Despite the limited number of signalized points and the small field of view of the scene ($30° \times 30°$) the accuracy of the panorama camera model is $\sigma \approx 3$ image pixel of the camera. To improve the accuracy a model with following features was used (Schneider, 2003).

- Exterior and interior orientation
- Eccentricity of projection center
- Non-parallelism of CCD line

- Lens distortion
- Affinity Non-uniform rotation (periodical deviations)

With this model an accuracy of better than one pixel can be achieved.

3.3. FUSION OF PANORAMIC- AND LASER SCANNER DATA

Before the data of M2 and 3D-LS can be fused, the calibration of the 3D-LS must be checked. The test field shown in Figure 4 was used for this purpose. The 3D-LS delivers a 3D point cloud. The mean distance between points is about 2-3 mm at the wall. As the depth and image data do not fit to a regular grid they cannot be compared with rasterized image data of a photogrammetric survey without additional processing.

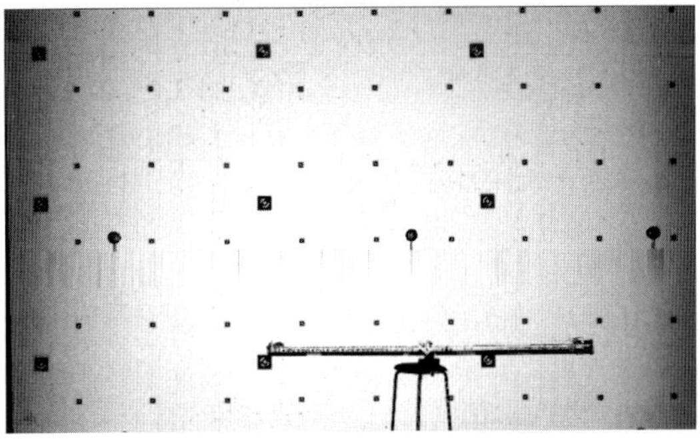

Figure 7. Laser image data.

The irregularly gridded 3D-LS data are triangulated and then interpolated to a regular grid (Figure 7). This procedure is implemented e.g. in the program ENVI (www.rsinc.com/envi/). The 3D-LS data can now be compared with the calibrated 3D reference frame. The absolute coordinate system is built up by an additional 2 m reference. In order to compare object data the following coordinate transform is required:

$$\begin{bmatrix} X_i \\ Y_i \\ Z_i \end{bmatrix} = \begin{bmatrix} r_{11} & r_{12} & r_{13} \\ r_{21} & r_{22} & r_{32} \\ r_{31} & r_{32} & r_{33} \end{bmatrix} \cdot \begin{bmatrix} x_i \\ y_i \\ z_i \end{bmatrix} + \begin{bmatrix} t_x \\ t_y \\ t_z \end{bmatrix} \tag{8}$$

where $\underline{x}_i$ are the points in the laser coordinate system and $\underline{X}_i$ in the camera system. $\underline{X}_0$ and r_{ij} are the unknown transform parameter, which can be derived by a least square fit, using some reference points. The calibration procedure, as shown in Section 3.2 delivers a relation between image coordinates (i, j) and object points (X, Y, Z). Now, all 3D-LS distance data can be transformed in the panoramic coordinate system and by that its pixel position in the panoramic image can be computed. For this position the actual grey value of the panoramic camera is correlated to the instantaneous laser image point.

After the transformation the accuracy for the 3D-LS can be determined in horizontal direction to 0.5 mm or $\frac{1}{4}$pixel and in vertical direction to 1 mm or $\frac{1}{2}$pixel, if the photogrammetric survey is regarded as a reference. Only one outlier could be observed.

4. PLP-CAM

Before the PLP-CAM was used in field experiments, the recording principle had been studied in a laboratory environment.

4.1. EXTENDED MODELLING

The moving sensor platform requires a modelling of the exterior orientation of the laser and the imaging system with the POS. As described in 2.3 the inertial measurement systems is fixed with respect to a body coordinate system which coincides with the principal axes of the platform movement. The inertially measured heading and attitude data are determined in the body coordinate system and are necessary for the transformation into the navigation coordinate system. The definition of these coordinate systems (see Figure 8) and their corresponding roll, pitch and yaw angles (ϕ, θ, ψ) do not conform with photogrammetric coordinate systems and angles (ω, ϕ, κ). The axes of the body coordinate system and the imaging system have to be mounted parallel to each other (except rotations of $\pi/2$ or π). Small remaining angular differences (misalignments) have to be determined separately. Based on the approaches of airborne photogrammetry (Börner et al., 1997), (Cramer, 1999) the platform angles (ϕ, θ, ψ) describe the actual orientation between the POS (body coordinate system) and the horizontal system (object coordinate system).

$$\underline{x}^n = \underline{\underline{R}}_z(\psi) \cdot \underline{\underline{R}}_y(\theta) \cdot \underline{\underline{R}}_x(\phi) \cdot \underline{x}^b = \underline{\underline{R}}_b^n \cdot \underline{x}^b \tag{9}$$

where:
$\underline{x}^n$ navigation coordinate system
$\underline{x}^b$ body coordinate system

For image processing however the transformation matrix $\underline{\underline{R}}_p^n$ between camera- (photo-) and object (navigation) coordinate system must be computed.

$$\underline{\underline{R}}_p^n = \underline{\underline{R}}_z(\kappa) \cdot \underline{\underline{R}}_y(\phi) \cdot \underline{\underline{R}}_x(\omega) \tag{10}$$

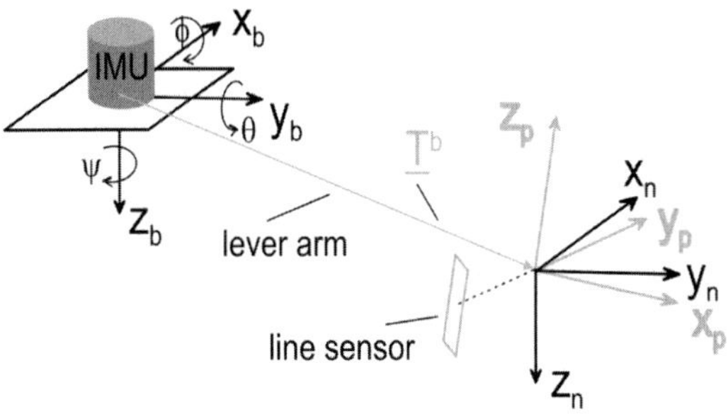

Figure 8. Definition of coordinate systems.

Introducing now possible misalignments between platform- (body-) and camera- (photo-) coordinate system the rotation matrix $\underline{\underline{R}}_p^b$ and the translation vector $\underline{T}^p$ of the CCD-line camera with respect to the body coordinate system have to be determined.

$$\underline{x}^b = \underline{\underline{R}}_p^b \cdot \underline{x}^p + \underline{T}^b \tag{11}$$

where:
$\underline{x}^p$ photo coordinate system
$\underline{T}^b$ Translation vector between photo- and body coordinate system (lever arm)

Insert Equation (11) into (9) results in:

$$\underline{x}^n = \underline{\underline{R}}_b^n \cdot \underline{\underline{R}}_p^b \cdot \underline{x}^p + \underline{\underline{R}}_b^n \cdot \underline{T}^b \tag{12}$$

Now the rotation matrix for the photo coordinate system consists of the platform rotation, modified by the misalignment matrix.

$$\underline{\underline{R}}_p^n = \underline{\underline{R}}_b^n \cdot \underline{\underline{R}}_p^b \tag{13}$$

Equation (13) is the required transformation for the photogrammetric image evaluation.

The following mathematical framework of data correction is based on the platform angels. This angels can be transformed into the photo-coordinate system, which is depicted in Figure (6), by rotation of $\pi/2$ around z-axis and a rotation around x-axis by π. This extends Equation 12. The misalignment is neglected and the matrix is replaced by the unit matrix.

The total 3D-rotation can be divided into 3 successive rotations:

$$\underline{\underline{R}}_x(\phi) = \begin{bmatrix} 1 & 0 & 0 \\ 0 & \cos\phi & -\sin\phi \\ 0 & \sin\phi & \cos\phi \end{bmatrix} \tag{14}$$

$$\underline{\underline{R}}_y(\theta) = \begin{bmatrix} \cos\theta & 0 & \sin\theta \\ 0 & 1 & 0 \\ -\sin\theta & 0 & \cos\theta \end{bmatrix} \tag{15}$$

$$\underline{\underline{R}}_z(\psi) = \begin{bmatrix} \cos\psi & -\sin\psi & 0 \\ \sin\psi & \cos\psi & 0 \\ 0 & 0 & 1 \end{bmatrix} \tag{16}$$

Combining all three rotations ($\underline{\underline{R}} = \underline{\underline{R}}_z(\psi) \cdot \underline{\underline{R}}_y(\theta) \cdot \underline{\underline{R}}_x(\phi)$) leads to the following rotation matrix (fixed axes):

$$\underline{\underline{R}} = \begin{bmatrix} \cos\theta\cos\psi & -\cos\theta\sin\psi & \sin\theta \\ \cos\phi\sin\psi + \sin\phi\sin\theta\cos\psi & \cos\phi\cos\psi - \sin\phi\sin\theta\sin\psi & -\sin\phi\cos\theta \\ \sin\phi\sin\psi - \cos\phi\sin\theta\cos\psi & \sin\phi\cos\psi + \cos\phi\sin\theta\sin\psi & \cos\phi\cos\theta \end{bmatrix} \tag{17}$$

The correction process is equivalent to the projection of each image point onto the $x-z$-plane in a certain distance y_0, which gives the corrected image points i' and j'.

$$\begin{pmatrix} j'\cdot\Delta \\ y \\ i'\cdot\Delta \end{pmatrix} = \begin{pmatrix} x_0 \\ y_0 \\ z_0 \end{pmatrix} + \lambda\cdot\underline{\underline{R}}\cdot\begin{pmatrix} 0 \\ -f \\ i\cdot\delta \end{pmatrix} \tag{18}$$

where:
f = focal length
δ = pixel distance in the image space
Δ = pixel distance in the object space

$$\begin{pmatrix} j'\cdot\Delta \\ y \\ i'\cdot\Delta \end{pmatrix} = \begin{pmatrix} x_0 \\ y_0 \\ z_0 \end{pmatrix} + \lambda\cdot\begin{pmatrix} a \\ b \\ c \end{pmatrix} \tag{19}$$

The scale factor λ results in:

$$\lambda = \frac{y - y_0}{b}, \tag{20}$$

and the corrected image points are:

$$j' = \frac{x_0 + \lambda \cdot a}{\Delta} = \frac{x_0}{\Delta} + \frac{(y - y_0) \cdot a}{\Delta \cdot b} \tag{21}$$

$$i' = \frac{z_0 + \lambda \cdot c}{\Delta} = \frac{z_0}{\Delta} + \frac{(y - y_0) \cdot c}{\Delta \cdot b} \tag{22}$$

4.2. PLP-CAM IN LABORATORY

The functioning of PLP-CAM is first verified by surveying the test field described in Section 3. During this experiment a robot is used as a moving platform. As GPS reception is impossible in the laboratory the position data and orientation data are obtained from the infrared camera tracking system ARTtrack2 (www.ar-tracking.de/) which comprises two CCD-cameras. ARTtrack is a position and orientation measurement system with high accuracy. The system has passive targets with 4 or more retro-reflective markers (rigid bodies), which provide the 6 degree of freedom (DOF) tracking. Up to 10 targets are simultaneously usable, each target with individual identification. The IMU measurement data is also recorded at the same time. This means that redundant orientation information is available and the accuracy of the orientation system can be verified. Figure 9 shows the robot with PLP-CAM. Figure 10 depicts one of the two tracking cameras. The robot is remotely controlled by a joystick.

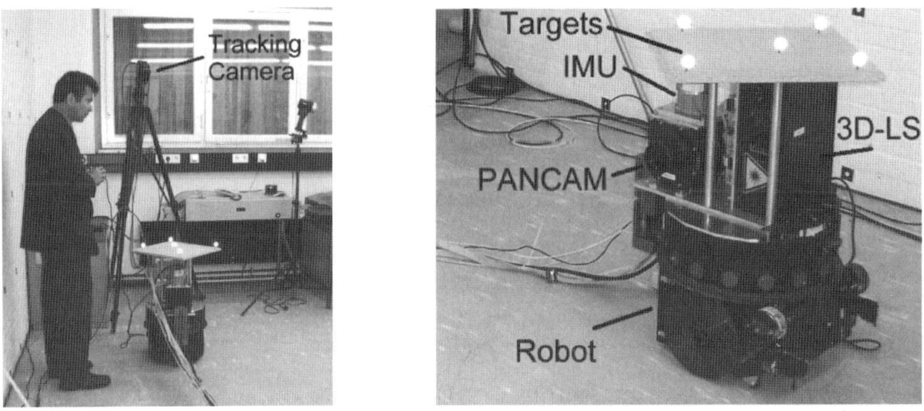

Figure 10. PLP-CAM carried by robot.

The results of these experiments were used to develop algorithms to integrate the data of the three independently working systems. It can be shown, that the data sets can be well synchronized. Furthermore, the whole system could be calibrated by using the targets (Figure 4).

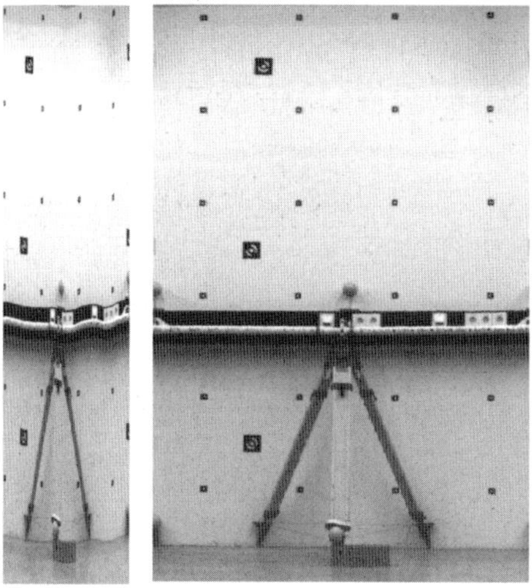

Figure 11. Disturbed- and corrected image.

4.3. PLP-CAM IN THE FIELD

For a field experiment the PLP-CAM was mounted in a surveying van. The GPS-antenna of POS was installed on top of the vehicle. The car drove along the facade of the Neue Schloss in Stuttgart (Figure 12).

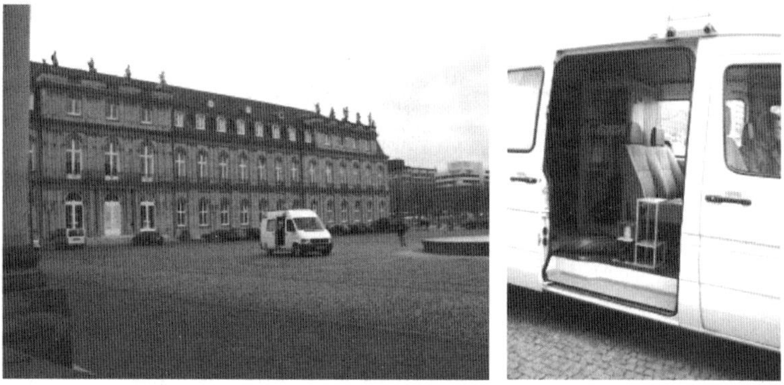

Figure 12. PLP-CAM in front of Neues Schloss Stuttgart.

As the range performance of the 3D-LS was too low, only image data of the CCD-line camera and the POS-data were recorded. The left image in Figure 13 shows the rectification result on the basis of POS-data alone. By applying image processing algorithms the oscillation can be reduced and a comprehensive correction is achieved by using external laser scanner data recorded independently during another survey (right image in Figure 13). The high performance of the line scan camera is documented in Figure

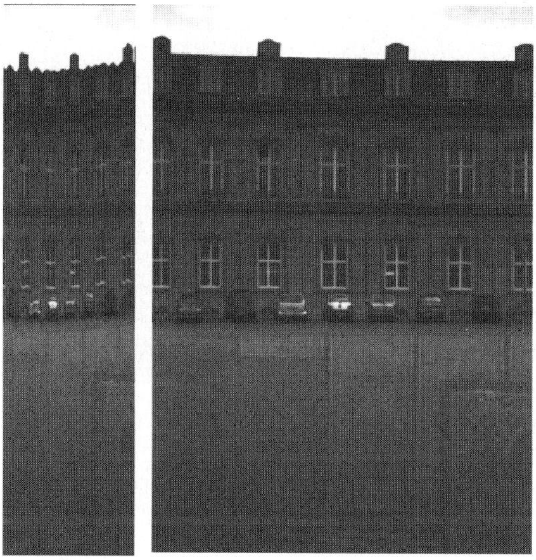

Figure 13. Survey with PLP-CAM.

14 and Figure 15. A heraldic animal at Schloss Solitude in Stuttgart was surveyed by PLP-Cam. The object is hardly recognizable (Figure 15) from the original PLP-CAM-data. However, after correcting the data a high quality image is obtained. The zoomed in part illustrates the high camera performance.

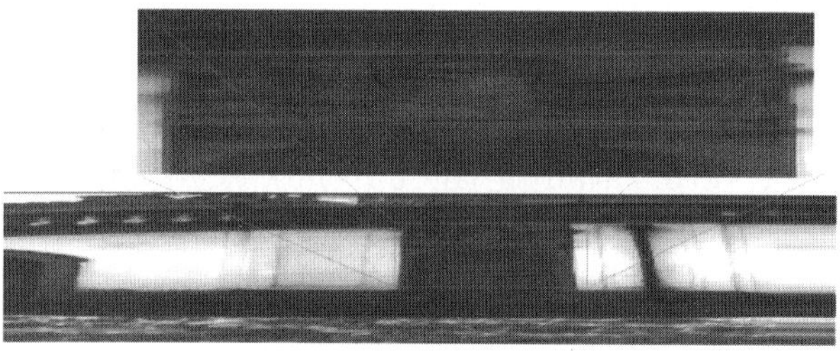

Figure 14. Original scanned data with panoramic camera.

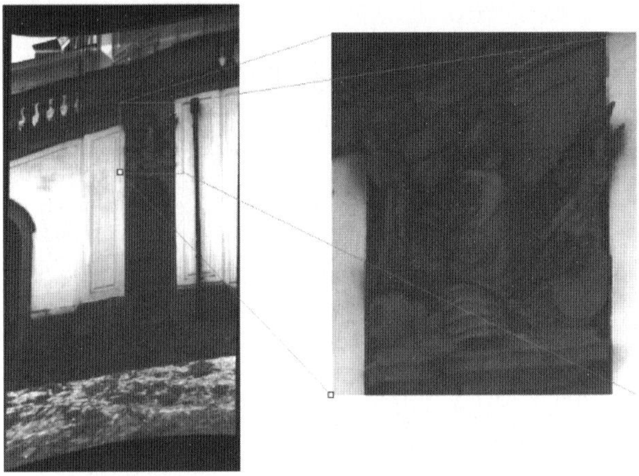

Figure 15. Result after correction.

5. Conclusions

The experiments fusing M2-data with 3D-LS data show that by using such an integrated system, high resolved 3D-images can be computed. The processing of the two independent data sets makes clear that a well defined and robust assembly is required, because it benefits from the well defined locations of the different origins and the relative orientation of the different devices with respect to each other. The system can be calibrated very precisely by using a sophisticated calibration field equipped with targets that could be identified and located very accurately with both PANCAM and 3D-LS. The field experiments with PLP-CAM demonstrated that in courtyards and in narrow streets with high buildings only a poor GPS signal is is available. Here, the POS-AV system of Applanix company worked very degraded, because it is designed for airborne applications, where one does not have to regard obscuration and multipath effects. For this application independent location measurement systems will deliver improved results. Next steps will be the further improvements of calibration and alignment and the verification of the absolute accuracy of the whole system. The presented examples makes clear that very detailed illustrations of facades including 3D-information can be obtained by fusing POS-, M2- and 3D-LS-data.

Acknowledgements

The authors would like to thank Prof. P. Levi Institute of Parallel and Distributed Systems, University of Stuttgart for making available the robot, Prof. H.-G. Maas and D. Schneider Institute of Photogrammetry and Remote

mote Sensing TU-Dresden for processing PLP-CAM data, Dr. M. Schneberger Advanced Realtime Tracking GmbH, Herrsching making available the camera tracking system ARTtrack2 and Mr. M. Thomas Institute of Navigation University Stuttgart for his outstanding support during the laboratory and field experiments and in processing the laser data and realizing the synchronization.

References

Börner, A., Reulke, R., Scheele, M., and Terzibaschian, T.: Stereo processing of image data from an airborne three line ccd scanner. In Proc. *Int. Conf. and Exhibition Airborne Remote Sensing*, Volume I, pages 423–430, 1997.

Cramer, M.: Direct geocoding - is aerial triangulation obsolete? In Proc. *Photogrammetric Week '99*, pages 59–70, 1999.

Klette, R., Gimel'farb, G., and Reulke, R.: Wide-angle image acquisition, analysis and visualization. In Proc. *Vision Interface*, pages 114–125, 2001.

Klette, R., Gimel'farb, G., Wei, S., Huang, F., Scheibe, K., Scheele, M., Brner, A., and Reulke, R.: On design and applications of cylindrical panoramas. In Proc. *CAIP*, 2003.

Reulke, R., Scheele, M., and Scheibe., K.: Multi-Sensor-Ansätze in der Nahbereichsphotogrammetrie. In Proc. *Jahrestagung DGPF*, Konstanz, 2001.

Scheele, M., Börner, A., Reulke, R., and Scheibe, K.: Geometrische Korrekturen: Vom Flugzeugscanner zur Nahbereichskamera; Photogrammetrie. *Photogrammetrie, Fernerkundung, Geoinformation*, **5**: 13–22, 2001.

Scheibe, K., Korsitzky, H., Reulke, R., Scheele, M., and Solbrig, M.: Eyescan - a high resolution digital panoramic camera. In Proc. *Robot Vision*, pages 77–83, 2001.

Schneider, D.: Geometrische Modellierung und Kalibrierung einer hochauflösenden digitalen Rotationszeilenkamera. In Proc. *Oldenburger 3D-Tage*, 2003.

Schneider, D. and Maas, H.-G.: Geometrische Modellierung und Kalibrierung einer hochauflösenden digitalen Rotationszeilenkamera. In Proc. *DGPF-Tagung*, 2002.

Wehr, A.: 3d-imaging laser scanner for close range metrology. In Proc. *SPIE*, volume 3707, pages 381–389, 1999.

MULTI-SENSOR PANORAMA FUSION AND VISUALIZATION

KARSTEN SCHEIBE
Optical Information Systems German Aerospace Center (DLR), Berlin Germany
REINHARD KLETTE
Department of Computer Science
The University of Auckland Auckland, New Zealand

Abstract. The paper describes a general approach for scanning and visualizing panoramic (360°) indoor scenes. It combines range data acquired by a laser range finder with color pictures acquired by a rotating CCD line camera. The paper defines coordinate systems of both sensors, specifies the fusion of range and color data acquired by both sensors, and reports about different alternatives for visualizing the generated 3D data set. Compared to earlier publications, the recent approach also utilizes an improved method for calculating the spatial (geometric) correspondence between laser diode of the laser range finder and the focal point of the rotating CCD line camera. Calibration is also a subject in this paper. A least-square minimization based approach is proposed for the rotating CCD line camera.

Key words: panoramic imaging, line-based camera, laser range finder, multi-sensor systems, panorama fusion, 3D visualization

1. Introduction

Laser range finders (LRFs) have been used for close-range photogrammetry (e.g., acquisition of building geometries) for several years, see (Niemeier, 1995; Wiedemann, 2001). An LRF, which utilizes the frequency-to-distance converter technique, has sub-millimeter accuracies for sensor-to-surface distances which are between less than one meter and up to 15 meters, and accuracies of 3 to 4 mm for distances less than 50 meters. It also captures intensity (i.e., gray-level) images. However, our projects require true-color surface textures.

In earlier publications (Huang et al., 2002) we demonstrated how to fuse LRF data with pictures (i.e., colored surface texture) obtained by a rotating CCD line camera (which we sometimes call *camera* for short in

K. Daniilidis and R. Klette (eds.), Imaging Beyond the Pinhole Camera, 185–206.

this paper). To be precise, the camera combines three CCD lines (i.e., one each for the red, green or blue channel) which capture a color picture; the length of these lines is in the order of thousands of cells (pixels).

Altogether, we use a *cloud of points* in 3D space (i.e., a finite set of 3D points in a defined coordinate system, on or near to the given object surfaces), produced by the LRF, and a *surface texture* (typically several gigabytes of color image data) produced by the camera during a single 360° scan. Both devices are independent systems and can be used separately. Our task is to combine both outputs into unified triangulated and textured surfaces.

The fusion of range data and pictures is a relatively new approach for 3D scene rendering; see, for example, (Kern, 2001) for combining range data with images acquired by a video camera. Combinations of panoramic images (Benosman and Kang, 2001) and LRF data provide a new technology for high-resolution 3D documentation and visualization. The fusion of range data and panoramic images acquired by rotating CCD line cameras has been discussed in (Huang et al., 2002; Klette et al., 2003). Calibrations of range sensors (Huang et al., 2002) and of rotating CCD line cameras (Huang et al., 2002a) provide necessary parameters for this process of data fusion. In this paper we introduce a last-square minimization approach as a new method for the calibration of a rotating CCD line camera, which also allows to estimate the parameters of exterior and interior orientation.

The main subject of this paper is a specification of coordinate transformations for data fusion, and a discussion of possible ways of visualizations (i.e., data projections). Possible applications are the generation of orthophotos, interactive 3D animations (e.g., for virtual tours), and so forth. Orthophotos are pictorial representations of orthogonal mappings of textured surfaces onto specified planes (also called *orthoplanes* in photogrammetry, see Figure 1). High-accuracy orthophotos are a common way of documenting existing architecture. Range data mapped into an orthoplane identify an *orthosurface* with respect to this plane.

Note that range data, acquired at one LRF viewpoint, provide 2.5 D surface data only, and full 3D surface acquisitions can only be obtained by merging data acquired at several LRF viewpoints.

The approach in (Huang et al., 2002) addresses multi-view data acquisition. It combines several clouds of points (i.e., LRF 3D data sets) with several surface textures (i.e., camera data sets) by mapping all data into specified orthoplanes. This simplified approach utilizes a 2.5 D surface model for the LRF data, and no complex ray tracing or volume rendering is needed. This simplified approach assumes the absence of occluding objects between LRF or camera and the orthosurface. In a first step we determine the viewing direction of each pixel of the camera (described by a formalized sensor model) towards the 2.5 D surface sampled by the LRF data. This can be done if both devices are calibrated (e.g., orientations of the systems in 3D space are known in relation to one world coordinate system) with sufficient accuracy. Requirements for accuracy are defined by the desired resolution in 3D scene space. Orientations (i.e., affine transforms) can be specified using control points and standard photogrammetry software. The 2.5 D model of orthosurfaces is generated by using several LRF scans to reduce the influence of shadows. More than a single camera viewpoint can be used for improved coloration (i.e., mapping of surface texture). Results can be mapped into several orthoplanes, which can be transformed into a unified 3D model in a second step. See Figure 1.

In this paper we discuss a more advanced approach. For coloration of a finite number of clouds of points (i.e., several LRF data sets, generated within one 3D scene), we use captured panoramic images obtained from several camera scans. This requires an implementation of a complex and efficient raytracing algorithm for an extremely large data set. Note that this raytracing cannot assume ideal correspondences between points defined by LRF data and captured surface texture; we have to allow assignments within local neighborhoods for identifying correspondences between range data and surface texture. Figure 2 illustrates this problem of local uncertainties.

There are different options to overcome this problem. A single LRF scan is not sufficient to generate a depth map for a complex 3D scene. Instead of fusing a single LRF scan with color information, followed by merging all these fused scans into a single 3D model, we prefer that all

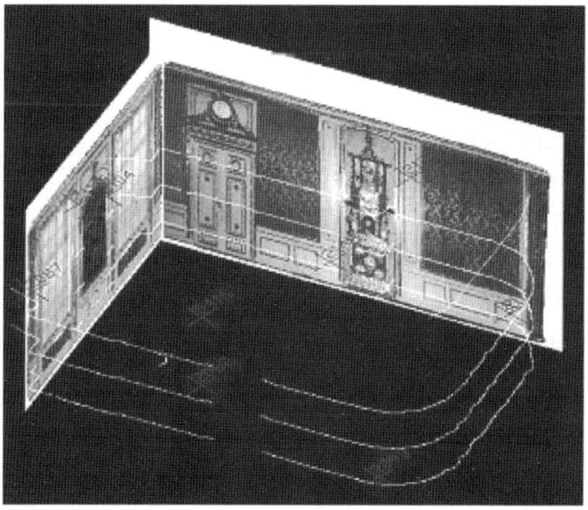

Figure 1. A (simple) 3D CAD model consisting of two orthoplanes.

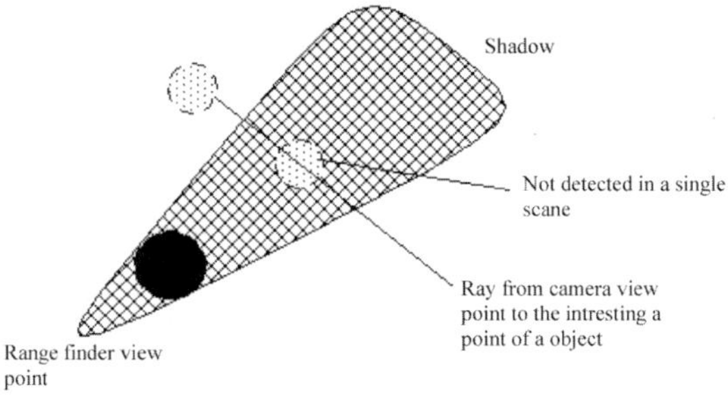

Figure 2. Raytracing problem when combining one LRF scan with data from one camera viewpoint. A 3D surface point P scanned by the LRF may actually (by surface geometry) generate a "shadow", and rays of the camera passing close to P may actually capture color values at hidden surface points.

LRF scans are merged first into one unified depth representation of the 3D scene, and then all camera data are used for coloration of this unified depth representation. Of course, this increases the size of data sets extremely, due to the high resolution of LRF and camera. For simplification of raytracing, the generated clouds of points can first be used to create object surfaces by triangulation, applying standard routines of computer graphics. This can then be followed by raytracing, where parameterizations, obtained by triangulation (including data reductions by simplification and uniform coloring of individual triangles), reduce the size of the involved sets of data.

LRF and camera have different viewpoints or positions in 3D space, even when we attempt to have both at about the same physical location. A simple approach for data fusion could be as follows: for a ray of the camera map the picture values captured along this ray onto a point P calculated by the LRF if P is the only point close (with respect to Euclidean distance) to this ray. An octree data structure can be used for an efficient implementation. However, this simplified approach never colorizes the whole laser scan, because surface edges or detailed structures in the 3D scene always create very dense points in the LRF data set.

As a more advanced approach assume that we are able to arrange that the main point (i.e., the origin of measurement rays) of the LRF and the projection center of the camera are (nearly) identical, and that orientations of both rotation axes coincide, as well as of both optical axes. Then, processing of the data is straightforward and we can design rendering algorithms that work in (or nearly in) real time. Intensity (i.e., gray-level) data of the LRF will be simply replaced by color information of the camera. No ray tracing algorithm is necessary for this step because occlusions do not need to be considered. The result is a colored cloud of points in world coordinates. Nevertheless, to model the data it is necessary to triangulate the LRF points into a mesh (because LRF rays and camera rays do not ideally coincide). A triangulation reduces the number of points and makes it possible to texture the mesh. Note that using this approach the same shadow problem can occur as briefly discussed above for single LRF scans.

This more advanced approach requires to transform the panoramic camera data into the LRF coordinate system. In order to cover the 3D scene completely, several scans are actually required from different viewpoints, which need to be merged to create a 3D mesh (also called *wireframe*). A cloud of points obtained from one LRF scan is merged with a cloud of points obtained from another LRF scan. In this case the advantage of unique ray-to-ray assignments (assuming aligned positions and directions of LRF and camera) is lost. It is again necessary to texture a 3D wireframe by data obtained from different camera viewpoints (i.e., a raytracing routine is again required). We describe a time-efficient raytracing approach for such a static texturing situation in this paper. We report about advantages of applying independent LRF and camera devices, and illustrate by examples obtained within our "Neuschwanstein project".

The Neuschwanstein project is directed on a complete 3D photogrammetric documentation of this Bavarian castle. Figures in this paper show the Thronsaal of this castle as scanned from the viewpoint (i.e., LRF and camera in about the same location) about at the center of the room. For more complete photogrammetric documentation we used more viewpoints to reduce the impact of hidden areas. The paper describes all transformations and algorithms applied in this process.

2. Coordinate Systems

LRF and camera scans are in different independent coordinate systems. To fuse both systems it is necessary to transform the data into one primary reference system, called the *world coordinate system*.

Rays of the panoramic camera are defined by image rows i (i.e., this is the horizontal coordinate) and pixel position j in the CCD line (i.e., this is the vertical coordinate). Similarly, we identify rays of the LRF by an index i and a constant angular increment φ_0 which defines the absolute horizontal rotation angle $\varphi = i \cdot \varphi_0$, and an index j and an angle increment ϑ_0 which defines the absolute vertical angle $\vartheta = j \cdot \vartheta_0$. Note that these absolute angles are also the same for the panoramic camera. However, the possible range of vertical angles of the camera is typically reduced compared to that of a LRF, and the possible range of horizontal angles of the LRF is typically reduced compared to that of a panoramic camera.

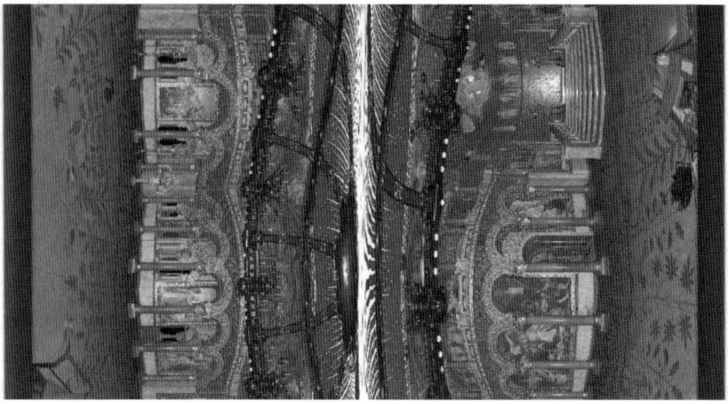

Figure 3. Raw data of an uncalibrated LRF image.

2.1. LRF

A LRF scans in two dimensions, vertically by a deflecting mirror and horizontally by rotating the whole measuring system. The vertical scan range is 310° (which leaves 50° uncovered), and the horizontal scan range is 180°. The LRF scans overhead, therefore a whole sphere can be scanned if using all 180°. Figure 3 depicts an LRF raw data set and the uncalibrated image.

Rays and detected surface points on these rays (which define the LRF data set) can be described in a polar coordinate system. According to our application of the LRF, it makes sense to transform all LRF data at one view point into a normal polar coordinate system with an horizontal range of of 360° and a vertical range of 180° only. At this step all LRF calibration data are available and required.

Photogrammetry specifies for rotating measuring devices (e.g., theodolite systems), how to measure errors along rotating axes. Those are classified into *vertical and horizontal collimation errors.* The pole columns describe the column around the *zenith*, which is the highest point in the image. To determine the collimation errors, typically a to be measured point will be determined from two sides (i.e., the point will be measured in two steps): first measured on side one, then both rotation axes are turned by 180°, and the same point is measured again (Däumlich and Steiger, 2002). Figure 4 depicts the optical Z-axis as an axis orthogonal both to the corresponding horizontal rotation axis and to the tilt-axis (i.e., the vertical rotation axis K).

The horizontal and vertical collimation errors are calculated by determining the pole column (this can be done in the LRF image based on two rows or layers, and identical points at the horizon). This provides offsets to the zenith and to the *equator* (i.e., the horizon). Secondly, the horizontal

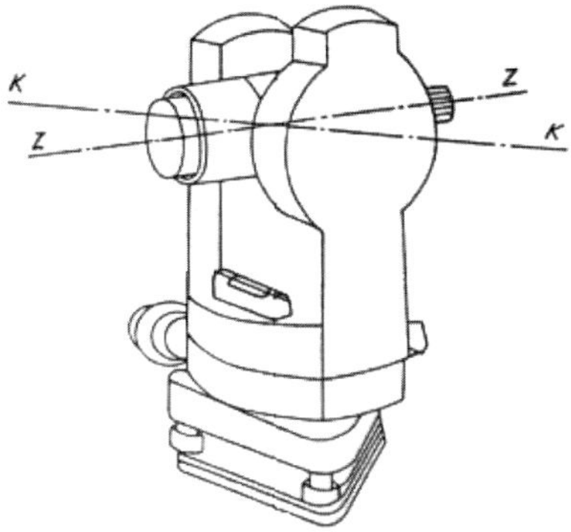

Figure 4. Theodolite with two axes: the (German) terms 'Zielachse' and 'Kippachse' specify in photogrammetry the optical Z-axis and an orthogonal K-axis. A range finder measures along a variable Z-axis, which may be effected by horizontal (i.e., along the Z-axis) or vertical (i.e., along the K-axis) errors.

collimation error can be calculated by control points along the equator. The vertical collimation error can be determined based on these results. As an important test we have to confirm that the zenith is uniquely defined in 3D space for the whole combined scan of 360°.

Each point in the LRF coordinate system is described in polar or Cartesian coordinates as a vector $\vec{p}$, which is defined as follows:

$$\begin{aligned} p_x &= R \cdot \sin\vartheta \cdot \cos\varphi \\ p_y &= R \cdot \sin\vartheta \cdot \sin\varphi \\ p_z &= R \cdot \cos\vartheta \end{aligned}$$

The orientation and position with respect to a reference vector $\vec{r}$ in the world coordinate system is defined by one rotation matrix $\mathbf{A}$ and a translation vector $\vec{r_0}$:

$$\vec{r} = \vec{r_0} + \mathbf{A} \cdot \vec{p} \tag{1}$$

We define all coordinate systems to be right-hand systems. The laser scanner rotates clockwise. The first scan line starts at the positive y-axis in the LRF coordinate system at the horizontal angle of 100gon[1] The rotation matrix combines three rotations around all three axes for the right hand system:

$$\mathbf{A} = \mathbf{A}_\omega \cdot \mathbf{A}_\phi \cdot \mathbf{A}_\kappa \tag{2}$$

[1] The unit gon is defined by $360° = 400$gon.

The resulting matrix $\mathbf{A}$ is then given as

$$\begin{pmatrix} C\varphi \cdot C\kappa & S\varphi \cdot S\kappa & S\varphi \\ C\omega \cdot S\kappa + S\omega \cdot S\varphi \cdot C\kappa & C\omega \cdot C\kappa - S\omega \cdot S\varphi \cdot S\kappa & -S\omega \cdot S\varphi \\ S\omega \cdot S\kappa - C\omega \cdot S\varphi \cdot C\kappa & S\omega \cdot C\kappa + C\omega \cdot S\varphi \cdot S\kappa & C\omega \cdot C\varphi \end{pmatrix}$$

where κ, ϕ, ω are the rotation angles around the z-, y-, and x-axis, respectively, and C stands short for the cosine and S for the sine.

2.2. CAMERA

The panoramic camera is basically a rotating CCD line sensor. Three CCD lines (i.e., Red, Greeen and Blue channels) are mounted vertically and rotate clockwise. The scanned data are stored in cylindrical coordinates. In an ideal focal plane each pixel of the combined (i.e., all three color channels) line is defined by the vector $\vec{r_d}$. The rotation axis of the camera is incident with the main point of the optics. The focal plane is located at focal length f, without any offset $\vec{\Delta}$. Scans begin at the horizontal angle of 100gon. We have the following:

$$\vec{r_d} = \begin{pmatrix} r_{dx} \\ r_{dy} \\ r_{dz} \end{pmatrix} = \begin{pmatrix} 0 \\ f \\ j \cdot \delta \end{pmatrix} \tag{3}$$

In our Neuschwanstein project, the used CCD line had a length of approximately 70mm and 10,296 pixels, with a pixel size $\delta = 7\mu m$, indexed by j. Each scanned surface point is identified by the camera rotation $\mathbf{A}_\varphi$.

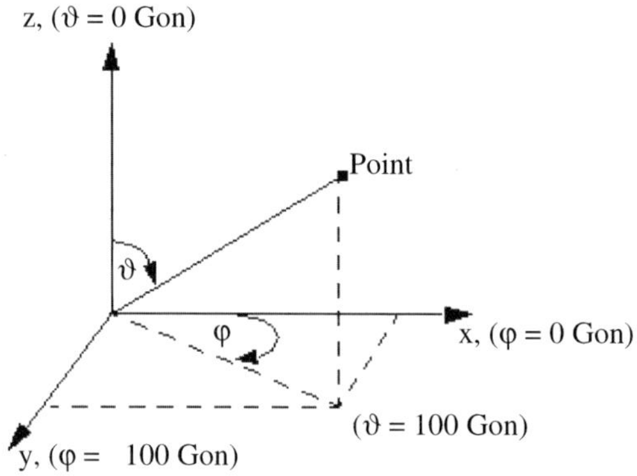

Figure 5. Range finder xyz-coordinate system: the Z-axis of Fig. 4 points towards p, and is defined by slant ϑ and tilt φ.

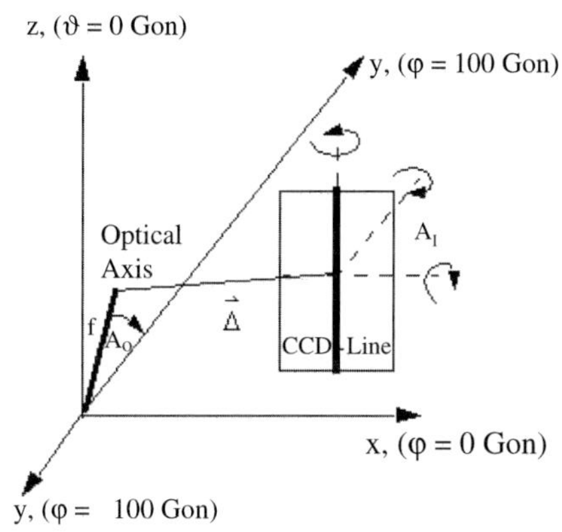

Figure 6. Rotating line camera xyz-coordinate system: the effective focal length f defines the position of an image column (i.e., the position of the CCD line at this moment) parallel to the z-axis, with an assumed offset Δ for the center of this image column.

In analogy to the LRF, a reference vector (in world coordinates) for the camera coordinate system is described by the rotation matrix **A** as follows:

$$\vec{r} = \vec{r}_0 + \mathbf{A} \cdot \lambda \cdot \mathbf{A}_\varphi \cdot \vec{r}_d \tag{4}$$

λ is an unknown scale factor of the camera coordinate system (for the 3D scene). If LRF and camera coordinate systems have the same origin, then λ correspondents to the distance measured by the laser scanner. We also model the following deviations from an ideal case:

- The CCD line is tilted by three angles $\mathbf{A}_I$ regarding the main point.
- The CCD line has an offset vector $\vec{\Delta}$ regarding the main point.
- The optical axis is rotated by $\mathbf{A}_O$ regarding the rotation axis.

These deviations are depicted in Figure 6 and described in the following equation:

$$\vec{r} = \vec{r_0} + \lambda \cdot \mathbf{A}\mathbf{A}_\varphi\mathbf{A}_O \left(\mathbf{A}_I \begin{pmatrix} 0 \\ 0 \\ j \cdot \delta \end{pmatrix} + \begin{pmatrix} \Delta_x \\ f + \Delta_y \\ \Delta_z \end{pmatrix} \right) \tag{5}$$

For the calculation of calibration parameters $\mathbf{A}_{opt.}$, $\mathbf{A}_{in}$ and the offset $\vec{\Delta}$, see (Huang et al., 2002). An adjustment calculation for rotating CCD line cameras is introduced in Section 3.

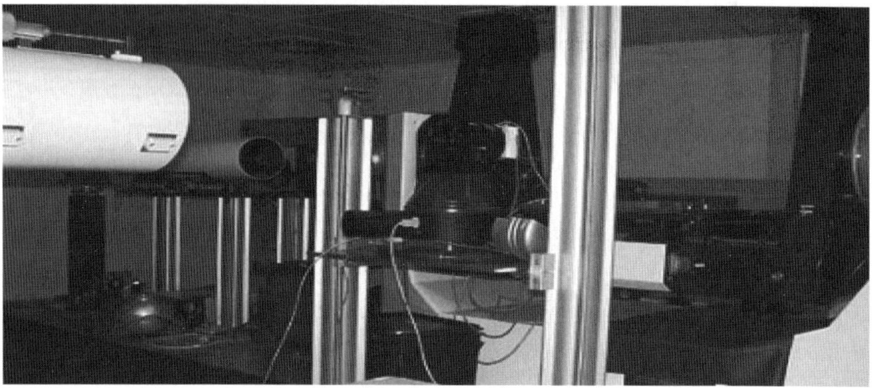

Figure 7. Panoramic camera mounted on a manipulator for measuring geometric or photogrammetric properties of single pixels.

3. Calibration

In earlier publications we have briefly described how to calibrate rotating line cameras in a specially designed calibration site. The camera is positioned on a *manipulator*, which is basically a high-precession turn table, which can measure in thousandth of a degree. Each pixel can be illuminated by a *collimator ray*, which is parallel light, approximating an endless focus. Figure 7 depicts (in a simplified scheme) the setup.

After measuring each pixel about two axes (α, β), the horizontal and vertical axes of the manipulator, the spatially attitude of the CCD line will be mapped into an ideal focal plane, where $x' = \frac{f \cdot \tan(\beta)}{\cos(\alpha)}$ and $y' = f \cdot \tan(\alpha)$ are the positions of each pixel in the ideal focal plane, and f is the focal length.

3.1. ADJUSTMENT CALCULATION FOR ROTATING CCD LINES

In close range photogrammetry its also important to use non-endless focusing. (For example, in the project *bb-focal* an approach was examined, which is using holographic optical elements to calibrate non-endless focused cameras.) However, this section describes a standard least-square approach, but adapted to rotating CCD lines. Based on the general Equation (4), expanded by an *off-axis parameter* (i.e., the camera is on a lever, see (Klette et al., 2003)) the following equations results:

$$\vec{r} = \vec{r}_0 + \mathbf{A} \cdot \mathbf{A}_\varphi \cdot \lambda \cdot \left(\vec{r}_d + \frac{1}{\lambda} \cdot \vec{\Delta} \right) \tag{6}$$

$$(\vec{r} - \vec{r}_0) \cdot \mathbf{A}^{-1} \cdot \mathbf{A}_\varphi^{-1} - \vec{\Delta} = \lambda \cdot \vec{r}_d \tag{7}$$

with

$$\vec{r_d} = \begin{pmatrix} r_{dx} \\ r_{dy} \\ r_{dz} \end{pmatrix} = \begin{pmatrix} \Delta_{xj} \\ f \\ j \cdot \delta + \Delta zj \end{pmatrix} \tag{8}$$

$$\vec{r}_d = \frac{1}{\lambda} \cdot \left(\mathbf{A}^{-1} \cdot \mathbf{A}_\varphi^{-1} \cdot (\vec{r} - \vec{r_0}) - \vec{\Delta}_{Off} \right) \tag{9}$$

and the following three components:

$$\Delta x_j = \frac{1}{\lambda} \cdot (a_{11}(r_x - r_{x0}) + a_{21}(r_y - r_{y0}) + a_{31}(r_z - r_{z0}) - \Delta_{Off_x}) \tag{10}$$

$$f = \frac{1}{\lambda} \cdot \left(a_{12}(r_x - r_{x0}) + a_{22}(r_y - r_{y0}) + a_{32}(r_z - r_{z0}) - \Delta_{Off_y} \right) \tag{11}$$

$$j \cdot \delta + \Delta y_j = \frac{1}{\lambda} \cdot (a_{13}(r_x - r_{x0}) + a_{23}(r_y - r_{y0}) + a_{33}(r_z - r_{z0})) \tag{12}$$

The reals $a_{11}..a_{33}$ are elements of the rotation matrices $\mathbf{A}$ and $\mathbf{A}_\varphi$. Therefore, the collinearity equations are defined as follows:

$$\Delta x_j = \frac{a_{11}(r_x - r_{x0}) + a_{21}(r_y - r_{y0}) + a_{31}(r_z - r_{z0}) - \Delta_{Off_x}}{a_{12}(r_x - r_{x0}) + a_{22}(r_y - r_{y0}) + a_{32}(r_z - r_{z0}) - \Delta_{Off_y}} \cdot f \tag{13}$$

and

$$j \cdot \delta + \Delta y_j = \frac{a_{13}(r_x - r_{x0}) + a_{23}(r_y - r_{y0}) + a_{33}(r_z - r_{z0})}{a_{12}(r_x - r_{x0}) + a_{22}(r_y - r_{y0}) + a_{32}(r_z - r_{z0}) - \Delta_{Off_y}} \cdot f \tag{14}$$

The unknown parameters are functions of these collinearity equations and of the focal length f:

$$\Delta x_j = F_x \cdot f$$

$$j \cdot \delta + \Delta y_j = F_z \cdot f$$

By linearization of these equations it is possible to estimate iteratively the unknown parameters:

$$\begin{aligned} \Delta x_j \; = \; & \Delta x_j^k + f \cdot \left(\frac{\partial F_x}{\partial r_{x0}} \cdot \Delta r_{x0}^k + \frac{\partial F_x}{\partial r_{y0}} \cdot \Delta r_{y0}^k + \frac{\partial F_x}{\partial r_{z0}} \cdot \Delta r_{z0}^k + \frac{\partial F_x}{\partial \omega} \cdot \Delta \omega^k \right. \\ & \left. + \frac{\partial F_x}{\partial \phi} \cdot \Delta \phi^k + \frac{\partial F_x}{\partial \kappa} \cdot \Delta \kappa^k + \frac{\partial F_x}{\partial Off_x} \cdot \Delta Off_x^k + \frac{\partial F_x}{\partial Off_y} \cdot \Delta Off_y^k \right) \end{aligned}$$

$$\begin{aligned} j \cdot \delta + \Delta y_j &= (j \cdot \delta + \Delta y_j)^k + f \cdot \left(\frac{\partial F_z}{\partial r_{x0}} \cdot \Delta r_{x0}^k + \frac{\partial F_z}{\partial r_{y0}} \cdot \Delta r_{y0}^k + \frac{\partial F_z}{\partial r_{z0}} \cdot \Delta r_{z0}^k \right. \\ &\quad + \frac{\partial F_z}{\partial \omega} \cdot \Delta \omega^k + \frac{\partial F_z}{\partial \phi} \cdot \Delta \phi^k + \frac{\partial F_z}{\partial \kappa} \cdot \Delta \kappa^k \\ &\quad \left. + \frac{\partial F_z}{\partial Off_x} \cdot \Delta Off_x^k + \frac{\partial F_z}{\partial Off_y} \cdot \Delta Off_y^k \right) \end{aligned}$$

The equations can be extended also modelling any interior orientation, such as $\mathbf{A}_{opt}$ and $\mathbf{A}_{in}$ (as defined above). Based on the matrix equation $l = \mathbf{A} \cdot x$, the solution is $x = \mathbf{A}^{-1} \cdot l$. – For $n > u$ observations, the following equation is known: $v = \mathbf{A}\hat{x} - l$.

By applying the method of least-square minimization, the minimum error is defined as follows:

$$min = v^T v = (A\hat{x} - l)^T (A\hat{x} - l) = \hat{x}^T A^T A\hat{x} - 2l^T A\hat{x} + l^T l$$

We obtain

$$\frac{\partial \left(v^T v\right)}{\partial \hat{x}} = 2\hat{x}^T A^T A - 2l^T A = 0$$

which leads to the following solution:

$$\hat{x} = \left(A^T A\right)^{-1} A^T l \tag{15}$$

4. Fusion

The fusion of our data sets starts with transforming both coordinate systems (i.e., those of LRF and camera viewpoints) into one world coordinate system. For this step, the orientation of both system needs to be known (see Section 3.1). A transformation of LRF data into the world coordinate system is then simple because all required parameters of the equation are given. The known object points $\vec{r}$ are now given by the LRF system and must be textured with color information of the panoramic image. By applying all parameters of the interior orientations to the vector $\vec{r_d}$, the following simplified equation results:

$$(\vec{r} - \vec{r_0}) \cdot \mathbf{A}^{-1} \cdot \mathbf{A}_{\varphi}^{-1} = \lambda \vec{r_d} \tag{16}$$

We apply the calculated exterior orientation $\mathbf{A}^{-1}$ to the camera location. This allows to specify the horizontal pixel column i in the panoramic image. Note that we choose to focus on the right quadrant in the image because of the following arcus tangent:

$$(r_x - r_{x0})' = -sin(i \cdot \Delta\varphi) \cdot \lambda \cdot f$$

$$(r_y - r_{y0})' = cos(i \cdot \Delta\varphi) \cdot \lambda \cdot f$$

$$i \cdot \Delta\varphi = -arctan\left(\frac{(r_x - r_{x0})'}{(r_y - r_{y0})'}\right) \tag{17}$$

By substituting Equation (16), now with the known parameters of the exterior orientation, and due to the fact that the rotation of the CCD line corresponds to index i, given by Equation (17), the vertical pixel row j can now be estimated as follows:

$$(r_y - r_{y0})'' = \lambda \cdot f$$

$$(r_z - r_{z0})'' = \lambda \cdot j \cdot \delta$$

$$j \cdot \delta = \frac{(r_z - r_{z0})''}{(r_y - r_{y0})''} \cdot f \tag{18}$$

But any ray between a pixel and a 3D point in the LRF data set can be disturbed by obstacles in the scene, and a raytracing routine has to check whether the LRF point can be colored properly. Here it is useful that we use such an LRF and camera setup which allows to center both main points in such a way that we are able to map any LRF point or camera ray into the world coordinate system. Equations (1) and (5), now reduced by the term $\vec{r_0} + \mathbf{A}$, are combined in the following equation:

$$\vec{p} = \lambda \mathbf{A}_\varphi \mathbf{A}_O \left(\mathbf{A}_I \begin{pmatrix} 0 \\ 0 \\ j \cdot \delta \end{pmatrix} + \begin{pmatrix} \Delta_x \\ f + \Delta_y \\ \Delta_z \end{pmatrix}\right) \tag{19}$$

By applying all parameters of the interior orientations to the vector $\vec{r_d}$, the following simplified equation results. $\vec{r_d}$ now describes the viewing direction of each pixel like being on an ideal focal plane (see Equation (4)), and we obtain the following:

$$\vec{p} = \lambda \cdot \mathbf{A}_\varphi \cdot \vec{r_d} \tag{20}$$

Note that λ corresponds to the distance R of the LRF to the scanned point. $\mathbf{A}_\varphi$ contains the rotation angle φ and represents an image column i. The transformed vector represents the image row j and the number of the pixel in the CCD line. Therefore, each point in the LRF coordinate system has an assigned pixel value in the panoramic image. Figure 8 depicts an "open sphere" mapped into a rectangular image. Horizontal coordinates represent angle φ, and vertical coordinates represent the angle ϑ of the LRF coordinate system.

5. Visualization

We discuss a few aspects of visualizations, relevant to the generated data, and where we added new aspects or modified existing methods.

5.1. PROJECTION

Projections can be comfortably implemented with OpenGL, which is an interface which stores all transformations in different types of matrixes. All other important information can be saved in arrays (e.g., object coordinates, normal vectors, or texture coordinates). The rendering engine multiplies all matrices with a transformation matrix and transforms each object coordinate by multiplying the current transformation matrix with the vector of the object's coordinates. Different kinds of matrixes can be stored in stacks to manipulate different objects by different matrices. The main transformation matrix $\mathbf{M}_T$ is given as follows:

$$\mathbf{M}_T = \mathbf{M}_V \cdot \mathbf{M}_N \cdot \mathbf{M}_P \cdot \mathbf{M}_M \tag{21}$$

$\mathbf{M}_V$ is the view port matrix, which is the transformation to the final window coordinates. $\mathbf{M}_N$ is the normalization matrix of the device coordinates, $\mathbf{M}_P$ the projection matrix and $\mathbf{M}_M$ the matrix to transform model coordinates (e.g., a rotation, scaling, or translation).

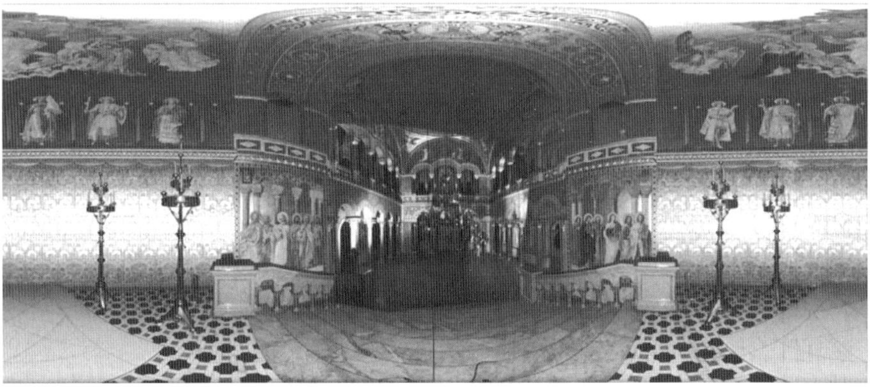

Figure 8. Panoramic image data have been fused in a subwindow near the center of the shown range image. (The figure shows the Thronsaal of castle Neuschwanstein.)

5.2. CENTRAL PROJECTION

Consider central projection of an object or scene on a perspective plane. The actual matrix for projection is the matrix

$$\mathbf{M}_p = \begin{pmatrix} \cot\frac{\theta}{2}\cdot\frac{h}{w} & 0 & 0 & 0 \\ 0 & \cot\frac{\theta}{2} & 0 & 0 \\ 0 & 0 & \frac{Z_F+Z_N}{Z_F-Z_N} & -\frac{2\cdot Z_F\cdot Z_N}{Z_F-Z_N} \\ 0 & 0 & -1 & 0 \end{pmatrix} \tag{22}$$

It results using the dependencies illustrated in Figure 9 and stated in Equation (22). In Figure (9), the clipping planes are drawn as *zFar* (we will use the symbol Z_F) and *zNear* (we use the symbol Z_N). The clipping planes can be seen as defining a bounding box which specifies the depth of the scene.

All matrices can be set in OpenGL comfortably by functions. Figure 10 depicts a 3D model rendered by central projection based on image data as shown in Figure 8. The figure shows the measured 3D points with measured (LRF) gray levels.

5.3. ORTHOGONAL PROJECTION

An orthogonal projection considers the projection of each point orthogonally to a specified plane. Figure 11 and Equation (23) illustrate and represent the dependencies. The matrix

$$\mathbf{M}_P = \begin{pmatrix} \frac{2}{R-L} & 0 & 0 & \frac{R+L}{R-L} \\ 0 & \frac{2}{T-B} & 0 & \frac{T+B}{T-B} \\ 0 & 0 & \frac{2}{F-N} & \frac{F+N}{F-N} \\ 0 & 0 & 0 & 1 \end{pmatrix} \tag{23}$$

is defined by the chosen values for F (far) and N (near), L (left) and R (right), and T and B.

A common demand is that high-resolution orthophotos (as the final product) are stored in an common file format independent from the resolution of the viewport of OpenGL. The first step is to determine the parameter (i.e., the altitude) of the orthoplane with respect to the 3D scene. A possible correction of the attitude can be included in this step (i.e., often a ceiling or a panel, the xy-plane, a wall, or the xz-plane is parallel to the chosen orthoplane in world coordinates). Equation (1), expanded by

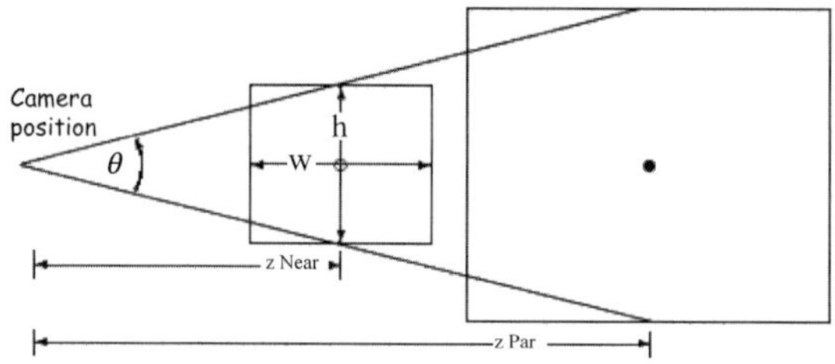

Figure 9. Central projection of objects in the range interval $[Z_N, Z_F]$ into a screen (or window) of size $w \times h$.

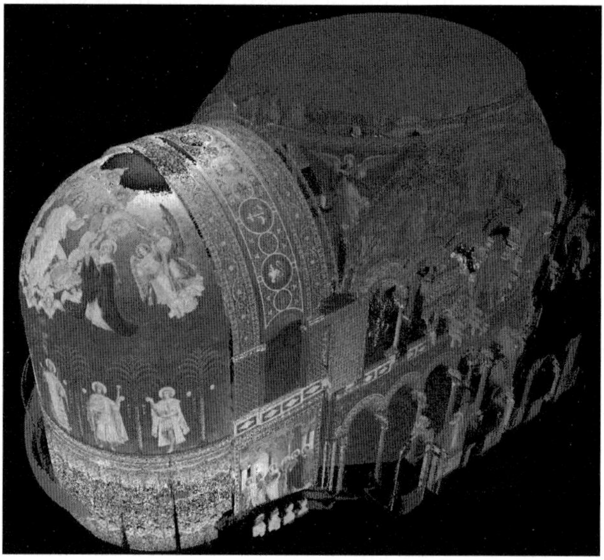

Figure 10. Central projection of the same hall as shown in Figure 8.

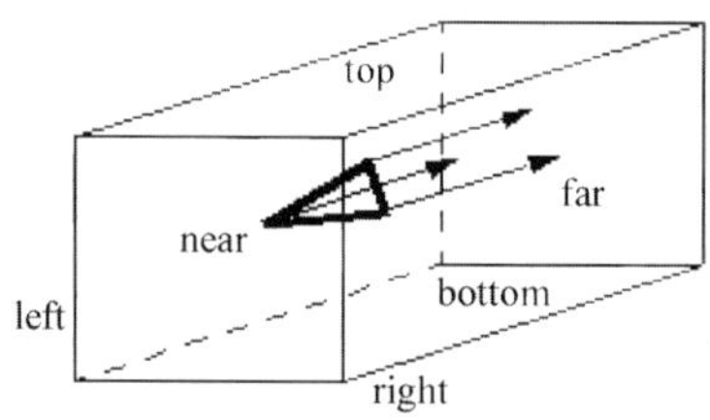

Figure 11. Orthogonal parallel projection: the screen (window) can be assumed at any intersection coplanar to the front (or back) side of the visualized cuboidal scene.

parameter $\mathbf{A}_{ortho}$ (i.e., the altitude of the orthoplane) and a factor t for the resolution, is shown in the following Equation 24. In this case we have that both systems are already fused into on joint image:

$$\vec{o} = t \cdot \mathbf{A}_{ortho} \cdot (\vec{r_0} + \mathbf{A} \cdot \vec{p}) \tag{24}$$

o_x and o_z specify a position in the orthoplane. If necessary then o_y can be used as the altitude in the orthosurface. A digital surface model (DSM) can be used to generate orthophotos from independent cameras Figures 12 and 13 illustrate spatial relations and a grey coded surface model, respectively.

5.4. STEREO PROJECTION

Model viewing can be modified by changing the matrix $\mathbf{M}_V$; this way the 3D object can rotate or translate in any direction. The camera view point also can be modified. It is possible to fly into the 3D scene, and to look around from a viewpoint within the scene. Furthermore, it is possible to render more than one viewpoint in the same rendering context, and to create (e.g., anaglyphic) stereo pairs this way. There are different methods for setting up a virtual camera, and for rendering stereo pairs. Actually, many methods are basically incorrect since they introduce an "artificial" vertical parallax. As an example, we cite the *toe-in method* (see Figure 14). Despite being incorrect it is still often in use because a correct asymmetric frustum method requires features not always supported by rendering packages (Bourke, 2004).

In the *toe-in* projection the camera has a fixed and symmetric aperture, and each camera is pointed at a single focal point. Images created using the *toe-in method* will still appear stereoscopic but the vertical parallax it

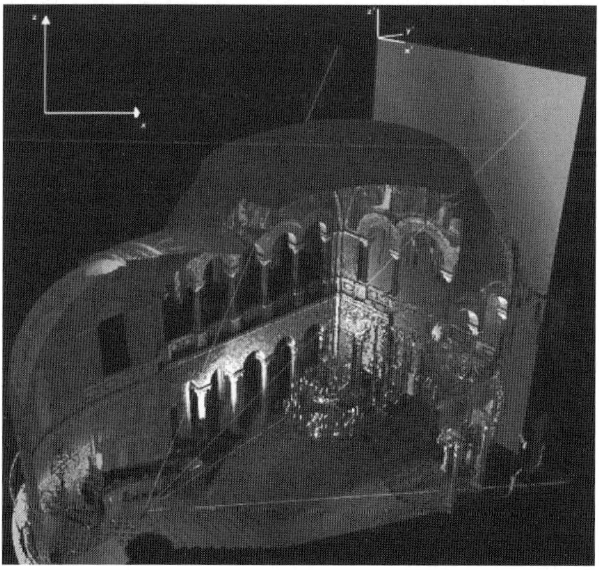

Figure 12. A defined ortho plane 'behind' the generated 3D data.

introduces will cause increased discomfort levels. The introduced vertical parallax increases with the distance to the center of the projection plane, and becomes more disturbing as the camera aperture increases.

The correct way to create stereo pairs is the *asymmetric frustum* method. It introduces no vertical parallax. It requires an asymmetric camera frustum, and this is supported by some rendering packages (e.g., by OpenGL).

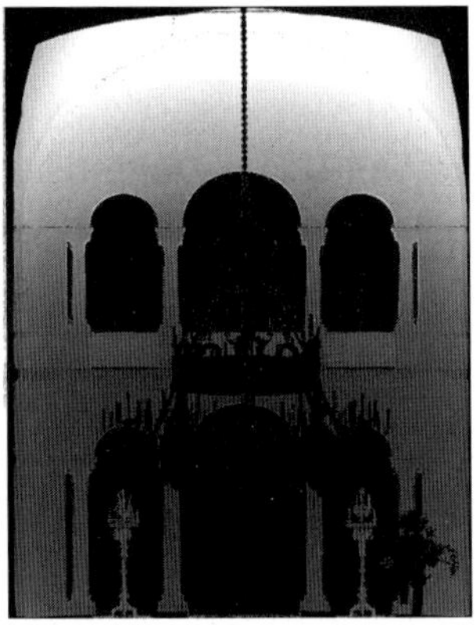

Figure 13. Gray-value encoded and orthogonally projected range data of those surface points which are in 2 meter distance to the defined (see Fig. 12) orthoplane.

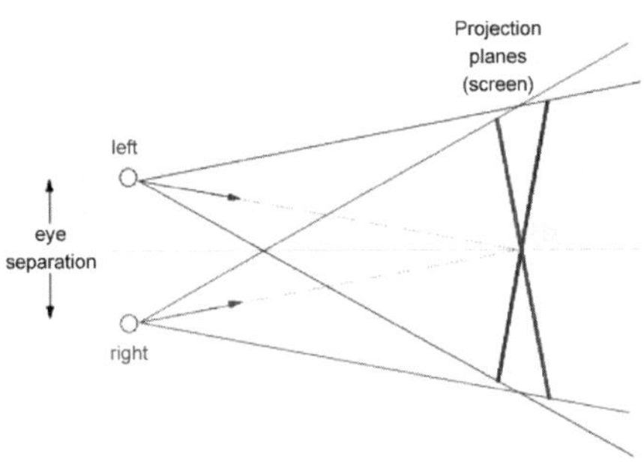

Figure 14. (Incorrect) toe-in stereo projection.

5.5. TRIANGULATION

Figure 10 shows the measured 3D points with (LRF) gray levels. High point density makes the point cloud look like a surface. (But the single points become visible when zooming in.) An other disadvantage of clouds of points is that modern graphic adapters with build-in 3D acceleration only support fast rendering of triangles or triangulated surfaces. Polygons are tessellated by the graphic adapter. These arguments show that it is necessary to triangulate clouds of points for appropriate viewing.

Initially, a dense triangular mesh is generated due to the high density of the available clouds of points (e.g., using the algorithm proposed by Bodenmueller (Bodenmueller and Hirzinger, 2001)). Originally, this approach was developed for online processing of unorganized data from hand-guided

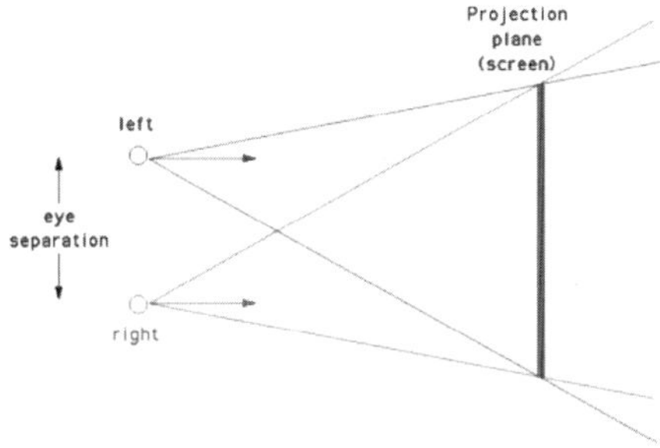

Figure 15. Correct stereo projection based on asymmetric camera frustums.

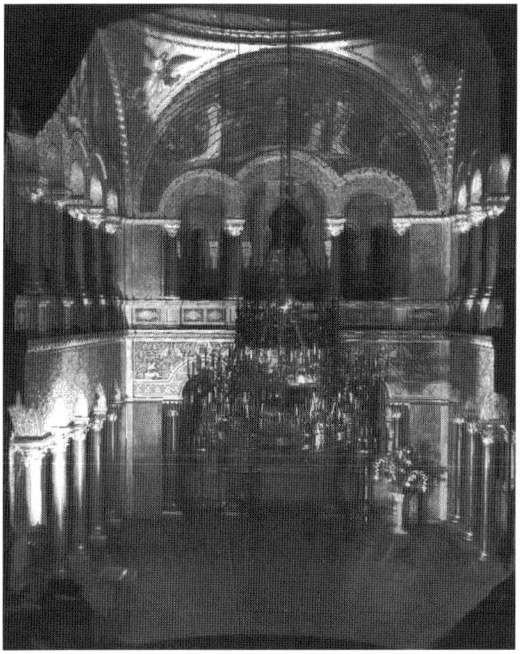

Figure 16. Correct stereo projection of the same hall as shown in Figure 8; the anaglyph uses red for the left eye.

scanner systems (tactile sensors). But the method is also suitable for the processing of laser scanner data because it uses a sparse, dynamic data structure which can hold larger data sets, and it is also able to generate a single mesh from multiple scans. The following work flow briefly lists the steps of triangulation:

- thinning of points (based on density check),
- normal approximation (local approximation of the surface),
- point addition (insert points, dependent on normals and density),
- estimation of Euclidean neighborhood relations,
- neighborhood projection to tangent planes (i.e., from 3D to 2D points), and
- calculation of Delaunay triangulations for those.

Another important relation is the connectivity (based on edge adjacency) of triangles, which is commonly used for defining strips of triangles, shadows, or to prepare meshing of points prior to triangulation. The following section describes a fast way to do connectivity analysis, which we designed for our purposes (i.e., dealing with extremely large sets of data).

5.6. CONNECTIVITY

Connectivity is defined as the transitive closure of edge adjacency between polygons. In "standard" computer graphics it is not necessary to improve provided algorithms for calculating connect components, because models have only a feasible number of polygons, given by static pre-calculations, mostly already given by an initialization of the object. Then it is straightforward to check every edge of an polygon against every other edges of all the other polygons (by proper subdivision of search spaces).

In our case we have many millions of polygons just for a single pair of one panoramic image and one LRF scan. The implementation of the common connectivity algorithm based on Gamasutra's article (Lee, 2004) lead to connected component detections with more than one hour for a one-viewpoint situation. Our idea for improving speed was to hash point indices to one edge index. Figure 17 illustrates this hashing of edges. Every edge has two indices n, m. Important is that (by sorting of indices) the first

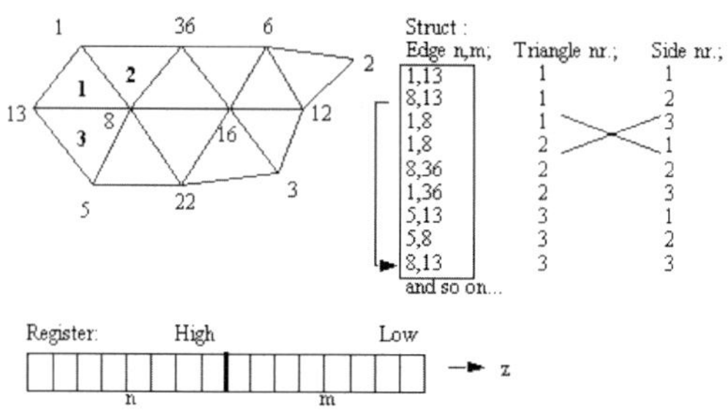

Figure 17. Fast connectivity calculation of triangles.

column represents the smaller index n; let m be the larger index. Every pair n, m has a unique address z by pushing the n value into the higher part of a register and m into the lower part. Now we can sort the first column of our structure by z. One loop is sufficient to identify all dependencies. If row i and row $i + 1$ have the same z value then the dependencies are directly given by the second and third column of our structure. Row three and four in Figure 17 must have the same z value, and connectivity can be identified in column two and three: triangle one, side three is connected to triangle two, side one. Using this algorithm we needed only about 10 seconds compared to the more than one hour before.

6. Concluding Remarks

This paper introduced an algorithm how to fuse laser scanning data and images captured by a rotating line camera. The coordinate systems of both sensors and the transformation of both data sets into one common reference system (world coordinate system) are described.

We also briefly discussed issues of the visualization of the data and different possibilities of projection. For a more realistic view some light effects and shadow calculations are needed, which will be reported in a forthcoming article. We also reported on a fast connectivity algorithm for achieving real-time analysis of very large sets of triangles.

There are several important subjects for future research: filtering of LRF data (e.g., along object edges), creation of sharp object edges based on analysis of color textures, avoidance of irregularities in LRF data due to surface material properties, detection of holes in created triangulated surfaces for further processing, adjusting color textures under conditions of inhomogeneous lighting, elimination of shadows from surface textures, and so forth. The size of the data sets defines an important aspect of the challenges; only efficient algorithms allow to follow calculations by subjective evaluation.

Acknowledgment

The authors thank Ralf Reulke for ongoing collaboration on the discussed subjects, and Bernd Strackenburg for supporting the experimental parts of the project.

References

Benosman, R. and S. B. Kang, editors: *Panoramic Vision: Sensors, Theory, and Applications*. Springer, Berlin, 2001.

Bodenmueller, T. and G. Hirzinger: Online surface reconstruction from unorganized 3d-points for the DLR hand-guided scannersystem. In Proc. *Eurographics*, pages 21-42, 2001.

Bourke, P.: http://astronomy.swin.edu.au/pbourke/stereographics/stereorender/(last visit: September 2004).

Crow, F. C.: Shadow algorithms for computer graphics, parts 1 and 2. In Proc. *SIGGRAPH*, Volume 11-2, pages 242–248 and 442–448, 1977.

Däumlich, F. and R. Steiger, editors: *Instrumentenkunde der Vermessungstechnik*. H. Wichmann, Heidelberg, 2002.

Huang, F., S. Wei, R. Klette, G. Gimel'farb, R. Reulke, M. Scheele, and K. Scheibe: Cylindrical panoramic cameras - from basic design to applications. In Proc. *Image and Vision Computing New Zealand*, pages 101–106, 2002.

Huang, F., S. Wei, and R. Klette: Calibration of line-based panoramic cameras. In Proc. *Image and Vision Computing New Zealand*, pages 107–112, 2002.

Kern, F.: Supplementing laserscanner geometric data with photogrammetric images for modelling. In Proc. *Int. Symposium CIPA*, pages 454–461, 2001.

Lee, A.: gamasutra.com/features/20000908/lee_01.htm (last visit: September 2004).

Niemeier, W.: Einsatz von Laserscannern für die Erfassung von Gebäudegeometrien. *Gebäudeinformationssysteme*, **19**: 155–168, 1995.

Klette, R., G. Gimel'farb, S. Wei, F. Huang, K. Scheibe, M. Scheele, A. Börner, and R. Reulke: On design and applications of cylindrical panoramas. In Proc. *Computer Analysis Images Patterns*, pages 1–8, LNCS 2756, Springer, Berlin, 2003.

Wiedemann, A.: Kombination von Laserscanner-Systemen und photogrammetrischen Methoden im Nahbereich. *Photogrammetrie Fernerkundung Geoinformation*, Heft 4, pages 261–270, 2001.

MULTI-PERSPECTIVE MOSAICS FOR INSPECTION AND VISUALIZATION

A. KOSCHAN, J.-C. NG and M. ABIDI
The Imaging, Robotics, and Intelligent Systems Laboratory
The University of Tennessee, Knoxville, 334 Ferris Hall
Knoxville, TN 37996-2100

Abstract. In this chapter, we address the topic of building multi-perspective mosaics of infra-red and color video data acquired by moving cameras under the constraints of small and large motion parallaxes. We distinguish between techniques for image sequences with small motion parallaxes and techniques for image sequences with large motion parallaxes and we describe techniques for building the mosaics for the purpose of under vehicle inspection and visualization of roadside sequences. For the under vehicle sequences, the goal is to create a large, high-resolution mosaic that may used to quickly inspect the entire scene shot by a camera making a single pass underneath the vehicle. The generated mosaics provide *efficient* and *complete* representations of video sequences.

Key words: mosaic, panorama, optical flow, phase correlation, infra-red

1. Introduction

In this chapter, we address the topic of building multi-perspective mosaics of infra-red and color video data acquired by moving cameras under the constraints of small and large motion parallaxes. We distinguish between techniques for image sequences with small motion parallaxes and techniques for image sequences with large motion parallaxes and we describe techniques for building the mosaics for the purpose of under vehicle inspection and visualization of roadside sequences. For the under vehicle sequences, the goal is to create a large, high-resolution mosaic that may used to quickly inspect the entire scene shot by a camera making a single pass underneath the vehicle. The generated mosaics provide *efficient* and *complete* representations of video sequences (Irani et al., 1996; Zheng, 2003). The concept is illustrated in Figure 1. Several constraints are placed on the video data in order to facilitate the assumption that the entire scene in the sequence

K. Daniilidis and R. Klette (eds.), Imaging Beyond the Pinhole Camera, 207–226.

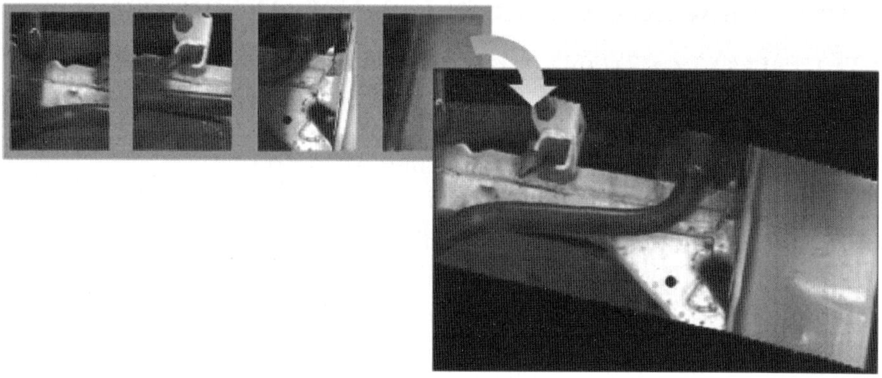

Figure 1. Mosaics as concise representations of video sequences.

exists on a single plane. Thus, a single mosaic is used to represent a single video sequence. Motion analysis is based on phase correlation in this case.

For roadside video sequences, it is assumed that the scene is composed of several planar layers, as opposed to a single plane. Layer extraction techniques are implemented in order to perform this decomposition. Instead of using phase correlation to perform motion analysis, the Lucas-Kanade motion tracking algorithm is used in order to create dense motion maps. Using these motion maps, spatial support for each layer is determined based on a pre-initialized layer model. By separating the pixels in the scene into motion-specific layers, it is possible to sample each element in the scene correctly while performing multi-perspective mosaic building. Moreover, this technique provides the ability to fill the many holes in the mosaic caused by occlusions, hence creating more complete representations of the objects of interest. The results are several mosaics with each mosaic representing a single planar layer of the scene.

2. Multi-perspective Mosaic Building

The term "multi-perspective mosaic" originates from the aim to create mosaics from sequences where the optical center of the camera moves; hence, the mosaic is created from camera views taken from multiple perspectives. This is opposed to panoramic mosaic building techniques, which aim to create mosaics traditionally taken from a panning, stationary camera. In other words, panoramic mosaic construction techniques create 360° surround views for stationary locations while the objective of multi-perspective mosaic building is to create very large high-resolution, billboard-like images from moving camera imagery. The paradigms associated with building multi-perspective mosaics, as described by Peleg and Herman (Peleg and

Herman, 1997), are straightforward. For a video sequence, the motion exhibited in the sequence must first be determined. Then, strips are sampled from each video frame in the sequence with the shape, width, and orientation of the strip chosen according to the motion in the sequence. These strips are then arranged together to form the multi-perspective mosaic.

For instance, for a camera translating sideways past a planar scene that is orthogonal to the principal axis of the camera, the dominant motion visible in the scene would be translational motion in the opposite direction of the camera's movement. A strip sampled from each frame in the sequence must be oriented perpendicular to the motion; therefore, in this case, the strip is vertically oriented. The width of a strip would be determined by the magnitude of the motion detected for the frame associated with that strip. The analysis of additional instrumentation data from GPS (global positioning system) and INS (inertial navigation system) can significantly simplify the alignment of images (Zhu et al., 1999). However, GPS and INS data are not always available and therefore, our mosaic building is exclusively based on video data.

2.1. CONSTRAINTS

Certain restrictions are placed on the movement of the camera to greatly simplify the mosaic construction process. Firstly, it is assumed that the camera is translated solely on a single plane that is parallel to the plane of the scene. Furthermore, it is assumed that the viewing plane of the camera is parallel to this plane of the scene and that the camera does not rotate about its principal axis. The collective effect of these constraints is that motion between frames is restricted to pure translational motion. An ideal video sequence would come from a camera moving in a constant direction while the camera's principal axis is kept orthogonal to the scene of interest. A camera placed on a mobile platform may be used for this purpose. The platform may then be moved in a straight line past the scene. If the scene is larger than the camera's vertical field of view, several straight line passes may be made to ensure the entire scene is captured. A single pass will produce one mosaic. Figure 2 illustrates a characteristic acquisition setup.

To accelerate mosaic construction, we suppose that the scene is roughly planar. This simplifies the processing to finding only one dominant motion vector between two adjacent frames, and using that motion as the basis for registration of the images. The assumption of a planar scene, of course, does not hold for most under vehicle scenes, as there will always be some parts under the vehicle closer to the camera than others. This situation results in a phenomenon called motion parallax: objects closer to the camera will move past the camera's field of view faster than objects in the background.

We assume, however, that these effects are negligible and will not adversely affect the goal of creating a summary of the under vehicle scene.

2.2. PERSPECTIVE DISTORTION CORRECTION

The purpose of perspective distortion correction is to make it appear as though the scene's motion is orthogonal to the principal axis of the camera. A similar procedure is employed by Zhu et al. (Zhu et al., 1999; Zhu et al., 2004) as an image rectification step. This procedure is required if the camera was viewing the scene of interest at an angle, for example, looking at a mirror. To perform perspective distortion correction, a projective warp is applied to each frame in the video sequence. Suppose we have a point in the original image $m_1 = (x_1 y_1 z_1)^t$, and a point in the corrected image $m_2 = (x_2 y_2 z_2)^t$. Perspective distortion correction is performed using

$$m_2 = VRm_1, \tag{1}$$

where

$$V = \begin{bmatrix} f & 0 & 0 \\ 0 & f & 0 \\ 0 & 0 & 1 \end{bmatrix} \tag{2}$$

and R, which is equal to

$$\begin{bmatrix} \cos\phi\cos\kappa & \sin\omega\sin\phi\cos\kappa + \cos\omega\sin\kappa & -\cos\omega\sin\phi\cos\kappa + \sin\omega\sin\kappa \\ -cos\phi\cos\kappa & -\sin\omega\sin\phi\sin\kappa + \cos\omega\cos\kappa & \cos\omega\sin\phi\sin\kappa + \sin\omega\cos\kappa \\ \sin\phi & -\sin\omega\cos\phi & \cos\omega\cos\phi \end{bmatrix},$$

are the scaling and 3D rotation matrices, with ω, ϕ, and κ being the pan, tilt, and rotation angles of the image plane and f is the focal length. The warp parameters are determined manually, using visual cues in the scene in question. If the angle at which the camera was viewing the scene is known, this could be translated into the warp parameters as well. Resampling of the images is done using nearest-neighbor interpolation.

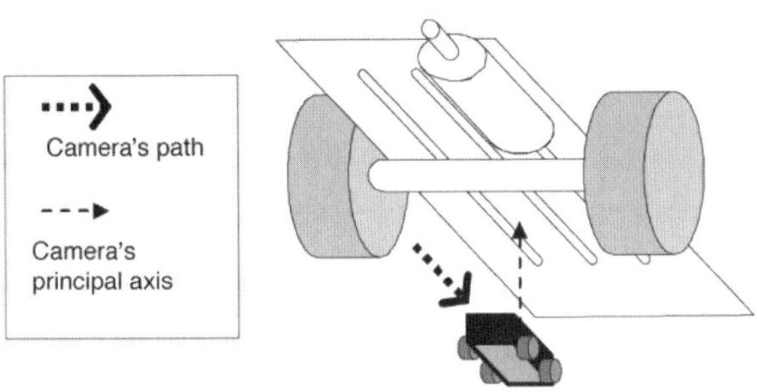

Figure 2. Video acquisition setup using a camera mounted on a mobile platform.

2.3. REGISTRATION USING PHASE CORRELATION

The registration step consists of computing the translational motion for each frame in the sequence. For any frame in the sequence, its motion vector is computed relative to the next frame the sequence. The motion vector (u, v) may consist of shifts in the horizontal (u) and vertical (v) directions. Due to motion parallax, there may be more than one motion vector present between two adjacent frames. Our aim is to compute, for a pair of adjacent frames, one dominant motion that may be used as the representative motion. Dominant motion is computed by adopting the phase correlation method described by Kuglin and Hines (Kuglin and Hines, 1975), since this technique is capable of extracting dominant inter-frame translation even in the presence of many smaller translations.

Phase correlation relies on the time shifting property of the Fourier transform. The Fourier transform of an image produces a spectrum of frequencies measuring the rate of change of intensity across the image. High frequencies correspond to sharp edges, low frequencies to gradual changes in intensity, such as lighting changes on large, angled planar surfaces. The spectrum $F(\xi, \eta)$ is a frequency-signature of the contents of the image. By correlating the spectra of two images, the lines along which they match can be established, and the translation between the two can be found.

According to the property of the Fourier transform, a translation within the image plane corresponds to an exponential factor in Fourier domain. Suppose we have two images, one being a translated version of the other, with a displacement vector (x_0, y_0). Given the Fourier transforms of the two images, F_1 and F_2, then the cross-power spectrum of these two images is defined as

$$\frac{F_1(\xi,\eta)F_2^*(\xi,\eta)}{F_1(\zeta,\eta)F_2(\xi,\eta)} = e^{j2\pi(\xi x_0+\eta y_0)}, \tag{3}$$

where F_2^* is the conjugate of F_2 and ξ and η are variables in the frequency domain corresponding to the displacement variables x, y in the spatial domain. The inverse Fourier transform of the cross-power spectrum, ideally, is zero everywhere except at the location of the impulse indicating the displacement (x_0, y_0) that corresponds to the translation motion between the two images.

The inverse Fourier transform of the cross-power spectrum is also referred to as the phase correlation surface. If there are several elements moving at different velocities in the picture, the phase correlation surface will produce more than one peak, with each peak corresponding to a motion vector. By isolating the peaks, a group of dominant motion vectors can be identified. This information does not specify individual pixel-vector relationships, but does provide information concerning motions in the frame as a whole. In our case, the strongest peak is selected as being representative of the dominant motion. One remarkable property of the phase correlation method is the accuracy of detecting the peak of the correlation function even with subpixel accuracy (Foroosh et al., 2002).

A simple extension to the phase correlation technique, proposed by Reddy and Chatterji (Reddy and Chatterji, 1996), allows for the rotation and scale changes between two images to be recovered as well. By remapping the Fourier transforms of two adjacent images to log-polar coordinates, and then performing phase correlation on the images of the remapped Fourier transforms, it is possible to recover the scale and rotation factors between those two images. Once the scale and rotation changes have been compensated for, then phase correlation can be performed again to recover the translation between those images. This extension may be useful if there is a large amount of zoom or directional change exhibited by a video sequence. Furthermore, background segmentation can be performed on the image to enhance the results (Hill and Vlachos, 2001).

Phase correlation may be affected by a phenomenon called *Discrete Fourier Transform leakage*, or DFT leakage. DFT leakage occurs in most Fourier transforms of real images, and is caused by the discontinuities between the opposing edges of the original image. In order to avoid DFT leakage, a mask based on the Hamming function is applied to each image prior to calculating its Fourier transform. The equation for the 1-dimensional Hamming function, which would provide the 1D weights of the tapering window, is

$$H(x) = 0.54 + 0.46 \cos\left(\frac{\pi x}{a}\right). \tag{4}$$

The resulting tapering window removes the discontinuities at the sides of the image while preserving a majority of the information towards the center of the images. In addition, we apply restrictions to the search region within the phase correlation surface, based on the motion we would expect in the video sequence. The search region parameters are determined by minimum and maximum values for the horizontal and vertical motion vectors, u_{min}, u_{max}, v_{min}, and v_{max}. These search region boundaries serve in reducing incorrect inter-frame motion estimates.

2.4. MERGING AND BLENDING

Once the horizontal and vertical motions between two images have been computed using phase correlation, strips are acquired from one of the images based on those motions. One of the motions will correspond to the direction in which the camera moved during acquisition; this is called the *primary motion*. The other motion, which may be due to the camera deviating from a straight path, or the camera's tilt, will be orthogonal to the primary motion and is called the *secondary motion*. The width of the strips is directly related to the primary motion. Adjacent strips on the mosaic are aligned using the secondary motion.

Although the strips may be properly aligned, seams may still be noticeable due to small motion parallax, rotation, or inconsistent lighting. A simple blending scheme is used in order to reduce the visual discontinuity caused by seams. Suppose in the mosaic D_m we have two strips sampled from two consecutive images, D_1 (the image on the left) and D_2 (the image on the right). The blending function is a one-dimensional function that is applied along a line orthogonal to the seam of the strips. For a coordinate i along this line, the intensity of its pixel in D_m is determined by

$$D_m\left(b-\frac{w}{2}+i\right) = \overbrace{\left(1-\frac{i}{w}\right)}^{A_1}\overbrace{D_1\left(c_1+\frac{w_1}{2}-\frac{w}{2}+i\right)}^{B_1} + \underbrace{\left(\frac{i}{w}\right)}_{A_2}\underbrace{D_2\left(c_2-\frac{w_1}{2}-\frac{w}{2}+i\right)}_{B_2},\quad \mathrm{i{=}1..w} \tag{5}$$

where c_1 and c_2 are the coordinates corresponding to the centers of D_1 and D_2, respectively, w_1 and w_2 are the widths of the strips sampled from D_1 and D_2,$w = min(w_1, w_2)$, and b is the mosaic coordinate corresponding to the boundary between the two strips. The terms A_1 and A_2 are weights for the pixel intensities for D_1 and D_2, while B_1 and B_2 are the pixel intensities themselves. For color images, this function is applied to the red, green, and blue component of the image. This simple blending technique has been chosen to accelerate the mosaic building process. Note that results of higher image fidelity may be obtained for the color image mosaic when applying (the more computationally costly) technique of Hasler and Süsstrunk (Hasler and Süsstrunk, 2004). However, their technique cannot be applied to the IR video sequence.

After the blending is complete, the two strips have been successfully merged. The process is then repeated for each subsequent frame in the video sequence. After each cycle of the merging process, the vertical and horizontal displacement of the last strip in the mosaic is recorded, and this information is used as the anchor for the next strip in the mosaic. Once every frame in the video sequence has been processed, the mosaic is complete.

2.5. EXPERIMENTAL RESULTS FOR UNDER VEHICLE INSPECTION

Two image modalities were used for the purpose of under vehicle inspection: color video (visible-spectrum) and infrared video. The color video sequences were taken using a Polaris Wp-300c Lipstick video camera mounted on a

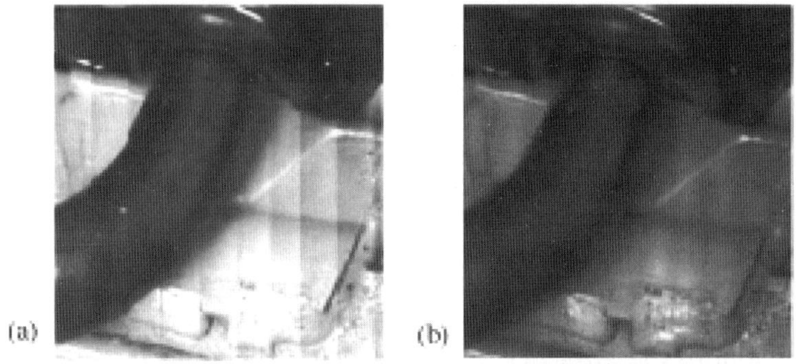

Figure 3. Results of mosaic building (a) without blending and (b) with blending

mobile platform. Infrared video was taken using a Raytheon PalmIR PRO thermal camera mounted on the same platform. The Lipstick camera has a focal length of 3.6mm, a 1/3" interline transfer CCD with 525-line interlace and 400-line horizontal resolution, while the Raytheon thermal camera has a minimum 25mm focal length. The tapering window parameter was set to $a = 146.286$ for both sequences and the search region parameters were set to $u_{min} = -30$, $u_{max} = 30$, $v_{min} = 170$, and $v_{max} = 0$

Here we present the results of our mosaic building algorithm for the visible-spectrum color video sequence UnderV4 (183 frames) and the infrared color video sequence IR1 (679 frames). The necessity of applying a blending technique to the stitched mosaic for creating visible appealing mosaics is shown by example in Figure 3. The figure shows the results of creating mosaics (a) without blending and (b) with blending. Note the reduced discontinuities at the seams separating each strip in the mosaic after blending.

Figures 4 and 5 show the results of constructing mosaics of the UnderV4 and IR1 video sequences. Figure 4(a) shows four sample frames from color video sequence UnderV4 which has been acquired with a camera pointing to the undercarriage of a Dodge Ram. One part of the constructed mosaic of sequence UnderV4 is shown in Figure 4(b). Figure 5(a) shows four sample frames from infra-red video sequence IR1 which has been acquired in the same manner as the color video sequence UnderV4 but with an infra-red camera.

From these results, it can be seen that our algorithm is capable of providing a good summary of these video sequences. There are still discontinuities visible in the mosaic due to motion parallax or absence of visual details that can be used to compute inter-frame motion (most noticeable in a large portion of the IR1 mosaic). Still, this algorithm performs well considering there are many parts of the IR1 sequence that display large homogenous areas. Local-motion analysis techniques such as the Lucas and

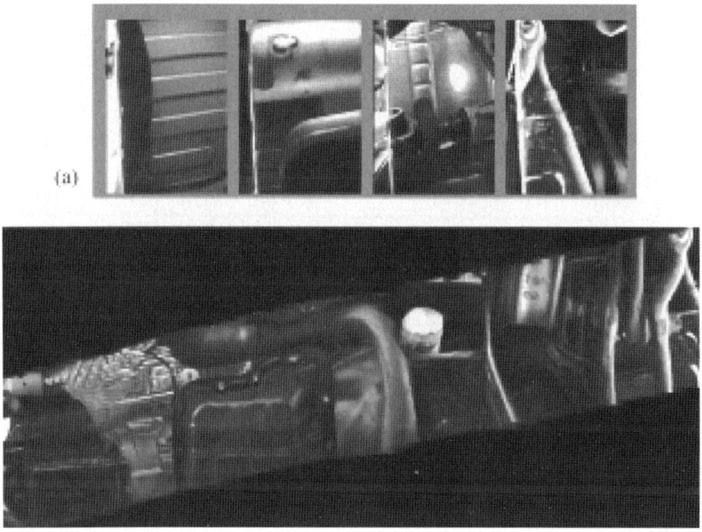

Figure 4. (a) Sample frames from sequence UnderV4 and (b) mosaic of sequence UnderV4

Kanade motion analysis algorithm (Lucas and Kanade, 1981) may have problems identifying good global motion vectors for these sequences.

3. Multi-Layer Mosaic Representation

The principles used to create single-mosaic representation are now extended to the process of creating multi-layered-mosaic representation (Peleg et al., 2000). For the single-mosaic representation, it was assumed that the scene exists entirely on a single plane parallel to the viewing plane. The extension to layered-mosaics representation is straightforward: it is now assumed that the scene is composed of several planar layers that are at varying distances from and parallel to the viewing plane. Suppose we have three points M_1, M_2, and M_3 on three planes of the scene P_1, P_2, and P_3 respectively (see Figure 6), and that these three points lie on a ground plane orthogonal to P_1, P_2, and P_3. The distance between the points m_1 and m_2 and the distance between their corresponding points m_1' and m_2' are not equal. This is caused by the disparity in the normal distance of the planes P_1 and P_2 from the viewing planes. In a video sequence, this is observed as motion parallax; objects in the foreground move past the camera's field of view faster than objects in the distance. Also, it is observed that there is no projection of the point M_3 on the viewing plane of C, due the occluding plane P_2.

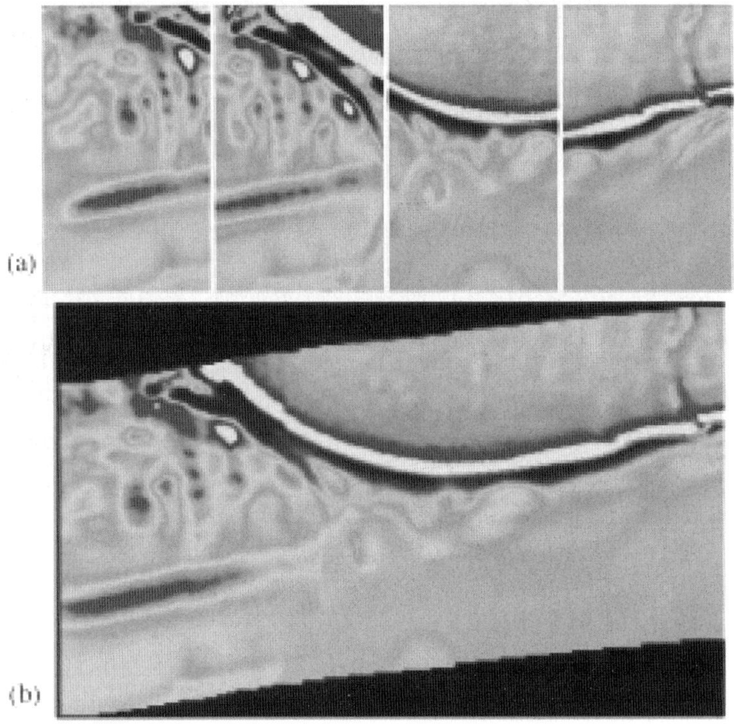

Figure 5. (a) Sample frames from infra-red video sequence IR1 which has been acquired with a camera pointing to the undercarriage of a Dodge Ram and (b) mosaic of IR1 sequence.

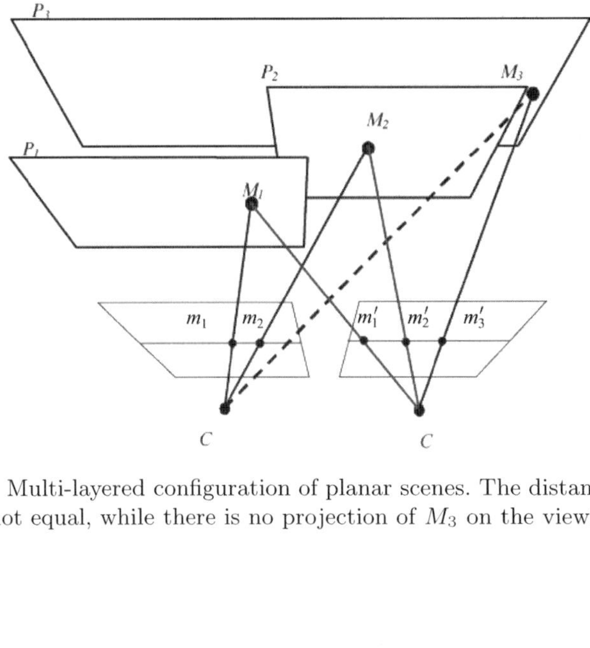

Figure 6. (a) Multi-layered configuration of planar scenes. The distances $m_1 - m_2$ and $m_1' - m_2'$ are not equal, while there is no projection of M_3 on the viewing plane of C at all.

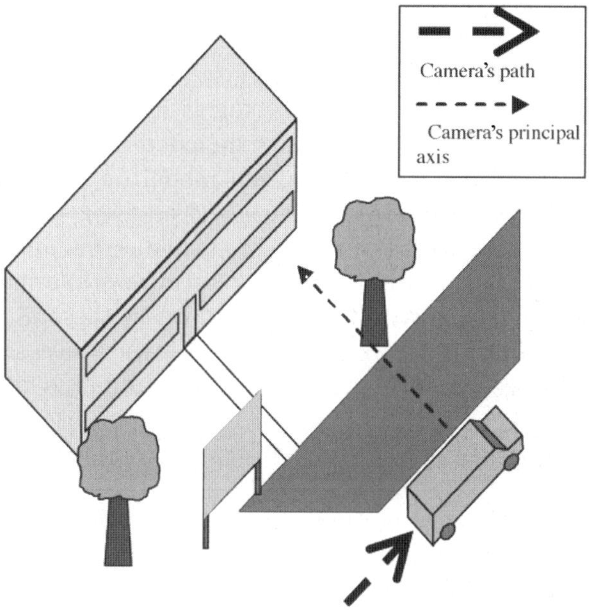

Figure 7. Video acquisition for outdoor/road scenes.

The disparity between the distances $m_1 - m_2$ and $m'_1 - m'_2$ is directly related to the disparity in the normal distances of P_1 and P_2 from the viewing planes. Therefore, assuming the scene and camera's movement constraints are met, the spatial support for each layer may be inferred by obtaining the translation velocities of pixels between consecutive frames. Pixels exhibiting the same translation are assigned to the same layer.

Video acquisition for the multi-layered mosaic representation requires that the camera, placed on a mobile platform, moves in a straight line past the scene while the camera is pointed towards the scene. For the sake of simplification we assume that the speed of the moving platform remains fairly constant throughout the entire acquisition process. Figure 7 illustrates a typical acquisition setup.

The mosaic construction process for the layered-mosaic representation is similar to the single-mosaic process for each individual layer mosaic. The differences are a) motion analysis is now performed using the Lucas-Kanade method and b) pixels are divided amongst the mosaics according to their velocities during the merging process. In addition to the mosaic building modules, model initialization for the layer representation is performed manually beforehand, and occluded sections of the mosaics are filled in using a mosaic composition module.

3.1. MULTI-LAYER MOSAIC CONSTRUCTION

For the layered-mosaic representation, registration is also performed using motion analysis, but this time using the Lucas-Kanade motion tracking algorithm. Spatial support for each layer is then determined using the motion analysis results, based on a pre-initialized model for layer representation. Image merging again consists of selecting and aligning strips on each individual mosaic. To deal with occlusions, multiple strips are obtained from different points in each frame and used to form multiple mosaics for each layer. It is possible to combine the spatial data in these multiple mosaics to fill in occluded areas in the final mosaics. A layer composition module is used to fill in the occluded areas and produce the final layered mosaics.

3.2. MOTION ANALYSIS USING THE LUCAS-KANADE METHOD

We apply a Lucas-Kanade motion tracking algorithm based on (Barron et al., 1994). This implementation performs a weighted least-squares fit of local first-order constraints to a constant model for the velocity, V, in each small spatial neighborhood (denoted by Ω) by minimizing

$$\sum_{x \in \Omega} W^2(x) \left[\nabla I(x,t) \cdot V + I_t(x,t) \right]^2 , \qquad (6)$$

where $W(x)$ is a window function that gives more influence to the constraints at the center of the window than to the ones at the periphery, x and t are spatial and time variables, and I and ∇I are the pixel intensity and pixel intensity gradient, respectively. In short, we find the velocity model that best describes the spatial and temporal intensity gradients for a given pixel.

Suppose for each pixel in an image frame, the velocity associated with that pixel is (u, v), which describes the horizontal and vertical velocity components. To compute these velocities, we need not only the current image frame, but the two image frames before and the two image frames after the current image frame in the sequence. The intensity gradients along the x-axis, y-axis, and along the five consecutive frames are ∇I_x, ∇I_y, and ∇I_t, respectively. We need to solve the linear system

$$\begin{bmatrix} \sum w \nabla I_x^2 & \sum w \nabla I_x \nabla I_y \\ \sum w \nabla I_x \nabla I_y & \sum w \nabla I_y^2 \end{bmatrix} \begin{bmatrix} u \\ v \end{bmatrix} = - \begin{bmatrix} \sum w I_x I_t \\ \sum w I_y I_t \end{bmatrix}, \qquad (7)$$

which is a solution derived from Equation (6). Before the gradients are calculated, spatial smoothing is performed by averaging the pixel values in an eight-neighborhood. Moreover, temporal smoothing is computed using a Gaussian mask convolved with the intensities of the current pixel and its corresponding pixels in the last six frames. Once spatiotemporal smoothing is complete, the intensity gradients ∇I_x, ∇I_y, and ∇I_t are calculated for each pixel in the current image frame. After the smoothed gradients have been obtained, they are used to solve for u and v in Equation (8). Once these have been calculated for each pixel in the image, the result is a flow field with velocity information for each pixel in the image.

So far, we have described the Lucas-Kanade motion analysis algorithm with respect to I, the pixel intensity only. However, we are using color images, defined by the three R, G, and B channels. The Lucas-Kanade algorithm is applied to all three channels separately. Different velocity measurements may be obtained for each channel. We pick the highest velocity estimate among the three as the correct estimate, with the reasoning that intensity changes due to motion may be less apparent in one or two channels, but if there is actual intensity change due to motion, at least one of the channels will exhibit a sharp change, resulting in a high velocity estimate. However, in general there are no significant differences in the results for the R, G, and B channels (Barron and Klette, 2002).

3.3. MODEL INITIALIZATION AND SPATIAL SUPPORT DETERMINATION

Layer extraction is split into two distinct processes: model initialization and spatial support determination. Both processes are based on a) the number of layers in the scene, and b) the velocities associated with each layer. All layers are assumed to follow the same motion model, which is purely translational motion of a rigid plane. Therefore, it is not required to specify separate motion models for each layer. Here, determination of the model initialization parameters is performed manually by the user. The video sequence is observed to choose a number of layers that would adequately represent the scene. An estimate of the inter-frame motion for each layer is also obtained through observation of the video, and these estimates are used as the layer velocities. For a layer P_n, a velocity (u_n, v_n) is associated with it, with the component representing secondary motion. Model initialization using two frames as a reference is illustrated in Figure 8.

The layer representation model may be initialized at any point before spatial support is determined. In this work, model initialization was performed before any other processing of the video frames. Once motion analysis of the frames has been performed, as described above, we may determine spatial support for each layer. For a pixel in a given image, the Euclidean distance between its motion vector, (x, y), in 2D space and each of the layer-assigned motion vectors $(u_0, v_0...u_N, v_N)$, with N being the number of layers, is calculated. The shortest distance found indicates

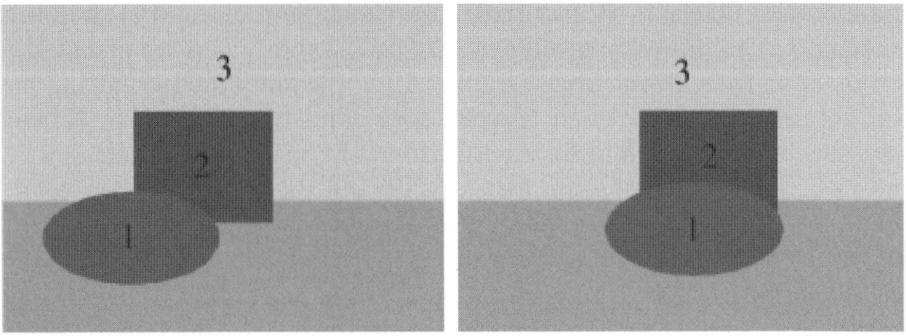

Figure 8. Model initialization of layers. Two mock video frames, (a) and (b), are used as a visual reference to perform model initialization. In this scene, a natural choice would be to designate separate layers to the plane of the object labeled 1, the object as labeled 2, and the background labeled as 3. The surface on which objects 1 and 2 lie on will most likely display non-translational affine motion, or, if the entire surface is homogenous, no apparent motion at all. No layer is initialized to represent this surface.

the layer that pixel is assigned to. In this manner, each frame is segmented according to the spatial support for each layer. This is repeated until each frame in the video sequence has been processed.

Note that we do not update the layer model after it has been initialized, and recall that one of the constraints placed on the camera movement was that the speed of the camera must remain fairly constant throughout the entire sequence. Because we do not update the layer model or any of the motion vectors associated with each layer during the spatial support determination process, the speed of the camera should not vary greatly, so that each layer displays the same motion properties throughout the entire sequence. If the motion of the camera varies throughout the sequence, the algorithm will lose track of many of the initialized layers, which will result in incorrect layer assignments during the spatial support determination process.

In a given frame, the collection of pixels assigned as belonging to a layer is henceforth referred to as that layer's *support region* within that frame. Motion analysis has provided an estimate for each layer's support region in each frame in the video sequence. However, there may still be noticeable errors present in these support regions, due to inaccurate motion estimates. For layers whose velocities are relatively low, these errors tend to be small or nonexistent. Layers with higher velocities, however, tend to have large gaps in their support regions, where pixels have been assigned incorrectly to other layers. In order to reduce these incorrect assignments in a given frame, dilation and erosion operations are performed in that order to form a closing operator on each layer's support region. Once the morphological operations have been applied to each frame in the video sequence, the process of determining spatial support for each layer is complete. This information may now be used to form the layered mosaics.

3.4. COMPOSITION OF MULTI-LAYERED MOSAICS

The challenge of representing partially occluded background elements in their entirety is dealt with using a layer composition method. To explain how this is done, we discuss the composition of a mosaic for a given planar layer, P_n, with partial occlusion. Again, strips are sampled from each frame from the video sequence, as was done for the single-mosaic representation. This time, however, there is no longer one global motion associated which each frame. Instead, each frame has been segmented according to the spatial support determination for each layer. So for a layer P_n, only those pixels that have been assigned to P_n, using the spatial support determination algorithm, are referenced. For a given image frame, we wish to determine (x_0, y_0), the primary and secondary motions, which will determine the width and alignment of the strip. For each pixel assigned to P_n, the vector computed for that pixel is (x, y). To find (x_0, y_0), the average value of (x, y) for all pixels assigned to P_n are calculated. Hence,

$$\begin{aligned} x_0 &= \frac{1}{m}\sum x,\ x \in P_n \text{ and} \\ y_0 &= \frac{1}{m}\sum y,\ y \in P_n, \end{aligned}$$

where m is the number of pixels in the given frame assigned to P_n. Strips are sampled from the frame according to (x_0, y_0), again with the width of the strip corresponding to the width of the primary motion. As it was in the single-mosaic representation, images are oriented so that the primary motion corresponds to y_0, and images are rotated accordingly if needed prior to processing. Only the intensity information of pixels belonging to the layer P_n is retrieved, while information from pixels belonging to other layers is ignored. This will result in mosaics that have 'gaps' where there were occluding or background elements that did not belong to the layer P_n. Figure 9 illustrates this process.

The discussion of strip sampling above does not address one possible scenario: what if, for a particular layer, there are parts of the sequence that do not clearly exhibit the motion associated with that layer? In other words, layers containing disparate elements such as signboards and trees may not have elements representative of its motion at some point in the sequence. However, we still need strips to build the mosaic representing this layer, or the distances between these elements within a mosaic of that layer would be inaccurate. Currently, in this work, we do not attempt to accurately determine this distance, but instead use the most recently computed value

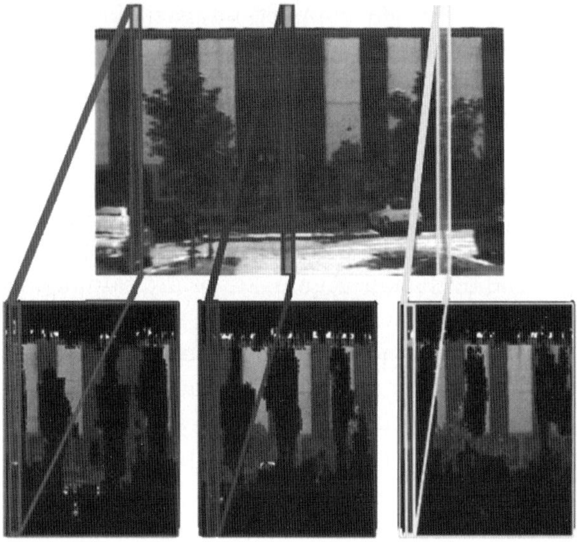

Figure 9. Creation of a reference mosaic and peripheral mosaics by sampling strips from different points in a frame.

of (x_0, y_0) for that layer if there are no vectors associated to a layer with which to compute (x_0, y_0). As it happens, in our current implementation, there is never an occasion when there are no vectors associated with a particular layer, since all vectors are assigned based on minimum distance to the layer vectors, not distance within a threshold.

In order to acquire a more complete representation of elements in the layer P_n, we create more than one mosaic of that layer. Each mosaic is created from strips sampled at different points in each frame. These strips are spaced apart evenly, and the pixel-wise distances of each strip from one another are known. Therefore, for P_n, we now have several mosaics M_1, M_2... M_k, where k is the number of mosaics that will be used in order to compose P_n. One of these mosaics, typically the mosaic composed from strips sampled closest to the center of each frame, (usually $M_{k/2}$) is used as a reference mosaic for composing P_n. The rest of the mosaics, because they are formed from strips sampled from either side of the center strip of each image frame, are referred to here as peripheral mosaics. Three parameters are used to determine how the strips for the peripheral and reference mosaics are sampled. The first parameter is k, the number of mosaics used to compose the layer. The other parameter is $dist$, the pixel-wise distance between the corresponding edges of the strips. The strips are always sampled with the reference strip close to the center of the image.

Given the horizontal dimension of an image frame, width, the horizontal position of the edge of the first strip, y_a, is determined by

$$y_a = \frac{width - ((k-1)\, dist)}{2}, \tag{8}$$

after which consecutive strips are sampled at intervals of *dist* pixels. After the reference and peripheral mosaics have been created, there will still be noticeable 'noise' in the resulting mosaics, where local incorrect assignments of pixels will produce inconsistencies in the layers. To reduce these inconsistencies, we perform a simple morphological closing operation on each mosaic. This time, however, the operation is performed on the *null* regions of each mosaic, i.e. the regions that were assigned as *not* belonging to that layer. The resulting, noise reduced mosaics are then used to perform the actual composition of the layer mosaic.

Now, since *dist*, the pixel-wise distance separating the strips sampled from each frame, is known, it is also known how the peripheral mosaics spatially correspond to the reference mosaic. This knowledge is used to fill in the 'gaps' in the reference mosaic, by equationing pixel intensity information from the peripheral mosaics that were created. First, the peripheral mosaics are ordered by the pixel-wise distance of their strips from the strips of the reference mosaic, from the smallest distance to the largest distance. Since the strips were sampled at equal distances apart, there will be two mosaics created from strips at the same pixel-wise distance from the reference strip; it does not matter which mosaic comes first in this order.

Then, starting with the first peripheral mosaic, its pixel information is used to fill in the gaps of our reference mosaic. In most cases, the gaps in this mosaic will overlap with the gaps in our reference mosaic, so once all available pixel information has been obtained, the process is repeated for the next peripheral mosaic, and so on until all available pixel information from all the peripheral mosaics have been referenced. If the occlusions were not too large, and a sufficient number of mosaics were used, then the reference mosaic should now have all its gaps filled, making it a complete representation of our object of interest. Figure 10 illustrates this process.

The video sequences used in this work were captured using a Sony DCR-TRV730 Digital 8 Camcorder, which uses a 1/4" 1.07 mega pixel color CCD. Figure 11 shows five frames of the BBHall scene and one of the mosaics resulting from multi-layer composition of the video sequence.

4. Summary and Conclusion

In one aspect, we have loosened the constraints placed on the data in the multi-layer representation, as opposed to the restrictions placed on the data of the single-mosaic representation: we no longer require that motion

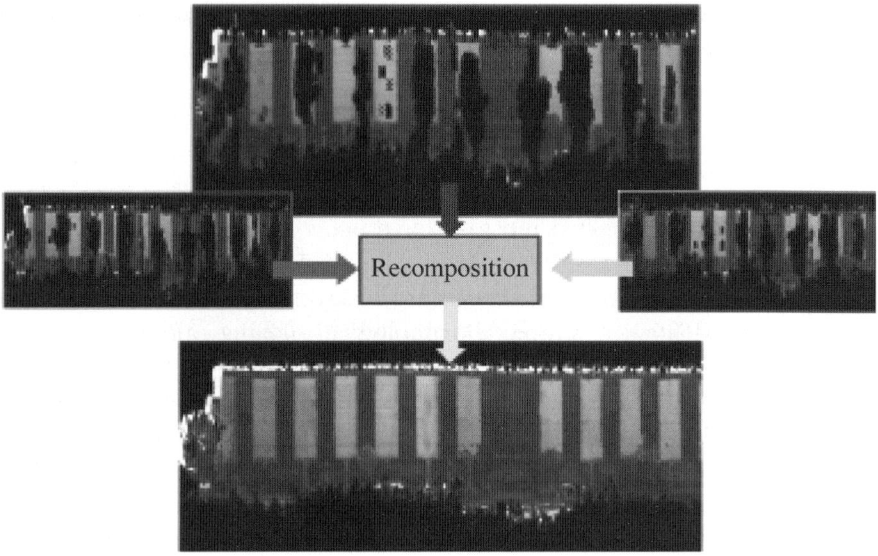

Figure 10. Recomposing the reference mosaic using pixel data from the peripheral mosaics.

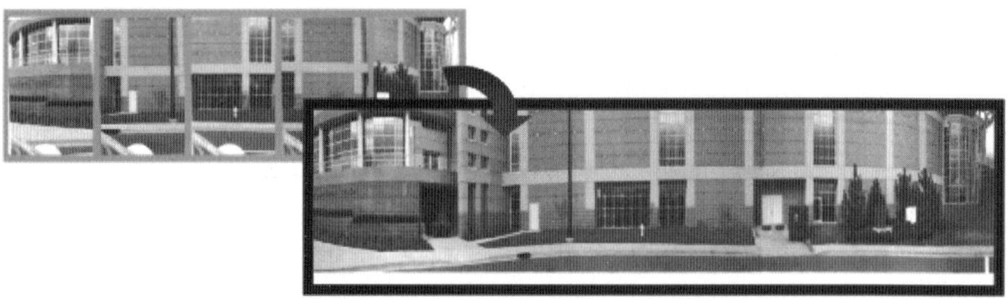

Figure 11. Five original frames of the BBHall scene and one of the mosaics resulting from multi-layer composition of the video sequence.

parallax in the scene be small. However, we have placed a constraint on the data for this algorithm that was not present before, which is the constraint that the speed of the moving platform does not vary greatly throughout the video sequence. Zhu's 3D LAMP representation (Zhu and Hanson, 2001) places a similar constraint on the data for their algorithm. The reason in both cases is the same: to simplify the tracking of layers throughout the entire sequence. If the speed of the platform were to vary greatly throughout the sequence, a more advanced feature tracking algorithm would have to implemented, as opposed to the straightforward motion analysis performed here, in conjunction with some framework for updating the motion models for each layer. As it stands, we have not addressed this problem yet in our implementation.

One question that may arise is, why do we not use the layered-mosaics representation to process the under vehicle data, and therefore have just one unified method of dealing with both cases? The short answer is that it is possible to use the layered-mosaics representation to process the under vehicle data, but because of the nature of that data and the purpose of those mosaics, it is not efficient to do so. We do not require a layered representation of the underside of a vehicle because there are very few occlusions that can be removed to any meaningful degree, because motion parallax in the sequences is small. We only require a single overview of the scene for inspection purposes, and any objects hidden behind large under vehicle components cannot be detected in the visible spectrum. Also, creating a single mosaic between frames is much faster than attempting to compute spatial support from several layers. If we wish to extend the system to real time use in order to inspect several vehicles, say, in a parking lot, then the speed of the algorithm becomes an issue.

On the other hand, why aren't we applying the registration methods developed for the single-mosaic representation to the layered-mosaics representation? The largest difference between the two techniques lies in the registration method: phase correlation only gives us global motion estimates, whereas the Lucas-Kanade algorithm gives us local motion estimates. With phase correlation, we cannot directly infer layer assignments; some additional processing steps, including perhaps a block-based matching algorithm, are required to acquire layer assignments. Lucas-Kanade gives us layer assignment estimates right from the beginning, and the only challenge left is to refine those estimates.

In summary, we have presented the efforts made to combine and implement several paradigms and techniques used in building digital image mosaics and layer extraction to support the tasks of inspection and scene visualization. Two closely related solutions were tailored to the specific needs for which the data was acquired. For the under vehicle inspection effort, a single-mosaic representation was devised to ease the process of inspection, and for the outdoor roadside scanning effort, a layered-mosaics representation was devised to remove occlusions from objects of interest and recreate elements in the presence of motion parallax. Given that many of the image sequences used here often display large homogenous areas with little visual detail, the phase correlation method is demonstrated to be a fairly robust registration method. Future research and development will address the fine tuning of this system.

Acknowledgements

This work is supported by the University Research Program in Robotics under grant DOE-DE-FG02-86NE37968, by the US Army under grant Army-W56HC2V-04-C-0044, and by the DOD/RDECOM/NAC/ARC Program, R01-1344-18.

References

Barron, J., Fleet, D., and Beauchemin, S.: Performance of optical flow techniques. *Int. J. Computer Vision*, **12**: 43–77, 1994.

Barron, J. and Klette, R.: Quantitative color optical flow. In Proc. *Int. Conf. Pattern Recognition*, Volume IV, pages 251–255, 2002.

Foroosh, H., Zerubia, J., and Berthod, M.: Extension of phase correlation to sub-pixel registration. *IEEE Trans. Image Processing*, **11**: 188–200, 2002.

Hasler, D. and Süsstrunk, S.: Mapping colour in image stitching applications. *J. Visual Communication and Image Representation*, **15**: 65–90, 2004.

Hill, L. and Vlachos, T.: Motion measurement using shape adaptive phase correlation. *IEEE Electronics Letters*, **37**: 1512–1513, 2001.

Irani, M., Anandan, P., Bergen, J., Kumar, R., and Hsu, S.: Efficient representations of video sequences and their applications. *Signal Processing: Image Communication*, **8**: 327–351, 1996.

Kuglin, C. D. and Hines, D. C.: The phase correlation image alignment method. In Proc. *Int. Conf. on Cybernetics and Society*, Volume IV, pages 163–165, 1975.

Lucas, B. and Kanade, T.: An iterative image registration technique with an application to stereo vision. In Proc. *Int. Joint Conf. on Artificial Intelligence*, pages 674–679, 1981.

Peleg, S. and Herman, J.: Panoramic mosaics by manifold projection. In Proc. *Int. Conf. Computer Vision Pattern Recognition*, pages 338–343, 1997.

Peleg, S., Rousso, B., Rav-Acha, A., and Zomet, A.: Mosaicking on adaptive manifolds. *IEEE Trans. Pattern Analysis Machine Intelligence*, **22**: 1144–1154, 2000.

Reddy, B. S. and Chatterji, B. N.: An FFT-based technique for translation, rotation, and scale-invariant image registration. *IEEE Trans. Image Processing*, **5**: 1266–1271, 1996.

Zheng, J. Y.: Digital route panoramas. *IEEE Multimedia*, **10**: 57–67, 2003.

Zhu, Z. and Hanson, A. R.: 3D LAMP: a new layered panoramic representation. In Proc. *Int. Conf. Computer Vision*, Volume 2, pages 723–730, 2001.

Zhu, Z., Hanson, A. R., Schultz, H., Stolle, F., and Riseman, E. M.: Stereo mosaics from a moving camera for environmental monitoring. In Proc. *Int. Workshop on Digital and Computational Video*, pages 45–54, 1999.

Zhu, Z., Riseman, E. M., and Hanson, A. R.: Generalized parallel-perspective stereo mosaics from airborne videos. *IEEE Trans. Pattern Analysis Machine Intelligence*, **26**: 226–237, 2004.

Part IV

Navigation

EXPLOITING PANORAMIC VISION FOR BEARING-ONLY ROBOT HOMING

KOSTAS E. BEKRIS
Computer Science Department, Rice University,
Houston, TX, 77005, USA

ANTONIS A. ARGYROS
Institute of Computer Science, Foundation for Research and Technology - Hellas (FORTH),
Heraklion, Crete, Greece

LYDIA E. KAVRAKI
Computer Science Department, Rice University,
Houston, TX, 77005, USA

Abstract. Omni-directional vision allows for the development of techniques for mobile robot navigation that have minimum perceptual requirements. In this work, we focus on robot navigation algorithms that do not require range information or metric maps of the environment. More specifically, we present a homing strategy that enables a robot to return to its home position after executing a long path. The proposed strategy relies on measuring the angle between pairs of features extracted from panoramic images, which can be achieved accurately and robustly. In the heart of the proposed homing strategy lies a novel, local control law that enables a robot to reach any position on the plane by exploiting the bearings of at least three landmarks of unknown position, without making assumptions regarding the robot's orientation and without making use of a compass. This control law is the result of the unification of two other local control laws which guide the robot by monitoring the bearing of landmarks and which are able to reach complementary sets of goal positions on the plane. Long-range homing is then realized through the systematic application of the unified control law between automatically extracted milestone positions connecting the robot's current position to the home position. Experimental results, conducted both in a simulated environment and on a robotic platform equipped with a panoramic camera validate the employed local control laws as well as the overall homing strategy. Moreover, they show that panoramic vision can assist in simplifying the perceptual processes required to support robust and accurate homing behaviors.

Key words: panoramic vision, robot homing, bearing

K. Daniilidis and R. Klette (eds.), Imaging Beyond the Pinhole Camera, 229–251.

1. Introduction

Vision-based robot navigation is an important application of computer vision techniques and tools. Many approaches to this problem either assume the existence of a geometric model of the environment (Kosaka and Pan, 1995) or the capability of constructing an environmental map (Davison and Murray, 2002). In this context, the problem of navigation is reduced to the problem of reconstructing the workspace, computing the robot's pose therein and planning the motion of the robot between desired positions. Probabilistic methods (Thrun, 2000) have been developed in robotics that deal with this problem, which is usually referred to as the simultaneous localization and mapping (SLAM) problem.

Catadioptric sensors have been proposed as suitable sensors for robot navigation. A panoramic field of view is advantageous for the achievement of robotic navigational tasks in the same way that a wide field of view facilitates the navigational tasks of various biological organisms such as insects and arthropods (Srinivasan et al., 1997). Many robotic systems that use panoramic cameras employ a methodology similar to the one employed in conventional camera systems. Adorni et al. discuss stereo omnidirectional vision and its advantages for robot navigation (Adorni et al., 2003). Correlation techniques have been used to find the most similar prestored panoramic image to the current one (Aihara et al., 1998). Winters et al. (Winters et al., 2000) qualitatively localize the robot from panoramic data and employ visual path following along a pre-specified trajectory in image coordinates.

Panoramic cameras, however, offer the possibility of supporting navigational tasks without requiring range estimation or a localization approach in the strict sense. Methods that rely on primitive perceptual information regarding the environment are of great importance to robot navigation because they pose minimal requirements on a-priori knowledge regarding the environment, on careful system calibration and, therefore, have better chances to result in efficient and robust robot behaviors. This category includes robot navigation techniques that mainly exploit angular information on image-based features that constitute visual landmarks. Several such methods exist for addressing a specific navigation problem, the problem of homing (Hong et al., 1991). Homing amounts to computing a path that returns a robot to a pre-visited "home" position (see Figure 1). One of the first biologically-inspired methods for visual homing was based on the "snapshot model" (Cartwright and Collett, 1983). A snapshot represents a sequence of landmarks labeled by their compass bearing as seen from a position in the environment. According to this model, the robot knows the difference in pose between the start and the goal and uses this information

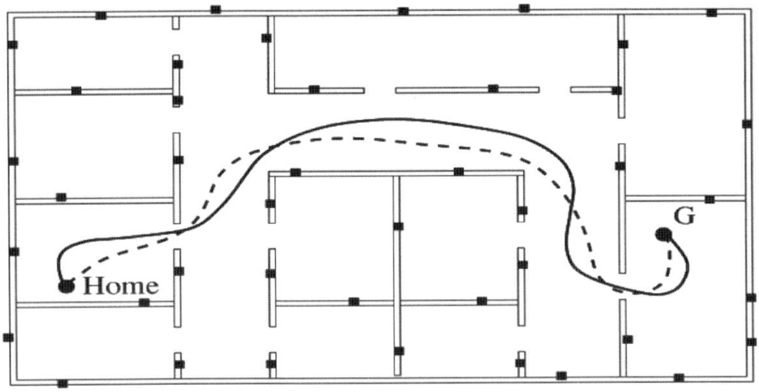

Figure 1. The robot acquires a snapshot of the environment at home position. Then, it wanders in its environment (solid line) and, at some position G homing is initiated so as to return to home (dashed line) by making use of the landmarks available in the workspace (small black rectangles).

to match the landmarks between the two snapshots and to compute its path. There have been several implementations of snapshot-based techniques on real mobile robots. Some of the implemented methods rely on the assumption that the robot has constant orientation or can make use of a compass (Lambrinos et al., 2000; Moller, 2000). These approaches are not able to support robot homing for any combination of goal (home) snapshot, current position and landmark configuration. Furthermore, the conditions under which the related control laws are successful are not straightforward and cannot be directly inferred from the visual information available at the current and the goal snapshots.

In this work, we present a complete long-range homing strategy for a robot equipped with a panoramic camera. The robot does not have to be aware of its position and orientation and does not have to reconstruct the scene. At the core of the proposed strategy lies a snapshot-based local control law (Argyros et al., 2001), which was later further studied and extended (Bekris et al., 2004). The advantage of this particular local control law is that it can guide a robot between two positions provided that three landmarks can be extracted and corresponded in the panoramas acquired at these two positions. This implies that there is no inherent control-related issue that restricts the set of position pairs that the algorithm can accommodate. Constraints are only related to difficulties in corresponding features in images acquired from different viewpoints.

Establishing feature correspondences in images acquired from adjacent viewpoints is a relatively easy problem. Thus, short-range homing (i.e., homing that starts at a position close to home) can be achieved by directly applying the proposed local control law as it is described in (Argyros et al., 2005). In the case of long-range homing (i.e., homing that starts at a position far from home), prominent features are greatly displaced and/or occluded, and the correspondence problem becomes much more difficult to solve (Lourakis et al., 2003). Therefore, control laws based on the comparison of two snapshot are only local in nature and they cannot support long-range homing. To overcome this problem, the proposed method decomposes homing into a series of simpler navigational tasks, each of which can be implemented based on the proposed local control law. More precisely, long-range homing is achieved by automatically decomposing the path between the current robot position and the home position with the aid of a set of milestone positions. The selection process guarantees that pairs of milestone positions view at least three common landmarks. The local control law can then be used to move the robot between consecutive milestone positions. The overall mechanism leads the robot to the home position through the sequential application of the control law. Note that using only the basic control law to move between adjacent milestone positions leads to a more conservative selection of such intermediate goals. With the introduction of the complementary control law (Bekris et al., 2004) and its unification with the basic one, the only constraints on the selection of the milestone positions are due to landmark visibility.

The proposed method for robot homing has been implemented and extensively tested on a robotic platform equipped with a panoramic camera in a real indoor office environment. Different kinds of visual features have been employed and tested as alternative landmarks to the proposed homing strategy. In all experiments the home position could be achieved with high accuracy after a long journey during which the robot performed complex maneuvers. There was no modification of the environment in order to facilitate the robot's homing task. The proposed method can efficiently achieve homing as long as enough features exist in the world. Homing will fail only if three robust features cannot be extracted and tracked at any time.

Our approach of robot navigation is similar to that of purposive vision (Aloimonos, 1993). We use information specific to our problem which is probably not general enough to support many other navigational tasks. We derive partial representations of the environment by employing retinal motion-based quantities which, although sufficient for the accomplishment of the task at hand do not allow for the reconstruction of the state of the robot. Similar findings have been reported for other robotic tasks such as robot centering in the middle of corridors (Argyros et al., 2004).

The rest of the work is organized as follows. Section 2 focuses on the local control strategy that enables a robot to move between adjacent positions provided that a correspondence between at least three features has been established in panoramas acquired at these positions. Section 3 describes our approach on how to automatically decompose a long-range homing task into a series of short-range navigation tasks each of which can be implemented through the proposed local control law. In Section 4 we present alternative panoramic image features that can be used to perceptually support the homing strategy. Extensive experimental results from implementations of the proposed homing strategy on a robotic platform are provided in Section 5. Moreover, the benefits stemming of the use of panoramic cameras compared to conventional ones are described in Section 6. The work concludes in Section 7 with a brief discussion on the key contributions of this work.

2. Control Law

In the following, the robot is abstracted as a point on the 2D plane. The objective of the local control law is to use angular information related to features extracted in panoramic images in order to calculate a motion vector $\vec{M}$ that, when updated over time, drives the robot to a pre-visited goal position. A *snapshot* of the workspace from a configuration $P \in (\mathbb{R}^2 \times S^1)$, corresponds both to the sequence of visible landmarks and the bearings with which the landmarks are visible from P. The current and the goal position of the robot, together with the corresponding snapshots, will be denoted as A and T, respectively.

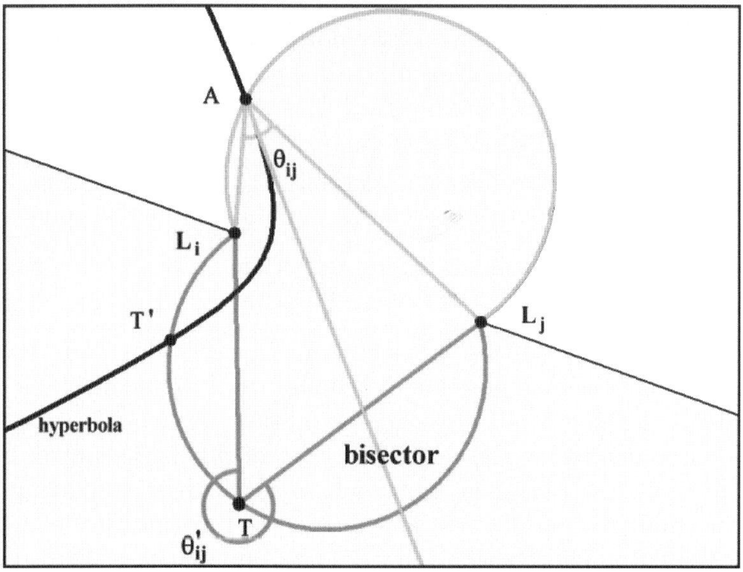

Figure 2. The definition of the motion vector for two landmarks.

2.1. BASIC CONTROL LAW

We will first consider the case of two landmarks L_i and L_j. The *angular separations* $\theta_{ij}, \theta'_{ij} \in [0, 2\pi)$ correspond to the angles between L_i and L_j as measured at A and T respectively. If $\Delta\theta_{ij} = \theta'_{ij} - \theta_{ij}$ is positive, then the robot views the two landmarks from position T with a greater angle than from position A. The robot will move in a direction that increases the angle θ_{ij}. If $0 \leq \theta_{ij} \leq \pi$ and $\Delta\theta_{ij} \geq 0$, the robot should move closer to the landmarks. All directions that are in the interior of the angle between vectors $\overrightarrow{AL_i}$ and $\overrightarrow{AL_j}$ will move the robot to a new position with greater θ_{ij} including the direction of the angle bisector $\overrightarrow{\delta_{ij}}$. Similarly, when $\theta_{ij} \geq \pi$, moving on the direction of $\overrightarrow{\delta_{ij}}$ increases θ_{ij}. When $\Delta\theta_{ij}$ is negative, the robot should follow the inverse of $\overrightarrow{\delta_{ij}}$. A motion vector that has the above properties and has magnitude that is a continuous function over the entire plane is given by the following equation:

$$\overrightarrow{M_{ij}} = \begin{cases} \Delta\theta_{ij} \cdot \overrightarrow{\delta_{ij}}, & \text{if } -\pi \leq \Delta\theta_{ij} \leq \pi \\ (2\pi - \Delta\theta_{ij}) \cdot \overrightarrow{\delta_{ij}}, & \text{if } \Delta\theta_{ij} > \pi \\ (-2\pi - \Delta\theta_{ij}) \cdot \overrightarrow{\delta_{ij}}, & \text{if } \Delta\theta_{ij} < -\pi. \end{cases} \tag{1}$$

If the robot moves according to the motion vector $\overrightarrow{M_{ij}}$ as this is described in Equation (1), it is guaranteed to reach the point of intersection of the circular arc (L_iTL_j) and the branch of the hyperbola that goes through A and has points L_i and L_j as foci. An example of such a point is T' in Figure 2. If a third landmark, L_k, exists in the environment, then every position T is constrained to lie on two more circular arcs. A partial motion vector $\overrightarrow{M_{ij}}$ is then defined for each possible pair of different landmarks L_i and L_j. By taking the vector sum of all these vectors the resultant motion vector $\overrightarrow{M}$ is produced. Figure 3 gives an example where $\overrightarrow{M_{ki}}$ and $\overrightarrow{M_{jk}}$ have the same direction as the bisector vectors. $\overrightarrow{M_{ij}}$ is opposite to $\overrightarrow{\delta_{ij}}$ because $\Delta\theta_{ij}$ is negative. The control law can be summarized in the equation

$$\overrightarrow{M} = \overrightarrow{M_{ij}} + \overrightarrow{M_{jk}} + \overrightarrow{M_{ki}}, \tag{2}$$

where the component vectors are defined in Equation (1). Note that when the robot reaches the goal position, it is guaranteed to remain there because at that point the magnitude of the global motion vector $\overrightarrow{M}$ is equal to zero.

In order to determine the reachability set of this basic control law, i.e., the set of points of the plane that can be reached by employing it in a particular configuration of three landmarks, we ran extensive experiments using a simulator as computed by detailed simulations. The gray area in Figure 4(a) shows the reachability area of the basic control law. The sets of points that are always reachable, independently of the robot's start position, are summarized below:

- The interior $\hat{C}$ of the circle defined by L_1, L_2 and L_3.
- The union $\hat{H}$ of all sets H_j. A set H_j is the intersection of two half-planes. The first half-plane is defined by line (L_iL_j) and does not include landmark L_k, while the second is defined by the line L_jL_k and does not include landmark L_i, where $k \neq i \neq j \neq k$. In Figure 4(b) the white area outside the circle defined by the three landmarks corresponds to the set $\hat{H}$.

2.2. COMPLEMENTARY CONTROL LAW

We now present the complementary control law, that reaches the positions that are unreachable by the basic law. As in the case of the basic control law, the complementary control law exploits the bearings of three landmarks.

We first define the *π-difference* of an angular separation θ_{ij} to correspond to $|\pi - \theta_{ij}|$. Points on the line segment (L_iL_j) will have π-difference of θ_{ij} equal to zero. The *nearest landmark pair* (`NLP`) to the goal is the pair of landmarks (L_iL_j), that has the minimum *π-difference*. The corresponding motion vector will be called the *nearest motion vector* (`NMV`). From the study of the basic control law, it can be shown that for an unreachable point T, the dominating component vector is the `NMV`. The robot follows a curve that is close to the hyperbola with the `NLP` landmarks L_i and L_j as the foci, until it approaches the circular arc (L_iTL_j). Close to the arc, the `NMV` stops dominating, because $\Delta\theta_{ij}$ approaches zero. If the goal position is located at the intersection of the curve and the arc (L_iTL_j), then the robot reaches the goal. Otherwise, the robot reaches the arc and follows the

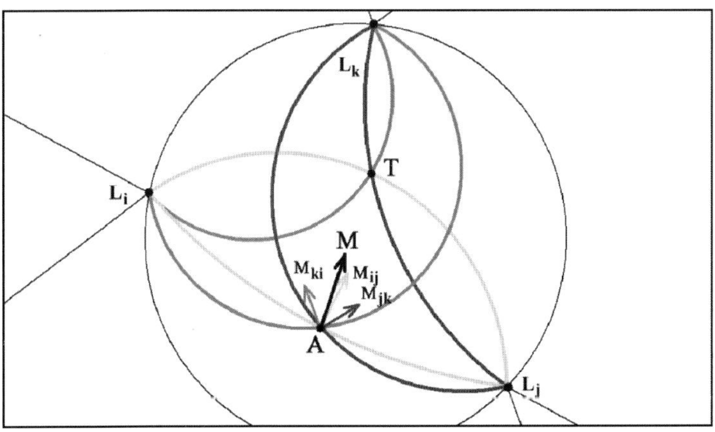

Figure 3. The definition of the motion vector for three landmarks.

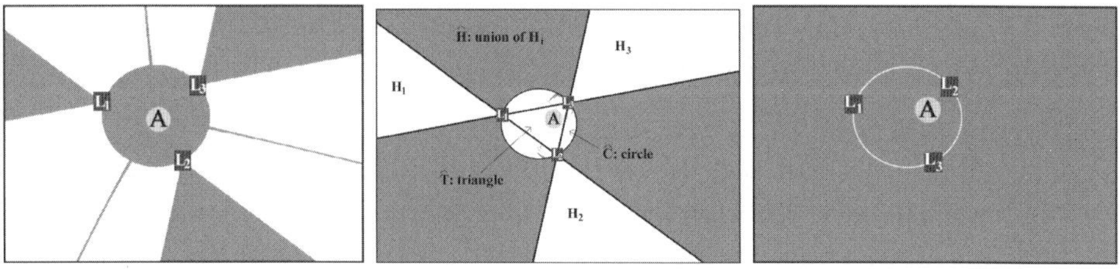

(a) (b) (c)

Figure 4. Simulation results. The robot's initial position is point A and three landmarks L_1, L_2, L_3 exist in the scene. Every point is painted gray if it constitutes a reachable destination by employing (a) the basic control law, (b) the complementary law or (c) the unified control law.

opposite direction from the goal. Notice that the robot can easily detect which landmark pairs do not correspond to the NLP. When the robot is close to the circular arc defined by the NLP, those two vectors guide the robot away from the goal.

In order to come up with a control law that reaches the complementary set of points to that of the basic control law, the two component motion vectors that are not the NMV vectors should be inverted. The gray area in Figure 4(b) shows the reachability set of this new law.

2.3. THE UNIFICATION OF THE TWO LOCAL CONTROL LAWS

In this section we show how to unify the two control laws that have complementary reachability areas in a single law with a reachability area that equals the entire plane. The previous discussion suggests that in order to decide which is the appropriate algorithm to use, the robot must distinguish whether the goal is located in the set $\hat{C}$ or in the set $\hat{H}$ so as to use the basic control law or whether it is located somewhere in the rest of the plane and the complementary law must be used. Deciding whether a snapshot has been taken from the interior of the circle of the landmarks based only on angular information is impossible. Nevertheless, the robot can always move towards the goal by employing the basic algorithm and, while moving, it can collect information regarding the goal snapshot. Based on a set of geometric criteria it is possible to infer whether the basic algorithm was the right choice or if the robot should switch to the complementary law. The geometric criteria consider only the bearings of the landmarks and in one case their rate of change.

For the description of the geometric criteria, we will denote the interior of the landmark's triangle as $\hat{T}$ and the circumscribed circle of two landmarks and the goal as a landmark-goal circle. If the landmarks that correspond to a landmark-goal circle belong to the NLP pair then the circle is called the NLP landmark-goal circle. The geometric criteria that can be used to infer which control law to use based on angular measurements are the following:

1. $\mathbb{T} \in \hat{\mathbb{T}}$? The goal snapshot T is in the set $\hat{T}$ if and only if $\theta'_{ij} < \pi$, $\forall i, j \in [1, 3]$, where L_i and L_j are consecutive landmarks as they are seen from T.
2. $T \in \hat{H}$ and $A \in \hat{T}$? The goal snapshot T is in the set $\hat{H}$ if and only if T can see the landmarks with a different order than A does when A is in $\hat{T}$.
3. $T \notin \hat{T}$ and A on opposite half-plane defined by NLP pair? The robot will then enter $\hat{T}$. If it is going to exit $\hat{T}$ then:
   If the last landmark-goal circle intersected by the robot before leaving $\hat{T}$ is the NLP circle then: $T \notin \hat{C}$.
4. A is on the NLP landmark-goal circle? The goal T is reachable by the basic control law if the non-NLP differences in angular separation are decreasing when the robot has reached the NLP landmark-goal circle.

The overall algorithm that is used for the navigation of the robot is described in Algorithm 1. The robot can be in three possible states: `UNCERTAIN`, `BASIC` and `COMPLEMENTARY`. When in `BASIC` the robot moves according to the basic control law and when in `COMPLEMENTARY` the complementary control law is applied.

The initial state is the `UNCERTAIN` one. The robot is applying the basic control law, but also continuously monitors whether any of the above geometric conditions have been met. If the goal is located in the interior of the landmark's triangle then the unified algorithm will immediately switch to `BASIC`. The second criterion can be checked if the robot enters the landmarks' triangle while the third one only upon exiting this triangle. The last criterion is used only if none of the previous ones has given any information and the robot has reached the NLP landmark-goal circle. At this point, the robot can switch behavior by tracking the change in angular separations. These criteria guarantee that the appropriate control law will be used, regardless of the location of the goal.

3. The Strategy for Long-Range Homing

The presented unified local control law may support homing when the latter is initiated from a position close to home. However, in the case that home is far apart from the position where homing is initiated, it may be the case that these two positions do not share any visual feature in common and, therefore, the unified local control strategy cannot support homing. In the

Algorithm II Unified Control Law

```
status = UNCERTAIN;
repeat
  if status is UNCERTAIN then
    if T ∈ T̂ then
      status = BASIC;
    else if T ∈ Ĥ and A ∈ T̂ then
      status = BASIC;
    else if T ∉ T̂ and A on opposite half-plane defined by NLP pair then
      if last landmark-goal circle intersected before leaving T̂ is the NLP circle
      then
        status = COMPLEMENTARY
      else
        status = BASIC
      end if
    else if A is on the NLP landmark-goal circle then
      if the non-NLP differences in angular separation are increasing then
        status = COMPLEMENTARY
      end if
    end if
  end if

  if status is BASIC or status is UNCERTAIN then
    compute motion vector M with Basic Control Law
  else
    compute motion vector M with Complementary Control Law
  end if

  move according to M
until current snapshot A and goal snapshot T are similar
```

following, we propose a memory-based extension to the local control law which enables it to support such a type of long range homing.

The proposed approach operates as follows. Initially the robot detects features in the view acquired at its home position. As it departs from this position, it continuously tracks these features in subsequent panoramic frames. During its course, some of the initially selected features may not be visible anymore while other, new features may appear in the robot's field of view. In the first case the system "drops" the features from subsequent tracking. In the second case, features start being tracked. This way, the system builds an internal "visual memory" where information regarding the "life-cycle" of features is stored.

A graphical illustration of this type of memory is provided in Figure 5. The vertical axis in this figure corresponds to all the features that have

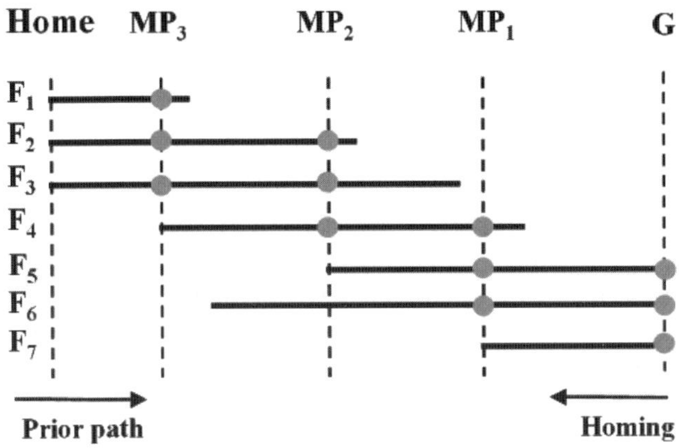

Figure 5. Graphical illustration of the memory used in long-range homing.

been identified and tracked during the journey of the robot from its home position to the current position G. The horizontal dimension corresponds to time. Each of the horizontal black lines corresponds to the life cycle of a certain feature. In the particular example of Figure 5, the home position and position G do not share any common feature and, therefore, the local control law presented in Section 2 cannot be employed to directly support homing. In order to alleviate this problem, milestone positions (MPs) are introduced. Being at the end position G, the method first decides how far the robot can go towards home based on the extracted and tracked features. A position with these characteristics is denoted as MP_1 in Figure 5. Achieving MP_1 from the goal position is feasible (by definition) by employing features F_5, F_6 and F_7 in the proposed local control law. The algorithm proceeds in a similar manner to define the next MP towards home. The procedure terminates when the last MP achieved coincides with the home position.

The local control law of Section 2 guarantees the achievement of a target position but not necessarily the achievement of the orientation with which the robot has previously visited this position. This is because it takes into account the differences of the bearings of features and not the bearings themselves. This poses a problem in the process of switching from the features that drove the robot to a certain MP to the features that will drive the robot to the next MP. This problem is solved as follows. Assume that the robot has originally visited a milestone position P with a certain orientation and that during homing it arrives at position P' where P' denotes position P, visited under a different orientation. Suppose that the robot arrived at P' via features F_1, F_2, ..., F_n. The bearings of these features as observed from position P are $A_p(F_1)$, $A_p(F_2)$, $\cdots$, $A_p(F_n)$ and the bearings of the same features as observed from P' are $A_{P'}(F_1)$, $A_{P'}(F_2)$, $\cdots$, $A_{P'}(F_n)$. Then, it holds that

$$A_P(F_i) - A_{P'}(F_i) = \phi, \ \forall i, 1 \leq i \leq n,$$

where ϕ is constant and equal to the difference in the robot orientation at P and P'. This is because panoramic images that have been acquired at the same location but under a different orientation differ by a constant rotational factor ϕ. Since both $A_P(F_i)$ and $A_{P'}(F_i)$ are known, ϕ can be calculated. Theoretically, one feature suffices for the computation of ϕ. Practically, for robustness purposes, all tracked (and therefore corresponded) features should contribute to the estimation of ϕ. Errors can be due to the inaccuracies in the feature tracking process and/or due to the non-perfect achievement of P during homing. For the above reasons, ϕ is computed as:

$$\phi = median\{A_P(F_i) - A_{P'}(F_i)\}, 1 \leq i \leq n.$$

Having an estimation of the angular shift ϕ between the panoramas acquired at P and $P^{'}$, it is possible to start a new homing procedure. The retinal coordinates of all features detected during the visit of P can be predicted based on the angular displacement ϕ. Feature selection is then applied to small windows centered at the predicted locations. This calculation results in registering all features acquired at P and $P^{'}$ which permits the identification of a new MP and the continuation of the homing procedure. Moreover, if the robot has already arrived at the home position it can align its orientation with the original one by rotating according to the computed angle ϕ.

An important implementation decision is the selection of the number of features that should be corresponded between two consecutive MPs. Although three features suffice more features can be used, if available. The advantage of considering more than three corresponded features is that reaching MPs (and consequently reaching the home position) becomes more accurate because feature-tracking errors are smoothed-out. However, as the number of features increases, the number of MPs also increases because it is less probable for a large number of features to "survive" for a long period. In a sense, the homing scheme becomes more conservative and it is decomposed into a larger number of safer, shorter and more accurate reactive navigation sessions. Specific implementation choices are discussed in the experimental results section of this work.

4. Extracting and Tracking Landmarks

The proposed bearing-only homing strategy assumes that three landmarks can be detected and corresponded in panoramic images acquired at different robot positions and that the bearings of these features can be measured. Two different types of features have been employed in different experiments, namely image corners and centroids of color blobs.

4.1. IMAGE CORNERS

One way to achieve feature correspondence is through the detection and tracking of image corners. More specifically, we have employed the KLT tracking algorithm (Shi and Tomasi, 1993). KLT starts by identifying characteristic image features, which it then tracks in a series of images. The KLT corner detection and tracking is not applied directly on the panoramic images provided by a panoramic camera (e.g., the image of Figure 7) but on the cylindrical image resulting by unfolding such an image using a polar-to-Cartesian transformation (Argyros et al., 2004) (see for example the image in Figure 6). In the resulting cylindrical image, the full 360° field of view is mapped on the horizontal image dimension. Once a corner feature F is detected and tracked in a sequence of such images, its bearing $AP(F)$ can be computed as $AP(F) = 2\pi x_F/D$ where x is the x-coordinate of feature F and D is the width of this panoramic image in pixels.

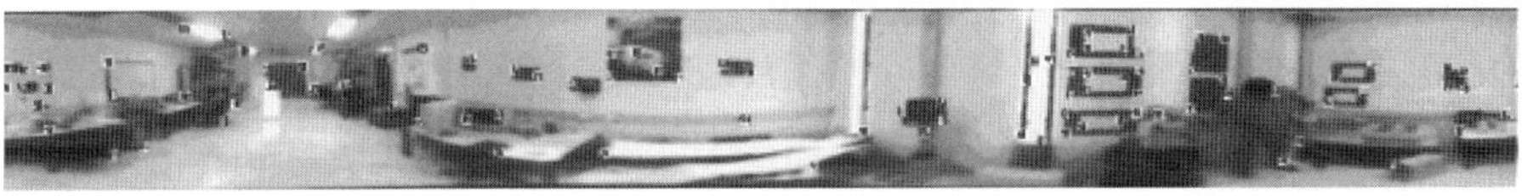

Figure 6. Cylindrical panoramic view of the workspace from the home position that the robot is approaching in Fig. 13. The features extracted and tracked at this panorama are also shown as numbered rectangles.

4.2. CENTROIDS OF COLORED BLOBS

The detection and tracking of landmarks can also be accomplished with the aid of a blob tracker (Argyros and Lourakis, 2004). Although originally developed for tracking skin-colored regions, this tracker may track multiple colored objects in images acquired by a possibly moving camera. The method encompasses a collection of techniques that enable the modeling and detection of colored objects and their temporal association in image sequences. In the employed tracker, colored objects are detected with a Bayesian classifier which is bootstrapped with a small set of training data. A color model is learned through an off-line procedure that permits the avoidance of much of the burden involved in the process of generating training data. Moreover, the employed tracker adapts the learned color model based on the recent history of tracked objects. Thus, without relying on complex models, is able to robustly and efficiently detect colored objects

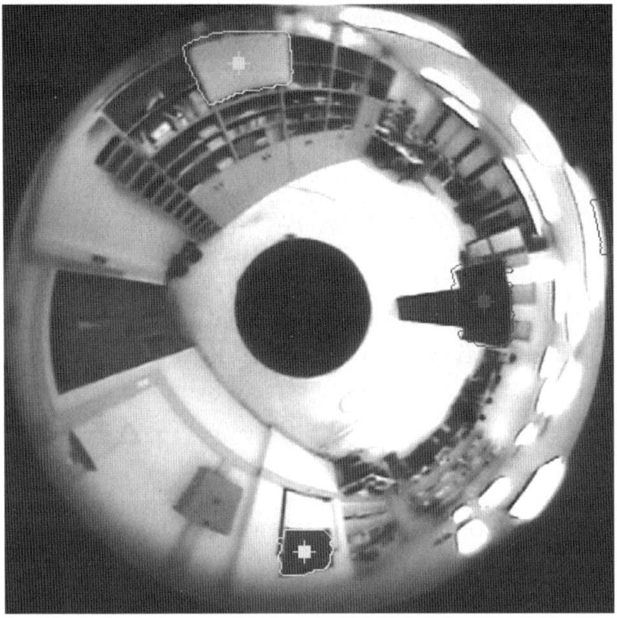

Figure 7. Sample panoramic image with extracted landmarks. Small squares represent the position of the detected and tracked landmarks. The contour of each detected landmark is also shown.

even in the case of changing illumination conditions. Tracking in time is performed by employing a novel technique that can cope with multiple hypotheses which occur when a time-varying number of objects move in complex trajectories and occlude each other in the field of view of a moving camera.

For the purposes of the experiments of this work, the employed tracker has been trained with color distributions corresponding to three colored posters (Figure 7). These posters are detected and subsequently tracked in the panoramic images acquired during a navigation session. A byproduct of the tracking process is the coordinate (x_{F_i}, y_{F_i}) of the centroid of each tracked landmark F_i. Then, assuming that the center of the panoramic image is (x_p, y_p), the bearing of landmark F_i can easily be computed as $\tan^{-1}\left(\frac{y_p - y_{F_i}}{x_p - x_{F_i}}\right)$. Landmarks that appear natural in indoor environments, such as office doors and desks, have also been successfully employed in our homing experiments.

5. Experiments

A series of experiments have been conducted in order to assess qualitatively and quantitatively the performance of the proposed homing scheme.

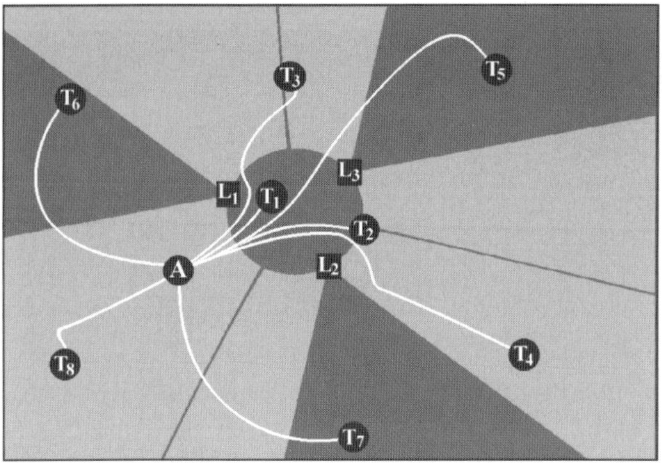

Figure 8. Paths computed by the unified local control law. The reachability sets of the basic and the complementary control laws are shown as dark and light gray regions, respectively.

5.1. VERIFYING THE LOCAL CONTROL LAWS

Towards verifying the developed local control strategies, a simulator has been built which allows the design of 2D environments populated with landmarks. The simulator was used to visualize the path of a simulated robot as the latter moves according to the proposed local control laws. Examples of such paths as computed by the simulator can be seen in Figure 8. Additionally, the simulator proved very useful in visualizing and verifying the shape of the reachability areas for the basic, the complementary and the unified local control laws.

Although simulations provide very useful information regarding the expected performance of the proposed local control laws, it is only experiments employing real robots in real environments that can actually test the performance of the proposed navigational strategy. For this reason, another series of experiments employ an I-Robot, B21R robot equipped with a Neuronics, V-cam360 panoramic camera in a typical laboratory environment. Figure 9(a) illustrates the setting where the reported experiments were conducted. As it can be seen in the figure, three distinctive colored panels were used as landmarks. Landmarks were detected and tracked in the panoramic images acquired by the robot using the method described in Section 4.2. The floor of the workspace was divided into the sets $\hat{C}$, $\hat{H}$ and the rest of the plane for the particular landmark configuration that was used. It should be stressed out that this was done only to visually verify that the conducted experiments were in agreement with the results from simulations. The workspace also contains six marked positions. Figure 9(b) shows a rough drawing of the robot's workspace where the sets $\hat{C}$, $\hat{H}$

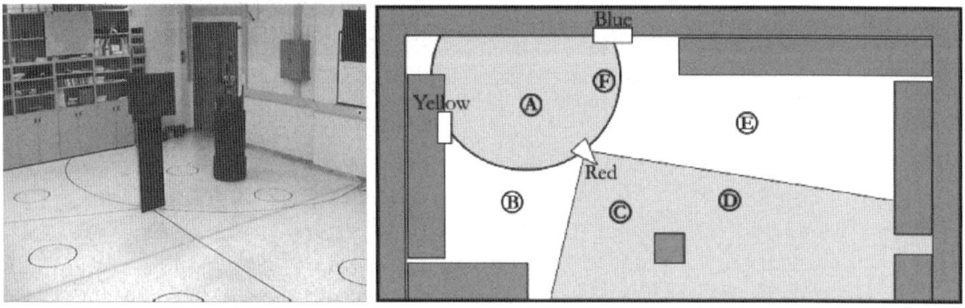

(a) (b)

Figure 9. The environment where the experiments were conducted.

as well as the marked positions are shown. Note that these six positions are representative of robot positions of interest to the proposed navigation algorithm, since $A \in \hat{T}$, $F \in \hat{C} - \hat{T}$, $C, D \in \hat{H}$ and B, E are positions in the rest of the plane.

In order to assess the accuracy of the tracking mechanism in providing the true bearings of the detected and tracked landmarks, the robot was placed in various positions in its workspace and was issued a variety of constant rotational velocities (0.075 rad/sec, 0.150 rad/sec). Since this corresponds to a pure rotational motion of the panoramic camera, it was expected for the tracker to report landmark positions changing at a constant rate, corresponding to the angular velocity of the robot. For all conducted experiments the accuracy in estimating the bearing was less than 0.1 degrees per frame, with a standard deviation of less than 0.2.

A first experiment was designed so as to provide evidence regarding the reachability sets of the three control strategies (basic, complementary and unified). For this reason, each algorithm has been tested for various start and goal positions (3 different starting positions $\times$ 3 different types of starting positions $\times$ 3 different goal positions $\times$ three algorithms). The table in Figure 10 summarizes the results of the 81 runs by providing the accuracy in reaching goal positions, measured in centimeters.

The main conclusions that can be drawn from this table are the following:

- The basic control law fails to reach certain goal positions, independently of the starting position. The reachability set is in agreement with simulation results.
- The complementary control law fails to reach certain goal positions, independently of the starting position. The reachability set is in agreement with simulation results.

- The unified control law reaches all goal positions.
- The accuracy in reaching a goal position is very high for all control laws.

To further assess the accuracy of the unified algorithm in reaching a goal position, as well as the mechanisms that the algorithm employs to switch between the complementary and the basic control law, the unified control law was employed 30 times to reach each of the 6 marked positions, resulting in 180 different runs. Figure 11 shows the results of the experiments and summarizes them by providing the mean error and the standard deviation of the error in achieving each position. As it can be verified from Figure 11, the accuracy of the unified law in reaching a goal position is very high as it is in the order of a very few centimeters for all goal positions.

Additional experiments have been carried out for different landmark configurations, including the special case of collinear landmarks. It is important to note that except from different landmark configurations, different landmarks have been also used. These landmarks were not specially made features such as the colored panels but corresponded to objects that already existed in the laboratory (e.g. the door that can be seen in Figure 9(a), the surface of an office desk, a pile of boxes, etc). The algorithm was also successful in the case that a human was moving in the environment occasionally occluding the landmarks for a number of frames. The tracker was able to recapture the landmark as soon as it reappeared in the robot's visual field. Finally, if the robot's motion towards the goal was interrupted by another process, such as manual control of the robot, the algorithm was able to continue guiding the robot as soon as the interrupting process completed. Sample representative videos from such experiments can be found in http://www.ics.forth.gr/cvrl/demos. In all the above cases the accuracy in reaching the goal position was comparable to the results reported in Figures 10 and 11.

Algorithm		Basic Law			Complementary			Combination		
Attempt	Positions	A	C	E	A	C	E	A	C	E
1st	Initial point in $\hat{C}$	3.5	3.0	Fail	Fail	Fail	4.5	1.0	4.5	5.5
2nd		2.0	1.0	Fail	Fail	Fail	5.5	2.0	3.5	8.5
3rd		0.0	1.5	Fail	Fail	Fail	4.0	4.0	3.0	3.0
1st	Initial point in $\hat{H}$	3.5	11.5	Fail	Fail	Fail	6.0	2.0	9.0	1.5
2nd		1.5	1.5	Fail	Fail	Fail	2.5	3.5	3.0	6.5
3rd		2.5	2.0	Fail	Fail	Fail	8.5	2.0	3.0	3.5
1st	Initial point not in $\hat{C}$ or , $\hat{H}$	2.0	2.0	Fail	Fail	Fail	2.5	1.5	2.0	2.0
2nd		4.0	0.0	Fail	Fail	Fail	9.0	3.5	2.0	5.5
3rd		0.5	5.5	Fail	Fail	Fail	3.0	1.5	3.5	8.0

Figure 10. Experiments testing the reachability area and the accuracy of the proposed local control laws.

Position:	A	B	E	D	F	C
Mean Val.	1.45	4.65	3.22	2.55	2.28	2.85
St. Dev.	1.13	2.10	1.96	1.35	1.22	1.41

Figure 11. Accuracy of the proposed local control laws in reaching a desired position (distance from actual position, in centimeters)

5.2. VERIFYING THE STRATEGY FOR LONG-RANGE HOMING

Besides verifying the proposed local control strategy in isolation, further experiments have been carried out to assess the accuracy of the full, long-range navigation scheme. Figure 12 gives an approximate layout of the robot's workspace and starting position in a representative long-range homing experiment. The robot leaves its home position and after executing a predetermined set of motion commands, reaches position G, covering a distance of approximately eight meters. Then, homing is initiated, and three MPs are automatically defined. The robot sequentially reaches these MPs to eventually reach the home position. Note that the properties of the local control strategy applied to reaching successive MPs are such that the homing path is not identical to the prior path. During this experiment, the robot has been acquiring panoramic views and processing them on-line. Image preprocessing involved unfolding of the original panoramic images and Gaussian smoothing ($\sigma = 1.4$). The resulting images were then fed to the KLT corner tracker to extract features as described in Section 4.1. Potential features were searched in 7 x 7 windows over the whole image. The robots maximum translational velocity was 4.0 cm/sec and its maximum rotational velocity was 3 deg/sec. These speed limits depend on the image acquisition and processing frame rate and are set to guarantee small inter-frame feature displacements which, in turn, guarantee robust feature tracking performance. The 100 strongest features were tracked at each time. After the execution of the initial path, three MPs were automatically defined by the algorithm so as to guarantee that at least 80 features would be constantly available during homing.

Figure 13 shows snapshots of the homing experiment as the robot reaches the home position. Figure 6 shows the visual input to the homing algorithm after image acquisition, unfolding and the application of the KLT tracker. The tracked features are superimposed on the image. It must be emphasized that although the homing experiment has been carried out in a single room, the appearance of the environment changes substantially between home position and position G. As it can be observed, the robot has achieved the home position with high accuracy (the robot in Figure 13(c) covers exactly the circular mark on the ground).

6. Advantages of Panoramic Vision for Bearing-Only Navigation

A major advantage of panoramic vision for navigation is that by exploiting such cameras, a robot can observe most of its surroundings without the need for elaborate, human-like gaze control. An alternative would be to use perspective cameras and alter their gaze direction via pan-tilt platforms, manipulator arms or spherical parallel manipulators. Another alternative would be to use a multi-camera system in which cameras jointly provide a wide field of view. Both alternatives, however, may present significant mechanical, perceptual and control challenges. Thus, panoramic cameras, which offer the possibility to switch the looking direction effortlessly and instantaneously, emerge as an advantageous solution.

Besides the practical problems arising when navigational tasks have to be supported by conventional cameras, panoramic vision is also important because the accuracy in reaching a goal position depends on the spatial arrangement of features around the target position. To illustrate this, assume a panoramic view that captures 360 degrees of the environment in a typical 640×480 image. The dimensions of the unfolded panoramic images produced by such panoramas are 1394×163, which means that each pixel represents 0.258 degrees of the visual field. If the accuracy of landmark localization is 3 pixels, the accuracy of measuring a bearing of a feature is 0.775 degrees or 0.0135 radians. This implies that the accuracy in determining the angular extent of a pair of features is 0.027 radians, or, equivalently, that all positions in space that view pair of features within the above bounds cannot be distinguished. Figure 14 shows results from related simulation experiments. In Figure 14(a), a simulated robot, equipped with

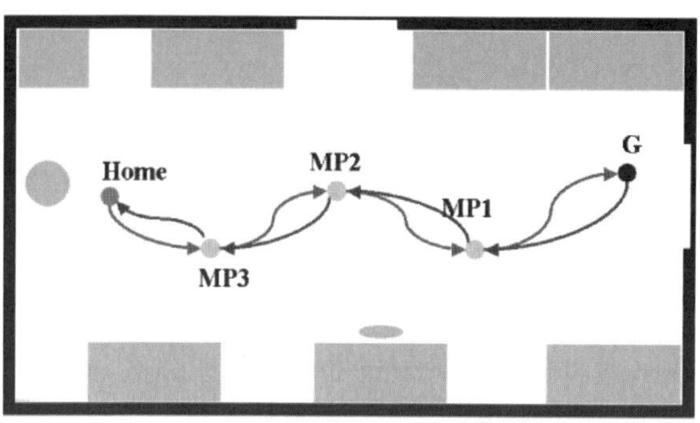

Figure 12. Workspace layout of a representative long-range homing experiment.

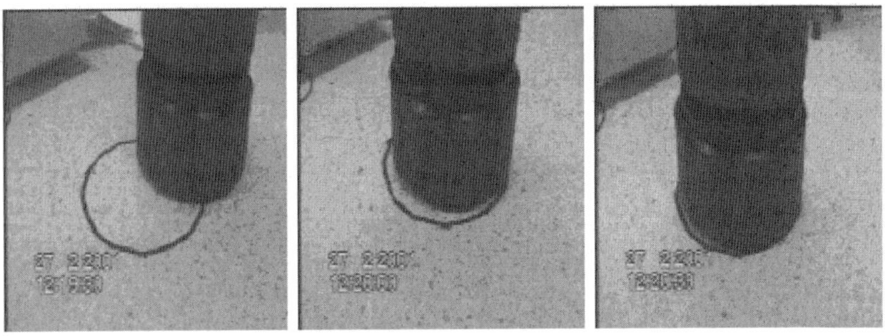

(a) (b) (c)

Figure 13. Snapshots of the long-range homing experiment, as the robot approaches home.

a panoramic camera, observes the features in its environment with the accuracy indicated above. Then the set of all positions that the robot would stop by the proposed control strategy are shown in the figure in dark gray color. It is evident that all such positions are quite close to the true robot location. Figure 14(b) shows a similar experiment but involves a robot that is equipped with a conventional camera with limited field of view that observes three features. Because of the limited field of view, features do not surround the robot. Due to this fact, the uncertainty in determining the true robot location has increased substantially although that the accuracy in measuring each landmark's direction is higher.

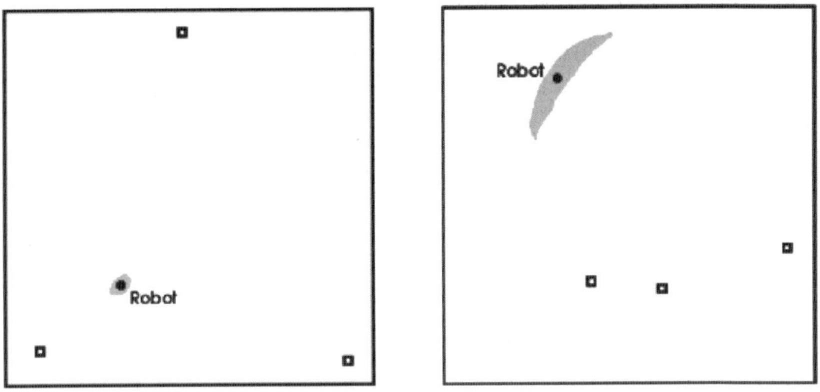

(a) (b)

Figure 14. Influence of the arrangement of features on the accuracy of reaching a desired position. The darker area represents the uncertainty in position due to the error in feature localization (a) for a panoramic camera and (b) for a 60° f.o.v. conventional camera, and the corresponding landmark configuration.

In current implementations of panoramic cameras, however, the omnidirectional field of view is achieved at the expense of low resolution, in the sense of low visual acuity. This reduced acuity could be a significant problem for tasks like fine manipulation. For navigation tasks, however, it seems that acuity could be sacrificed in favor of a wide field of view. For example, the estimation of 3D motion is facilitated by a wide field of view, because this removes the ambiguities inherent in this process when a narrow field of view is used (Fermuller and Aloimonos, 2000). As an example, in the experiment of Figure 14(b), the camera captures 60 degrees of the visual field in a 640×480 image. Thus, each pixel represents 0.094 degrees of the visual field and the accuracy of measuring a bearing of a feature is 0.282 degrees or 0.005 radians. Consequently, accuracy in determining the angular extend of a pair of features is 0.01 radians, which is almost three times better compared to the accuracy of the panoramic camera. Still, the accuracy in determining the goal position is larger in the case of panoramic camera.

7. Discussion

This work has shown that panoramic vision is suitable for the implementation of bearing-only robot navigation techniques. These techniques are able to accurately achieve a goal position as long as the visual input is able to provide angular measurements without having to reconstruct the robot's state in the workspace. Compared to the existing approaches to robot homing, the proposed strategy has a number of attractive properties. The requirement for an external compass is no longer necessary. The proposed local control strategy does not require the definition of two types of motion vectors (tangential and centrifugal), as in the original "snapshot model" (Cartwright and Collett, 1983) and, therefore, the definition of motion vectors is simplified. We have extended the capabilities of the local control law strategy so that the entire plane is reachable as long as the features are visible by the robot while executing homing. This fact greatly simplifies the use of the proposed local strategy as a building block for implementing long-range homing strategies. In this work we have also presented one such long-range homing algorithm that builds a memory of visited positions during an exploration step. By successively applying the local control strategy between snapshots stored in memory the robot can return to any of the positions it has visited in the past. Last, but certainly not least, it has been shown that panoramic vision can be critically important in such navigation tasks because a wide field of view corresponds to greater accuracy in the achievement of the goal position compared to the increased resolution that pinhole cameras offer. Both the local control laws and the long-range strategy have been validated in a series of experiments which have shown that homing can be achieved with a remarkable accuracy, despite the fact that primitive visual information is employed in simple mechanisms.

References

Adorni, G., Mordonini, M., and Sgorbissa, A.: Omnidirectional stereo systems for robot navigation. In Proc. *IEEE Workshop Omnidirectional Vision and Camera Networks*, pages 79–89, 2003.

Aihara, N., Iwasa, H., Yokoya, N., and Takemura, H.: Memory-based self localization using omnidirectional images. In Proc. *Int. Conf. Pattern Recognition*, Volume 2, pages 1799–1803, 1998.

Aloimonos, Y.: *Active Perception.* Lawrence Erlbaum Assoc., 1993.

Argyros, A. A., Bekris, K. E., Orphanoudakis, S. C., and Kavraki, L. E.: Robot homing by exploiting panoramic vision. *Autonomous Robots*, **19**: 7–25, 2005,

Argyros, A. A., Bekris, K. E., and Orphanoudakis, S. E.: Robot homing based on corner tracking in a sequence of panoramic images. In Proc. *CVPR*, Volume 2, pages 3–10, 2001.

Argyros, A. A. and Lourakis, M. I. A.: Real-time tracking of skin-colored regions by a Ppotentially moving camera. In Proc. *Europ. Conf. Computer Vision*, Volume 3, pages 368–379, 2004.

Argyros, A. A., Tsakiris, D. P., and Groyer, C.: Bio-mimetic centering behavior: mobile robots with panoramic sensors. *IEEE Robotics and Automation Magazine*, special issue on *Panoramic Robotics*, pages 21–33, 2004.

Bekris, K. E., Argyros, A. A., and Kavraki, L. E.: New methods for reaching the entire plane with angle-based navigation. In Proc. *IEEE Int. Conf. Robotics and Automation*, pages 2373–2378, 2004.

Cartwright, B. A. and Collett, T. S: Landmark learning in bees: experiments and models. *Computational Physiology*, **151**: 521–543, 1983.

Davison, A. J. and Murray, D. W.: Simultaneous localization and map-building using active vision. *IEEE Trans. Pattern Analysis Machine Intelligence*, **24**: 865–880, 2002.

Fermller, C. and Aloimonos, Y.: Geometry of eye design: biology and technology. In *Multi-Image Analysis* (R. Klette, T.S. Huang, and G.L. Gimel'farb, editors), LNCS 2032, pages 22–38, 2000.

Hong, J., Tan, X., Pinette, B., Weiss, R., and Riseman, E. M.: Image-based homing. In Proc. *IEEE Int. Conf. Robotics and Automation*, pages 620–625, 1991.

Kosaka, A. and Pan, J.: Purdue experiments in model-based vision for hallway navigation. In Proc. *Workshop on Vision for Robots*, pages 87–96, 1995.

Lambrinos, D., Moller, R., Labhart, T., Pfeifer, R., and Wehner, R.: A mobile robot employing insect strategies for navigation. *Robotics and Autonomous Systems*, **30**: 39–64, 2000.

Lourakis, M. I. A., Tzourbakis, S., Argyros, A. A., and S. C., Orphanoudakis: Feature transfer and matching in disparate views through the use of plane homographies. *IEEE Trans. Pattern Analysis Machine Intelligence*, **25**: 271–276, 2003.

Moller, R.: Insect visual homing strategies in a robot with analog processing. *Biological Cybernetics*, special issue on *Navigation in Biological and Artificial Systems*, **83**: 231–243, 2000.

Shi, J. and Tomasi, C.: Good features to track. TR-93-1399, Department of Computer Science - Cornell University, 1993.

Srinivasan, M., Weber, K., and Venkatesh, S.: *From Living Eyes to Seeing Machines.* Oxford University Press, 1997.

Thrun, S.: Probabilistic algorithms in robotics. *AI Magazine*, **21**: 93–109, 2000.

Winters, N., Gaspar, J., Lacey, G., and Santos-Victor, J.: Omni-directional vision for robot navigation. In Proc. *IEEE Workshop Omnidirectional Vision*, pages 21–28, 2000.

CORRESPONDENCELESS VISUAL NAVIGATION UNDER CONSTRAINED MOTION

AMEESH MAKADIA
GRASP Laboratory
Department of Computer and Information Science
University of Pennsylvania

Abstract. Visual navigation techniques traditionally use feature correspondences to estimate motion in the presence of large camera motions. The availability of black-box feature tracking software makes the utilization of correspondences appealing when designing motion estimation algorithms. However, such algorithms break down when the feature matching becomes unreliable. To address this issue, we introduce a novel approach for estimating camera motions in a correspondenceless framework. This model can be easily adapted to many constrained motion problems, and we will show examples of pure camera rotations, pure translations, and planar motions. The objective is to efficiently compute a global correlation grid which measures the relative likelihood of each camera motion, and in each of our three examples we show how this correlation grid can be quickly estimated by using generalized Fourier transforms.

Key words: correspondenceless motion, visual navigation, harmonic analysis, spherical Fourier transform

1. Introduction

The general algorithmic pipeline for estimating the 3D motion of a calibrated camera is well-established: features are matched between image pairs to find correspondences, and a sufficient number of correspondences allows for a linear least-squares estimate of the unknown camera motion parameters (usually as the Essential matrix). However, most correspondence-based algorithms relying on least-squares solutions become unreliable in the presence of noisy or outlying feature matches.

Sophisticated feature extractors (Shi and Tomasi, 1994; Lowe, 2004) are often application or scene-dependent in that many parameters must be tuned in order to obtain satisfactory results for a particular data set. Although the tracking of features is considered a familiar and well-understood

K. Daniilidis and R. Klette (eds.), Imaging Beyond the Pinhole Camera, 253–268.

problem, there are many practical scenarios (depending on properties of the imaging sensor, or scenes and objects with repeated textures) for which features cannot be successfully matched. Take for example omnidirectional camera systems, which have become synonymous with mobile robots. The panoramic view which makes such sensors so appealing is also being represented by relatively fewer pixels (per viewing angle). This fact, combined with the projection geometry of such sensors, makes the problem of matching points between images quite difficult under many circumstances. Due to the geometry of perspective projection, a global image transformation which models rigid motions of a camera does not exist, and so we cannot altogether abandon the calculation of localized image characteristics. Previously, in the area of correspondenceless motion, Aloimonos and Hervé (Aloimonos and Hervé, 1990) showed the rigid motion of planar patches can be estimated without correspondences using a binocular stereo setup. Antone and Teller (Antone and Teller, 2002) use a Hough transform on lines in images to identify vanishing points (which are used in rotational alignment). A subsequent Hough transform on feature pairs in rotationally aligned images is used to estimate the direction of translation. The computational complexity of a direct computation is circumvented by pruning possible feature pairs and only desiring an rough estimate of the solution, which is used to initialize an EM algorithm. Roy and Cox (Roy and Cox, 1996) contributed a correspondenceless motion algorithm by statistically modeling the variance of intensity differences between points relative to their Euclidean distance. This model is then used to estimate the likelihood of assumed motions. Makadia et al. (Makadia et al., 2005) proposed a 5D Radon transform on the space of observable camera motions to generate a likelihood for all possible motions.

To address the issues presented above, namely the large motions and noisy feature matches, we propose a general correspondence-free motion estimation approach which is easily adaptable to various constrained motion problems. We study three constrained motions which commonly present themselves in practical situations: purely rotational motion, purely translational motion, and planar motions. We will examine in detail how each of the three constrained motions fall within our general framework. In the instances where the camera motion includes a translational component, we avoid finding feature correspondences by processing the entire set of possible feature pairs between two images. The underlying principle to our approach is the general idea that the Fourier transform of a correlation (or convolution) of functions can be obtained directly from the pointwise multiplication of the Fourier transforms of the individual correlating (or convolving) functions. This general principle generated from a group theoretic approach produces a very powerful computational tool with which we can develop novel motion estimation algorithms. For the case of pure rotation, we can frame our estimation problem as a correlation of two spherical images. In the case of translational motion we can frame the problem as the pure convolution of two spherical signals which respectively encode feature pair information and the translational epipolar constraint. A similar procedure is also used for planar motion, where we correlate two functions (each defined on the direct product of spheres) encoding feature pair similarities and the planar epipolar constraint.

In the three subsequent sections we present in order the theory behind the rotational, translational, and planar motion estimation solutions, followed by some concluding remarks.

2. Rotations

The simplest rigid motion of a camera, when considering the problem of visual navigation, is arguably a pure rotation (a rotation of a camera is any motion which keeps the effective viewpoint of the imaging system fixed in space). Given two images I and J, a straightforward algorithm to find the rotation between the two would be to *rotate image I* for every possible 3D rotation and compare the result to image J. The rotation which matches the closest can be considered the correct rotation of motion. Surprisingly, as we will see, this naive approach turns out to be a very effective motion estimator for purely rotational motions. This approach is only viable because rotational image transformations are scene and depth-independent. This means we can correctly warp an image to reflect a camera rotation. We define our image formation model to be spherical perspective, where the image surface takes the shape of a sphere and the single viewpoint of the system lies at the center of the sphere. The spherical perspective projection model maps scene points $P \in \mathbb{R}^3$ to image points $p \in \mathbb{S}^2$, where $p = P/||P||$. Our choice of a spherical projection is motivated in part by the large class of Omnidirectional sensors which can be modeled by projections to the sphere followed by stereographic projections to the image plane (Geyer and Daniilidis, 2001). By parameterizing the group of 3D rotations $SO(3)$ with ZYZ Euler angles α, β, and γ, any $R \in SO(3)$ can be written as $R = R_z(\gamma)R_y(\beta)R_z(\alpha)$, where R_z and R_y represent rotations about the Z and Y axes respectively. We define rotation with the operator Λ so that the rotation of a point p becomes $\Lambda_R p = R^T p$, and the rotation of an image I is $\Lambda_R I(p) = I(R^T p)$.

If we associate the similarity of two spherical images with the correlation of their image intensities, then we can write our search for the rotation of motion as the search for the global maximum of the following correlation function:

$$f(R) = \int_p I(p)J(R^T p)dp \tag{1}$$

This formulation is quite similar to the correlation techniques applied to planar pattern matching problems (Chirikjian and Kyatkin, 2000). In such problems, the search is for a planar shift (translation and/or rotation) which aligns a pattern with its target location within an image. Although the search for the correct shift is global, a fast solution is obtained by exploiting the computational benefits of evaluating the correlation and convolution of planar signals as pointwise multiplications of the signals' Fourier transforms. We wish to expedite the computation of (1) using similar principles. Such an improvement is possible if we recognize that analyzing the spectral information of images defined on planes or spheres is part of the same general framework of harmonic analysis on homogeneous spaces.

2.1. THE SPHERICAL FOURIER TRANSFORM

The treatment of spherical harmonics is based on (Driscoll and Healy, 1994; Arfken and Weber, 1966). In traditional Fourier analysis, periodic functions on the line are expanded in a basis obtained by restricting the Laplacian to the unit circle. Similarly, the eigenfunctions of the spherical Laplacian provide a basis for $f(\eta) \in \mathbb{S}^2$. These eigenfunctions are the well known spherical harmonics ($Y_m^l : \mathbb{S}^2 \mapsto \mathbb{C}$), which form an eigenspace of harmonic homogeneous polynomials of dimension $2l+1$. Thus, the $2l+1$ spherical harmonics for each $l \geq 0$ form an orthonormal basis for any $f(\eta) \in \mathbb{S}^2$. The $(2l+1)$ spherical harmonics of degree l are given as

$$Y_m^l(\theta, \phi) = (-1)^m \sqrt{\frac{(2l+1)(l-m)!}{4\pi(l+m)!}} P_m^l(\cos\theta)e^{im\phi}$$

where P_m^l are the associated Legendre Functions and the normalization factor is chosen to satisfy the orthogonality relation

$$\int_{\eta\in\mathbb{S}^2} Y_m^l(\eta) Y_{m'}^{l'}(\eta) d\eta = \delta_{mm'}\delta_{ll'},$$

where δ_{ab} is the Kronecker delta function. Any function $f(\eta) \in \mathcal{L}^2(\mathbb{S}^2)$ can be expanded in a basis of spherical harmonics:

$$f(\eta) = \sum_{l\in\mathbb{N}} \sum_{|m|\leq l} \hat{f}_m^l Y_m^l(eta)$$

$$\hat{f}_m^l = \int_{\eta\in\mathbb{S}^2} f(\eta)\overline{Y_m^l}(\eta)d\eta \tag{2}$$

The $\hat{f}_{lm}$ are the coefficients of the Spherical Fourier Transform (SFT). Henceforth, we will use $\hat{f}^l$ and Y^l to annotate vectors in $\mathbb{C}^{2l+1}$ containing all elements of degree l.

2.2. THE SHIFT THEOREM

Since we are also interested in studying the Fourier transform of spherical images undergoing rotations, we would like to understand how the spectrum of a function $f \in \mathcal{L}^2(\mathbb{S}^2)$ changes when the function itself is rotated. Analogous to functions defined on the real line, where Fourier coefficients of shifted functions are related by modulations, rotated spherical coefficients are connected by modulations of all coefficients of the same degree. This linear transformation is realized by observing the effect of rotations upon the spherical harmonic functions:

$$Y^l(R^T\eta) = U^l(R)Y^l(\eta). \tag{3}$$

U^l is the irreducible unitary representation of the rotation group, $SO(3)$, whose matrix elements are given by:

$$U^l_{mn}(R(\alpha,\beta,\gamma)) = e^{-im\gamma}P^l_{mn}(\cos(\beta))e^{-in\alpha}.$$

The P^l_{mn} are generalized associated Legendre polynomials which can be calculated efficiently using recurrence relations. Substituting (3) into the forward SFT, we obtain the spectral relationship between rotated functions:

$$\begin{aligned}
\Lambda_R \hat{f}^l_m &= \int_{\eta' \in \mathbb{S}^2} f(\eta')\overline{Y^l_m}(R\eta')d(\eta'), \eta' = R^{-1}\eta \\
&= \int_{\eta' \in \mathbb{S}^2} f(\eta') \sum_{|p|\le l} U^l_{mp}(R^{-1})\overline{Y^l_p}(\eta')d(\eta') \\
&= \sum_{|p|\le l} U^l_{mp}(R^{-1}) \int_{\eta' \in \mathbb{S}^2} f(\eta')\overline{Y^l_p}(\eta')d(\eta') \\
&= \sum_{|p|\le l} \hat{f}^l_p U^l_{pm}(R). \qquad (4)
\end{aligned}$$

In matrix form, our shift theorem becomes $\Lambda_R \hat{f}^l = U^l(R)\hat{f}^l$. Note that the U^l matrix representations of the rotation group SO(3) are the spectral analogue to 3D rotations. As vectors in $\mathbb{R}^3$ are rotated by orthogonal matrices, the $(2l+1)$-length complex vectors $\hat{f}^l$ are transformed under rotations by the unitary matrices U^l. An important byproduct of this transformation is that the rotation of a function does not alter the distribution of spectral energy among degrees:

$$||\Lambda_R \hat{f}^l|| = ||\hat{f}^l||, \forall R \in SO(3)$$

2.3. DISCRETE SPHERICAL FOURIER TRANSFORM

Before going further, we must mention some details regarding the computation of a discrete SFT. Assuming our spherical images are represented on a uniformly sampled angular grid (polar coordinates θ, ϕ), we would like to perform the SFT of these images directly from the grid samples. Driscoll and Healy have shown that if a band-limited function $f(\eta)$ with band limit b ($\hat{f}^l_m = 0, l \geq b$), is sampled uniformly $2b$ times in both θ and ϕ, then spherical coefficients can be obtained using only these samples:

$$\hat{f}^l_m = \frac{\pi^2}{2b^2} \sum_{j=0}^{2b} \sum_{k=0}^{2b-1} a_j f(\eta_{jk}) \overline{Y^l_m}(\eta_{jk}), l \leq b \text{ and } |m| \leq l$$

where $\eta_{jk} = \eta(\theta_j, \phi_k)$, $\theta_j = \frac{\pi j}{2b}$, $\phi_k = \frac{\pi k}{b}$, and the a_j are the grid weights. These coefficients can be computed efficiently with an FFT along ϕ and a Legendre Transform along θ for a total computational complexity of $O(n(\log n)^2)$, where n is the number of sample points ($n = 4b^2$). For more information, readers are referred to (Driscoll and Healy, 1994).

2.4. ROTATION ESTIMATION AS CORRELATION

We may now return our attention to the problem of estimating the rotation between two spherical images. If we examine (1) more closely, we see that we have developed the necessary tools to expand both $I(p)$ and $J(R^T p)$ with their respective Spherical Fourier expansions:

$$f(R) = \sum_l \sum_{|m| \leq l} \sum_{|p| \leq l} \hat{g}^l_m \overline{\hat{h}^l_p U^l_{pm}(R)} \quad (5)$$

where we have replaced images I and J with more generic labels $g(\eta), h(\eta) \in \mathcal{L}^2(\mathbb{S}^2)$. In matrix form the computation for $f(R)$ reduces to

$$f(R) = \sum_l (\hat{g}^l)^T (\overline{U^l(R)\hat{h}^l}) \quad (6)$$

$f(R)$ can be estimated using only the Fourier transforms of the spherical functions g and h. Computationally, this is appealing because in general the number of coefficients $\hat{g}^l$ to retain from the SFT (the maximum value of l) to represent the function g with sufficient accuracy is quite small compared to the number of function samples available. However, for each desired sample of $f(R)$, we still must recompute the summation in (6), and we would like to improve on this result.

As defined, $f(R)$ is a function on the rotation group $f(R) \in \mathcal{L}^2(SO(3))$, and thus we would like to explore the Fourier transform over $SO(3)$. This avenue has been made feasible by the recent development of a fast algorithm to compute the inverse SO(3) Fourier Transform (SOFT, (Kostelec and Rockmore, 2003)).

The SOFT for any function $f(R) \in \mathcal{L}^2(SO(3))$ with bandlimit L is given as

$$f(R) = \sum_l \sum_{|m|\leq l} \sum_{|p|\leq l} \hat{f}^l_{mp} U^l_{mp}(R) \tag{7}$$

$$\hat{f}^l_{mp} = \int_{R\in SO(3)} f(R)\overline{U^l_{mp}(R)}dR \tag{8}$$

Given the orthogonality of the matrices $U^l(R)$ $(\int U^l_{mp}(R)\overline{U^q_{sr}(R)dR} = \delta_{ql}\delta_{mr}\delta_{ps})$, it is clear to see that the SOFT of (6) reduces to

$$\hat{f}^l_{mp} = \hat{g}^l_m \overline{\hat{h}^l_p} \tag{9}$$

As we had initially desired, the correlation of two spherical functions reflects the similar properties of a generalized convolution: the $SO(3)$ Fourier coefficients of the correlation of two spherical functions can be obtained directly from the pointwise multiplication of the individual Spherical Fourier coefficients.

In vector form, the $(2l+1) \times (2l+1)$ matrix of SOFT coefficients $\hat{f}^l$ is equivalent to the outer product of the coefficient vectors $\hat{g}^l$ and $\hat{h}^l$. Given the $\hat{f}^l$, the inverse SOFT retrieves the desired function $f(R)$, with $(2L+1)$ samples in each of the three Euler angles. By generating $f(R)$ by first computing directly the SOFT coefficients of $f(R)$, we avoid calculating (6) for every R in a discretized $SO(3)$. Because the sampling of $f(R)$ depends on the number of coefficients we retain from the SFT of g and h, this computation is accurate up to $\pm\left(\frac{180}{2L+1}\right)^\circ$ in α and γ and $\pm\left(\frac{90}{2L+1}\right)^\circ$ in β. See Figure 2.4 for an example of a 2D slice of the recovered correlation function f(R).

3. Translations

Another typical camera motion encountered in systems requiring visual navigation is a purely translational motion. Although 3D translations form a 3-dimensional space like rotations, there does not exist a global image transformation which can map one image into its translated counterpart without knowing precisely the depth of the scene points. We can begin by exploring the geometric interpretation behind the traditional epipolar constraint in the specific case of translational motion. With a spherical perspective projection, knowing the translational direction restricts the

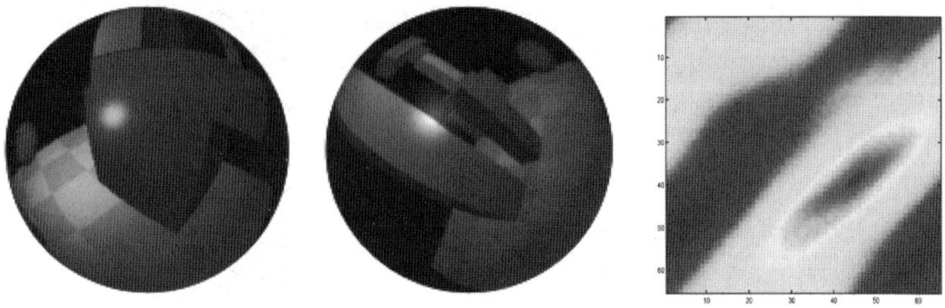

Figure 1. Left and Center: Two artificial images separated by a large camera rotation. The simulated motion contains also a small translational component. On the right is a 2D slice of the estimated function G(R) at the location of the global maximum. The peak is easily distinguishable (at the correct location) even in the presence of the small translational motion.

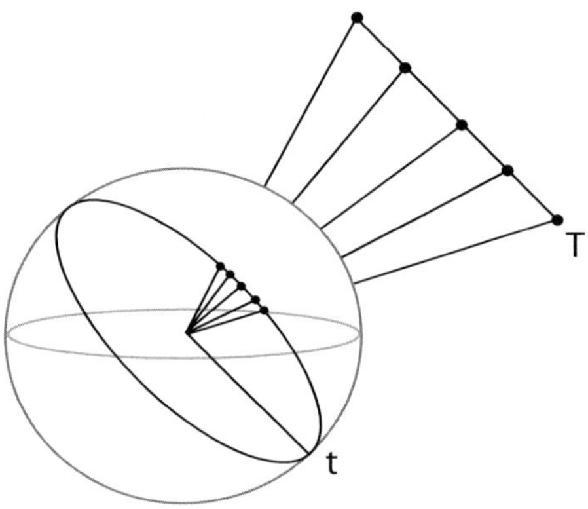

Figure 2. Epipolar circles: for a point translating along a line T, its projection onto an image will remain on a great circle intersecting the translation direction vector t.

motion of image points to great circles (the spherical version of epipolar arcs) on the image surface (see Figure 3).

Observe that the geometric constraint for points after a purely translational motion is that the image projections of a world point before and after the camera motion (p_i and q_i, respectively) are coplanar with the translation vector t. This is equivalent to saying q_i resides on the great circle intersecting t and p_i (which is unique only when $p_i \neq t, -t$). Furthermore, we can say that $p_i \times q_i$ resides on the great circle defining the plane orthogonal to t. This last observation is clearly true for all matching point pairs between two images, and so we can formulate our motion estimation problem as a search for the great circle which intersects the greatest number of matched point pairs $\frac{(p_i \times q_i)}{||p_i \times q_i||} \in S^2$.

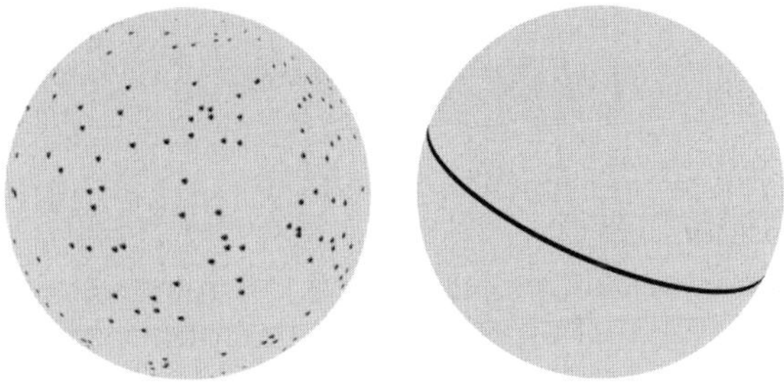

Figure 3. Left: An example of the weighting function g. Each nonzero point ω in the spherical signal (marked by a dot) holds the similarity between two features $p \in I_1$ and $q \in I_2$ such that $\omega = \frac{p \times q}{||p \times q||}$. Right: An image of the equatorial great circle. The goal is to find the relative orientation of the two images so that the circle intersects the most points (weighted).

Of course, the one hurdle is that we cannot always identify matching points between two images. Furthermore, as we have discussed above, we also cannot rely on global image characteristics such as frequency information (SFT coefficients) because there is no model to relate such information between a translated pair of images. So, given that we are essentially restricted to generate some form of local image characteristics, and that we cannot rely on feature correspondences, we are inclined to examine all possible point pairs between two images. However, using image intensity information poses the opposite problem of not providing a sufficiently distinguishing characteristic. A happy medium can be obtained by extracting image *features* from both images and considering the set of *all possible feature pairs* (which clearly contain as a subset the true feature correspondences). We opt to use the black-box feature extractor SIFT (Lowe, 1999), which computes distinguishing characteristics such as local gradient orientation distributions. Using SIFT features we propose to find the great circle which intersects the greatest number of all feature pairs ($p_i \times q_i$), weighted by the similarity of the features p_i, q_i (see Figure 3). This formulation can be expressed with the following integral:

$$G(t) = \int_p \int_q g((p \times q))\delta((p \times q)^T t)dpdq \qquad (10)$$

Here δ is nonzero only if $p \times q$ resides on the great circle orthogonal to t, and the weighting function g stores the similarity of the features p and q at the sphere point $\left(\frac{p \times q}{||p \times q||}\right)$.

Since we are concerned only with the great circle orthogonal to the translation t, our formulation is (as expected) independent of the translational vector's scale. To reflect this we can write t as a unit vector explicitly defined by a 2-parameter rotation: $T = \frac{t}{||t||} = Re_3, R \equiv R_z(\gamma)R_y(\beta)$, where e_3 is the north pole (Z-axis) basis vector. We can rewrite G(T) as [1]:

$$G(R) = \int_p \int_q g(p \times q)\delta(((p \times q)^T R\vec{e_3})dpdq \quad (11)$$

$$= \int_p \int_q g(p \times q)\delta((R^T(p \times q))^T \vec{e_3})dpdq \quad (12)$$

Following the framework developed in the previous section, we would like the functions g and δ to be defined on the sphere $\mathbb{S}^2$. To this end, we can equivalently consider normalized points $\omega = \frac{p \times q}{||p \times q||}, \omega \in \mathbb{S}^2$ such that $(R_2^T \omega)^T \vec{e_3} = 0$. ω is ill-defined when $q = \pm p$, but this can occur for only a negligible subset of possible point pairs, which are easily omitted. Our similarity function $g(w) = g(p \times q)$ must take into account the fact that the projection $(p \times q) \in \mathbb{R}^3 \mapsto \omega \in \mathbb{S}^2$ is not unique. Our weights are generated by summing over all pairs which are equivalent in this mapping:

$$g(\omega) = \sum_{p \in I_1} \sum_{q \in I_2} e^{-||p-q||}\delta(||\omega \times (p \times q)||) \quad (13)$$

Notice that the similarity between any two features is captured by the term $e^{-||p-q||}$. When using SIFT features, the feature characteristics are usually given as vectors in $\mathbb{R}^{128}$, so we can simple define the distance $||p - q||$ to be the Euclidean distance between the two feature vectors generated for p and q.

Our integral now becomes

$$G(R) = \int_\omega g(\omega)\delta((R^T \omega)^T \vec{e_3})d\omega. \quad (14)$$

This looks suspiciously similar to the correlation integral we developed to identify purely rotational motion, and indeed we have been able to write the translational estimation problem as a correlation of two spherical signals. However, instead of matching image intensities, we are using the same framework to maximally intersect an image of a great circle $(\delta(\omega^T e_3))$ with a signal consisting of feature pair similarities $(g(\omega))$.

We could easily follow the derivation presented in the rotational case to obtain an estimate for the translation t, but instead we can take advantage of the fact that the rotation R is only a partial (2-parameter) rotation. Recall that this came about since we defined $T = R\vec{e_3}$, and the first rotational term $R_z(\alpha)$ leaves $\vec{e_3}$ unchanged. We will now see how this helps to rephrase our correlation integral as a convolution of two spherical signals.

[1] Readers familiar with the Radon transform will recognize the form of $G(R)$ as a generalized version of this integral transform. Here we can treat g as a weighting function on the data space and δ as a soft characteristic function which embeds some constraint (in this case the epipolar constraint) determined by the parameter R.

Our characteristic function $\delta(\omega^T \vec{e_3})$ is just the image of the equatorial great circle, which corresponds to a camera translating along the Z-axis. Now consider what happens to δ as it is rotated by an element of $SO(3)$. We can write $\omega \in \mathbb{S}^2$ as a rotation of the north pole vector $\vec{e_3}$, just as we did for the translation vector T. By making the substitution $\omega = R_2\vec{e_3}, R_2 \in SO(3)$, we have

$$G(R) = \int_{R_2} g(R_2\vec{e_3})\delta((R^T R_2\vec{e_3})^T \vec{e_3} dR_2 \qquad (15)$$

Since δ is just the image of the equator, a rotation of δ by an element $R \in SO(3)$ is equivalent to a rotation by its inverse R^T:

$$\delta((R^T R_2)\vec{e_3})^T \vec{e_3}) = \delta((R_2^T R)\vec{e_3})^T \vec{e_3}) \qquad (16)$$

Remember that $R = R_z(\gamma)R_y(\beta)$ is the rotation that determines the direction of camera translation as $T = R\vec{e_3}$. (15) becomes

$$G(T) = \int_{R_2} g(R\vec{e_3})\delta((R_2^T T)^T \vec{e_3})dR_2, \qquad (17)$$

which is the exact definition of the convolution of the two spherical signals g and δ. From the convolution theorem of spherical signals (obtained directly from the SFT and shift theorems), we can generate the Spherical Fourier coefficients of $G(T)$ from the pointwise multiplication of the SFT coefficients of g and δ:

$$\hat{G}^l_m = 2\pi\sqrt{\frac{4\pi}{2l+1}}\hat{g}^l_m \hat{\delta}^l_0 \qquad (18)$$

Notice the subtle differences with this result and the result obtained from the pure rotation estimation (9). In the latter, the correlation grid was defined over the full $SO(3)$. Here, the set of translation directions does not extend to the full $SO(3)$. In fact, this set can be identified with the sphere $\mathbb{S}^2$, and thus the matching function $G(T) \in \mathcal{L}^2(\mathbb{S}^2)$ can be expressed as a true convolution of spherical functions. The computational effect of this difference can be seen immediately from the inverse Fourier transforms required to generate the correlation results. In (9), an inverse $SO(3)$ Fourier transform is needed to generate the full grid $f(R)$, and here only an inverse Spherical Fourier transform is required to obtain the function samples of $G(T)$.

4. Planar Motion

The final rigid motion we will consider is planar motions, which incorporate both rotational and translational components of motion. We define a planar motion to be any rigid motion where the axis of rotation is orthogonal to the direction of translation. This type of motion is typical of omnidirectional cameras mounted on a mobile robot navigating through flat terrain (here the rotation axis would be the $\vec{e_3}$ and the translation direction would lie along the equator).

As we have done in the two previous sections, we will begin by examining the effect of planar motions on transformation of image points. For starters, we consider the plane of motion to be known, and fixed to be the equatorial plane of the spherical camera system. Hence, for the time being, we are only considering rotations around the Z-axis and translations in the equatorial plane. The rotational component of motion is given by $R = R_z(\alpha)$, and the translational component by $t = R_z(\theta)\vec{e_1}$, where $\vec{e_1}$ is the basis vector associated with the X axis. With such a parameterization we have identified this set of planar motions with the rotation pair $(R_z(\alpha), R_z(\theta))$. Since rotations around the Z axis can be associated with elements of the rotation group $SO(2)$, we can identify planar motions with the rotation pair $(R_z(\alpha), R_z(\theta)) \in SO(2) \times SO(2)$, which is in effect the direct product group of $SO(2)$ with itself. We will now make a brief interlude to examine the relevance of this fact regarding our immediate motion estimation concerns. Although we have only considered constrained camera motions to this point, it is worthwhile to examine the role of general 3D motions in the framework developed. The full range of 3D rigid motions is captured by the group $SE(3)$ (a semi-direct product between $SO(3)$ and $\mathbb{R}^3$). However, we are concerned here with understanding motion from visual input, so we can only capture the translational component of motion up to scale. By fixing this scale to 1, the set of translations is equivalent to the set of unit vectors in $\mathbb{R}^3$ which, as we have utilized earlier, can be identified with $\mathbb{S}^2$. So, we can identify the space of motions with elements of $SO(3) \times \mathbb{S}^2 \cong SO(3) \times SO(2)/SO(3)$. This reinforces the fact that the planar motions for a fixed plane form a closed subset of the visually observable motions.

Returning to the effect of planar motions on image pixels, the epipolar constraint in this restricting case is given as

$$(Rp \times q)^T t = 0 \quad (19)$$

$$(R_z(\alpha)p \times q)^T R_z(\theta) e_1 = 0 \quad (20)$$

As we learned in the previous section, the presence of a translational component of motion requires the consideration of local image characteristics, and once again we opt to use the SIFT image features.

This time we are searching for the motion parameters α, θ which constrain the largest subset of feature pairs given by the planar constraint (20). Since we are considering all possible feature pairs, we must once again weight our calculations by the similarity of the features under observation. We can write such a calculation with the following Radon integral:

$$G(R_z(\alpha), R_z(\theta)) = \int_p \int_q g(p,q)\delta((R_z(\alpha)p \times q)^T R_z(\theta)\vec{e_1})dpdq \quad (21)$$

$$= \int_p \int_q g(p,q)\delta((R_z(\theta-\alpha)^T p \times R_z(\theta)^T q)^T \vec{e_1})dpdq \quad (22)$$

Here the weighting function once again measures the likelihood two features represent the projections of the same world point:

$$g(p,q) = \begin{cases} e^{-\|p-q\|} & \text{if features have been extracted at } p \text{ and } q \\ 0 & \text{otherwise} \end{cases}$$

Notice that the domain of both our weighting function and characteristic function is the manifold $\mathbb{S}^2 \times \mathbb{S}^2$, since (p,q) is an ordered pair of points on the sphere $\mathbb{S}^2$. Similarly, points in our parameter space can be identified with elements of the direct product group $SO(3) \times SO(3)$ (as noted earlier, we can also make a stronger statement identifying the planar motions with $SO(2) \times SO(2)$, and we will revisit this fact later). Thus, the functions g, δ are defined on the homogeneous space $\mathbb{S}^2 \times \mathbb{S}^2$ of the Lie group $SO(3) \times SO(3)$. Analogous to what we observed in the previous sections, we are considering here a correlation of functions on the product of spheres, where the correlation *shift* comes from the rotation group $SO(3) \times SO(3)$. The theory previously developed to derive the Fourier transforms of spherical signals extends directly to the direct-product groups and spaces.

The expansion for functions $f(\omega_1,\omega_2) \in \mathcal{L}^2(\mathbb{S}^2 \times \mathbb{S}^2)$ is given as

$$f(\omega_1,\omega_2) = \sum_{l\in\mathbb{N}} \sum_{|m|\leq l} \sum_{n\in\mathbb{N}} \sum_{|p|\leq n} \hat{f}^{ln}_{mp} Y^l_m(\omega_1) Y^n_p(\omega_2)$$

$$\hat{f}^{ln}_{mp} = \int_{\omega_1} \int_{\omega_2} f(\omega_1,\omega_2)\overline{Y^l_m}(\omega_1)\overline{Y^n_p}(\omega_2)d\omega_1 d\omega_2,$$

with a corresponding Shift theorem (in matrix form):

$$h(\omega_1,\omega_2) = f(R_1^T\omega_1, R_2^T\omega_2) \Leftrightarrow \hat{h}^{ln}_{mp} = U^l(R_1)^T \hat{f}^{ln} U^n(R_2) \quad (23)$$

We are now prepared to extend the expression for G into the spectral domain. By substituting the Fourier transforms of g and δ into 22, we will find

$$G(R_z(\theta-\alpha), R_z(\theta)) = \sum_l \sum_n \sum_{|m|\leq l} \sum_{|p|\leq n} \hat{g}^{ln}_{mp} \hat{\delta}^{ln}_{mp} e^{i(m(\alpha-\theta)-p\theta)}, \quad (24)$$

At this point the result of the planar motions as elements of $SO(2) \times SO(2)$ has presented itself. Notice that the modulation or shift of δ by the rotation pair $(R_z(\theta - \alpha), R_z(\theta)$ is exposed in the term $e^{-i(m(\alpha-\theta)-p\theta)}$. Remember that the complex exponentials form the basis for periodic functions on the circle (the traditional Fourier basis). The fact that the full $SO(3) \times SO(3)$ modulation terms $(U^l(R_z(\theta - \alpha)), U^n(R_z(\theta)))$ are reduced to the simpler complex exponentials is a direct result of the planar motions being identified with $SO(2) \times SO(2)$. Thus, by taking the traditional 2D Fourier transform of G, we find the coefficients $\hat{G}$ are simply

$$\hat{G}_{k_1 k_2} = \sum_l \sum_n \hat{g}^{ln}_{k_1 k_2} \hat{\delta}^{ln}_{k_1 k_2} \tag{25}$$

The Fourier coefficients $\hat{G}$ can be computed directly from $\hat{g}$ and $\hat{\delta}$. As we have experienced with the previous correlation computations, the resolution of our correlation grid directly depends upon the band-limit we assume for g and δ. If our band-limit is chosen to be L, we will obtain a result that is accurate up to $\pm \left(\frac{180}{2L+1}\right)^\circ$ for each parameter.

Described above is a fast and robust algorithm to estimate the parameters of a planar motion when the plane of motion is known. If, however, the plane of motion is unknown, we can extend our existing algorithm with minimal effort. The critical observation is that the "difference" between planar motion in an unknown plane versus the equatorial plane is just a change of basis (which can be effected by a rotation). Clearly, if the plane of motion is known (one other than the equatorial plane), then our spherical images could be *registered* (via rotation) so that the effective plane of motion is the equatorial plane. Furthermore, this rotational registration can be performed directly on the coefficients $\hat{g}^{ln}$ via the SFT shift theorem (23). In this manner we could feasibly trace through the possible planes of motion by registering the images at each plane (via the shift of $\hat{g}$) and recomputing G. The global maximum over all planes will identify the correct planar motion.

One of the benefits of this straightforward approach is that it lends itself to simple hierarchical search methods in the space of planes. Since we will deal with each plane using a rotational registration, we should identify planes with the angles $\beta \in [0, \frac{\pi}{2}]$, $\gamma \in [0, 2\pi)$, so that searching through the space of planes is equivalent to searching on the hemisphere. A fast multiresolution approach to localize the plane of motion requires an equidistant distribution of points on the sphere, and here we adopt a method based on the subdivision of the icosahedron (Kobbelt, 2000).

5. Conclusion

Fourier techniques conventionally attempt to perform a computation on the global spectral content of an image. In cases where camera motions can be effected in the image domain by global transformations, these techniques are quite effective. Indeed, in the case of pure rotation, we find that the correlation of two spherical images can be computed efficiently as a product of Fourier coefficients of the correlating functions.

Approaches which seek to match global image characteristics are limited because as global operators they cannot account for signal alterations introduced by occlusion, depth-variations, and a limited field of view. Instead of trying to estimate translational motion using the spectral components of the intensity images, we perform our Fourier decomposition on the feature information stored within the images. In the case of planar motion, a similar result was obtained by formulating a correlation between a signal encoding feature pair similarities with a signal encoding the planar motion epipolar constraint.

We have successfully developed a framework for constrained motion estimation which treats the search for motion parameters as a search for the global maximum of a correlation grid. In all three cases of constrained motion (rotational, translational, planar), this correlation grid can be obtained via a direct pointwise multiplication of the Fourier coefficients of the correlating signals and an inverse Fourier transform on the appropriate space.

Furthermore, because we are computing a correlation grid, we are effectively scoring each possible camera motion independently. This strengthens our formulation to the presence of multiple motions or a dynamic scene. If the image regions involved in these secondary motions are sufficiently large and textured, their motions may also be recovered as local maxima in the correlation grid.

References

Aloimonos, J. and Hervé, J. Y.: Correspondenceless stereo and motion: Planar surfaces. *IEEE Trans. Pattern Analysis Machine Intelligence*, **12**: 504–510, 1990.

Antone, M. and Teller, S.: Scalable, extrinsic calibration of omni-directional image networks. *Int. J. Computer Vision*, **49**: 143–174, 2002.

Arfken, G. and Weber, H.: *Mathematical Methods for Physicists*. Academic Press, 1966.

Chirikjian, G. and Kyatkin, A.: *Engineering Applications of Noncommutative Harmonic Analysis: WIth Emphasis on Rotation and Motion Groups*. CRC Press, 2000.

Driscoll, J. and Healy, D.: Computing fourier transforms and convolutions on the 2-sphere. *Advances in Applied Mathematics*, **15**: 202–250, 1994.

Geyer, C. and Daniilidis, K.: Catadioptric projective geometry. *Int. J. Computer Vision*, **43**: 223–243, 2001.

Kobbelt, L.: $\sqrt{3}$ subdivision. In Proc. *SIGGRAPH*, pages 103–112, 2000.

Kostelec, P. J. and Rockmore, D. N.: FFTs on the rotation group. In *Working Paper Series, Santa Fe Institute*, 2003.

Lowe, D.: Sift (scale invariant feature transform): Distinctive image features from scale-invariant keypoints. *Int. J. Computer Vision*, **60**: 91–110, 2004.

Lowe, D. G.: Object recognition from local scale-invariant features. In Proc. *Int. Conf. Computer Vision*, pages 1150–1157, 1999.

Makadia, A., Geyer, C., Sastry, S., and Daniilidis, K.: Radon-based structure from motion without correspondences. In Proc. *Int. Conf. Computer Vision Pattern Recognition*, 2005.

Roy, S. and Cox, I.: Motion without structure. In Proc. *Int. Conf. Pattern Recognition*, 1996.

Shi, J. and Tomasi, C.: Good features to track. In Proc. *Int. Conf. Computer Vision Pattern Recognition*, 1994.

NAVIGATION AND GRAVITATION

S.S. BEAUCHEMIN
The University of Western Ontario
London, Canada

M.T. KOTB
The University of Western Ontario
London, Canada

H.O. HAMSHARI
The University of Western Ontario
London, Canada

Abstract. We propose a mathematical model for vision-based autonomous navigation on general terrains. Our model, a generalization of Mallot's inverse perspective, assumes the direction of gravity and the speed of the mobile agent to be known, thus combining visual, inertial, and navigational information into a coherent scheme. Experiments showing the viability of this approach are presented and a sensitivity analysis with random, zero-mean Gaussian noise is provided.

Key words: autonomous navigation, optical flow, perspective mapping, inverse perspective mapping

Introduction

Needless to say, there is a growing interest in the field of vision-based autonomous navigation, partly due to its important applications in natural and man-made environments (Batavia et al., 2002; Baten et al., 1998; Choi et al., 1999; Desouza and Kak, 2002; Tang and Yuta, 2001; Tang and Yuta, 2002; Wijesoma et al., 2002).

The complexity of the navigation problem increases with that of the terrain and the environment in general. Navigation over rough terrains requires a vision system to react correctly with respect to the conditions posed by navigational surfaces with significant irregularities.

In general, perception systems rely on sensors such as sonar, lasers, or range finders. In addition, their outputs may be fused to increase the

K. Daniilidis and R. Klette (eds.), Imaging Beyond the Pinhole Camera, 269–282.

reliability of the perception process. Environmental data captured and fused in this way may then be used for essential navigation tasks such as relative position and egomotion estimation (Jin et al., 2003; Kim and Kim, 2003), obstacle detection and avoidance (Ku and Tsai, 1999), and path planning (Desouza and Kak, 2002).

Relative position may be estimated through spatial relations to external objects such as land-marks or through incremental movement estimation using odometry and gyroscopes. Path planning methods depend on many factors, such as the complexity of the navigational tasks, the level of knowledge about the environment, and the dimension of the navigational problem. For instance, in the 1-dimensional case, the navigation is kept with a fixed distance to a reference line. In 2 and 3-dimensional navigation, landmarks are commonly used for estimating the current position and performing local path planning. Topological and geometrical relations between environmental elements and features are represented by various spatial maps that are established prior to the navigational task. For instance, landmark maps hold the information about the position of landmarks on the terrain, whereas passability maps represent the traversable paths on the terrain, or the location of obstacles in the environment. With the knowledge of the relative position of the moving sensor and the information held in the landmark and passability maps, navigating becomes a relatively trivial task. However, solving this problem with potentially unreliable information about the environment or the location of obstacles is very challenging.

The use of motion information for navigational purposes such as optical flow poses significant problems in general. The difficulty of obtaining numerically accurate and meaningful optical flow measurements has been known for some time (Barron et al., 1994). For this and other reasons, if one could impose additional constraints onto the spatiotemporal structure of optical flow, one could most probably obtain better flow estimation. For instance, Mallot's inverse perspective mapping model eliminates optical flow divergence, provided that the navigational path on the terrain remains perfectly flat. As a result, when the sensing agent moves in a straight line, the optical flow estimates are then isotropically parallel and their magnitudes describe the corresponding terrain heights.

In this contribution, we propose a generalization of this model for uneven terrains, modeled as triangulations of randomly generated height points. As we demonstrate, it is possible to maintain a correct optical flow pattern in spite of the motion experienced by the visual sensor while navigating on an uneven terrain. We also provide noise analysis to the reconstructed 3d world model. Our proposed model will be used without being provided with landmark or passability maps. Ultimately, the mobile agent is required to make real-time navigational decisions, using the perceived information from the scene. Incremental movement estimation using odometers and gyroscopes will be used for relative position estimation and the determination of the direction of the gravity field.

This contribution is organized as follows: section 1 defines the coordinate systems involved, section 2 is a synopsis of Mallot's perspective and inverse perspective mapping model, section 4 outlines the problems encountered while applying this model on uneven terrains, section 5 is a description of our proposed perspective and inverse perspective mathematical models, and section 6 presents a noise sensitivity analysis for our proposed model.

1. Coordinate Systems

The projection of a 3d world point onto the image plane involves three coordinate systems and two transformations. The world coordinate system W is described with 3 primary axes, X, Y, and Z. A point in the 3d world is denoted by P_w and the coordinates of this point are $(P_{w_x}, P_{w_y}, P_{w_z})$. The point P_w is transformed from the world coordinate system W into the camera coordinate system C giving a point $P_c = (P_{c_x}, P_{c_y}, P_{c_z})$, where c_x, c_y, and c_z are the sensor axes defined in the world coordinate system. The point P_c is projected into the image plane giving a corresponding point P_i. This point is described in an image plane coordinate system $I(a, b)$.

2. Mallot's Model

Mallot's model presents an inverse perspective scheme for navigation on flat terrains. It is a bird's eye model where the imagery recorded by the visual sensor undergoes a mathematical transformation such that the sensor's gaze axis becomes perpendicular to the navigational surface. This transformation effectively nulls the perspective effects within the resulting optical flow and allows for a simple procedure to estimate obstacle locations.

2.1. PERSPECTIVE MAPPING

Perspective mapping or projection may be written in the following way:

$$\begin{pmatrix} P_{I_a} \\ P_{I_b} \\ -f \end{pmatrix} = \frac{-f}{P_{c_z}} \begin{pmatrix} P_{c_x} \\ P_{c_y} \\ P_{c_z} \end{pmatrix} \qquad (1)$$

where f is the focal length. Figure 1 shows the world map of a triangulated flat terrain captured by a perspective visual sensor.

Figure 2a shows the perspective mapping image from the visual sensor specified in Equation (1), moving along the diagonal of the terrain. The

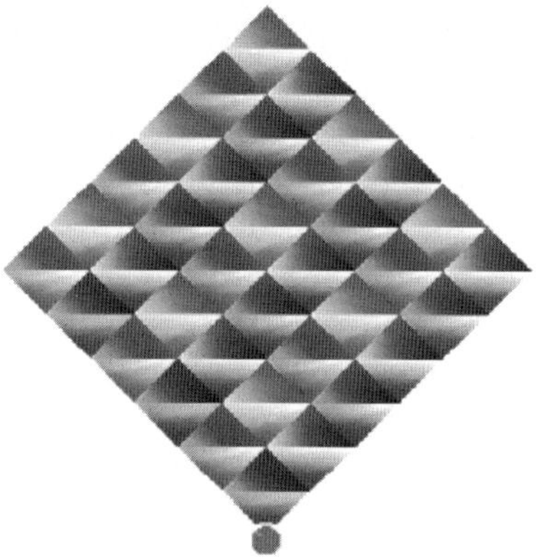

Figure 1. The map of a flat terrain, where the circle represents the position of the mobile agent.

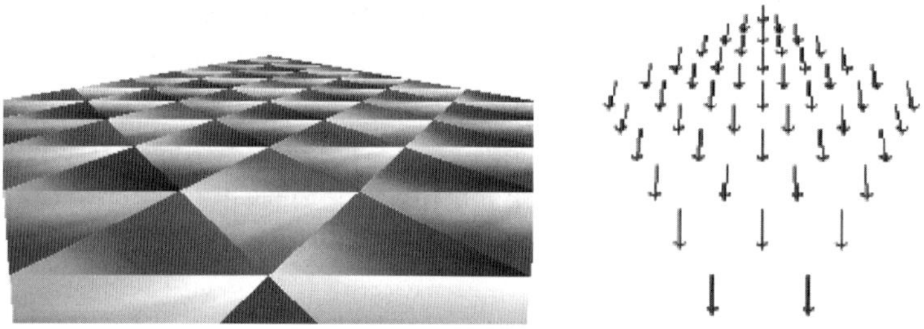

Figure 2. **a) Left:** Perspective mapping from the visual sensor, moving along the diagonal of the terrain. **b) Right:** The optical flow of the perspective mapping in **a)**.

terrain in the image is a square surface, as shown in Figure 1. The obvious perspective effects resulting from projection are noted in Figure 2a. Figure 2b shows the optical flow of the perspective mapping from Figure 2a as the visual sensor moves along a straight line on the terrain. It can be easily seen from Figure 2b that the Focus Of Expansion (FOE) is located at the horizon. In addition, from Equation (1) and Figure 2b, it can be understood that perspective effects are in direct relation with, among other things, the relative height of the visual sensor from the navigational surface.

Applying the transform T from Mallot's model results in the correct, perspective free, optical flow vector field. The transformation T is shown in Figure 3, where P is the point which the camera looks at. Figures 4a and 4b show the perspective mapping and optical flow respectively, after applying the transformation T onto the sensor imagery.

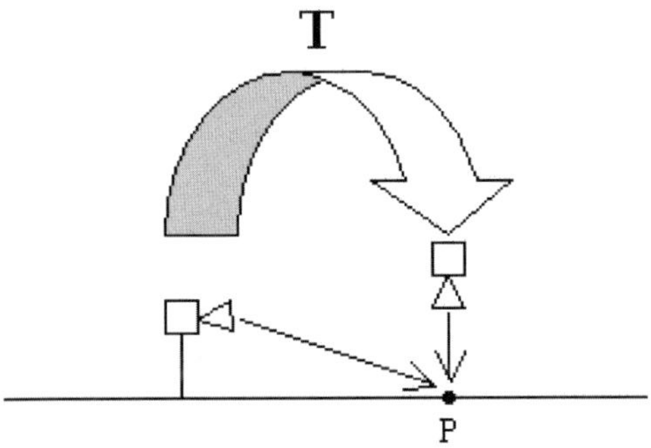

Figure 3. Camera transformation T.

Since inverse-perspective optical flow is a function of depth, then different terrain heights have different optical flow vector magnitudes. Figure 5a shows a global map that has some spikes in the middle of the terrain. Figures 5b and 5c show the perspective mapping and the optical flow respectively. As shown in Figure 5c, the optical flow vectors that represent the motion of the spikes with respect to the camera are longer than those which represent the flat part of the terrain.

2.2. INVERSE PERSPECTIVE MAPPING

Equation (2) presents the inverse perspective mapping as per Mallot's model. This mapping gives a point P_w which corresponds to a point P_i in the image plane. The inverse perspective mapping involves two transformations, one from the image plane coordinate system to the camera coordinate system, and a second transform from the camera coordinate system to the world coordinate system:

$$\begin{pmatrix} W_x \\ W_y \end{pmatrix} = \beta \cdot \gamma \tag{2}$$

where

$$\beta = \frac{-h}{N_x P_{I_a} + N_y P_{I_b} - N_z f}$$

and

$$\gamma = \begin{pmatrix} U_x P_{i_a} + U_y P_{i_b} - U_z f \\ V_x P_{i_a} + V_y P_{i_b} - V_z f \end{pmatrix}$$

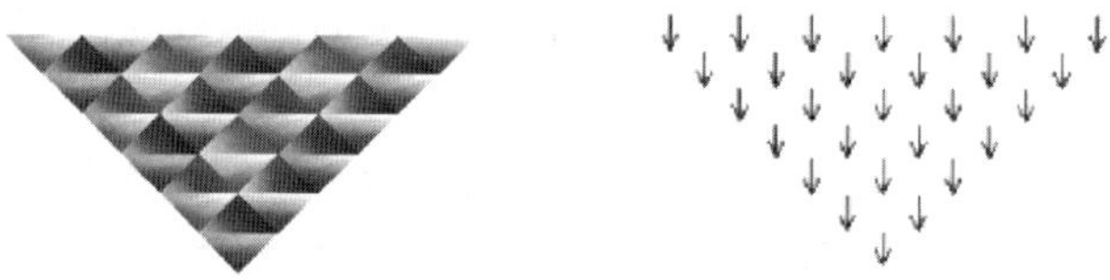

Figure 4. **a) Left:** Perspective mapping taken by the visual sensor, moving along the diagonal of the terrain after applying the transformation T. **b) Right:** The optical flow of the perspective mapping in a).

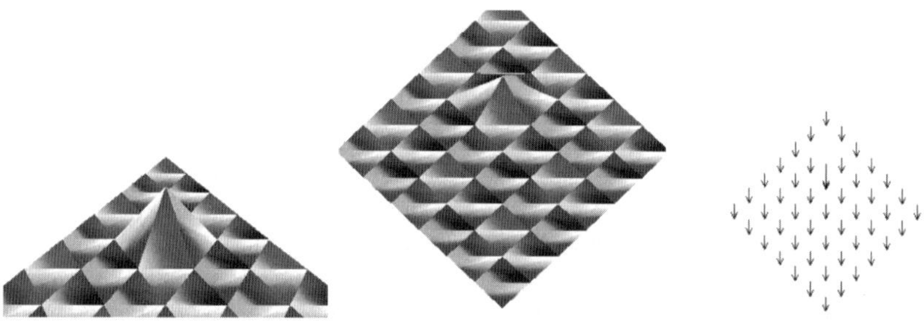

Figure 5. **a) Left:** Camera view from an arbitrary point for a terrain that contains a spike. **b) Center:** Perspective mapping of the image perceived by the visual sensor, pictured at the start of the simulation. **c) Right:** Optical flow obtained from the perspective mapping in **b)**.

Here, (N_x, N_y, N_z), (U_x, U_y, U_z), and (V_x, V_y, V_z) are the sensor axial components described in the world coordinate system W, (P_{i_a}, P_{i_b}) is a point in the image plane described by the image plane coordinate system $I(a, b)$, and h is the height of the visual sensor from the ground. Figure 6 shows the inverse perspective mappings corresponding to the images in Figure 5.

The result of this transformation on the optical flow field displayed in Figure 3 is shown in Figure 5c, where the totality of optical flow vectors are parallel to each other, as expected from the application of the inverse perspective mapping.

3. Mallot's Model and Uneven Terrain

Generally, applying Mallot's model from a mobile agent moving on an uneven terrain yields optical flow fields in which vectors may not be exhibiting parallelism among their constituent vectors. This is exemplified by the

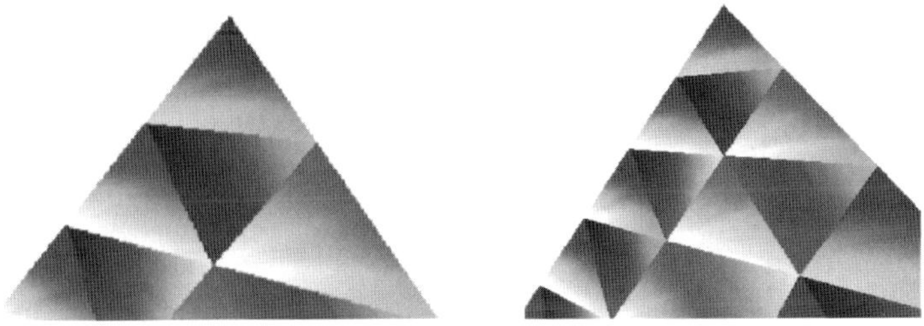

Figure 6. **a) Left**: Inverse perspective mapping for the image in Figure 5a. **b) Right:** Inverse perspective mapping for the image in Figure 5b.

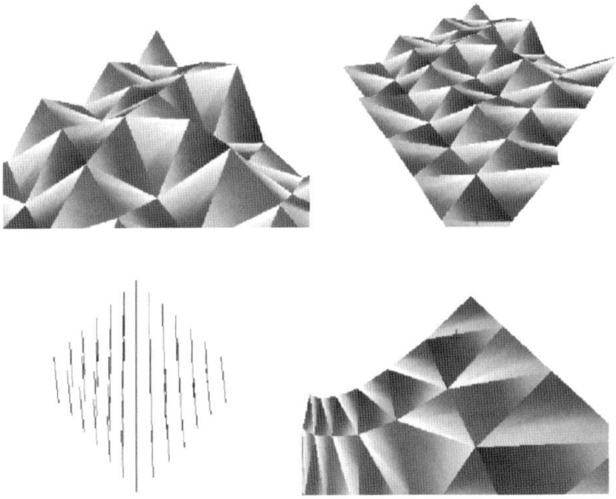

Figure 7. **a) Top-left:** Camera view from an arbitrary point for a terrain. **b) Top-Right**: Perspective mapping of the image perceived by the visual sensor, at the start of the simulation. **c) Bottom-Left:** Optical flow obtained from the perspective mapping in b). **d) Bottom-Right:** Inverse Perspective mapping for the image in b).

following case, where Figure 7a shows a 3d surface of irregular terrain and Figures 7b, 7c, and 7d display the perspective mapping, resulting optical flow, and the inverse perspective mapping respectively.

Figure 8 shows the reason behind the incorrect optical flow of Figure 7c. The point P in Figure 8 is on the terrain and the dashed line represents the path the agent must follow to keep the angle between its sensor and the horizon constant as it travels on the surface. Because the surface is uneven, this angle varies and the optical flow vectors deviate from the parallelism they should exhibit. This demonstrates the inadequacy of Mallot's model on irregular navigational terrains.

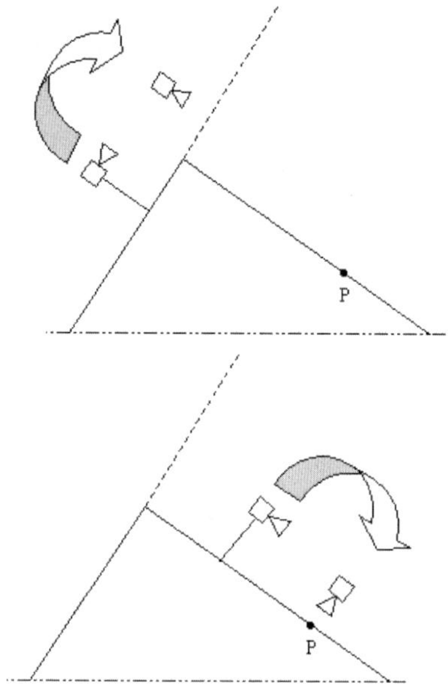

Figure 8. Mallot's inverse perspective on rough terrain.

4. The Proposed Model

As previously stated and under the conditions created by an uneven navigational surface, Equation (2) yields an incorrect optical flow, and a further transformation T is needed to null its effects. Hence, Equation (2) may be rewritten as:

$$\begin{pmatrix} Q_{i_a} \\ Q_{i_b} \\ 1 \end{pmatrix} = \frac{-f}{P_{c_z}} \begin{pmatrix} P_{c_x} \\ P_{c_y} \\ P_{c_z} \end{pmatrix} T(\theta) \tag{3}$$

where $T(\theta)$ is a rotation matrix, and θ is the angle between the optical axis of the camera and the perpendicular to the absolute horizon[1]. For Mallot's inverse perspective to be valid under the hypothesis of an uneven

[1] We define the absolute horizon as the plane perpendicular to the vector describing the direction of the gravitational field.

navigational terrain, one must find the transformation T which allows the visual sensor's angle relative to the absolute horizon to remain constant regardless of the slope of the terrain over which the agent moves.

As the agent navigates, the transformation $T(\theta)$ evolves in relation to the angle that the sensor makes with the direction of the gravitational field. Provided that the agent is fitted with adequate gyroscopic equipment, then the vector describing the direction of gravity is available and the plane to which this vector is perpendicular represents the flat navigational surface which Mallot's model requires to perform adequately.

Assuming that the agent is so equipped as to instantaneously measure the pitch and roll angles it makes with respect to the aforementioned plane, then the model can be generalized in the following fashion:

$$\begin{pmatrix} P_{i_a} \\ P_{i_b} \\ 1 \end{pmatrix} = \begin{pmatrix} Q_{i_a} \\ Q_{i_b} \\ 1 \end{pmatrix} \cdot \mathrm{P}(\alpha) \cdot \mathrm{R}(\phi) \tag{4}$$

where α and ϕ are the respective pitch and roll angles:

$$\mathrm{P}(\alpha) = \begin{pmatrix} 1 & 0 & 0 \\ 0 & \cos\alpha & \sin\alpha \\ 0 & -\sin\alpha & \cos\alpha \end{pmatrix}$$

$$\mathrm{R}(\phi) = \begin{pmatrix} \cos\phi & \sin\phi & 0 \\ -\sin\phi & \cos\phi & 0 \\ 0 & 0 & 1 \end{pmatrix}$$

As it navigates on an uneven terrain, the mobile agent experiences height variations with respect to any arbitrarily determined reference point on the terrain. This, of course, introduces unwanted perspective effects, even while pitch and roll are being corrected in the imagery acquired by the sensor. Therefore, a third transformation, this time requiring both the gravimeter and the speed of the sensory agent as inputs, needs to be formulated.

Figure 11 shows the agent moving on such a rough terrain. As the camera moves further down, the height of the camera with respect to a terrain point P decreases, thus creating a perspective effect. The following Equation shows the transformation $T_{h'}$ which compensates for the perspective:

$$T_{h'} = \begin{pmatrix} 1 & 0 & 0 \\ 0 & 1 & 0 \\ 0 & -h' & 1 \end{pmatrix} \tag{5}$$

where h' is the difference in camera height with respect to a virtual plane, normal to the direction of gravity. It is obtained in the following way:

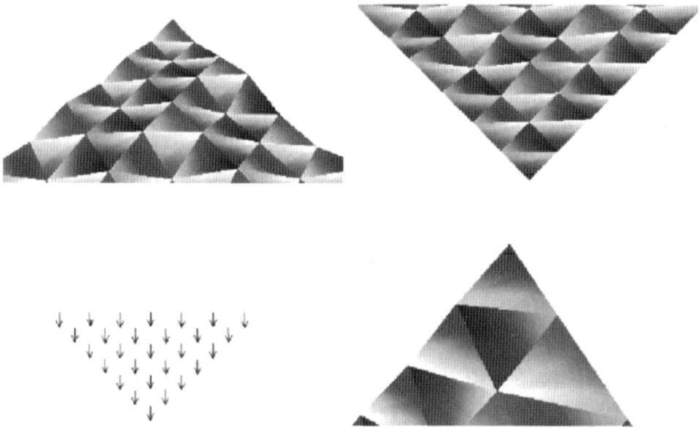

Figure 9. **a) Top-left:** Camera view from an arbitrary point about a moderately rough terrain. **b)Top-Right:** Perspective mapping of the image perceived by the visual sensor for the camera view in a). **c) Bottom-Left:** Optical flow obtained from the perspective mapping in b). **d) Bottom-Right:** Inverse Perspective mapping for the image in b).

assuming that the robot is moving with velocity V, then the distance per time interval traversed by the robot is equal to:

$$\delta S = Vt \tag{6}$$

Given that the angle of the terrain surface is known to be ρ by way of a gravimeter, then the change in camera height h' with respect to the virtual plane is obtained as follows:

$$h' = \delta S \sin \rho \tag{7}$$

The next Equation shows how this last transformation is combined with the two previous ones:

$$\begin{pmatrix} P_{i_a} \\ P_{i_b} \\ 1 \end{pmatrix} = \begin{pmatrix} Q_{i_a} \\ Q_{i_b} \\ 1 \end{pmatrix} \cdot T_{h'} \cdot \mathrm{P}(\alpha) \cdot \mathrm{R}(\phi) \tag{8}$$

Figures 9a and 10a show the camera view for different terrains with different roughness. Figures 9b and 10b are the perspective mapping; Figures 9c and 10c are the optical flow; and Figures 9d and 10d are the inverse perspective mapping, respectively.

5. Noise Analysis and Sensitivity

The orientation and magnitude of ground-truth optical flow fields were corrupted by two independent, zero-mean Gaussian distributions. Consider

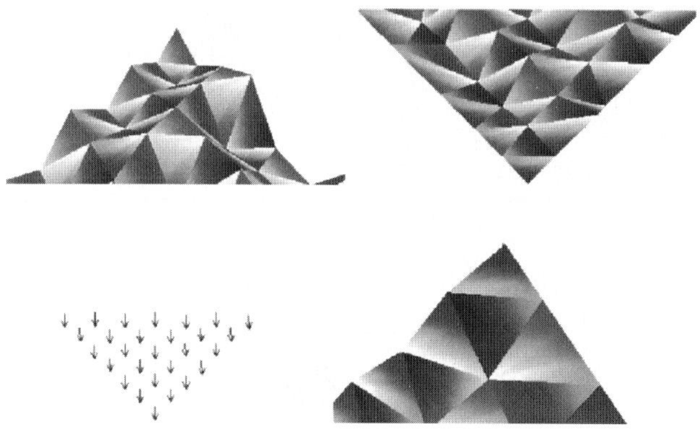

Figure 10. **a) Top-Left:** Camera view from an arbitrary point about a very rough terrain. **b) Top-Right:** Perspective mapping of the image perceived by the visual sensor for the camera view in a). **c) Bottom-Left:** Optical flow obtained from the perspective mapping in b). **d) Bottom-Right:** Inverse Perspective mapping for the image in b).

ϵ_{angle}, a randomly generated number from a zero-mean Gaussian distribution with standard deviation σ_{angle}. We formed the disturbance angle θ_d as:

$$\theta_d = \epsilon_{angle} 2\pi. \tag{9}$$

Consider ϵ_{mag}, a randomly generated number from a zero-mean Gaussian distribution with standard deviation σ_{mag}. We formed the disturbance value to be added to the magnitudes of optical flow vectors as:

$$\ell_{noisy} = \epsilon_{mag} \times \ell_{orig}. \tag{10}$$

The output noise in the terrain reconstruction process is represented by the Sum of Squared Errors (SSE) between a noise-free inverse perspective mapping and the noisy one, reconstructed with the corrupted optical flow vectors. The following Equation represents our noise metric:

$$\text{SSE} = \sum_{i=1}^{n} \sqrt{(x_i - \bar{x}_i)^2 + (y_i - \bar{y}_i)^2} \tag{11}$$

where x_i and y_i are the reconstructed coordinates of a point P_i in the image, and $\bar{x}_i$ and $\bar{y}_i$ are the corresponding noisy ones.

Figure 12 shows the relation between the two standard deviations σ_{angle}, and σ_{mag}, within the range 0.0001 and 0.05 with step 0.01 and the SSE metric. We observe that the error increases non-linearly with the progression of the standard deviation that corrupts the magnitude of the optical

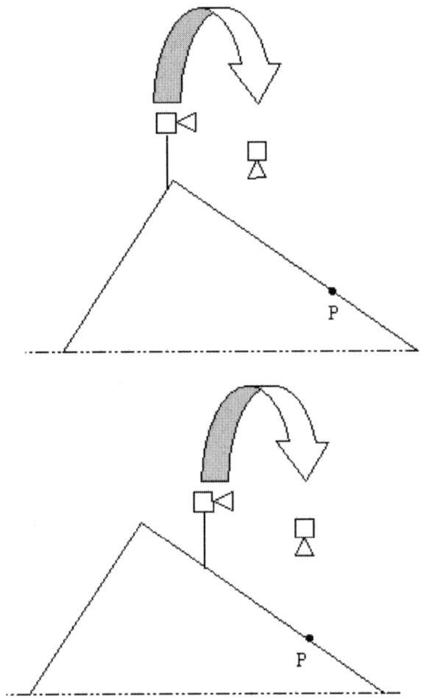

Figure 11. The camera, for the proposed model.

flow vectors. However, the output error behavior for the input optical flow directional error appears to be linear.

It is apparent from this analysis that linear input noise generates non-linear output noise in the terrain reconstruction process. We believe this effect to be mainly due from expected sources, including the behavior of perspective projection equations and the relationship between optical flow from a bird's eye perspective and the depth of environmental surfaces.

6. Conclusion

We proposed a mathematical model for optical flow-based autonomous navigation on uneven terrains. We provided a detailed explanation on the inadequacy of Mallot's inverse perspective scheme for uneven navigational surfaces. The model was extended to include these types of surfaces.

Our generalization of Mallot's model relies on the knowledge of the direction of the gravitational field and the speed of the mobile agent. We believe that visual information must be fused with other sources of information, such as one's position with respect to the direction of gravity, odometry, and inertial information. In addition, our model can be further

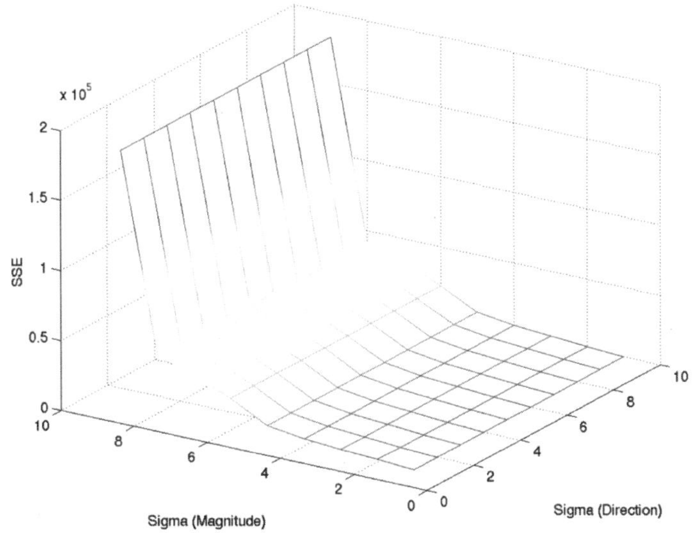

Figure 12. SSE versus standard deviation, representing the noise in optical flow vector magnitudes and directions. Each unit in the graph represents 0.01 standard deviation. The experiment displays a standard deviation range from 0.0001 to 0.05.

extended to compensate for acceleration, as long as this information is made available to the vision system through odometry.

We are currently working towards generalizing our approach to stereo vision systems, so as to obtain multiple channels of visual information, onto which cue selection and integration could be performed, thus enhancing the robustness of the approach.

References

Barron, J. L., D. J. Fleet, and S. S. Beauchemin: Performance of optical flow techniques. *IJCV*, **12**: 43–77, 1994.

Batavia, P. H., S. A. Roth, and S. Singh: Autonomous coverage operations in semi-structured outdoor environments. In *IEEE RSJ Int. Conf. Intelligent Robots and Systems*, October 2002.

Baten, S., M. Lutzeler, E. D. Dickmanns, R. Mandelbaum, and P. J. Burt: Techniques for autonomous, off-road navigation. *IEEE Intelligent Systems*, **13**, 1998.

Choi, W., C. Ryu, and H. Kim: Navigation of a mobile robot using mono-vision and mono-audition. In *IEEE Int. Conf. Systems, Man and Cybernetics*, 1999.

Desouza, G. N. and A. C. Kak: Vision for mobile robot navigation: a survey. *IEEE Trans. Pattern Analysis Machine Intelligence*, **24**, 2002.

Jin, T., S. Park, and J. Lee: A study on position determination for mobile robot navigation in an indoor environment. In Proc. *IEEE Int. Symp. Computational Intelligence in Robotics and Automation*, 2003.

Kim, Y. and H. Kim: Dense 3d map building for autonomous mobile robots. In Proc. *IEEE Int. Symp. Computational Intelligence in Robotics and Automation*, 2003.

Ku, C. and W. Tsai: Obstacle avoidance for autonomous land vehicle navigation in indoor environments by quadratic classifiers. *IEEE Trans. Systems, Man and Cybernetics*, **29**, 1999.

Tang, L. and S. Yuta: Vision-based navigation for mobile robots in indoor environments by teaching and playing-back scheme. In Proc. *IEEE Int. Conf. Robotics and Automation*, 2001.

Tang, L. and S. Yuta: Indoor navigation for mobile robots using memorized omnidirectional images and robot's motion. In Proc. *IEEE RSJ Int. Conf. Intelligent Robots and Systems*, 2002.

Wijesoma, W. S., K. R. S. Kodagoda, and A. P. Balasuryia: A laser and a camera for mobile robot navigation. In Proc. *Int. Conf. Control, Automation, Robotics and Vision*, 2002.

Part V

Sensors and Other Modalities

BEYOND TRICHROMATIC IMAGING *

ELLI ANGELOPOULOU
Computer Science Department
Stevens Institute of Technology
Hoboken, NJ 07030, USA

Abstract. An integral part of computer vision and graphics is modeling how a surface reflects light. There is a substantial body of work on models describing surface reflectance ranging from purely diffuse to purely specular. One of the advantages of diffuse reflectance is that the color and the intensity of the reflected light are separable. For diffuse materials, the objective color of the surface depends on the chromophores present in the material and is described by its albedo. We will show that for diffuse reflectance, multispectral image analysis allows us to isolate the albedo of a surface. By computing the spectral gradients, i.e. evaluating the partial derivatives with respect to wavelength at distinct wavelengths, one can extract a quantity that is independent of the incident light and the scene geometry. The extracted measurement is the partial derivative of the albedo with respect to wavelength.

In specular highlights the color and the intensity of a specularity depend on both the geometry and the index of refraction of the material, which in turn is a function of wavelength. Though the vision and graphics communities often assume that for non-conductive materials the color of the specularity is the color of the light source, we will show that under multispectral imaging this assumption is often violated. Multispectral image analysis supports the underlying theory which predicts that even for non-metallic surfaces the reflectivity ratio at specularities varies with both wavelength and angle of incidence. Furthermore, the spectral gradients of specular highlights isolate the Fresnel term up to an additive constant.

Key words: multispectral, albedo, specular highlights, Fresnel, spectral gradients

1. Introduction

The starting point of most computer vision techniques is the light intensity reflected from an imaged scene. The reflected light is directly related to the geometry of the scene, the reflectance properties of the materials in the scene and the illumination under which the scene was captured. There

* This material is based upon work supported by the National Science Foundation under Grant No. ITR-0085864 and Grant No. CAREER-0133549

K. Daniilidis and R. Klette (eds.), Imaging Beyond the Pinhole Camera, 285–306.

is a considerable body of work which attempts to isolate at least one of these factors for further scene analysis. In this work we will show how multispectral imaging can assist in isolating reflectance properties like the albedo of a diffuse surface or the Fresnel term at specular highlights.

A closely related topic is that of color constancy, the task of consistently identifying colors, despite changes in illumination conditions. (Maloney and Wandell, 1986) were the first to develop a tractable color constancy algorithm by modeling both the surface reflectance and the incident illumination as a finite dimensional linear model. This idea was further explored by (Forsyth, 1990), (Ho et al., 1990), (Finlayson et al., 1994), (Funt and Finlayson, 1995), (Finlayson, 1996), (Barnard et al., 1997), and (Healey and Slater, 1994). Color is a very important cue in object identification. (Swain and Ballard, 1991) showed that objects can be recognized by using color information alone. Combining color cues with color constancy ((Healey and Slater, 1994), (Healey and Wang, 1995), (Funt and Finlayson, 1995), (Finlayson, 1996)) generated even more powerful color-guided object recognition systems.

In general, extracting reflectance information (whether it is recovery of surface color or reliable identification of specular highlights or computation of other surface reflectance properties) is an under-constrained problem. All the afore-mentioned methodologies had to introduce some additional constraints that may limit their applicability. For example, most color techniques assume that the spectral reflectance functions have the same degrees of freedom as the number of photo-receptor classes (typically three.) Thus, none of these methods can be used in grey-scale images for extracting illumination invariant color information. Furthermore, a considerable body of work on color assumes that the incident illumination has two or three degrees of freedom. However, (Slater and Healey, 1998) showed that for outdoor scenes, the illumination functions have seven degrees of freedom.

Specularity detection is even more complex that analyzing diffuse surfaces, because unlike diffuse reflectance, the color and the intensity of the specular highlights are not separable. Rather, they both depend on the angle of incidence as well as the index of refraction of the material at the surface of an object, which, in turn, is a function of wavelength (see (Hechts, 1998)). The reflectance models developed by (Phong, 1975) and (Blinn, 1977) though popular, ignore the effects of wavelength in specular regions. In comparison, the (Cook and Torrance, 1982) model predicts both the directional and the spectral composition of specularities. It describes the light and surface interaction, once the light reaches the surface, through the use of the Fresnel reflectance equations. These equations relate specular reflection to the refractive indices of the two media at the interface, the angle of incidence and the polarization of the incoming light (Hechts, 1998).

The Cook-Torrance model places emphasis on the specular color variations caused by changes in the angle of incidence. The model clearly acknowledges that the specular reflectivity of a surface depends on the index of refraction, which is a function of wavelength and states that the specularity response varies over the light spectrum. However, it assumes that for dielectric materials, particularly plastics and ceramics, the specular reflectance varies only slightly with wavelength and consequently its color can be considered the same as the color of the light source. This assumption has been widely adopted by the computer graphics and vision communities ((Bajcsy et al., 1990), (Blinn, 1977), (Cook and Torrance, 1982), (Klinker et al., 1992), (Shafer, 1985)). As a result, many specular detection algorithms are searching for regions whose color signature is identical to that of the incident light.

We will show that multispectral imaging clearly indicates that the color at specular highlights is (a) not the color of incident light and (b) material dependent. By taking advantage of the dense spectral sampling, we developed a new technique based on spectral derivatives for analyzing reflectance properties. We examine the rate of change in reflected intensity with respect to wavelength over the visible part of the electromagnetic spectrum. Our methodology extracts color information which is invariant to geometry and incident illumination. For diffuse surfaces, independent of the particular model of reflectance, the only factor that contributes to variations over the wavelength is the albedo of the surface. Thus, what we end up extracting is the reflectivity profile of the surface. For specular surfaces, our technique extracts the Fresnel term, up to an additive term.

Multispectral imaging combined with spectral derivatives creates a flexible, more information rich scene analysis tool. Unlike the more traditional band-ratios, spectral derivatives are used on a per pixel basis. They do not depend on neighboring regions, an assumption that is common in other photometric methods, which use logarithms and/or narrow-band filters like (Funt and Finlayson, 1995). The only assumption that we make is that incident illumination remains stable over small intervals in the visible spectrum. It will be demonstrated that this is a reasonable assumption.

Experiments on diffuse surfaces of different colors and materials demonstrated the ability of spectral gradients to: a) identify surfaces with the same albedo under variable viewing conditions; b) discriminate between surfaces that have different albedo; and c) provide a measure of how close the colors of the two surfaces are. Our experimental analysis on specular regions showed that we can compute the spectral profile of the Fresnel term with an accuracy of well under 2%. Further experimentation with everyday objects demonstrated that the extracted term is not constant with respect to wavelength and differs with both the surface material and the angle of incidence.

2. Spectral Derivatives

The intensity images that we process in computer vision are formed when light from a scene falls on a photosensitive sensor. The amount of light reflected from each point $\vec{p} = (x, y, z)$ in the scene depends on the light illuminating the scene, E, and the surface reflectance, S, of the surfaces in the scene:

$$I(\vec{p}, \lambda) = E(\vec{p}, \lambda)S(\vec{p}, \lambda) \tag{1}$$

where λ, the wavelength, shows the dependence of incident and reflected light on wavelength. The reflectance function $S(\vec{p}, \lambda)$ depends on the surface material, the scene geometry and the viewing and incidence angles.

When the spectral distribution of the incident light does not vary with the direction of the light, the geometric and spectral components of the incident illumination are separable:

$$E(\theta_i, \phi_i, \lambda) = e(\lambda)E(\theta_i, \phi_i) \tag{2}$$

where (θ_i, ϕ_i) are the spherical coordinates of the unit-length light-direction vector and $e(\lambda)$ is the illumination spectrum. Note that, the incident light intensity is included in $E(\theta_i, \phi_i)$ and may vary as the position of the illumination source changes. The scene brightness then becomes:

$$I(\vec{p}, \lambda) = e(\vec{p}, \lambda)E(\vec{p}, \theta_i, \phi_i)S(\vec{p}, \lambda) \tag{3}$$

Before we perform any analysis we simplify the scene brightness equation by taking its logarithm. The logarithmic brightness equation reduces the product into a sum:

$$L(\vec{p}, \lambda) = \ln e(\vec{p}, \lambda) + \ln E(\vec{p}, \theta_i, \phi_i) + \ln S(\vec{p}, \lambda) \tag{4}$$

In order to analyze the behavior of the surface reflectance over the various wavelengths we compute the *spectral derivative*, which is the partial derivative of the logarithmic image with respect to the wavelength λ:

$$L_\lambda(\vec{p}, \lambda) = \frac{e_\lambda(\vec{p}, \lambda)}{e(\vec{p}, \lambda)} + \frac{S_\lambda(\vec{p}, \lambda)}{S(\vec{p}, \lambda)} \tag{5}$$

where $e_\lambda(\vec{p}, \lambda) = \partial e(\vec{p}, \lambda)/\partial\lambda$ is the partial derivative of the spectrum of the incident light with respect to wavelength and $S_\lambda(\vec{p}, \lambda) = \partial S(\vec{p}, \lambda)/\partial\lambda$ is the partial derivative of the surface reflectance with respect to wavelength.

Our work concentrates on the visible part of the electromagnetic spectrum, i.e. from 400nm to 700nm. (Ho et al., 1990) have shown, that for natural objects the surface spectral reflectance curves, i.e. the plots of $S(\vec{p}, \lambda)$ versus λ, are usually reasonably smooth and continuous over the visible spectrum.

2.1. INVARIANCE TO INCIDENT ILLUMINATION

Consider first the term of the spectral distribution of the incident light. For most of the commonly used indoor illumination sources one can safely assume that e increases at a relatively slow and approximately constant rate with respect to wavelength, λ, over the visible range (black body radiation, fluorescent light outside the narrow spikes). Thus:

$$\frac{e_\lambda(\vec{p}, \lambda)}{e(\vec{p}, \lambda)} \approx c \tag{6}$$

where c is a small constant determined by the specific illumination conditions. This implies that one can safely assume that in general the partial derivative of the logarithmic image depends mainly on the surface reflectance:

$$L_\lambda(\vec{p}, \lambda) \approx \frac{S_\lambda(\vec{p}, \lambda)}{S(\vec{p}, \lambda)} + c \tag{7}$$

3. Diffuse Reflectance

For diffuse surface reflectance, independent of the particular model of reflectance, the only term that depends on wavelength is the albedo of the surface. Albedo $\rho(\lambda)$ is the ratio of electromagnetic energy reflected by a surface to the amount of electromagnetic energy incident upon the surface (see (Sabins, 1997)). It is a color descriptor which is invariant to viewpoint, scene geometry and incident illumination. A profile of albedo values over the entire visible spectrum is a physically based descriptor of color.

Consider for example one of the most complex diffuse reflectance model, the Generalized Lambertian model developed by (Oren and Nayar, 1995) (for other diffuse reflectance models see (Angelopoulou, 2000) . Their model describes the diffuse reflectance of surfaces with substantial macroscopic surface roughness. The macrostructure of the surface is modeled as a collection of long V-cavities. (Long in the sense that the area of each facet of the cavity is much larger than the wavelength of the incident light.) The modeling of a surface with V-cavities is a widely accepted surface description as in (Torrance and Sparrow, 1967), (Hering and Smith, 1970).

The light measured at a single pixel of an optical sensor is an aggregate measure of the brightness reflected from a single surface patch composed of numerous V-cavities. Each cavity is composed of two planar Lambertian facets with opposing normals. All the V-cavities within the same surface patch have the same albedo, ρ. Different facets can have different slopes and orientation. Oren and Nayar assume that the V-cavities are uniformly distributed in azimuth angle orientation on the surface plane, while the facet tilt follows a Gaussian distribution with zero mean and standard deviation σ. The standard deviation σ can be viewed as a roughness parameter. When $\sigma = 0$, all the facet normals align with the mean surface normal and produce a planar patch that exhibits an approximately Lambertian reflectance. As σ increases, the V-cavities get deeper and the deviation from Lambert's law increases. Ignoring interreflections from the neighboring facets, but accounting for the masking and shadowing effects that the facets introduce, the Oren-Nayar model approximates the surface reflectance as:

$$\begin{aligned} S(\vec{p}, \lambda, \sigma) &= \frac{\rho(\vec{p}, \lambda)}{\pi} \cos\theta_i(\vec{p}) \Big[C_1(\sigma) \\ &+ \cos(\phi_r(\vec{p}) - \phi_i(\vec{p})) C_2(\alpha; \beta; \phi_r - \phi_i; \sigma; \vec{p}) \tan\beta(\vec{p}) \\ &+ (1 - |\cos(\phi_r(\vec{p}) - \phi_i(\vec{p}))|) \\ & \quad C_3(\alpha; \beta; \sigma; \vec{p}) \tan\left(\frac{\alpha(\vec{p}) + \beta(\vec{p})}{2}\right) \Big] \end{aligned} \tag{8}$$

where $\rho(\vec{p}, \lambda)$ is the albedo or diffuse reflection coefficient at point $\vec{p}$, and $(\theta_i(\vec{p}), \phi_i(\vec{p}))$ and $(\theta_r(\vec{p}), \phi_r(\vec{p}))$ are the spherical coordinates of the angles of incidence and reflectance accordingly, $\alpha(\vec{p}) = \max(\theta_i(\vec{p}), \theta_r(\vec{p}))$ and $\beta(\vec{p}) = \min(\theta_i(\vec{p}), \theta_r(\vec{p}))$. $C_1()$, $C_2()$ and $C_3()$ are coefficients related to the surface macrostructure. The first coefficient, $C_1()$ depends solely on the distribution of the facet orientation, while the other two depend on the surface roughness, the angle of incidence and the angle of reflectance:

$$C_1(\sigma) = 1 - 0.5 \frac{\sigma^2}{\sigma^2 + 0.33} \tag{9}$$

$$\begin{aligned} & C_2\ (\alpha; \beta; \phi_r - \phi_i; \sigma; \vec{p}) \\ &= \begin{cases} 0.45 \frac{\sigma^2}{\sigma^2 + 0.09} \sin\alpha(\vec{p}) & \text{if} \cos(\phi_r(\vec{p}) - \phi_i(\vec{p})) \geq 0 \\ 0.45 \frac{\sigma^2}{\sigma^2 + 0.09} (\sin\alpha(\vec{p}) - (\frac{2\beta(\vec{p})}{\pi})^3) & \text{otherwise} \end{cases} \end{aligned} \tag{10}$$

$$C_3(\alpha; \beta; \sigma; \vec{p}) = 0.125 \left(\frac{\sigma^2}{\sigma^2 + 0.09} \right) \left(\frac{4\alpha(\vec{p})\beta(\vec{p})}{\pi^2} \right)^2 \tag{11}$$

For clarity of presentation, we define the term $V(\vec{p},\sigma)$ which combines the terms that accounts for all the reflectance effects which are introduced by the roughness of the surface:

$$\begin{aligned} V(\vec{p},\sigma) &= C_1(\sigma) \\ &+ \cos\left(\phi_r(\vec{p}) - \phi_i(\vec{p})\right) C_2(\alpha;\beta;\phi_r - \phi_i;\sigma;\vec{p}) \tan\beta(\vec{p}) \\ &+ (1 - |\cos\left(\phi_r(\vec{p}) - \phi_i(\vec{p})\right)|) C_3(\alpha;\beta;\sigma;\vec{p}) \tan\left(\frac{\alpha(\vec{p}) + \beta(\vec{p})}{2}\right) \end{aligned} \quad (12)$$

The angles of incidence and reflectance, as well as the distribution of the cavities affect the value of the function $V(\vec{p},\sigma)$. The Oren-Nayar reflectance model can then be written more compactly as:

$$S(\vec{p},\lambda,\sigma) = \frac{\rho(\vec{p},\lambda)}{\pi} \cos\theta_i(\vec{p}) V(\vec{p},\sigma) \quad (13)$$

The spectral derivative (see Equation 7) of a surface that exhibits Generalized Lambertian reflectance is a measure of how albedo changes with respect to wavelength:

$$L_\lambda(\vec{p},\lambda) \approx \frac{S_\lambda(\vec{p},\lambda)}{S(\vec{p},\lambda)} + c = \frac{\rho_\lambda(\vec{p},\lambda)}{\rho(\vec{p},\lambda)} + c \quad (14)$$

where $\rho_\lambda(\vec{p},\lambda)$ is the partial derivative of the surface albedo with respect to wavelength. The scene geometry, including the angle of incidence $\theta_i(\vec{p})$ and the constant π, are independent of wavelength. None of the terms in the function $V(\vec{p},\sigma)$ vary with wavelength. As a result, when we have the dense spectral sampling of multispectral imaging and we compute the spectral derivative for diffuse surfaces we obtain a color descriptor which is a purely material dependent. An important advantage of the extracted albedo profile is that since the dependence on the angle of incidence gets canceled out, there is no need for assuming an infinitely distant light source. The incident illumination can vary from one point to another, without affecting the resulting spectral derivative.

Thus, for diffuse surfaces, the spectral derivative of an image $L_\lambda(\vec{p},\lambda)$ is primarily a function of the albedo of the surface, independent of the diffuse reflectance model. Specifically, the spectral derivative is the normalized partial derivative of the albedo with respect to wavelength $\rho_\lambda(\vec{p},\lambda)/\rho(\vec{p},\lambda)$ (normalized by the magnitude of the albedo itself) offset by a term which is constant per illumination condition.

4. Diffuse Surface Experiments

Our multispectral sensor was constructed by placing a filter wheel with narrow bandpass filters in front of a grey-scale camera. Each of these filters has a bandwidth of approximately 10nm and a transmittance of about 50%. The central wavelengths are at 450nm, 480nm, 510nm, 540nm, 570nm, 600nm, 630nm and 660nm respectively. If one were to assign color names to these filters, he/she could label them as follows: 450nm = blue, 480nm = cyan, 510 = green, 540 = yellow, 570 = amber, 600 = red, 630 = scarlet red, 660 = mauve. The use of narrow bandpass filters allowed us to closely sample almost the entire visible spectrum. The dense narrow sampling permitted us to avoid sampling (or ignore samples) where the incident light may be discontinuous. (Hall and Greenberg, 1983) have demonstrated that such a sampling density provides for the reproduction of a good approximation of the continuous reflectance spectrum.

In practice, differentiation can be approximated by finite differencing, as long as the differencing interval is sufficiently small. Thus, we computed the spectral derivative of a multispectral image, by first taking the logarithm of each color image and then subtracting pairs of consecutive color images. The resulting spectral gradient is an M-dimensional vector $(L_{\lambda_1}, L_{\lambda_2}, \ldots, L_{\lambda_M})$. Specifically, in our setup each L_{λ_k} was computed over the wavelength interval $\delta\lambda = 30nm$ by subtracting two logarithmic images taken under two different color filters which were 30nm apart:

$$L_{\lambda_k} = L_{w+30} - L_w \tag{15}$$

where $k = 1, 2, \ldots, 7$ and $w = 450, 480, 510, 540, 570, 600, 6300$ accordingly. In our setup the spectral gradient was a 7-vector:

$$(L_{\lambda_1}, L_{\lambda_2}, \ldots, L_{\lambda_7}) = (L_{480} - L_{450}, L_{510} - L_{480}, \ldots, L_{660} - L_{630}) \tag{16}$$

4.1. OBJECTS WITH DIFFUSE SURFACE

In our series of experiments with diffuse objects we took images of four different types of materials: foam, paper, ceramic and a curved metallic surface painted with flat (matte) paint. The foam and the paper sheets came in a variety of colors. The foam which was a relatively smooth and diffuse surface came in white, pink, magenta, green, yellow, orange and red samples. The paper had a rougher texture and came in pink, fuchsia, brown, orange, yellow, green, white, blue, and violet colors. We also took images of a pink ceramic plate and of two single albedo curved surfaces

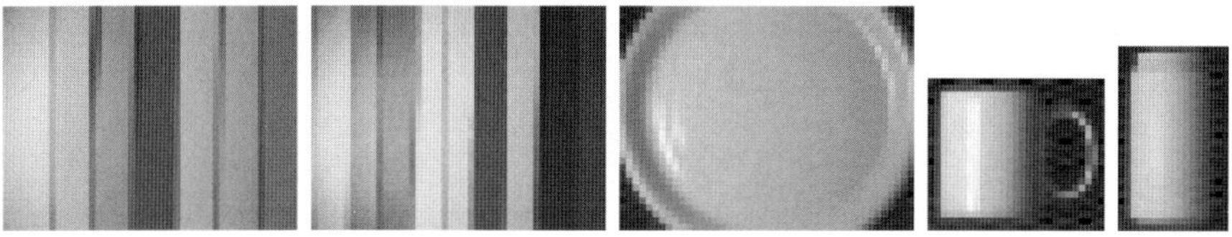

Figure 1. Sample filtered images of the objects and materials used in the experiments. From left to right: various colors of foam, various colors of paper, a pink ceramic plate, a white ceramic mug, a white spray-painted soda can. All the images in this figure were taken with the red 600nm filter.

(a mug and a painted soda-can). Figure 1 shows samples of the actual images taken using the 600nm filter.

In this series of experiments the only source of illumination was a single tungsten light bulb mounted in a reflected scoop. For each scene we used four different illumination setups, generated by the combination of two distinct light bulbs, a 150W bulb and a 200W bulb and two different light positions. One illumination position was to the left of the camera and about 5cm below the camera. Its direction vector formed approximately a 45° angle with the optic axis. The other light-bulb position was to the right of the camera and about 15cm above it. Its direction vector formed roughly a angle with the optic axis. Both locations were 40cm away from the scene.

For these objects, the spectral gradient vector was expected to remain constant for diffuse surfaces with the same albedo profile, independent of variations in viewing conditions. At the same time, the spectral gradient should differ between distinct colors. Furthermore, the more distant the colors are, the bigger the difference between the respective spectral gradients should be. The following figures show the plots of the spectral gradient values for each surface versus the wavelength. The horizontal axis is the wavelength, while the vertical axis is the spectral gradient which is also the normalized partial derivative of albedo. Figure 2 shows the plots of different colors of paper on the left and of different colors of foam on the right. Within each group, the plots are quite unique and easily differentiable from each other.

On the other hand, the spectral gradients of different surfaces of the same color, generate plots that look almost identical. Figure 3 on the left shows the gradient plots for the white paper, the white foam, the white mug, and the white painted soda can. In a similar manner, when we have similar but not identical colors, the spectral gradient plots resemble each other, but are not as closely clustered. The right side of Figure 3 shows the spectral gradients of various shades of pink and magenta. The closer the two shades are, the more closely the corresponding plots are clustered.

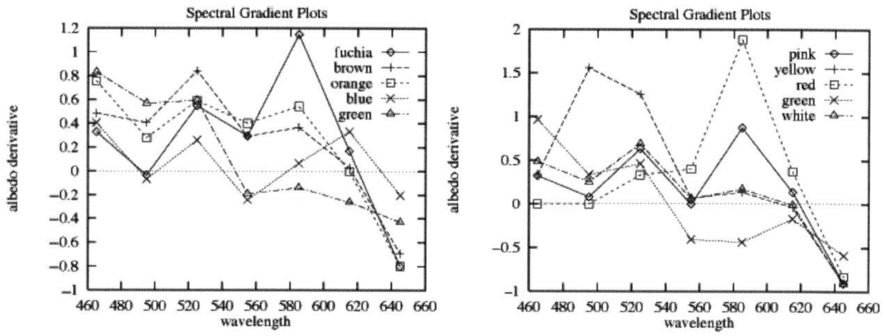

Figure 2. Spectral gradients of different colors of (left) paper and (right) foam under the same viewing conditions (same illumination, same geometry).

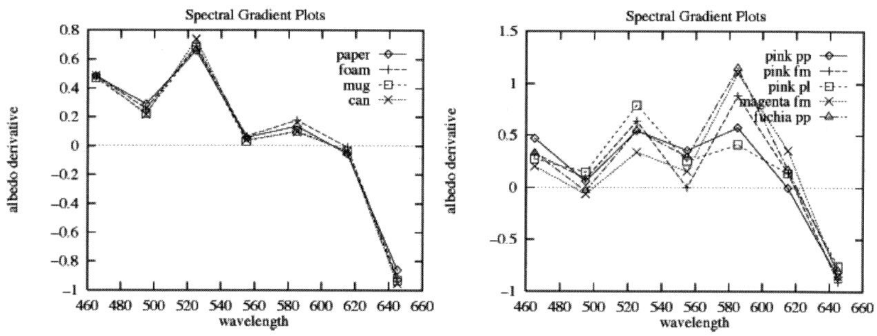

Figure 3. Spectral gradients of (left) different white surfaces (foam, paper, ceramic mug, diffuse can) and (right) different shades of pink and different materials: pink foam, magenta foam, pink paper, fuchsia paper and pink ceramic plate. All images were taken under the same viewing conditions (same illumination, same geometry).

The next couple of figures demonstrate that the spectral gradient remains constant under variations in illumination and viewing. This is expected as spectral gradients are purely a function of albedo. The plots in Figure 4 were produced by measuring the spectral gradient for the same surface patch while altering the position and intensity of the light sources.

We also tested the invariance of the spectral derivatives with respect to the viewing angle and the surface geometry. Figure 5 shows the plots of the spectral gradients produced by different patches of the same curved object (the painted soda can in this case). As can be seen in the left graph in Figure 5 for patches that are at mildly to quite oblique angles to the viewer and/or the incident light the spectral gradient plots remain closely

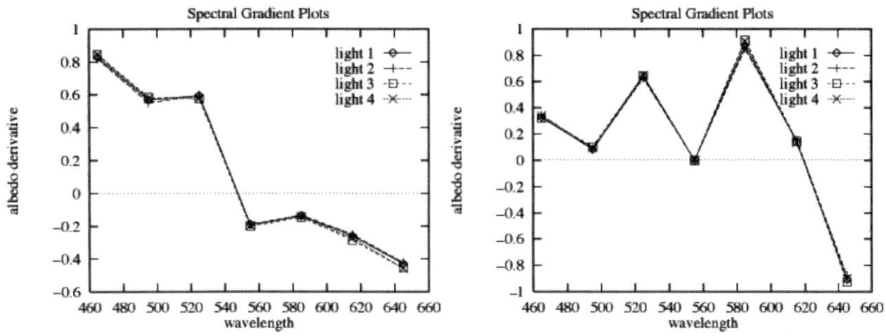

Figure 4. Spectral gradients of the same color (left) green and (right) pink under varying illumination. Both the position and the intensity of illumination is altered, while the viewing position remains the same.

clustered. However, as can be seen at the right graph of Figure 5, for almost grazing angles of incidence, the spectral gradients do not remain constant. Deviations at such large angles are a known physical phenomenon (see (Kortum, 1969)). (Oren and Nayar, 1995) also pointed out that in this special case, most of the light that is reflected from a surface patch is due to interreflections from nearby facets.

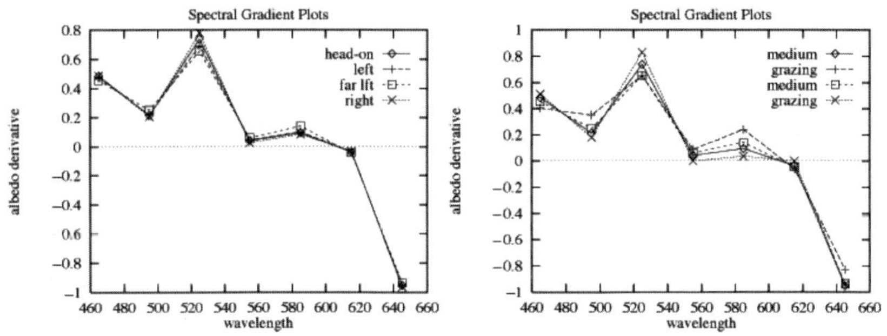

Figure 5. Spectral gradients of white color at different angles of incidence and reflectance. The spectral gradients at different surface patches of the white soda can are shown. The surface normals for the patches on the left vary from almost parallel to the optic axis, to very oblique, while on the right the incident light is almost grazing the surface.

5. Specular Reflectance

The analysis of specularly reflective surfaces is more complex, partly because the color and intensity of specular highlights is not separable. A physically-based specular reflectance model which captures quite accurately the directional distribution and spectral composition of the reflected light (as well as its dependence on the local surface geometry, on the surface roughness, and on the material properties) is that developed by (Cook and Torrance, 1982). In that model, the surface roughness is expressed as a collection of micro-facets, each of which is a smooth mirror. The dependence of specular reflectance on material properties is described using the Fresnel equations. Cook and Torrance define the fraction S of the incident light that is specularly reflected as:

$$S = \frac{DGF}{\pi(N \cdot L)(N \cdot V)} \tag{17}$$

where D is the micro-facet distribution term, G is the shadowing/masking term, F is the Fresnel reflectance term, L is the light direction vector, V is the viewing vector and N is the surface normal. All vectors are assumed to be unit length.

The terms D and G describe the light pathways and their geometric interaction with the surface microstructure. They do not capture how the surface and light geometry can affect the amount of light that is specularly reflected from a surface. It is the Fresnel reflectance term F in the Cook and Torrance model that describes how light is reflected from each smooth micro-facet. The Fresnel term encapsulates the effects of color, material and angle of incidence on light reflection.

5.1. THE FRESNEL TERM

A quantifiable measure of amount of light is *radiant flux density*, the rate of flow of radiant energy per unit surface area. Thus, an appropriate measurement of surface reflectance ratio, $F(\lambda)$, at each micro-facet is the ratio of reflected over incident radiant flux densities at different wavelengths. Radiant flux density itself is proportional to the square of amplitude reflection coefficient, r. Depending on the orientation of the electric field of the incident light's electromagnetic wave with respect to the plane of incidence (the plane defined by N and L), there exist two amplitude reflection coefficients, $r_\perp$ and $r_\parallel$. Based on the definition of radiant flux, the derived surface reflectance ratio is:

$$F = \frac{1}{2}(r_\perp^2 + r_\parallel^2) \tag{18}$$

The amplitude reflection coefficients themselves are given by the following Fresnel equations for details (Hechts, 1998). When the electric field is perpendicular ($\perp$) to the plane of incidence the amplitude reflection coefficient $r_\perp$ is:

$$r_\perp = \frac{n_i \cos\theta_i - n_t \cos\theta_t}{n_i \cos\theta_i + n_t \cos\theta_t} \tag{19}$$

where θ_i is the angle of incidence, θ_t is the angle of transmittance and n_i and n_t are the refractive indices of the incident and the transmitting media respectively. Similarly, when the electric field is parallel ($\|$) to the plane of incidence, the amplitude reflection coefficient $r_\|$ is:

$$r_\| = \frac{n_t \cos\theta_i - n_i \cos\theta_t}{n_i \cos\theta_t + n_t \cos\theta_i} \tag{20}$$

By combining Equations (18), (19), and (20) and employing trigonometric equalities, as well as Snell's Law ((Hechts, 1998)), $n_i \sin\theta_i = n_t \sin\theta_t$, the surface reflectance for non-monochromatic light can be rewritten as:

$$\begin{aligned} F(\lambda,\theta_i) &= \frac{1}{2}\frac{n_i^2(\lambda)\cos^2\theta_i + J(\lambda,\theta_i) - 2n_i(\lambda)\cos\theta_i\sqrt{J(\lambda,\theta_i)}}{n_i^2(\lambda)\cos^2\theta_i + J(\lambda,\theta_i) + 2n_i(\lambda)\cos\theta_i\sqrt{J(\lambda,\theta_i)}} \\ &+ \frac{1}{2}\frac{n_t^2(\lambda)\cos^2\theta_i + n_{it}^2(\lambda)J(\lambda,\theta_i) - 2n_i(\lambda)\cos\theta_i\sqrt{J(\lambda,\theta_i)}}{n_t^2(\lambda)\cos^2\theta_i + n_{it}^2(\lambda)J(\lambda,\theta_i) + 2n_i(\lambda)\cos\theta_i\sqrt{J(\lambda,\theta_i)}} \end{aligned} \tag{21}$$

where $J(\lambda,\theta_i) = n_t^2(\lambda) - n_i^2(\lambda) + n_i^2(\lambda)\cos^2\theta_i$ and $n_{it}(\lambda) = n_i(\lambda)/n_t(\lambda)$.

Because the values of the index of refraction and their variation with wavelength are not typically known ((Cook and Torrance, 1982), (Jähne and Haussecker, 2000), (Watt, 2000)) suggest using the following approximation for the Fresnel equations at normal incidence:

$$\begin{aligned} F_{CT}(\lambda,\theta_i) &= \frac{1}{2}\frac{(g(\lambda,\theta_i) - \cos\theta_i)^2}{(g(\lambda,\theta_i) + \cos\theta_i)^2} \\ &\left(1 + \frac{(\cos\theta_i(g(\lambda,\theta_i) + \cos\theta_i) - 1)^2}{(\cos\theta_i(g(\lambda,\theta_i) - \cos\theta_i) + 1)^2}\right) \end{aligned} \tag{22}$$

where $g(\lambda,\theta_i) = \sqrt{n_{it}^2(\lambda) + \cos^2\theta_i - 1}$. When the normal incidence reflectance is known, they suggest using Equation (23) to obtain an estimate of n_{it} and then substitute the derived estimate of n_{it} in the original Fresnel equations to obtain the Fresnel coefficients at other angles of incidence. Though Cook and Torrance used Equation (23) only to obtain an estimate of n_{it}, many implementations of their model replace the Fresnel term with the normal incidence approximation shown in Equation (23).

5.2. THE SENSITIVITY OF SURFACE REFLECTANCE TO WAVELENGTH

Equation (22) and its approximation by Cook and Torrance (see Equation 23)show the dependence of the Fresnel reflectance term on the angle of incidence and the indices of refraction and subsequently on wavelength. Thus, according to the specular reflectance model: (a) different materials due to the differences in their refractive index should have different surface reflectance and (b) since the index of refraction varies with wavelength, the reflectance value is expected to vary with wavelength itself. The latter implies that, independent of the angle of incidence, the color of specular highlights is not necessarily the color of incident light (which assumes constant reflectance across wavelengths).

It is common practice in the computer vision and graphics communities to place more emphasis on the effects of the incidence angle on the color of specularity and to assume that the color of specular highlights for dielectrics can be approximated by the color of the incident light as in (Blinn, 1977), (Cook and Torrance, 1982), (Klinker et al., 1992), (Phong, 1975), (Shafer, 1985). However, when we used Equation (22) to compute the expected Fresnel term at different wavelengths for various opaque plastics, grain and mineral oil, at wavelengths between 400nm and 660nm we observed that wavelength variations can be significant. The refractive indices of the opaque plastics were measured using a NanoView SE MF 1000 Spectroscopic Ellipsometer, while the ones for grain and mineral oil are publicly available. Because the index of refraction values are relatively small we calculated the percent change in the index of refraction in measurements taken at consecutive wavelengths. The total variation in the index of refraction in the visible wavelength, Δn, is given by the sum of the absolute values of the percent changes between consecutive wavelengths:

$$\Delta n = 100 \sum_{\lambda=400}^{600} \left(\frac{|n(\lambda + \delta\lambda) - n(\lambda)|}{n(\lambda)} \right) \tag{23}$$

where $\delta\lambda = 30nm$ for the plastics and $\delta\lambda = 48nm$ approximately for the grain and the mineral oil. We also computed in a similar manner the total variation in the Fresnel coefficients, ΔF, in the 400nm to 660nm range:

$$\Delta F = 100 \sum_{\lambda=400}^{600} \left(\frac{|F(\lambda + \delta\lambda) - F(\lambda)|}{F(\lambda)} \right) \tag{24}$$

As the table below demonstrates, even small variations in the index of refraction have a compound effect on surface reflectance. Our analysis shows that the Fresnel coefficient does change with respect to wavelength by amounts that may cause a visible change in the spectrum of specular highlights. An average 6.16% change in surface reflectance can be significant for specularity detection algorithms.

Materials	$\Delta n(\lambda)$	$\Delta F(\lambda)$
Pink Plastic (Cycolac RD1098)	1.17%	4.39%
Green Plastic (Lexan 73518)	0.94%	3.31%
Yellow Plastic (Lexan 40166)	4.89%	16.36%
Blue Plastic (Valox BL8016)	1.77%	6.12%
Beige Plastic (Noryl BR8267)	1.22%	4.32%
Grain	1.29%	5.49%
Mineral Oil	0.78%	3.16%

Table 1. Effects of the refractive index on the Fresnel coefficient]Changes in the value of the refractive index $\Delta n(\lambda)$ at different wavelengths between 400-660nm for various materials and the resulting changes in surface reflectance ratio $\Delta F(\lambda)$.

5.3. EXTRACTING THE FRESNEL TERM

The Fresnel term, with its dependence on wavelength, affects the color of the specular highlight to a high enough degree to make it distinct from the color of incident light. At specular regions the spectral derivatives isolate the effects of the Fresnel term on the color of specularities. More specifically, the spectral derivative measures how the Fresnel term changes with wavelength.

According to the specular component of the Cook and Torrance model (see Equation (17)), the logarithm of the surface reflectance term is:

$$\begin{aligned} \ln S(\vec{p}, \lambda) &= \ln F(\vec{p}, \lambda) + \ln D(\vec{p}) + \ln G(\vec{p}) \\ &- \ln \pi - \ln (N(\vec{p}) \cdot L(\vec{p})) - \ln (N(\vec{p}) \cdot V(\vec{p})) \end{aligned} \quad (25)$$

The Fresnel term can be either the approximation $F_{CT}(\ )$, suggested by Cook and Torrance (see Equation (23)) or our computation of surface reflectance ratio, $F(\ )$ (see Equation (22)). The only term that depends on the wavelength is the Fresnel term. Therefore, when we take the partial derivative with respect to wavelength we obtain:

$$L_\lambda(\vec{p},\lambda) \approx \frac{S_\lambda(\vec{p},\lambda)}{S(\vec{p},\lambda)} + c = \frac{F_\lambda(\vec{p},\lambda)}{F(\vec{p},\lambda)} + c \tag{26}$$

where $F_\lambda(\vec{p},\lambda) = \partial F(\vec{p},\lambda)/\partial\lambda$ is the partial derivative of the Fresnel term with respect to wavelength.

For specularities, the spectral derivative of an image $L_\lambda(\vec{p},\lambda)$ is primarily a function of the Fresnel term, independent of the particulars of the Fresnel term derivation. Specifically, the spectral derivative is the normalized partial derivative of the Fresnel term with respect to wavelength $F_\lambda(\vec{p},\lambda)/F(\vec{p},\lambda)$ (normalized by the magnitude of the Fresnel term itself) offset by a term which is constant per illumination condition.

6. Specular Regions Experiments

6.1. CAPTURING THE EFFECTS OF THE FRESNEL TERM

Our first test involved verifying whether the expected spectral shifts at specular regions can be registered by color cameras. We took images of different plastic and ceramic objects using 2 different color sensors: a) a traditional wide (70nm wide) bandpass Red, Green, and Blue camera and b) our multispectral sensor (described in the diffuse surface experiments section). We used a single fiber optic light source to illuminate the scene.

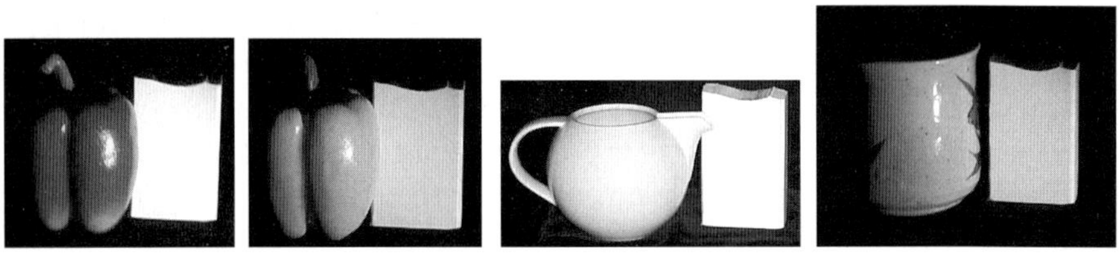

Figure 6. Two of the experimental objects were identically shaped peppers made of different types of plastic. Another set of experimental objects was composed of different quality of glossy ceramics: a white porcelain creamer and a grey earthenware mug.

Our experimental objects were composed of three different types of dielectric materials: smooth plastics, glossy ceramics and glossy paper. In order to isolate the effects of the refractive index, two of our objects, a yellow and a red plastic pepper had the same geometry (see left part of Figure 6). The ceramic objects also came in different colors and slightly different materials. One of the objects was a white porcelain creamer, while the other was a grey earthenware mug (see right part of Figure 6). We also took images of a paper plate which had a semiglossy off-white surface with some limited flower designs. All of the objects had a smooth surface and exhibited localized specularities. The paper plate was also exhibiting some self-shadowing at the rims. We always placed in the scene a block made of white Spectralon, a material that behaves like an ideal diffuse surface. The spectrum of the light reflected from the Spectralon block approximates the spectrum of the incident light and is, thus, used as a reference to the spectrum of the incident light.

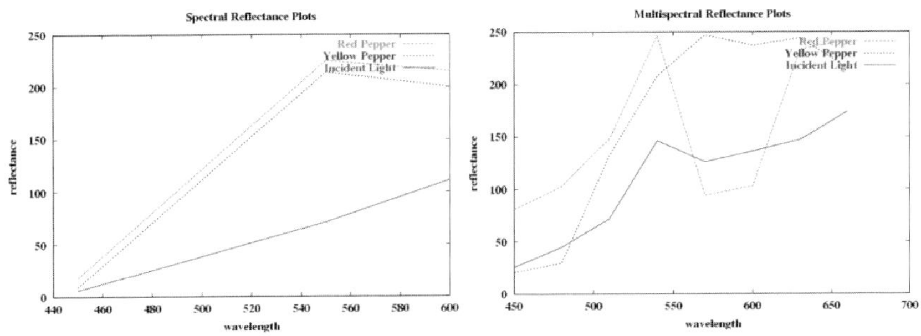

Figure 7. The specularity spectra at the same region of a red and a yellow plastic pepper as recorded by (left) our RGB sensor and (right) our multispectral sensor.

In the graphs of this subsection the horizontal axis represents wavelength, and the vertical axis represents the reflectance values measured by our sensor. In each graph we include the recorded reflected spectrum of the Spectralon block as a measurement of the spectrum of the incident light. Figure 7 shows the spectrum of the specularities in approximately the same region of the yellow and red peppers as captured by each of our color cameras. The RGB camera registers very similar responses for the two peppers but distinct from that of the incident light. Our multispectral sensor gives us distinct plots for the two pepper specular highlights.

The absence in the analyzed specular regions of any effects from the diffuse components of the reflectance is evidenced in Figure 8. This figure shows on the left the RGB response and on the right the multispectral response of specular highlights in two different white objects (creamer and paper plate), and a grey object (mug) next to the diffuse response of a white object (Spectralon block). The RGB sensor gave similar responses for the two ceramic objects but a different response from the white paper plate. All 3 specular color triplets are not the color of incident light. Our multispectral sensor gave us different plots for each specularity.

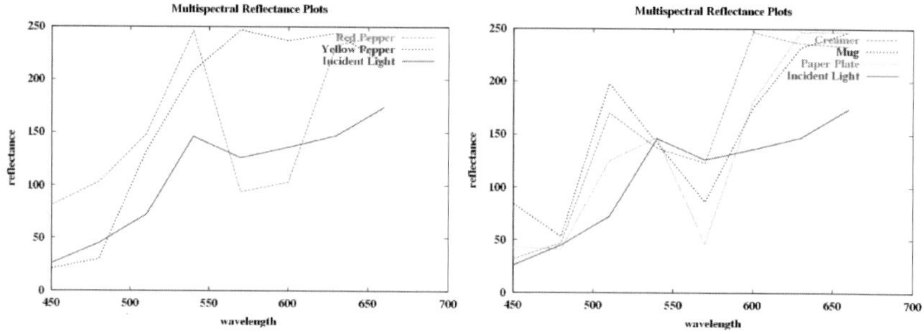

Figure 8. The specularity spectra of white porcelain, white glossy paper and grey earthenware as recorded by (left) our RGB sensor and (right) our multispectral sensor.

6.2. GROUND TRUTH PLASTICS

To test the validity of our claim that the spectral derivatives can be used for extracting the Fresnel term of specular reflectance, we performed a series of experiments on opaque plastics with known index of refraction. We used a collection of thin plastic tiles which: a) were made of different types of plastic composites (CYCOLAC, LEXAN, NORYL, VALOX); b) came in distinct colors; and c) were composed of a collection of surface patches each with a different degree of surface roughness, varying from very smooth to visibly textured (see Figure 9).

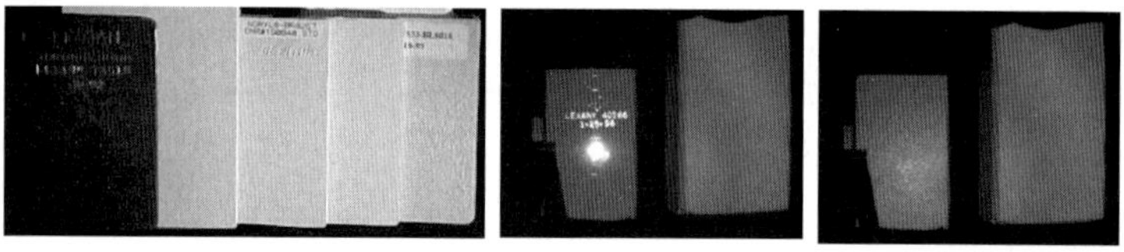

Figure 9. From left to right: a collection of opaque plastic tiles with known refractive index; image of the smooth side of the yellow tile taken using a narrow (10nm wide) red bandpass filter; image of the textured side of the same tile under the same color filter.

We took images of both sides of each plastic tile, one tile at a time. Each tile was positioned at the same location, next to the white Spectralon block, at an angle of approximately 15° to the fiber optic illumination source (see Figure 9). The camera's optic axis was roughly aligned with the reflection vector so as to maximize the visibility of the specularity. Each of the plastic tiles had distinct indices of refraction (see the left side of Figure 10). On the right side of Figure 10 one can see the Fresnel coefficient for each of the tiles. Note that, for each of the tiles the Fresnel term has the same shape with the index of refraction and both of them vary with respect to wavelength.

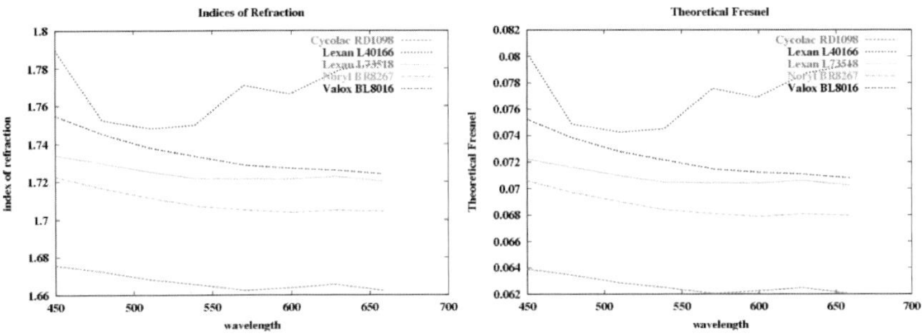

Figure 10. Left: The index of refraction of five different plastic tiles as a function of wavelength. Right: The Fresnel coefficient of the same five tiles as a function of wavelength.

Figure 11 shows the effect of the Fresnel term on specularities. The plot on the left displays the spectrum of the specularities for each of the 5 plastic tiles as recorded by our multispectral camera. The spectral profile for each of the specularities does not resemble that of the Fresnel term. This is expected as the Fresnel coefficient accounts for only part of the behavior of the light specularly reflected from a surface. The plot on the right side of Figure 11 shows the spectral gradient of the specularities for each of the 5 tiles. The spectral profile of the gradients exhibits the influence of the Fresnel term. For example, the spectral gradient of LEXAN 73518 is close to zero across all the wavelengths, while the gradient of CYCOLAC RD1098 increases at the 600 to 630nm interval. Note that the spectrum of the incident light and its spectral gradient is distinct from the specularity spectrum.

We also compared for each of the plastic tiles, the theoretical spectral gradient, which we computed using Equation (26), with the values we extracted from the images. In our comparisons we used the normalized magnitude of the spectral gradient because the light source spectral profile provided to us was also normalized. The theoretical and the image-extracted spectral gradients are very similar. The Percent Mean Squared Error in the recovery of the Fresnel term for each of the five plastics (in the order shown in Figure 9) is 0.9%, 1.1%, 2.3%, 2.9% and 1.7%.

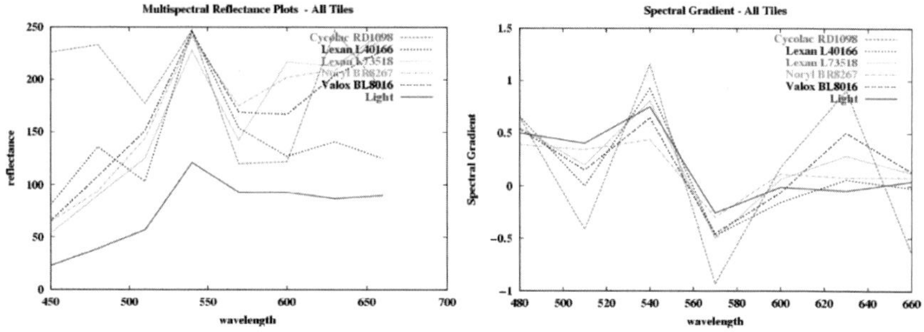

Figure 11. Left: The spectrum of specularities of five different opaque plastic tiles. Right: The spectral gradient of the same specularities of the five opaque plastic tiles.

6.3. COMMON PLASTICS AND CERAMICS

Similar behavior was also observed in our experiments with the uncalibrated, everyday items shown in Figure 6. The specular regions of these objects had spectral gradients which differed among the various materials and were also distinct from the spectral gradient of the incident light (Figure 12). However, as expected, pixels within the same specular region exhibited similar spectral gradients (Figure 13).

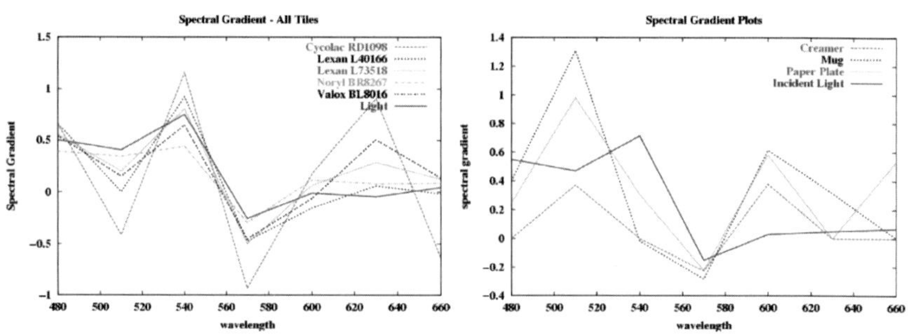

Figure 12. The spectral gradients of the specularities (left) at the same region of a red and a yellow plastic pepper and (right) of different ceramics and glossy paper.

7. Summary

Dense spectral sampling provides a rich description of surface reflectance behavior. One technique for analyzing surface reflectance is to compute the spectral derivatives at a per pixel basis. For diffuse surfaces, spectral

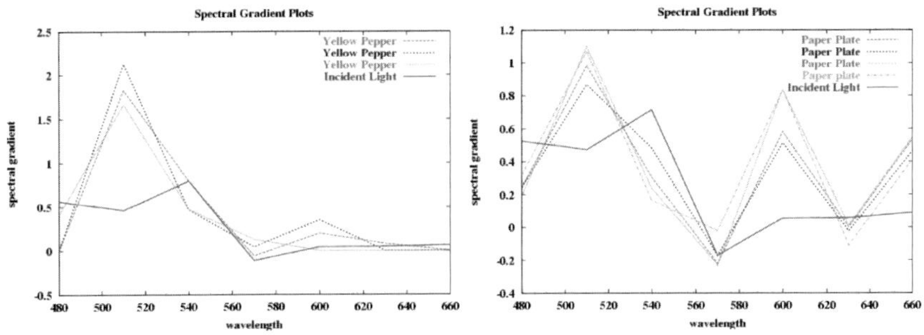

Figure 13. The spectral gradients of the specular pixels within the same region of (left) a yellow plastic pepper and (right) a white glossy paper plate.

derivatives extract surface albedo information which is purely a physical property independent of illumination and scene geometry. In a sense it is a descriptor of the objective color of the surface since it depends only on the chromophores of the material. For specular regions the spectral derivatives isolate the Fresnel term up to an additive illumination constant. Our experiments with opaque plastics of known refractive index demonstrated that the spectral gradient can be computed with an average accuracy of 1.78%.

Furthermore multispectral images make more evident the inaccuracy of the prevalent assumption that the color of specular highlights for materials like plastics and ceramics can be accurately approximated by the color of the incident light. As we showed, the sensitivity of the Fresnel term to the wavelength variations of the refractive index can be at least as large as 15%. Both an RGB sensor but particularly multispectral sensor can capture the deviation of the color of specular highlights from the color of the incident light.

References

Angelopoulou, E.: Objective colour from multispectral imaging. In Proc *European Conf. Computer Vision*, pages 359–374, 2000.

Blinn, J. F.: Models of light reflection for computer synthesized pictures. *Computer Graphics*, **11**: 192–198, 1977.

Cook, R. L. and K. E. Torrance: A reflectance model for computer graphics. *ACM Trans. Graphics*, **1**: 7–24, 1982.

Finlayson, G. D.: Color in perspective. *IEEE Trans. Pattern Analysis Machine Intelligence*, **18**: 1034–1038, 1996.

Forsyth, D.: A novel algorithm for color constancy. *Int. J. Computer Vision*, **5**: 5–36, 1990.

Funt, B. V. and G. D. Finlayson: Color constant color indexing. *IEEE Trans. Pattern Analysis Machine Intelligence*, **17**: 522–529, 1995.

Finlayson, G. D., M. S. Drew, and B. V. Funt: Color constancy: generalized diagonal transforms suffice. *J. Optical Society of America A*, **11**: 3011–3019, 1994.

Klinker, G. J., S. A. Shafer, and T. Kanade: The measurement of highlights in color images. *Int. J. Computer Vision*, **2**: 7–26, 1992.

Hall, R. A. and D. P. Greenberg: A testbed for realistic image synthesis. *IEEE Computer Graphics and Applications*, **3**: 10–19, 1983.

Healey, G. and D. Slater: Global color constancy: recognition of objects by use of illumination-invariant properties of color distribution. *J. Optical Society of America A*, **11**: 3003–3010, 1994.

Healey, G. and L. Wang: Illumination-invariant recognition of texture in color images. *J. Optical Society of America A*, **12**: 1877–1883, 1995.

Hechts, E.: *Optics*, 3rd edition. Addison Wesley Longman, 1998..

Hering, R. G. and T. F. Smith: Apparent radiation properties of a rough surface. *AIAA Progress in Astronautics and Aeronautics*, **23**: 337–361, 1970.

Ho, J., B. V. Funt, and M. S. Drew: Separating a color signal into illumination and surface reflectance components: theory and applications. *IEEE Trans. Pattern Analysis Machine Intelligence*, **12**: 966–977, 1990.

Jähne, B. and K. Haussecker: *Computer Vision and Applications: A Guide for Students and Practitioners.* Academic Press, 2000.

Barnard, K., G. Finlayson, and B. Funt: Color constancy for scenes with varying illumination. *Computer Vision Image Understanding*, **65**: 311–321, 1997.

Kortum, G.: *Reflectance Spectroscopy.* Springer, 1969.

Maloney, L. T. and B. A. Wandell: A computational model of color constancy. *J. Optical Society of America A*, **3**: 29–33, 1986.

Oren, M. and S. K. Nayar: Generalization of the Lambertian model and implications for machine vision. *Int. J. Computer Vision*, **14**: 227–251, 1995.

Phong, B. T.: Illumination for computer generated pictures. *Comm. ACM*, **18**: 311–317, 1975.

Bajcsy, R., S. W. Lee, and A. Leonardis: Color image segmentation with detection of hghlights and local illumination induced by inter-reflection. In Proc. *Int. Conf. Pattern Recognition*, pages 785–790, 1990.

Sabins, F. F.: *Remote Sensing - Principles and Interpretation*, 3rd edition. W. H. Freeman and Co., 1997.

Shafer, S. A.: Using color to separate reflection components. *J. Color Research and Application*, **10**: 210–218, 1985.

Slater, D. and Healey, G. (). What is the spectral dimensionality of illumination functions in outdoor scenes? In Proc. *Computer Vision Pattern Recognition*, pages 105–110, 1998.

Swain, M. J. and D. H. Ballard: Color indexing. *Int. J. Computer Vision*, **7**: 11–32, 1991.

Torrance, K. E. and E. M. Sparrow: Theory for off-specular reflection from rough surfaces. *J. Optical Society of America*, **67**: 1105–1114, 1967.

Watt, A.: *3D Computer Graphics*, 3rd edition. Addison-Wesley, 2000.

UBIQUITOUS AND WEARABLE VISION SYSTEMS

TAKASHI MATSUYAMA
Graduate School of Informatics
Kyoto University
Sakyo, Kyoto, 606-8501, Japan

Abstract. Capturing multi-view images by a group of spatially distributed cameras is one of the most useful and practical methods to extend utilities and overcome limitations of a standard pinhole camera: limited size of visual field and degeneration of 3D information. This paper gives an overview of our research activities on multi-view image analysis. First we address a *ubiquitous vision system*, where a group of network-connected active cameras are embeded in the real world to realize 1) wide-area dynamic 3D scene understanding and 2) versatile 3D scene visualization. To demonstrate utilities of the system, we developed a cooperative distributed active object tracking system and a 3D video generation system. The latter half of the paper discusses a *wearable vision system*, where multiple active cameras are placed nearby around human eyes to share the visual field. To demonstrate utilities of the system, we developed systems for 1) real time accurate estimation of 3D human gaze point, 2) 3D digitization of a hand-held object, and 3) estimation of 3D human motion trajectory.

Key words: multi-camera systems, multi-view image, ubiquitous vision, wearable vision, camera network, 3D video, 3D gaze point detection, 3D object digitization

Introduction

Capturing multi-view images by a group of spatially distributed cameras is one of the most useful and practical methods to extend utilities and overcome limitations of a standard pinhole camera: limited size of visual field and degeneration of 3D information.

Figure 1 illustrates three typical types of multi-view camera arrangements:

(1) Parallel View: for wide area stereo vision (e.g. capturing 100m race at the Olympic game)

(2) Convergent View: for detailed 3D human action observation (e.g. digital archive of traditional dances)

(3) Divergent View: for omnidirectional panoramic scene observation

K. Daniilidis and R. Klette (eds.), Imaging Beyond the Pinhole Camera, 307–330.

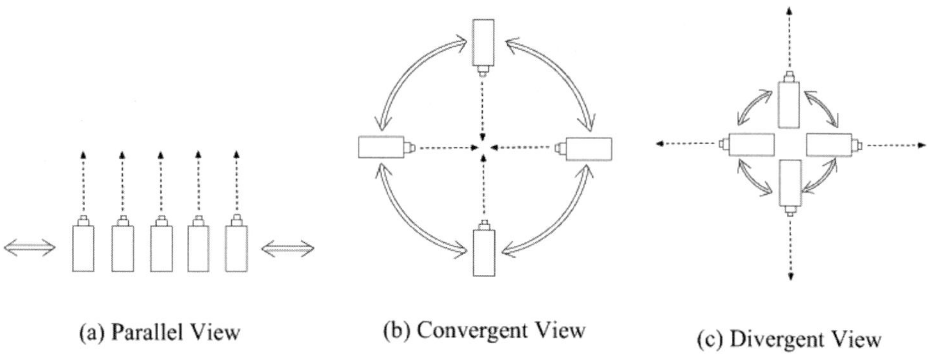

Figure 1. Types of multi-view camera arrangements.

This paper gives an overview of our research activities on multi-view image analysis. Following a brief introduction of our specialized active camera, the paper addresses a convergent view multi-camera system, where a group of network-connected active cameras are embedded in the real world to realize 1) wide-area dynamic 3D scene understanding and 2) versatile 3D scene visualization (Matsuyama, 1998). We may call such system a *ubiquitous vision system*. Based on this scheme, we developed a cooperative distributed active object tracking system (Matsuyama and Ukita, 2002) and a 3D video (Moezzi et al., 1997) generation system (Matsuyama et al., 2004). Experimental results demonstrated utilities of the ubiquitous vision system.

The latter half of the paper discusses a *wearable active vision system*, where multiple active cameras are placed nearby around human eyes to share the visual field. This system employs either convergent or divergent view observations depending on required tasks: the former for 1) real time accurate estimation of 3D human gaze point and 2) 3D digitization of a hand-held object, and the latter for 3) estimation of 3D human motion trajectory (Sumi et al., 2004).

Since the space is limited, the paper gives just a summary of our research attainments obtained so far. As for technical details, please refer to the references.

1. Fixed-Viewpoint Pan-Tilt-Zoom Camera for Wide Area Scene Observation and Active Object Tracking

First of all, to expand the visual field of a camera is an important issue in developing wide area scene observation and real time moving object tracking.

In (Wada and Matsuyama, 1996), we developed a *fixed-viewpoint pan-tilt-zoom (FV-PTZ, in short) camera*: as its projection center stays fixed irrespectively of any camera rotations and zoomings, we can use it as a pinhole camera with a very wide visual field. All the systems described in this paper employ an off-the-shelf active video camera SONY EVI-G20 since it can be well modeled as an FV-PTZ camera.

With an FV-PTZ camera, we can easily realize an active target tracking system as well as generate an wide panoramic image by mosaicking images taken with different pan-tilt-zoom parameters. Figure 2 illustrates the basic scheme of the active background subtraction for object tracking (Matsuyama, 1998):

1. Generate the *APpearance Plane* (APP) image: a wide panoramic image of the background scene.
2. Extract a window image from the APP image according to the current pan-tilt-zoom parameters and regard it as the current background image; with the FV-PTZ camera, there exists the direct mapping between the position in the APP image and pan-tilt-zoom parameters of the camera.
3. Compute difference between the current background image and an observed image.

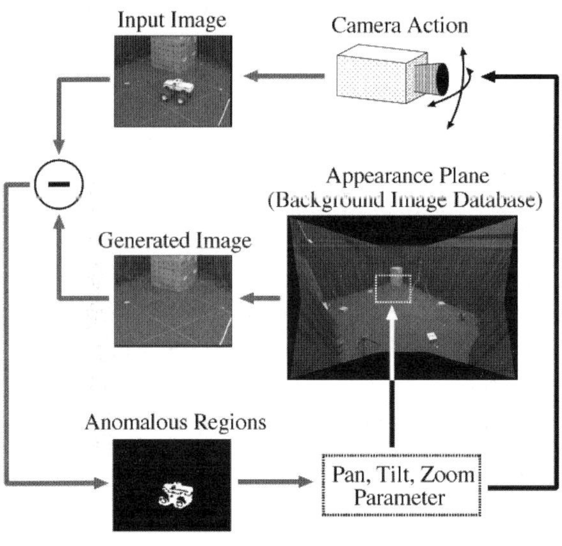

Figure 2. Active background subtraction with a fixed-viewpoint pan-tilt-zoom (FV-PTZ) camera.

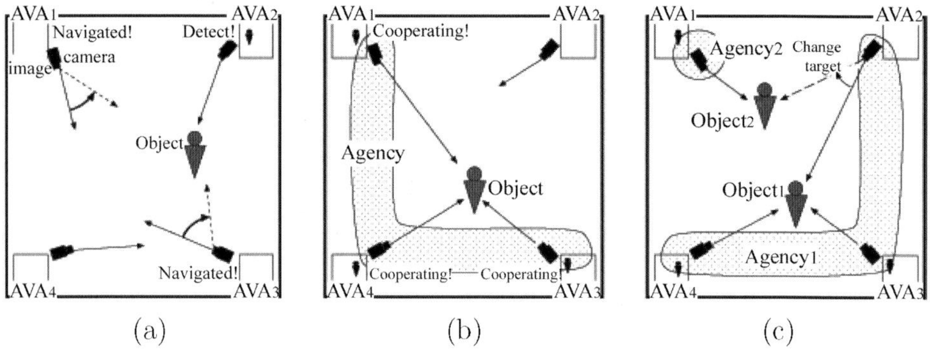

Figure 3. Basic scheme for cooperative tracking: (a) Gaze navigation, (b) Cooperative gazing, (c) Adaptive target switching.

4. If anomalous regions are detected in the difference image, select one and control the camera parameters to track the selected target.

Based on this scheme, we developed a real-time active moving object tracking system, where a robust background subtraction method (Matsuyama et al., 2000) and a sophisticated real-time camera control method (Matsuyama et al., 2000a) were employed.

2. Tracking and 3D Digitization of Objects by a Ubiquitous Vision System

2.1. COOPERATIVE MULTI-TARGET TRACKING BY COMMUNICATING ACTIVE VISION AGENTS

Since the observation from a single viewpoint cannot give us explicit 3D scene information or avoid occlusion, we developed a multi-viewpoint camera system (i.e. convergent view multi-camera system), where a group of network connected FV-PTZ cameras are distributed in a wide area scene. Each camera is controlled by its corresponding PC, which exchanges observed data with each other to track objects and measure their 3D information. We call such network-connected PC with an active camera *Active Vision Agent* (AVA, in short).

Assuming that the cameras are calibrated and densely distributed over the scene so that their visual fields are well overlapping with each other, we developed a cooperative multi-target tracking system by a group of communicating AVAs (Matsuyama and Ukita, 2002).

Figure 3 illustrates the basic tasks conducted by the cooperation among AVAs:

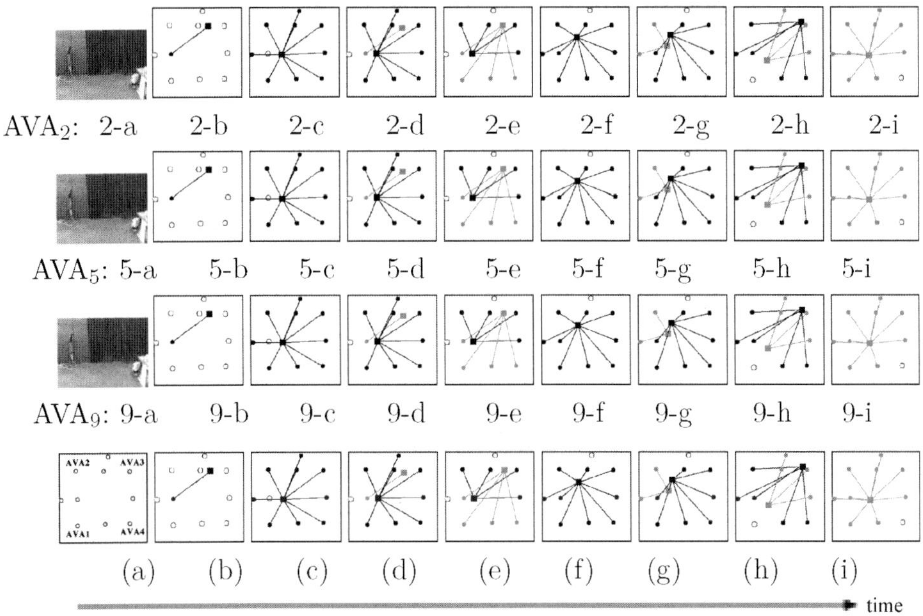

Figure 4. Experimental results.

1. Initially, each AVA independently searches for a target that comes into its observable area.
2. If an AVA detects a target, it navigates the gazes of the other AVAs towards that target (Figure 3(a)).
3. A group of AVAs which gaze at the same target form what we call an *Agency* and keep measuring the 3D information of the target from multi-view images (Figure 3(b)). Note that while some AVAs are tracking an object, others are still searching for new objects.
4. Depending on target locations in the scene, each AVA dynamically changes its target (Figure 3(c)).

To verify the effectiveness of the proposed system, we conducted experiments of multiple human tracking in a room (about $5m \times 5m$). The system consists of ten AVAs. Each AVA is implemented on a network-connected PC (Pentium III 600MHz $\times$ 2) with an FV-PTZ camera (SONY EVI-G20).

In the experiment shown in Figure 4, the system tracked two people. Target$_1$ first came into the scene and after a while, target$_2$ came into the scene. Both targets then moved freely. The upper three rows in Figure 4 show the partial image sequences observed by AVA$_2$, AVA$_5$ and AVA$_9$, respectively. The images on the same column were taken at almost the same time. The regions enclosed by black and gray lines in the images show the detected regions corresponding to $target_1$ and $target_2$ respectively. Note that the image sequences in Figure 4 are not recorded ones but captured real-time according to the target motions.

The bottom row in Figure 4 shows the dynamic cooperation process conducted by ten AVAs. White circles mean that AVAs are in the target search mode, while black and gray circles indicate AVAs are tracking $target_1$ or $target_2$ forming $agency_1$ or $agency_2$, respectively. Black and gray squares indicate computed locations of $target_1$ and $target_2$ respectively, toward which gazing lines from AVAs are directed.

The system worked as follows. Note that (a)-(i) below denote the situations illustrated in Figure 4.

(a) Initially, each AVA searched for an object independently.

(b) AVA_5 first detected $target_1$, and after the gaze navigation of the other AVAs, $agency_1$ was formed.

(c) After a while, all AVAs except AVA_5 were tracking $target_1$, since AVA_5 had switched its mode from tracking to searching, depending the target motion.

(d) Then, AVA_5 detected a new target, $target_2$, and generated $agency_2$.

(e) The agency restructuring protocol (i.e. adaptive target switching) balanced the numbers of member AVAs in $agency_1$ and $agency_2$. Note that AVA_9 and AVA_{10} were searching for still new objects.

(f) Since two targets came very close to each other and no AVA could distinguish them, the agency unification protocol merged $agency_2$ into $agency_1$.

(g) When the targets got apart, $agency_1$ detected a 'new' target. Then, it activated the agency spawning protocol to generate $agency_2$ again for $target_2$.

(h) $Target_1$ was going out of the scene.

(i) After $agency_1$ was eliminated, all the AVAs except AVA_4 came to track $target_2$.

These experiments proved that the cooperative target tracking by a group of multi-viewpoint active cameras is very effective to cope with unorganized dynamic object behaviors.

2.2. GENERATION OF HIGH FIDELITY 3D VIDEO

With the above mentioned tracking system, we can capture convergent multi-view video data of a moving object. To make full use of the captured video data, we developed a system for generating 3D video (Matsuyama et al., 2004) (Wada et al., 2000) (Matsuyama and Takai, 2002) (Matsuyama et al., 2004).

3D video (Moezzi et al., 1997) is NOT an artificial CG animation but a real 3D movie recording the full 3D shape, motion, and precise surface color & texture of real world objects. It enables us to observe real object behaviors from any viewpoints as well as to see pop-up 3D object images. Such new featured image medium will promote wide varieties of personal and social human activities: communication (e.g. 3D TV phone), entertainment (e.g. 3D game and 3D TV), education (e.g. 3D animal picture books), sports (e.g. sport performance analysis), medicine (e.g. 3D surgery monitoring), culture (e.g. 3D archive of traditional dances), and so on.

So far we developed

1. PC cluster system with distributed active cameras for real-time 3D shape reconstruction
2. Dynamic 3D mesh deformation method for obtaining accurate 3D object shape
3. Texture mapping algorithm for high fidelity visualization
4. User friendly 3D video editing system

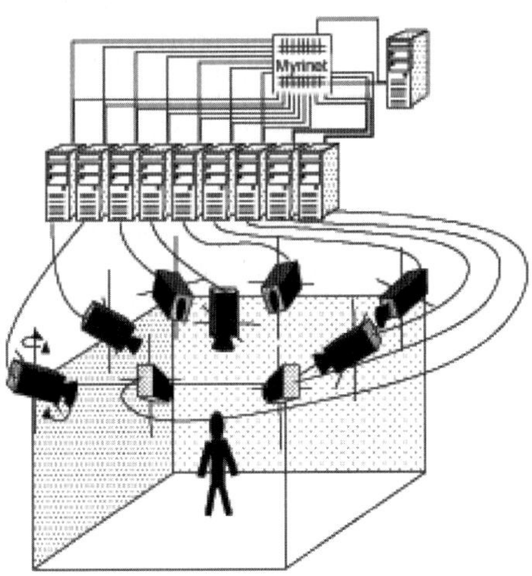

Figure 5. PC cluster for real-time active 3D object shape reconstruction.

2.2.1. *System Organization*
Figure 5 illustrates the architecture of our real-time *active* 3D object shape reconstruction system. It consists of

- PC cluster: 30 node PCs (dual Pentium III 1GHz) are connected through Myrinet, an ultra high speed network (full duplex 1.28Gbps), which enables us to implement efficient parallel processing on the PC cluster.
- Distributed active video cameras: Among 30, 25 PCs have Fixed-Viewpoint Pan-Tilt (FV-PT) cameras, respectively, for active object tracking and imaging.

Figure 6 shows a snapshot of multi-view object video data captured by the system. Note that since the above mentioned PC cluster is our second generation system and has just become in operation, all test data used in this paper are those taken by the first generation system (16PCs and 12 cameras) (Wada et al., 2000). We have verified that the second generation system can generate much more high quality 3D video in much less computation time. Experimental results by the second generation system will be published soon.

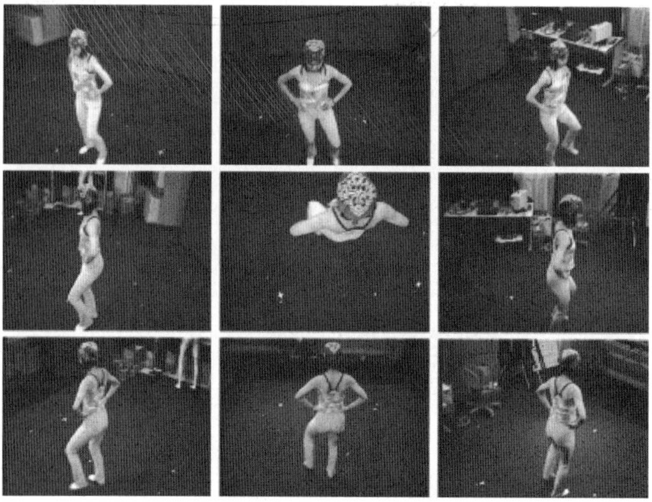

Figure 6. Captured multi-viewpoint images.

2.2.2. *Processing Scheme of 3D Video Generation*
Figure 7 illustrates the basic process of generating a 3D video frame in our system:

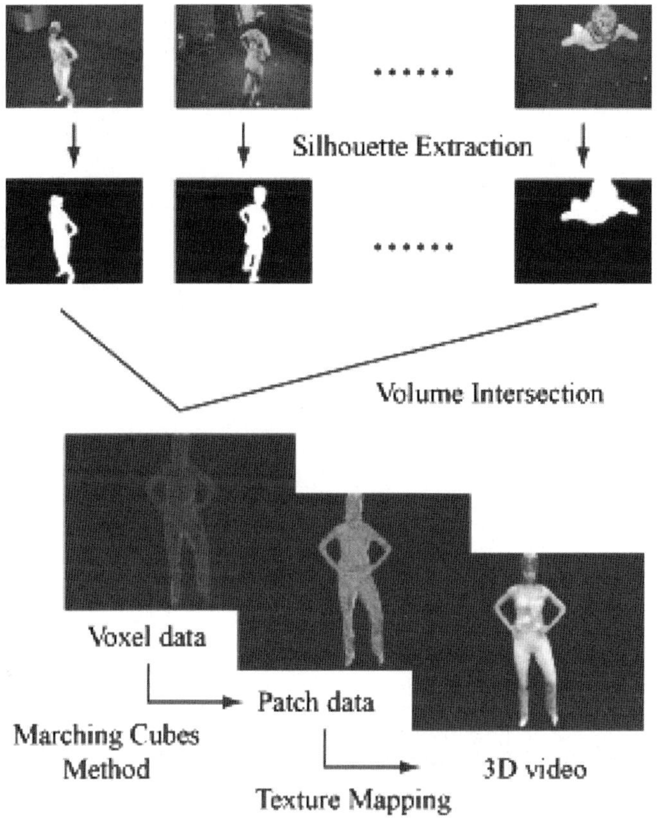

Figure 7. 3D video generation process.

1. **Synchronized Multi-View Image Acquisition**: A set of multi-view object images are taken simultaneously (top row in Figure 7).
2. **Silhouette Extraction**: Background subtraction is applied to each captured image to generate a set of multi-view object silhouettes (second top row in Figure 7).
3. **Silhouette Volume Intersection**: Each silhouette is back-projected into the common 3D space to generate a visual cone encasing the 3D object. Then, such 3D cones are intersected with each other to generate the visual hull of the object (i.e. the voxel representation of the rough object shape) (third bottom in Figure 7).
   To realize real-time 3D volume intersection,
   - we first developed the plane-based volume intersection method, where the 3D voxel space is partitioned into a group of parallel planes and the cross-section of the 3D object volume on each plane is reconstructed.

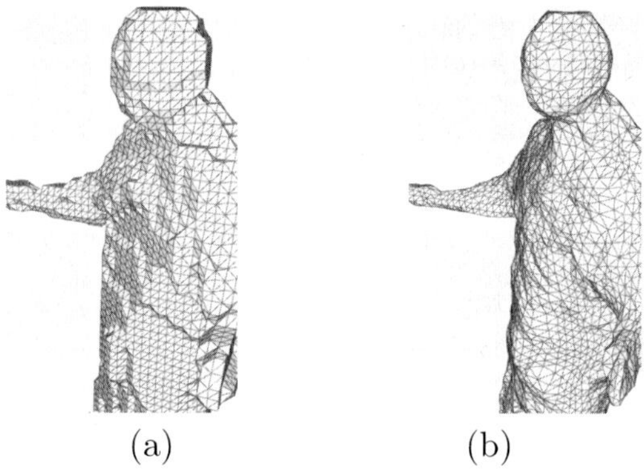

Figure 8. (a) surface mesh generated by the discrete Marching cube method and (b) surface mesh after the intra-frame mesh deformation.

- Secondly, we devised the Plane-to-Plane Perspective Projection algorithm to realize efficient plane-to-plane projection computation.
- And thirdly, to realize real-time processing, we implemented parallel pipeline processing on a PC cluster system (Wada et al., 2000).

Experimental results showed that the proposed methods works efficiently and the PC cluster system can reconstruct 3D shape of a dancing human at about 12 volume per second in the voxel size of 2cm$\times$ 2cm$\times$ 2cm contained in a space of 2m $\times$ 2m $\times$ 2m. Note that this result is by the first generation PC cluster system.

4. **Surface Shape Computation**: The discrete marching cubes method (Kenmochi et al., 1999) is applied to convert the voxel representation to the surface mesh representation. Then the generated 3D mesh is deformed to obtain accurate 3D object shape (second bottom in Figure 7).

We developed a deformable 3D mesh model which reconstructs both the accurate 3D object shape and motion (Matsuyama et al., 2004).

- For the initial video frame, we apply the intra-frame deformation method. Using the mesh generated from the voxel data as the initial shape, it deforms the mesh to satisfy the smoothness, silhouette, and photo-consistency constraints. The photo-consistency constraint enables us to recover concave parts of the object, which cannot be reconstructed by the volume intersection method. Figure 8 demonstrates the effectiveness of the mesh deformation.
- Using the result of the intra-frame deformation as the initial shape, we apply the inter-frame deformation method to a series of video frames. It additionally introduces the 3D motion flow and inertia

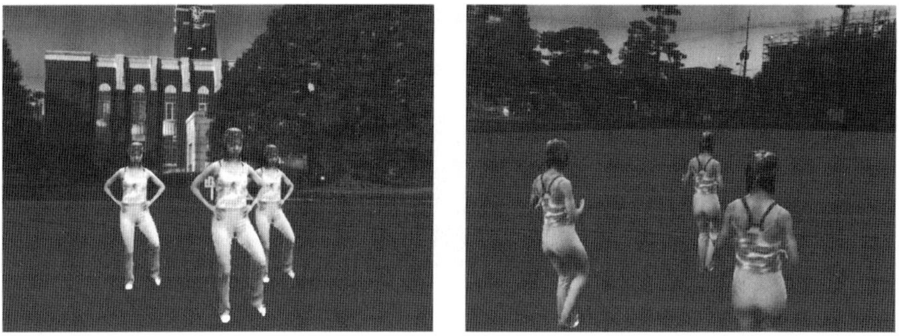

Figure 9. Visualized 3D video with an omnidirectional background

constraints as well as a stiffness parameter into the mesh model to cope with non-rigid object motion.

Experimental results showed that the mesh deformation methods can significantly improve the accuracy of the reconstructed 3D shape. Moreover, we can obtain a temporal sequence of 3D meshes whose topological structures are kept constant; the complete vertex correspondence is established for all the 3D meshes. Their computation speeds, however, are far from real-time: for both the intra- and inter-frame deformations, it took about 5 minutes for 12000 vertices with 4 cameras and 10 minutes for 12000 vertices with 9 cameras by a PC (Xeon 1.7GHz). The parallel implementation to speed up the methods is one of our future works.

5. **Texture Mapping**: Color and texture on each patch are computed from the observed multi-view images (bottom in Figure 7).

   We proposed the viewpoint dependent vertex-based texture mapping method to avoid jitters in rendered object images which are caused due to the limited accuracy of the reconstructed 3D object shape (Matsuyama et al., 2004). Experimental results showed that the proposed method can generate almost natural looking object images from arbitrary viewpoints. By compiling a temporal sequence of reconstructed 3D shape data and multi-view video into a temporal sequence of vertex lists, we can render arbitrary VGA views of 3D video sequence at video rate by an ordinary PC.

By repeating the above process for each video frame, we have a live 3D motion picture.

We also developed a 3D video editing system, with which we can copy and arrange a foreground 3D video object in front of a background omnidirectional video. Figure 9 illustrates a sample sequence of an edited 3D video.

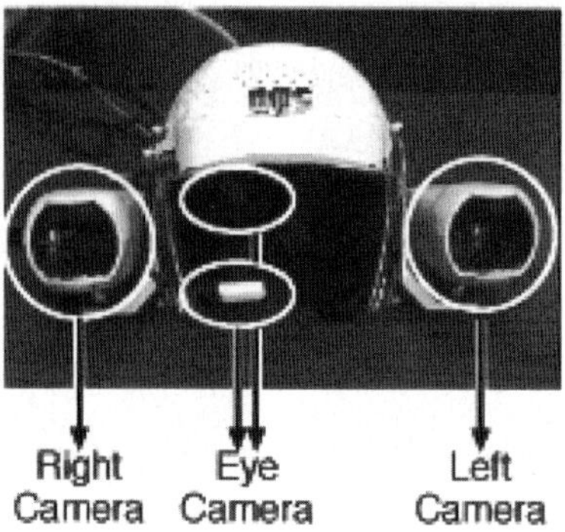

Figure 10. Active wearable vision sensor

3. Recognition of Human Activities and Surrounding Environments by an Active Wearable Vision System

The ubiquitous vision systems described so far observe people from outside to *objectively* analyze their behaviors and activities. In this section, on the other hand, we introduce a wearable vision system (Figure 10) (Sugimoto et al., 2002) to observe and analyze *subjective* view of a human; viewpoints of cameras are placed nearby around human eyes and moves with human behaviors. The system is equipped with a pair of FV-PTZ stereo cameras and a gaze-direction detector (i.e. eye camera in Figure 10) to monitor human eye and head movements. Here we address the methods to realized the following three functionalities: 1) 3D gaze point detection and focused object imaging, 2) 3D digitization of a hand-held object, and 3) 3D human motion trajectory measurement.

3.1. 3D GAZE POINT DETECTION AND FOCUSED OBJECT IMAGING

Here, we present a method to capture a close-up image of a human focusing object by actively controlling cameras based on 3D gaze point detection.

Since the gaze-direction detector equipped can only measure the human gaze direction, we control the FV-PTZ cameras to detect where he/she is looking at in the 3D space. Figure 11 illustrates a method to measure a 3D gaze point, which is defined by an intersection point between the gaze-direction line and an object surface. Assuming the cameras and the gaze-direction detector have been calibrated in advance, the viewing line is projected onto a pair of stereo images captured by the cameras. Then, we apply stereo matching along the pair of the projected lines.

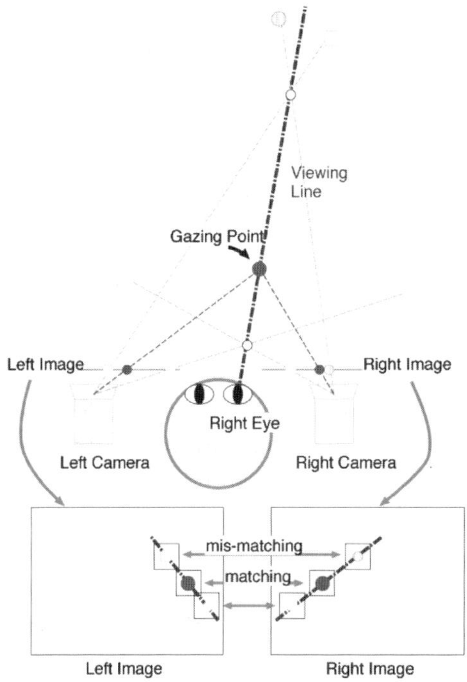

Figure 11. Stereo matching along the gaze-direction line to detect a 3D human gazing point.

Based on the measured 3D gaze point, we control pan, tilt, and zoom parameters of the active cameras to capture detailed target object images:

- If the human gaze direction is moving, the cameras are zoomed out to capture images of wide visual field. Pan and tilt are controlled to follow the gaze motion.
- If the human gaze direction is fixed, the camera is zoomed in to capture detailed images of the target object. The pan and tilt are controlled to converge toward the 3D gaze point.

We have implemented the above camera control strategy with a dynamic memory architecture (Matsuyama et al., 2000a), with which smooth reactive (without delay) camera control can be realized (Figure 12).

Figure 13 demonstrates the effectiveness of this active camera control. The upper and lower rows show pairs of stereo images captured without and with the gaze navigated camera control, respectively. A straight line and a dot in each image illustrate a projected view direction line and a human gazing point, respectively.

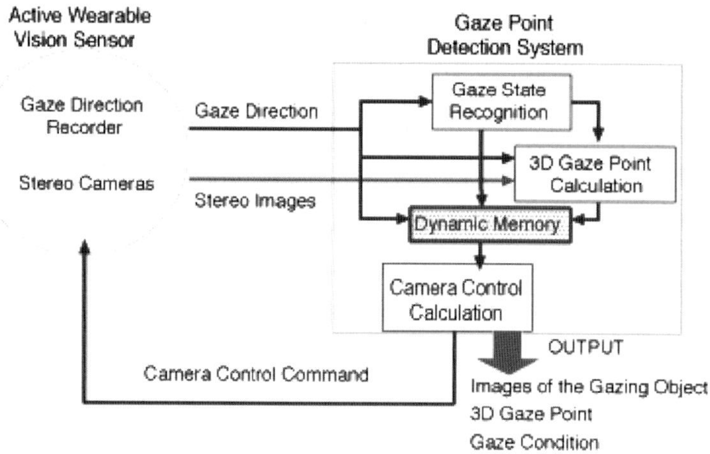

Figure 12. Control scheme of 3D gaze point detection and camera control.

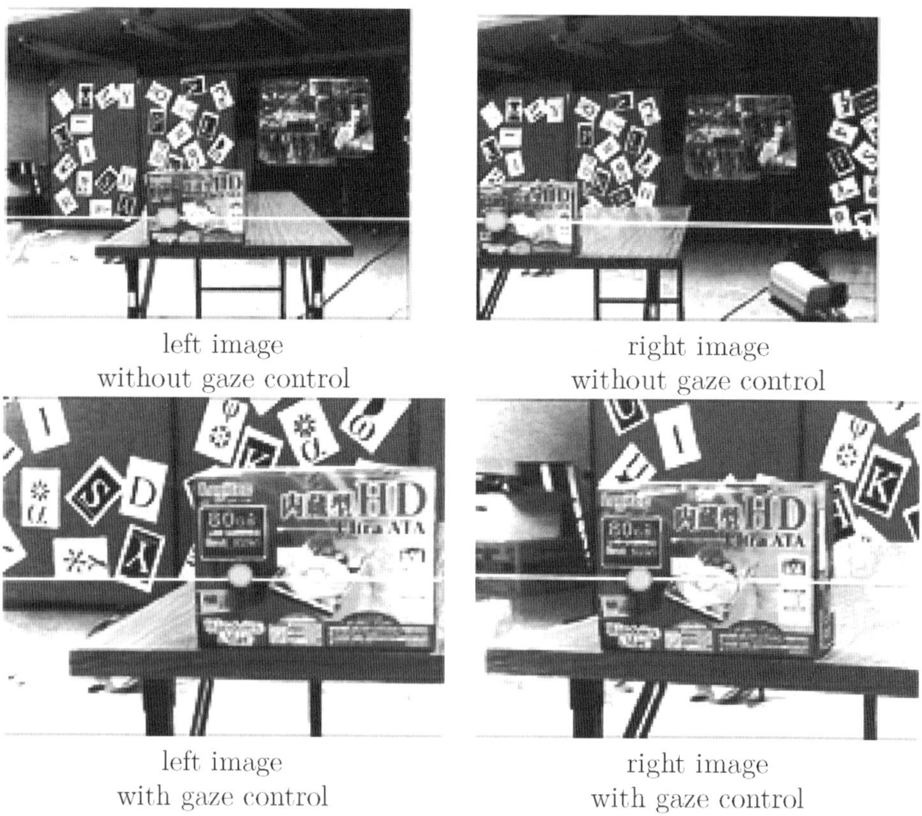

Figure 13. Results of 3D gaze point detection and camera control.

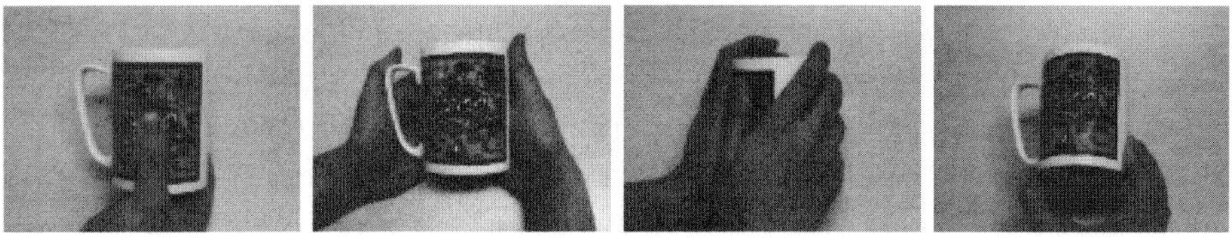

(a) Shape Acquisition (b) Surface Texture Acquisition (c) Haptic Texture Acquisition (d) Total Appearance Acquisition

Figure 14. Categorization of hand-object relationships.

3.2. 3D DIGITIZATION OF A HAND-HELD OBJECT

Suppose we are in a department store and checking a coffee cup to buy. In such a situation, we manipulate an object to examine its shape, color, and surface painting from various viewpoints. With the wearable vision system, we developed a method to obtain a full 3D object image from video data captured during this human action.

From a viewpoint of human action analysis, first, we classify hand-object relationships into four classes based on the information human can acquire:

Shape Acquisition: Examine the overall object shape, where most of the object silhouette is visible (Figure 14(a)).

Surface Texture Acquisition: Examine surface painting, where some parts of the object silhouette are covered by hands (Figure 14(b)).

Haptic Texture Acquisition: Examine surface smoothness, where the object is wrapped by hands and most of the object surface is invisible (Figure 14(c)).

Total Appearance Acquisition: Examine the balance between shape and surface painting, where the object is turned around and most of object shape and surface painting can be observed (Figure 14(d)).

Then, from a viewpoint of computer vision, the problems to be studied are characterized as follows:

1. Assuming an object is rigid, the wearable vision system can capture convergent multi-view stereo images of the object; that is, representing the object manipulation process in the object centered coordinate system, a pair of stereo cameras are dynamically moved around the object to observe it from multiple different viewpoints. Technically speaking, to determine 3D camera positions and motion in the object centered

coordinate system, we have to compute 3D relative position between the cameras and object at each captured video frame as well as conduct stereo camera calibration.

2. While the object shape and position stay fixed in the object centered coordinate system, human hands change their shapes and positions dynamically to occlude the object. That is, we have to recover the 3D object shape from convergent multi-view stereo images where the shape and position of an occluding object changes depending on the viewpoint. We may call this problem *shape from multi-view stereo images corrupted with viewpoint dependent occlusion.*

It is not always easy to distinguish between an object and hands, especially when the object is being held by hands. Moreover, due to the viewpoint dependent occlusion, we cannot apply such conventional techniques as shape from silhouettes (Hoppe et al., 1992) or space carving (Kutulakos and Seitz, 1999).

To solve the problem, we proposed a vacant space carving. That is, we first compute a vacant space, one that is not occupied by any object, from each viewpoint. Then, multiple vacant spaces from different viewpoints are integrated to generate a 3D object shape. The rationale behind this method is that a vacant space from one viewpoint can carve out a space occupied by hands at another viewpoint. This removes the viewpoint dependent occlusion, while the object space is left.

We developed the following method to recover 3D object shape from multi-view stereo images corrupted with viewpoint dependent occlusion:

1. **Capture** – A series of stereo images of a hand manipulated object are captured by the wearable vision sensor.
2. **Feature Point Detection** – From each frame of the dynamic stereo images, feature points on the object surface are detected by Harris Corner Detector (Harris and Stephens, 1988) and then, the 3D location of the feature points are calculated by stereo analysis.
3. **Camera Motion Recovery** – Based on 3D feature point data observed from multiple viewpoints, the 3D camera position and motion in the object centered coordinate system are estimated by an advanced ICP algorithm (Besl and McKey, 1992).
4. **Depth Map Acquisition** – For each viewpoint, a depth map is computed by region based stereo analysis. Then, based on the depth map, the vacant space is computed.
5. **Silhouette Acquisition** – For each viewpoint, an object & hand silhouette is computed by background subtraction. Then again, we compute the vacant space based on the silhouette.

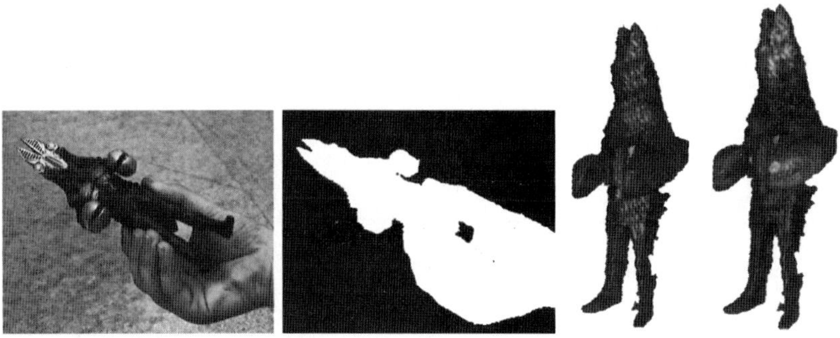

(a) (b) (c) (d)

Figure 15. 3D digitization of an alien figure: (a) captured image, (b) silhouette image, (c) 3D shape, and (d) digitized object.

6. **Vacant Space Carving** – The 3D block space is carved by a group of vacant spaces computed from multiple viewpoint to generate a 3D object shape.

Since the wearable vision system can capture video images to generate densely placed multi-view stereo images and hand shape and position changes dynamically to manipulate an object, the above method can generate the accurate 3D object shape.

We applied the method to a complex alien figure as shown in Figure 15(a). The images were captured from 13 viewpoints around the object. Figure 15(b) illustrates an extracted object & hand silhouette. Figure 15(c) shows the result of the vacant space carving. After mapping the texture, we obtained the 3D digitized object shown in Figure 15(d).

3.3. ESTIMATION OF 3D HUMAN MOTION TRAJECTORY BY BINOCULAR INDEPENDENT FIXATION CAMERA CONTROL

Here, we address 3D human motion trajectory estimation using the active wearable vision system. In the previous two methods, the active cameras work as stereo cameras sharing the visual field with human to understand what he/she is looking at. In other words, the cameras captured convergent multi-view images of a human interested object.

In this research, on the other hand, a pair of active cameras are used to get the 3D surrounding scene information, which enables us to estimate the 3D human motion (i.e. to be specific, camera motion) in the scene. That is, the cameras capture divergent multi-view images of the scene during human motion.

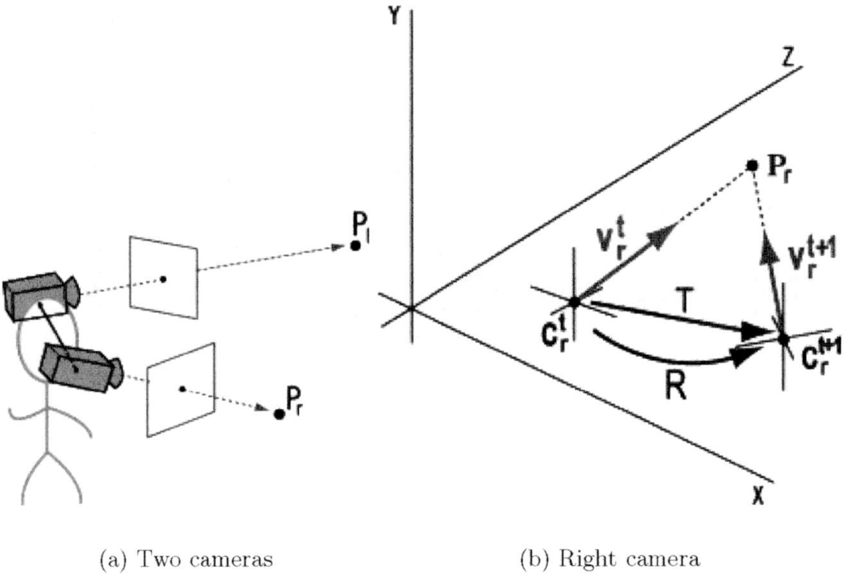

Figure 16. (a) Binocular independent fixation camera control. (b) Geometric configuration in the right camera fixation control.

To estimate the 3D human motion trajectory with a pair of active wearable cameras, we introduced what we call the *binocular independent fixation camera control* (Figure 16a): each camera automatically fixates its optical axis on a selected scene point (i.e. the *fixation point*) and keeps the fixation irrespectively of human motion. This may be called *the cross-eyed vision.*

Suppose a pair of wearable cameras are calibrated and their optical axes are fixated at a pair of corresponding scene points during human motion. Let $\boldsymbol{T}$ and R denote the translation vector and rotation matrix describing the human motion between t and $t + 1$, respectively.

Figure 16b shows the geometric configuration in the right camera fixation control: the projection center moves from C_{r}^{t} to C_{r}^{t+1} while keeping the optical axis fixated at P_{r}. From this configuration, we can get the following constraint on $\mathbf{T}$ and $\mathbf{R}$:

$$\lambda R_0 \boldsymbol{v}_{\mathrm{r}}^{t} \;=\; \lambda' R_0 R \boldsymbol{v}_{\mathrm{r}}^{t+1} + \boldsymbol{T},$$

where λ and λ' are non-zero constants, and $\boldsymbol{v}_{\mathrm{r}}^{t}$ and $\boldsymbol{v}_{\mathrm{r}}^{t+1}$ denote the viewing direction vectors at t and $t+1$, respectively. We assume that the orientation of the world coordinate system has been obtained by applying rotation matrix R_0^{-1} to the orientation of the right-camera coordinate system at time t. This equation is rewritten by

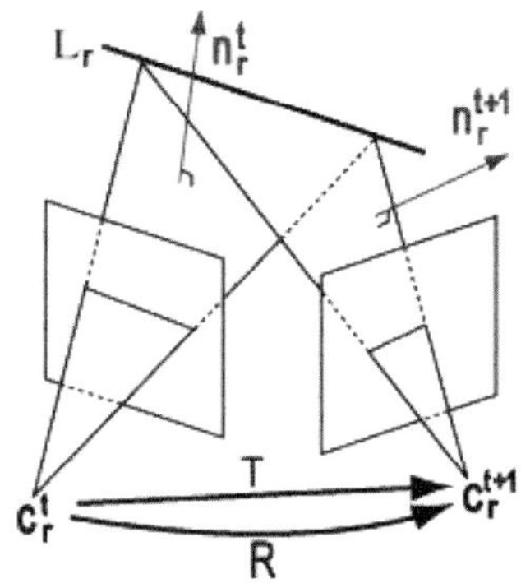

Figure 17. Geometry based on the line correspondence of the right camera.

$$\det\left[\, R_0 \boldsymbol{v}_{\mathrm{r}}^{t+1} \;\; R_0 R \boldsymbol{v}_{\mathrm{r}}^{t} \;\; \boldsymbol{T} \,\right] = 0, \tag{1}$$

which gives the constraint on the human motion. The constraint similar to (1) is obtained from the the fixation control of the left camera.

The human motion has 6 degrees of freedom: 3 for a rotation and 3 for a translation. The number of constraints on the human motion derived from the fixation control of two cameras, on the other hand, is two ((1) and that computed from the left camera). We therefore need to derive more constraints to estimate the human motion.

To derive sufficient constraints to estimate the human motion, we employ correspondences between lines located nearby around the fixation point.

We assume that we have established the image correspondence of a 3D line L_{r} at time t and $t+1$, where line L_{r} is selected from a neighborhood of the fixation point of the right camera (Figure 3.3). Based on this geometric configuration, we obtain the following constraint on the human motion from the line correspondence between two image frames captured by the right camera:

$$\mu_{\mathrm{r}} \boldsymbol{L}_{\mathrm{r}} = (R_0 \boldsymbol{n}_{\mathrm{r}}^{t}) \times (R_0 R \boldsymbol{n}_{\mathrm{r}}^{t+1}), \tag{2}$$

where $\boldsymbol{L}_{\mathrm{r}}$ denotes the unit direction vector of the focused line L_{r} in the world coordinate system, and $\boldsymbol{n}_{\mathrm{r}}^{t}$ and $\boldsymbol{n}_{\mathrm{r}}^{t+1}$ normal vectors of the planes formed by two projection centers C_{r}^{t} and C_{r}^{t+1} and 3D line L_{r}, respectively. μ_{r} is a non-zero constant and depends on the focused line. We see that this constraint is linear homogeneous with respect to the unknowns, i.e., R and the non-zero constant. In the similar way, we obtain the constraint on the human motion derived from the line correspondence of the left camera.

The constraints derived from the line correspondence depend only on the rotation of the human motion. We can thus divide the human motion estimation into two steps: the rotation estimation and the translation estimation.

The first step is the rotation estimation of the human motion. Suppose that we have correspondences of n focused lines between two temporal frames. Then, we have $n + 3$ unknowns (n scale factors and 3 rotation parameters) and $3n$ constraints. Therefore, we can estimate the rotation if we have correspondences of more than two focused lines.

Finishing the estimation of the rotation matrix, unknowns are only the translation vector. Given the rotation matrix, the constraint derived from the camera fixation becomes homogeneous linear with respect to the unknowns. Hence, we can obtain the translation of the human motion up to scale from two independent fixation points. That is, whenever we estimate the translation of the human motion over two frames, we have one unknown scale factor. The trilinear constraints (Hartley and Zisserman, 2000) on corresponding points over three frames enable us to adjust the unknown scales with only linear computation.

Comparing our binocular independent fixation camera control with ordinary stereo vision, ours has the following advantages:

- Since the image feature matching in the former is conducted between temporally separated image frames captured from almost the same viewpoint (i.e. by the same moving camera), image features to be matched have enough similar appearances to facilitate the matching. As is well known, on the other hand, matching in the latter is conducted between images captured from spatially separated viewpoints (i.e. different cameras), so that images feature appearances often become different, which makes the matching difficult. In other words, the former employs temporal image feature matching while the latter spatial image feature matching. Since the former method is much easier and more robust than the latter, our method can work better than stereo vision.
- The similar computational scheme as ours holds when we put cameras at the fixation points in the scene, which are looking at a person. Since the distance between the fixation points can be much longer than the baseline length of ordinary stereo cameras (for example, the baseline between a pair of cameras in our wearable vision system is about 27cm) and the accuracy in the 3D measurement depends on the baseline length between the cameras, our method can realize more accurate 3D position sensing than stereo vision.

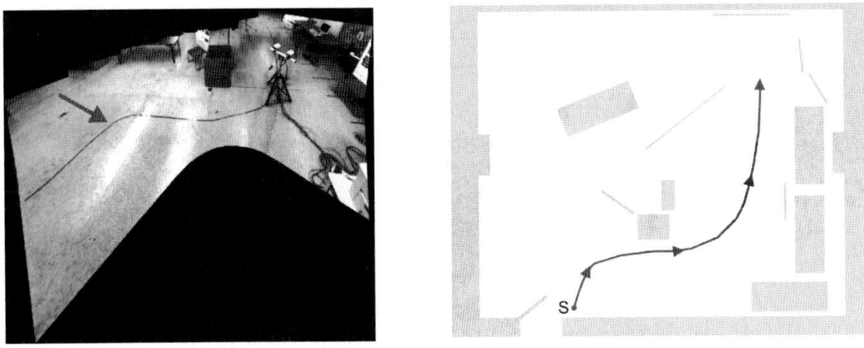

(a) wide view scene representation (b) top view of the scene

Figure 18. Camera motion trajectory.

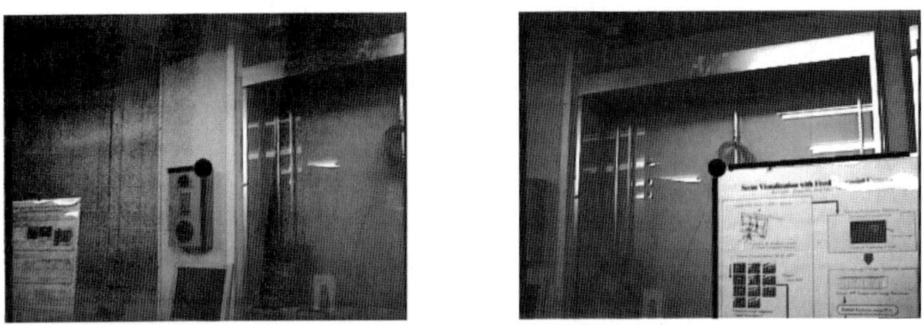

(a) left camera image (b) right camera image

Figure 19. Example images acquired for the binocular independent fixation.

To verify the effectiveness of the proposed method, we moved a pair of stereo cameras in a room and estimated their 3D motion trajectory. The trajectory of the right camera motion is shown in Figure 18, where the path length of the trajectory was about 6m. We marked 35 points on the trajectory and regarded them as sensing positions during the motion. We then applied the binocular independent fixation camera control at the sensing positions to estimate the right camera motion.

In the images captured by each camera at the starting point of the camera motion, we manually selected a fixation point. During the estimation, we manually updated fixation points 8 times; when the camera moves largely and the surrounding scene changes much, we have to change fixation points. We used two focused lines for each camera; edge detection followed by the Hough transformation is used for focused line detection. Figure 19 shows an example of image pairs captured at a sensing position. In the image, the fixation point (the black circle) and two focused lines (the thick black lines) are overlaid.

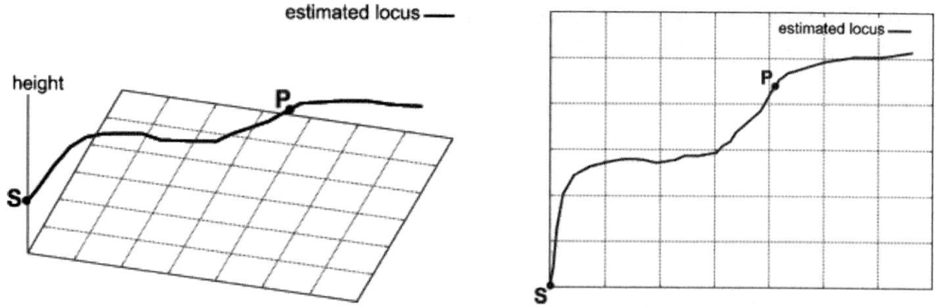

(a) 3D representation (b) top-view representation

Figure 20. Estimated trajectory of the camera motion.

Under the above conditions, we estimated the right camera motion at each sensing position. Figure 20 shows the estimated trajectory of the right camera motion, obtained by concatenating the estimated motions at the sensing positions. In the figure, S is the starting point of the motion.

The height from the floor, which is almost constant, was almost accurately estimated. As for the component parallel to the floor, however, while the former part (from S to P in the figure) of the estimated trajectory is fairly close to the actual trajectory, the latter part (after P) deviates from the actual trajectory. This is because the motion at P was incorrectly estimated; since the motion was incrementally estimated, an incorrect estimation at a sensing position caused a systematic deviation in the subsequent estimations. While it has not been implemented, this problem can be solved by introducing some global trajectory optimization using results obtained by local motion estimations.

4. Concluding Remarks

In this paper we discussed how we can extend visual information processing capabilities by using a group of multi-view cameras.

First we address a ubiquitous vision system, where a group of network-connected (active) cameras are embedded in the real world to observe dynamic events from various different viewpoints. We demonstrated its effectiveness with the cooperative distributed active multi-target tracking system and the high fidelity 3D video generation system.

In the latter half of the paper, we proposed a wearable active vision system, where multiple cameras are placed nearby around human eyes to share the viewpoint. We demonstrated its effectiveness with 1) accurate estimation of 3D human gaze point and close-up image acquisition of a focused object, 2) 3D digitization of a hand-held object, and 3) estimation of 3D human-motion trajectory.

We believe ubiquitous and wearable visions systems enable us to improve human-computer interfaces and support our everyday life activities.

Acknowledgements

This series of researches are supported by
· Grant-in-Aid for Scientific Research No. 13308017, No. 13224051 and No. 14380161 of the Ministry of Education, Culture, Sports, Science and Technology, Japan,
· National research project on Development of High Fidelity Digitization Software for Large-Scale and Intangible Cultural Assets of the Ministry of Education, Culture, Sports, Science and Technology, Japan, and
· Center of Excellence on Knowledge Society Infrastructure, Kyoto University.

Research efforts and supports to prepare the paper by all members of our laboratory and Dr. A. Sugimoto of the National Institute of Informatics, Japan are gratefully acknowledged.

References

Matsuyama, T.: Cooperative distributed vision - dynamic integration of visual perception, action, and communication. In Proc. *Image Understanding Workshop*, pages 365–384, 1998.

Matsuyama, T. and Ukita, N.: Real-time multi-target tracking by a cooperative distributed vision system. *Proc. IEEE*, **90**: 1136–1150, 2002.

Moezzi, S., Tai, L., and Gerard, P. Virtual: View generation for 3D digital video. In Proc. *IEEE Multimedia*, pages 18-26, 1997.

Matsuyama, T., Wu, X., Takai, T., and Wada, T.: Real-time dynamic 3D object shape reconstruction and high-fidelity texture mapping for 3D video. *IEEE Trans. Circuits Systems Video Technology*, **14**: 357–369, 2004.

Sumi, K., Sugimoto, A., and Matsuyama, T.: Active wearable vision sensor: recognition of human activities and environments. In Proc. *Int. Conf. Informatics Research for Development of Knowledge Society Infrastructure*, pages 15–22, Kyoto, 2004.

Wada, T. and Matsuyama, T.: Appearance sphere:background model for pan-tilt- zoom camera. In Proc. *ICPR*, pages A-718 – A-722, 1996.

Matsuyama, T., Ohya, T., and Habe, H.: Background subtraction for non-stationary scenes. In Proc. *Asian Conf. Computer Vision*, pages 662–667, 2000

Matsuyama, T., Hiura, S., Wada, T., Murase, K., and Yoshioka, A.: Dynamic memory: architecture for real time integration of visual perception, camera action, and network communication. In Proc. *Int. Conf. Computer Vision Pattern Recognition*, pages 728–735, 2000

Wada, T. and Wu, X. and Tokai, S. and Matsuyama, T.: Homography based parallel volume intersection: toward real-time reconstruction using active camera. In Proc. *Int. Workshop Computer Architectures for Machine Perception*, pages 331–339, 2000.

Matsuyama, T. and Takai, T.: Generation, visualization, and editing of 3D video. In Proc. *Symp. 3D Data Processing Visualization and Transmission*, pages 234–245, 2002.

Matsuyama, T. and Wu, X. and Takai, T. and Nobuhara, S.: Real-time 3D shape reconstruction, dynamic 3D mesh deformation, and high fidelity visualization for 3D video. *Int. J. Computer Vision Image Understanding*, **96**: 393-434, 2004.

Kenmochi, Y. and Kotani, K. and Imiya, A.: Marching cubes method with connectivity. In Proc. *Int. Conf. Image Processing*, pages 361–365, 1999.

Sugimoto, A., Nakayama, A., and Matsuyama, T.: Detecting a gazing region by visual direction and stereo cameras. In Proc. *Int. Conf. Pattern Recognition*, Volume III, pages 278–282, 2002.

Hoppe, H., DeRose, T., Duchamp, T., McDonald, J., and Stuetzle, W.: Surface reconstruction from unorganized points. In Proc. *SIGGRAPH*, Volume 26, pages 71–78, 1992.

Kutulakos, K.N. and Seitz, S. M.:A theory of shape by space carving. In Proc. *Int. Conf. Computer Vision*, pages 307–314, 1999.

Harris, C.J. and Stephens, M.: A combined corner and edge detector, In Proc. *Alvey Vision Conf.*, pages 147–151, 1988.

Besl, P.J. and McKey, N.D.: A method for registration of 3-D shapes, *IEEE Trans. PAMI*, **14**: 239–256, 1992.

Hartley, R. and Zisserman, A.: *Multiple View Geometry in Computer Vision*, Cambridge Univ. Press, 2000.

3D OPTICAL FLOW IN GATED MRI CARDIAC DATASETS

JOHN BARRON
Department of Computer Science
University of Western Ontario
London N6A 5B7, Ontario, Canada

Abstract. We report on the computation of 3D volumetric optical flow on gated MRI datasets. We extend the 2D "strawman" least squares and regularization approaches of Lucas and Kanade (Lucas and Kanade, 1981) and Horn and Schunck (Horn and Schunck, 1981) and show flow fields (as XY and XZ 2D flows) for a beating heart. The flow not only can captures the expansion and contraction of the various parts of the heart motion but also can capture the twisting motion of the heart while it is beating.

Key words: least squares/regularized 3D optical flow, 3D volumetric motion, gated MRI cardiac datasets

1. Introduction

It is now possible to acquire good gated MRI [Magnetic Resonance Imagery] data of a human beating heart. Such data has high resolution (compared to US [UltraSound] data), has good blood/tissue contrast and offers a wide topographical field of view of the heart. Unlike CT [Computed Tomography] it is also non-invasive (no radiation dose required). However, it is still challenging to measure the 3D motions that the heart is undergoing, especially any motions with a physiological basis. For example, heart wall motion abnormalities are a good indicator of heart disease. Physicians are greatly interested in the local motions of the left ventricular chamber which pumps oxygenated blood to the body, as these are good indicators of heart function. One obvious option for measuring 3D motion is to track 3D "interest" points. Unfortunately, MRI data allows tracking only for partial parts of the systole or diastole phases of the heart beat cycle because the magnetization signal weakens over time (Park et al., 1996). Nonetheless it can allow tracking via correspondence of tagged markers (Park et al., 1996). We note all the work on 2D motion analysis of heart data (see (Frangi et al., 2001) for a survey) but we believe the analysis must be 3D over time

K. Daniilidis and R. Klette (eds.), Imaging Beyond the Pinhole Camera, 331–344.

(some people call this 4D) to capture the true heart motions, for example, the twisting motion the heart undergoes in each beat cycle.

With increased computational resources and the availability of time-varying data, it is becoming more and more feasible to compute full 3D optical flow fields. We have already presented methods to compute 3D optical flow for 3D Doppler Radar data in a regularization framework constrained by the least squares velocities (Chen et al., 2001a; Chen et al., 2001b) and we have used this 3D optical flow to predict the locations of severe weather storms over time (Tang et al., 2003). We have also shown how to compute 3D range flow (Spies et al., 2002). Range flow is the 3D motion of points on a surface while generic 3D optical flow is 3D volumetric motion. We present two simple extensions to the 2D optical flows by (Lucas and Kanade, 1981) and (Horn and Schunck, 1981) here and elsewhere (Barron, 2004). We implement our algorithms in Tinatool (Pollard et al., 1999; Barron, 2003), an X windows based software package for Computer Vision algorithms.

2. Gated MRI Data and its Acquisition

We test our algorithms on gated MRI data obtained from the Robarts Research Institute at the University of Western Ontario (Moore et al., 2003). Various sets of this data each contain 20 volumes of 3D volumetric data for one synchronized heart beat, with each 3D volume dataset consisting of either $256 \times 256 \times 31$ (axial view) or $256 \times 256 \times 75$ (coronal view) with voxel intensities (unsigned shorts) in the range $[0-4095]$ (12 bits). For the smaller datasets the resolution is 1.25mm in the x and y dimensions and 5.0mm in the z dimension[1] while the larger datasets have 1.25mm resolution in all 3 dimensions. The heart motion is discontinuous in space and time: different chambers in the heart are contracting/expanding at different times and the heart as a whole undergoes a twisting motion as it beats. The word "gated" refers to the way the data is collected: 1 or a few slices of each volume set are acquired at the same time instance in a cardiac cycle. A patient lies in an MRI machine and holds his breath for approximately 42 second intervals to acquire each set of slices. This data acquisition method relies on the patient not moving or breathing during the acquisition (this minimizes heart motion caused by a moving diaphragm): the result can be misalignment in adjacent slices in the heart data at a single time. One way to correct this misalignment is presented in (Moore et al., 2003). Figures 6 and 7 below provides a good example of slice misalignment. For the **5phase.936** flows there is significant motion detected at the borders of

[1] This means z velocity magnitudes are actually 4 times larger than they appear.

the chest cavity. For the **10phase.16.36** flows there is little motion in this area as the adjacent slices in the data are better aligned (the flow for **10phase.936** also has no motion at the chest cavity borders). The MRI data is prospectively (versus retrospectively) acquired: the MRI machine uses an ECG for the patient to gate when to acquire a given phase. Thus it has to leave a gap between cycles while waiting for the next R wave. This means the data is not uniformly sampled in time; rather there is a different time interval between the last and first datasets then between the other datasets.

Although neither the acquisition or optical flow calculations are anywhere near real-time, we believe this type of processing will be quite feasible in the years to come, especially with advances in both computational resources and MRI technology. For example, recent advances in in MRI hardware have lead to parallel MRI acquisition strategies (Sodickson, 2000; Weiger et al., 2000) and that plus the use of a SIMD parallel computer may lead to near "real-time" 3D MRI optical flow.

3. The 3D Motion Constraint Equation

Differential optical flow is always based on some version of the **motion constraint equation**. In 3D, we assume that $I(x, y, z, t) = I(x + \delta_x, y + \delta t, z + \delta z, t + \delta t)$. That is, a small $n \times n \times n$ 3D neighborhood of voxels centered at (x, y, z) at time t translate to $(x + \delta x, y + \delta y, z + \delta z)$ at time $t + \delta t$. A 1st order Taylor series expansion of $I(x + \delta x, y + \delta y, z + \delta z, t + \delta t)$ yields:

$$\begin{aligned} I(x + \delta x, y + \delta y, z + \delta z, t + \delta t) &= I(x, y, z, t) + \\ & \frac{\partial I}{\partial x}\delta x + \frac{\partial I}{\partial y}\delta y + \frac{\partial I}{\partial z}\delta z + \frac{\partial I}{\partial t}\delta t. \end{aligned} \quad (1)$$

Since $I(x + \delta x, y + \delta y, z + \delta z, t + \delta t) = I(x, y, z, t)$ we have:

$$\frac{\partial I}{\partial x}\frac{\delta x}{\delta t} + \frac{\partial I}{\partial y}\frac{\delta y}{\delta t} + \frac{\partial I}{\partial z}\frac{\delta z}{\delta t} + \frac{\partial I}{\partial t} = 0. \quad (2)$$

or

$$I_x U + I_y V + I_z W + I_t = 0, \quad (3)$$

where $U = \frac{\delta x}{\delta t}$, $V = \frac{\delta y}{\delta t}$ and $W = \frac{\delta y}{\delta t}$ are the three 3D velocity components and I_x, I_y, I_z and I_t denote the partial spatio-temporal intensity derivatives. Equation (3) is 1 equation if 3 unknowns (a plane).

4. 3D Normal Velocity

The 2D aperture problem (Marr and Ullman, 1981) means that locally only the velocity normal to the local intensity structure can be measured. The aperture problem in 3D actually yields two types of normal velocity: **plane normal** velocity (the velocity normal to a local intensity planar structure) and **line normal** velocity (the velocity normal to a local line intensity structure caused by the intersection of 2 planes) and full details can be found in other papers (Spies et al., 1999; Spies et al., 2002)[2] Plane and Line normal velocities are illustrated in Figure 1 and explained briefly as follows. If the spatio-temporal derivative data best fits a single plane only,

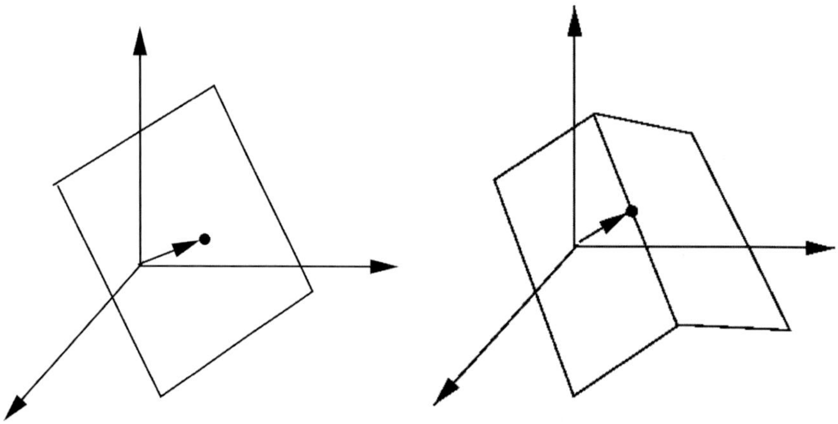

Figure 1. Graphical illustrations of the 3D plane and line normal velocities.

we have plane normal velocity. The point on the plane closest to the origin $(0, 0, 0)$ is its magnitude and the plane surface normal is it direction. If the spatio-temporal derivative data best fit two separate planes (perhaps found by an EM calculation) than the point on their intersection line closest to the origin $(0, 0, 0)$ is the line normal velocity. Of course, if the spatio-temporal derivative data fits 3 or more planes we have a full 3D velocity calculation (the best intersection point of all the planes via a (total) Least Squares fit). We are concerned only with the computation of full 3D velocity for the programs described in this paper but plane and line normal velocities may be of use in future MRI optical flow work.

[2] These papers describe the 3D aperture problems and the resulting types of normal velocity and their computation for 3D range flow [which is just 3D optical flow for points on a moving surface) and, with only minor changes, applies to 3D (volumetric) optical flow, which we are interested in here.]

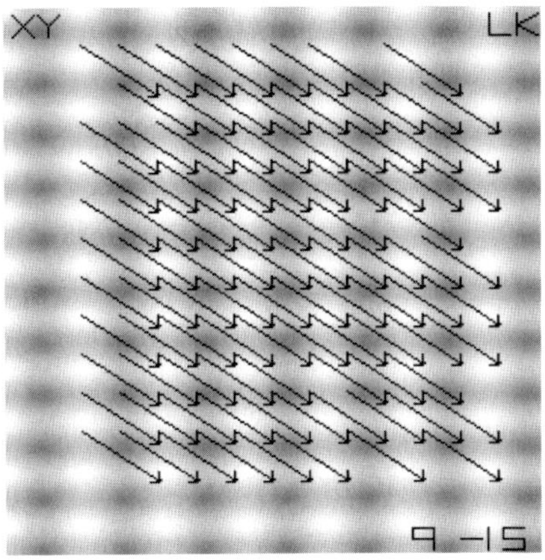

LK-XY-9-15

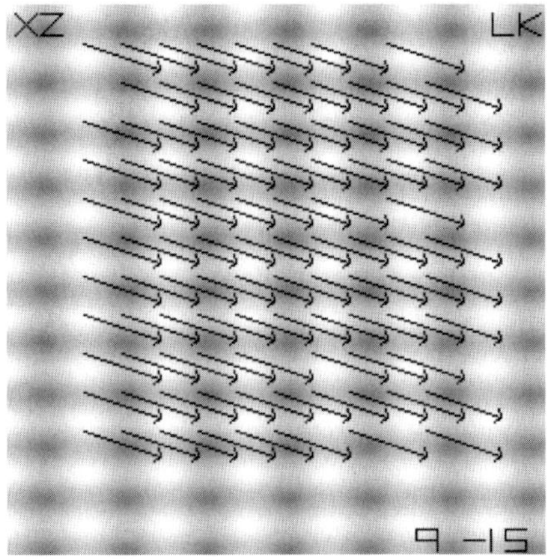

LK-XZ-9-15

Figure 2. The Lucas and Kanade XY and XZ flow fields superimposed on the 15th slice of the 9th volume of sinusoidal data for 50 and 100 iterations. $\alpha = 1.0$.

5. 3D Lucas and Kanade

Using the 3D motion constraint equation, $I_xU + I_yV + I_zW = -I_t$, we assume a constant 3D velocity, $\vec{V} = (U, V, W)$, in a local $n \times n \times n$ 3D neighborhood and solve:

$$\vec{V} = [A^T W^2 A]^{-1} A^T W B, \tag{4}$$

where, for $N = n \times n \times n$:

$$\begin{aligned} A &= [\nabla I(x_1, y_1, z_1), ..., \nabla I(x_N, y_N, z_N)], & (5)\\ W &= \text{diag}[W(x_1, y_1, z_1), ..., W(x_N, y_N, z_N)], & (6)\\ B &= -(I_t(x_1, y_1, z_1), ..., I_t(x_N, y_N, z_N)). & (7) \end{aligned}$$

$A^T W^2 A$ is computed as:

$$A^T W^2 A = \begin{pmatrix} \sum W^2(x,y,z) I_x(x,y,z)^2 & \sum W^2(x,y,z) I_x(x,y,z) I_y(x,y,z) \\ \sum W^2(x,y,z) I_y(x,y,z) I_x(x,y,z) & \sum W^2(x,y,z) I_y(x,y,z)^2 \\ \sum W^2(x,y,z) I_z(x,y,z) I_x(x,y,z) & \sum W^2(x,y,z) I_z(x,y,z) I_y(x,y,z) \end{pmatrix}$$

$$\begin{pmatrix} \sum W^2(x,y,z) I_x(x,y,z) I_z(x,y,z) \\ \sum W^2(x,y,z) I_y(x,y,z) I_z(x,y,z) \\ \sum W^2(x,y,z) I_z(x,y,z)^2 \end{pmatrix}. \tag{8}$$

W is a weighting matrix (all elements 1.0 for now). Alternatively, we could have the W diagonal elements to contain 3D Gaussian coefficient value that weight derivative values less when they are further they are from the

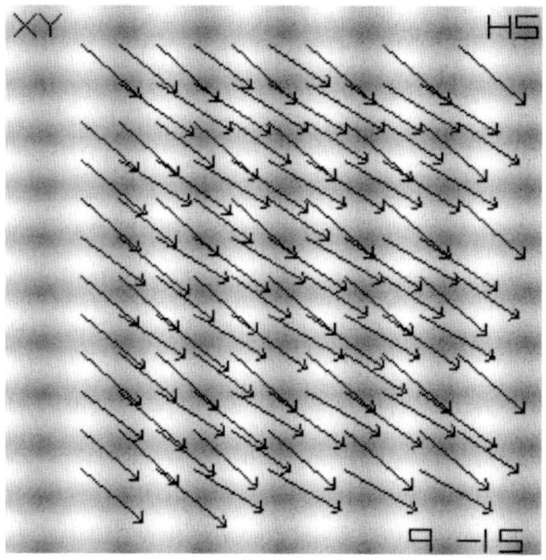

HS-XY-9-15 (50 iterations)

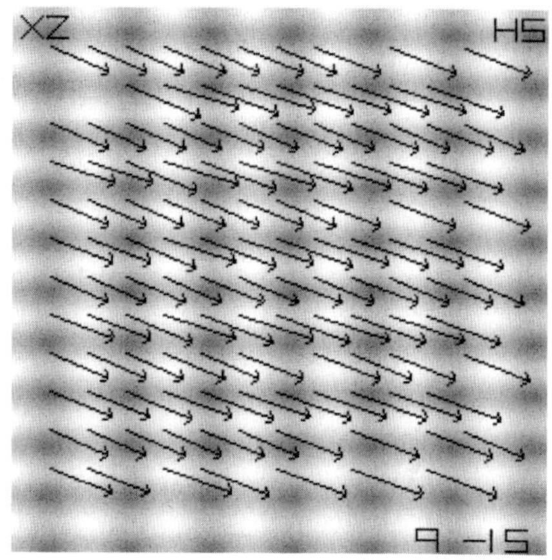

HS-XZ-9-15 (50 iterations)

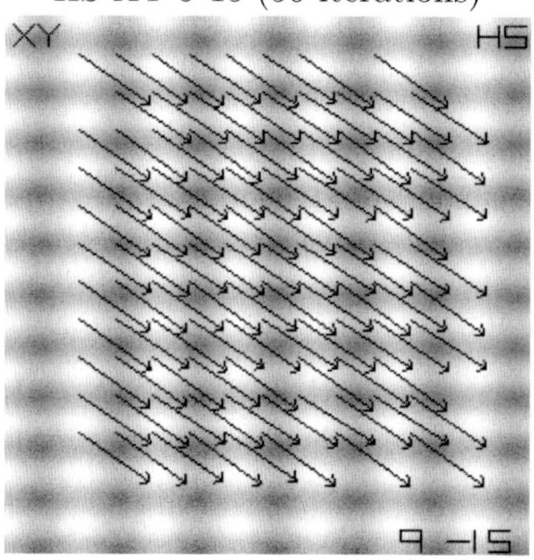

HS-XY-9-15 (100 iterations)

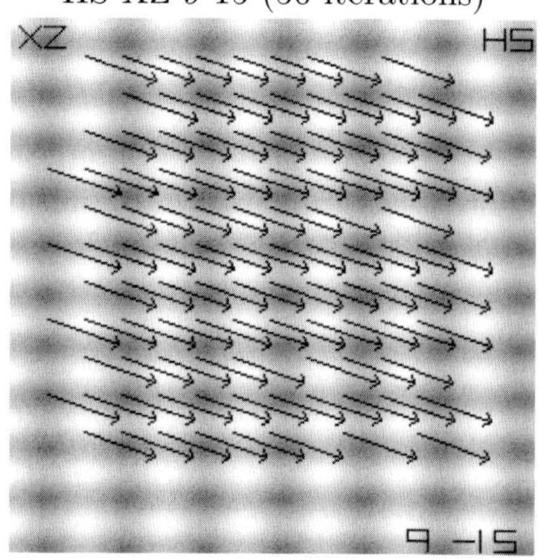

HS-XZ-9-51 (100 iterations)

Figure 3. The Horn and Schunck XY and XZ flow fields superimposed on the 15th slice of the 9th volume of sinusoidal data for 50 and 100 iterations. $\alpha = 1.0$.

neighborhood's center or to derivative certainty values which would weight the equations' influence on the final result by the computed derivatives' quality (Spies, 2003; Spies and Barron, 2004). The latter will be incorporated in later work. We perform eigenvalue/eigenvector analysis of $A^T W^2 A$ to compute eigenvalues $\lambda_3 \geq \lambda_2 \geq \lambda_1 \geq 0$ and accept as reliable full 3D velocities those velocities with $\lambda_1 > \tau_D$. τ_D is 1.0 here. We didn't compute line normal velocities (when $\lambda_1 < \tau_D$ and $\lambda_3 \geq \lambda_2 \geq \tau_D$) or plane normal velocities (when $\lambda_1 \leq \lambda_2 < \tau_D$ and $\lambda_3 \geq \tau_D$) here as they didn't seem useful. We did compute the two type of 3D normal velocity in earlier work using an eigenvector/eigenvalue analysis in a total least square framework for range flow [3D optical flow on a moving (deformable) surface) (Spies

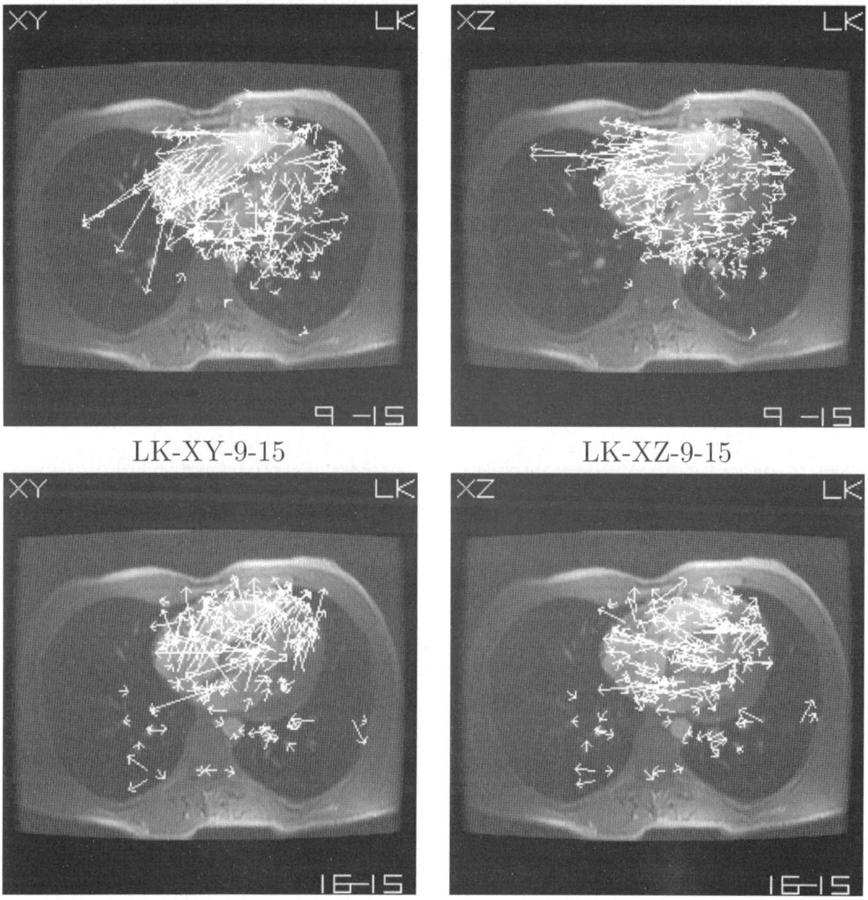

LK-XY-9-15 LK-XZ-9-15

LK-XY-16-15 LK-XZ-16-15

Figure 4. The Lucas and Kanade XY and XZ flow fields superimposed on the 15th slice of the 9th and 16th volumes of MRI data for $\tau_D = 1.0$.

et al., 1999; Spies et al., 2002)]. In this paper we are solely interested in full 3D volumetric optical flow.

6. 3D Horn and Schunck

We extend the 2D Horn and Schunck regularization to:

$$\sum_R (I_x U + I_y V + I_z W + I_t) + \alpha^2 \left[\left(\frac{\partial U}{\partial x} \right)^2 + \left(\frac{\partial U}{\partial y} \right)^2 + \left(\frac{\partial U}{\partial z} \right)^2 + \right.$$

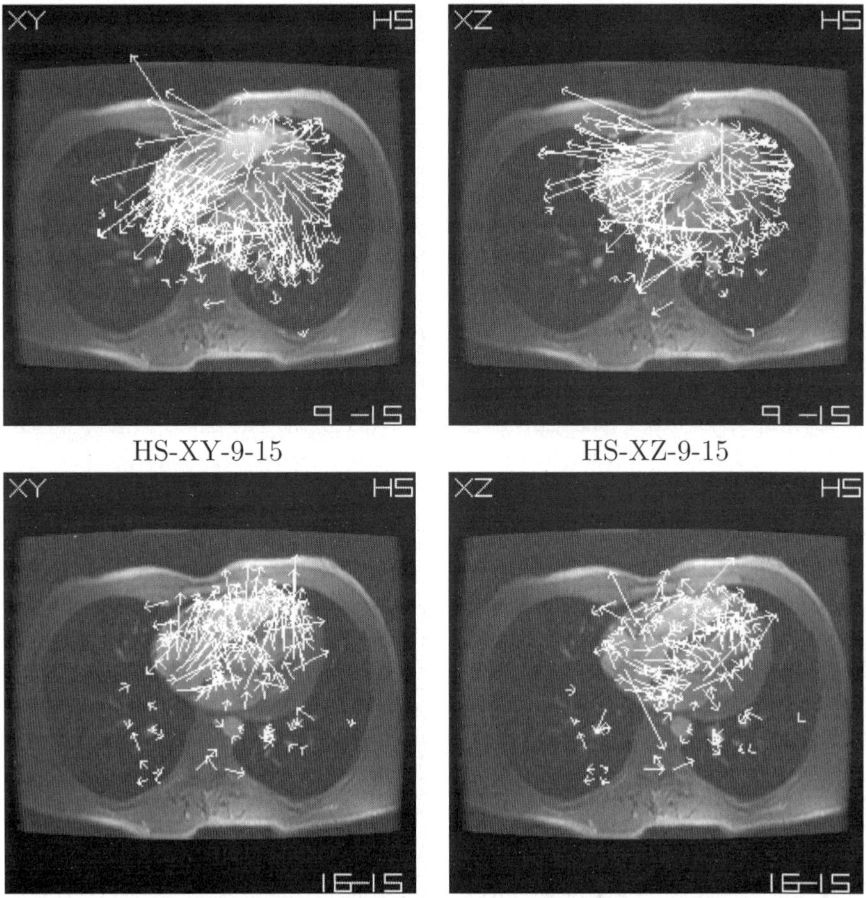

HS-XY-9-15 HS-XZ-9-15

HS-XY-16-15 HS-XZ-16-15

Figure 5. The Horn and Schunck XY and XZ flow fields superimposed on the 15th slice of the 9th and 16th volumes of MRI data for 100 iterations. $\alpha = 1.0$.

$$\left(\frac{\partial V}{\partial x}\right)^2 + \left(\frac{\partial V}{\partial y}\right)^2 + \left(\frac{\partial V}{\partial z}\right)^2 + \left(\frac{\partial W}{\partial x}\right)^2 + \left(\frac{\partial W}{\partial y}\right)^2 + \left(\frac{\partial W}{\partial z}\right)^2 \Bigg] \quad (9)$$

where $\vec{V} = (U, V, W)$ is the 3D volumetric optical flow and $\left(\frac{\partial U}{\partial x}\right)$, $\left(\frac{\partial U}{\partial y}\right)$ and $\left(\frac{\partial U}{\partial z}\right)$ are the partial derivative of U with respect to x, y and z, etc. The iterative Gauss Seidel equations that solve the Euler-Lagrange equations derived from this functional are:

$$U^{k+1} = \bar{U}^n - \frac{I_x \left[I_x \bar{U} + I_y \bar{V} + I_z \bar{W} + I_t\right]}{(\alpha^2 + I_x^2 + I_y^2 + I_z^2)}, \quad (10)$$

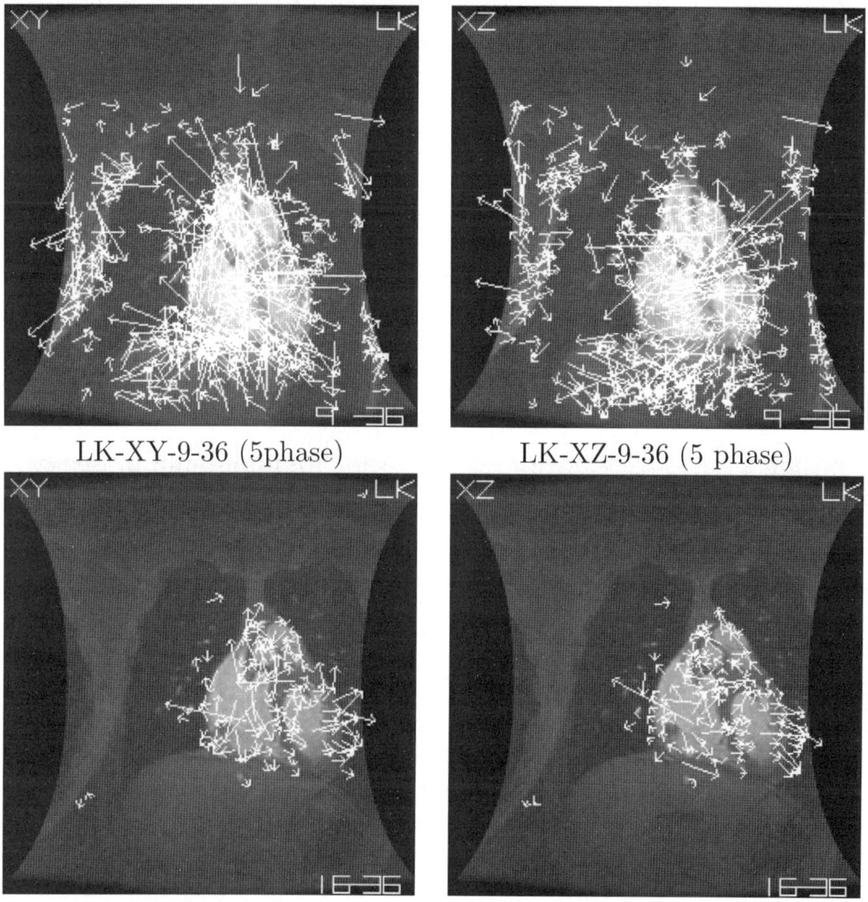

LK-XY-9-36 (5phase) LK-XZ-9-36 (5 phase)

LK-XY-16-36 (10phase) LK-XZ-16-36 (10phase)

Figure 6. The Lucas and Kanade XY and XZ flow fields superimposed on the 36th slice of the 9th and 16th volumes of the 5phase and 10phase data for $\tau_D = 1.0$.

$$V^{k+1} = \bar{V}^k - \frac{I_y \left[I_x \bar{U} + I_y \bar{V} + I_z \bar{W} + I_t \right]}{(\alpha^2 + I_x^2 + I_y^2 + I_z^2)}, \tag{11}$$

$$W^{k+1} = \bar{W}^k - \frac{I_z \left[I_x \bar{U} + I_y \bar{V} + I_z \bar{W} + I_t \right]}{(\alpha^2 + I_x^2 + I_y^2 + I_z^2)}. \tag{12}$$

Again α was typically 1.0 or 10.0 and the number of iterations was typically 50 or 100.

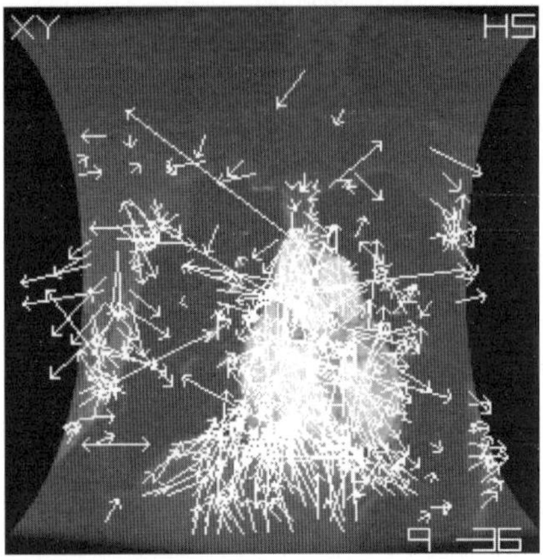

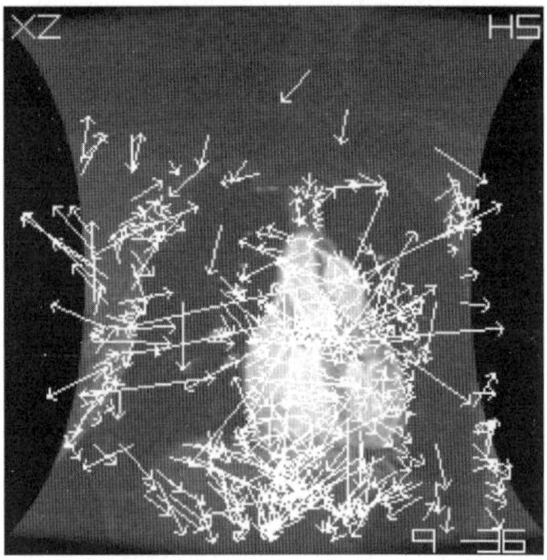

HS-XY-9-36 (5phase) HS-XZ-9-36 (5phase)

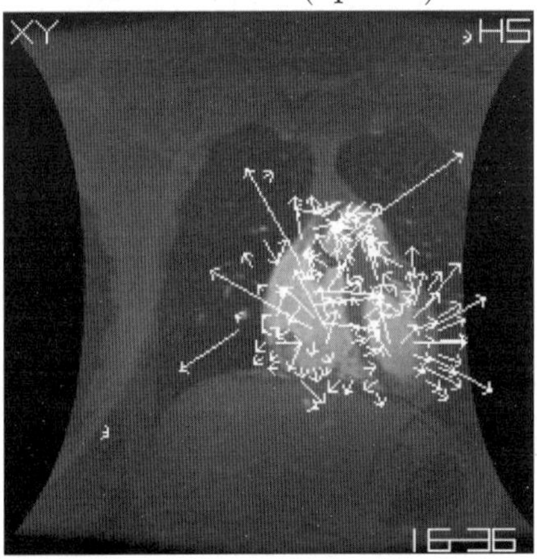

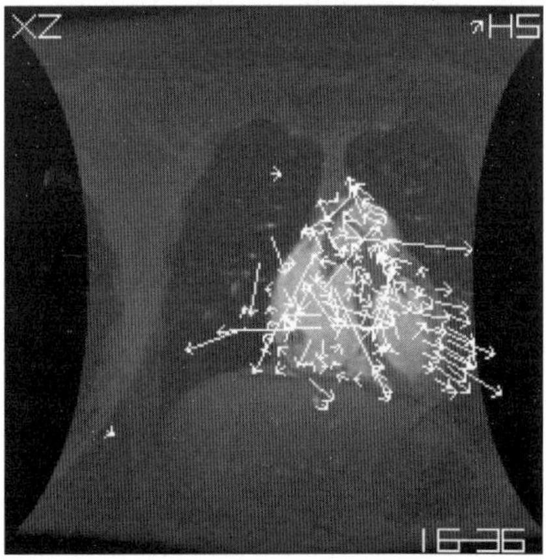

HS-XY-16-36 (10phase) HS-XZ-16-36 (10phase)

Figure 7. The Horn and Schunck XY and XZ flow fields superimposed on the 36th slice of the 9th and 16th volumes of the 5phase and 10phase data for 100 iterations. $\alpha = 1.0$.

7. 3D Differentiation

Regardless of the optical flow method used, we need to compute image intensity derivatives. Differentiation was done using Simoncelli's (Simoncelli, 1994) matched balanced filters for low pass filtering (blurring) [p_5 in Table 1] and high pass filtering (differentiation) [d_5 in Table 1]. Matched filters allow comparisons between the signal and its derivatives as the high pass filter is simply the derivative of the low pass filter and, from experimental observations, yields more accurate derivative values.

Before performing Simoncelli's filtering we use the simple averaging filter suggested by Simoncelli, $[\frac{1}{4}, \frac{1}{2}, \frac{1}{4}]$, to slightly blur the images. Simoncelli

Table 1. Simoncelli's 5-point Matched/Balanced Kernels.

n	p_5	d_5
0	0.036	−0.108
1	0.249	−0.283
2	0.431	0.0
3	0.249	0.283
4	0.036	0.108

claims that, because both of his filters were derived from the same principles, more accurate derivatives result.

To compute I_x in 3D, we first smooth in the t dimension first using p_5 (to reduce the 5 volumes of 3D data to 1 volume of 3D data), then smooth that result in the y dimension using p_5 and then smooth that new result in the z dimension, again using p_5, and finally differentiate the $y - z$ smoothed result in the x dimension using d_5. Similar operations are performed to compute I_y and I_z. To compute I_t in 3D, we smooth each of the 5 volumes, first in the x dimension, then that result in the y dimension and finally that new result in the z dimension, using p_5 (theoretically the order is not important). Lastly, we differentiate the 5 volumes of $x - y - z$ smoothed data using d_5 in the t dimension (this computation is a CPU intensive operation).

8. Experimental Results

The first step in the programs' evaluation is to test it with synthetic data where the correct flow is known. We choose to generate 20 volumes of $256 \times 256 \times 31$ sinusoidal data sets using a 3D version of the formula used to generate 2D sinusoidal patterns in (Barron et al., 1994). The correct constant velocity is $\vec{V} = (3, 2, 1)$. At places, especially at the beginning and the end slices of the datasets, the differentiation was a little poorer but still acceptable. Figure 2 shows the sinusoidal flow for Lucas and Kanade with $\tau_D = 1.0$ while Figure 3 shows the sinusoidal flow field after 50 and 100 iterations of Horn and Schunck with $\alpha = 1.0$ (because of space limitations, we do not show the Lucas and Kanade sinusoidal flow, which looks like the 100 iteration Horn and Schunck sinusoidal flow). The overall error (including velocities computed from poor derivative data) for Lucas and Kanade was $0.339790\% \pm 0.002716\%$ in the velocity magnitudes and $0.275550^\circ \pm 0.000760^\circ$ in the velocity directions while for the 100 iterations Horn and Schunck it was $0.044190\% \pm 0.003558\%$ in the velocity magnitudes and $0.195305° \pm 0.000949°$ in the velocity directions. The flow fields and the overall accuracy show the correctness of the two 3D algorithms. Note that the sinusoidal flow for 50 iterations of Horn and Schunck is definitely inferior to the flow for 100 iterations of Horn and Schunck; we use 100 iterations in all subsequent Horn and Schunck flow calculations.

Figures 4 and 5 show the XY and XZ flow fields for the 15th slice of the $256 \times 256 \times 31$ axiel MRI datasets (**mri.9** and **mri.16**) for the Lucas and Kanade and Horn and Schunck algorithms. We see that the flow field smoothing in Horn and Schunck make the flow fields visibly more pleasing. There are obvious outliers due to poor differentiation results that are not completely eliminated by Horn and Schunck smoothing. Figures 6 and 7 show the XY and XZ flow fields for the 36th slice of the $256 \times 256 \times 75$ coronal MRI datasets (**5phase.9** and **10phase.16**) for Lucas and Kanade and Horn and Schunck. Again, there are many outliers and obviously incorrect flow vectors. Nevertheless, the flows capture the essential heart motion, which includes expansion and contraction of its 4 chambers plus a twisting motion. The flow on the chest cavity for the 36th slice of the **5phase.9** data indicates that the data is not registered. Indeed the diaphragm that the heart is resting on has significant motion in the **5phase.9** data. Flow at the chest cavity borders is not present in the 36th slice of the **10phase.16** data, indicating this data is better registered and the flow more reliable.

The computational times for these flow calculations are large. We report typical times for a 750MHz laptop having 256MB of main memory and running RedHat linux. For the **mri.9** and **mri.16** datasets, 10 minutes was required for differentiation of a single volume and 5 minutes for a Lucas and Kanade flow calculation and 20 minutes for a 100 iteration Horn and Schunck flow calculation. For the **5phase.9** and **10phase.9** datasets things were considerably worse. Significant paging and virtual memory use was obvious and differentiation took about 1 hour, a Lucas and Kanade calculation about 0.5 hours and a 100 iteration Horn and Schunck calculation about 2 hours. These calculations are not real time!

9. Conclusions

The results in this paper are a preliminary start to measuring the complex motions of a beating heart. Subjectively, the 3D Horn and Schunck flows often look better that the 3D Lucas and Kanade flows. One problem is that the quality of the flow is directly dependent on the quality of the derivatives (the sinusoidal derivatives were quite good and hence their flow fields were quite accurate). The coarse sampling nature of the data and the registration misalignments in adjacent slices of the data probably cause serious problems for differentiation. A spline based approach to differentiation may overcome these problems and is currently under investigation. Another problem with the MRI data is that the 3D motion is discontinuous at places in space and time (after all, different but adjacent parts of the heart are moving differently). A 3D algorithm, based on Nagel's 2D optical flow algorithm (Nagel, 1983; Nagel, 1987; Nagel, 1989), where a Horn and Schunck-like smoothing is used but additionally the smoothing is inhibited across intensity discontinuities and enhanced at locations where the 3D aperture can be robustly overcome, may better be able to handle discontinuous optical flow fields. A version of this algorithm is currently under implementation. Lastly, we are considering the use of 2-frame optical flow in an attempt to register adjacent frames in a volumetric dataset. Towards this end, we are implementing a 2-frame optical algorithm by (Brox et al., 2004). A successful completion of this project would allow us to measure 3D heart motions using optical flow with a physiological basis.

We close with a comment on the current computational resources required for one of these 3D flow calculations. If Moore's law (processing power doubles every 18 months) continues then by 2010 we'll easily have 20GHz laptops with 32GB of main memory. This would allow a reasonable time analysis of these datasets (≤ 5 minutes) using these current algorithm implementations (which are correct but not optimal). Both of these algorithms also can easily be implemented on a SIMD parallel machine, where, given sufficient individual processor power, could make these calculations "real-time".

Acknowledgments

The author gratefully acknowledges financial support from a Natural Science and Engineering Council of Canada (NSERC) Discovery Grant.

References

Pollard, S., J. Porrill, and N. Thacker: TINA programmer's guide. Medical Biophysics and Clinical Radiology, University of Manchester, UK. (www.niac.man.ac.uk/Tina/docs/programmers_guide/programmers_guide.html).

Simoncelli, E.P. : Design of multi-dimensional derivative filters. *IEEE Int. Conf. Image Processing*, Vol. 1, pages 790–793, 1994.

Horn, B.K.P. and B.G. Schunck: Determining optical flow. *Artificial Intelligence*, **17**: 185–204, 1981.

Lucas, B.D. and T. Kanade: An iterative image registration technique with an application to stereo vision. In Proc. DARPA *Image Understanding Workshop*, pages 121–130, 1981 (see also *IJCAI'81*, pages 674–679, 1981).

Barron, J.L., D.J. Fleet, and S.S. Beauchemin: Performance of optical flow techniques. *Int. J. Computer Vision*, **12**: 43–77, 1994.

Spies, H., H. Haußecker, B. Jähne, and J.L. Barron: Differential range flow estimation. In Proc. *DAGM*, pages 309-316, 1999.

Spies, H., B. Jähne, and J.L. Barron: Range flow estimation'. *Computer Vision Image Understanding*, **85**:209–231, 2002.

Spies, H.: Certainties in low-level operators. In Proc. *Vision Interface*, pages 257–262, 2003.

Spies, H. and J.L. Barron: Evaluating certainties in image intensity differentiation for optical flow. In Proc. *Canadian Conf. Computer and Robot Vision*, pages 408–416, 2004.

Nagel, H.H.: Displacement vectors derived from second-order intensity variations in image sequences. *Computer Graphics Image Processing*, **21**: 85–117, 1983.

Nagel, H.-H.: On the estimation of optical flow: relations between different approaches and some new results. *AI*, **33**: 299–324, 1987.

Nagel, H.-H.: On a constraint equation for the estimation of displacement rates in image sequences. *IEEE Trans. PAMI*, **11**: 13–30, 1989.

Marr, D. and Ullman S.: Directional selectivity and its use in early visual processing. *Proc. Royal Society London*, **B211**: 151–180, 1981.

Tang, X., J.L. Barron, R.E. Mercer, and P. Joe: Tracking weather storms using 3D doppler radial velocity information. In Proc. *Scand. Conf. Image Analysis*, pages 1038–1043, 2003.

Park, J., D. Metaxas, and L. Axel: Analysis of left ventricular wall motion based on volumetric deformable models and MRI-SPAMM. *Medical Image Analysis*, **1**: 53–71, 1996.

Park, J., D. Metaxas, A.Young, and L. Axel: Deformable models with parameter functions for cardiac motion analysis from tagged MRI Data. *IEEE IEEE Trans. Medical Imaging*, **15**: 278–289, 1996.

Frangi, A.F., W.J. Niessen, and M.A. Viergever: Three-dimensional modelling for functional analysis of cardiac images: a review. *IEEE Trans. Medical Imaging*, **20**: 2–25, 2001.

Chen, X., J.L. Barron, R.E. Mercer, and P. Joe: 3D regularized velocity from 3D doppler radial velocity. In Proc. *Int. Conf. Image Processing*, Volume 3, pages 664–667, 2001.

Chen, X., J.L. Barron, R.E. Mercer, and P. Joe: 3D least squares velocity from 3D doppler radial velocity. In Proc. *Vision Interface*, pages 56–63, 2001.

Moore, J., M. Drangova, M. Wiergbicki, J. Barron, and T. Peters: A high resolution dynamic heart model. *Medical Image Computing and Computer-Assisted Intervention*, **1**:549–555, 2003.

Brox, T., A. Bruhn, N. Paperberg, and J. Weickert. High accuracy optical flow estimation based on a theory of warping. In Proc. *ECCV*, pages 25–36, 2004.

Barron, J.L.: The integration of optical flow into Tinatool. Dept. of Computer Science, The Univ. of Western Ontario, TR601 (report Open Source Medical Image Analysis), 2003.

Barron, J.L.: Experience with 3D optical flow on gated MRI cardiac datasets. In Proc. *Canadian Conf. Computer and Robot Vision*, pages 370–377, 2004.

Sodickson, D.K.: Spatial encoding using multiple RF coils. In *SMASH Imaging and Parallel MRI Methods in Biomedical MRI and Spectroscopy*, (E. Young, editor), pages 239–250, Wiley, 2000.

Weiger, M., K.P. Pruessmann, and P. Boesiger: Cardiac real-time imaging using SENSE. *Magn. Reson. Med.*, **43**: 177–184, 2000.

IMAGING THROUGH TIME: THE ADVANTAGES OF SITTING STILL

ROBERT PLESS
Department of Computer Science and Engineering
Washington University in St. Louis

Abstract. Many classical vision algorithms mimic the structure and function of the human visual system — which has been an effective tool for driving research into stereo and structure from motion based algorithms. However, for problems such as surveillance, tracking, anomaly detection and scene segmentation; problems that depend significantly on local context, the lessons of the human visual system are less clear. For these problems, significant advantages are possible in a "persistent vision" paradigm that advocates collecting statistical representations of scene variation from a single viewpoint over very long time periods. This chapter motivates this approach by providing a collection of examples where very simple statistics, which can be easily kept over very long time periods, dramatically simplify scene interpretation problems including segmentation and feature attribution.

Key words: time, segmentation, statistics

1. Introduction

The goal of much computer vision research is to provide the foundation for visual systems that function unattended for days, weeks or years — but machine vision systems perform dismally, compared to biological systems, at the task of interpreting natural environments. Why? Two answers are that biological vision systems are optimized for the specific questions they need to address and the biological computational methods are more effective than current algorithms at interpreting new data in context. While much of the work on omnidirectional, catadioptric or otherwise non-pinhole cameras supplies the first answer, here we address the second; for the limited case of a static video camera that observes a changing environment.

The definition of context, from Miriam Webster, is:

Context: The interrelated conditions in which something exists or occurs, from Latin contextus: connection of words, coherence.

K. Daniilidis and R. Klette (eds.), Imaging Beyond the Pinhole Camera, 345–363.

This work progresses from the literal reading of this definition, suggesting that context be derived from representing simple correlations — the interrelated conditions and coherence. Simple correlations ground approaches to visual analysis from the most local, such as Reichardt detectors for motion estimation ((Poggio and Reichardt, 1973)) to the very global correlations that underlie Principle Components Analysis. Creating these correlations during very long time sequences defines a structure under which new images can be more easily interpreted.

Here we introduce a small collection of case studies which apply simple statistical techniques over very long video sequences. These case studies span variations in the spatial and temporal scale of the relevant context. For each case study, the statistical properties (both the local and global properties) can be updated with each new frame, describe properties at each pixel location, and can be visualized as images. This is "imaging beyond the pinhole camera", where *beyond* is a temporal extent. As CMOS imaging sensors push more and more processing onto the imaging chip itself, it is correct to consider these statistical measures as alternative forms of imaging: especially the consistent, everywhere uniform processing that underlies our approach.

2. Spatio-Temporal Context and Finding Anomalies

Anomaly detection is a clean first problem on which to focus. Anomaly detection, in video surveillance, is the problem of defining the common features of a video stream in order to automatically identify unusual objects or behaviors. The problem inherently has two parts. First, for an input video stream, develop a statistical model of the appearance of that stream. Second, for new data from the same stream, define a likelihood (or, if possible, a probability) that each pixel arises from the appearance model. That is, we want to gather statistics from a long video sequence in order to determine — in the context of that scene — what parts of a new frame are unusual.

There is today a compelling need to automatically identify unusual events in many scenes, including those that include both significant natural background motions of water, grass or trees moving in the wind, and human motions of people, cars and aircraft. These scenes require the analysis of new video within the context of the motion that is typical for that scene.

Several definitions serve to make this presentation more concrete, and will hold throughout this presentation. The input video is considered to be a function I, whose value is defined for different pixel locations (x, y), and different times t. The pixel intensity value at pixel (x, y) during frame t, will be denoted $I(x, y, t)$. This function is a discrete function, and all image processing is done and described here in a discrete framework, however, the justification for using discrete approximations to derivative filters is based on the view of I as a continuous function. Spatio-temporal image derivative filters are particularly meaningful in the context of analyzing motion on the image. Considering a specific pixel and time (x, y, t), we can define $I_x(x, y, t)$ to be the derivative of the image intensity as you move in the x-direction of the image. $I_y(x, y, t)$, and $I_t(x, y, t)$ are defined similarly. Dropping the (x, y, t) component, the optic flow constraint equation gives a relationship between I_x, I_y, and I_t, and the optic flow, (the 2D motion at that part of the image) ((Horn, 1986)):

$$I_x u + I_y v + I_t = 0. \tag{1}$$

Since this gives only one equation per pixel, many classical computer vision algorithms assume that the optic flow is constant over a small region of the image, and use the (I_x, I_y, I_t) values from neighboring pixels to provide additional constraints.

However, if the camera is static, and viewing repeated natural motions in the image, instead of combining data from a spatially extended region of the image, we can instead combine equations through *time*. This allows one to compute the optic flow at a single pixel location without any spatial smoothing. Figure 1 shows one frame of a video sequence of a traffic intersection, and the flow field that best fits the data for each pixel over time. The key to this method is that the distribution of intensity derivatives, (I_x, I_y, I_t) — only the distribution, and not, for instance the time sequence — encodes several important parameters of the underlying variation at each pixel. Fortunately, simple parametric representations of this distribution have the dual benefits of (1) the parameters are efficient to update and maintain, allowing real-time systems, and (2) the set of parameters for the entire image efficiently summarize the local motion context at each pixel.

Formally, let

$$\nabla I(x, y, t) = (I_x(x, y, t), I_y(x, y, t), I_t(x, y, t))^T$$

be the spatio-temporal derivatives of the image intensity $I(x, y, t)$ at pixel x, y and time t. At each pixel, the structure tensor, Σ, accumulated through time, is defined as:

$$\Sigma(x, y) = \frac{1}{f} \sum_{t=1}^{f} \nabla I(x, y, t) \nabla I(x, y, t)^T,$$

where f is the number of frames in the sequence and (x, y) is hereafter omitted. We consider these distributions to be independent at each pixel. To focus on scene motion, the measurements are filtered to only considering measurements that come from change in the scene, that is, measurements for which $|I_t| > 0$. For the sake of the clarity of the following exposition, the mean of ∇I is assumed to be 0 (which does not specify that the mean motion is zero. For instance, if an object appears with $I_x > 0$ and $I_t > 0$, and disappears with $I_x < 0$ and $I_t < 0$, then the mean of these measurements is zero even though there is a consistent motion.).

Under this assumption, Σ defines a Gaussian distribution $\mathcal{N}(0, \Sigma)$. Previous work in anomaly detection can be cast nicely within this framework: anomalous measurements can be detected by comparing either the Mahalanobis distance, $\nabla I^T \Sigma^{-1} \nabla I$, or the negative log-likelihood:

$$ln((2\pi)^{3/2}|\Sigma|^{1/2}) + \frac{1}{2}\nabla I^T \Sigma^{-1} \nabla I,$$

to a preselected threshold ((Pless et al., 2003)).

In real-time applications, computing with the entire sequence is not feasible and the structure tensor must be estimated online. Assuming the distribution is stationary, Σ can be estimated as the sample mean of $\nabla I \nabla I^T$,

$$\Sigma_t = \frac{(n-1)}{n}\Sigma_{t-1} + \frac{1}{n}\nabla I \nabla I^T.$$

This maintains the weighted average over all data collected, but the relative weights of the new data and existing average can be changed to provide an exponentially weighted moving average. This gives a more localized temporal context, where choice of the value ϵ defines the size of the temporal window.

$$\Sigma_t = \Big(\frac{(n-1)}{n} - \epsilon\Big)\Sigma_{t-1} + \Big(\frac{1}{n} - \epsilon\Big)\nabla I \nabla I^T.$$

Relationship to 2-D Image Motion: The value of the structure tensor as a background model comes from the strong relationship between optic flow and the spatio-temporal derivatives. Equation 1 constrains all gradient measurements produced by a flow (u, v) to lie on a plane through the origin in I_x, I_y, I_t-space. The vector $(u, v, 1)$ is normal to this plane.

Suppose the distribution of ∇I measurements comes from different textures with the same flow, and one models this distribution as a Gaussian, $\mathcal{N}(0, \Sigma)$. Let $\vec{x_1}, \vec{x_2}, \vec{x_3}$ be the eigenvectors of Σ and $\lambda_1, \lambda_2, \lambda_3$ the corresponding eigenvalues. Then $\vec{x_1}$ and $\vec{x_2}$ will lie in the optic flow plane, with $\vec{x_3}$ normal to the plane and $\lambda_1, \lambda_2 \gg \lambda_3$. In fact, the third eigenvector, $\vec{x_3}$, is the total least-squares estimate of the homogeneous optic flow, $\frac{(u,v,1)}{\|(u,v,1)\|}$ ((Nagel and Haag, 1998)). Figure 1 shows the best fitting optic flow field of a traffic intersection, computed by combining measurements at each

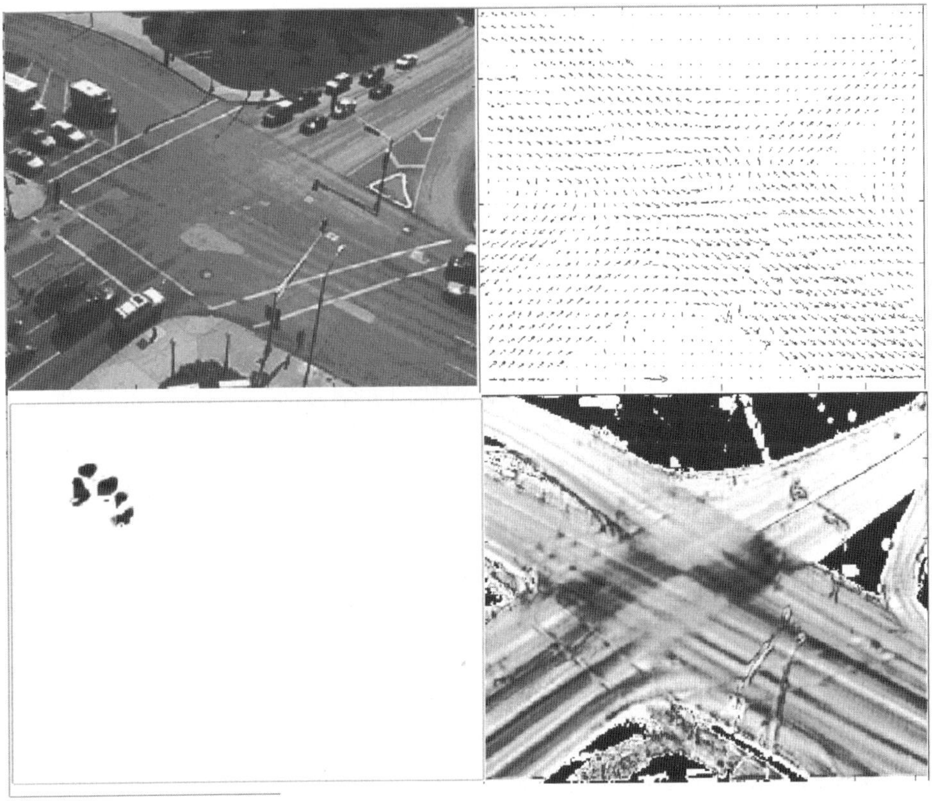

Figure 1. (top left) One frame of a 19,000 frame video sequence of an intersection with normal traffic patterns. (top right) The best fitting optic flow field, fitted at each pixel location by temporally combining all image derivative measurements at that pixel with $|I_t| > 0$. (bottom right) A map of the third eigenvector of the structure tensor, a measure of the residual error of fitting a single optic flow vector to all image derivative measurements at each pixel. (bottom left) The Mahalanobis distance of each image derivative measurement from the accumulated model, during the passing of an ambulance— an illustration that this vehicle motion does not fit the motion context defined by the sequence.

pixel over 10 minutes. This optic flow field is a partial visualization of the structure tensor field which defines the background spatio-temporal derivative distribution. This allows the detection of an ambulance that is moving abnormally — by marking local image derivative measurements that do not fit the distribution at that pixel.

More generally, the structure tensor field is a local context for interpreting the local image variation and identifying anomalies within that context. The same code can be directly applied in other cases to build a local model of image motion to identify anomalous objects (such as ducks) moving in a lake scene with consistent motion everywhere in the image, or infrared

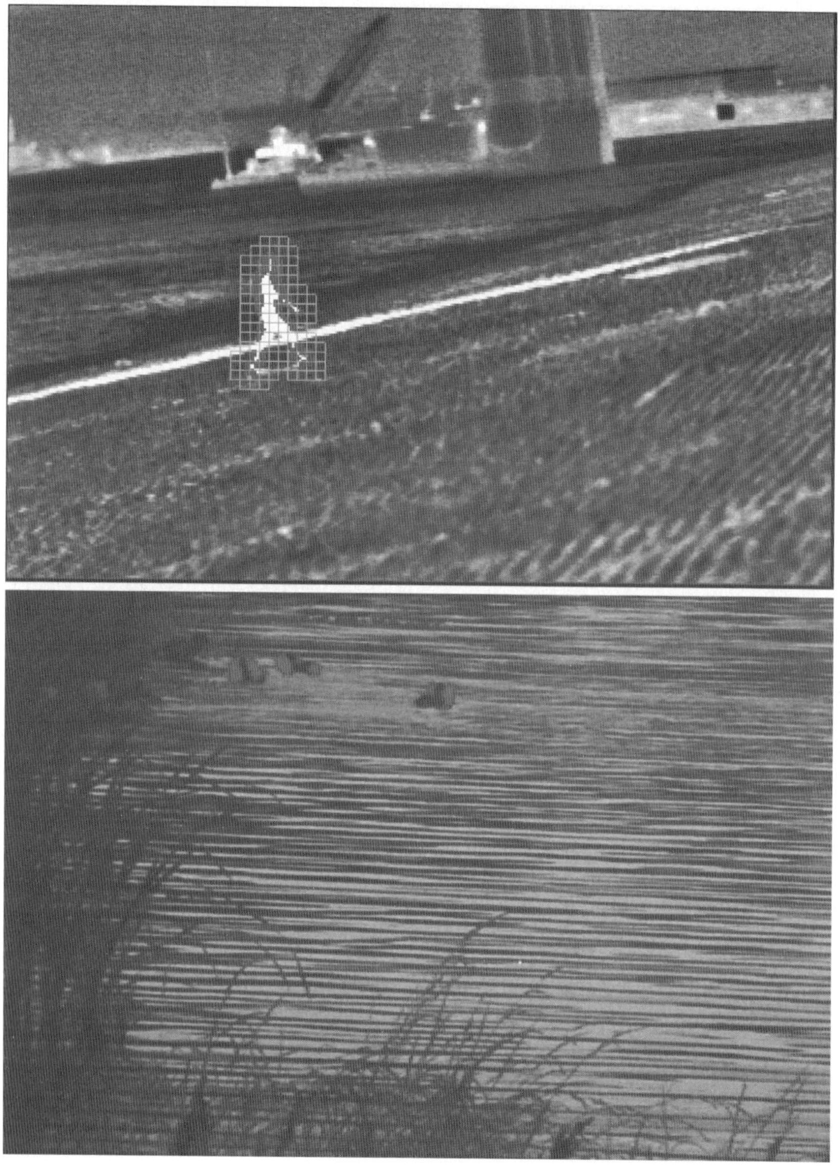

Figure 2. Example anomaly detection using the spatio-temporal structure tensor defined over long time periods. (top) Detection of a man walking along a river bank, during a 25 minute IR video surveillance sequence. (bottom) Detection of ducks swimming in a lake scene with significant motion over the entire image. Identical code runs in either case, builds a model of the local context for that scene as the distribution of spatio-temporal derivatives, and identifies anomalous pixels as those whose derivative measurements do not fit the model.

surveillance video of a river-bank scene. Figure 2 gives examples of anomaly detection in each of these cases.

3. A Static Interlude

Spatio-temporal derivatives give a good basis for representing local motion properties in a scene, but what about global properties? PCA is one of a family of methods that find global correlations in an image set, by decomposing the images into a mean image and basis vectors which account for most image variation. PCA (also called the Karhunen-Loeve transform) is most commonly used as a data-reduction technique — which maps each image in the original set to a low dimensional coordinate specified by its coefficients.

If consider the view of our input video sequence as an intensity function $I(x, y, t)$, these approaches consider a single frame, and create a vector of the intensity values in that frame. Here we will write $\vec{I}(t)$ as the vector of the intensity measurements at all (x, y) pixel locations as time t. Then, PCA is one method of defining a linear basis function v_i such that each image $\vec{I}(t)$ can be expressed in terms of those basis functions:

$$\vec{I}(t) \approx \mu + \alpha_1(t)v_1 + \alpha_2(t)v_2 + \alpha_3(t)v_3 + \ldots,$$

where $(\alpha_1(t), \alpha_2(t), \alpha_3(t), \ldots)$ are the coefficients used to approximately reconstruct frame $\vec{I}(t)$, and define the low-dimensional projection of that image. Classical work in face recognition then compares and clusters these low-dimensional projections ((Turk and Pentland, 1991)), and more recent work seeks to understand and interpret and extend video data by modeling the time course of these coefficients ((Soatto et al., 2001; Fitzgibbon, 2001)). But considering the *coefficients* themselves to interpret single images, or the time series in the analysis of video, ignores the information that lies within the basis images. For images from different viewpoints, the statistics of natural imagery ((Huang and Mumford, 1999)) gives insights into what basis functions are generally good for image representation, but for a static camera viewing an environment over a very long time period, these basis images defined by PCA $(v_1, v_2, v_3, \ldots)$ are independent of time, capture the variation of the sequence as a whole, and provide significant insight into the segmentation and interpretation of the scene.

For instance, Figure 3 shows one image of a time lapse video (one frame captured every 45 seconds), taken from a static camera over the course of 5 hours in the afternoon. The principle images can be estimated online (following (Weng et al., 2003)), although it is infeasible to store the complete covariance matrix, so these principle images only approximate the basis function of the optimal KL-transform. The procedure very loosely follows

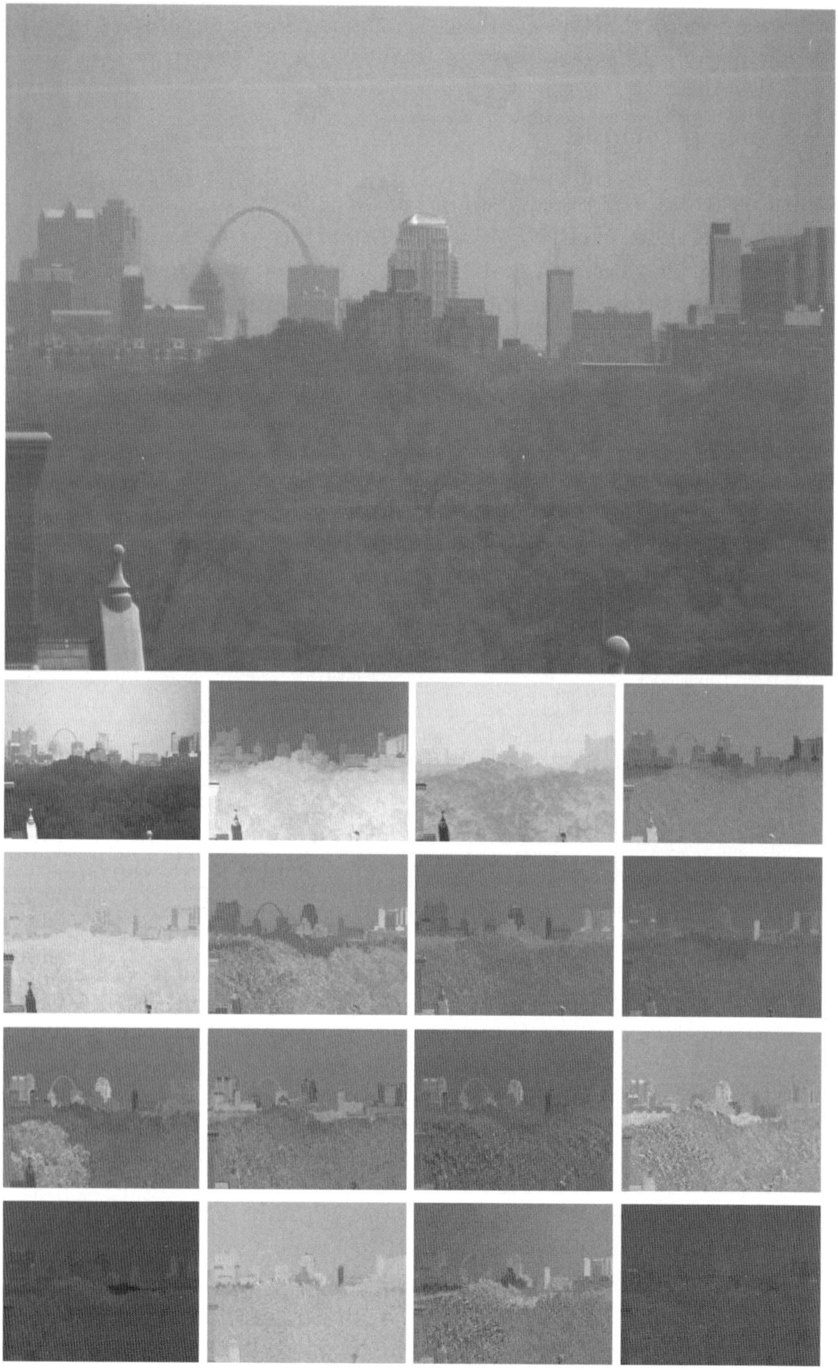

Figure 3. One frame of a time lapse video taken over several hours. Also shown are the mean and first 15 principle images. Note the scene segmentation easily visible in the

the following algorithm (which is presented primarily to give intuition and guide later developments):

Given image $\vec{I}$, the (n+1)-th image.

$\mu_{new} = \frac{n}{n+1}\mu + \frac{1}{n+1}I$	update the mean image.
$\vec{I} = \vec{I} - \mu_{new}$	subtract off the updated mean image.
$v_1(n+1) = \frac{n}{n+1}v_1(n) + \frac{1}{n+1}(\vec{I}^\top \frac{v_1(n)}{\|\|v_1(n)\|\|})\vec{I}$	update the n-th estimate of the first eigenvector as the weighted average of the previous estimate and the current residual image, with the residual image having a larger effect if it has a high correlation with v_1.
$\vec{I} = \vec{I} - \vec{I}^\top \frac{v_1(n+1)}{\|\|v_1(n+1)\|\|} \frac{v_1(n+1)}{\|\|v_1(n+1)\|\|}$	Recreate the residual image to be orthogonal to the new eigenvector v_1.
	loop through the last two steps for as many eigenvectors as desired.

The advantage to this procedure is that memory requirements are strictly limited to storing the principle images themselves, and empirically and theoretically can be shown to be an efficient estimator of the KL-transform with the addition of some constraints on the distribution from which the initial images are drawn ((Weng et al., 2003)).

4. Principle Motion Fields

The principle images identify image regions whose variation is correlated. Do these methods carry past the analysis of scene appearance into the analysis of scene motion? Two factors complicate the direct application of iterative PCA algorithm to the structure tensor fields defined earlier. First, the motion fields are sparse (as they are only defined for parts of the image containing, at that frame, moving objects), and second, each image gives only a set of image derivative measurements, and it is the

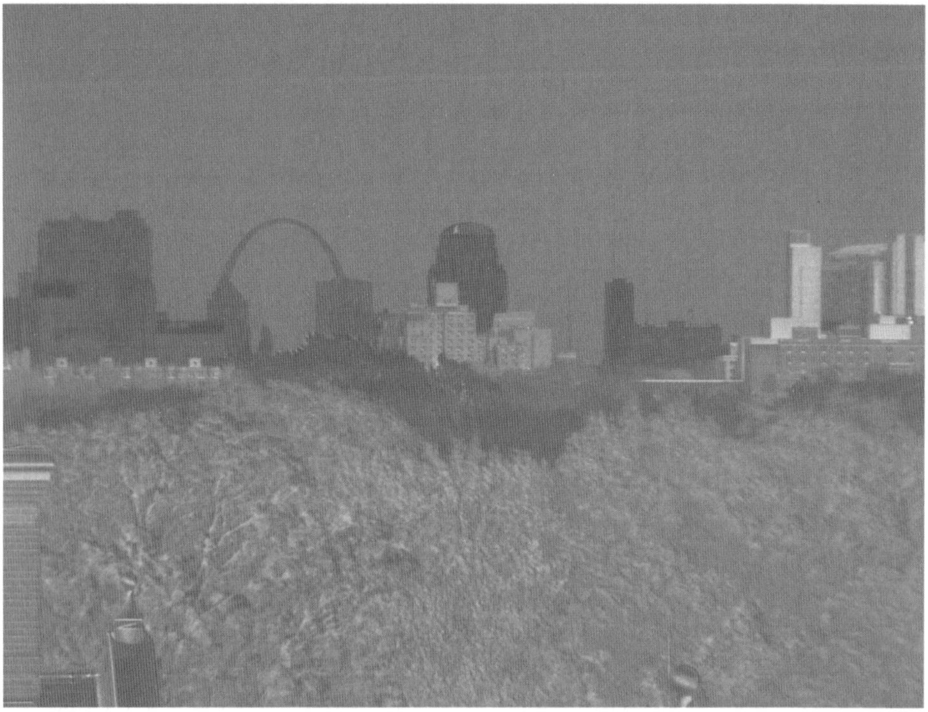

Figure 4. False color image using 3 principle images from the set shown as the red, green, and blue color components. Compelling in this picture is the segmentation of the scene, where dark blue are building that are in downtown St. Louis (about 10 miles away), in dark green are buildings of St. Louis University (about 6 miles away), and in yellow-green are buildings from the Washington University Medical School (about 3 miles away). These buildings are clustered because natural scene intensity variations (for instance, from clouds) tend to have a consistent effect locally, by vary in larger geographic regions.

distribution of these measurements that defines the structure tensor. This section illustrates an approach to addressing both these problems from ((Wright and Pless, 2005)).

The spatio-temporal image variations at each pixel are collected using the structure tensor. The structure tensor field defines a zero-mean Gaussian joint distribution of the image derivatives, which is independent at each pixel. This set of distributions may also be considered as a single (constrained) joint Gaussian, $\mathcal{N}_{global}$ over the entire image. Let Σ_i be the structure tensor at the i-th pixel. Then the covariance matrix of the global distribution is the block-diagonal matrix:

$$\tilde{\Sigma}_{global} = \begin{pmatrix} \Sigma_1 & & & \mathbf{0} \\ & \Sigma_2 & & \\ & \mathbf{0} & \ddots & \\ & & & \Sigma_p \end{pmatrix}$$

As the structure tensor field can be nicely visualized as a motion field, we use these terms interchangeably. This background model can be modified to handle multiple motions. Each motion field is treated as a joint Gaussian distribution over the entire image as described above. These large Gaussians are combined in a single mixture model,

$$w_1 \mathcal{N}_1(0, \tilde{\Sigma}_1) + \ldots + w_M \mathcal{N}_M(0, \tilde{\Sigma}_M) + w_{unk} \mathcal{M}_{unk}$$

where M is the number of unique background motions. This model loosely resembles the representation of single images as a linear combination of principle images, with the addition of $\mathcal{M}_{unk}$ as the prior distribution of (I_x, I_y, I_t) vectors for motions not fitting any background model – including anomalous events and objects that do not follow the background. $\mathcal{M}_{unk}$ may be chosen as a uniform distribution, or as an isotropic Gaussian, with little qualitative effect on the mixture estimated. One advantage of choosing a uniform foreground prior is that anomalous objects can be detected by simply thresholding the negative log-likelihood of the backgrounds.

Let $\tilde{\nabla} I$ be the concatenation of the gradient vector at each individual pixel:

$$\tilde{\nabla} I = (I_x^{(1)}, I_y^{(1)}, I_t^{(1)}, I_x^{(2)}, \ldots).$$

Then, the likelihood of the observation at a given frame is

$$P(\tilde{\nabla} I | \mathcal{N}_{global}) = k \exp(-\frac{1}{2} \tilde{\nabla} I^T \tilde{\Sigma}_{global}^{-1} \tilde{\nabla} I)$$

where k is a normalizing constant. Because $\tilde{\Sigma}$ is block diagonal, this can be rewritten as:

$$P(\tilde{\nabla} I | \mathcal{N}_{global}) = \prod_i P(\nabla I_i | \mathcal{N}_i(0, \Sigma_i)),$$

Online update rules: The model is a Gaussian mixture model and can be updated according to the standard adaptive mixture model update equations (as used, for example, in ((Stauffer and Grimson, 1999))), although here it is applied to a very high-dimensional distribution. The special block-diagonal structure simplifies the computations. The mixture model can be updated online with an online update rule that mimics the update rule for online PCA detailed in Section 3).

The update process proceeds by first calculating the likelihoods:

$$P(\mathcal{N}_i|\tilde{\nabla} I) = \frac{w_i P(\tilde{\nabla} I|\mathcal{N}_i)}{w_{unk} P(\tilde{\nabla} I|\mathcal{M}_{unk}) + \sum_{j=1}^{M} w_j P(\tilde{\nabla} I|\mathcal{N}_j)},$$

then each of the fields can be updated as:

$$\tilde{\Sigma}_{i,t} = (1 - \beta_i)\tilde{\Sigma}_{i,t-1} + \beta_i \tilde{\nabla} I \tilde{\nabla} I^T$$

with a weighting factor $\beta_i = P(\mathcal{N}_i|\tilde{\nabla} I)$, which is the probability that $\mathcal{N}_i$ is the correct model, and is analogous to the part of the iterative PCA algorithm which weights the update of the principle image by the correlation between the image and that principle image. However, if the maximum likelihood model is $\mathcal{M}_{unk}$, there is a strong probability that the image motion does not come from any of the current models, and so we use this measurement to initialize a new tensor field, $\mathcal{N}_{M+1}(0, \Sigma_{M+1})$. The complete update of the adaptive mixture model requires that the weights of the components be adjusted. The weights w_i can be updated as $w_{i,t} = (1 - \beta_i)w_{i,t-1} + \beta_i$.

The constraint on the derivative measurements at each pixel represented by the structure tensor is independent of the measurements at other pixels, and the block-diagonal form of each of the components of the mixture model maintains this independence. The mixture model implies that all measurements at a given time in the image come from one of the components. Let $W_i(t)$ be the event "the motion in the world comes from model i at time t". Then for pixels $p, p', p \neq p'$, our covariance constraint can be rewritten as

$$P_{p,p'}(\nabla I_p, \nabla I_{p'}|W_i(t)) = P_p(\nabla I_p|W_i(t))P_{p'}(\nabla I'_p|W_i(t)).$$

That is, measurements at different pixels are conditionally independent, given that motion in the world comes from model i. This is a plausible assumption for the example shown in Figure 5 in which one intersection fills the field of view, but a scene with multiple different independent motion patterns would require a multi-resolution extension of these techniques. However, using this choice of a global model to express all of our knowledge about inter-pixel dependencies allows the model to be maintained efficiently. One final note, because the motion fields are generated by discrete objects, in no frame is the entire component motion field visible, even if single frame optic flow measurements were reliable, it would not be possible to generate these components with a standard EM type approach.

When blindly applying this adaptive mixtures model for clustering scene motion, finer features such as cars turning left are lost in the clustering process. The main difficulty in producing a clean segmentation is that while flow fields are defined over the entire scene, at any given frame there is

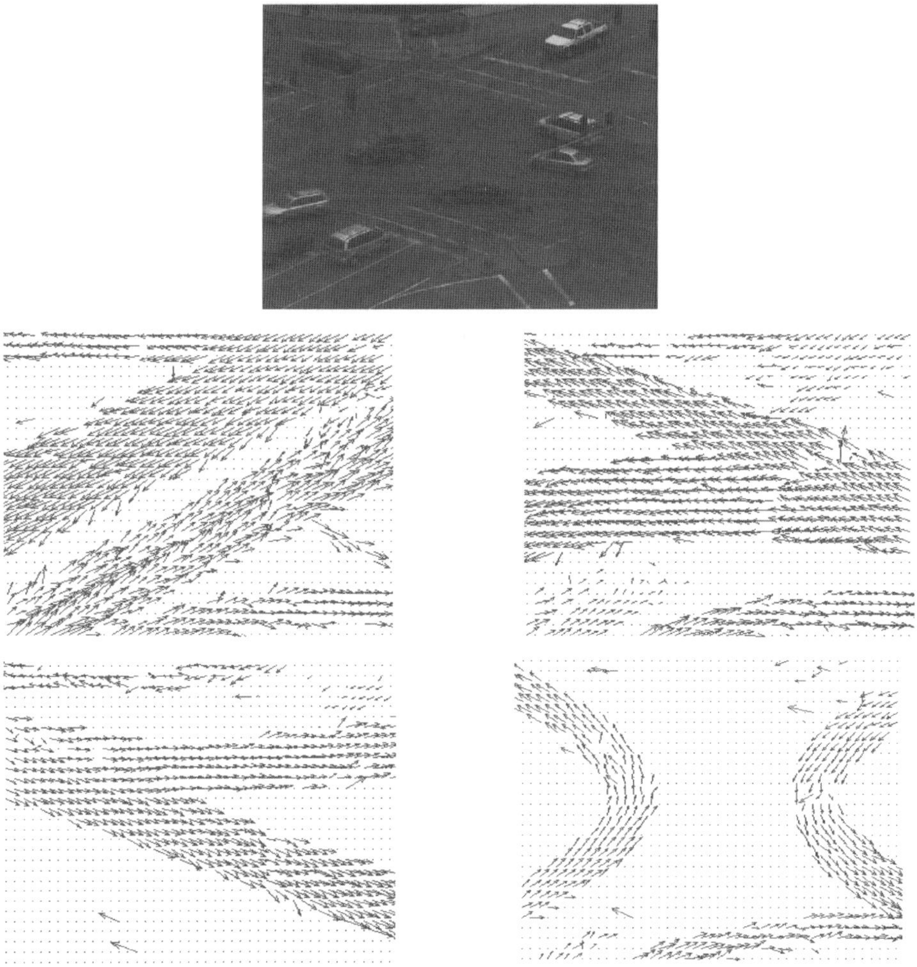

Figure 5. Flow field visualization of the automatically extracted four mixture components comprising the adaptive mixtures model of global structure tensor fields.

unlikely to be motion everywhere. This leads to difficulties in bootstrapping and initializing new models.

We address this problem by grouping consecutive frames. As consecutive frames are more likely to contain motion from the same motion field, these can be jointly assigned to a single model. Suppose measurements $A = \{\tilde{\nabla} I_{t-L}, \tilde{\nabla} I_{t-L+1}, \ldots, \tilde{\nabla} I_{t-1}\}$ have already been judged to come from a single motion. We can determine whether the next measurement, $\tilde{\nabla} I_t$, comes from the same discrete mode by first aggregating the measurements A into a single Gaussian $\mathcal{N}_{new}(0, \Sigma_{new})$. Then, $\tilde{\nabla} I_t$ is judged to belong to the same discrete motion if $P(\tilde{\nabla} I_t | \mathcal{N}_{new}) > P(\tilde{\nabla} I_t | \mathcal{M}_{unk})$. If $\tilde{\nabla} I_t$ is judged to come from $\mathcal{N}_{new}$, we use it to update $\mathcal{N}_{new}$. Otherwise, we initialize a new Gaussian $\mathcal{N}'_{new} = \mathcal{N}(0, \tilde{\nabla} I \tilde{\nabla} I^T)$ and assign A to one of the mixture components, $\mathcal{N}_1, \ldots, \mathcal{N}_M$.

Treating frames as independent, the negative log-likelihood $-\log P(A|\mathcal{N}_i)$ is just $\sum_{i=t-L}^{t-1} -\log P(\tilde{\nabla} I_i|\mathcal{N}_i)$. The posteriors $P(\mathcal{N}_i|A)$ can then be calculated as in the previous section. All of A can be assigned to the mixture component that maximizes the posterior or used to initialize a new mixture component, if $\mathcal{M}_{unk}$ is the maximum aposteriori mixture component. Let $\mathcal{N}_j(0, \tilde{Sigma}_j)$ be the best mixture component. We can update $\mathcal{N}_j$ wholesale as $\tilde{\Sigma}'_j = \gamma\tilde{\Sigma}_j + (1-\gamma)\tilde{\Sigma}_{new}$. Since $\tilde{\Sigma}_j$ can be updated directly from covariance $\tilde{\Sigma}_{new}$, it is not necessary to keep, in memory, every $\tilde{\nabla} I_i \in A$.

This process of factoring motion fields leads to the decomposition of the traffic patterns in an intersection, cleanly and automatically capturing the four major motion patterns 5. This mixture model of spatio-temporal structure tensor fields can only be generated by rather long input sequences (at least tens of minutes). However, it segments very cleanly the typical motion patterns, could be used to improve the anomaly detection discussed earlier, and could serve as a powerful prior model for tracking within the scene.

5. Scene Context Attribution

These principle motion fields illuminate the areas of the scene that have correlated local motion measures. While the inspiration for this study of local motion patterns was an attempt at background modeling for anomaly detection, the background models themselves define the motion context of the scene. This context facilitates the definition of semantic descriptors of different scene regions. In particular, we consider the problem of automated road detection extraction, following the work of ((Pless and Jurgens, 2004)). Capturing the distribution and correlations of spatio-temporal image derivatives gives a powerful representation of the scene variation and motion typical at each pixel. This allows a functional attribution of the scene; a "road" is defined as paths of consistent motion — a definition which is valid in a large and diverse set of environments.

The spatio-temporal structure tensor — the covariance matrix of the intensity derivatives at a pixel — has a number of interesting properties that are exposed through computation of its eigenvalues and eigenvectors. In particular, suppose that the structure tensor (a 3×3 matrix) has eigenvectors $(\vec{v}_1, \vec{v}_2, \vec{v}_3)$ corresponding to eigenvalues (e_1, e_2, e_3), and suppose that the eigenvalues are sorted by magnitude with v_1 as the largest magnitude. The following properties hold:

- The vector $\vec{v}_3$ is a homogeneous representation of the total least squares solution ((Huffel and Vandewalle, 1991)) for the optic flow. The 2-d flow vector (f_x, f_y) can be written:

$$(f_x, f_y) = (v_3(1)/v_3(3), v_3(2)/v_3(3))$$

- If, for all the data at that pixel, the set of image intensity derivatives exactly fits some particular optic flow, then e_3 is zero.
- If, for all the data at that pixel, the image gradient is in exactly the same direction, then e_2 is zero. (This is the manifestation of the aperture problem).
- The value $(1 - e_3/e_2)$ varies from 0 to 1, and is an indicator of how consistent the image gradients are with the best fitting optic flow, with 1 indicating perfect fit, and 0 indicating that many measurements do not fit this optic flow. We call this measure c, for consistency.
- The ratio e_2/e_1, varies from 0 to 1, and is an indicator of how well specified the optic flow vector is. When this number is close to 0, the image derivative data could fit a family of optic flow vectors with relatively low error, when this ratio is closer to 1, then the best fitting optic flow is better localized. We call this measure s, for specificity.

The analysis of optic flow in terms of the eigenvalues and eigenvectors of the structure tensor has been considered before ((Jähne, 1997; Haussecker and Fleet, 2001)). In the typical context of computer vision the covariance matrix is made from measurements in a region of the image that is assumed to have constant flow. Since this assumption breaks down as the patch size increases, there is strong pressure to use patches as small as possible, instead of including enough data to validate the statistical analysis of the covariance matrix. However, in stabilized video analysis paradigm, we can collect sufficient data at each pixel by aggregating measurements through time, and this analysis becomes more relevant.

The claim is that these variables capture and represent the local motion information contained in a video sequence. Moreover, the analysis of these scalar, vector, and tensor fields turns out to be an effective method for extracting road features from stabilized video — video which is either captured from a static camera, or has been captured from a moving platform (such as an airplane) and warped to appear static.

Figure 6 shows two frames from a stabilized aerial video of an urban scene with several roads which have significant traffic. For each pixel, a score is calculated to measure how likely that pixel is to come from a road. This score function (graphically displayed at the bottom right for Figure 6) is:

$$sc\Sigma I_t^2,$$

which is the intensity variance at that pixel, modulated by the previously defined scores that measure how well the optic flow solution fits the observed

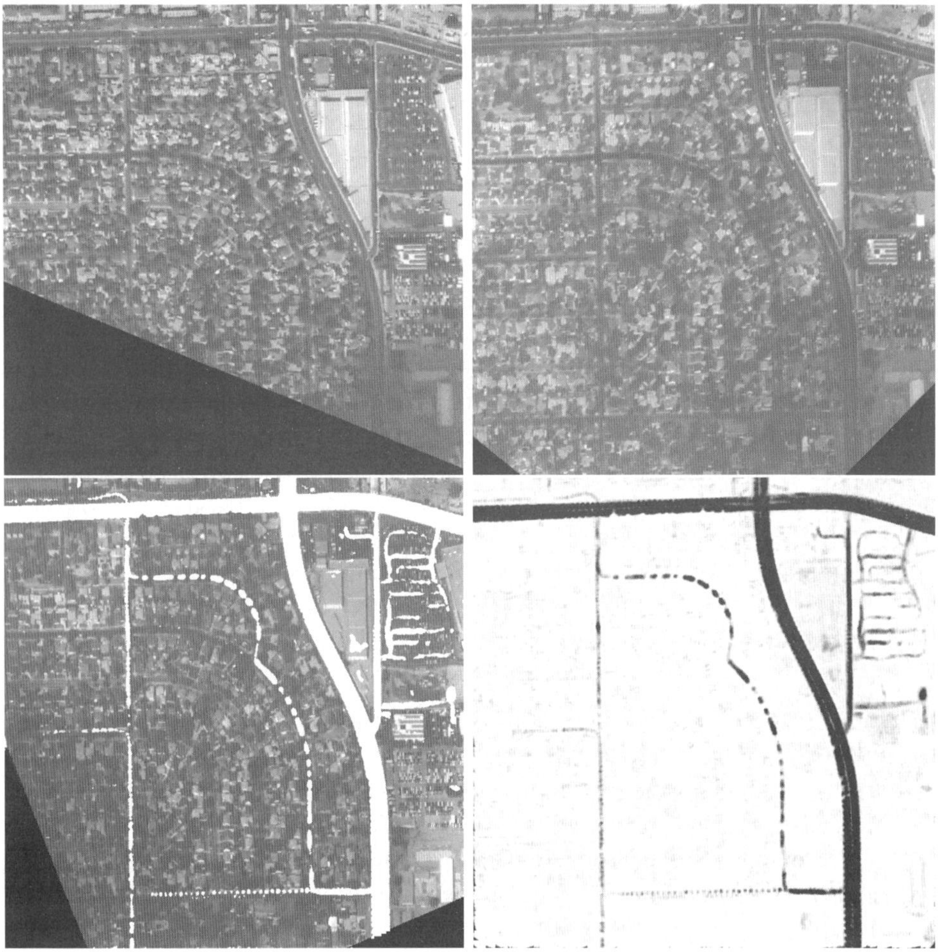

Figure 6. The top row shows frames 1 and 250 of a 451 frame stabilized aerial video (approximately 2:30 minutes long, 3 frames per second). The black in the corners are areas in this geo-registered frame that are not captured in these images, these areas are in view for much of the sequence. The bottom right shows the amount of image variation modulated by the motion consistency — a measure of how much of the image variation is caused by consistent motion as would be the case for a road (black is more likely to be a road).

data (c) and how unique that solution is (s). This score is thresholded (threshold value set by hand), and overlayed on top of the original image in the bottom left of Figure 6.

However, the motion cues provide more information than simply a measure of whether the pixel lies on a road. The best fitting solution for the optic flow also gives the direction of motion at each pixel. The components of the motion vectors are shown as the top row of Figure 7. There is significant noise in this motion field because of substantial image noise and the fact that for some roads the data included few moving vehicles. A longer image sequence would provide more data and make flow fields that are well constrained and largely consistent. The method would continue to fail in regions that contain multiple different motion directions or where the optic flow constraint equations fail. To make this analysis feasible with shorter stabilized video segments, it is necessary to combine information between nearby pixels.

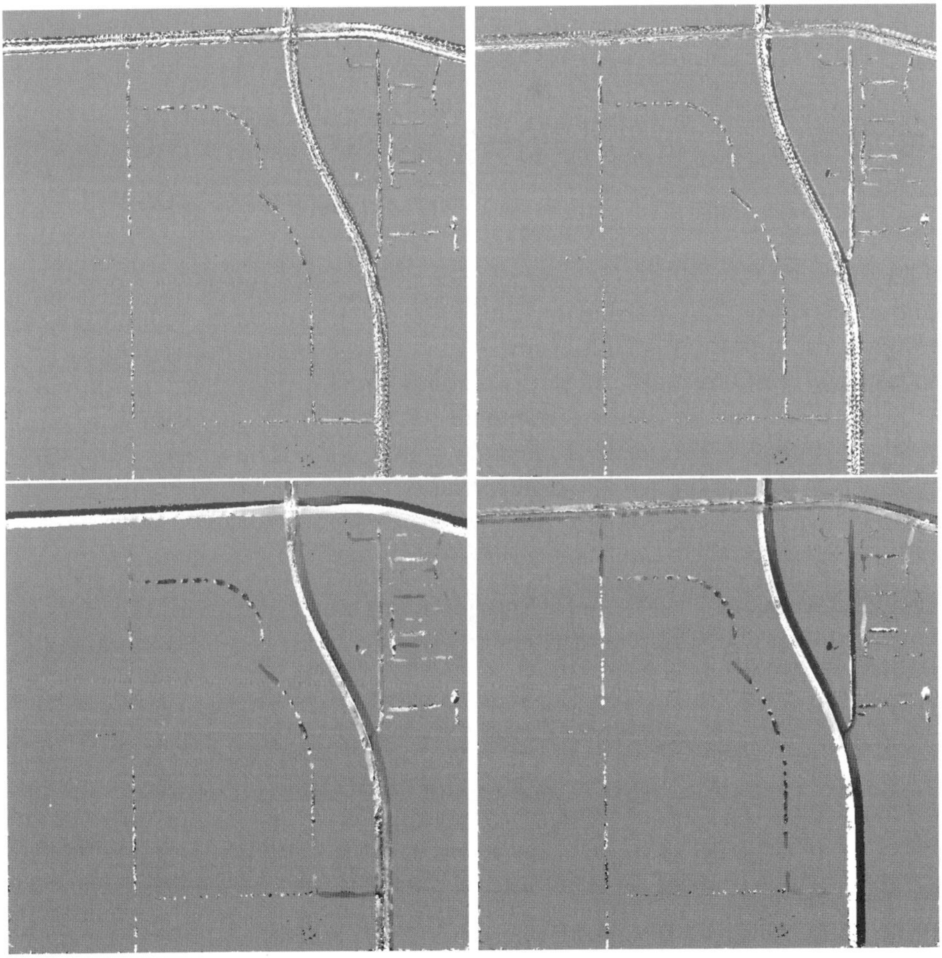

Figure 7. The top row show the x and y components of the best fitting optic flow vectors for the pixels designated as roads in figure 2. The flow fields are poorly defined, in part because of noisy data, and in part because there were few cars that move along some roads. These (poor) flow estimates were used to define the directional blurring filters that combine the image intensity measurements from nearby pixels (forward and backwards in the direction of motion). Using the covariance matrix data from other locations along the motion direction gives significantly better optic flow measurements (bottom row). In these images, black is negative and white is positive, relative to the origin in the top left corner of the image.

Typically, combining information between pixels leads to blurring of the image and a loss of fidelity of the image features. However, the flow field that is extracted gives a best fitting direction of travel at each pixel. We use this as a direction in which we can combine data without blurring features - that is, we use the estimate of the motion to combine data along the roads, rather than across roads. This is a variant of motion oriented averaging ((Nagel, 1990)). The results of this process (detailed more rigorously in (Pless and Jurgens, 2004)) is illustrated on the bottom row of Figure 7.

This road annotation uses simple statistical properties that are maintained in real time over long video sequences. As the types of statistics that can be maintained in real time grows, methods to automatically label other scene features may also effectively make use of data from very long video sequences.

6. Final Thoughts

These three case studies of anomaly detection, static scene segmentation, and scene structure attribution illustrate a vast amount of information available in maintaining simple statistics over very long time sequences. As many video cameras operating in surveillance environments are static, they view the same part of their environment for their entire operating lives. Exploiting statistical properties to define a visual context over these long time ranges will unlock further possibilities in autonomous visual algorithms.

Acknowledgments

Daily interactions with Leon Barrett, John Wright and David Jurgens the and David Jurgens provided the context wherein these ideas came to light.

References

Fitzgibbon, A.: Stochastic rigidity: image registration for nowhere-static scenes. In Proc. *Int. Conf. Computer Vision*, pages 662–670, 2001.

Haussecker, H. and Fleet, D.: Computing optical flow with physical models of brightness variation. *IEEE Trans. Pattern Analysis Machine Intelligence*, **23**: 661–673, 2001.

Horn, B. K. P.: *Robot Vision*. McGraw Hill, New York, 1986.

Huang, J. and Mumford, D.: Statistics of natural images and models. In Proc. *Int. Conf. Computer Vision*, pages 541–547, 1999.

Huffel, S. V. and Vandewalle, J.: *The Total Least Squares Problem: Computational Aspects and Analysis*. Society for Industrial and Applied Mathematics, Philadelphia, 1991.

Jähne, B.: *Digital Image Processing: Concepts, Algorithms, and Scientific Applications*. Springer, New York, 1997.

Nagel, H. H.: Extending the 'oriented smoothness constraint' into the temporal domain and the estimation of derivatives of optical flow. In Proc. *Europ. Conf. Computer Vision*, pages 139–148, 1990.

Nagel, H.-H. and Haag, M.: Bias-corrected optical flow estimation for road vehicle tracking. In Proc. *Int. Conf. Computer Vision*, pages 1006–1011, 1998.

Pless, R. and Jurgens, D.: Road extraction from motion cues in aerial video. In Proc. *Int. Symp. ACM GIS*, Washington DC, 2004.

Pless, R., Larson, J., Siebers, S., and Westover, B.: Evaluation of local models of dynamic backgrounds. In Proc. *Int. Conf. Computer Vision Pattern Recognition*, 2003.

Poggio, T. and Reichardt, W.: Considerations on models of movement detection. *Kybernetik*, **13**: 223–227, 1973.

Soatto, S., Doretto, G., and Wu, Y. N.: Dynamic textures. In Proc. *Int. Conf. Computer Vision*, pages 439–446, 2001.

Stauffer, C. and Grimson, W. E. L.: Adaptive background mixture models for real-time tracking. In Proc. *Int. Conf. Computer Vision Pattern Recognition*, 1999.

Turk, M. and Pentland, A.: Eigenfaces for recognition. *J. Neuroscience*, **3**: 71–86, 1991.

Weng, J., Zhang, Y., and Hwang, W.-S.: Candid covariance-free incremental principal component analysis. *IEEE Trans. Pattern Analysis Machine Intelligence*, **25**: 1034–1040, 2003.

Wright, J. N. and Pless, R.: Analysis of persistent motion patterns using the 3d structure tensor. In Proc. *IEEE Workshop Motion Video Computing*, Breckenridge, Colorado, 2005.

Index

Computational Imaging and Vision

1. B.M. ter Haar Romeny (ed.): *Geometry-Driven Diffusion in Computer Vision.* 1994 ISBN 0-7923-3087-0
2. J. Serra and P. Soille (eds.): *Mathematical Morphology and Its Applications to Image Processing.* 1994 ISBN 0-7923-3093-5
3. Y. Bizais, C. Barillot, and R. Di Paola (eds.): *Information Processing in Medical Imaging.* 1995 ISBN 0-7923-3593-7
4. P. Grangeat and J.-L. Amans (eds.): *Three-Dimensional Image Reconstruction in Radiology and Nuclear Medicine.* 1996 ISBN 0-7923-4129-5
5. P. Maragos, R.W. Schafer and M.A. Butt (eds.): *Mathematical Morphology and Its Applications to Image and Signal Processing.* 1996 ISBN 0-7923-9733-9
6. G. Xu and Z. Zhang: *Epipolar Geometry in Stereo, Motion and Object Recognition.* A Unified Approach. 1996 ISBN 0-7923-4199-6
7. D. Eberly: *Ridges in Image and Data Analysis.* 1996 ISBN 0-7923-4268-2
8. J. Sporring, M. Nielsen, L. Florack and P. Johansen (eds.): *Gaussian Scale-Space Theory.* 1997 ISBN 0-7923-4561-4
9. M. Shah and R. Jain (eds.): *Motion-Based Recognition.* 1997 ISBN 0-7923-4618-1
10. L. Florack: *Image Structure.* 1997 ISBN 0-7923-4808-7
11. L.J. Latecki: *Discrete Representation of Spatial Objects in Computer Vision.* 1998 ISBN 0-7923-4912-1
12. H.J.A.M. Heijmans and J.B.T.M. Roerdink (eds.): *Mathematical Morphology and its Applications to Image and Signal Processing.* 1998 ISBN 0-7923-5133-9
13. N. Karssemeijer, M. Thijssen, J. Hendriks and L. van Erning (eds.): *Digital Mammography.* 1998 ISBN 0-7923-5274-2
14. R. Highnam and M. Brady: *Mammographic Image Analysis.* 1999 ISBN 0-7923-5620-9
15. I. Amidror: *The Theory of the Moiré Phenomenon.* 2000 ISBN 0-7923-5949-6; Pb: ISBN 0-7923-5950-x
16. G.L. Gimel'farb: *Image Textures and Gibbs Random Fields.* 1999 ISBN 0-7923-5961
17. R. Klette, H.S. Stiehl, M.A. Viergever and K.L. Vincken (eds.): *Performance Characterization in Computer Vision.* 2000 ISBN 0-7923-6374-4
18. J. Goutsias, L. Vincent and D.S. Bloomberg (eds.): *Mathematical Morphology and Its Applications to Image and Signal Processing.* 2000 ISBN 0-7923-7862-8
19. A.A. Petrosian and F.G. Meyer (eds.): *Wavelets in Signal and Image Analysis.* From Theory to Practice. 2001 ISBN 1-4020-0053-7
20. A. Jaklič, A. Leonardis and F. Solina: *Segmentation and Recovery of Superquadrics.* 2000 ISBN 0-7923-6601-8
21. K. Rohr: *Landmark-Based Image Analysis.* Using Geometric and Intensity Models. 2001 ISBN 0-7923-6751-0
22. R.C. Veltkamp, H. Burkhardt and H.-P. Kriegel (eds.): *State-of-the-Art in Content-Based Image and Video Retrieval.* 2001 ISBN 1-4020-0109-6
23. A.A. Amini and J.L. Prince (eds.): *Measurement of Cardiac Deformations from MRI: Physical and Mathematical Models.* 2001 ISBN 1-4020-0222-X

Computational Imaging and Vision

24. M.I. Schlesinger and V. Hlaváč: *Ten Lectures on Statistical and Structural Pattern Recognition*. 2002 ISBN 1-4020-0642-X
25. F. Mokhtarian and M. Bober: *Curvature Scale Space Representation: Theory, Applications, and MPEG-7 Standardization*. 2003 ISBN 1-4020-1233-0
26. N. Sebe and M.S. Lew: *Robust Computer Vision*. Theory and Applications. 2003 ISBN 1-4020-1293-4
27. B.M.T.H. Romeny: *Front-End Vision and Multi-Scale Image Analysis*. Multi-scale Computer Vision Theory and Applications, written in Mathematica. 2003 ISBN 1-4020-1503-8
28. J.E. Hilliard and L.R. Lawson: *Stereology and Stochastic Geometry*. 2003 ISBN 1-4020-1687-5
29. N. Sebe, I. Cohen, A. Garg and S.T. Huang: *Machine Learning in Computer Vision*. 2005 ISBN 1-4020-3274-9
30. C. Ronse, L. Najman and E. Decencière (eds.): *Mathematical Morphology: 40 Years On*. Proceedings of the 7th International Symposium on Mathematical Morphology, April 18–20, 2005. 2005 ISBN 1-4020-3442-3
31. R. Klette, R. Kozera, L. Noakes and J. Weickert (eds.): *Geometric Properties for Incomplete Data*. 2006 ISBN 1-4020-3857-7
32. K. Wojciechowski, B. Smolka, H. Palus, R.S. Kozera, W. Skarbek and L. Noakes (eds.): *Computer Vision and Graphics*. International Conference, ICCVG 2004, Warsaw, Poland, September 2004, Proceedings. 2006 ISBN 1-4020-4178-0
33. K. Daniilidis and R. Klette (eds.): *Imaging Beyond the Pinhole Camera*. 2006 ISBN 1-4020-4893-9